A History of
Civilization
1815 to the Present

A History of Civilization

1815 to the Present

Fifth Edition

46809

Crane Brinton

John B. Christopher
University of Rochester

Robert Lee Wolff
Archibald Cary Coolidge Professor of History
Harvard University

Prentice-Hall, Inc., Englewood Cliffs, New Jersey

Library of Congress Cataloging in Publication Data

Brinton, Clarence Crane, 1898–1968.
   A history of civilization.

   Contents: v.1. Prehistory to 1300 v.2. 1300 to
1815 v.3. 1815 to the present.
   Includes bibliographies and index.
   1. Civilization—History. I. Christopher, John B.,
joint author. II. Wolff, Robert Lee, joint author.
III. Title
CB69.B74 1976   909   75-21293
ISBN 0-13-389791-5 (vol. 1) pbk.
0-13-389817-2 (vol. 2)
0-13-389825-3 (vol. 3)

Printed in the United States of America

10 9 8 7 6 5 4 3 2 1

Design by A Good Thing, Inc.

Art research by Roberta Guerrette and Olivia Beuhl

Maps by Vincent Kotschar

Prentice-Hall International, Inc., London
Prentice-Hall of Australia, Pty. Ltd., Sydney
Prentice-Hall of Canada, Ltd., Toronto
Prentice-Hall of India Private Limited, New Delhi
Prentice-Hall of Japan, Inc., Tokyo
Prentice-Hall of Southeast Asia (Pte.) Ltd., Singapore

Contents

Preface

With this fifth edition *A History of Civilization* is available for the first time in a choice of paperback formats—two volumes, with the break at 1715, and three volumes, breaking at about 1300 and 1815. Readers familiar with earlier hard-cover editions will find that their generous allotment of maps, the end-of-chapter reading suggestions, and most of their other features have weathered the paperback revolution; the illustrations have been selected with particular care to tie in closely with the text. Throughout the book we have endeavored to take account of new historical evidence and interpretations that have appeared since the fourth edition as well as of increasing student interest in social and cultural history. We have reorganized some chapters to attain greater clarity and coherence, and sharpened the introductory sections of many chapters to provide a simplified chart of a particular historical terrain before elaborating on its detailed typography.

To summarize the most significant changes: We have revised Chapter 1 in the light of recent archaeological finds and of advances in deciphering languages. Chapter 4 includes a new section on the immediate background of Christianity as well as added material on Augustine, the most celebrated of the early Church fathers. We have completely revamped the chapters on the medieval West to aid the reader's understanding of a complex and often bewildering period. Chapter 7 discusses the Church and ecclesiastical culture together with the great confrontation between the papacy and the Holy Roman Empire, and Chapter 8 the English and French monarchies plus secular literature. To enlarge the treatment of the forces that made possible the birth of modern western civilization, discussion of the burgeoning money economy has been shifted to chapter 11 (The Renaissance) from Chapter 10 (War and Politics in the Late Middle Ages). The much-debated crises of the fourteenth and seventeenth centuries receive augmented treatment in Chapters 10 and 15, respectively, and many sections on the arts are enriched, in Chapter 6 (Islam), 11 (Renaissance), 15 (Baroque) and 23 (19th century). We have added an entirely new chapter (32) on the major political developments since 1970 and have incorporated substantial new material in the final chapter (33) recapitulating the intellectual and cultural history of the twentieth century.

The successful completion of a complicated project requires help from many people. We wish to acknowledge our debt to our senior co-author, the late Crane Brinton, whose gift for catching the essential style of a civilization still informs this history; to readers who have taken the trouble to write down their specific suggestions for improving the text; and to the men and women of Prentice-Hall, Inc., for their patience and expertise in the lengthy process of converting manuscript into book form.

John B. Christopher
Robert Lee Wolff

A Note on the Reading Suggestions

A list of suggestions for additional reading is appended to each chapter of these volumes (except that the bibliographies for Chapters 30, 31, and 32 are consolidated into a single list). Since such brief bibliographies must be highly selective, we therefore stress four different categories of works: (1) standard authorities, both older and recent, and both concise and detailed; (2) diverse interpretations representing a spectrum of views, enabling the reader to realize that the past often provokes as much controversy as the present; (3) collections of source materials—texts of laws and decrees, memoirs, letters, chronicles and other items to help a student formulate his own interpretation of events; (4) historical novels and dramas that reflect with reasonable faithfulness the externals of the past and, what is even more difficult, its internal features as well, the motivations, values, and lifestyles of bygone generations.

Our lists star with an asterisk all titles available in paperbacks. New titles are constantly appearing in paperback, and old ones vanishing, so that an indispensable tool is the latest volume of *Paperbound Books in Print* (R. R. Bowker Co.), which lists tens of thousands of items by title, author and subject and is usually to be found in most libraries and bookstores. For a fuller list of works on a given topic, particularly scholarly books published only in hard covers, the handiest tool is the subject cards in a library catalog. In addition, useful up-to-date bibliographies may be found in the two volumes of P. Gay and R. Webb, *Modern Europe* (*Harper & Row), and in the revised *Harvard Guide to American History* (Harvard University Press, 1974).

New scholarly books are often reviewed in the Sunday book section of *The New York Times, The New York Review of Books,* and the London weekly, *The Times Literary Supplement.* Almost all scholarly titles are eventually reviewed in at least one of the major professional journals, such as *The American Historical Review* and *The Journal of Modern History,* or one of the more specialized ones, such as *The Middle East Journal* or *Speculum* (for medieval studies). Three periodicals consist entirely of critiques—*History: Reviews of New Books, Reviews in American History,* and *Reviews in European History.* Journals occasionally publish review articles evaluating at length a book of especial significance or assessing all the major recent publications in a given field, the French Revolution, for instance. Finally, the latest discoveries of historical evidence and innovations in interpretation appear frequently in journal articles months or even years before they do in books. A complete list of the journals concerned with history would itself require an article; a few useful titles, in addition to those already cited, include *History and Theory, The Journal of Interdisciplinary History, The Journal of the History of Childhood* (for psychohistory), *The Journal of the History of Ideas, The Journal of Medieval and Renaissance Studies, The Renaissance Quarterly, The Journal of British Studies, French Historical Studies,* and two British publications, *Past and Present* and *History Today.*

Maps

A History of
Civilization
1815 to the Present

1815 to the Present

Revolution and Counterrevolution
1815-1850

I Introduction

Although the half century after Napoleon recorded no crisis comparable to that of 1789 and produced no personality so dominant as Bonaparte, it was crowded with major developments. Between 1815 and 1870 the Industrial Revolution came of age, modern doctrines of socialism were born, and Darwin's evolutionary hypothesis revolutionized the social sciences as well as biology. In politics, Great Britain and the United States moved steadily, and France more erratically, toward the practical establishment of democracy; Italy and Germany at last achieved national unification. All these developments, though they were well under way by 1850, reached a climax after the mid-century mark and will therefore be postponed to later chapters. The present chapter focuses on the interaction of cultural and political forces, particularly in continental Europe, during the post-Napoleonic generation from 1815 to 1850.

The labels "reaction" and "counterrevolution" are often applied to this generation. By 1815, Europe was reacting strongly against the French Revolution, which had made Napoleon possible, and against the Enlightenment, which had made the Revolution possible. The reaction against the Enlightenment took the form of the romantic movement. Romantic writers and artists protested against the rationalism and classicism of the eighteenth century and championed faith, emotion, tradition, and other values slighted by many philosophes. The political counterrevolution came of age at the Congress of Vienna in 1814–1815, where the leaders of the last coalition against Napoleon reestablished the European balance of power and repudiated the revolutionary principles, though not all the revolutionary achievements, that had shattered the eighteenth-century balance. Reason and natural law, in the judgment both of political leaders and of many romantics, had led not only to progress but also to the Reign of Terror and Napoleonic imperialism.

Yet, despite the ascendancy of counterrevolutionary forces, the spirit of 1789 did not die in 1815. It inspired new and progressively more intense outbreaks of revolution in the 1820s, in 1830, and in 1848. The revolutions of 1848, though put down by the forces of order, marked a critical turning point in the development of the liberalism and nationalism bequeathed by the great French Revolution.

II The Romantic Protest

It may seem paradoxical to bracket the romantic movement together with counterrevolution. We tend to have the image of the romantic as the rebel or the gallant defender of a cause—Shelley preaching anarchism, Byron dying in the Greek War of Independence, Victor Hugo forced into exile because he championed the cause of the short-lived Second French Republic against the dictatorship of a new Bonaparte. But the image is misleading. In a gallery of romantic figures Shelley and Byron should stand alongside Wordsworth and Coleridge, whose youthful enthusiasm for the French Revolution soon evaporated, leaving them rather stodgy defenders of established political and ecclesiastical institutions. Hugo should be flanked by Chateaubriand, who published the *Genius of Christianity* during Napoleon's Consulate. It is true that the romantics' stress on the individual ultimately enriched the doctrines of liberalism and their emphasis on the historical evolution of communities strengthened nationalism. Yet the immediate political influence of romanticism was exerted in the main in support of God and king and in opposition to republicanism and anticlericalism.

On the other hand, the revolutionary qualities of the romantics were always evident in literature and the arts, where they rebelled against the devotion of Jacobin and Napoleonic France to the cult of classical an-

Byron in Greek dress.

tiquity. Here we encounter another paradox: Revolutionary regimes tend to be quite unrevolutionary in aesthetic realms, clinging to traditional canons of expression, and cool or hostile toward innovation and experiment. This was to be true of the Communist revolutionaries in Russia and the Nazis in Germany; it had been true of revolutionary France with its attachment not only to Roman names, furniture, and fashions but also to neoclassical painting and architecture. The romantics were truly revolutionary in their disdain for the literary and artistic canons of neoclassicism and their attraction to the medieval and the Gothic, to the colorful and the exotic, and to the undisciplined and the irrational.

The protest against reason reached full force during the first third of the nineteenth century—the romantic decades of 1800 to 1830 or 1840—but it had been building up for a long time in the mounting challenges to the Enlightenment. Before 1750, Wesley in England and the Pietists in Germany were protesting against the deism of the philosophes and preaching a religion of the heart, not the head. Soon Rousseau proclaimed conscience, not reason, the "true guide of man"; Hume fastened on men's "sentiments and affections" as the mainsprings of their actions. Kant elevated intuition over the commonsense reason of the Enlightenment and restated, in very philosophical language, the Platonic belief in a noumenal realm of eternal verities beyond the world of transient phenomena.

In 1790 Edmund Burke's *Reflections on the Revolution in France* neatly turned against the philosophes their favorite appeal to the simple mathematical laws of Newtonian science. Natural rights, Burke argued,

entering into common life, like rays of light which pierce into a dense medium, are, by the laws of nature, refracted from their straight line. Indeed in the gross and complicated mass of human passions and concerns, the primitive rights of men undergo such a variety of refractions and reflections, that it becomes absurd to talk of them as if they continued in the simplicity of their original direction. The nature of man is intricate; the objects of society are of the greatest possible complexity. . . .*

The protest against the oversimplification of man and society, and the insistence on the intricacy and complexity of humanity, formed one common denominator of romanticism. Other common denominators of this complicated and contradictory movement will emerge from a survey of the achievements of the romantics, beginning with their most characteristic realm of activity—literature.

An Age of Feeling and of Poetry

Literary romanticism may be traced back to the mid-eighteenth century—to novels of "sensibility" like Richardson's *Clarissa* and Rousseau's *La Nouvelle Héloïse* and to the sentimental "tearful comedies" of the French stage. In the 1770s and 1780s a new intensity appeared in the very popular works of the German Sturm und Drang—Goethe's *Werther,* and *The Robbers,* a drama of social protest by Schiller that later won him the award of honorary French citizenship from the Convention. Schiller (1759–1805) went on to write a series of dramas with exceedingly romantic heroes and heroines—William Tell, Wallenstein, Joan of Arc, Mary Stuart.

Goethe (1749–1832), whose career extended through the whole romantic era, was himself no romantic hero. In many respects he was a good eighteenth-century man of reason, interested in natural science, comfortably established in Weimar at the enlightened court of a small German state, and quite detached from the political passions sweeping Germany and Europe in the revolutionary and Napoleonic age. He wrote an epic in the neoclassical manner, *Herman and Dorothea* (1797). Yet romantic values lie at the heart of his most famous writings—his short lyrics and, above all, *Faust,* which many have called the greatest work in the German language. Begun when he was in his twenties, and finished only when he was eighty, this long poetic drama was less a play than a philosophical commentary on the main currents of European thought. According to the traditional legend, the aged Faust, weary of book learning and pining for eternal youth, sold his soul to the Devil, receiving back the enjoyment of his youth for an allotted time, and then, terror-stricken, went to the everlasting fires. Goethe partially transformed the legend. Faust makes his infernal compact with Mephistopheles, who points out how disillusioning and profit-less intellectual pursuits are: "Grey, dear friend, is all theory, but the golden tree of life is green!" But Faust

*E. Burke, *Reflections on the Revolution in France,* Everyman ed. (New York, 1910), p. 59.

is ultimately saved through his realization that he must sacrifice selfish concerns to the welfare of others. A drama of man's sinning, striving, and redemption, Goethe's *Faust* is a reaffirmation of the Christian way that the Enlightenment had belittled.

The Enlightenment had also belittled any poetry except that following very strict forms, like the heroic couplets of Racine and Pope. The romantics decried this neoclassicism as stilted and artificial and praised the vigor, color, and freedom of the Bible, Homer, and Shakespeare. The result was a great renaissance of poetry all over Europe, especially in England, which produced a galaxy of great poets—Byron, Shelley, Keats, Wordsworth, Coleridge, and others.

Of them all, Wordsworth (1770–1850) and Coleridge (1772–1834) pressed furthest in reaction against classicism and rationalism. In 1798, the two men published *Lyrical Ballads,* the first great landmark of English romanticism. As Coleridge later explained, their purpose was explicitly anticlassical:

In the present age the poet . . . seems to propose to himself as his main object . . . new and striking images; with incidents that interest the affections or excite the curiosity. Both his characters and his descriptions he renders, as much as possible, specific and individual, even to a degree of portraiture. In his diction and metre, on the other hand, he is comparatively careless.*

To *Lyrical Ballads* Coleridge contributed the *Rime of the Ancient Mariner,* a supernatural tale of the curse afflicting a sailor who slays an albatross. Later he created the very "striking images" of *Kubla Khan,* which has a surrealistic quality and has been likened to an experience on a drug-induced "trip."

Among Wordsworth's contributions to *Lyrical Ballads* was an attack on conventional learning:

Come forth into the light of things,
Let Nature be your teacher.

. . .

One impulse from a vernal wood
May teach you more of man,
Of moral evil and of good,
Than all the sages can.

Sweet is the lore which Nature brings;
Our meddling intellect
Mis-shapes the beauteous forms of things:—
We murder to dissect.

Enough of Science and of Art;
Close up those barren leaves;
Come forth, and bring with you a heart
That watches and receives.†

For Wordsworth nature was no longer something to be analyzed and reduced to laws but a mysterious, vitalizing force that had to be sensed and experienced. Two passages from his long autobiographical *Prelude* express his beliefs:

Ye Presences of Nature in the sky
And on the earth! Ye Visions of the hills!
And Souls of lonely places! can I think
A vulgar hope was yours when you employed
Such ministry, when ye, through many a year
Haunting me thus among my boyish sports,
On caves and trees, upon the woods and hills,
Impressed, upon all forms, the characters
Of danger or desire; and thus did make
The surface of the universal earth,
With triumph and delight, with hope and fear,
Work like a sea?

. . .

Dust as we are, the immortal spirit grows
Like harmony in music; there is a dark
Inscrutable workmanship that reconciles
Discordant elements, makes them cling together
In one society.*

"Presences," "Visions," "Souls," "haunting"—this is truly romantic language. In place of the light shed by Newton's laws, Wordsworth finds "a dark inscrutable workmanship," and in place of a mathematically ordered world machine there is the Xanadu of Coleridge's *Kubla Khan:*

Where Alph, the sacred river, ran
Through caverns measureless to man,
Down to a sunless sea.

To the Enlightenment all caverns could be measured and all seas could be sunny. Wordsworth, who had lived in France during the early years of the Revolution and been disillusioned by the failure of rational reform, abandoned the philosophes' confidence in the perfectibility of man through reason to put his faith in the "immortal spirit" of the individual.

The Return to the Past

It may seem a long leap from the almost pantheistic universe of Wordsworth to the romantics' enthusiasm for the Middle Ages in general and for the earlier history of their own nations in particular. And yet nationalism is an irrational, almost mystical Wordsworthian force that—so its devotees believe—"reconciles discor-

Biographia Literaria, Everyman ed. (New York, 1908), p. 173.
† *The Tables Turned,* ll 15–16, 21–32.

*Book I, ll 464–475, 340–344.

dant elements, makes them cling together in one society." The heightened sense of nationalism evident almost everywhere in Europe by 1815 was in part a matter of political self-preservation. In the crisis of the Napoleonic wars, for example, the Spaniards became more aware of their Spanish heritage and the Germans of their Germanic one. The romantic return to the national past, however, though intensified by French imperialism, had begun before 1789 as a facet of the retreat from the Enlightenment. The pioneers of romanticism tended to cherish what the philosophes detested, notably the Middle Ages and the medieval preoccupation with religion.

The German writer Herder (1744–1803) provided intellectual justification for medieval studies with his theory of cultural nationalism. Each separate nation, he argued, like any organism, had its own distinct personality, its *Volksgeist* or "folk spirit," and its own pattern of growth. The surest measure of a nation's growth was its literature—poetry in youth, prose in maturity. Stimulated by Herder, students of medieval German literature collected popular ballads, and the

Beethoven in 1820.

brothers Grimm compiled their *Fairy Tales.* In 1782, the first complete text of the *Nibelungenlied* (Song of the Nibelungs) was published, a heroic saga of the nation's youth that had been much admired in the later Middle Ages only to be forgotten in succeeding centuries. By putting a new value on the German literature of the past, Herder helped to free the German literature of his own day from its bondage to French culture. He was no narrow nationalist, however, and asserted that the cultivated man should know cultures other than his own. So Herder also helped to loose the flood of translations that poured over Germany beginning about 1800—translations of Shakespeare, of *Don Quixote,* of Spanish and Portuguese poetry, even of works in Sanskrit.

Some German romantics, stirred by the patriotic revival after the humiliations of Jena and Tilsit, carried national enthusiasm to an extreme that Herder would have deplored. Thus the Grimms claimed preeminence for the German language, and the dramatist Kleist (1777–1811) was sounding the trumpet for the defeat of the new Caesar in his *Battle of Arminius,* boasting of the prowess of the ancient Germans in defeating the legions of Augustus. For the romantic extremists, the mere fact of being German appeared to be a cardinal virtue. By contrast, many German writers struck Herder's happy balance between national and cosmopolitan concerns; Goethe, for example, prided himself on being a good European, not simply a German.

Other nations, too, demonstrated that the return to the past meant veneration of the Middle Ages rather than classical antiquity. In Britain, Sir Walter Scott (1771–1832) assisted in collecting the vigorous medieval folk ballads and went on to write more than thirty historical novels, of which *Ivanhoe,* set in the days of Richard the Lionhearted and the Crusades, is the best known. In Russia, the poet Pushkin (1799–1837) deserted the archaic Slavonic language of the Orthodox church to write the first major literary works in the national vernacular. He took subjects from Russia's past and introduced local color from its newly acquired provinces in the Crimea and the Caucasus. He also celebrated his own exotic grandfather, Hannibal, the African Negro slave of Peter the Great.

In France, the home of the "classical spirit," the romantic reaction gathered slowly, beginning in the first years of the new century with Chateaubriand's *Genius of Christianity* and his Rousseau-like tales, *Atala* and *René.* In 1813 Madame de Staël, who was the daughter of the banker Necker, published *De l'Allemagne* (*Concerning Germany*), a plea for the French to remember that they were the descendants not only of ancient Romans but also of Teutonic Franks, from whom they had inherited a quite unclassical heritage. The great blow against classicism came early in 1830 at the first night of *Hernani,* by Victor Hugo (1802–1885), who deliberately flouted the classical rules of dramatic verse. When one of the characters uttered a line ending in the middle of a word, traditionalists in the audience set off a riot, and the issues were fought and refought at the theater and in the press for weeks to come, with the composer Berlioz and the painter Delacroix coming to Hugo's defense. In the next year Hugo published his great historical novel, *Notre Dame de Paris,* set in the dying days of Gothic France under Louis XI.

Music

Romantic musicians, like romantic poets, sought out the popular ballads and tales of the national past; they too were inventive and imaginative, seeking to release their compositions from the constraints of classical rules. For color and drama, composers of opera and song turned to literature—Shakespeare's plays, Scott's novels, Byron's poetry, and the poems and tales of Goethe and Pushkin. Yet, although literature and music often took parallel paths during the romantic era, the parallel was far from complete. Romantic musicians did not revolt against the great eighteenth-century composers in the way that Wordsworth and Coleridge revolted against their predecessors. Rather, romantic music evolved peacefully out of the older classical school.

Berlioz in 1845: a wood engraving from a French newspaper.

The composer who played the commanding part in this evolution was Beethoven (1770–1827), a Fleming by ancestry and a Viennese by adoption. Whereas Coleridge had said that the romantic artist might be careless in matters of diction and meter, Beethoven showed a classical concern for the forms and techniques that were the musical counterparts of diction and meter. Yet his innovations also enriched the great tradition that he inherited from Bach, Haydn, and Mozart. For example, where Mozart and Haydn had used the courtly minuet for the third movement in a symphony, Beethoven introduced the more plebeian and rollicking scherzo. Where earlier composers had indicated the tempo with a simple "allegro" (fast) or "andante" (slow), Beethoven added such designations as "appassionato" and "Strife between Head and Heart." Part of the color and passion of Beethoven's works derived from his skill in exploiting the resources of the piano, which was perfected during his lifetime. He also scored his orchestral compositions for a greater number of instruments, especially winds, percussion, and double basses, than had been the practice of Mozart and Haydn.

In his Ninth (and final) symphony, Beethoven introduced a chorus in the last movement to sing his setting of Schiller's *Ode to Joy.* After Beethoven, orchestral works took on increasingly heroic dimensions. The French composer Berlioz (1803–1869) projected an orchestra of 465 pieces, including 120 violins, 37 double basses, and 30 each of pianos and harps. Although this utopian scheme remained on paper, Berlioz made some spectacular experiments with the theatrical potentialities of orchestral music. The *Fantastic Symphony,* which he supposedly based on Goethe's *Werther,* was completed appropriately in 1830, the year of Hugo's *Hernani* and

of the July Revolution in Paris. Later, he produced an interpretation of *Romeo and Juliet* that combines symphony and cantata, and *The Damnation of Faust,* based on the original legend without Goethe's happy ending, that fuses symphony and opera. Berlioz' *Requiem* called for a full orchestra, a great pipe organ, four brass choirs, and a chorus of two hundred. Incidentally, the romantic propensity for bigness also affected the presentation of Bach's choral works like *The Passion According to St Matthew,* originally composed for relatively few performers but revived with a full orchestra and a large chorus in a precedent-setting performance directed by Felix Mendelssohn in 1829.

Music for the human voice reflected both the increased enthusiasm for instruments, particularly the piano, and the general romantic nostalgia for the past. In composing songs and arias, romantic musicians devoted as much skill to the accompaniment as to the voice part itself. Franz Schubert (1797–1826), Beethoven's Viennese contemporary, made a fine art of blending voice and piano in more than six hundred sensitive lieder (songs), seventy of them musical settings of poems by Goethe. Meantime, Weber (1786–1826) was striving to create a truly German opera, taking an old legend as the libretto for *Der Freischütz* (The Freeshooter, 1820). Its plot ran the good romantic gamut of an enchanted forest, a magic bullet, and an innocent maiden outwitting the Devil, and its choruses and marches employed many folklike melodies. Weber was by no means the only serious composer to utilize national folk tunes. In Russia, Glinka (1804–1857) cast aside the Italian influences that had previously dominated the secular

The Houses of Parliament, London.

music of his country. He based his opera, *Russlan and Ludmilla* (1842), on a poem by Pushkin and embellished it with dances and choruses derived from the native music of Russia's Asian provinces.

The Arts

In the fine arts, the forces of romanticism gained no such triumph as they won in literature and music. The virtual dictator of European painting during the first two decades of the nineteenth century was the French neoclassicist David (1748–1825). A deputy to the Convention, president of the Paris Jacobin club, and member of the Committee of General Security, David organized many of the great ceremonies of the Revolution, notably Robespierre's Festival of the Supreme Being (June 1794). He became Napoleon's court painter, then was sent into exile by the restored Bourbons. David's canvases formed a capsule history of the rise and decline of revolutionary fervor—before 1789, Roman republican heroes and victims of aristocratic persecution like Socrates; after 1789, dramatic moments like the Tennis Court Oath and the death of Marat; and, after Brumaire, Napoleon's crossing of the Alps and his coronation, both somewhat misrepresented, incidentally, to tally with the impression the publicity-conscious Bonaparte wanted to make. No matter how revolutionary the subject, David employed traditional neoclassical techniques, stressing form, line, and perspective.

The works of David's Spanish contemporary Goya (1746–1828) were much less conventional and much closer to the romantic temper with their warmth and passion and sense of outraged patriotism. No one could

have any illusions about Spanish royalty after looking at Goya's revealing portraits of the enlightened Charles III and his successors. After viewing Goya's etchings of French actions against the Madrid insurgents of May 1808, one can understand the story that Goya made his preliminary sketches in the very blood of the executed Spanish patriots whose agonies he was portraying.

Romantic painting did not acquire formal recognition until the official Paris exhibition of 1824. Although many of the pictures hung in the salon of 1824 came from the school of David, the two leaders of romantic painting were also represented—the Englishman, Constable (1776–1837), and the Frenchman, Delacroix (1799–1863). Constable took painting out of doors, studied nature afresh, and produced a series of landscapes that stressed light and color more than classical purity of line, and paved the way for the impressionists of the later nineteenth century. Delacroix, too, championed color and light and urged young painters to study the flamboyant canvases of Rubens, whom David had banished from the ranks of orthodox artists. The purpose of art, Delacroix claimed in a good romantic definition, was "not to imitate nature but to strike the imagination." His painting *The Massacre of Scio,* depicting a bloody episode in the Greek War of Independence, which seems conventional enough today, was denounced at the salon of 1824 as "barbarous, drunken, delirious"—the "massacre of painting." Delacroix's celebration of the French revolution of 1830, *Liberty Leading the People,* might almost be a campaign poster, but his paintings of Algerian women, a Moroccan Jewish wedding, and other subjects encountered on a trip to North Africa really do strike the imagination with their color and their emancipation from the artificial atmosphere of the classicist's studio. By the 1830s, French painters were divided into opposing schools: the still influential disciples of David, and the romantic followers of Delacroix.

In architecture, also, two schools flourished during the first half of the nineteenth century—the neoclassical, looking to Greek and Roman antiquity, and the neo-Gothic, or Gothic revival, looking to the Middle Ages. Significantly, the label "Gothic" was no longer derogatory, as it had once been when employed by rationalist haters of things medieval. While there were obvious differences between the two schools, the contrast was not total. Many architects of the early 1800s mastered both styles; moreover, they did not so much copy ancient or medieval structures outright as adapt them to the needs and tastes of the day. Generally, the basic design was classical in its proportions, even if the external shell and decoration were medieval. The Houses of Parliament in London, rebuilt in the 1830s and '40s after a disastrous fire, seem very Gothic at first glance with their spires and towers. But a longer look shows that they also embody classical principles of balance and symmetry. Romantic architecture antici-

pated the eclecticism, the wide range of inspiration and style, characteristic of the later nineteenth century.

As the nineteenth century began, the Roman vogue, so firmly set by the French Revolution, reached a peak in Napoleonic Paris with triumphal arches patterned after those of Roman emperors, the Vendôme column modeled on Trajan's in Rome, and the Church of the Madeleine, which was an enlarged copy of an actual Roman temple surviving at Nîmes, in southern France, the Maison Carrée (square house). In America, the versatile Thomas Jefferson, who was a gifted designer, pronounced the Maison Carrée a perfect example of "cubical" architecture and adapted it to secular purposes for the Virginia capitol building at Richmond. At Charlottesville, about 1820, Jefferson provided the University of Virginia with a most distinguished group of academic buildings focused on a circular library, derived from the Roman Pantheon (the perfect example of "spherical" architecture). From the library, somewhat in the manner of a large Roman villa, he extended two rows of smaller structures, each recalling a different Roman temple and interconnected by colonnades. By the second quarter of the nineteenth century, neo-Roman was yielding place to the "Greek revival," stirred in part by the wave of Philhellenic

The library of the University of Virginia, designed by Thomas Jefferson.

enthusiasm then sweeping the Western world in the wake of the Greek independence movement. London's British Museum and Philadelphia's Girard College are two of many splendid examples of the Greek revival.

Meantime, especially in Britain, the Gothic revival was gaining ground, stimulated by the wealth of medieval architectural lore in Scott's novels, by the revival of religion, and by buildings like Fonthill Abbey, which had been started in 1797 and boasted an immensely long and high hall. Though it cost its owner, an eccentric millionaire, £500,000, it was so shoddily built that the central tower collapsed twenty-five years later. Undeterred, British architects applied the Gothic manner to every kind of structure after 1820, to the embellishment of public buildings like the Houses of Parliament, to churches, to elaborate villas and modest cottages. Excessive "gloomth" often resulted, and the fad for "medieval" furniture, bristling with spikes, prompted one critic to warn that the occupant of a neo-Gothic room would be lucky to escape being "wounded by some of its minutiae." Though the Gothic revival prompted some monstrosities, it also fostered the preservation or restoration of medieval masterpieces half ruined by neglect or by anticlerical vandalism.

Religion and Philosophy

The romantic religious revival was marked at the institutional level by the pope's reestablishment in 1814 of the Jesuit order, whose suppression in 1773 had been one of the great victories of the Enlightenment. On the whole, the romantics were horrified by the religious skepticism of the philosophes; Shelley, an outspoken atheist, was an isolated exception. While Catholicism gained many converts among romantic writers, particularly in Germany, the Protestants also made gains. Pietism found a new leader in Schleiermacher, a professor at the University of Berlin, who preached man's utter dependence on God, and as we have already noted, there was a large element of Pietism in the devout practices of Madame de Krüdener, the friend of Czar Alexander I. In England, Wordsworth wrote *Ecclesiastical Sonnets,* and Coleridge also vigorously defended the established Church.

It was Coleridge who introduced his countrymen to the new philosophies of idealism expounded in Germany. Chief among these romantic German philosophers was Hegel (1770–1831), a follower of Kant and a professor at the University of Berlin. Like his master, Hegel attacked the tendency of the Enlightenment to see in human nature and human history only what first met the eye. The history of mankind, properly understood, was the history of human efforts to attain the good, and this in turn was the unfolding of God's plan for the world. For Hegel, history was a *dialectical* process—that is, a series of conflicts. The two elements in the conflict were the *thesis,* the established order of life, and the *antithesis,* the challenge to the old order. Out of the struggle of thesis and antithesis emerged the

synthesis, no mere compromise between the two but a new and better way, another step in man's slow progression toward the best of all possible worlds. The synthesis, in turn, broke down; a new thesis and antithesis became locked in conflict; the dialectic produced another synthesis—and so on.

The death throes of the Roman Republic afforded Hegel an illustration of the dialectic at work. The thesis was represented by the decadent republic, the antithesis by oriental despotism, and the synthesis by the Caesarism of the early Roman Empire. Hegel explained that "This important change must not be regarded as a thing of chance; it was *necessary,*" a part of God's grand design. Julius Caesar himself Hegel called a "hero," one of the few "world-historical individuals" who "had an insight into the requirements of the time" and who knew "what was ripe for development." This concept of the hero as the agent of a cosmic process is another characteristic of the romantic temper.

The dialectical philosophy of history was the most original and influential element in Hegel's thought; it helped, for example, to shape the dialectical materialism of Karl Marx. It is perhaps difficult for citizens of a twentieth-century democracy to appreciate that Hegel was once even more famous as a liberal idealist. His emphasis on duty, his choice of Alexander the Great, Caesar, and Napoleon as "world-historical" heroes, his assertion that the state "existed for its own sake"—all suggest a link with authoritarianism. Yet Hegel himself seems to have foreseen the final synthesis of the dialectic not as a brutal police state but as a liberalized version of the Prussian monarchy.

The Romantic Style

Thus Hegel, like the philosophes, believed in progress and the perfectibility of man, though he also believed that the process would require far more time and struggle than an optimist like Condorcet had ever imagined. Indeed, the style of romanticism by no means contrasted in every particular with that of the Enlightenment. Not only a modified doctrine of progress but also eighteenth-century cosmopolitanism lived on into the nineteenth. Homer, Cervantes, Shakespeare, and Scott won appreciative readers in many countries; the giants of the age, men like Beethoven and Goethe, were not merely Austrian or German citizens but citizens of the world.

These similarities and continuities notwithstanding, romanticism did have a decided style of its own—imaginative, emotional, and haunted by the supernatural and by history. The romantics could no longer view history in Gibbon's terms of a classical golden age followed by long centuries of benighted superstition. Rather history was, as Herder and Hegel had argued, an organic process of growth and development, which was indebted to the Middle Ages for magnificent Gothic buildings, religious enthusiasm, folk ballads, and heroic epics. Just as the romantics rejected the Enlightenment's view of the past, so they found the Newtonian world-machine an entirely inadequate interpretation of the universe. It was too static, too drab and materialistic, and in its place they put the neo-Gothic world of religious mystery, the Hegelian world of dialectic and heroes, the poetic and artistic world of feeling, color, and "impulses from the vernal wood."

III   The Reconstruction of Europe

The romantic movement, by the very diffuseness of its nature, could scarely have been expected to provide blueprints for the reconstruction of Europe after the defeat of Napoleon. The general guidelines, though not the specific details, for reconstruction lay at hand in the writings of Edmund Burke (1729–1797), the Whig politician and publicist, who set the tone of counter-revolutionary conservatism. Unlike the champions of revolution, Burke could not accept simple black-and-white assumptions about the goodness of man and the unmitigated evil of the Old Regime. He revered the social and political institutions so painstakingly built up over the centuries yet also believed that they could be changed, provided it was done gradually. Reforms had to be introduced so that "the useful parts of the old establishment" might be preserved; they had to be managed "with circumspection and caution"—in short, conservatively.

Burke welcomed American independence, which he viewed not so much as a revolution as a reaffirmation of the glorious English tradition of 1688. The same reasoning drove him to violent condemnation in his *Reflections on the Revolution in France* (1790). The men of 1789 destroyed everything, good, bad, and indifferent. Rage and frenzy, he observed, "pull down more in half an hour, than prudence, deliberation and foresight can build up in a hundred years";* thereby society itself is jeopardized. "Society is indeed a contract," Burke wrote, but he did not mean what Rousseau had meant:

> The state ought not to be considered as nothing better than a partnership agreement in a trade of pepper and coffee, calico or tobacco, or some such other low concern, to be taken up for a little temporary interest, and to be dissolved by the fancy of the parties. It is to be looked on with other reverence, because it is not a partnership in things subservient only to the gross animal existence of a temporary and perishable nature. It is a partnership in all science; a partnership in all art; a partnership in every virtue, and in all perfection. As the ends of such a partnership cannot be obtained in many generations, it becomes a partnership not only between those who are living, but between those who are living, those who are dead, and those who are to be born.†

Burke's doctrines were especially welcomed by the

émigrés. Among them was Joseph de Maistre (1753–1821), a diplomat in the service of the king of Sardinia, who had been forced into exile when the French overran Savoy and Piedmont. De Maistre combined Burke's conservatism with a Hobbesian view of the viciousness of the state of nature and a traditional Catholic view of man's depravity and need for discipline. The French Revolution, he believed, had been God's punishment of the philosophes' effrontery in believing that society could be remade without divine assistance. What men would need in the postrevolutionary world was firm control by an absolute monarch and inspired guidance from the Church. De Maistre carried the revival of Catholicism to an extreme of Ultramontanism, asserting for the papacy a universal authority the popes themselves had not claimed since the days of Innocent III and Boniface VIII.

The force of tradition revered by Burke and De Maistre bore heavily upon the politics of post-Napoleonic Europe. Yet it was not so much ideological conviction as political pragmatism that accounted for the conservatism of the man who presided over the actual reconstruction of Europe. This was Metternich, Prince Clement Wenceslas Lothair Népomucène Metternich (1773–1859), Austrian foreign minister from 1809 to 1848 and the chief figure in European diplomacy during most of his long career. Handsome, dashing, an aristocrat through and through, Metternich retained some of the eighteenth century's belief in reform through enlightened despotism. But, he also believed, reform should proceed with Burkean caution, not at a revolutionary pace. His family's estates in the German Rhineland had suffered severely during the French Revolution. Moreover, Metternich served a state that was particularly susceptible to injury by the liberal and nationalist energies released by the Revolution. Tradition, he knew, was the cement that held together the disparate parts of the Austrian Hapsburg realm; it should be fortified as much as possible.

The Congress of Vienna

In 1814 and 1815, Metternich was host to the Congress of Vienna, which approached its task of rebuilding Europe with truly conservative deliberateness. For the larger part of a year, the diplomats indulged to the full in balls and banquets, concerts and hunting parties; "Congress dances," quipped an observer, "but it does not march." Actually, the brilliant social life distracted the lesser fry while the important diplomats settled things in private conference.

Four men made most of the major decisions at Vienna—Metternich; Czar Alexander I; Viscount Castlereagh, the British foreign secretary; and Talleyrand, the foreign minister of Louis XVIII, the restored Bourbon king of defeated France. Castlereagh, who shared the conservative outlook of Metternich, was less concerned with punishing the French for their past sins than with preventing the appearance of new Robe-

*Burke, *Reflections*, p. 164.
†Ibid., p. 93.

Statesmen at the Congress of Vienna. Talleyrand is seated at the right with his arm on the table; Metternich is standing prominently at the left.

spierres and Bonapartes. He was at Vienna, he said, "not to collect trophies, but to bring the world back to peaceful habits." The best way to do this, he believed, was to restore the balance of power and keep any of the major states, including France, from becoming either too strong or too weak. "No arrangement could be wise that carried ruin to one of the countries between which it was concluded."

Talleyrand: a drawing made in 1833.

Talleyrand scored at Vienna the greatest success of his long career. Originally a worldly bishop of the Old Regime, he had in succession rallied to the Revolution in 1789, become one of the very few bishops to support the Civil Constitution of the Clergy, served as Napoleon's foreign minister, and then, while still holding office, intrigued against him during the years after Tilsit. This supremely adaptable diplomat soon maneuvered himself into the inner circle at Vienna, and the representatives of the victorious powers accepted the emissary of defeated France as their equal. Talleyrand was particularly adept in exploiting his nuisance value—acting as the spokesman of lesser diplomats who resented being shoved aside, and making the most of the differences that divided the victors.

To these differences Alexander I contributed greatly. Metternich actually called the czar a Jacobin, although Alexander's reputation for enlightenment was only partially deserved, as we have already seen. By 1814, the czar had acquired a thoroughly romantic enthusiasm for religion, spending hours on end praying and reading the Bible in the company of Madame de Krüdener. Under her influence he prepared a Holy Alliance whereby all states would regenerate their policies by following Christian teachings. In the first months at Vienna, it was not Alexander's scheme of a Holy Alliance but rather his Polish policy that nearly disrupted the congress. He proposed a partial restoration of prepartition Poland, with himself as its monarch; Austria and Prussia would lose the Polish lands they had grabbed late in the preceding century. Alexander won the support of Prussia by backing her demands for the annexation of Saxony, whose king had remained loyal to Napoleon. Metternich, however, did not want Austria's traditional Prussian rival to make such a substantial gain. Moreover, both Metternich and Castlereagh disliked the prospect of a large, Russian-dominated Poland.

The dispute over Saxony and Poland gave Talleyrand a magnificent chance to fish in troubled waters. Thus it was that in January 1815 the representative of defeated France joined Metternich and Castlereagh in threatening both Prussia and Russia with war unless they moderated their demands. The threat produced an immediate settlement. Alexander obtained Poland but agreed to reduce its size and allow Prussia and Austria to keep part of their loot from the partitions. Prussia took about half of Saxony; the king of Saxony retained the balance.

Once the Saxon-Polish question was out of the way, the congress was able to resolve other important dynastic and territorial questions. According to what Talleyrand christened "the sacred principle of legitimacy," thrones and frontiers were to be reestablished as they had existed in 1789. In practice, however, legitimacy was ignored almost as often as it was applied, since the diplomats realized that they could not undo all the changes worked by the Revolution and Napoleon. Although they sanctioned the return of the Bourbons to the thrones of France, Spain, and Naples in the name of legitimacy, they did not attempt to resurrect the Republic of Venice or to revive all the hundreds of German states that had vanished since 1789. In Germany, the congress provided for thirty-nine states, loosely grouped in a weak confederation, which came close to reincarnating the impotent Holy Roman Empire. The chief organ of the German Confederation, the diet, was to be a council of diplomats from sovereign states rather than a representative national assembly. Its most important members were Prussia and Austria, for the German-speaking provinces of the multinational Hapsburg realm were considered an integral part of Germany.

Prussia, in addition to annexing part of Saxony, added the lands of the Napoleonic kingdom of Westphalia to her old scattered lands in western Germany, thus creating the imposing Rhine Province. Austria lost Belgium, which was incorporated into the Kingdom of the Netherlands in order to strengthen the northern buffer against France. But she recovered the Illyrian provinces on the eastern Adriatic shore and the old Hapsburg possession of Lombardy, to which Venetia was now joined. By holding Lombardy-Venetia and exploiting the close family ties between the Hapsburgs and the ruling dynasties in other Italian states, Austria was in a position to dominate Italy. The Congress of Vienna restored the Bourbon Kingdom of Naples, the States of the Church and, on their northern flank, the Grand Duchy of Tuscany and the smaller duchies of Modena and Parma (where Marie-Louise, Napoleon's wife, was eventually installed).

In northwestern Italy, the Kingdom of Piedmont-Sardinia acquired Genoa as a buttress against France. Another buttress was established in the Republic of Switzerland, now independent once again and slightly enlarged. The congress confirmed the earlier transfer of Finland from Sweden to Russia, and compensated Sweden by the transfer of Norway from the rule of Denmark to that of Sweden. This last punished the Danes for their pro-French policy and rewarded Bernadotte, former marshal in Napoleon's army and now Swedish crown prince, for the anti-French course he had pursued after Napoleon's seizure of Swedish Pomerania on the Baltic coast of Germany in 1812. Finally, Great Britain received the strategic little Mediterranean island of Malta and, outside Europe, the former Dutch colonies of Ceylon and the Cape of Good Hope plus a few insignificant French outposts.

France at first was given her boundaries of 1792, which included the minor territorial acquistions made during the early days of the Revolution. Then came Napoleon's escape from Elba and the Hundred Days. The final settlement reached after Waterloo assigned France the frontiers of 1790, substantially those of the Old Regime plus Avignon. In addition, the French were to return Napoleon's art plunder to its rightful owners, pay the victorious allies an indemnity of 700,000,000 francs (roughly $140,000,000), and finance allied military occupation of seventeen frontier fortresses on French soil for not more than five years.

To quarantine any possible new French aggression, Castlereagh conceived the policy of strengthening France's neighbors so that they would be able to restrain the troublemaker in the future. Thus to the north the French faced the Belgians and the Dutch combined in the single Kingdom of the Netherlands. On the northeast they encountered the Rhine Province of Prussia, and on the east the expanded states of Switzerland and Piedmont. The Quadruple Alliance, signed in November 1815, constituted the second great measure of quarantine. The four allies—Britain, Prussia, Austria, and Russia—agreed to use force, if necessary, to preserve the Vienna settlement. At Castlereagh's insistence, the allies further decided on periodic conferences to consider the measures "most salutary for the repose and prosperity of Nations, and the maintenance of the Peace of Europe."

Public opinion, especially in the English-speaking countries, unfortunately confused the Quadruple Alliance with Alexander's Holy Alliance, which it identified with the blackest reaction. The Holy Alliance, signed in September 1815, was actually a fairly harmless document dedicated to the proposition that "the policy of the powers . . . ought to be guided by the sublime truths taught by the eternal religion of God our Saviour." Although most of the major European rulers signed the Holy Alliance, only Czar Alexander seems to have taken it seriously. Castlereagh called it "a piece of sublime mysticism and nonsense," and Britain declined to participate—the first sign of the rift that was to open between her and the continental powers. The pope, refusing an invitation to join, remarked tartly that the Vatican needed no new interpretations of Christian doctrine by the laity.

Neither the Holy Alliance nor the Quadruple Alliance fulfilled the expectations of their architects. At the first meeting of the Quadruple Alliance, at Aix-la-Chapelle in 1818, the allies agreed to withdraw their occupation forces from France, which had paid up the indemnity imposed upon her. Then Czar Alexander pressed the other allies to participate in a vague international union with the contradictory goals of promoting constitutional monarchy everywhere, repressing revolution, fostering disarmament, and supporting an international army to sustain governments and defend existing frontiers. Metternich and Castlereagh demurred, the latter deploring the czar's effort "to endow the transparent soul of the Holy Alliance with a body." At the next meeting of the allies, two years later, Metternich and Castlereagh would find themselves ranged on opposite sides on the issue of putting down revolutions under international auspices.

For these revolutions of 1820–1821 the Congress of Vienna was itself partly to blame, through its attempt to stifle both liberal and nationalist aspirations. Yet, as major international settlements go, that of Vienna was a good one, in many respects more success-

UNITED KINGDOM
OF GREAT BRITAIN
AND IRELAND

KINGDOM OF
NORWAY
AND SWEDEN

SCOTLAND

North Sea

IRELAND

DENMARK

Baltic

WALES

ENGLAND

London

The Hague

Brussels

K. OF NETHERLANDS

Aachen

Rhine R.

P R U S S I A

Berlin

Oder R.

Atlantic Ocean

LUX.

Wartburg

Weser R.

Frankfurt

SAXONY

Carlsbad

Prague

Tropp

Seine R.

Paris

GERMAN

Hambach

BOHEMIA

Elbe R.

Loire R.

Meuse R.

CONFEDERATION

Danube R.

AUSTRIA

E M

FRANCE

Vienna

SWITZERLAND

TYROL

A

Garonne R.

Rhône R.

LOMBARDY

Novara

Milan

Custozza

VENETIA

Venice

Turin

PIEDMONT

Genoa

PARMA

MODENA

PORTUGAL

Ebro R.

SPAIN

Madrid

Barcelona

CORSICA

(Fr.)

KINGDOM OF SARDINIA

TUSCANY

Florence

PAPAL

Adriatic Sea

Lisbon

Tagus R.

STATES

Rome

Guadalquivir R.

BALEARIC IS.

SARDINIA

Naples

Cadiz

KINGDOM OF THE
TWO SICILIES

Algiers

Mediterranean Sea

B A R B A R Y   S T A T E S

SICILY

0   500

Miles

MALTA
(Br.)

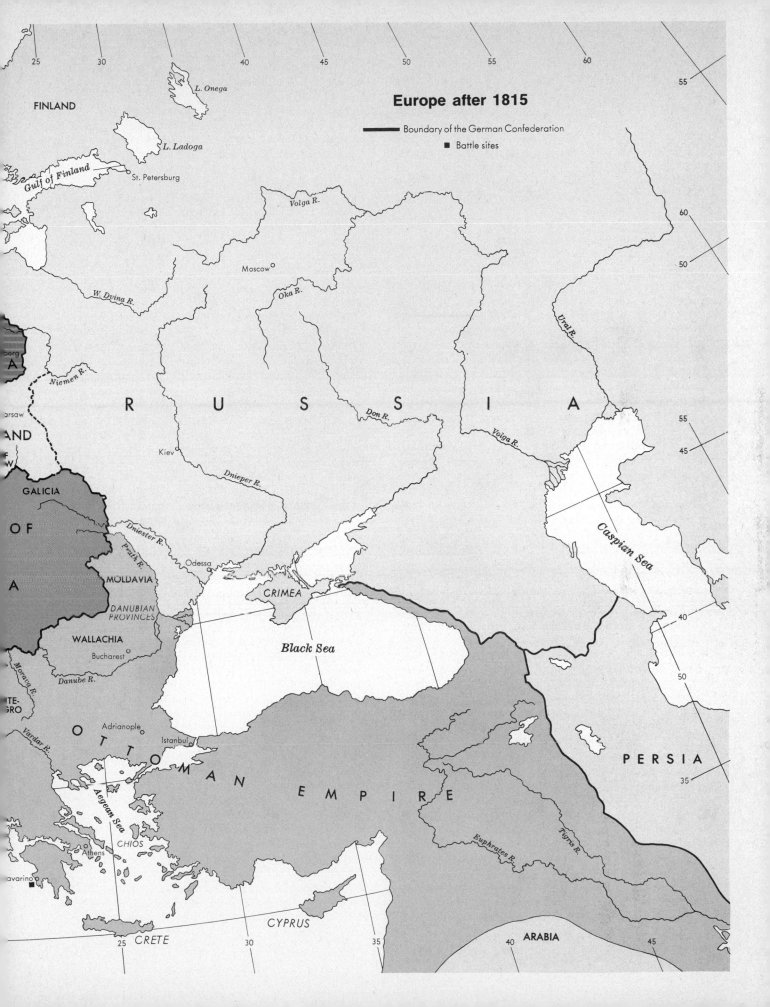

Europe after 1815

— Boundary of the German Confederation
■ Battle sites

FINLAND

L. Onega

L. Ladoga

Gulf of Finland

St. Petersburg

Volga R.

Moscow ○

W. Dvina R.

Oka R.

Ural R.

60

50

borg

Niemen R.

R   U   S   S   I   A

arsaw

55
45

Don R.

AND

Voiga R.

EW

Kiev

Dnieper R.

Caspian Sea

GALICIA

Dniester R.

OF

Prath R.

Odessa

40

A

MOLDAVIA

CRIMEA

DANUBIAN
PROVINCES

Black Sea

50

WALLACHIA

Bucharest ○

Morava R.

Danube R.

TE-
GRO

Adrianople ○

O   T   T   O   M   A   N   E   M   P   I   R   E

35

Vardar R.

Istanbul ○

PERSIA

Aegean Sea

Euphrates R.

Tigris R.

CHIOS

Athens ○

avarino ■

CYPRUS

25

CRETE

30

35

40 ARABIA

45

ful than its two predecessors—Westphalia (1648) and Utrecht (1713)—and the Versailles settlement of 1919–1920. There was to be no war involving several powers until the second-rate Crimean conflict of the 1850s, and no major war embroiling the whole of Europe until a century after 1815. Seldom have victors treated a defeated aggressor with the wisdom and generosity displayed in 1815. Most of the leading diplomats at Vienna could have said with Castlereagh that they acted "to bring the world back to peaceful habits."

The Persistence of Revolution, 1820–1823

The revolutionary leaders of the post-Napoleonic generation despised the traditions so revered by conservatives. Opposing the counterrevolutionary alliance of throne and altar, they stood for liberty, equality, and fraternity. The first two words of the great revolutionary motto continued to signify the abolition of noble and clerical privileges in society and, with few exceptions, the application of laissez faire to the economy. They also involved the broadening of civil rights, the institution of representative assemblies, and the granting of constitutions, which would bring limited monarchy or possibly even a republic. Almost every leader of revolution proclaimed himself a liberal although, as we shall soon see, the kind of liberalism actually practiced varied from the narrow to the sweeping.

Fraternity, intensified by the romantic cult of the nation, continued to evolve into the formidable doctrine of nationalism. The nationalists of the post-1815 generation dreamed of a world in which each nation would be free of domination by any other, and all nations would live together harmoniously. In practical terms, this signified movements toward national unity and national independence. It meant growing pressure for the unification of Germany and Italy. And it inspired demands for freedom by peoples living under the control of a foreign power—by Belgians against their Dutch rulers, by Poles against Russians, by Greeks and Serbs against Turks, and by Italians, Hungarians, and Czechs against the Hapsburgs of Vienna.

The first revolutionary outbreaks after 1815 took place in Spain, Portugal, and the Kingdom of the Two Sicilies. In all three states legitimacy meant a return to the Old Regime at its least enlightened. Yet the great majority of the population responded calmly, even enthusiastically, for the aristocracy were delighted to recover their ancient privileges and the peasantry welcomed the return of familiar traditions. A small minority, drawn chiefly from the middle class, the intellectuals, and the army, dissented; in Spain and Italy, they regretted the abrogation of the Code Napoléon, and of the antifeudal and anticlerical legislation introduced by the French. In all three states the discontent of the liberal minority produced the revolutionary movement of 1820.

The trouble began in Spain. During the war against Napoleon, representatives from the liberal middle class of Cadiz and other commercial towns had framed the Constitution of 1812. Based on the French Constitution of 1791, this document limited greatly the power of the monarchy, gave wide authority to a Cortes elected on a broad suffrage, and deprived the Spanish Church of some of its lands and privileges. This constitution was doubtless too liberal to be very workable in traditionalist Spain, and the Bourbon Ferdinand VII soon suspended it after he assumed the Spanish crown in 1814. Ferdinand also restored the social inequalities of the Old Regime and reestablished not only the Jesuits but also the Inquisition. Army officers, alienated by his highhandedness and clericalism, and merchants, facing ruin because of the revolt of Spanish colonies in the New World, joined the political clubs and Masonic lodges that formed the liberal opposition.

It was Ferdinand's attempt to subdue the rebellious colonies that triggered revolution at home. The independence movement in Spanish America had been the outcome of the refusal of the colonial populations either to recognize Napoleon's brother Joseph as their king or to accept the closer ties between colonies and mother country proposed by patriots in Spain and implicit in the Constitution of 1812. Behind the Spanish-American independence movement lay several other factors: the powerful examples of the American and French revolutions; the sympathetic interest of Great Britain, anxious to release lucrative markets from Spanish mercantilist restrictions; and the accumulated resentment of colonial peoples at the centuries of indifferent rule by Spanish governors. The colonial rebels won their initial success at Buenos Aires in 1810, and their movement spread rapidly to Spain's other American possessions.

Ferdinand now determined to crush the rebels by force; to transport troops he augmented the small Spanish fleet with three leaky hulks purchased from Russia. At the end of 1819, this motley new armada, carrying 20,000 men, was about to sail from Cadiz. It never sailed, for on January 1, 1820, a mutiny broke out at Cadiz led by the liberal colonel Riego. Uprisings soon followed in Madrid, in Barcelona, and in other Spanish cities. The revolutionaries sang "Riego's Hymn," with the refrain "Swallow it, you dog" (the "it" referred to the Constitution of 1812). Ferdinand surrendered.

The liberal minorities in Portugal and Naples followed the Spanish lead. An army faction seized control of the Portuguese government in 1820, abolished the Inquisition, and set up a constitution on the Spanish model of 1812. In Naples, the revolution was the work of General Pepe, backed by the Carbonari (charcoal burners). This secret society, with a membership exceeding 50,000, had been opposed to the French and their reforms in the days of Napoleon's hegemony but now sponsored a vaguely liberal program inspired by the French Revolution and the Spanish Constitution of 1812. King Ferdinand I of the Two Sicilies, who was

Centers of Revolution

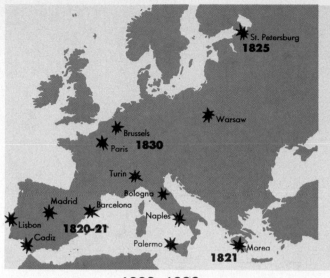

1820–1830

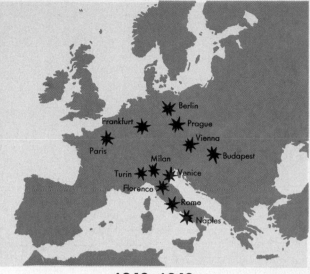

1848–1849

the uncle of the Spanish Ferdinand VII, gave in at the first sign of opposition in 1820 and accepted a constitution of the Spanish type.

The strength of the revolutionary movement of 1820 ebbed as quickly as it had risen. The reforms introduced precipitately by the inexperienced liberal leaders in Spain and Naples alienated the bulk of the population at home and so alarmed the conservative leaders of the great powers that they sponsored counterrevolutionary intervention. The Spanish revolutionaries were further weakened by a split between *moderados,* who wanted to keep the Constitution of 1812, and *exaltados,* led by Colonel Riego, who wanted to go much further and set up a violently anticlerical republic. Only in Portugal did the revolutionary regime survive, and only because it had British protection. Even so, there was enough confusion to enable the great Portuguese colony of Brazil to declare itself independent of the mother country (1822).

The revolutions of 1820 tested both the stability of the Vienna settlement and the solidarity of the Quadruple Alliance of Britain, Prussia, Austria, and Russia. Legitimacy was again restored in Spain and Italy, but in the process the Quadruple Alliance was split in two. While the continental allies increasingly favored armed intervention to suppress revolution, Britain inclined more and more toward the principle of nonintervention. The split became evident at the conference of the Quadruple Alliance meeting at Troppau in Silesia late in 1820. Castlereagh, the British foreign minister, knowing that the Neapolitan revolution threatened the Hapsburg hegemony in Italy, was willing to see Austria intervene in Naples, but without the backing of the alliance. The alliance, Castlereagh declared, was never designed "for the superintendence

of the internal affairs of other states," and Britain refused to participate formally in the Troppau meeting. Metternich, supported by Alexander, pressed for a blanket commitment from the alliance, and the result was the Troppau Protocol (November 1820), signed by Austria, Prussia, and Russia. It declared that

> States which have undergone a change of Government, due to revolution, the results of which threaten other states, *ipso facto* cease to be members of the European Alliance, and remain excluded from it until their situation gives guarantees for legal order and stability. If, owing to such alterations, immediate danger threatens other states, the Powers bind themselves, by peaceful means, or if need be by arms, to bring back the guilty state into the bosom of the Great Alliance.*

Under the terms of the Troppau Protocol, an Austrian army duly toppled the revolutionary government of Naples in 1821. In 1823, a French army crossed the Pyrenees and restored the absolute authority of Ferdinand VII, who proceeded to execute Colonel Riego and hundreds of his followers.

French intervention in Spain provoked the strong opposition of Great Britain and ended the Quadruple Alliance. Canning, who had succeeded Castlereagh as British foreign minister in 1822, suspected that the continental powers might now aid Spain to recover her former American colonies. So also did the United States, which had recognized the independence of the Latin-American republics. But America also feared both a possible Russian move southward from Alaska along the Pacific coast and an attempt by Britain to

*Quoted in W. A. Phillips, *The Confederation of Europe* (New York, 1920), pp. 208–209.

extend her sphere of control in the Caribbean. Therefore, when Canning proposed a joint Anglo-American statement to ward off any European interference in Latin America, the government of President Monroe refused the invitation. However, in a message to the American Congress in December 1823, the President included the statement that is known to history as the Monroe Doctrine:

> In the wars of the European powers, in matters relating to themselves, we have never taken any part, nor does it comport with our policy so to do. It is only when our rights are invaded, or seriously menaced, that we resent injuries or make preparation for our defence. With the movements in this hemisphere, we are, of necessity, more immediately connected, and by causes which must be obvious to all enlightened and impartial observers. The political system of the allied powers is essentially different, in this respect, from that of America. . . . We owe it, therefore, to candor, and to the amicable relations existing between the United States and those powers, to declare, that we should consider any attempt on their part to extend their system to any portion of this hemisphere, as dangerous to our peace and safety. With the existing colonies or dependencies of any European power, we have not interfered, and shall not interfere. But with the governments who have declared their independence, and maintained it, and whose independence we have, on great consideration, and on just principles, acknowledged, we could not view any interposition for the purpose of oppressing them, or controlling, in any other manner, their destiny, by an European power, in any other light than as the manifestation of an unfriendly disposition towards the United States.

Although this document marked an important assertion of policy on the part of the youthful American republic, it had little immediate international significance. The European powers were not fully committed to the project of restoring Spain's American empire. And, so far as they were deterred from that venture, they were deterred not by President Monroe but by Canning and the possible actions of the British fleet.

Serbian and Greek Independence

The British fleet was soon to take an important role in the Greeks' bid for national independence. The Greek revolt was part of the general movement of the Balkan nations for emancipation from their Turkish overlords. During the last quarter of the eighteenth century, the Christian peoples of the Balkan peninsula were awakening to their national identities under the impulse of French Revolutionary and romantic ideas. They examined their national past with new interest and affection and put particular stress on their native languages.

The first outbreak against the Turkish authorities came in 1804 among the Serbs, today one of the component peoples of Yugoslavia. Led by a prosperous pig farmer named Karageorge, these early Serbian nationalists knew they would need outside help to win their independence. Some of them turned to Austria, which was nearby and ruled over their fellow Yugoslavs, the Croats and Slovenes; others looked to distant Russia, which attracted them because it was both Slavic in language and Orthodox in religion, for the Serbs were Orthodox, unlike the other Yugoslavs, who were Catholic. Thus was established a pattern of conflicting Austrian and Russian interests that ultimately led to World War I. Napoleon's venture in the Illyrian provinces gave the Yugoslavs a taste of the Enlightenment and stimulated their desire for independence. After Karageorge's defection in 1813, leadership of Serb nationalism passed to his rival, Milosh Obrenovich, who won Russian support and succeeded by 1830 in becoming prince of an autonomous Serbia. Although he still paid tribute to the Ottoman emperor and a Turkish garrison remained in the Serb capital of Belgrade, a major step toward eventual independence had been completed.

Meantime, the Greeks had launched a revolution. Leadership came from two groups—the Phanariot Greeks, named for the quarter where they lived in Istanbul, and the Island Greeks, merchants from the ports and islands of the Aegean. The Phanariots had long held positions of power and responsibility in governing the Orthodox subjects of the Ottoman Empire. The Island Greeks dominated the commerce of the Near East and had business outposts at Vienna, Marseilles, London, and Russia's Black Sea port of Odessa. The Island Greeks revived not only the old Greek mercantile tradition but also some of the old Greek zeal for self-government. From their home islands and from their merchant colonies abroad they poured forth a stream of patriotic exhortation. Greek nationalists sponsored a campaign to purge the modern Greek language of its Turkish and Slavic words and to return it to the classical tongue of the Age of Pericles. A revolutionary secret society was formed in Odessa, patterned after the Carbonari of Italy and headed by Ypsilanti, a Phanariot who was a general in the Russian army.

In 1821, Ypsilanti led an expedition into the Danubian provinces of the Ottoman Empire but failed in his aim to stir up a major revolt. The conspirators were more successful in the Morea (the ancient Peloponnesus) where they fomented an uprising among the peasants. The ensuing war for independence was a ferocious conflict: the Morean peasants slaughtered every Turk they could lay their hands on; the Ottoman government retaliated by killing or selling into slavery thirty thousand Greeks from the prosperous Aegean island of Chios (Scio), an atrocity that inspired Delacroix's famous painting. In the work of repression, the Ottoman emperor supplemented his own inadequate forces by those of his vassal, the governor of Egypt, Muhammad Ali. By 1827, it appeared likely that the Egyptian expedition would recapture the last rebel strongholds. Then Britain, France, and Russia intervened to save the Greek independence movement at its darkest hour.

The three-power action resulted from the combined pressures of public opinion and strategic interests. In Britain and France, and also in Germany and the United States, the Philhellenic (pro-Greek) movement had won legions of supporters. Philhellenic committees sent supplies and money and demanded that civilized governments intervene directly. Intervention hinged on the action of Russia, for Greek patriots had formed their secret society at Odessa, on Russian soil and with Russian backing. For a time, Metternich was able to restrain Russia by pointing out the dangers to the European balance in supporting revolution in one country and repressing it in others. Ultimately, however, Russia's aspirations for hegemony over the Balkans won out over her concern for preserving the status quo, and she rallied openly to the Greek cause. Britain and France now felt obliged to take action because of Philhellenic pressure and, still more, because they feared to let Russia act alone lest she gain mastery over the whole Near East. A three-power intervention seemed the only course that would both rescue the Greeks and check the Russians.

Neither aim was fully achieved. In October 1827, Russian, British, and French squadrons sank the Turkish and Egyptian vessels anchored at Navarino, on the southwest corner of the Morea, and thus destroyed the chief Ottoman base. The subsequent Treaty of Adrianople (1829), while allowing Russia to annex outright only a little Turkish territory, arranged that the Ottoman Danubian provinces of Moldavia and Wallachia (the heart of present-day Romania) should become a virtual Russian protectorate. After considerable wrangling, the European powers accorded formal recognition to an independent Greek kingdom of very modest size, which left many Greeks still within the Ottoman Empire. Neither nationalism nor liberalism had won a complete victory in the Greek war. Greek patriots now schemed for the day when they might enlarge the boundaries of their new kingdom. And Greek politicians were to threaten its stability and disillusion Philhellenists abroad by continuing the bitter feuds that had divided them even in the midst of their desperate struggle for independence.

The Decembrist Revolt in Russia

Russia, which did so much to determine the outcome of revolutions elsewhere, herself felt the revolutionary wave, but with diminished force. A brief uprising took place after the death of Czar Alexander I (December 1825), as the Decembrists vainly attempted to apply and extend the program of liberal reforms apparently promised by the czar but seldom implemented by him.

The last period of Alexander's reign, marked by the influence of the unpopular Arakcheev and by the establishment of the hated military colonies, had thoroughly disappointed Russian liberals. Liberal ideas, however, continued to penetrate the country, disseminated by the secret societies that flourished in Russia after 1815. The introduction of Freemasonry during the

eighteenth century and the secret ritual connected with many of the lodges had given jaded nobles a thrill and had also enabled them to meet on equal terms with men from other ranks of society. Masonry aroused humanitarian urges; it also afforded a cover of secrecy under which subversive ideas might be incubated. Moreover, the contrast between the relatively enlightened West and backward Russia made a deep impression on officers who had served in the campaigns against Napoleon. One of the future Decembrist leaders left this report of his reactions upon returning home:

> From France we returned to Russia by sea. The First Division of the Guard landed at Oranienbaum and listened to the *Te Deum.* . . . During the prayer the police were mercilessly beating the people who attempted to draw nearer to the lined-up troops. . . . Finally the Emperor appeared, accompanied by the Guard, on a fine sorrel horse, with an unsheathed sword, which he was ready to lower before the Empress. But at that very moment, almost under his horse, a peasant crossed the street. The Emperor spurred his horse and rushed with the unsheathed sword toward the running peasant. The police attacked him with their clubs. We did not believe our own eyes and turned away, ashamed for our beloved Tsar.*

High-ranking officers at St. Petersburg secretly formed the Northern Society, which aimed to make Russia a limited, decentralized monarchy, with the various provinces enjoying rights somewhat like those of the states in the American republic. The serfs would receive their freedom but no land, and the whole series of reforms would be achieved by peaceful means. A second secret organization, the Southern Society, with headquarters at Kiev, included many relatively impoverished officers among its members; its leader was Colonel Pestel, a Jacobin in temperament and an admirer of Napoleon. On every main issue the program of the Southern Society went beyond that of the Petersburg group. It advocated a highly centralized republic, the granting of land to liberated serfs, and the use of violence—specifically, assassination of the czar—to gain its ends. Pestel himself planned to install a dictatorship, supported by secret police, as an interim government between the overthrow of the czardom and the advent of the republic.

Both the Northern Society and the Southern Society tried to profit by the political confusion following the death of Alexander I. Since Alexander left no son, the crown would normally have passed to his younger brother, Constantine, his viceroy in Poland. Constantine, however, had relinquished his rights to a still younger brother, Nicholas, but in a document so secret that Nicholas never saw it. On the death of Alexander, Constantine declared that Nicholas was the legal czar, and Nicholas declared that Constantine was. While the two brothers were clarifying their status, the Northern

Society summoned the Petersburg garrison to revolt against Nicholas. Throughout the day of December 26, 1825, the rebels stood their ground in Russia's capital city until Nicholas subdued them. Two weeks later, the Southern Society launched a movement that was doomed from the start because its leader, Pestel, had already been placed under arrest.

The Decembrist revolt, for all its ineffectiveness, was an important episode. It throughly alarmed Czar Nicholas I (1825–1855), who now resolved to follow a severely autocratic policy. Although Nicholas dismissed the unpopular Arakcheev and put an end to the military colonies, he also had five of the Decembrists executed and exiled more than one hundred others to Siberia, where many of them contributed to the advance of local government and education. The Decembrists were the first in the long line of modern Russia's political martyrs, and the program of Pestel's Southern Society may now be seen as a kind of early blueprint for the revolutionary dictatorship that was to come to Russia as a consequence of the Bolshevik uprising of 1917.

IV The Revolutions of 1830
France

The next revolutionary wave—that of 1830—swept first over the traditional home of revolution, France. King Louis XVIII (1814–1824) had given the Bourbon restoration an ambiguous start. By personal inclination he would have preferred to be an absolute ruler, but he was sensible enough to know that a full return to the Old Regime was impractical, especially since he was declining in years and in health and suffered from the

"Liberty Guiding the People (July 28, 1830)": a painting by Delacroix.

additional political handicap of having been imposed on the French by their enemies.

The ambiguities of Louis XVIII's policies were evident in the constitutional charter that he issued in 1814, before the Hundred Days. Some sections sounded like the unreconstructed absolute monarchy of Louis XIV. The charter was "granted in the nineteenth year of our reign," and the preamble asserted the royal prerogative: "The authority in France resides in the person of the king." But the charter then proceeded to grant a measure of constitutional monarchy. There was a legislature, composed of a Chamber of Peers appointed by the king, and a Chamber of Deputies elected on a very restricted suffrage that allowed fewer than 100,000 of France's thirty million the right to vote. "In the king alone is vested the executive power," the charter stated, and the Chambers had no formal right to confirm the king's choices as ministers. Yet since Louis tended to select ministers acceptable to majority opinion in the legislature, this was a kind of backhanded parliamentary government. The charter confirmed many of the decisive changes instituted in France since 1789. It guaranteed religious toleration, a measure of freedom for the press, equality before the law, and equal eligibility to civil and military office; it likewise accepted the Code Napoléon and, still more important, the revolutionary property settlement.

The charter, however, greatly irritated the ultra-royalist faction, drawn from the noble and clerical émigrés, who had returned to France after their revolutionary exile. These Ultras, grouped around the king's brother and heir, the Count of Artois, were determined to recover both the privileges and the property they had lost during the Revolution. Louis XVIII held the Ultras at bay for five years. When the election of 1815 gave them control of the Chamber of Deputies, they proposed legislation to outlaw divorce and to institutionalize the "white terror" already launched by setting up special courts to deal with suspected revolutionaries. At the insistence of the allies, Louis XVIII dismissed the Chamber and held a new election, which returned a less fanatical majority. He chose moderate ministers who worked to pay off the indemnity to the victorious allies and, in general, to put French finances in good order.

Events, however, soon strengthened the Ultras' hand. Antirevolutionary fears swept France in the wake of the Spanish uprising of 1820 and of the assassination of the Duke of Berri, the king's nephew (February 1820), stabbed by a fanatic who hoped to extinguish the Bourbon line (the widowed duchess, however, gave birth to a son seven months later). The Ultras won control of the Chamber of Deputies, clamped controls on the press, and put through a law giving extra weight to the votes of the wealthiest 25 percent of the very restricted electorate. They also pressed Louis XVIII to appoint a reactionary ministry, which sent French troops to aid Ferdinand VII against the Spanish revolutionaries.

The tempo of the reaction quickened when Louis died and the Ultra leader, Artois, became King Charles X (1824–1830). Though a man of charm, Charles had little sense of political realities. He tried to revive some of the medieval glamor of monarchy by staging an elaborate coronation ceremony—and arranged a nine-month prison term for the witty poet who called it "the consecration of Charles the Simple." He greatly extended the influence of the Church by encouraging the activities of the Jesuits, who were still legally banned from France, and by appointing clerics as teachers and administrators in the state school system. He also sponsored a law of indemnification granting state annuities to the émigrés as compensation for their confiscated property. The measure could be defended as a sensible political move that lifted the last threat of confiscation from those who had acquired property during the Revolution. But it was widely, if inaccurately, believed that a concurrent reduction of the annual interest on government obligations from 5 to 3 percent was intended to defray the cost of the annuities. Many influential Parisian bourgeois were infuriated by the move as well as by the clericalism of the king.

The Ultras, therefore, lost ground in the elections of 1827, and Charles for a time endeavored to put up with a moderate ministry. But in 1829 he appointed as his chief minister the Prince of Polignac, an Ultra of Ultras, who claimed to have had visions in which the Virgin Mary promised him success. Polignac hoped to bolster the waning prestige of his monarch by scoring a resounding diplomatic victory. He therefore attacked the dey of Algiers (a largely independent vassal of the Ottoman emperor), who was notorious for his collusion with the hated Barbary pirates and who had insulted the French consul by striking him with a flywhisk. The capture of Algiers (July 5, 1830) laid the foundation of the French empire in North Africa. Meanwhile, the liberal majority in the Chamber of Deputies had attacked Polignac's ministry as unconstitutional because it did not command the confidence of the legislature. In the hope of securing a more tractable Chamber, Charles X arranged new elections for late June and early July; the opposition won. On July 25, 1830, without securing the legislature's approval Charles and Polignac issued ordinances muzzling the press, dissolving the newly elected Chamber, ordering a fresh election, and introducing new voting qualifications that would have disenfranchised the bourgeois who were the mainstay of the opposition. The king and his chief minister believed that public opinion, mollified by the recent victory at Algiers, would accept these July Ordinances calmly. They miscalculated utterly.

Aroused by the protests of liberal journalists, and encouraged by the hot summer weather, the Parisians staged a riot that became a revolution. During *les trois glorieuses* (the three glorious days of July 27, 28, and 29) they threw up barricades, captured the Paris city hall, and hoisted the tricolor atop Notre Dame. When Charles X saw the revolutionary flag through a spyglass from his suburban retreat, he arranged to abdicate on behalf of his grandson, the posthumous son of the Duke of Berri, and sailed to exile in England. Contrary to an impression often held, the July revolution was not bloodless: some 1,800 insurgents and 200 soldiers were slain.

Contrary to another widespread impression, the revolutionaries were not the poor and the downtrodden. Although there was unemployment, as a result of bank failures, and although poor harvests created high food prices, suffering remained in the background. The revolutionary rank and file in 1830 came mainly from the lower bourgeoisie and the skilled workers, whose numbers were increasing with the growth of industry in Paris. These were essentially the same social groups who had furnished the Vainqueurs de la Bastille in 1789. Revolutionary leadership came from the parliamentary opponents of Charles X and from cautious young liberals like Adolphe Thiers (1797–1877) and François Guizot (1787–1874), both destined to play important political roles in the future. Thiers edited the paper *Le National,* which spearheaded the opposition; he had also written a history of the great revolution to show that it had not been all bloodshed but had had a peaceful, constructive side. Guizot, too, had written history, a survey of civilization focused on the rise of the bourgeoisie, and he had been active in an organization called Aide-toi, le Ciel t'aidera! (heaven helps those who help themselves) instrumental in getting out the vote to defeat the Ultras in the elections of 1827 and 1830.

The revolutionaries of 1830, like those of 1789, were not agreed on the kind of regime they wanted. A minority would have liked a democratic republic with universal suffrage; they rallied around that venerable symbol of revolution, Lafayette, who was now in his seventies. But many others, who identified a republic with the Terror, wanted a safe and sane constitutional monarchy with a suffrage restricted to those with substantial wealth; for them France's 1830 should be the counterpart of England's 1688. The moderate leaders were Thiers, the banker Laffitte, and Talleyrand, who was also in his seventies but as astute as ever. The moderates had the money, they had the brains, and they had the support not only of the parliamentary opponents of Charles X but also of veteran Napoleonic officials, weary of languishing in the political wasteland. And they had the perfect candidate for the throne— Louis Philippe, the duke of Orléans.

Louis Philippe's father had participated in the Paris demonstrations of 1789, had assumed the revolutionary name of Philippe Egalité, and voted for the execution of Louis XVI, only to be guillotined during the Terror. Louis Philippe himself had fought in the revolutionary army at Valmy in 1792, then had emigrated in 1793 before the worst of the Terror. He claimed to have little use for the pomp of royalty and dressed and acted like a sober and well-to-do businessman. Having deceived the gullible Lafayette into thinking he was a republican, he accepted the crown

Louis Philippe crying at the funeral of Lafayette: the monarch sheds crocodile tears in this lithograph by Daumier.

at the invitation of the Chamber that had been elected in early July.

The Chamber also revised the Charter of 1814, which now allowed the legislature more initiative, deleted references to royal absolutism, and implied that the charter was not a grant by the monarch but a pact between him and the nation. Significantly, the revised charter called Louis Philippe not king of France but, following the precedent of 1791, king of the French. It also substituted the revolutionary tricolor for the white flag of the Bourbons. The suffrage, though doubled in size, was still highly restricted; in 1831 only 166,000 Frenchmen had the right to vote. The July Monarchy, as the new regime was termed, left France far short of realizing the democratic potential of liberty, equality, and fraternity. The 166,000 men who paid the minimum annual tax of 200 francs ($40) to qualify for the vote were divided between the business and professional men of the bourgeoisie and the large rural landowners. The France of Louis Philippe, rather like Whig Britain of the eighteenth century, functioned on the narrow social base of landed gentry and funded gentry.

Belgium

Within a month of the July uprising in Paris, a revolution began in Belgium. The union of Belgium and the Netherlands, decreed by the peacemakers of 1815, worked well only in economics. The commerce and colonies of Holland supplied raw materials and markets for the textile, glass, and other manufactures of Belgium, at that time the most advanced industrial area of the Continent. In the very sensitive areas of language,

politics, and religion, however, King William I of the Netherlands exerted arbitrary power where he might better have made tactful concessions. He made Dutch the official language throughout his realm, including the French-speaking Walloon provinces. He denied the pleas of Belgians to rectify the "Dutch arithmetic" that gave the Dutch provinces, with two million inhabitants, and the Belgian, with three and a half million, an equal number of seats in the States-General. He refused to grant special status to the Catholic church in Belgium and particularly offended the faithful by insisting that the education of priests be subject to state supervision. All these grievances tended to create a Belgian nationalism and to forge common bonds between the Catholic Dutch-speaking Flemings of the provinces north of Brussels and the Catholic French-speaking Walloons of the highly industrialized southern provinces. In later years, however, the Flemish-Walloon partnership was to be strained by differences in language and also by the divergence between the devout Flemings and the increasingly anticlerical Walloons, much influenced by the example of the French.

The revolution broke out in Brussels on August 25, 1830, at a performance of Auber's *La Muette de Portici*, an opera about a revolt in Naples. Headed by students, inspired by the example of Paris—and perhaps incited by French agents—the audience rioted against Dutch rule. By the end of September, Dutch troops had been driven out of Brussels, and Dutch rule was collapsing. The insurgents recruited their fighters chiefly from the industrial workers, many of whom complained of low pay and frequent unemployment. The better-organized middle-class leadership soon controlled the revolutionary movement and predominated in the Belgian national congress that convened in November 1830.

This congress proclaimed Belgium independent and made it a constitutional monarchy. The new constitution granted religious toleration, provided for wide local self-government, always a touchy issue in Flanders, and put rigorous limits on the king's authority. Although it did not establish universal suffrage, the financial qualifications for voting were lower in Belgium than they were at the time in Britain or France. When the congress chose as king the duke of Nemours, a son of Louis Philippe, the British protested vehemently at what appeared to them an effort to place Belgium within the French orbit. The congress then picked Leopold of Saxe-Coburg, a German princeling, the widowed son-in-law of George IV of Britain. Leopold was well fitted for the exacting role of a constitutional monarch in a brand-new kingdom. He had already shown his political shrewdness by refusing the shaky new throne of Greece; he now demonstrated it by marrying a daughter of Louis Philippe, thus mitigating French disappointment over the aborted candidacy of the duke of Nemours.

The Belgian revolution made the first permanent breach in the Vienna settlement. King William, stubborn as the proverbial Dutchman, tried to retake Belgium by force in 1831–1832. A French army and British fleet successfully defended the secessionists, and prolonged negotiations resulted in Dutch recognition of Belgium's new status in 1839. In 1839 also, representatives of Britain, France, Prussia, Austria, and Russia guaranteed both the independence and the neutrality of Belgium in a document that the German Empire was to term "a scrap of paper" when it invaded Belgium in 1914. In the 1830s Metternich and Czar Nicholas I of Russia were disturbed by Belgian independence but too distracted by revolutions on their own Italian and Polish doorsteps, respectively, to do very much about it.

Poland

The course of revolution in Poland contrasted tragically with that in Belgium. In 1815, the Kingdom of Poland possessed the most liberal constitution on the Continent; twenty years later, it had become a mere colony of the Russian Empire. The constitution given to the Poles by Czar Alexander I preserved the Code Napoléon and endowed the diet with limited legislative power. A hundred thousand Poles received the franchise, more than the total number of voters in the France of Louis XVIII, which had a population ten times greater. In practice, however, difficulties arose. Many of the men chosen for official posts in Poland were not acceptable to the Poles; indeed, one may doubt that any government imposed by Russia would have satisfied them. Censorship, unrest, and police intervention appeared during the last years of Alexander I.

The advent of the highly conservative Nicholas I in 1825 increased political friction, although the new czar at first abided by the Polish constitution. Meantime, romantic doctrines of nationalism made many converts at the universities of Warsaw and Vilna (in Lithuania). Polish nationalists demanded the transfer from Russia to Poland of provinces that had belonged to the prepartition Polish state—Lithuania, White Russia, and the Ukraine. Secret societies on the Carbonari model arose in these provinces and in the Kingdom of Poland.

A secret society of army cadets in Warsaw launched a revolution in November 1830. Leadership of the movement was assumed by Polish nobles, but they were at best reluctant revolutionaries who had no intention of emancipating the Polish peasants, so long the victims of oppressive landlords. This was a revolution for national independence, not for righting the wrongs of the Old Regime. Radicals in Warsaw and other cities disrupted the revolutionary government, which collapsed in September 1831. Polish misery was intensified by a terrible epidemic of cholera, the first outbreak of this Asian disease in Europe. Once the Russians were in control again, Nicholas I scrapped the Polish constitution, imposed a regime of martial law that was to continue for a quarter of a century, and closed the universities of Warsaw and Vilna, the chief

centers of Polish nationalist propaganda. To escape the vengeance of Nicholas, some revolutionaries fled the country, and Paris soon became the capital of these Polish exiles. Romantic tradition and Western sympathy for the underdog have often exaggerated the number of these expatriates, which was less than ten thousand.

Italy and Germany

In Italy and Germany the excitement of the July Revolution in Paris set off revolutionary fireworks that soon fizzled out. In 1831, Carbonari insurgents in north-central Italy briefly controlled the little duchies of Parma and Modena and a sizable part of the Papal States, including the city of Bologna. Among the participants was the youthful Louis Napoleon Bonaparte, nephew of Napoleon I, who was later to become Emperor Napoleon III. The revolutionaries counted on French assistance, but the July Monarchy had no intention of risking war with Austria by poaching on the Hapsburg preserve. Again, as in 1821, Metternich sent troops to restore legitimacy in Italy.

Metternich did not require soldiers to preserve legitimacy in Germany; whenever a crisis arose, the Diet of the German Confederation obediently followed the Austrian lead. In Prussia, King Frederick William III (1797–1840) had never fulfilled his promise to grant a constitution, though he did set up provincial diets. Only Weimar and a few south German states enjoyed liberal constitutions, on the order of the French Charter of 1814. Political agitation came almost entirely from the small minority of intellectuals who had roused national resistance to Napoleon—journalists, romantic writers, university professors, and students.

After 1815, German university students formed a new organization, the Burschenschaft (Students' Union). In October 1817 students of the University of Jena held a rally on the Wartburg, where Luther had worked on his German translation of the Bible, to celebrate both the tercentenary of the Ninety-Five Theses and the fourth anniversary of the battle of Leipzig. During the rally the Burschenschaft burned a diplomat's wig, a Prussian officer's corset, and books by reactionary writers. In March 1819 one of the writers, Kotzebue, who was also a Russian agent, was assassinated by a demented theological student. Metternich, already alarmed by the student prank of 1817, now got the Diet of the German Confederation to approve the Carlsbad Decrees (September 1819), which stiffened press censorship, dissolved the Burschenschaft, and curtailed academic freedom.

Despite the Carlsbad Decrees, mild political ferment continued in Germany, and the Burschenschaft reorganized underground. In 1830 and the years following, a few rulers in northern Germany, notably in Saxony and Hanover, were forced to grant constitutions. Excited by these minor successes, and by the appearance of Polish refugees, thirty thousand revolutionary sympathizers, including many students from Heidelberg and other universities in the region, gathered at Hambach in the Palatinate in May 1832. There they toasted Lafayette and demanded the union of the German states under a democratic republic. Effective action toward unification was another matter. In 1833 some fifty instructors and students tried to seize Frankfurt, the capital of the German Confederation and seat of its Diet. The insurgents, together with hundreds of other students accused of Burschenschaft activities, were given harsh sentences by courts in Prussia and other German states.

The Lessons of 1830

The revolutionary wave of the 1830s revealed two great facts of political life. First, it widened the split between the West and the East already evident in the wake of the revolutions of 1820. Britain and France were committed to support cautiously liberal constitutional monarchies both at home and in neighboring Belgium. On the other hand, Russia, Austria, and Prussia were more firmly committed than ever to the counterrevolutionary principles of the Troppau Protocol. In 1833, Czar Nicholas I, Metternich, and King Frederick William III formally pledged their joint assistance to any sovereign threatened by revolution, though they were unable to help King William of the Netherlands.

Second, revolution succeeded in 1830 only in France and Belgium, only where it enlisted the support of a substantial segment of the population, thanks in part to the dislocations caused by the Industrial Revolution. It failed in every country where the revolutionaries represented only a fraction of the people. In Poland, the reactionary social policies of aristocratic nationalist leaders alienated them from the peasants. Italian revolutionaries still relied on their romantic Carbonari tradition and on flimsy hopes of foreign aid. In Germany, revolution was a matter of student out-

bursts, toasts to Lafayette, and other gestures by a small minority. Conspirators and intellectuals needed to make their doctrines penetrate to the grass roots of society; they needed to develop able political leaders and to mature well-laid plans for political reform. These were the tasks which they undertook after 1830; their success was to be tested in the most formidable and the most extensive chain of political uprisings in the history of nineteenth-century Europe—the revolutions of 1848.

V The Revolutions of 1848

Nationalism was a common denominator of several revolutions in 1848. It prompted the disunited Germans and Italians to attempt political unification, and it inspired the subject peoples of the Hapsburg Empire to seek political and cultural autonomy. The French Revolutionary and Napoleonic upheavals together with the romantic movement had stimulated a nationalistic renaissance among most peoples in central and eastern Europe. For the national minorities within the Hapsburg Empire, as for the Christian nationalities within the Ottoman Empire, the new nationalism tended to be focused on language. The Czech language, for example, was on the verge of extinction in the later eighteenth century; the population of Bohemia increasingly used the German of their Austrian rulers. By 1848, however, a Czech linguistic and literary revival was in full swing. Patriotic histories of Bohemia and collections of Czech folk poetry kindled a lively interest in the national past and fostered dreams of a Pan-Slavic awakening in which the Czechs would lead their brother Slavs.

The nationalists of 1848 did not necessarily preach the brotherhood of man. Although some of them agreed with Mazzini, the democratic Italian patriot, that each nation's "special mission" fulfilled the "general mission of humanity," others held less generous views. John Stuart Mill, the English liberal observer, deplored those who ignored the welfare "of any portion of the human species, save that which is called by the same name and speaks the same language as themselves." * There were many self-styled Chosen People in the revolutions of 1848.

Liberalism, the second common denominator of the revolutions, also encompassed a wide range of programs. In central and eastern Europe, where much of the Old Regime survived, liberals demanded constitutions to limit absolute monarchy and to liquidate feudal rights and manorial dues. In France, which already had a constitutional monarchy, many liberals sought to replace the July Monarchy with a democratic republic. But what did they mean by "democratic?" For some, democracy meant that every man should

"Behind the Barricade": wood engraving depicting the Revolution of 1848 in France, from a contemporary English newspaper.

*J. S. Mill, "The French Revolution and Its Assailants," *Westminster Review*, II (1849), 17.

have not only the right to vote but also the "right to work," a phrase that implied the need for government action to do something about unemployment and other social ills aggravated by the alternating prosperity and depression of this early period of industrial growth.

In the Europe of 1848, as in the France of 1789, an economic crisis helped to catalyze discontent into revolution. A blight ruined the Irish potato crop in 1845 and soon spread to the Continent; the grain harvest of 1846 also failed in western Europe. The consequences were a sharp rise in the price of bread and resulting bread riots; mass starvation occurred in Ireland, and widespread misery affected France, Germany, and Austria. The food crisis was compounded by an industrial depression, touched off in 1847 by the collapse of a boom in railroad construction. The number of unemployed mounted just as food prices were rising, thus intensifying popular suffering.

France

The economic crisis hit France with particular severity. Railroad construction almost ceased, throwing more than half a million out of work; coal mines and iron foundries, in turn, laid men off. Unemployment increased the discontent of French workers already embittered by their low wages and by the still lower esteem in which they were held by the government of Louis Philippe. Under the July Monarchy, French agriculture experienced a golden age, at the same time that industrialization was beginning to develop. The government, however, appeared to be indifferent to the social misery that accompanied the new prosperity. In eighteen years, it took only two steps to improve the welfare of the industrial working class: an extension of state aid to primary schools in 1833 and a laxly enforced law in 1841 limiting child labor. There was a great deal of truth in the famous judgment passed by Alexis de Tocqueville, himself a member of the Chamber, that "Government in those days resembled an industrial company whose every operation is undertaken for the profits which the stockholders may gain thereby."

The "stockholders" of the July Monarchy were the Napoleonic veterans who emerged as prefects and diplomats after a wholesale overturn of official personnel, and the social and economic elite who had the right to vote. Demands for liberalization of the suffrage were met with Guizot's injunction: *Enrichissez-vous!*—make yourself rich enough to meet the stiff fiscal qualifications for voting. The government banned labor organizations and repressed harshly the workmen of Paris and Lyons who demonstrated in the early 1830s to demand a republic and higher wages. The symbol of this repression was the massacre of the rue Transnonain (April 1834), when soldiers killed fourteen residents of a Paris house thought to be harboring a sniper. The press mercilessly caricatured the pear-shaped head, obese figure, and inevitable umbrella of Louis Philippe, until censorship was imposed.

Opposition to the July Monarchy, though stifled in the 1830s, revived during the next decade. It was nourished in part by the humiliation suffered by France when international pressure forced her withdrawal of support from the empire-building of her protégé, the ambitious Egyptian governor Muhammad Ali. The opposition, however, was far from united—a fact that goes far to explain the erratic course of the revolution it set off. Heading what might be termed the official or loyal opposition was Adolphe Thiers, identified with the July Monarchy from its beginning, but a victim of the collapse of France's Egyptian venture. Shelved by Louis Philippe in favor of Guizot, the chief minister from 1840 until 1848, Thiers continued to support the principle of constitutional monarchy. Cynics claim that the chief difference between him and Guizot was the fact that he was out of office while Guizot was in.

The republicans formed a second opposition group, which increased in numbers with the growing political awareness and literacy of the working classes (in 1847 two out of three men mustered into the army could read). The third, and smallest, group took in the exponents of various doctrines of socialism, which the next chapter examines in more detail; the socialists gained recruits from the economic depression of the late 1840s, and their influence is reflected in the slogan, the "right to work." Potentially more formidable than any of these, but as yet representing only a vague, unorganized sentiment, were the Bonapartists. The return of the emperor's remains from St. Helena to Paris in 1840, arranged by Thiers as an expedient to improve the image of a sagging regime, revived and renewed the legend of a glorious and warlike Napoleon, so different from the uninspiring Louis Philippe.

In the summer of 1847, constitutional monarchists of the Thiers faction joined with republicans to stage a series of political banquets throughout France calling for an extension of the suffrage and the resignation of Guizot. This campaign appeared comparatively harmless until a particularly huge banquet was announced for February 22, 1848, to be held in Paris. When the Guizot ministry forbade the banquet, the Parisians substituted a large demonstration. On February 23, Louis Philippe dismissed Guizot and prepared to summon Thiers to the ministry. But his concessions came too late. Supported by workers, students, and the more radical republican leaders, the demonstration of February 22 turned into a riot on the 23rd, in which more than fifty of the rioters were killed or wounded. The number of casualties intensified the revolutionary atmosphere, barricades were thrown up, and Thiers was so unnerved he made no attempt to form a ministry.

On the next day, February 24, 1848, Louis Philippe abdicated, and the Chamber set up a provisional government headed by an eloquent but cautious advocate of a republic, the romantic poet Lamartine. Popular unrest, mounting along with unemployment (more than half the work force in some trades had been laid off), virtually obliged the provisional government to take in a few socialists. Notable among these was Louis Blanc (1811–1882), an advocate of social workshops, which the workers themselves would own and run with the financial assistance of the state. As a gesture toward the "right to work," and also as a measure to restore calm in Paris, the provisional government authorized the establishment of national workshops in the capital. These national workshops, however, were not a genuine attempt to implement the blueprint of Louis Blanc but a relief project organized along semimilitary lines, and enrolling more than a hundred thousand unemployed persons from Paris and the provinces. About ten thousand of the recruits received two francs (about 40 cents) a day for working on municipal improvements; the rest did no work and received a dole of one franc a day. Meantime, the provisional government was also trying to discount the international repercussions of flamboyant promises by left-wing politicians to the effect that a democratic and republican France would help to liberate the other peoples of Europe. Lamartine was particularly concerned to reassure Britain that, while French words might be bellicose, French actions would be moderate.

The future shape of France now hinged on the outcome of the elections of April 23, 1848, when all adult males—nine million as opposed to a quarter of a million in the last days of the July Monarchy—would be qualified to vote for the National Assembly, which would draw up a constitution for the Second French Republic. (The First Republic had lasted from September 1792 down to Napoleon's coronation in 1804; the second had existed in fact, if not formally, since Louis Philippe's abdication on February 24.) In this momentous election—the first in European history when there was real universal manhood suffrage—eight million Frenchmen went to the polls, 84 percent of the potential electorate. The conservative peasants, who still made up the bulk of the population, approved the fall of the July Monarchy but dreaded anything resembling an attack on private property. Of the almost 900 deputies elected, therefore, most were either monarchists or conservative republicans; only a hundred or so sympathized with the Paris radicals.

The latter, however, refused to accept the decision of the country. On May 15, a huge crowd of noisy but unarmed demonstrators invaded the National Assembly and proposed its dissolution and the formation of a new provisional government at the Paris City Hall. The moderates, now thoroughly alarmed, arrested radical leaders and decided that the national workshops threatened law and order because they had attracted so many economically desperate men to Paris. The Assembly decreed the orderly closing of the workshops, with their recruits given the alternatives of enlistment in the army or accepting work in the provinces. The poor districts of the capital responded by rising in insurrection, from June 23 to June 26, 1848, when they were subdued by the troops brought in by General Cavaignac, the energetic minister of war.

These June Days were a landmark in modern history, the first large-scale outbreak with overtones of class warfare which have become exaggerated in later socialist tradition. Most of the insurgents seem to have come not from members of the national workshops, who still received their dole, but from the unemployed who had tried vainly to enroll in the workshops and were now at the end of their tether, motivated more by desperation than by any hope of attaining a socialist millennium. Among them were men of the new industrial age—mechanics, railroad men, stevedores—as well as winesellers, masons, locksmiths, cabinetmakers, and other craftsmen of the type who had been prominent in the capture of the Bastille in 1789. The prospect of a social revolution, though it may have been remote as a practical matter, terrified the propertied classes, and Tocqueville reported that "peasants, shopkeepers, landowners, and nobles" were all pouring into Paris by the new railroads to quell the uprising. The spirit of panic accounted for the severe repression: about ten thousand were killed or wounded, and about the same number were subsequently deported, chiefly to Algeria. All socialist clubs and newspapers were padlocked, and Louis Blanc fled to England. France became a virtual military dictatorship under General Cavaignac.

The fears of the moderates were evident in the constitution of the Second French Republic which the National Assembly completed in November 1848. The Assembly declared property inviolable and rejected a motion to list the right to work among the fundamental rights of French citizens. In other respects the constitution seemed to be a daring venture in representative democracy and in experimenting with the combination of a strong president and a powerful legislature. The president was to be chosen by popular election every four years, and the legislature, a single chamber, was to be elected every three years. Perhaps the venture was not quite so daring as it seemed, since the universal male suffrage it provided had already shown in the elections of 1848 that it could enable conservatives to outvote radicals.

Circumstances did not favor the success of the now formally constituted Second Republic. The military rule exercised by Cavaignac while the Assembly was drafting the constitution was one ominous sign. Another was the outcome of the presidential election in December 1848, in which fewer than half a million votes were polled by the three genuinely republican candidates, a million and a half were cast for General Cavaignac, and some five and a half million votes and the presidency of the republic went to Louis Napoleon Bonaparte (1808–1873). This nephew of the great Napoleon, the son of his troublesome brother Louis, was not a prepossessing figure. He spoke haltingly in heavily accented French, the result of his boyhood exile in the Germanic part of Switzerland, and he was known for his association with disreputable people and ill-conceived projects. Yet he had the enormous asset of bearing the magical Bonaparte name and tapping all the accumulated glamor of the Napoleonic legend. In 1848 he staged a clever campaign to identify himself with the cause of order and stability—for example, volunteering to serve as a constable in London during the spring when a mass demonstration was anticipated. Back in France, he contested and won several by-elections to fill vacancies in the National Assembly, where he took his seat in September. In domestic politics, as a later chapter will show, he proved a true successor of his uncle, subverting the constitution of the Second Republic in a coup d'état late in 1851 and proclaiming himself Emperor Napoleon III a year later. The French Revolution of 1848, like that of 1789, had established a republic that ended in a Napoleonic empire.

Italy

In Italy, where the youthful Louis Napoleon had taken part in the mini-revolution of 1831, new reform movements now supplanted the discredited Carbonari. By the 1840s three movements were competing for the leadership of Italian nationalism; their rivalry and the fact that none of them commanded wide popular allegiance did not augur well for the success of an Italian revolution. Two of the reforming groups were moderate, agreeing that political power in an Italy emancipated from Hapsburg control should be limited to the nobility and the bourgeoisie, but at odds over the form that a united Italian nation should assume. One group, based in the north, favored the domination of Piedmont; its leader was the eventual unifier of Italy, Count Cavour, who was a great admirer of British and French liberal ways. Cavour was the editor of an influential newspaper in Turin, the capital of Piedmont—*Il Risorgimento* ("resurgence" or "regeneration"), which gave its name to the whole process of unification. The other moderate group called themselves Neo-Guelfs because, like the Guelf political faction of the Middle Ages, they hoped to engage the pope in the task of freeing Italy from the control of a German emperor. The Neo-Guelf leader, the priest Gioberti, declared that the future depended on "the union of Rome and Turin." The pope would head, and the army of Piedmont would defend, a federation of Italian states, each with its monarch and its cautiously liberal constitution.

The third group of liberals, Young Italy, so named because only those under the age of forty were eligible for membership, asserted that Italy should be unified as a democratic republic. Its founder, Mazzini (1805–1872), hoped to create an organization more effective than the Carbonari but was frustrated by his own prolonged exile and by the frequent ineptitude of his lieutenants. Nevertheless, Mazzini did win an enduring reputation as the great democratic idealist of modern Italian politics. Here is a statement of his political credo:

We believe, therefore, in the Holy Alliance of the Peoples

Portrait of Napoleon III by Chappel.

as being the vastest formula of association possible in our epoch;—in the *liberty* and *equality* of the peoples, without which no true association can exist;—in *nationality,* which is the *conscience* of the peoples, and which, by assigning to them their part in the work of association, . . . constitutes their mission upon earth, that is to say, their *individuality,* without which neither liberty nor equality are possible;—in the sacred *Fatherland,* cradle of nationality; altar and workshop of the individuals of which each nation is composed.*

A good European as well as an ardent Italian nationalist, Mazzini inspired the formation of Young Germany, Young Poland, and similar movements, all joined together in a federation called Young Europe.

The prospects for reform in Italy brightened a little in the years immediately preceding 1848. In 1846, a new pope was elected, Pio Nono (Pius IX, 1846–1878), whose initial progressive actions, like the release of political prisoners and some rather haphazard steps to modernize the antiquated administrative machinery of the Papal States, aroused great expectations of a thorough liberalization of papal government. In the next year, King Charles Albert of Piedmont relaxed the traditionally tight censorship of a conservative monarchy sufficiently to permit *Il Risorgimento* to publicize

*"Faith and the Future," in *Life and Writings of Joseph Mazzini* (London, 1905), 3:129.

Cavour's program for economic and political improvements.

Actual revolution occurred in Italy before it did in Paris. In January 1848, an uprising in the Two Sicilies forced King Ferdinand II to grant a constitution on the pattern of the French Charter of 1814, as revised by the July Monarchy; in mid-February, the Grand Duke of Tuscany was forced to follow suit. News of the rising in Paris quickened the pace of the Italian revolutions, as Charles Albert of Piedmont (March 5) and Pius IX (March 15) agreed to become constitutional rulers in the manner of Louis Philippe. Next came the turn of Lombardy and Venetia, where Hapsburg rule had been relatively mild but where the ideas of Young Italy had inspired revolutionary movements. Ever since January 1, 1848, citizens of Milan, the capital of Lombardy, had been boycotting cigars as a protest against the Austrian tax on tobacco—a maneuver suggested by a professor's lecture on the Boston tea party; severe rioting resulted. News of a revolution in Vienna and the departure of Metternich (March 12–13) touched off five days of heavy fighting in Milan (March 18–22) which forced the Austrians to withdraw their forces. The Milanese improvised some extraordinary barricades, utilizing pianos, sentry boxes, and omnibuses in addition to the usual paving blocks. At the same time, Venice, the capital of Austria's other Italian province, proclaimed herself the independent Republic of St. Mark.

The rapid collapse of Hapsburg rule in Lombardy-Venetia inspired a national crusade against the Austrians. Charles Albert of Piedmont assumed command of the Italian forces, which included contingents from Naples, Tuscany, and even the Papal States. He refused an offer of help from the provisional government of the French republic with the ill-fated prediction, *Italia farà da se* ("Italy will do it alone"). For the moment it seemed possible that the Piedmontese and Neo-Guelf forces would unite to assure the victory of both nationalism and moderate liberalism in Italy.

But only for the moment. During the spring and early summer of 1848, Piedmont annexed Lombardy and the two small north Italian duchies of Parma and Modena. The other Italian states, jealous of their particularist traditions, commenced to fear the imperialism of Piedmont more than they desired the unification of Italy. On April 29, 1848, Pius IX announced that his "equal affection" for all peoples obliged him to adopt a neutral position in the war with Austria and to recall his soldiers. The pope could not act both as an Italian patriot and as an international spiritual leader. Moreover, Pius was alarmed by the threats of Austrian and German bishops to create an anti-pope and by the increasingly radical political temper of the Roman population. The Neo-Guelf cause had received a fatal blow. In the Two Sicilies, the king scrapped the constitution and followed the papal example in withdrawing his contingents from the war (May 1848). The Austrians, taking the offensive, reconquered Lombardy and crushed the forces of Charles Albert at Custozza (July 1848). Italy had not been able to do it alone.

A few months later, the revolutionary movement got a brief second wind. In Rome, adherents of Young Italy, dissatisfied with the constitution of March, rose up in November 1848. After Pius IX fled to Neapolitan territory early in the next year, they transformed the Papal States into a democratic Roman Republic, headed by Mazzini himself, who proved to be rather authoritarian in a position of power. In March 1849 radicals in Piedmont forced the reluctant Charles Albert to renew the war with Austria, but within the month Austria again prevailed, at the battle of Novara. In August 1849 the Austrians put an end to the Republic of St. Mark after a prolonged siege and bombardment of Venice, which suffered acutely from famine and cholera. Meanwhile (July 1849), Mazzini's Roman Republic had surrendered to French troops sent by President Bonaparte in a bid for Catholic gratitude.

Except for the French garrison stationed in Rome, Italy returned almost completely to its prerevolutionary status, again subdivided into many sovereign units, again dominated by the Hapsburgs. Both the Neo-Guelfs and Young Italy were discredited. The only bright spot in the picture was the emergence of Piedmont as the natural leader of Italian nationalism and liberalism. Despite the defeats at Custozza and Novara, despite the loss of the territories momentarily annexed in 1848, Piedmont enjoyed the prestige of having twice defied the hated Austrians. Moreover, it was also the only Italian state to retain the constitution granted in 1848. When Charles Albert, whose enthusiasm for change was tepid, abdicated to retire to a monastery after the defeat of Novara, the crown passed to Victor Emmanuel II, who was to have the distinction of becoming the first king of modern Italy.

Germany

The course of the German revolutions in 1848 roughly paralleled that of the Italian. In Germany, too, liberalism and nationalism won initial victories and then collapsed in the face of internal dissension and Austrian resistance. The failure in Germany was the more surprising—and ominous—since the revolutionary movement had begun to recruit support at the grass roots among industrial workers, craftsmen fearing industrial competition, and peasants seeking to abolish the relics of manorialism. Liberal and nationalist agitation, however, was centered in the well-to-do business and professional classes, especially university professors, who enjoyed more influence and respect in Germany than anywhere else in Europe. Except for a few republicans and socialists, the German liberals were moderates. They wanted constitutional monarchies in the various German states, the strengthening of the German Confederation, and an end to the repressive hegemony of Metternich.

The hero of German liberals was King Frederick

William IV of Prussia (1840–1861). Attractive and cultivated, but unstable and infatuated with romantic concepts of divine-right kingship, Frederick William promised much and delivered little. He promised to carry out his father's unhonored pledge to give Prussia a constitution and an elected assembly; however, the meeting of representatives from the provincial diets he convoked at last in 1847 was a great disappointment.

Not this royal knight-errant, but the architects of the Zollverein (customs union) constituted Prussia's most solid contribution to German unification before 1848. In 1818, Prussia had abolished internal tariffs within its scattered territories and applied a uniform tariff schedule to imports. The first states to join the Zollverein were small neighbors of Prussia, already surrounded by her territories. Membership proved so profitable that by 1844 almost all the German states, except Austria, had joined. The Zollverein liberated Germany from an oppressive burden of local tolls and taxes and cleared the way for her phenomenal economic development later in the century. Although it did not exercise a decisive influence on politics, it suggested that the state which had fostered German economic unification might naturally take the initiative in political unification.

Unification seemed almost a certainty in 1848. Stimulated by the example of Paris, the revolutionaries scored their first successes in the western German states early in March. From there, the demands for the granting of constitutions and civil liberties, the suppression of feudal and manorial remnants, and the strengthening of the German Confederation fanned out rapidly. By mid-March most of the rulers of the smaller German states had yielded to the pressure, and in the Prussian capital demonstrators were erecting barricades. Frederick William IV accepted some of the liberals' demands and appealed for calm in Berlin; but before his appeal could be publicized, rioting broke out with redoubled violence, and more than two hundred rioters, chiefly workingmen, were killed. The mob broke into the royal palace and forced the king to go through a grotesque ceremony of saluting the corpses of the victims. Overwrought by the humiliation to himself and by the death of his subjects, Frederick William accepted all the demands of liberals and nationalists. He summoned an assembly to draw up a constitution, declared Prussia "merged in Germany," and proclaimed himself "king of the free regenerated German nation."

Drastic reform of the German Confederation now

"Storming the Arsenal": revolutionary outbreaks in Berlin 1848: wood engraving from an English newspaper.

began. In May 1848 a constitutional convention held its first session in the Church of St. Paul at Frankfurt, the capital of the confederation. Its 830 members were elected throughout Germany but often by electoral colleges and with suffrage restrictions that made the results fall short of being a true popular mandate. The members did represent the flower of the German intelligentsia—18 doctors, 33 clergymen, 49 university professors, 57 schoolteachers, 223 lawyers and judges. While some 140 deputies could be placed in the loose category of businessmen, there were only four artisans and a single dirt farmer. The Frankfurt Assembly lacked a broad popular base, and, as events soon demonstrated, many of its members also lacked political experience and talent for practical statesmanship.

The Frankfurt Assembly had to decide the geographical limits of Germany. The confederation included Austria proper but excluded most of the non-German Hapsburg territories. Neither did it include the eastern provinces of Prussia, notably those acquired in the partitions of Poland. The Austrian issue divided the assembly into two camps: the "Big Germans" who favored the inclusion of Austria and of Bohemia, with its large Czech population, in the projected German state, and the "Little Germans," who opposed the idea. Austrian objections to a "Big Germany" ensured the assembly's adoption of the "Little Germany" proposal.

On the question of Prussian Poland, the nationalism of the Frankfurt Assembly overcame its liberalism. By a large majority it voted to include some Prussian areas in which the Poles formed the majority of the population. The arguments advanced against the Poles in the debates revealed German nationalism at its most superheated. One orator declared that the minority of Germans had a natural right to rule the Poles, who had "less cultural content":

> It is high time for us . . . to wake to a wholesome national egotism, to say the word right out for once, which in every question places the welfare and honour of the fatherland uppermost. . . . Our right is none other than the right of the stronger, the right of conquest.*

In contrast, the national constitution promulgated by the Frankfurt Assembly in March 1849 was a decidedly liberal document, a combination of principles drawn from the American federal system and British parliamentary practice. The individual states were to surrender many of their powers to the German federal government. The federal legislature would consist of a lower house, elected by universal male suffrage, and an upper house, chosen by the governments and the legislatures of the constituent states. Ministers responsible to the legislature would form the federal executive.

*Quoted in J. G. Legge, *Rhyme and Revolution in Germany* (London, 1918), p. 397.

Over all would preside a constitutional monarch, the German emperor.

The Frankfurt constitution died aborning. The assembly elected the king of Prussia to be emperor, but Frederick William, ignoring his fine promises of March 1848 and alarmed by Austrian opposition, rejected the offer. He called the Frankfurt constitution a "bastard" product:

> The crown is no crown. The crown which a Hohenzollern could accept . . . is not one created by an Assembly born of revolutionary seed. . . . It must be a crown set with the seal of the Almighty. . . .*

Since the major candidate for the imperial office had balked, the Frankfurt Assembly soon came to an end. It had never secured recognition from foreign governments, had never raised a penny in taxes, and had never exerted real sovereignty over Germany. The couplet mocking the plethora of academic deputies, though it exaggerated their numbers, had been justified:

> *Hundert fünfzig Professoren!*
> *Lieber Gott, wir sind verloren!*
> [*A hundred and fifty professors!*
> *Good God, we're sunk!*]

German liberalism had suffered a major defeat. After the initial shock of the revolutions, the comfortably situated professional and business classes began to fear the radicalism of the workers and artisans. The German princes soon either revoked or abridged the constitutions that they had granted in 1848. In Prussia, Frederick William and his conservative advisers repeatedly doctored the work of the constitutional assembly summoned in 1848. The end product, the Constitution of 1850, as a later chapter shows, made Prussia relatively safe for autocracy and aristocracy down to World War I.

The Hapsburg Domains

The fate of German and Italian nationalism in 1848 hinged partly on the outcome of the revolutions in the Hapsburg Empire. If these revolutions had immobilized the Hapsburg government for a long period, then Italian and German unification might have been realized. But Austria, though buffeted by wave after wave of revolution, rode out the storm. The success of the counterrevolution in the Hapsburg Empire assured its victory in Italy and Germany.

The nature and the outcome of the Hapsburg revolutions depended in turn on the complex structure of nationalities within the Austrian Empire. Here are the nationalities under Hapsburg rule in 1848:

*Ibid., pp. 516–517.

Nationality	Percentage of Total Population
German	23
Magyar (Hungarian)	14
Czech and Slovak	19
South (Yugo-) Slav	
Slovene	4
Croat	4
Serb	5
Pole	7
Ruthenian (Little Russian)	8
Romanian	8
Italian	8

These national groups were not always neatly segregated geographically, each in its own compartment. For instance, in the Hungarian part of the empire, which had important minorities of Slovaks, Romanians, Serbs, Croats, and Germans, the dominant Magyars fell just short of a numerical majority. Throughout the empire, moreover, the German element, chiefly bureaucrats and tradesmen, predominated in most of the towns and cities, even in the Czech capital of Prague and the Magyar capital of Budapest.

Among the component peoples of the Hapsburg realm in 1848, nationalism ran strongest among the Italians of Lombardy-Venetia, the Czechs of Bohemia, and the Magyars and Croats of Hungary. Language was an important issue with the Magyars as it was with Czechs; the replacement of Latin by Hungarian as the official tongue of the eastern part of the empire in 1844 marked a victory for Magyar nationalism. Since Hungary was overwhelmingly an agricultural land, nationalism, like all other aspects of political life, was dominated by nobles and country squires who monopolized the seats in the county assemblies and the central diet. One group of Magyar nationalists aimed at the gradual modernization of Hungary's culture and economy along moderate English lines. A more extreme group, whose spokesman was the spell-binding orator Louis Kossuth (an ardent nationalist, though he was of Slovak rather than Magyar background), regarded the linguistic reform of 1844 as but the first in a series of revolutionary projects cutting all ties with the Vienna government. Magyar nationalists bitterly opposed the satisfaction of the growing national aspirations of their Slavic subjects. The most discontented were the Croats, whose national awakening had begun when their homeland was absorbed into the Illyrian provinces of Napoleon's empire.

The antagonism between Croats and Magyars revealed an all-important fact about the nationalistic movements within the Hapsburg Empire. Some groups—Italians, Magyars, Czechs, Poles—resented the German-dominated government in Vienna. Others, notably the Croats and Romanians, were not so much anti-German as anti-Magyar. Here was a situation where the central government in Vienna might apply the policy of "divide and conquer," pitting the anti-Magyar elements against the anti-German Magyars, and subduing both. This was substantially what happened in 1848. A similar policy had already been used in 1846 to suppress a revolt in Galicia, the province that Austria had acquired in the partitions of Poland. When the Polish landlords revolted, their exploited Ruthenian peasants rose against them and received the backing of Vienna.

Liberalism also played a significant part in the Hapsburg revolutions, especially in Austria proper. The expanding middle class desired civil liberties, a voice in government, and the lifting of mercantilist restrictions on business. In Vienna, as in Paris and Berlin, some workers went further and demanded radical democratic reforms.

From 1815 to 1848, the Hapsburg government virtually ignored the grumblings and protests that arose in almost every quarter of the empire. If Prince Metternich had had his way, he would probably have made some concessions to liberal and nationalist aspirations. But Metternich, though he enjoyed a nearly free hand in foreign affairs, did not have his way in domestic policy. He was blocked by the emperors—the bureaucratic Francis I (1792–1835) and the feeble-minded Ferdinand I (1835–1848)—and by the vested interests of the aristocracy. The Hapsburg government, though buttressed by an army of censors and spies, was at best an inefficient autocracy; Austria, Metternich accurately stated, was "administered, but not ruled."

The news of the February revolution in Paris shook the empire to its foundations. Four separate revolutions broke out almost simultaneously in March 1848—in Milan and Venice, in Hungary, in Vienna itself, and in Bohemia. In Hungary, Kossuth and his ardent Magyar supporters forced Emperor Ferdinand to accept the March Laws, which gave Hungary political autonomy. The March Laws instituted parliamentary government and substituted an elected legislature for the feudal Hungarian diet. They abolished serfdom and ended the immunity of nobles and gentry from taxation. But they rode roughshod over the rights of non-Magyars by making use of the Hungarian language a requirement for election as a deputy to the legislature.

Aroused by the Hungarian revolt, university students, together with workingmen dismayed by growing unemployment, rose in Vienna on March 12. On the next day, Prince Metternich resigned from the post he had held for thirty-nine years and fled to Britain. Although the imperial government repeatedly promised reforms, the constitution it granted seemed a half-measure at best to the Viennese insurgents. Rioting continued in Vienna, and by May the political atmosphere was so charged that Emperor Ferdinand and his family left the capital for Innsbruck in the Tyrol. Pending the meeting of a constituent assembly in July, a revolutionary council ran affairs in Vienna.

Meanwhile, in Prague, Czech nationalists were demanding rights similar to those granted the Magyars in the March Laws. Discontent mounted with the news that the "Big German" faction in the Frankfurt Assembly was contemplating the inclusion of Bohemia in a German federation. In June 1848 the Czechs organized a Pan-Slav Congress to promote the solidarity of Slavic peoples against "Big German" encroachments. The Pan-Slav Congress set off demonstrations, in the course of which the wife of Prince Windischgrätz, the commander of the Austrian garrison of Prague, was accidentally killed (June 12, 1848). Five days later, Windischgrätz, after bombarding Prague, dispersed the Czech revolutionaries and established a military regime in Bohemia. The counterrevolution was beginning.

In July, the Austrian forces in Italy defeated Piedmont at Custozza. In September the Vienna Constituent Assembly, which represented all the provinces of the empire except the Italian and Hungarian, passed a great reform measure that actually accelerated the counterrevolution. It emancipated the peasants from their last remaining servile obligations, notably the requirement to work for their landlords. The peasants, the core of the Hapsburg population, had achieved their main goal; they now tended to withhold support from further revolutionary activities.

The time was ripe for the policy of "divide and conquer." In Hungary, the Germans, Slovaks, Romanians, Serbs, and Croats, all outraged by the discrimination against them in the March Laws, had risen up against the Magyars. In September 1848 the imperial government authorized Jellachich, the governor of Croatia, to invade central Hungary. While the hard-fighting Magyars held off the forces of Jellachich, the radicals of Vienna revolted again, proclaiming their support of the Magyars and declaring Austria a democratic republic. But the armies of Jellachich and Windischgrätz crushed the Vienna revolution (October 31, 1848) and executed the radical leaders.

The counterrevolution was hitting its full stride. In November 1848 the energetic and unscrupulous prince Felix Schwarzenberg, the brother-in-law of Windischgrätz, became chief minister of the Hapsburg government. Schwarzenberg arranged the abdication of the incapable Ferdinand I in December and the accession of Ferdinand's eighteen-year-old nephew, the emperor Francis Joseph (1848–1916). Schwarzenberg declared that the promises made by the old emperor could not legally bind his successor and therefore shelved the projects of the Austrian Constitutent Assembly, though he honored the assembly's emancipation of the peasantry. Schwarzenberg's high-handedness infuriated the Magyars, who fought on like tigers. In April 1849 the Parliament of Hungary declared the country an independent republic and named Kossuth its chief executive. Russia now offered Austria military assistance, for Czar Nicholas I feared that the revolutionary contagion might spread to Russian Poland unless it was checked. Schwarzenberg accepted the czar's offer, and in August 1849 Russian troops helped to subjugate the Hungarian republic.

"The Peoples' Springtime"?

The czar boasted in 1850 that Providence had assigned him "the mission of delivering Europe from constitutional governments." By 1850, almost the whole Continent was in the process of being delivered from the regimes of 1848. In France, the Second Republic faced a very uncertain future under an ambitious president and a conservative assembly, both very much concerned with preserving order against liberty. In Prussia, Frederick William IV, and in Austria and Italy, Prince Schwarzenberg, guided the triumphant course of the counterrevolution. Kossuth, Mazzini, and other revolutionaries went into exile. In the early months of 1848, enthusiastic liberals had hailed the arrival of "the peoples' springtime." It had been a false spring.

Mazzini undertook to explain why. In 1850, he wrote from London:

> Why, then, has *reaction* triumphed?
>
> Yes: the cause is in ourselves; in our want of organisation; . . . in our ceaseless distrust, in our miserable little vanities, in our absolute want of that spirit of discipline which alone can achieve great results; in the scattering and dispersing of our forces in a multitude of small centres and sects, powerful to dissolve, impotent to found.
>
> The cause is in the gradual substitution of the worship of material interests . . . for the grand problem of education, which alone can legitimatise our efforts. . . . It is in the narrow spirit of *Nationalism* substituted for the spirit of Nationality; in the stupid presumption on the part of each people that they are capable of solving the political, social, and economical problem alone; in their forgetfulness of the great truths that the cause of the peoples is one; that the cause of the Fatherland must lean upon Humanity. . . . The language of narrow nationalism held at Frankfurt destroyed the German Revolution; as the fatal idea of aggrandisement of the House of Savoy [Piedmont] destroyed the Italian Revolution.*

The revolutionaries of 1848 had not fully learned the lessons of 1830. They relied on moral exhortation and pinned their hopes on spontaneous uprisings when they would have done better to concentrate on discipline and organization. Many of them were either too doctrinaire or too idealistic to make practical politicians. The strength of the revolutionary forces was sapped by the tensions between artisans and industrial workers, between radicals and moderates, between the followers of Mazzini and those of Gioberti, between "Big" and "Little" Germans, and between Magyars and Slavs.

"The narrow spirit of nationalism" deplored by Mazzini was to grow ever more intense after 1848. It

Life and Writings of Joseph Mazzini (London, 1905), 3:76–77.

was to haunt the Hapsburg Empire for the rest of its days and eventually destroy it. The failure of the liberals to unify Italy and Germany in 1848 transferred the leadership of the nationalist movements from the amateur revolutionaries to the professional politicians of Piedmont and Prussia. In the case of Italy, the transfer augured well; Piedmont, alone among the Italian states, retained the moderate constitution it had secured in 1848; in the case of Germany, the antiliberal Bismarck was to achieve through "blood and iron" what the Frankfurt Assembly had not accomplished by peaceful means.

Equally prophetic was the role of the working class, particularly in the French campaign for the right to work and in the June Days with their long roster of casualties and exiles. Europe was experiencing the challenge of the forces released by the Industrial Revolution, and new demands for drastic social and economic improvement were arising alongside the older demands for political liberties, constitutions, and the end of peasant servitude. The year 1848 was not only the year of abortive revolution but also the year when Marx and Engels published their guidelines for future revolutions in *The Communist Manifesto*

Reading Suggestions
on Revolution and Counterrevolution, 1815–1850
General Accounts

F. B. Artz, *Reaction and Revolution, 1814–1832,* and W. L. Langer, *Political and Social Upheaval, 1832–1852* (*Torchbooks). Comprehensive volumes in the series Rise of Modern Europe; with very full bibliographies. The chapters in Langer's volume treating the midcentury upheaval are available separately: *Revolutions of 1848* (*Torchbooks).

The New Cambridge Modern History, Vols. IX and X (Cambridge Univ. Press, 1965, 1960). Chapter by many scholars, uneven in quality, but providing information on topics and areas often neglected in general surveys.

Jacques Droz, *Europe between Revolutions, 1815–1848* (*Torchbooks). A survey by a French scholar stressing the working of economic and social forces and their political consequences.

J. L. Talmon, *Romanticism and Revolt, 1815–1848* (*Harcourt). Stressing social and intellectual developments.

E. J. Hobsbawm, *The Age of Revolution, 1789–1848* (*Mentor). Provocative survey stressing economic and political developments from the Marxian point of view.

The Romantic Protest
The full texts of almost all the landmarks in romantic literature mentioned in this chapter are available in paperbound editions.

J. B. Halsted, ed., *Romanticism: Problems of Definition, Explanation, Evaluation* (*Heath). Informative samplings of many different points of view. Halsted has also edited a good anthology of romantic writing, *Romanticism* (*Torchbooks), a volume in The Documentary History of Western Civilization series.

H. Hugo, ed., *The Romantic Reader* (*Viking). Imaginatively arranged anthology with an enlightening introduction.

Lilian R. Furst, *Romanticism in Perspective* (St. Martin's, 1969). Helpful interpretation, with chapters on the historical perspective and on individualism, imagination, and feeling.

J. Bronowski and B. Mazlish, *The Western Intellectual Tradition from Leonardo to Hegel* (*Torchbooks); C. Brinton, *The Shaping of Modern Thought* (*Prentice-Hall); W. H. Coates and H. V. White, *The Ordeal of Liberal Humanism* (*McGraw-Hill). Three lucid reviews of intellectual history.

G. Brandes, *Main Currents in Nineteenth Century Literature,* 6 vols. (Heinemann, 1901–1905). A celebrated detailed study.

George Boas, *French Philosophies of the Romantic Period* (Johns Hopkins Univ. Press, 1934). Sympathetic and instructive study.

C. Brinton, *Political Ideas of the English Romanticists* (*Ann Arbor). A perceptive analysis.

Kuno Francke, *A History of German Literature as Determined by Social Forces,* 4th ed. (Holt, 1931). Old-fashioned and very informative.

M. Reynal, *The Nineteenth Century* (Skira, 1951). Handsomely illustrated survey of painting.

W. Friedlaender, *David to Delacroix* (Harvard Univ., 1952). Good study of neoclassical and romantic painting in France.

D. L. Dowd, *Pageant-Master of the Republic* (Univ. of Nebraska, 1948). David's role as propagandist of the revolution.

T. Prideaux, *The World of Delacroix* (Time-Life Books, 1966).

K. Clark, *The Gothic Revival* (*Penguin). Entertaining essay, focused on architecture in Britain.

H.-R. (Henry-Russell) Hitchcock, *Architecture: Nineteenth and Twentieth Centuries* (Penguin, 1958) and F. Novotny, *Painting and Sculpture in Europe, 1780–1880* (Penguin, 1960). Two detailed and comprehensive volumes in "The Pelican History of Art."

A. Einstein, *Music in the Romantic Era* (Norton, 1947). Standard introduction.

K. B. Klaus, *The Romantic Period in Music* (Allyn & Bacon, 1970). Another useful introduction, which goes well beyond the chronological limits of this chapter.

C. Rosen, *The Classical Style* (*Norton). Treats Beethoven in addition to Mozart and Haydn.

J. Barzun, *Berlioz and the Romantic Century,* 2 vols. (Little, Brown, 1950). Detailed examination of the career of a most characteristically Romantic composer.

The Reconstruction of Europe
G. Bertier de Sauvigny, *Metternich and His Times* (Darton, Longman, and Todd, 1962). By a French expert on conservatism.

A. J. May, *The Age of Metternich,* rev. ed. (*Holt). Brief appraisal by an American expert on Hapsburg history.

H. F. Schwarz, ed., *Metternich, the Coachman of Europe: Statesman or Evil Genius?* (*Heath). Instructive cross section of contradictory interpretations.

Mack Walker, ed., *Metternich's Europe* (*Torchbooks). Useful collection of sources; a volume in The Documentary History of Western Civilization series.

E. L. Woodward, *Three Studies in European Conservatism* (Constable, 1929). Thoughtful essays on Metternich, Guizot, and the Catholic Church in the nineteenth century.

P. Viereck, *Conservatism Revisited* (*Free Press). Sympathetic reappraisal.

H. Nicolson, *The Congress of Vienna* (*Harcourt); G. Ferrero, *The Reconstruction of Europe* (*Norton). Detailed studies of the settlement of 1814–1815.

H. A. Kissinger, *A World Restored* (*Universal). Efforts of the conservative forces to restore the European balance, 1812–1822.

Works on Individual States

G. Bertier de Sauvigny, *The Restoration* (Univ. of Pennsylvania Press, 1966). Sympathetic detailed interpretation of France under Louis XVIII and Charles X.

F. B. Artz, *France under the Bourbon Restoration, 1814–1830* (Harvard Univ. Press, 1931). Less friendly analysis from the liberal standpoint.

D. H. Pinkney, *The French Revolution of 1830* (Princeton Univ. Press, 1972). Important scholarly study revising many older ideas about the nature of the July Revolution.

M. R. D. Leys, *Between Two Empires* (Longmans, 1955). Brief survey of French social and political history, 1814–1848.

I. Collins, *Government and Society in France, 1814–1848* (Edward Arnold, 1970). Very useful collection of documents.

T. E. B. Howarth, *Citizen-King* (Eyre & Spottiswoode, 1961). Biography of Louis Philippe.

D. Johnson, *Guizot: Aspects of French History, 1787–1874* (Routledge, 1963). Illuminating biography of the French conservative liberal.

R. Carr, *Spain, 1808–1939* (Clarendon, 1966). Scholarly account.

A. J. Whyte, *The Evolution of Modern Italy* (*Norton). Sound introduction.

D. Mack Smith, ed. *The Making of Italy, 1796–1870* (*Torchbooks). Excellent volume in The Documentary History of Western Civilization; compiled by a ranking expert on the subject.

G. T. Romani, *The Neapolitan Revolution of 1820–1821* (Northwestern Univ. Press, 1950). A scholarly monograph.

G. Salvemini, *Mazzini* (*Collier). Sympathetic analysis. May be supplemented by the selections from Mazzini's writings in I. Silone, ed., *The Living Thoughts of Mazzini* (Longmans, 1939).

H. Treitschke, *History of Germany in the Nineteenth Century*, 7 vols. (McBride, Nast, 1915–1919). Very detailed and colorful, very Prussian and nationalistic in tone. A good brief antidote is A. J. P. Taylor, *The Course of German History* (*Capricorn).

T. S. Hamerow, *Restoration, Revolution, Reaction* (*Princeton Univ. Press). Scholarly reevaluation of German economics and politics, 1815–1871.

R. H. Thomas, *Liberalism, Nationalism, and the German Intellectuals* (Cambridge Univ. Press, 1952). Good study of the period 1822–1847.

W. O. Henderson, *The Zollverein* (Univ. of Chicago Press, 1959). The standard work on the subject.

J. C. Legge, ed., *Rhyme and Revolution in Germany* (Constable, 1918). Lively anthology of German history and literature, 1813–1850.

C. A. Macartney, *The Habsburg Empire, 1790–1918* (Macmillan, 1969). By a ranking expert in the field.

A. J. P. Taylor, *The Habsburg Monarchy, 1809–1918* (*Torchbooks). Spirited brief treatment.

R. F. Leslie, *Polish Politics and the Revolution of 1830* (Athlone Press, 1956). Detailed analysis of the stresses and antagonisms that doomed the Polish movement.

D. Dakin, *The Struggle for Greek Independence, 1821–1833* (Univ. of California Press, 1973) Definitive scholarly study.

A. G. Mazour, *The First Russian Revolution* (*Stanford Univ. Press), and Marc Raeff, *The Decembrist Movement* (Prentice-Hall, 1966). Valuable studies of the abortive coup of 1825 and its background.

The Revolutions of 1848

G. Fasel, *Europe in Upheaval: the Revolutions of 1848* (*Rand McNally). Up-to-date concise account.

J. Sigman, *1848: The Romantic and Democratic Revolutions in Europe* (Harper, 1973). Revisionist study by a Frenchman, focused particularly on the economic, social, and political difficulties during 1846 and 1847.

Priscilla Robertson, *Revolutions of 1848: A Social History* (*Princeton Univ. Press). Uneven narrative, valuable for stressing the role taken by women and by students.

R. Postgate, *Story of a Year: 1848* (Oxford Univ. Press, 1956). A lively and well-illustrated chronicle.

M. Kranzberg, ed., *1848: A Turning Point?* (*Heath). Diverse evaluations as to whether or not Europe failed to turn.

G. Rudé, *The Crowd in History, 1730–1884* (*Wiley). Includes a chapter on the socioeconomic background of the Parisian demonstrators of 1848.

G. Duveau, *1848: The Making of a Revolution* (*Vintage). By a leading French scholar.

L. B. Namier, *1848: The Revolution of the Intellectuals* (*Anchor). Trenchant essay castigating liberals, especially in Germany, for their illiberal attitudes.

P. H. Noyes, *Organization and Revolution* (Princeton Univ. Press, 1966). Enlightening study of working-class disunity in Germany.

R. J. Rath, *The Viennese Revolution of 1848* (Univ. of Texas Press, 1957). Detailed monograph.

The Industrial Revolution

I Introduction

On May 1, 1851, in London, Queen Victoria opened the Great Exhibition of the Works of Industry of All Nations. The first of many world's fairs, this international exposition displayed the latest mechanical marvels in a setting that was itself a marvel of engineering—the Crystal Palace, a structure of iron and glass stretching like a mammoth greenhouse for more than a third of a mile in Hyde Park. To the visitors who thronged the Crystal Palace it was evident that Britain was, as she claimed, the workshop of the world. Her exhibits featured mechanical wonders, while those of the continental states stressed traditional arts and crafts. To succeeding generations the London exhibition marked the heyday of British leadership in the Industrial Revolution. Machines and factories had already begun to change the face of Britain in the late eighteenth century; since 1851 they have transformed not only Britain and the Western nations generally but also Japan, Russia, and still others.

By the mid-nineteenth century revolutionary changes in technology and business organization were exerting a revolutionary impact on politics and society. Industrialism bound nations closer together by stimulating international trade and by lowering the barriers of distance through improved transport and communication. Yet it heightened international tensions by fortifying nationalism with economic appetite and by insuring a bloodless war for markets and raw materials. Businessmen demanded that governments pursue policies that would augment profits, and they sought the political rights that would give them a voice in determining those policies. By making goods cheaper and more plentiful, industrialism raised standards of living and enabled increasing numbers of men to enjoy the decencies and comforts of existence. But it also created problems of unemployment, low wages, and bad living and working conditions. Laborers clamored for the right to work and to organize, to strike, and to vote.

The rise of industry and labor inspired divergent schools of economic and social thought. The classical economists advocated laissez faire, preaching that the state should let the economy regulate itself, and that what was good for business was bound to be good for labor, too. If a worker wanted economic security and political status, he should win them through his own efforts, by getting rich, as Guizot had advised the citizens of the July Monarchy. Humanitarian liberals, exemplified by John Stuart Mill, on the other hand, believed that state intervention in economic life might sometimes be justified to protect or assist the working class. The prospect of moderate reform and of gradual advance toward democracy offered by these liberals satisfied some workers. Others, however, hoping for swifter achievement of their goals, favored the more drastic but still peaceful changes of the type recommended in Louis Blanc's social workshops and in the blueprints of his fellow utopian socialists. Still others embraced revolutionary socialism, which would be the outcome of the violent and inevitable class war predicted by Marx and Engels.

The Industrial Revolution thus brought to the fore economic and political issues still alive today. It created a new labor problem and intensified the older farm problem. It sharpened the differences between the champions of relatively free international trade and the economic nationalists who demanded protective tariffs. It divided liberals into the opponents and the defenders of the benevolent or welfare state. It created a radical wing of the working class, soon to be split between the rival schools of utopian and Marxian socialism. It altered the course of human history even more profoundly than did a great political upheaval like the French Revolution. The British economic historian E. J. Hobsbawm calls it "probably the most important

The main corridor at London's Great Exhibition of the Works of Industries of All Nations, Crystal Palace, 1851: an engraving after a daguerreotype.

overcome, production expands rapidly, and the economy moves into a long period of sustained growth. This crucial phase may be compressed into a relatively short period: In Britain, Rostow concludes, the economy "took off" in the two decades following 1783, a time span not greatly exceeding that of the American or French revolutions.

The relative abruptness of the take-off contrasted with the centuries of preparation that preceded it. The preparatory stage has been traced all the way back to the monasteries of the early Middle Ages, which, by their insistence on discipline and on the performance of specified tasks at specified times, have been likened to a model for the organization of the labor force in a mine or mill. The factors that prepared Europe and America for industrialism included, obviously, the capitalism of medieval and Renaissance bankers and merchants, and the colonialism and mercantilism of the sixteenth and subsequent centuries. Less obviously, they also included most of the forces that shaped the early modern world. The rise of the competitive state system, the Protestant stress on hard work, the brushing aside of tradition by the scientists of the seventeenth century and by the philosophes of the eighteenth—all played their part in creating a society ready for sweeping economic changes.

Britain Takes Off

Why was Britain the first state to take off? Why not France, which was richer and much more populous, or the Dutch Republic, the "economic schoolmaster" of seventeenth-century Europe? Rostow summarizes the answers:

> The Dutch became too committed to finance and trade, without an adequate manufacturing base. . . .
>
> What about the French? They were too rough with their Protestants. They were politically and socially too inflexible. . . . The best minds and spirits of eighteenth-century France . . . had to think about political, social and religious revolution rather than economic revolution. Moreover, the French were committed heavily to ground warfare in Europe; and they cheated on shipping and naval strength at an historical moment when ships mattered greatly.
>
> And so Britain, with more basic industrial resources than the Netherlands; more nonconformists, and more ships than France; with its political, social, and religious revolution fought out by 1688—Britain alone was in a position to weave together cotton manufacture, coal and iron technology, the steam-engine and ample foreign trade to pull it off.*

event in world history, at least since the invention of agriculture and cities." *

Not all historians agree with Hobsbawm. 1776 and 1789 still have their champions, and others, including the present authors, suggest that the Industrial Revolution was only one facet of a great modern revolution that also involved European expansion overseas, the great leap forward made by science during the century of genius, and the ideals of the Enlightenment, together with the attempts of Americans and Frenchmen to translate them into reality. In any case, it cannot be denied that the changes launching industry on its modern course had a revolutionary impact on Western history.

II The Stages of Economic Growth

What has made some historians shy away from the term "Industrial Revolution" is the fact that these economic changes occurred both too slowly and too peacefully to be called revolutionary. But the American economic historian W. W. Rostow, in his influential analysis *The Stages of Economic Growth*, has introduced the idea of an economic "take-off," when old inhibiting factors are

Rostow also suggests that English victories over a series of foreign enemies and competitors—over the Church of Rome and the Spain of Philip II in the sixteenth century, the Dutch in the seventeenth, and the French

*E. J. Hobsbawm, *The Age of Revolution, 1789–1848* (Mentor), p. 46.

The Stages of Economic Growth (Cambridge, 1960), p. 33.

in the eighteenth—gave English national self-confidence and drive a major boost.

More particular factors also accounted for Britain's head start in industrial development. She had ample supplies of capital from the profits of foreign and colonial trade. She possessed large and easily available deposits of coal and iron; the geographical compactness of the British Isles made shipments from mine to smelter and from mill to seaport short and cheap. Britain had a large reservoir of potential factory labor in the marginal farmers, driven off the land by the enclosure movement, and in the Irish, emigrating from their poverty-ridden and overcrowded island. The commercial and naval leadership gained by Britain in the eighteenth century and fortified by the French Revolutionary and Napoleonic wars paved the way for her industrial leadership. It facilitated the search for raw materials and markets, and the profits from overseas trade and the empire swelled investment in industry. The wars themselves stimulated demand for metal goods and the invention of new machines. And the construction of great docks along the lower Thames during the wars entrenched London in its position as the greatest economic center in Europe.

Finally, it has also been argued that the absence in Britain of the rigid and elaborate centralized administrative structure found in France and other continental countries permitted more flexibility in accepting new enterprises. While this argument probably exaggerates the rigidity of the Old Regime on the Continent, the fact remains that the casual, almost slipshod, quality of British local government could be an asset. If, for example, a capitalist who wanted to set up a factory found himself blocked by vested interests in one locality, he simply went to another, where the local authorities were more agreeable. Thus it was that Manchester, which had the barest minimum of governmental apparatus in the eighteenth century, became the textile capital not only of Lancashire but also of the world.

Cotton Manufacture and the Steam Engine

The textile industry was the first to exploit the potentialities of power-driven machinery. Beginning with the spinning jenny of the 1760s the use of machinery gradually spread to other processes. In 1793, the American Eli Whitney devised the cotton gin, an engine that separated the fibers of the raw cotton from the seeds and enabled a single slave to do what had previously required the hand labor of fifty slaves. Meanwhile, British inventors perfected a power-driven loom for weaving cotton thread into cloth. By 1830, Britain operated more than 50,000 power looms, and cotton goods accounted for half of her exports. By 1851 the British census listed more than half a million workers employed in cotton manufacturing alone.

Advances in mechanical engineering made this rapid expansion possible. Earlier, for instance, the difficulty of procuring exactly fitting parts had restricted the output of Watt's steam engine. Then British engineers, by studying the precision techniques of watchmakers, devised a lathe that turned screws of almost perfect regularity. They also developed machines for sawing, boring, and turning the pulley blocks used by British vessels in the Napoleonic wars. In North America, meantime, Eli Whitney undertook important experiments at his arms factory in Connecticut. He explained that he planned to "make the same parts of different guns, as the locks, for example, as much like each other as the successive impressions of a copperplate engraving." In other words, Whitney was utilizing the concept of standardized parts, one of the basic principles of mass production.

It is important to realize that not all processes in an industry "took off" at the same time. The revolutionary implications of Whitney's experiments with standardization, for example, were long ignored by manufacturers; the survival of handicraft techniques also slowed down the process of mechanization. Even in the cotton industry, weaving on the hand loom continued in districts with a large reservoir of cheap labor, like Ireland and central Europe, where peasants could produce cloth in their cottages. In the woolen and clothing industries mechanization did not come until the 1850s, when Britain produced a machine for woolcombing and an American, Isaac Singer, popularized the sewing machine.

Coal and Iron

Coal ranked with cotton as an industry that pioneered in the solution of technical problems. Steam engines

Mule spinning in a Lancashire mill, 1834.

pumped water from the mines; ventilating shafts and power fans supplied them with fresh air; and safety lamps gave miners protection against dangerous underground gases. The coal output of Britain, then the world's leading producer, rose steadily from about 16 million tons in 1816, to 30 million in 1836, and 65 million in 1856. The consumption of coal mounted because of its increased use as a household fuel in wood-short Britain, its importance in producing steam power, and its vital contribution to the expanding iron industry, which required large quantities of coal to make the coke used in smelting.

The efficiency of smelting advanced rapidly after the development of the blast furnace (1828), in which fans provided a blast of hot air to intensify the action of the hot coke on the iron. Thanks to the blast furnace, Britain produced iron strong enough for use in bridges and in factory buildings. Yet the best grade of iron lacked the tremendous strength of steel, which is iron purified of all but a minute fraction of carbon by a process of prolonged, intensive heating. Steel for industrial purposes could be made in the early 1800s, but only by ruinously expensive methods. Then in 1856 Bessemer, an Englishman of French extraction, invented the converter, which accelerated the removal of impurities by shooting jets of compressed air into the molten metal. A decade later, Siemens, a German living in England, devised the open-hearth process, which utilized scrap as well as new iron, and which handled larger amounts of metal than the converter could. The inventions of Bessemer and Siemens lowered the cost of making steel so substantially that the world output increased tenfold between 1865 and 1880.

Transport and Communication

The railroad consumed large amounts of iron and steel (on the average, 300 tons were required for a single mile

The Soho Engineering Works at Birmingham, England, where James Watt and Matthew Boulton manufactured steam engines, 1775–1800.

of track). The revolution in transport, which culminated in the railroad, began early in the nineteenth century with the proliferation of canals and hard-surfaced roads. During the century's first three decades many hundreds of miles of canals were dug in Europe and in North America, and highway construction was improved by a Scot, McAdam, who devised the durable road surface of broken stones that still bears his name. Shippers, however, also required a way of conveying overland coal, iron, and other heavy shipments; the railroad furnished the solution. In the 1820s, methods of rolling rails and constructing sturdy roadbeds were already known, and only mechanization remained to be accomplished. George Stephenson and others put the steam engine on wheels and created the locomotive. In 1830, Stephenson's "Rocket" traversed twelve miles in fifty-three minutes on the new Liverpool and Manchester Railway, the first line to be operated entirely by steam. The railroad building boom was soon in full swing: Britain had 500 miles of track in 1838, 6,600 miles in 1850, and 15,500 in 1870.

Steam also affected water transport, though at a less revolutionary pace. Fulton's steamboat, the *Clermont,* made a successful trip on the Hudson River in 1807, and soon paddle-wheel steamers plied the inland waterways of the United States and Europe. Ocean-going steamships, however, were uneconomical to operate because of the inefficiency of the marine engine. When the Scot Samuel Cunard inaugurated the first regular transatlantic steamer service (between Liverpool and Boston in 1840), the coal required for the voyage took up almost half of the space on his vessels. Consequently, only passengers and mails went by steamship; most freight was still handled in sailing ships, like the beautiful and efficient American clippers. Finally, in the 1860s, the development of improved marine engines and the substitution of the screw propeller for the cumbersome paddle wheel forecast the eventual doom of the commercial sailing vessel. All these improvements in transport by sea and land promoted industrial expansion by facilitating shipments of raw materials and finished products and by opening up almost the whole world as a potential market.

Communications also experienced radical improvements. A beginning was made in 1840, when Great Britain inaugurated the penny post, which enabled a letter to go from London to Edinburgh, for instance, at the cost of a penny (about four cents), less than a tenth of the old rate. More dramatic was the utilization of electricity for instantaneous communication. An impressive series of "firsts" started with the first telegraph message, from Baltimore to Washington in 1844. Then came the first submarine cable, under the English Channel in 1851; the first transatlantic cable, 1866; and the first telephone, 1876.

Money, Banking, and Limited Liability

The exploitation of all these new inventions and discoveries required a constant flow of fresh capital. From the first, the older commercial community supported the young industrial community. The slave traders of Liverpool financed the cotton mills of Manchester and other nearby towns in Lancashire, thereby increasing the demand for American cotton fiber and for slaves to work the plantations. Tobacco merchants of Glasgow provided the funds that made their city the foremost industrial center of Scotland, and tea merchants in London and Bristol aided the ironmasters of South Wales. Bankers played such an important role that Disraeli, the British politician, listed the Barings of London and the international house of Rothschild among the great powers of Europe. In the early nineteenth century each of the five Rothschild brothers, sons of a German Jewish banker, established himself in an important economic center—London, Paris, Frankfurt, Naples, and Vienna. The Rothschilds prospered because, in an age of frequent speculation, they avoided unduly risky undertakings, and because they facilitated investment by residents of one state in the projects of other states. The Paris Rothschild, for instance, negotiated the investment of British capital in the construction of French railroads during the 1840s.

Banks further assisted economic expansion by promoting the use of checks and banknotes in place of specie. During the Napoleonic wars, when the shortage of coins forced some British millowners to pay their workers in goods, the British government empowered local banks to issue paper notes supplementing the meager supply of coins. But whenever financial crises occurred—and they came frequently before 1850—dozens of local banks failed and their notes became valueless. Parliament therefore encouraged the absorption of small shaky banks by the larger and more solid institutions, and in 1844 it gave the Bank of England a virtual monopoly of the issuing of banknotes, thus providing a very reliable paper currency. It also applied, first to railroads and then to other companies, the principle of limited liability, indicated by the familiar "Ltd." after the name of British firms. Earlier, the shareholders in most British companies had incurred unlimited liability: they might find their personal fortunes appropriated to satisfy the creditors of an unsuccessful company. The practice of limiting each shareholder's liability to the par value of his shares encouraged investment by diminishing its risks.

Others Take Off

In the mid-nineteenth century, the tangible signs of Britain's economic predominance were evident on every hand—in the teeming London docks, in the thriving financial houses of the City, in the exhibits at the Crystal Palace, in the mushrooming factory and mining towns of the Midlands, the North of England, and Scotland, and in other quarters of the globe as well. British capital and thousands of skilled British workers participated in the construction of French railroads. American trains ran on rails rolled in British mills and

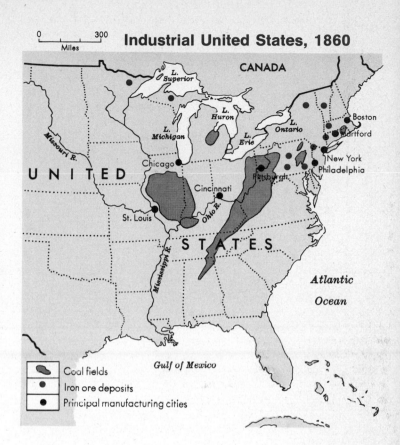

Industrial United States, 1860

0   300
Miles

CANADA

L. Superior
L. Huron
L. Michigan
L. Ontario
L. Erie

Missouri R.

UNITED

Chicago

Cincinnati

St. Louis

Ohio R.

Mississippi R.

STATES

Boston
Hartford
New York
Philadelphia
Pittsburgh

Atlantic

Ocean

Gulf of Mexico

Coal fields
Iron ore deposits
Principal manufacturing cities

on the capital from British investors. Cotton goods made in Lancashire clothed a sizable part of the world's population, and British entrepreneurs and inventors brought the Industrial Revolution to Belgium and parts of Germany.

Yet Britain, even in the heyday of her leadership, did not monopolize inventive skill. Frenchmen, for example, devised the chlorine process of bleaching cloth and the Jacquard loom for weaving intricate patterns. German technicians led the world in agricultural chemistry and in the utilization of the valuable byproducts of coal. And from the United States came Eli Whitney and the cotton gin, Morse and the telegraph, Singer and the sewing machine, and Cyrus McCormick, whose reaper (1831) was the first of many agricultural machines developed in America.

In a sense, the whole North Atlantic world, European and American, constituted an economic community. As one member of that community, Britain, matured, other members would be going through the stage of take-off. After 1850, therefore, Britain began to lose the advantage of her head start and soon began to feel with increasing sharpness the pinch of competition. W. W. Rostow estimates that by 1850 three states were in the process of take-off—Belgium, France, and the United States, or more exactly the northeastern and midwestern states, which enjoyed an immense economic advantage over the South in the Civil War. Germany's

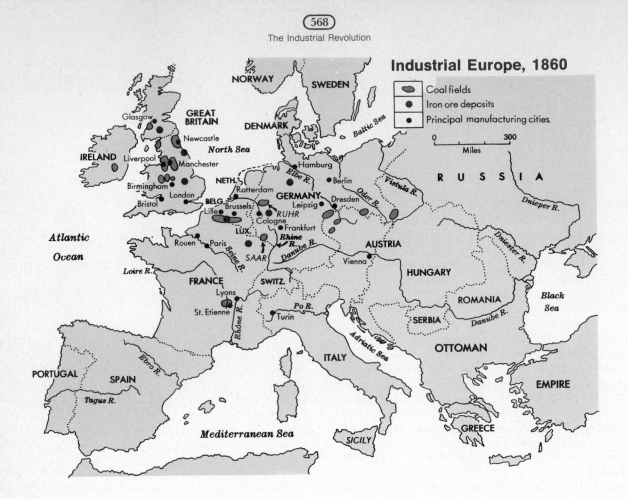

Industrial Europe, 1860

take-off began about 1850 and was completed after the lift provided by the country's triumphant unification as the German Empire in 1871. By the turn of the century the North Atlantic world was facing the prospect of losing the advantages of its head start as Japan and czarist Russia were engaged in take-off.

The details of Rostow's timetable of industrialization do not satisfy all the experts, who suggest some shifts in dates and modifications that would underline the fact that take-off was often a rather lopsided and undramatic affair. This, of course, is the normal academic way of testing and refining a hypothesis. The figure of take-off remains a very useful one because it expresses so well the fact that economic growth proceeded erratically, with sudden bursts of activity. And in our own century the idea of take-off has fired the imagination of people in less developed countries all over the world, who yearn to share in the greater prosperity and enhanced status enjoyed by industrial states.

III The Economic and Social Impact of Industrialization
The Agricultural Revolution

The industrial and agricultural revolutions have usually been mutually dependent. To take off into sustained growth, industry relies on a more efficient agri-culture for raw materials and for additions to its labor force, recruited from surplus workers no longer needed on mechanized farms. Agriculture depends on industry for the tools and fertilizers that enable fewer and fewer men to produce more and more and transform farms into agrarian factories. In the nineteenth century, factory-made implements like the steel plow and the reaper improved the cultivation of old farmlands and permitted the opening of vast new areas, like the North American prairies, that could scarcely have been touched if the pioneers had had to rely on hand labor alone. The mechanical cream separator raised the dairy industry to a big business, and railroads and steamers sped the transport of produce from farm to market. The processes of canning, refrigeration, and freezing, all industrial in origin and all first applied on a wide scale during the last third of the century, permitted the preservation of many perishable commodities and their shipment halfway around the world.

Farmers found steadily expanding markets both in industrial demand for raw materials and in the food required by mining and factory towns. International trade in farm products increased rapidly during the second half of the nineteenth century. The annual export of wheat from the United States and Canada rose from 22,000,000 bushels in the 1850s to 150,000,000 in 1880. Imported flour accounted for a quarter of the bread consumed in Britain during the 1850s and for half in the 1870s. Denmark and the Netherlands increasingly furnished the British table with bacon, butter, eggs, and cheese; Australia supplied its mutton and Argentina its beef.

Germany now partly assumed Britain's old role as the pioneer of scientific agriculture. German experimenters, shortly after 1800, extracted sugar from beets in commercially important quantities, thus ending Europe's dependence on the cane sugar of the West Indies. In the 1840s the German chemist Liebig published a series of influential works on the agricultural applications of organic chemistry. Plant growth, Liebig argued, depended on three basic elements—nitrogen, potassium, and phosphorus. But the production of crops and fodder leached these elements from the soil: unless they could be returned to it, fertile lands might go the way of "the once prolific soil of Virginia, now in many parts no longer able to grow its former staple productions—wheat and tobacco." Liebig's warnings promoted the wide use of fertilizers—guano from the nesting islands of sea birds off the west coast of South America, nitrate from Chile, and potash from European mines.

Farming progressed and prospered in the nineteenth century as never before. Yet the agricultural revolution exacted a price, sometimes a very high price. Faced with the competition of beet sugar, the sugarcane islands of the West Indies went into a depression from which some of them have never fully recovered. In the highly industrialized countries the social and political importance of agricultural interests began to decline. Farming was no longer the principal occupation of Englishmen in the nineteenth century, and land was no longer the almost universal yardstick of wealth and power. The manufacturers and merchants of Britain scored a decisive victory over the landed gentry in the campaign to repeal the Corn Laws, the tariffs on the importation of the wheat and other cereals which the English term collectively "corn." The powerful Anti-Corn Law League protested that the tariffs "artificially enhance the price of food," and "prevent the exchange of the products of industry for the food of other countries." Free trade was the remedy prescribed by the Anti-Corn Law League, and free trade came when Parliament repealed the Corn Laws in 1846. The decisive factor was the disastrous attack of black rot that ruined the Irish potato crop two years running and made the importation of cheap grain imperative to prevent the worsening of an already disastrous famine in Ireland.

The Population Explosion and the Standard of Living

When Britain thus abandoned any pretense of growing all the basic foods her people needed, her population was growing so rapidly that self-sufficiency was no longer possible. Despite substantial emigration, the number of inhabitants in England and Wales more than tripled during the course of the nineteenth cen-

tury, from about 9,000,000 in 1800 to 32,500,000 in 1900. Scholars are still arguing about the reasons why and whether the Industrial Revolution was responsible. Some demographers have claimed that the British population explosion in the nineteenth century may be attributed not to a higher birth rate but to the lowered death rate resulting from the improved food and sanitation—especially cheap washable cotton materials— brought by industrialism. Others claim that neither diet nor sanitation improved until the second half of the century and that the population increase in the first half may be attributed to the rural areas and not to the cities, which had a much higher death rate. It is also pointed out that in Russia, still an agrarian country in the preparatory preindustrial stage, the population increased proportionately (36,000,000 in 1800, about 100,000,000 in 1900) almost as fast as it did in Britain.

A similar controversy is focused on the extent to which the Industrial Revolution improved the standard of living not just of the new capitalist and managerial classes, but of the workers themselves. So far as the facts can be determined from the rather sketchy statistical data, they suggest that the overall standard of living in Britain did not begin a steady improvement until after the Napoleonic wars and the immediate postwar slump. From about 1820 on the purchasing power of the worker seems to have grown very gradually, as more goods and cheaper ones became available. At the same time, opportunities for steady regular employment also grew, as did the chances for the laborer to climb up the economic ladder a rung or two by mastering a skill enabling him to hold a better-paying job. But all these factors varied in their effect from industry to industry and from one locality to another; they also fluctuated with the ups and downs of the economic cycle. Many people, consequently, appear to have felt that their standard of living was declining.

There is little debate about one most important social result of industrialism—the truly revolutionary changes it caused in the structure and distribution of the population. Wherever mines and factories were opened, towns and cities appeared. Large areas of once-rural England became urban England, and a similar transformation was beginning in the lowlands of Scotland around Glasgow, in the northern French plain around Lille, in the German Rhineland, and along the rivers of the northeastern United States. The growth of an urban population increased the numbers and influence of the two social classes that form the backbone of an industrial society. These are the businessmen and the workingmen. Industrialists, bankers, investors, managers, and promoters of every sort joined the already established capitalists to form the modern middle class or bourgeoisie. Millhands, railwaymen, miners, clerks, and a host of other recruits swelled the ranks of wage-earning workers.

The impact of capital and labor upon the life of industrial nations was becoming increasingly evident by the middle of the nineteenth century. Some of the signs pointed to steady material progress—the wonders of the Crystal Palace, or the conquest of space by the railroad, the steamship, and the telegraph. Other signs, however, portended serious dislocation and violent change. The repeal of the Corn Laws buried an old agrarian way of life in Britain. The collapse of the French railroad boom in the late 1840s suggested that in an industrial society economic slumps might have alarming consequences, for as we have seen, the hundreds of thousands thrown out of work aggravated the political unrest that culminated in the June Days of 1848 in Paris.

Middle-Class Grievances and Aspirations

Both businessmen and workingmen nourished grievances—and aspirations. A revealing view of middle-class complaints and hopes is given in a famous parable published in 1819 by the French social planner, Saint-Simon. Saint-Simon supposed that France suddenly lost fifty of her best mechanical engineers, of her finest architects, doctors, bankers—and so on through a long list comprising the three thousand leading men in business, science, and the arts. These men, Saint-Simon stated, are "the most useful to their country"; "the nation would become a lifeless corpse as soon as it lost them."

> Let us pass on to another assumption. Suppose that France preserves all the men of genius that she possesses in the sciences, fine arts and professions, but has the misfortune to lose in the same day Monsieur the King's brother [and many other members of the royal family]. Suppose that France loses at the same time all the great officers of the royal household, all the ministers (with or without portfolio), all the councillors of state, all the chief magistrates, marshals, cardinals, archbishops, bishops, vicars-general, judges, and, in addition, ten thousand of the richest proprietors who live in the style of nobles.
>
> This mischance would certainly distress the French, because they are kind-hearted, and could not see with indifference the sudden disappearance of such a large number of their compatriots. But this loss of thirty thousand individuals, considered to be the most important in the State, would only grieve them for purely sentimental reasons and would result in no political evil for the State.
>
> These suppositions underline the most important fact of present politics. . . . that our social organization is seriously defective. . . .
>
> The scientists, artists, and artisans, the only men whose work is of positive utility to society, and cost it practically nothing, are kept down by the princes and other rulers who are simply more or less incapable bureaucrats. Those who control honours and other national awards owe, in general, the supremacy they enjoy, to the accident of birth, to flattery, intrigue and other dubious methods. . . .
>
> These suppositions show that society is a world which is upside down.*

*H. de Saint-Simon, *Selected Writings*, ed. F. M. H. Markham (New York, 1952), pp. 72–74.

To the men of the middle class, society indeed seemed upside down. In the Britain of the 1820s the new industrialists had small opportunity to mold national policy. Booming industrial cities like Manchester and Birmingham sent not a single representative to the House of Commons. A high proportion of businessmen belonged not to the Church of England but to non-Anglican Protestant "chapels"; nonconformists, as these dissenters were now termed, still suffered discrimination when it came to holding public office or sending their sons to Oxford or Cambridge. Even in France, despite the gains made since 1789, the bourgeois often enjoyed only the second-class status sketched by Saint-Simon.

In western Europe, the middle classes very soon won the place in the sun which they felt they deserved. In Britain, the gradual process of reform gave them substantially all they wanted. The high spot, higher even than the repeal of the Corn Laws, was the Reform Bill of 1832, which extended the suffrage to the middle class, as the next chapter will show. In 1830, the French bourgeois got their citizen-king, and their Belgian counterparts scored a very great advance in political power. In Piedmont the middle class found a sympathetic leader in the aristocratic Cavour and secured at least a narrowly liberal constitution in 1848. In southern and central Europe, by contrast, the waves of revolution that crested in 1848 left the bourgeoisie with unfinished political business, to which we shall turn in a subsequent chapter.

Working-Class Grievances and Hopes

The grievances of workingmen were more numerous than those of their masters, and they were harder to satisfy. The difficulties may be illustrated by the protracted struggle of laborers to secure the vote and to obtain the right to organize and to carry on union activities. In Britain, substantial numbers of workers first won the vote in 1867, a generation after the enfranchisement of the wealthier middle class. In France, universal male suffrage was tried for a brief period starting in 1848; it became permanent only with the establishment of the Third Republic after 1870. The unified German Empire had a democratic suffrage from its inception in 1871, but without some other institutions of democracy. Elsewhere, universal manhood suffrage came slowly—not until 1893 in Belgium, and not until the twentieth century in Italy, Austria, Russia, and even in Sweden, Denmark, and the Netherlands, which we are apt to assume have always been in the van of democratic progress.

During most of the nineteenth century, labor unions and strikes were regarded as improper restraints on the free operation of natural economic laws. Hence the specific ban on such combinations, as they were termed, imposed by the British Combination Acts at the close of the eighteenth century. Parliament moderated the effect of the acts in the 1820s but did not repeal them until 1876. Continental governments imposed similar restrictions, and the July Monarchy, in particular, repressed strikes with great brutality. France's Le Chapelier Law of 1791 was only relaxed in the 1860s and repealed in 1884. Everywhere it took labor a long time to win full legal recognition of union activities—until 1867 in Austria, for instance, 1872 in the Netherlands, and 1890 in Germany.

Labor's drive for political and legal rights, however, was only a side issue during the early days of the Industrial Revolution. Many workers faced the more pressing problems of finding jobs and making ends meet on inadequate wages. The modern Western world had long experienced the business cycle, with its alternations of full employment and drastic layoffs. The Industrial Revolution intensified the cycle, making boom periods more hectic and widespread depressions, such as the one in the late 1840s, more frequent and more severe. At first factories made little attempt to provide a fairly steady level of employment. When a batch of orders came in, machines and men were worked to capacity until the orders were filled; then the factory simply shut down to await the next batch.

A century and more ago labor sometimes got such low wages that a family man might have to put both his children and his wife to work as a matter of sheer economic necessity. Humanitarian tradition probably exaggerates the extent to which industry exploited and degraded women and children, probably tends to view the exceptional instance of extreme hardship as the average situation. Nevertheless, exploitation and degradation did occur. Here is the testimony of a factory worker, Samuel Coulson, before a British parliamentary committee in 1831–1832:

At what time in the morning, in the brisk time, did those girls go to the mills? *In the brisk time, for about six weeks, they have gone at 3 o'clock in the morning, and ended at 10, or nearly half-past, at night.*

What intervals were allowed for rest or refreshment during those nineteen hours of labour? *Breakfast a quarter of an hour, and dinner half an hour, and drinking a quarter of an hour.*

Was any of that time taken up in cleaning the machinery? *They generally had to do what they call dry down; sometimes this took the whole of the time at breakfast or drinking, and they were to get their dinner or breakfast as they could; if not, it was brought home.*

Had you not great difficulty in awakening your children to this excessive labour? *Yes, in the early time we had them to take up asleep and shake them when we got them on the floor to dress them, before we could get them off to their work; but not so in the common hours.*

What was the length of time they could be in bed during those long hours? *It was near 11 o'clock before we could get them into bed after getting a little victuals, and then at morning my mistress used to stop up all night, for fear that we could not get them ready for the time. . . .*

So that they had not above four hours' sleep at this time? *No, they had not.*

For how long together was it? *About six weeks it held; it*

"Hurrying Coal": a girl drawing a loaded wagon of coal weighing between 200 and 500 pounds in a Yorkshire mine, 1842.

was only done when the throng was very much on; it was not often that.

The common hours of labour were from 6 in the morning till half-past eight in night? *Yes.*

With the same intervals for food? *Yes, just the same.*

Were the children excessively fatigued by this labour? *Many times; we have cried often when we have given them the little victualling we had to give them; we had to shake them, and they have fallen to sleep with the victuals in their mouths many a time.*

Did this excessive term of labour occasion much cruelty also? *Yes, with being so very much fatigued the strap was very frequently used.*

What was the wages in the short hours? *Three shillings a week each.*

When they wrought those very long hours what did they get? *Three shillings and sevenpence halfpenny.*

For all that additional labour they had only sevenpence halfpenny a week additional? *No more.**

Excessively long hours, low pay, rigorous discipline, and subhuman working conditions were the most common grievances of early industrial workers. Many plants neglected hazards to their employees, few had safety devices to guard dangerous machinery, and cotton mills maintained both the heat and the humidity at an uncomfortable level because threads broke less often in a hot, damp atmosphere. Many workers could not afford decent housing, and if they could afford it, they could not always find it. Some of the new factory towns were reasonably well planned, with wide streets and space for yards and parks. Some even had a copious supply of good water and arrangements for disposing of sewage. But many had none of these necessities, and in rapidly growing London the Thames soon became an open sewer so foul that riverside dwellers were reluctant to open their windows. Fantastic numbers of human beings were jammed into the overcrowded slums of Lille in France and of Liverpool and Manchester in Lancashire.

Lord Shaftesbury, an English reformer of the 1840s, predicted that, unless conditions were improved, Lancashire would soon become a "province of pigmies."

*A. Bland, P. Brown, and R. Tawney, *English Economic History: Select Documents* (London, 1915), pp. 510–513. Three shillings were equivalent to about 75 cents, and sevenpence halfpenny to about 15 cents.

It was estimated that the life expectancy of a boy born to a working-class family in Manchester was only half that of one born to rural laborers. The industrial nations also threatened to remain nations of semiliterates. Until they made provisions for free public schools, during the last third of the nineteenth century, education facilities were grossly inadequate. In England, as often as not, only the Sunday school gave the millhand's child a chance to learn his ABCs. The millhand himself, if he had great ambition and fortitude, might attend one of the adult schools known as "mechanics' institutes." No wonder that in the 1840s a third of the men and half of the women married in England could not sign their names on the marriage register and simply made their mark. And no wonder that Disraeli, the Tory reformer, in his novel *Sybil* (1845), called Britain "two nations"—the rich and the poor.

IV The Responses of Liberalism
"The Dismal Science"

Faced with the widening cleavage between rich and poor, nineteenth-century liberals at first held to the doctrine of laissez faire.

> Suffering and evil are nature's admonitions; they cannot be got rid of; and the impatient attempts of benevolence to banish them from the world by legislation . . . have always been productive of more evil than good.*

Such was the argument advanced by liberals in the British Parliament against the first piece of legislation proposed to safeguard public health. The men who advanced these ideas in the early nineteenth century are known to history as the classical economists; to their enemies they were the architects of "the dismal science." The most famous of them were two Englishmen, Thomas Malthus (1766–1834) and David Ricardo (1772–1823).

"Dismal science" is hardly too strong a term for the theories of Malthus. Educated for the ministry, Malthus became perhaps the very first professional economist in history; he was hired by the East India Company to teach its employees at a training school in England. In 1798 he published the famous *Essay on Population*, a dramatic warning that the human species would breed itself into starvation. In the *Essay*, Malthus formulated a series of natural laws:

> The power of population is indefinitely greater than the power in earth to produce subsistence for man.
>
> Population, when unchecked, increases in a geometrical ratio. Subsistence only increases in an arithmetical ratio. . . . Through the animal and vegetable kingdoms, nature has scattered the seeds of life abroad with the most profuse and liberal hands. She has been comparatively sparing in the room and the nourishment necessary to rear

them. . . . Necessity, that imperious, all-pervading law of nature, restrains them within the prescribed bounds. Among plants and animals its effects are waste of seed, sickness, and premature death. Among mankind, misery and vice.*

Misery and vice would spread, Malthus believed, because the unchecked increase in human numbers would lower the demand for labor and therefore lower the wages of labor.

> When the wages of labour are hardly sufficient to maintain two children, a man marries and has five or six. He of course finds himself miserably distressed. He accuses the insufficiency of the price of labour to maintain a family. . . . He accuses the partial and unjust institutions of society, which have awarded him an inadequate share of the produce of the earth. He accuses perhaps the dispensations of Providence, which have assigned to him a place in society so beset with unavoidable distress and dependence. In searching for objects of accusation, he never adverts to the quarter from which his misfortunes originate. The last person that he would think of accusing is himself, on whom in fact the whole of the blame lies. . . .†

The reduction of the human birth rate was the only hope that this prophet of gloom held out to suffering humanity. It was to be achieved by "moral restraint," that is, by late marriage and by "chastity till that period arrives."

Ricardo, too, was a prophet of gloom. He attributed economic activity to three main forces: there was rent, paid to the owners of great natural resources like farmland and mines; there was profit, accruing to the enterprising individuals who exploited these resources; and there were wages, paid to the workers who performed the actual labor of exploitation. Of the three, rent was in the long run the most important. Farms and mines would become depleted and exhausted, but their produce would continue in great demand. Rent, accordingly, would consume an ever larger share of the "economic pie," leaving smaller and smaller portions for profit and wages.

Ricardo tempered his grim forecasts with qualifications and reservations. For instance, he did not believe that the size of the economic pie was necessarily fixed and thus did not subscribe entirely to the mercantilist idea that the total wealth of mankind was severely limited, so that more for one human unit meant less for another. And yet he did sketch a picture of eventual stagnation. While Adam Smith had cheerfully predicted an increasing division of labor, accompanied by steadily rising wages, Ricardo, in contrast, brought labor and wages under the Malthusian formula:

> The market price of labour is the price which is really paid for it, from the natural operation of the proportion of the

*The Economist, May 13, 1848.

*T. Malthus, First Essay on Population (reprinted, New York, 1965), pp. 13–15.
†An Essay on the Principles of Population (London, 1888), pp. 404–405.

supply to the demand; labour is dear when it is scarce, and cheap when it is plentiful. . . . It is when the market price of labour exceeds its natural price, that the condition of the labourer is flourishing and happy. . . . When, however, by the encouragement which high wages give to the increase of population, the number of labourers is increased, wages again fall to their natural price, and indeed . . . sometimes fall below it.*

Ricardo's disciples hardened this principle into the Iron Law of Wages, which bound workmen to an everlasting cycle of high wages and large families, followed by an increase in the labor supply, a corresponding increase in the competition for jobs, and an inevitable slump in wages. The slump would lead workers to have fewer children, a shortage of labor would develop, wages would rise, and the whole cycle would begin again. Ricardo himself, however, regarded the cycle not as an Iron Law but simply as a probability. Unforeseen factors might in the future modify its course and might even permit a gradual improvement of the worker's lot.

What particularly separated the classical economists of the early nineteenth century from their eighteenth-century predecessors was their overall pessimism. Like the philosophes, they did not doubt that natural laws were superior to manmade laws and that laissez faire was the best policy, but, unlike them, they no longer viewed nature as the creation of the beneficent God of the deists. To these adherents of the "dismal science" nature was at best a neutral force and at worst a sinister one. Man himself—wasteful, careless, improvident—seemed once more afflicted with a kind of original sin. The classical economists supplied a needed corrective to the naïve optimism of the philosophes, one that has acquired fresh cogency in a world concerned with shortages of food and fuel.

Yet the classical economists, too, had their naïve faith. They viewed the economy as a world-machine governed by a few simple, almost unalterable laws—Malthusian laws of population, Ricardian laws of rent and wages. The history of the next hundred years would demonstrate the inadequacy of their view. The size of the economic pie expanded far beyond the expectations of Ricardo, and so did the portions allotted to rent, to profit, and to wages. Malthus did not foresee that scientific advances would make the output of agriculture expand at a nearly geometrical ratio. He did not foresee that the perils of increasing birth rates would sometimes be averted by the use of contraceptives, first popularized during the nineteenth century, or by recourse to emigration. Many millions of people moved from crowded Europe to lightly populated America during the nineteenth century. The exodus from overcrowded Ireland, in particular, continued so briskly after the famine of the 1840s that by 1900 the Irish population was little more than half what it had been fifty years earlier.

*On the Principles of Political Economy, chap. 5 in The Works and Correspondence of David Ricardo, ed. P. Sraffa (Cambridge, England, 1951), 1:94.

Although the classical economists did not take sufficient account of the immense changes being worked by the agricultural and industrial revolutions, their laissez faire liberalism won particular favor with the new industrial magnates. The captains of industry were perhaps disturbed by Ricardo's prediction that profits would inevitably shrink; but they could take comfort from the theory that "suffering and evil" were "nature's admonitions." It was consoling to the rich to be told, in effect, that the poor deserved to be poor because they had indulged their appetites to excess, that whatever was, was right, or at any rate ordained by nature. To the working class, the vaunted freedom of laissez faire often meant freedom to be undernourished, ill-housed, and alternately overworked and unemployed. The poor did not like to hear that they deserved to be poor, and they sometimes felt that whatever was, was wrong and needed to be remedied, if necessary by interference with natural laws, no matter how sacred.

To sum up: in the face of positive social evils, the classical economists offered only the essentially negative policy of laissez faire. They were often very earnest men, honestly convinced that letting nature take her course was the only thing to do. Yet they were open to the accusation of acting without heart and without conscience, and of advancing economic theories that were only rationalizations of their economic interests. It is not surprising that, as a practical and social political philosophy, strict laissez faire liberalism today is almost extinct.

Bentham and Utilitarianism

The retreat from laissez faire originated with a man who was himself the friend and patron of the classical economists—Jeremy Bentham (1748–1832). Bentham behaved as popular opinion expects an eccentric philosopher to behave, astonishing his guests by trotting and bobbing about the garden before dinner, or, as he put it, performing his "anteprandial circumgyrations." He directed that at death his body be mummified and kept at the University College of London, which he had helped to found. In life, he projected dozens of schemes for the improvement of the human race, among them a model prison and reformatory which he called the Panopticon, because guards stationed in a central block could survey the activities of all the inmates. He coined new words by the dozen, too; some of them have been happily forgotten but others have made valuable contributions to the language, like "minimize," "codify," and "international."

Bentham founded his social teachings on the concept of utility, a modern form of the Epicurean doctrines of antiquity:

Nature has placed mankind under the governance of two sovereign masters, *pain* and *pleasure*. It is for them alone to point out what we ought to do. . . . They govern us in all we can do, in all we say, in all we think: every effort we can make to throw off our subjection, will serve but to demonstrate and confirm it. . . . The *principle of utility* recognizes this subjection, and assumes it for the foundation of that system, the object of which is to rear the fabric of felicity by the hands of reason and of law. . . .

The interest of the community is one of the most general expressions that can occur in the phraseology of morals: no wonder that the meaning of it is often lost. . . . The community is a fictitious *body,* composed of the individual persons who are considered as constituting as it were its *members.* The interest of the community then is, what?—the sum of the interests of the several members who compose it.

It is in vain to talk of the interest of the community without understanding what is the interest of the individual. A thing is said to promote the interest, or to be *for* the interest of an individual, when it tends to add to the sum total of his pleasures: or, what comes to the same thing, to diminish the sum total of his pains.*

Bentham listed a dozen or so simple pleasures and pains—the pleasures of the senses and the pains of deprivation, the pleasure of wealth and the pain of impoverishment, the pleasure of skill and the pain of awkwardness, and so on. Each category was subdivided, the pleasures of the senses, for instance, into those of taste, intoxication, smelling, touching, hearing, seeing, sex, health, and novelty. And each pleasure or pain could be evaluated according to its intensity, its duration, its certainty or uncertainty, its propinquity or remoteness, its fecundity, and its purity. This "felicific calculus," as Bentham termed it, was a good example of the Enlightenment's attempts to measure the immeasurable and to apply the exact methods of natural science to the subtleties of human behavior.

Nevertheless, Bentham was no doctrinaire philosophe and had no patience with attempts to equate ethical principles with nature's laws. He made short work of the French revolutionaries' Declaration of the Rights of Man: "*Natural rights* is simple nonsense: natural and imprescriptible rights, rhetorical nonsense,—nonsense upon stilts." He dismissed the eighteenth-century theory of political contracts as a mere fiction. Ordinarily, he believed, governments could best safeguard the well-being of the community by following a hands-off policy. In social and economic matters, they should act as "passive policemen," and give private initiative a generally free hand. Here a close and sympathetic relationship existed between Bentham and the classical economists. Yet Bentham realized that the state might become a more active policeman when the pursuit of self-interest by some individuals worked against the best interest of other individuals. If the pains endured by the many exceeded the pleasures enjoyed by the few, then the state should step in. In such a situation Bentham believed the state to be, in a word of his own devising, "omnicompetent," fit to undertake anything for the general welfare. Twentieth-century doctrines of

the welfare state owe a considerable debt to his utilitarianism.

By the time of his death, Bentham was already gaining an international reputation. He had advised reformers in Portugal, Russia, Greece, and Egypt, and his writings were to exert a broad influence, particularly in France, Spain, and the Spanish-American republics. As late as 1920, his Panopticon provided the plan for an American prison (in Joliet, Illinois). His most important English disciples, the Philosophic Radicals, pressed for reform of court procedures, local government, and poor relief, as the next chapter will show. But their aims were sometimes so narrowly utilitarian that critics claimed they wanted to drain life of all its savor and variety.

Mill and Humanitarian Liberalism

Charles Dickens, an informed and compassionate observer of industrial England, stated most eloquently the case against the dehumanized sameness implicit in the teachings of the utilitarians and the laissez faire liberals. Here from his novel *Hard Times* (1854), is his famous description of Coketown, which might have been any one of England's burgeoning industrial cities:

It contained several large streets all very like one another, and many small streets still more like one another, inhabited by people equally like one another, who all went in and out at the same hours, with the same sound upon the same pavements, to do the same work, and to whom every day was the same as yesterday and to-morrow, and every year the counterpart of the last and the next.

You saw nothing in Coketown but what was severely workful. If the members of a religious persuasion built a chapel there—as the members of eighteen religious persuasions had done—they made it a pious warehouse of red brick. . . . All the public inscriptions in the town were painted alike, in severe characters of black and white. The jail might have been the infirmary, the infirmary might have been the jail, the town-hall might have been either, or both, or anything else, for anything that appeared to the contrary in the graces of their construction. Fact, fact, fact, everywhere in the material aspect of the town; fact, fact, fact everywhere in the immaterial. The M'Choakumchild school was all fact, and the relations between master and man were all fact, and everything was fact between the lying-in hospital and the cemetery, and what you couldn't state in figures, or show to be purchaseable in the cheapest market and saleable in the dearest, was not, and never should be, world without end, Amen.*

Dickens saw what was wrong; John Stuart Mill (1806–1873) thought he knew what could be done to put it right. Mill grew up in an atmosphere dense with the teachings of utilitarianism and classical economics. From his father, who worked closely with Bentham and was a good friend of Ricardo, he received an education almost without parallel for intensity and speed. He

*J. Bentham, *An Introduction to the Principles of Morals and Legislation,* ed. W. Harrison (New York, 1948), pp. 125–127.

*Book 1, chap. 5.

"Over London by Rail": an 1872 engraving after Gustave Doré showing the living conditions of the working class.

began the study of Greek at three, was writing history at twelve, and at sixteen organized an active Utilitarian Society. At the age of twenty the overworked youth suffered a breakdown; as Mill relates in his *Autobiography,* he had become "a mere reasoning machine." So Mill turned for renewal to music and to the poetry of Wordsworth and Coleridge; presently he fell in love with Mrs. Taylor, a woman of warm personality, to whom he assigned the major credit for his later writings. They remained friends for twenty years until the death of Mr. Taylor at length enabled them to marry. Mill's personal history is important, for it goes far to explain why he endowed the liberal creed with the warmth and humanity it had lacked.

Mill's humane liberalism was expressed most clearly in his essay *On Liberty* (1859) and his *Autobiography* (1873). But it is evident, too, in his more technical works, notably *The Principles of Political Economy.* He first

published this enormously successful textbook in 1848 and later revised it several times, each revision departing more and more from the "dismal science" of Ricardo and Malthus. The first edition of the *Principles* rejected the gloomy implications of the Iron Law of Wages:

> By what means, then, is poverty to be contended against? How is the evil of low wages to be remedied? If the expedients usually recommended for the purpose are not adapted to it, can no others be thought of? Is the problem incapable of solution? Can political economy do nothing, but only object to everything, and demonstrate that nothing can be done?*

Of course something could be done, and Mill proceeded to outline schemes for curbing overpopulation by pro-

*J. S. Mill, *The Principles of Political Economy* (Boston, 1848), book 2, chap. 13.

moting emigration to the colonies and by "elevating the habits of the labouring people through education."

This one example is typical of the way in which Mill's quest for positive remedies led him to modify the laissez faire attitude so long associated with liberalism. Although he did not accept the ultimate socialistic solution of abolishing private property, he sympathized with the French national workshops of 1848 and with some of the socialistic blueprints that we shall examine shortly. He asserted that the workers should be allowed to organize trade unions, form cooperatives, obtain higher wages, and even receive a share of profits. These changes could best be secured within the framework of private enterprise, Mill believed, and not by public intervention. But he also believed that there were some matters so pressing that the state would have to step in. He read the reports of parliamentary investigating committees, like that on child labor cited earlier in this chapter, and he was shocked by their accounts of human degradation. So he recommended legislation to protect children and to improve intolerable living and working conditions.

Whereas Bentham had expected universal suffrage and universal education would be possible only in the distant future, Mill made them immediate objectives. All men, he believed, should have the right to vote; all should be prepared for it by receiving a basic minimum of schooling, if need be at state expense. Moreover, women should have the same rights—for Mill was a pioneer in the movement for their liberation, thanks in part to his esteem for Mrs. Taylor. He also proposed the introduction of proportional representation in the House of Commons, so that political minorities might be sure of a voice and might not be overwhelmed by the tyranny of the majority. The proposal and the fears that actuated it are particularly characteristic of Mill. He made protection of the individual's rights the basis of his famous essay *On Liberty:*

A government cannot have too much of the kind of activity which does not impede, but aids and stimulates, individual exertion and development. The mischief begins when, instead of calling forth the activity and powers of individuals and bodies, it substitutes its own activity for theirs; when, instead of informing, advising, and, upon occasion, denouncing, it makes them work in fetters, or bids them stand aside and does their work instead of them. The worth of a State, in the long run, is the worth of the individuals composing it . . . a State which dwarfs its men, in order that they may be more docile instruments in its hands even for beneficial purposes—will find that with small men no great thing can really be accomplished. . . .*

Critics have claimed that Mill's eloquent defense of the dissenting individual had undemocratic implications, for he seemed to mistrust the opinions of the majority and to favor those of the intellectual elite. Yet Mill's fear of excessive state power and the hopes he

*Utilitarianism, Liberty, and Representative Government, Everyman ed. (New York, 1910), pp. 169–170.

placed in enlightened individuals kept him firmly in the liberal tradition. He did not so much reject laissez faire liberalism as endow it with new sensitivity and flexibility. He had a more tender conscience than Adam Smith, Ricardo, or Bentham, and he lived at a later age, when the defects of industrialism were plainer. Therefore he found the exceptions to the rule of laissez faire more numerous and urgent than had his predecessors. Liberalism, as we understand the term today, is the legacy not of the "dismal scientists" but of Mill and other political thinkers and of the enlightened politicians who have shaped modern Western democracies.

V The Socialist Responses

In his later years, Mill referred to himself as a socialist; by his standard, however, most of us are socialists today. Universal suffrage for men and for women, universal free education, the curbing of laissez faire in the interests of the general welfare, the use of the taxing power to limit the accumulation of masses of private property—all these major reforms foreseen by Mill are now widely accepted. But they are not authentically socialistic. The authentic socialist does not stop, as Mill did, with changes in the *distribution* of wealth; he goes on to propose a radical change in arrangements for the *production* of goods. The means of production are to be transferred from the control of individuals to the control of the community as a whole.

Socialism—like fascism, liberalism, democracy—is one of those words in the political vocabulary so laden with moral connotations and personal conviction that their real meaning is often obscured. Everyone uses the word, yet mostly to indicate emphatic approval or disapproval of a given policy. The historian attempts to use the word neutrally, for purposes of description and not of passing judgment. Historically, socialism denotes any philosophy that advocates the vesting of production in the hands of society and not those of private individuals. In practice, it usually means that the state, acting as the trustee of the community, owns major industries like coal, railroads, and steel. Socialism in its most complete form involves public ownership of almost all the instruments of production including the land itself, virtually eliminating private property.

Today we tend to call this complete form communism. In the mid-nineteenth century, however, the terms "socialism" and "communism" were used almost interchangeably. Over a hundred years of history have gone into making the distinction now usually drawn between the two, which is not simply a matter of more and less complete versions of the same thing. Especially since the Bolshevik revolution in Russia in 1917, a communist has come to mean someone who believes that the collectivization of property can only be accomplished swiftly and violently, by revolution and outright seizure, while a socialist has come to mean someone who believes that it should be accomplished gradually and peacefully through normal political procedures and with compensation to private owners. Though the ends have their similarities, the means are worlds apart. This highly significant difference started to appear long before 1917, with the development of two divergent schools of socialist thought in the mid-nineteenth century, the Utopian and the Marxian.

The Utopians

The Utopian socialists were essentially good sons of the Enlightenment. If only men would apply their reason to solving the problems of an industrial economy, if only they would wipe out manmade inequalities by letting the great natural law of brotherhood operate freely—then utopia would be within their grasp, and social and economic progress would come about almost automatically. This is the common belief linking together the four chief Utopians of the early nineteenth century—Saint-Simon, Fourier, Robert Owen, and Louis Blanc.

Henri, count of Saint-Simon (1760–1825), belonged to a family so old and aristocratic that it claimed direct descent from Charlemagne. Educated by philosophes, Saint-Simon fought with the French army in the American War of Independence. During the French Revolution he made a large fortune by speculating in lands expropriated from the Church and the émigrés, then lost most of it through the trickery of an unscrupulous partner. Despite his own reverses, he never lost his enthusiasm for the enormous potentialities of the industrial age.

In accordance with the parable about the three thousand real leaders of France quoted earlier in this chapter, Saint-Simon would have given supreme political authority to a Parliament of Improvements, composed of ten industrialists and five each of artists, philosophers, chemists, physiologists, physicists, astronomers, and mathematicians, and presided over by one of the mathematicians. He admonished the members of the new elite: "Christianity commands you to use all your powers to increase as rapidly as possible the social welfare of the poor!"* Reform should come peacefully, through "persuasion and demonstration," and it should affect particularly the rich drones of society, "parasites" who "prey" on the actual producers. Combining the Enlightenment's respect for science with romanticism's zeal for the community, Saint-Simon proclaimed the one science transcending all others to be the application of the Golden Rule. Since even men of different nations were brothers, Saint-Simon envisaged a federation of European states. It would start with a union of the most advanced countries, France and Britain, under the Council of Newton, and would culminate in the establishment of a European parliament when all states had been "organized" to the point where they could live together in "harmony."

"Organization," "harmony," and "industry" were three of Saint-Simon's catchwords. When all three elements were coordinated, he believed, mankind could achieve some of the major improvements he proposed, among them great networks of highways and waterways. After Saint-Simon's death, his followers focused on the strain of social Christianity in his teaching and formed a fantastic though short-lived religious cult under the leadership of an engineer, "Father" Prosper Enfantin (1796–1864). Saint-Simon's enthusiasm for public improvements proved more lasting. Enfantin combined local railroads into the Paris-Lyons-Mediterranean trunk line and another Saint-Simonian, Ferdinand de Lesseps (1805–1894), promoted the building of the Suez Canal and made an abortive start at digging across the Isthmus of Panama. The very vagueness of Saint-Simon's concepts, and his failure to define them precisely, permitted almost every kind of social thinker, from laissez faire liberal to communist, to cite him with approval. Among his disciples were Mazzini, Louis Blanc, the Russian revolutionary pioneer Herzen, and the French positivist philosopher Comte. What was socialistic about Saint-Simon was his goal of achieving the reorganization and harmony of society as a whole, rather than merely improving the well-being of some of its individual members.

Fourier and Owen

Saint-Simon's compatriot and contemporary, Fourier (1772–1837), also extolled harmony, and drew up an elaborate blueprint for achieving it. At the French textile center of Lyons, Fourier was shocked by the wealth of the silk manufacturers and the misery of their workmen. At Paris, he was shocked when he found that a single apple cost a sum that would have bought a hundred apples in the countryside. Clearly, he concluded, something was amiss in a society and economy that permitted such fantastic divergences. He compared the historical importance of his apple with that of Newton, and honestly believed himself to be the Newton of the social sciences. Just as Newton had found the force holding the heavenly bodies in a state of mutual attraction, so Fourier claimed to have discovered the force holding the individuals of human society in a state of mutual attraction.

This force was *l'attraction passionnelle:* human beings are drawn to one another by their passions. Fourier drew up a list of passions, rather like the list of pleasures in Bentham's "felicific calculus"—sex, companionship, food, luxury, variety, and so on, to a total of 810. Since existing society thwarted their satisfaction, Fourier proposed its remodeling into units that he called *phalanges,* "phalanxes," each containing 400 acres of land and accommodating 500 to 2,000 human beings. Volunteers would form a phalanx by setting up a community

*Saint-Simon, *Selected Writings*, p. 116.

Factory in Tewkesbury, England, around 1860. Note the rules posted on the wall.

company, agreeing to split its profits three ways—five-twelfths to those who did the work, four-twelfths to those who undertook the management, and three-twelfths to those who supplied the capital.

Fourier's phalanx, with its relatively generous rewards to managers and capitalists, fell short of complete equality. Yet it did assign labor the largest share of the profits, and it foreshadowed many other features of socialist planning. Each phalanx would be nearly self-sufficient, producing in its own orchards, fields, and workshops most of the things required by its inhabitants. Adult workers who performed the most dangerous or unpleasant tasks would receive the highest remuneration. The inhabitants of the phalanx were to live in one large building, a sort of apartment hotel, which Fourier called a *phalanstère*. The phalanstère would provide the maximum opportunity for the satisfaction of man's sociable passions, and it would also make the routine of daily living more efficient by substituting one central kitchen for hundreds of separate ones. The sordid features of housekeeping could be left to little boys, who loved dirt anyway and would cheerfully form squads to dispose of garbage and refuse.

Other details of the phalanx bore witness to Fourier's reaction against the kind of monotony pictured in Dickens' Coketown. Places of work would be made as pleasant as possible by frequent, colorful redecoration. Members of the phalanx would change their jobs eight times a day because of the human predisposition to the

passion papillonne ("butterfly passion")—"enthusiasm cannot be sustained for more than an hour and a half or two hours in the performance of one particular operation." They would work from four to five in the morning to eight or nine at night, enjoying five meals, plus snacks. They would need only five hours of sleep, since the delightful variety of work would not tire them and the days would not be long enough to permit them to taste all the pleasures of life. It would all be so healthy that physicians would be superfluous and everyone would live to the age of 140.

Underneath these colorful details lay substantial contributions to socialist theory and social psychology. Some of Fourier's recommendations, like higher pay for dangerous jobs and devices for relieving the tedium of work, have become common practice in the modern business world. In the short run, however, Fourier tended to make Utopian socialism seem identical with "free love" and therefore, in the popular mind, with the grossest immorality. Both to eliminate the evil of prostitution and to allow human association the fullest possible scope, Fourier advocated complete sexual freedom in the phalanx; he recommended marriage only for the elderly, whose passions had begun to cool.

Another Utopian and advocate of sexual emancipation was the self-made British businessman Robert Owen (1772–1858). When he was still in his twenties, Owen took over the large cotton mills at New Lanark in Scotland and found conditions that shook him to the marrow, even though the previous owner had been accounted benevolent by the standards of the day. A large part of the working force in the mills consisted of children who had been recruited from orphanages in Edinburgh when they were between six and eight years old. Although the youngsters did get a little schooling after hours, Owen found many of them "dwarfs in body and mind." Adult laborers at New Lanark fared little better.

Remaking New Lanark into a model industrial village, Owen set out to show that he could increase his profits and increase the welfare of his laborers at the same time. For the adults he provided better working conditions, a ten-and-a-half-hour day, higher pay, and cleaner and roomier housing. He restrained the traditional Scottish Saturday night brawl by closing down the worst drinking places, making good liquor available at cheap prices, and punishing offenders who made themselves a public nuisance. As for the children, he raised the minimum age for employment to ten, hoping ultimately to put it at twelve, and he gave his child laborers time for some real schooling. His educational preferences followed Rousseau; advanced bookish subjects were avoided, while crafts, nature study, and other utilitarian subjects received much attention. A properly educated nation, Owen believed, would confute the gloomy predictions of Malthus, who "has not told us how much more food an intelligent and industrious people will create from the same soil, than will be produced by one ignorant and ill-governed."*

Owen inherited much of the optimism of the philosophes; he also inherited some of their failures and disappointments. Despite his own success as a philanthropic capitalist, few businessmen followed his example. Disappointed but not disheartened, Owen drew up plans for an idealized version of New Lanark, very much like Fourier's phalanx. His "parallelogram" (named for the layout of its buildings) was to be a voluntary organization, relatively small in size, neatly balanced between farming and industry, and decidedly advanced in Owen's recommendation for the partial abandonment of conventional ties of marriage and the family. In the 1820s, Owen visited America to finance an abortive effort to set up a parallelogram at New Harmony, Indiana. Undaunted by this failure, he spent the rest of his career publishing and supporting projects for social reform. He advocated the association of all labor in one big union—an experiment that failed; and he sought to reduce the expenditures of workingmen by promoting the formation of consumers' cooperatives—an experiment that succeeded. He also offended many of his contemporaries by his advocacy of sexual freedom, by his Voltairean attacks on established religion, and by his enthusiasm for spiritualism.

Both Owen and Fourier attracted followers not only in their native lands but also in the United States,

*R. Owen, *A New View of Society* (Glencoe, Ill., 1948), pp. 174–175.

THE CRISIS,

OR THE CHANGE FROM ERROR AND MISERY, TO TRUTH AND HAPPINESS.

1832.

IF WE CANNOT YET   RECONCILE ALL OPINIONS,

LET US ENDEAVOUR   TO UNITE ALL HEARTS.

IT IS OF ALL TRUTHS THE MOST IMPORTANT, THAT THE CHARACTER OF MAN IS FORMED FOR—NOT BY HIMSELF.

Design of a Community of 2,000 Persons, founded upon a principle, commended by Plato, Lord Bacon, Sir T. More, & R. Owen.

EDITED BY
ROBERT OWEN AND ROBERT DALE OWEN.

London:
PRINTED AND PUBLISHED BY J. EAMONSON, 15, CHICHESTER PLACE, GRAY'S INN ROAD.
STRANGE, PATERNOSTER ROW. PURKISS, OLD COMPTON STREET, AND MAY BE HAD OF ALL BOOKSELLERS.
1833.

Title page of *The Crisis,* bearing Robert Owen's portrait and Stedman Whitwell's design for an Owenite community.

where religious sects were already launching ventures in communal living. The American Fourierists included many intellectuals, among them the crusading editor Horace Greeley and the poet John Greenleaf Whittier. They sponsored more than thirty attempts to set up phalanxes; two celebrated ones were Brook Farm, near Boston, and Phalanx, near Red Bank, New Jersey. America also witnessed more than half a dozen Owenite experiments in addition to New Harmony. Most of these utopias did not prosper very long, and the few that became firmly established returned to conventional ways of individual profit-taking and family life.

Louis Blanc

Both Owen and Fourier relied on private initiative to build their model communities, and the latter kept a daily office hour for ten years to receive the millionaire who would finance his phalanxes and who never appeared. In contrast, Louis Blanc (1811–1882) developed Saint-Simon's vaguely formulated principle of "organization" into a doctrine of state intervention to achieve Utopian ends. Author of a pioneering history of the French Revolution from the socialist standpoint and implacable critic of the July Monarchy, Blanc outlined his scheme for social workshops in a pamphlet, *The Organization of Labor* (1839).

"What proletarians need," he wrote, "is the instruments of labor; it is the function of government to supply these. If we were to define our conception of the state, our answer would be that the state is the banker of the poor." * The government would finance and supervise the purchase of productive equipment and the formation of social workshops; it would withdraw its support and supervision once the workshops were on their feet. As the workshops gradually spread throughout France, socialistic enterprise would replace private enterprise, profits as such would vanish, and labor would emerge as the only class left in society.

Much of Louis Blanc's socialism was characteristically Utopian, particularly in his reliance on the workers to make their own arrangements for communal living. The real novelty of his plan lay in the role he assigned to the state and in the fact that he began to move socialism out of the realm of philanthropy and into that of politics. Ironically, politics were to prove his undoing: as we have already seen, alarmed conservatives identified the national workshops of 1848 as an effort to implement his social workshops, and he himself was forced into exile after the June Days.

Marx

With Karl Marx (1818–1883) socialism assumed its most intense form—revolutionary communism. Whereas the early socialists had anticipated a gradual and peaceful evolution toward utopia, Marx forecast a sudden and violent proletarian uprising, by which

*"L'Organisation du Travail," in *The French Revolution of 1848,* ed. J. A. R. Marriott (Oxford, 1913), 1:14. Our translation.

Karl Marx.

the workers would capture governments and make them the instruments for securing proletarian welfare. Dogmatic and cocksure, Marx was certain that he alone knew the answers and that the future of mankind would develop inevitably according to the pattern which he found in human history. His self-confidence, his truculence, and the fact that he was born at Trier, in the Prussian Rhineland, have earned him the label "the Red Prussian."

Marx found three laws in the pattern of history. First, economic determinism: he believed that economic conditions largely determined the character of all other human institutions—society and government, religion and art. Second, the class struggle: he believed that history was a dialectical process, a series of conflicts between antagonistic economic groups. In his own day the antagonists were the "haves" and the "have-nots"—the propertied bourgeois and the propertyless proletarians, who, possessing nothing but their working skills, had nothing to fall back on in bad times and were thus at the mercy of their masters. Third, the inevitability of communism: he believed that the class struggle was bound to produce one final upheaval that would raise the victorious proletariat over the prostrate bourgeoisie in eternal triumph.

Although Marx was born and died in the nineteenth century, he belonged in spirit partly to the eighteenth. Both his grandfathers were rabbis, but his father was a deist and a skeptic who trained him in the rationalism of the Enlightenment. Marx early acquired the kind of faith in natural law that had characterized the philosophes. In his case it was faith in the natural laws of economic determinism and the class struggle, fortified by the materialistic teachings of the anti-Christian philosopher Feuerbach, who proclaimed that *Man ist was er isst* ("One is what one eats"). From all this followed the boast made by Marx and his disciples that their socialism alone was "scientific," as opposed to the romantic doctrines of the Utopians.

The romantic philosophy of Hegel, however, provided the intellectual scaffolding of Marxism. Although Hegel had died in 1831, his influence permeated the University of Berlin during Marx's student days (1836–1841). Marx translated the Hegelian dialectic into the language of economic determinism and the class struggle. In his own day he believed that capitalistic production and the bourgeoisie comprised the thesis; the antithesis was the proletariat; and the synthesis, issuing from the communist revolution, would be true socialism. In later years Marx summarized his relation to Hegel:

> My dialectic method is not only different from the Hegelian but is its direct opposite. To Hegel, the life-process of the human brain, . . . which, under the name of "the Idea," he even transforms into an independent subject, is the demiurgos of the real world, and the real world is only the external, phenomenal form of "the Idea." With me, on the contrary, the ideal is nothing else than the material world

reflected by the human mind, and translated into forms of thought. . . .

The mystification which dialectic suffers in Hegel's hands, by no means prevents him from being the first to present its general form of working in a comprehensive and conscious manner. *With him it is standing on its head. It must be turned right again,* if you would discover the rational kernel within the mystical shell.*

By the time Marx was thirty, he had completed the outlines of his theory of scientific, revolutionary socialism. He had also become a permanent exile from his native Germany. On leaving the University of Berlin, he worked for a newspaper at Cologne in the Prussian Rhineland, then moved to Paris in 1843 after his atheistic articles had aroused the authorities against him. Exiled again, because the government of Louis Philippe feared his antibourgeois propaganda, he went to Brussels in 1845. Wherever he happened to be, he read widely in the economists of the past and talked with the socialists and other radicals of his own generation.

Everything Marx read and everyone he met strengthened his conviction that the capitalistic order was unjust, rotten, doomed to fall. From Adam Smith's labor theory of value he concluded that only the worker should receive the profits from the sale of a commodity, since the value of the commodity should be determined by the labor of the man who produced it. The Iron Law of Wages, however, confirmed Marx's belief that capitalism would never permit the worker to receive this just reward. And from reading other economists and observing the depression of the late 1840s, he concluded that economic crises were bound to occur again and again under a system that allowed capital to produce too much and labor to consume too little.

Engels and "The Communist Manifesto"

Meanwhile, Marx began his friendship and collaboration with Friedrich Engels (1820–1895). In many ways, the two men made a striking contrast. Marx was poor and quarrelsome, a man of few friends; except for his devotion to his wife and children, he was utterly preoccupied with his economic studies. Engels, on the other hand, was the son of a well-to-do German manufacturer and represented the family textile business in Liverpool and Manchester. He loved sports, women, and high living. But he also hated the iniquities of industrialism and, when he met Marx, had already written a bitter study, *The Condition of the Working Class in England,* based on his first-hand knowledge of the situation in Manchester.

Both Engels and Marx took an interest in the Communist League, a small international organization of radical workingmen. In 1847, the London office of the Communist League requested them to draw up a

*Preface to the second edition of *Capital,* Modern Library ed. (New York, n.d.), p. 25. Our italics.

Friedrich Engels.

program. Engels wrote the first draft, which Marx revised from start to finish; the result, published in January 1848, was *The Manifesto of the Communist Party.* Today, more than a century later, it remains the classic statement of Marxian socialism.

The *Manifesto* opens with the dramatic announcement that "A spectre is haunting Europe—the spectre of Communism." It closes with a stirring and confident appeal:

Let the ruling classes tremble at a Communist revolution. The proletarians have nothing to lose but their chains. They have a world to win.

Workingmen of all countries, unite!

In the few dozen pages of the *Manifesto,* Marx and Engels rapidly block in the main outlines of their theory. "The history of all hitherto existing society," they affirm, "is the history of class struggle." Changing economic conditions determined that the struggle should develop successively between "freeman and slave, patrician and plebeian, lord and serf, guildmaster and journeyman." The guild system gave way first to manufacture by large numbers of small capitalists and then to "the giant, modern industry."

Modern industry will inevitably destroy bourgeois society. It creates a mounting economic pressure by producing more goods than it can sell; it creates a mounting social pressure by narrowing the circle of capitalists to fewer and fewer individuals and depriving more and more people of their property and forcing them down to the proletariat. These pressures increase to the point where a revolutionary explosion occurs, a massive assault on private property. Landed property will be abolished outright; other forms of property are to be liquidated more gradually through the imposition of severe income taxes and the abolition of inherited wealth. Eventually, social classes and tensions will vanish, and "we shall have an association in which the free development of each is the condition for the free development of all."

"The free development of each is the condition for the free development of all"—the *Manifesto* provides only this vague description of the situation that would exist after the revolution. Since Marx defined political authority as "the organized power of one class for oppressing another," he apparently expected that, in the famous phrase, "the state would wither away" once it had created a classless regime. He also apparently assumed that the great dialectical process of history, having achieved its final synthesis, would then cease to operate in its traditional form. But, readers of the *Manifesto* may inquire, how is this possible? Will not the dialectic continue forever creating economic and political theses and antitheses? Will not the state always be with us? To these questions Marx offered no answer except the implication that somehow the liquidation of bourgeois capitalism would radically alter the course of history and transform humanity.

Marx oversimplified the complexities of human nature by trying to force it into the rigid mold of economic determinism and ignoring the nonmaterial motives and interests of men. Neither proletarians nor bourgeois have proved to be the simple economic stereotypes Marx supposed them to be. Labor has often behaved in scandalously un-Marxian fashion and assumed a markedly bourgeois outlook and mentality. Capital has put its own house in better order and eliminated the worst injustices of the factory system. No more than Malthus did Marx foresee the notable rise in the standard of living that began in the mid-nineteenth century and has continued, with an occasional backward slip, down to our own day.

Since Marx failed to take into account the growing strength of nationalism, the *Manifesto* confidently expected the class struggle to transcend national boundaries. In social and economic warfare, nation would not be pitted against nation, nor state against state; the proletariat everywhere would fight the bourgeoisie. "Workingmen have no country" and "national differences and antagonisms are vanishing gradually from day to day." In Marx's own lifetime, however, national differences and antagonisms were increasing rapidly from day to day. Within a few months of the publication of the *Manifesto,* the revolutions of 1848 disclosed the antagonism between Italians and Austrians, Austrians and Hungarians, Hungarians and Slavs, Slavs and Germans.

The *Communist Manifesto* anticipated the strengths as well as the weaknesses of the communist movement. First, it foreshadowed the very important role to be played by propaganda, supplying the earliest of those effective catch phrases that have become the mark of Marxism—the constant sneering at bourgeois morality, bourgeois law, and bourgeois property, and the dramatic references to the "spectre haunting Europe" and to the proletarians who "have nothing to lose but their chains." Second, the *Manifesto* anticipated the emphasis to be placed on the role of the party in forging the proletarian revolution. The communists, Marx declared in 1848, were a spearhead, "the most advanced section of the working class parties of every country." In matters of theory, "they have over the great mass of the proletariat the advantage of clearly understanding the line of march, the conditions, and the ultimate general results of the proletarian movement."

Third, the *Manifesto* assigned the state a great role in the revolution. Among the policies recommended by Marx were "centralization of credit in the hands of the state," and "extension of factories and instruments of production owned by the state." Thus, despite the supposition that the state would wither away, the *Manifesto* faintly anticipated the totalitarian regime of the Soviet Union. And, finally, it clearly established the line dividing communism from the other forms of socialism. Marx's dogmatism, his philosophy of history, and his belief in the necessity for a "total" revolution made his brand of socialism a thing apart. Like a religious prophet granted a revelation, Marx expected his gospel to supplant all others. He scorned and pitied the Utopian socialists. They were about as futile, he wrote, as "organizers of charity, members of societies for the prevention of cruelty to animals, temperance fanatics, hole-and-corner reformers of every kind."

Marxism after 1848

Age neither mellowed Marx nor greatly altered his views. From 1849 until his death in 1883, he lived in London, where, partly because of his own financial mismanagement, his family experienced the misery of a proletarian existence in the slums of Soho. After poverty and near-starvation had caused the death of three of his children, he eventually obtained a modest income from the generosity of Engels and from his own writings.

Throughout the 1850s Marx contributed a weekly article on British politics or international affairs to Horace Greeley's radical paper, *The New York Tribune.* He produced a series of pamphlets, of which the most famous was *The Eighteenth Brumaire of Louis Napoleon,* a study of the fall of the short-lived Second French Republic. Meantime, he spent his days in the British Museum, reading the reports of parliamentary investigating committees and piling up evidence on the condition of miners and factory hands. Thus Marx accumulated the material for his full-dress economic study, *Das Kapital.* The first volume of this massive analysis of capitalism appeared in 1867; two further volumes, pieced together from his notes, were published after his death.

In *Das Kapital,* Marx elaborated, but did not substantially revise, the doctrines of the *Communist Manifesto.* He spelled out the labor theory of value according to which the worker created the total value of the commodity that he produced, yet received in the form of wages only a part of the price for the item. The difference between the sale price and the worker's wages constituted *surplus value,* something actually created by labor but appropriated by capital as profit. *Das Kapital* goes on to relate surplus value to the ultimate doom of capitalism. It is the nature of capitalism, Marx insists, to diminish its own profits by replacing human labor with machines and thus gradually choking off the source of surplus value. Hence will arise the mounting crises of overproduction and underconsumption predicted by the *Manifesto.* In a famous passage toward the close of Volume I of *Das Kapital,* Marx compared capitalism to an integument, a skin or shell, increasingly stretched and strained from within. One day these internal pressures would prove irresistible: "This integument is burst asunder. The knell of capitalist private property sounds. The expropriators are expropriated." *

In 1864, three years before the first volume of *Das Kapital* was published, Marx joined in the formation of the First International Workingmen's Association. This was an ambitious attempt to organize workers of every country and of every variety of radical belief. A loose federation rather than a coherent political party, the First International soon began to disintegrate, and expired in 1876. Increasing persecution by hostile governments helped to bring on its end; but so, too, did the factional quarrels that repeatedly engaged both its leaders and the rank and file of its members. And Marx himself set the example, both by his intolerance of disagreement and by his incapacity for practical politics.

In 1889, the Second International was organized; it lasted down to the time of World War I and the Bolshevik revolution in Russia. The Second International was more coherently organized and more political in character than the First International had been. It represented the Marxian socialist or Social Democratic parties, which, as we shall see in later chapters, were becoming important forces in the major countries of continental Europe. Among its leaders were men more adept than Marx himself at the political game. Yet the old spirit of factionalism continued to weaken the International. Some of its leaders tenaciously defended the precepts of the master and forbade any cooperation between socialists and the bourgeois political parties; these were the orthodox Marxists. Other leaders of the Second International were, from the orthodox standpoint, heretics. While calling themselves disciples of Marx, they revised his doctrines in the direction of moderation and of harmonization with the views of the Utopians. These "revisionists" believed in cooperation between classes rather than in a struggle to the death, and they trusted that human decency and intelligence, working through the machinery of democratic government, could avert the horrors of outright

*Modern Library ed., p. 837.

class war. Both orthodox and heretical Marxists have persisted to the present day, though the precise connotations of orthodoxy and heresy have varied with shifts in the Communist Party line.

VI Apostles of Violence—and Nonviolence

The various forms of liberalism and socialism by no means exhausted the range of responses to the economic and social problems created by the Industrial Revolution. As later chapters will show, nationalists reinvigorated old mercantilist ideas, not only advocating tariffs to protect agriculture and industry but also demanding empires abroad to provide new markets for surplus products, new fields for the investment of surplus capital, and new settlements for surplus citizens. Here we shall examine the responses made by the apostles of violence and by the nonviolent preachers of mutualism and of Christian good will and good works.

Blanquism and Anarchism

Left-wing tradition assigns the honor of being the first modern socialists to Gracchus Babeuf and his fellow conspirators under the French Directory in 1796–1797. The equalitarianism of Babeuf, though fervent, was too loosely formulated to be called truly socialist; the only direct link between him and later socialist doctrines came through the book about his attempted coup, *The Conspiracy of the Equals,* written thirty years after the event by his chief lieutenant, Filippo Buonarotti (the nephew several generations removed of Michelangelo). Buonarotti, who veiled the failure of the Equals in a romantic mist, fired a new generation of would-be revolutionaries with the conviction that the only way to improve the human condition lay through immediate violent action in the manner of the Reign of Terror.

The leader of these new terrorists was Auguste Blanqui (1805–1881), a professional revolutionary who participated in the Paris revolts of 1830, 1848, and 1870–1871 (in the wake of defeat in the Franco-Prussian War). Although Blanqui shared the socialists' sympathy with the exploited working class, he had none of their zeal for drawing up detailed blueprints and none of their patience in waiting until conditions for change were ripe. He was not an ideologist but an activist, believing that the imposition of a dictatorial regime by an elite vanguard of conspirators would be the only way to deal with a bourgeois capitalist society. An inveterate plotter of violence, he was put in jail by every regime in post-Napoleonic France, from the Bourbon restoration to the Third Republic, and spent forty years of his life span of seventy-six in prison. When his movement petered out in the 1870s, his followers tended to join the Marxian socialists. His dedication to activism made him a significant figure in left-wing history: it has been said that Lenin's formula for a successful Bolshevik revolution was Marxism plus Blanquism.

Other apostles of violence called themselves anarchists, believing that the best government is no government at all. Most of the recipes for socialism contained at least a dash of anarchism: witness the Utopians' mistrust of governments and the withering away of the state promised by the Marxists. For a handful of anarchists, however, it was not enough that the state should wither at some distant time; such an instrument of oppression should be annihilated at once. The weapon of the anarchist terrorists was the assassination of heads of state, and they provided the stereotype of the bearded, wild-eyed, bomb-toting radical. At the turn of the century, their assassinations levied an impressive toll—the French president Carnot in 1894, King Humbert of Italy in 1900, and the American president McKinley in 1901. Otherwise the terrorists accomplished little except to drive the governments they hated to more vigorous measures of retaliation.

The anarchist ideal, however, exerted an important influence on the proletarian movement. The Russian scientist and thinker Prince Peter Kropotkin (1842–1921) made the most complete statement of its theory and ideals in his book *Mutual Aid: A Factor in Evolution* (1902). Kropotkin foresaw a revolution that would abolish the state as well as private property and that would lead to a new society of autonomous groups wherein the individual would achieve greater fulfillment and would need to labor only four to five hours a day. Kropotkin's countryman and fellow anarchist, Bakunin (1814–1876), helped to shape the Russian revolutionary movement and won the attention of workers from many countries by his participation in the First International. Although Bakunin drew only a vague sketch of his utopia, he made it clear that the millennium was to be achieved through an international rebellion set off by small groups of anarchist conspirators.

Bakunin contributed to the formation of the program known as anarcho-syndicalism (from the French word *syndicat,* which means an economic grouping, particularly a trade union). The anarcho-syndicalists disbelieved in political parties, even Marxist ones; they believed in direct action by the workers to culminate in a spontaneous general strike that would free labor from the capitalistic yoke. Meantime, workers could rehearse for the great day by forming unions and by engaging in acts of anticapitalist sabotage. These theories received forceful expression in *Reflections on Violence* (1908) by a French engineer and anarcho-syndicalist, Georges Sorel, who declared that belief in the general strike constituted a kind of myth that would convert workers into saboteurs.

Proudhon and Mutualism

The writer most frequently cited by the anarcho-syndicalists was the French publicist Proudhon (1809–

1865). "What is property?" Proudhon asked in a famous pamphlet in 1840—"Property is theft." Although Marx predicted the pamphlet would rank in importance with Siéyès' *What Is the Third Estate?* his praise turned to contempt when he found that his own views no longer commanded Proudhon's allegiance. A second pamphlet by Proudhon, *The Philosophy of Poverty,* elicited a Marxian rebutal tartly entitled *The Poverty of Philosophy.* The property that Proudhon called "theft" was not all property but unearned income, the revenues that men gained from investing their wealth rather than from the sweat of their brows. Of all the forms of unearned income, the worst, in Proudhon's view, was the "leprosy of interest," and the most diabolical of capitalists was the moneylender. Under existing conditions, only the well-to-do could afford to borrow, but in the utopia envisaged by Proudhon all men would be able to secure credit. Instead of private banks and the Bank of France, there would be a People's Bank, lending to all without interest and issuing notes that would replace ordinary money. The credit provided by the People's Bank would enable each man to become a producer on his own.

Thus, where Marx foresaw a revolution in ownership of the means of production, Proudhon foresaw a "revolution of credit," a revolution in financing production. Where Marx proposed to have the proletariat liquidate the bourgeoisie, Proudhon proposed to raise the proletarian to the level of the bourgeois by making every worker an owner. Proudhon's utopia was not collectivized or socialized; it was a loose association of middle-class individualists. Because Proudhon dreaded restraints upon the individual, he opposed the social workshops of Louis Blanc and the phalanxes of Fourier as too restrictive. He projected, instead, a society founded upon mutualism. Economically, mutualism would take the form of associations of producers in agriculture and industry, not unlike the producers' cooperatives found among farmers today. Politically, it would take the form of federalism—that is, a loose federation of associations would replace the centralized state rather on the model of the Swiss confederation of local cantons.

Proudhon's doctrines exerted a strong appeal in France, with its devotion to individualism and with the legacy of federalism bequeathed by the Girondins of the Revolution. Tens of thousands of small businessmen in France were often denied financial credit by the bankers denounced by Proudhon, and thus always stood on the edge of being displaced from the lower fringes of the middle class to the proletariat. Proudhon's attacks on the state naturally fed the anarchist strain in anarcho-syndicalism. Yet much of his teaching contradicted the syndicalist strain. Not only did he dislike trade unions as unnatural restrictions on individual liberty; he deplored all activities suggesting class warfare, including the strikes so dear to the syndicalists. These views, together with his expressed hostility to Jewish moneylenders, have led some modern critics to call Proudhon an incipient fascist; other critics, however, have dismissed the charge as absurd because Proudhon seemed to reject entirely any kind of totalitarian state.

Christian Socialists and Christian Democrats

Another effort to mitigate class antagonisms came from the Christian Socialists, a small group of mid-nineteenth-century reformers from the Anglican clergy who urged the Church of England to put aside theological disputes and direct its efforts toward ending social abuses. One of these Christian Socialists was Charles Kingsley (1819–1875), remembered today chiefly as the author of children's fiction but more significant historically for his didactic social novel, *Alton Locke,* and the pamphlet, *Cheap Clothes and Nasty,* exposing the sweatshops where tailors and seamstresses worked long hours for meager pay, often in appallingly crowded and unsanitary surroundings. The Christian Socialists attacked materialism and championed brotherly love against unbrotherly strife, association and cooperation against exploitation and competition. They were, however, scarcely more socialistic than John Stuart Mill had been, and relied far more on private philanthropy than on state intervention. Kingsley, for instance, helped launch the Working Men's College in London and promoted other activities of the type later identified with the YMCA.

The Catholic counterparts of the Christian Socialists called their rather similar programs by the more accurate name of Christian Democracy or Social Christianity. By the second half of the nineteenth century an atmosphere of crisis was enveloping the Roman Church. A thousand years of papal rule in central Italy ended when the city of Rome passed to the newly unified Kingdom of Italy in 1870; anticlerical legislation threatened traditional Catholic bulwarks in Italy, France, and Germany; and the materialism of the Industrial Revolution and the new ideologies of science, nationalism, and socialism were all competing for the allegiance of Catholic workingmen. In the face of all these problems, the Church responded initially by seeking refuge in the past.

Pope Pius IX (1846–1878), whose experiences in 1848 and 1849 had ended his earlier flirtation with liberalism, issued in 1864 the *Syllabus of Errors,* condemning many social theories and institutions not consecrated by centuries of tradition. While Pius also condemned the materialism implicit in laissez faire, socially minded Catholics were disturbed by his apparent hostility to trade unions and democracy and by his statement that it was an error to suppose that the pope "can and ought to reconcile and harmonize himself with progress, liberalism, and modern civilization."

The successor of Pius, Leo XIII (1878–1903), recognized that the Church could hardly continue to turn its back on progress, liberalism, and modernity without suffering serious losses. Pope Leo fully recognized the rapid changes being worked by science and technology; as a papal nuncio he had witnessed them at first hand in the industrial regions of Belgium, France, and Germany. He knew that Catholicism was flourishing in the supposedly hostile climate of the democratic and largely Protestant United States. Moreover, his studies of Saint Thomas Aquinas convinced him that the Church had much to gain and little to lose by following the middle-of-the-road social and economic policies recommended by that great medieval Schoolman. Accordingly, Leo XIII issued a series of famous documents, notably the encyclical letter *Rerum Novarum* (Concerning New Things, 1891).

In *Rerum Novarum* Pope Leo exposed the defects of capitalism as vigorously as any socialist, and then attacked with equal vigor the socialist view of property and the socialist doctrine of class war. He pronounced it a "great mistake" to believe

> that class is naturally hostile to class, and that the wealthy and the workingmen are intended by nature to live in mutual conflict. . . . Each needs the other: Capital cannot do without Labor, nor Labor without Capital.

Leo therefore urged the economic man to act as a Christian man of good will:

> Religion teaches the laboring man . . . to carry out honestly and fairly all equitable agreements freely entered into; never to injure the property, nor to outrage the person, of an employer; never to resort to violence . . . ; and to have nothing to do with men of evil principles, who work upon the people with artful promises, and excite foolish hopes which usually end in useless regrets, followed by insolvency. Religion teaches the wealthy owner and the employer that their workpeople are not to be accounted their bondsmen; that in every man they must respect his dignity and worth as a man and as a Christian; that labor is not a thing to be ashamed of, if we lend ear to right reason and to Christian philosophy, but is an honorable calling, enabling a man to sustain his life in a way upright and creditable; and that it is shameful and inhuman to treat men like chattels to make money by, or to look upon them merely as so much muscle or physical power.*

While Leo XIII believed that the state must always remain subordinate to the interests of the individuals composing it, he did not necessarily defend laissez faire policies. On the contrary, he repeatedly cited Saint Thomas to prove that the state should take measures for the general welfare. On behalf of capital, it should discourage agitators and protect property from violence. On behalf of labor, it should work to remove "the causes which lead to conflict between employer and employed." For example, it might regulate child labor, limit the hours of work, and insist that Sundays be free for religious activity and for rest. Leo also believed that the workers must help themselves, and *Rerum*

The Great Encyclical Letters of Pope Leo XIII (New York, 1903), pp. 218, 219.

Novarum concluded with a fervent appeal for the formation of Catholic trade unions.

These Catholic unions exist today, but they are only a minority in the realm of organized labor. Neither the Christian democracy of Leo XIII nor the Christian socialism of the Anglican reformers has achieved all that the founders hoped. Yet the Christian democrats eventually came to play a central part in the politics of Germany, Italy, and other European states, particularly after World War II. And in Britain, at the beginning of the twentieth century, both Marxism and the Christian socialist tradition helped to attract workingmen and middle-class intellectuals to the developing Labor party.

Reading Suggestions on the Industrial Revolution

The Industrial Revolution

H. J. Habakkuk and M. Postan, eds., *The Cambridge Economic History of Europe,* Vol. 6, parts 1 and 2 (Cambridge Univ. Press, 1965). Essays on the Industrial Revolution by ranking scholars. The contribution by David Landes has been amplified and issued separately: *The Unbound Prometheus: Technological Change and Industrial Development in Western Europe from 1750 to the Present* (*Cambridge Univ. Press).

E. J. Hobsbawm, *The Pelican Economic History of Britain,* Volume 3; *Industry and Empire* (*Penguin). By a ranking Marxian scholar, author also of the provocative *Age of Revolution, 1789–1848* (*Mentor).

W. O. Henderson, *The Industrialization of Europe, 1780–1914* (*Harcourt) and T. Kemp, *Industrialization in Nineteenth-Century Europe* (*Humanities). Useful for developments on the Continent.

W. W. Rostow, *Stages of Economic Growth: A Non-Communist Manifesto* (*Cambridge Univ. Press). Stimulating essay on the timetable of industrialization. Its implications are discussed in W. W. Rostow, ed., *The Economics of Take-off into Sustained Growth* (St. Martin's, 1963).

P. M. Deane and W. A. Cole, *British Economic Growth, 1688–1959,* 2nd ed. (*Cambridge Univ. Press). Good introduction.

P. M. Deane, *The First Industrial Revolution* (*Cambridge Univ. Press); P. Mantoux, *The Industrial Revolution in the Eighteenth Century* (*Torchbooks); T. S. Ashton, *The Industrial Revolution, 1760–1830* (*Galaxy); R. M. Hartwell, ed., *The Causes of the Industrial Revolution in England* (Methuen, 1967). Four useful works on the early history of modern industrialism.

E. P. Thompson, *The Making of The English Working Class* (*Penguin). Detailed account of the impact of the French Revolution and the early Industrial Revolution.

J. Clapham, *An Economic History of Modern Britain,* rev. ed., 3 vols. (Cambridge Univ. Press, 1930–1938) and *Economic Development of France and Germany, 1815–1914* (*Cambridge Univ. Press). Older scholarly works that are still worth reading.

L. Mumford, *Technics and Civilization* (*Harbinger). A sweeping survey, first published in the 1930s; dated but still suggestive.

The Responses of Liberalism

C. Brinton, *English Political Thought in the Nineteenth Century* (Benn, 1933). Essays on Bentham, Mill, Owen, Kingsley, and other important figures.

W. H. Coates and H. V. White, *The Ordeal of Liberal Humanism* (*McGraw-Hill). Useful brief textbook account.

E. Halévy, *The Growth of Philosophic Radicalism* (*Macmillan, 1928). Celebrated older study of Bentham and his Utilitarian followers.

M. Mack, *Jeremy Bentham* (Heinemann, 1962). More recent biography.

T. R. Malthus, *Population: The First Essay* (*Ann Arbor). The original essay of 1798, stating Malthusianism in its most undiluted form.

R. Heilbroner, *The Worldly Philosophers,* rev. ed. (*Touchstone). A good introduction to the philosophy of laissez faire.

M. S. Packe, *The Life of John Stuart Mill* (Macmillan, 1954). Sound biography. For a psychohistory of the famous father and son, consult B. Mazlish, *James and John Stuart Mill* (Basic Books, 1975).

J. S. Mill, *Autobiography* (*several eds.); *Principles of Political Economy* (*Penguin); *On Liberty* (*Bobbs); *On the Subjection of Women* (*Fawcett World); *Utilitarianism* (*Bobbs). Major writings of the great Victorian liberal.

The Socialist Responses

A. Fried and R. Sanders, *Socialist Thought: A Documentary History* (*Anchor). Informative collection of source materials.

H. W. Laidler, *A History of Socialism* (*Apollo). Updated version of an older standard account.

G. D. H. Cole, *A History of Socialist Thought,* Vols. 1, 2 (St. Martin's, 1953–1960). Pedestrian but sensible detailed account.

G. Lichtheim, *Origins of Socialism* (*Praeger) and *A Short History of Socialism* (*Praeger). Highly useful introductions.

J. C. Schumpeter, *Capitalism, Socialism, and Democracy* (*Torchbooks). Thoughtful survey, extending into the present century.

Edmund Wilson, *To the Finland Station* (*Anchor). A sympathetic and balanced history of socialism.

F. Manuel, ed., *Utopias and Utopian Thought* (*Beacon). A useful documentary collection. Manuel has written several studies of the utopians, the most detailed being *The New World of Henri Saint-Simon* (*Univ. of Notre Dame Press).

H. de Saint-Simon, *Social Organization, The Science of Man, and Other Writings,* F. Markham, ed. (*Torchbooks). Well-edited anthology.

N. V. Riasanovsky, *The Teaching of Charles Fourier* (Univ. of California Press, 1969). Now the standard work on the French utopian.

J. F. C. Harrison, *Quest for the New Moral World: Robert Owen and the Owenites in Britain and America* (Routledge, 1969). Now the standard study of the radical British businessman and his impact.

K. Marx and F. Engels, *Basic Writings on Politics and Philosophy,* L. S. Feuer, ed. (*Anchor). Good selection.

I. Berlin, *Karl Marx: His Life and Environment* (*Galaxy). Brilliant study.

S. Avineri, *The Social and Political Thought of Karl Marx* (*Cambridge Univ. Press), and G. Lichtheim, *Marxism: An Historical and*

Critical Study, 2nd ed. (*Praeger). Thoughtful recent evaluations.

J. Braunthal, *History of the International,* 2 vols. (Praeger, 1967). Sound scholarly study.

Apostles of Violence—and Nonviolence

A. B. Spitzer, *The Revolutionary Theories of Auguste Blanqui* (Columbia Univ. Press, 1957). Good study of the perennial French agitator and prisoner.

P. A. Kropotkin, *Selected Readings on Anarchism and Revolution* (*MIT Press). Useful introduction to his ideas.

J. Joll, *The Anarchists* (Grosset and Dunlap, 1964). Helpful introduction.

G. Sorel, *Reflections on Violence* (*Collier). The famous defense of direct revolutionary action and the general strike.

Pope Leo XIII et al., *Seven Great Encyclicals* (*Paulist-Newman).

Basic statements of the new social and economic position taken by the Vatican in the late nineteenth century.

Historical Fiction

Charles Dickens, *Hard Times* (*several editions). The shortest of his great social novels, with memorable descriptions of Coketown and its citizens.

Mrs. Elizabeth Gaskell, *North and South* (Oxford Univ. Press, 1973) and *Mary Barton* (*Norton). Instructive social novels by a close associate of Dickens.

Emile Zola, *Germinal* (*Signet). Famous French novel about a strike in a coal mine; less inhibited than its English counterparts.

E. Bellamy, *Looking Backward, 2000–1887* (*several editions). Sensitive adaptation of socialist views by a late nineteenth-century American.

The Western Democracies in the Nineteenth Century

Introduction: Democracies Large and Small

For the historian the nineteenth century means the hundred years from Waterloo to the outbreak of World War I. This chapter follows down to 1914 the domestic history of the major self-governing Western nations—Great Britain, France, Italy, and the United States. They are all democracies today and, though they have all had their lapses from democratic standards, especially France and Italy, they are all relatively "old" democracies. But so are many of the smaller states of western and northern Europe. The Netherlands, Belgium, Switzerland, and the Scandinavian countries have all worked out their national variants of liberalism. In particular, Denmark, Norway, and Sweden, with their homogeneous populations, their common Lutheran religion, their common traditions, and their very high rate of literacy, have sometimes surpassed the larger states in making democracy function effectively. Visitors to Copenhagen, Oslo, or Stockholm are impressed not only by their tidiness but also by the absence of slums and other signs of poverty. And the cooperatives of Denmark and Sweden have received much praise as the "middle way" between welfare socialism and uncontrolled economic individualism.

The history of these smaller states is in no way insignificant or uninteresting, even though a book of this scope cannot treat it in any detail. They too underwent most of the stresses and strains of the rest of Europe. Belgium, notably, was divided—and still is—between French-speaking and Flemish-speaking areas, often in conflict. In 1847, Switzerland underwent a miniature civil war between the *Sonderbund* (Separate League), an alliance of the more conservative and rural Catholic cantons, and the more liberal and urban Protestant cantons. The Sonderbund was dissolved, and the Swiss federal government strengthened on the model of the United States. Sweden and Norway, yoked together in the Vienna settlement of 1815, parted com-

pany peacefully in 1907, after nearly a century of restive partnership.

These smaller states have also helped to maintain the balance of international politics and to shape European opinion, a role for which they are particularly well suited by their relative detachment from ambitious nationalist aspirations. They have collaborated effectively in many forms of international activity. The Hague, the Dutch capital, was the meeting place of two pioneering conferences (1899 and 1907) called to formulate rules and machinery for the regulation of international disputes; after World War I Geneva became the capital of the League of Nations; and after World War II a Norwegian, a Swede, and a representative of a newer small democracy, Austria, served the league's successor, the United Nations, as secretary-general. Moreover, Scandinavian contingents have been a mainstay of the peacekeeping forces stationed in trouble spots under United Nations auspices.

In many fields the citizens of the smaller European democracies have contributed proportionately more heavily to our modern Western culture than their numbers would suggest. To cite a few examples: Switzerland supplied the great historian of the Renaissance, Burckhardt, and Belgium, the poet and playwright Maeterlinck. From Finland came the composer Sibelius; from Norway, Ibsen and his modern social dramas; from Holland, the physicist Lorentz, winner of the Nobel Prize in 1902; and from Sweden, the novelist and playwright Strindberg as well as Nobel himself, the munitions king who endowed the prizes for peaceful achievement.

Spain, too, though not a democracy, had a varied and interesting history in the nineteenth century, swinging between conservative monarchy and radical republicanism after the revolution of 1820 had been suppressed. But Spain was now a minor power and, though her cultural achievements, especially the work

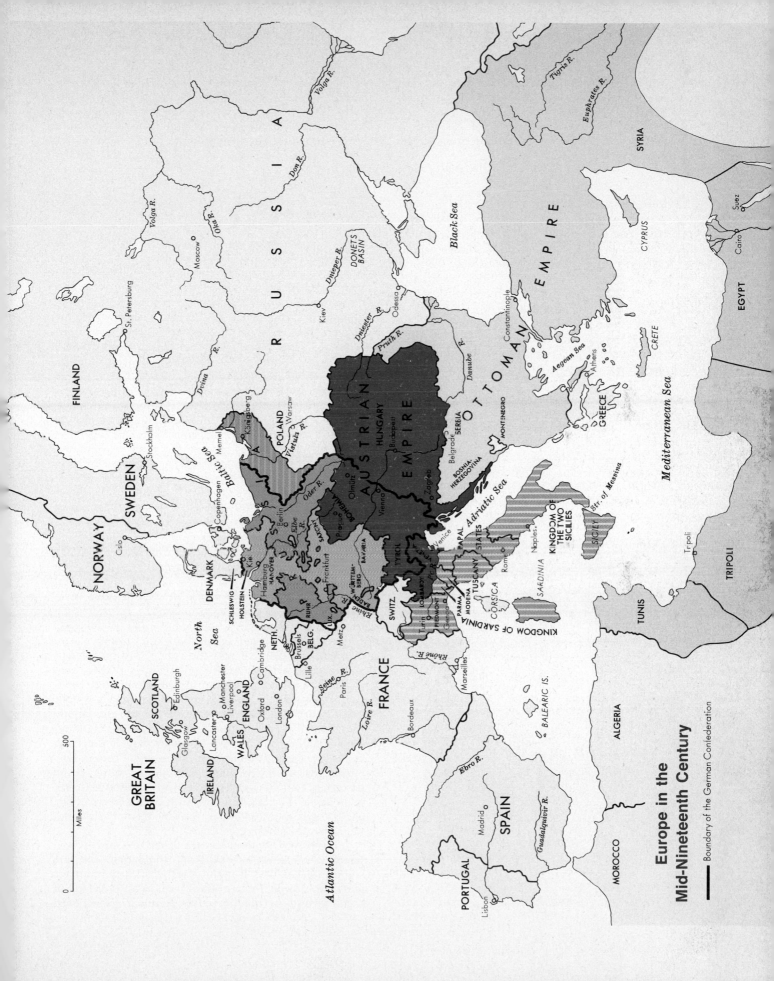

Europe in the
Mid-Nineteenth Century

Boundary of the German Confederation

GREAT
BRITAIN

SCOTLAND

Glasgow
Edinburgh

IRELAND
Lancaster
Liverpool Manchester
WALES
ENGLAND
Oxford Cambridge
London

NORWAY
Oslo

SWEDEN
Stockholm

FINLAND

P R U S S I A

Moscow

Oka R.

Volga R.

St. Petersburg

R U S S I A

Don R.

Volga R.

Dvina R.

Dnieper R.

Kiev

DONETS
BASIN

Odessa

Dniester R.

Pruth R.

Warsaw
POLAND
Vistula R.

Königsberg
Memel

Copenhagen
DENMARK
Baltic Sea

SCHLESWIG
HOLSTEIN
Kiel
Hamburg
HANOVER
Berlin
Elbe R.
Oder R.
SAXONY
BOHEMIA
Olmütz
Prague
Vienna
BAVARIA
Frankfurt
RUHR
BADEN WÜRTTEM-
BERG
Rhine R.
Lux.
Metz
SWITZ.
TYROL

AUSTRIAN
HUNGARY
EMPIRE

Budapest

Zagreb

Black Sea

Constantinople

O T T O M A N
E M P I R E

Danube R.

Belgrade
SERBIA
BOSNIA-
HERZEGOVINA
MONTENEGRO

Aegean Sea

Athens
GREECE

CRETE

CYPRUS

SYRIA

Suez

Cairo

EGYPT

NETH.
Brussels
BELG.
Lille

North
Sea

Atlantic
Ocean

Paris
Seine R.
Loire R.
FRANCE

Bordeaux

Ebro R.

SPAIN
Madrid

PORTUGAL
Lisbon

Guadalquivir R.

MOROCCO

ALGERIA

TUNIS

Rhone R.

Marseilles

Turin
PIEDMONT
Genoa
LOMBARDY
PARMA
MODENA
Venice
PAPAL
TUSCANY STATES
Rome
Naples
KINGDOM OF
THE TWO
SICILIES

KINGDOM OF SARDINIA

SARDINIA

CORSICA

BALEARIC IS.

Adriatic Sea

Str. of Messina

SICILY

Mediterranean Sea

Tripoli

TRIPOLI

Tigris R.

Euphrates R.

500
Miles
0

of her novelists, were distinguished, fuller consideration of Spanish history will be postponed until in the civil war of the 1930s Spain once more enters the mainstream of events. We must now turn to the states who have played the major roles in our story. Of these in the nineteenth century, Britain was unquestionably the first, the leading power.

II Britain, 1815–1914

In the years immediately after Waterloo, Britain went through a typical postwar economic crisis. Unsold goods accumulated, and the working classes experienced widespread unemployment and misery. Popular suffering increased as a result of the Corn Law of 1815, which was the latest in a series of protective tariffs on grain and forbade the importation of cheap foreign grain until the price of the home-grown commodity rose to a specified level. This assured the profits of the English grain farmer and raised the cost of bread for the average English family. Although trade unions were outlawed by the Combination Acts, workers nonetheless asserted themselves in strikes and in popular agitation that helped prepare the way for the parliamentary Reform Bill of 1832. By the 1820s, economic conditions were improving, and Britain embarked on the process of reform that was to make her a democratic state.

Into this process were fed the economic and social drives noted in the last chapter, and twentieth-century Britain was to become not only a very complete political democracy but also in part an economic and social

Queen Victoria and some of her children grouped around bust of "Dear Albert," 1867.

democracy. Yet reform focused always on concrete political action. It is a process of which the British are very proud, for it was achieved without revolution and almost without violence or any serious civil disturbance. The fruits of discussion, education, and propaganda were consolidated in a specific reform bill, followed by another stage of preparatory work and another reform bill.

Parliamentary Reform

The process is most clearly marked in the great milestones of parliamentary reform that transformed the government of Britain from an oligarchy into a political democracy. Britain emerged from the Napoleonic wars with its executive composed of a prime minister and his cabinet of ministers who were wholly under the control of Parliament. The Crown was now, as the nineteenth-century political writer Bagehot was to put it, largely "decorative." On that decorative post, held for most of the century (1837–1901) by Queen Victoria, who has given her name to an age and a culture, were centered the patriotic emotions of loyal British subjects. Victoria never thought of herself as a mere figurehead; she was a determined, sensible, emotional, conventional and intellectually unsophisticated Victorian lady.

Nevertheless, real power lay with Parliament, which in the early nineteenth century was very far from being a broadly representative body. The House of Lords, which had equal power with the lower house except over money bills, was composed of the small, privileged class of peers born to their seats in the Lords, with the addition of a relatively few new peers created by the crown from time to time. The House of Commons, its members unpaid, was recruited wholly from the gentry, the professional classes, and very successful businessmen, with a sprinkling of sons of peers (who were for electoral purposes commoners). It was chosen by less than one-sixth of the adult male population, voting without a secret ballot. Both the working classes in town and country and the run of prosperous but not spectacularly successful middle-class people were generally excluded from the franchise, although, with characteristic British lack of uniformity, some boroughs had a much broader electorate. Moreover, the largely rural south, once the most populous area of the kingdom, now had more representatives than it deserved, including a large contingent from the "rotten boroughs," towns of very small population or, as in the notorious Old Sarum, once a lively medieval town, none at all. The teeming new industrial centers of the north, such as Manchester, Liverpool, and Sheffield, were grossly underrepresented.

Projects to begin modernizing the structure of representation came close to being adopted in the late eighteenth century. But the wars with Revolutionary and Napoleonic France made reform impossible; in wartime and in the immediate postwar years, even moderate reformers were denounced as Jacobins. In August 1819 a nervous Tory government permitted the soldiery to break up a large and peaceful mass meeting assembled at St. Peter's Field near Manchester to hear speeches on parliamentary reform. Eleven persons died and several hundred were wounded in what was called, with an echo of Waterloo, the "Peterloo" massacre. In the aftermath of Peterloo, postwar repression reached its height with Parliament's approval of the Six Acts (December 1819), curtailing freedom of speech and of assembly and abrogating other civil rights. Fortunately, moderation soon prevailed once more in Britain, together with economic prosperity, and the peaceful campaign of agitation that produced the parliamentary reform of 1832 was resumed.

In this campaign the middle class did not hesitate to appeal to the lower classes for aid by using freely the language of popular rights, and even of universal suffrage. Many popular leaders talked as if the Reform Bill would bring political democracy to England at once. Yet much of the preparation for reform was actually the work not of liberal agitators, but of conservatives. Guided by enlightened individuals such as Canning and Robert Peel, the Tory governments of the 1820s lifted the restrictions on civil rights imposed during the long war with France and the postwar crisis. They weakened the Combination Acts to the extent of permitting laborers to organize into unions, though not to strike; they reformed the antiquated criminal code, so that, for example, the theft of a sheep no longer carried with it in theory a death penalty; and they began the reduction in protective tariffs (though not as yet affecting the Corn Laws) that was to lead to free trade. The seventeenth-century Test Act, which, though not observed, legally excluded Nonconformists from public life, was repealed. Also repealed, under the banner of "Catholic emancipation," were the laws that really did exclude Catholics from public life. In international politics, as we have already seen, Canning lined Britain up against the conservative monarchies of central and eastern Europe and their principle of intervention to suppress revolutions.

The Reform Bill itself was enacted under the leadership of the Whig Lord Grey, backed by a full apparatus of agitation and pressure groups. Tory opponents of parliamentary reform were won over—even the very Tory Duke of Wellington was converted at the last moment—until only the Tory House of Lords blocked the measure. At this climax, Lord Grey persuaded King William IV (1830–1837) to threaten the creation by royal prerogative of enough new Whig peers to put the reform through the Lords. This threat, combined with fears of a run on the Bank of England and of an outbreak of popular violence (street fighting had occurred in Bristol), resulted in passage of the bill on June 4, 1832.

The First Reform Bill is probably the most celebrated single act of legislation passed by Parliament because it accomplished a change of revolutionary potential without revolutionary violence. Yet it by no means brought political democracy to Britain. It did diminish the great irregularities of electoral districts, wiping out more than fifty rotten boroughs and giving seats in the Commons to more than forty hitherto unrepresented industrial towns. The number of voters was increased by about 50 percent so that virtually all the middle class got the vote, but the property qualifications for voting excluded the great mass of workers. Ironically, the new, more uniform qualifications actually took the franchise away from some men who had enjoyed it in a few exceptionally liberal boroughs.

From the new ground of the partly reformed Parliament, agitation went on for a wider suffrage. The middle class had won its gains not in the name of its own admission to an oligarchy, but in the name of the right of all competent men to have the vote. With the gradual spread of literacy to the lower classes and with their gradual political awakening, the numbers of competent men deserving the vote were steadily growing. Moreover, many middle-class Englishmen sincerely believed in gradually widening the franchise.

The more impatient workingmen, however, not content to wait for piecemeal reform, wanted immediate direct representation in Parliament in order to press for legislation that would mitigate the hardships imposed upon them by the Industrial Revolution. These demands were formally drawn up in a People's Charter calling for universal manhood suffrage, the secret ballot, abolition of property requirements for members of Parliament, payment of members, equal electoral districts, and annually elected Parliaments. The Chartists, who greatly alarmed the conservative classes, were the closest English equivalent of the radical parties that on the Continent carried on the Jacobin tradition of the French Revolution, mingled with elements of nascent socialism. Chartist strength lay in the urban industrial proletariat, particularly the union organizations, and was supported by many intellectuals of varied social and economic background. The movement presented to Parliament in 1839 a monster petition, with several hundred thousand signatures, urging adoption of the Charter. Parliament never considered the petition, even after two further Chartist initiatives in 1842 and 1848 (it was on this last occasion that Louis Napoleon served as one of the 150,000 special constables appointed to curb disorders that never materialized). Although Chartism petered out after 1848, all its major demands were to become law in the course of the next two generations.

By the 1860s the groundswell for more parliamentary reform was so powerful that Disraeli (1804–1881), the leader of the Conservatives (as the former Tories were now officially designated), decided that if his party did not put through the reform the Liberals (former Whigs) almost certainly would, and that his party might as well get the credit. Disraeli hoped that the newly enfranchised urban working class, hostile to

Benjamin Disraeli, Lord Beaconsfield.

still did not have the vote. In addition, the medieval constituencies of borough and shire were modernized, and many smaller boroughs were lumped together with surrounding county areas to form single constituencies. The political map of Britain was beginning to be redrawn so that all districts would have roughly the same population. Some striking inequalities continued, however. Workers could scarcely hope to become members of Parliament, for MPs served without pay; a few thousand voters with business property in one district and a home in another could vote twice; and graduates of Oxford and Cambridge could vote a second time for special university members (indeed, a university man with scattered property could, if he could get around to the polls fast enough, cast a dozen votes).

Still, by 1885 Britain was already a political democracy, in which the majority of the people, through their representatives in the House of Commons, were almost, but not quite, politically sovereign, since the House of Lords retained the right to veto most legislative acts. This last limitation was removed in 1911, when the Parliament Act of that year ended the real power of the Lords, leaving them with no more than a delaying or suspensive veto. Other codicils to the reforms of the nineteenth century were the institution of salaries for MPs (also in 1911) and a major act in 1918 that enfranchised all men over twenty-one, gave the vote to women over thirty, and limited plural voting to two votes—a property vote and a university vote. In 1928, women got the vote at twenty-one, and after World War II, the university votes were abolished, along with most of the few remaining powers of the Lords. Finally, in 1969 Britain, in common with other Western democracies, lowered the voting age to eighteen.

their middle-class employers, would vote for the Conservatives as good country gentlemen, responsible caretakers of the lower classes. But in 1868, in the first general election after the new reform, the Conservatives were turned out.

The Reform Bill of 1867 did not introduce full manhood suffrage. Like the first, it was a piecemeal change that brought the electoral districts into more uniformity and equality, but left them still divided into boroughs and shires as in the Middle Ages. It about doubled the number of voters in Britain by giving the vote to householders—that is, settled men owning or paying rent on their dwellings—in the boroughs. But this Second Reform Bill did not give the vote in rural areas to men without the "stake" of property—that is, men who did not own a piece of real estate or even have a bank account, men who were therefore felt by many upper-class Victorians to be irresponsible, willing to vote away other people's property.

The next reforms in the series were put through by the Liberal party, under the leadership of Gladstone (1809–1898). The bills of 1884 and 1885, while not yet introducing universal manhood suffrage, again doubled the size of the electorate, particularly by extending the franchise in rural areas. But migrant laborers, domestic servants, and bachelors living in parental households

Liberals, Conservatives, and the Two-Party System

The dynamics of the process of democratizing British politics are in part explicable in terms of the class struggle, as the bourgeoisie and then the proletariat gained the vote. But the central human institution working this change, the political party, was something more than an instrument for advancing narrow class interests. When the Conservative Disraeli took the "leap in the dark" in 1867, he hoped that the newly enfranchised workers would vote for their "betters" in his own party. Though he was proved wrong in 1868, in the long-run he was partly right, for after his death the Conservatives returned triumphantly to power for a whole decade (1895–1905) under the still wider franchise of 1885.

Both the Conservative and Liberal parties were by now very different from their ancestors, the oligarchical eighteenth-century factions of Tories and Whigs. The Conservatives, first under Peel and then under Disraeli, kept their old electoral following among country gentlemen, army and navy officers, and Anglican clergymen, but they added many new supporters among agricultural laborers, tradesmen, and even some of the urban working and white-collar classes. The Liberals, who in the early and middle parts of the century were still led by men like Grey and Palmerston from the great aristocratic Whig families, found many new supporters among businessmen, large and small, the Nonconformists, white-collar radicals, and politically conscious workers. Both parties frankly appealed to the "people"; and the Conservatives, with their Primrose League in memory of Disraeli's favorite flower, their appeal to love of queen and country, their record of social legislation against the worst evils of the new factory system, did at least as good a job in building a party machine and getting out the vote as did the Liberals. In the Victorian heyday, the librettist Gilbert was quite justified in having his guardsmen sing in *Iolanthe*:

> *That every boy and every gal*
> *That's born into the world alive*
> *Is either a little Liberal*
> *Or else a little Conservative.*

The two-party system was almost wholly confined to the English-speaking lands—Britain, the United States, and the British dominions. On the Continent, not only in France, Italy, and pre-Hitler Germany but also in the smaller democracies of Scandinavia, Switzerland, Holland, and Belgium, the multiparty system usually prevailed, and governments were generally coalitions of parties with separate organizations. While English-speaking opinion probably exaggerates the defects and dangers of multiparty democracy, a two-party democracy does have distinct advantages in the way of stability and continuity of policy, if only because a given group can enjoy a longer, more assured tenure of power.

In terms of political psychology, the two-party system means that the millions of individual voters who make up each party are in greater agreement than disagreement over what the party stands for; or at least that when they vote for a candidate they feel he stands more for what they want than for what they don't want. Each voter makes some kind of compromise within himself, takes something less in practice than he would ideally like, or else he abstains. This sort of compromise the French voter of the 1880s, for instance, did not have to make, for he could choose, from among a dozen or more platforms and candidates, the one closest to his own convictions.

The reasons why Englishmen made these compromises must be sought in British history. One reason lies in the relative security of the British Isles from external foes during the long years in which political habits of moderation and compromise could mature without the constant pressure of foreign wars. All the continental states were repeatedly exposed to the dangers of war and the threat of invasion—an experience that seemed to promote psychological tendencies to seek final and extreme solutions. This might have happened in Britain, too, had she undergone many repetitions of the kind of alarm raised over the possibilities of subversion by Jacobins and invasion by Napoleon.

Another reason may be found in the fact that continental states in the nineteenth century were still going through the popular revolutionary modification of royal absolutism. They were still torn by major class antagonisms between privileged nobles, backed usually by orthodox religion, and a middle class. In England, the struggle against absolutism had occurred a full century and a half earlier and had never been quite so bitter as it was on the Continent. It had left England in charge of a moderate ruling class that was itself the product of a compromise between the old landed gentry and the new commercial classes, a ruling class that would develop within itself habits of moderation and compromise. The deep abyss the French Revolution had dug on the Continent between royalists and republicans and between clericals and anticlericals did not exist in England.

Thus, even more important than the individual readiness of Liberals and Conservatives to support their party's policies was the fact that both parties had a wide area of mutual agreement above and beyond party. To put it quite baldly, there wasn't much difference between the Conservatives and the Liberals. When one

William Gladstone:
an 1869 caricature of the British prime minister.

went out of power and the other came in, the ship of state tacked a bit, but it did not change direction. The Conservative Disraeli and the Liberal Gladstone were perhaps not quite shadowboxing in their heated parliamentary exchanges, but they clearly were not fighting to kill, nor perhaps even for the knockout.

To sum up, government by discussion, Her Majesty's Government and Her Majesty's Opposition equally loyal to established ways, under the shelter of the English Channel and the British navy, in a prosperous land without deep-seated class antagonisms or insuperable class barriers and rigidities—all these helped to develop in the British people habits of compromise, of law-abidingness, a sort of political sportsmanship. And these habits survive today, when Victorian geographical security has gone with the airplane and Victorian economic preponderance has gone with the rise of competing industrial nations. The British, who once cut off the head of one king and drove another into exile, have for nearly two centuries enjoyed remarkable political stability.

Reforms of the Utilitarians

The Reform Bill of 1832 was soon followed by other measures that helped make over not merely British political life, but British economic and social life as well. The inspiration of these reforms came in large part from a small but influential middle-class group of Utilitarians, the Philosophic Radicals. These disciples of Bentham and of the Enlightenment believed that men, if properly educated, are impelled by rational self-interest and thus automatically do what is best for themselves and all their fellows. Under the influence of the Philosophic Radicals, English local government and the English legal system were made simpler and cleansed of some of the impediments to efficiency, the residue of centuries of red tape. Legal procedures, for instance, which had been so complicated that the Chancery Court was many years behind its backlog of cases, were gradually speeded up. The Municipal Corporations Act of 1835, though allowing medieval town and city offices to remain in name, vested basic authority in elective councillors who supervised professional civil servants. Among the latter were the recently established professional policemen, who got their nickname "bobby" from Robert Peel.

The middle-class radicals, believing that that government governs best which governs least, sought rather to expedite that minimum of government than to add to its tasks. They believed in education, but not in compulsory public education; private initiative would in their opinion do well what the government would do poorly and tyrannically. Large-scale government reform of British popular education had therefore to wait until 1870. Meanwhile, the private initiative preached by the Utilitarians sponsored mechanics' institutes and other means of adult and vocational education. It also sponsored all sorts of private schools and,

in London, Manchester, and some other cities, new universities that resembled in many ways American urban universities. These new "red-brick" institutions (so called in contrast to the medieval stones of Oxford and Cambridge) first broke into the centuries-old monopoly of "Oxbridge," though they did not then, and still do not, rank equally in prestige.

The most typical Utilitarian reform, the one that stirred up public opinion most thoroughly, was the New Poor Law of 1834. This bill codified, centralized, and made more coherent a complicated system of public relief that had originated in the Elizabethan Poor Law of 1601 and earlier Tudor legislation. But it did more. It shifted the base of this relief. The old methods of home relief, "outdoor relief," had gradually come to permit supplementary payments from the parishes to able-bodied poor working on low wages, supplements for children, and in general relatively easygoing "doles" direct to families in their homes. The new system would have none of this laxness, this encouragement of men in what the Utilitarian, in spite of his belief in human rationality, rather feared was "natural" human laziness. Poor Law unions united parishes for greater efficiency, permitted greater supervision by the central government in London, and supplied—in formidable poorhouses in which the sexes were firmly separated—the "indoor relief" by which able-bodied paupers were made as uncomfortable as decency would allow. These hardships, it was held, would encourage them to try to become self-supporting outside. The New Poor Law set off a controversy rather similar to that surrounding proposals for reforming welfare payments in twentieth-century America. Its poorhouses offended humanitarians in the upper classes, but to middle-class business interests it had the decided merit of making poor relief more efficient. The poor themselves managed to survive in the workhouses.

Greatest of the Utilitarian reforms in its long-run consequences was the repeal of the Corn Laws in 1846, after a long campaign headed by the Anti-Corn Law League. This pressure group wanted Britain to exploit her head start in the Industrial Revolution by adopting free trade so that she might use exports of manufactured goods to pay for imports of raw materials and food. The victory of the free traders was achieved in 1846 when they persuaded the Conservative leader Peel to abandon traditional Tory protectionism in the face of the tragic potato famine in Ireland and the urgent need for massive importation of cheap grain. Britain was now a free trade nation, the only major free trade nation in a world that never quite lost its mercantilist preconceptions and habits. The repeal of the Corn Laws had, however, temporarily split the Conservative party into two groups, one the Peelites, who accepted the repeal; the other, soon led by a brilliant young man named Disraeli, who continued to support high tariffs on wheat. Within a decade the Conservatives were once more united in a single party under Disraeli's leadership.

Labor, Education, and the Army

Still another series of reforms helped make the prosperous England of Gladstone and Disraeli. These were the Factory Acts, begun in 1802 and 1819 with bills sponsored by Peel's father. Addicts of the economic interpretation of history hold that middle-class people put through reforms like those of the Poor Law and the repeal of the Corn Laws, but that the landed gentry and upper-class intellectuals, jealous of the new city wealth and outraged by the ugliness of the new industrial towns, put through reforms like those of the Factory Acts regulating hours of work, sanitation, and the labor of women and children. It is true that many leaders of the movement for state regulation of economic life were either members of the Tory ruling class, like the Peels, or intellectuals, like Coleridge, Disraeli, Carlyle, Ruskin, and Matthew Arnold, who preached against the horrors of working-class life in prosperous Victorian England. And it is true that the economic and political philosophy of the business class was laissez faire.

But the practice was a different matter. None of the Factory Acts and similar reforms of the nineteenth century could have gone through Parliament successfully without some support from both political parties. Moreover, neither landed gentry nor industrialists and businessmen were mutually exclusive "classes" in a neat Marxist sense. Rather, they were thoroughly intermingled in education, marriage, and even in economic interests, since the gentry invested in stocks and bonds and the industrialists invested in landed estates. The elder Peel, father of the Factory Acts, was a self-made industrialist.

The Factory Acts followed a sequence not unlike the sequence of acts that reformed the suffrage. The first acts were modest indeed; they underlined the frightful conditions they were designed to remedy. That of 1819, for instance, applying only to the cotton industry, forbade night work for children, and limited day work to twelve hours. Even so, it provided for no really effective inspection, and was violated with impunity by many employers. The Act of 1833, forbidding child labor entirely below the age of nine, and restricting it to nine hours for those below thirteen, and twelve for those below eighteen, marked an important stage by setting up salaried inspectors to enforce the law.

By the end of the nineteenth century, there was on the books a whole code of labor legislation, regulating hours of labor for everyone, giving special protection to women and children, and including provisions that made the employer responsible for workmen's compensation in industrial accidents. Then in 1911 came the great National Insurance Act, which inaugurated compulsory health and unemployment insurance through combined payments from the state, employers, and employees.

The same story of piecemeal but cumulative reforms could be found in education. The commonly held Victorian idea that education was not properly a func-

"Disraeli Measuring the British Lion": cartoon from *Punch,* 1849, on the state of the nation three years after the repeal of the Corn Laws.

tion of the state postponed a general education act until 1870. The issue was complicated by the wrangling of Anglicans and Nonconformists, for many existing schools were controlled by a private society that required instruction in the doctrines of the Church of England. But even before 1870 a government committee had been aiding local education boards by grants from the national treasury (in 1860 they reached nearly a million pounds), by providing an inspection service, and by helping to organize teacher training. School attendance was not compulsory, however, and the average age for leaving school was eleven years. After many workers got the vote in 1867, worried Conservatives—and Liberals—began to urge the slogan "Educate your masters." The bill of 1870, put through under Gladstone's minister of education, William Forster, did not quite set up compulsory national education at the elementary level. It did permit the local school boards to compel attendance, and it did extend national aid and supervision. Church schools continued to get aid from taxes levied by the central government, an offense to radicals who wanted complete separation of church and state.

Beginnings were made in publicly supported schools at the secondary level, though the British "public school," which in American terms is a private school, continues until our own day to maintain a privileged position in the British social system. In comparison with the public school systems in Germany, France, and the United States, British education on the eve of World

War I was administratively complex and full of anomalies. On the whole, though, it got the job done, and the general level of popular education in the British Isles was at least as high as that of the other democracies at the time.

Gladstone's ministry also allowed the winds of modernization to enter other citadels of upper-class privilege. In 1871 the old requirement that both students and staff of Oxford and Cambridge had to take religious tests to confirm their Anglicanism was at last abolished. And in the same year, Cardwell, the secretary of war, put through a massive reorganization of the army, which had been discredited by its poor showing in the Crimean War of the 1850s. The ban on the sale of commissions weakened the virtual monopoly of the aristocracy and gentry over the higher grades of officers, and a reduction in the term of service made recruitment to the ranks more attractive.

Foreign and Imperial Policy

Nowhere does the basic unity that underlies the party strife of nineteenth-century Britain come out more clearly than in foreign relations. Almost everyone was agreed on the fundamental position of Britain: maintain the European state system in balance, preferably by diplomatic rather than military action; police the seas with the British navy; open world markets to British goods; maintain—and in Africa extend—the vast network of the British Empire. The Liberals were more likely to side with the democratic and nationalist movements in Europe than the Conservatives were. They sympathized with the struggling Italians, Greeks, and Poles, and disliked the old Metternichian powers, especially Russia. In mid-century the Liberal Palmerston pursued an active policy of near intervention in behalf of oppressed nationalities, and British benevolence was a factor in the attainment of Italian unity.

Yet emotional and verbal partisanship had very little to do with Britain's entry into the only European war in which she was directly involved between 1815 and 1914. The Crimean War of 1854–1856 was fought to maintain the balance of power, as England joined France in opposing what they judged to be a Russian threat to their Near Eastern interests. They supported the Ottoman Empire, whose treatment of her own Christian minorities was a chronic source of Liberal indignation under other circumstances. While the war was mismanaged on both sides, it at least checked Russian advances for a time and made the ultimate disposition of the Balkan regions of the decaying Turkish Empire a matter for joint action by all the great powers.

On imperial policy, it seems at first glance as though British public opinion really was deeply divided. Disraeli and Gladstone were never so gladiatorially fierce as when the Conservative defended the greatness of the empire and the Liberal attacked imperialism at home and abroad as un-Christian, illiberal, and unprofitable. And it would be absurd to maintain that in action there was no real difference between the two. Disraeli bought up the financially embarrassed Egyptian khedive's shares in the French-built Suez Canal (1875), a step toward eventual British control of Egypt, and triumphantly made Queen Victoria empress of India (1876). Gladstone, in his succeeding ministry, withdrew British troops from Afghanistan in 1880, conceded virtual independence to the Boer Republics in South Africa by the Pretoria Convention of 1881, and in 1884–1885 neglected General Gordon surrounded by rebels in the Sudan, then a southern outpost of Egyptian territory. Yet Gladstone kept British armies on the northwest frontier of India, abutting Afghanistan. It was under his administration in 1882 that the British actually bombarded Alexandria and established a protectorate over Egypt. Gladstone finally sent troops to rescue Gordon, though they arrived too late, and even in South Africa the Boer Republics were freed only under the "suzerainty" of Britain. In short, Gladstone regretted and no doubt even neglected the Empire; but he kept it.

The Irish Problem

Much nearer home, a nationality problem grew more acute as the nineteenth century came to a close, and did draw something more than a verbal line between Conservatives and Liberals. This was the Irish problem, which had beset the English ever since the Norman-English conquest of Ireland in the twelfth century. The English, and the Scots who came to settle in the northern Irish province of Ulster in the sixteenth and seventeenth centuries, had remained as privileged Protestant landowners in the midst of a subject population of Catholic Irish peasants. Although there were also native Irish among the ruling classes, many of them had been Anglicized and had turned Protestant.

For three centuries, religious, political, and economic problems in Ireland had remained unsolved. As the nineteenth century opened, the English attempted to solve the political problem by a formal union of the two kingdoms, with Irish members admitted to the British Parliament, in which they were of course a minority. On January 1, 1801, the United Kingdom of Great Britain and Ireland came into being. Beginning with the Catholic Emancipation Act of 1829, which allowed Irish voters to elect Catholics to office, most of the English reforms we have outlined above were extended to Ireland. The Irish, led by Daniel O'Connell, the Great Emancipator, organized politically to press for more thoroughgoing changes and, eventually, for home rule. They sought not only for self-government but also for land reforms to break the economic dominance of the Protestant minority and for disestablishment of the Anglican church in Ireland—that is, abolition of a state church supported by taxes levied on both members and nonmembers.

Irish hatred for the English was fanned by the

disastrous potato famine of the 1840s, when blight ruined a crop essential to the food supply. The British government with its instinctive laissez faire reaction to an emergency, did not provide prompt and efficient relief, nor was there any international organization like the Red Cross to step in. Twenty-one thousand Irish deaths were attributed directly to starvation, and at least a million, weakened by malnutrition, succumbed to typhus, cholera, and other diseases. Many of these deaths occurred on emigrant ships, for hundreds of thousands of Irish emigrated and, if they survived, carried their hatreds with them. They formed pressure groups such as the Fenian Brotherhood, organized in New York in 1858 to raise funds to aid Irish resistance and to make trouble generally for the British.

Over the next decades, British governments made piecemeal reforms. In 1869 the Anglican church was disestablished in Ireland, and in the next year the Irish Land Act began a series of agrarian measures that were designed to protect tenants from "rack-renting" (we would say "rent-gouging") by landlords, many of them absentee members of the British "garrison." The reforms were neither far-reaching nor rapid enough to satisfy the Irish. Moreover, the Irish question was not just a matter of land, or of religion, but also of a peculiarly intense form of underdog awareness of cultural differences and of nationality. Then in the 1870s a brilliant Irish leader arose, Charles Parnell, himself a Protestant descendant of the "garrison," but a firm Irish patriot. Under the leadership of Parnell in the British Parliament, the Irish nationalists were welded into a firm, well-disciplined party which, though it held less than a hundred seats in the House of Commons of the United Kingdom, could often swing the balance between Liberals and Conservatives.

The critical step came when in 1885 Gladstone was converted to home rule, and introduced a bill providing for a separate Irish parliament with some restrictions on its sovereignty, and of course under the Crown. Gladstone's decision split his own Liberal party in something like the way Peel's conversion to free trade had split the Conservatives in 1846. A group led by Joseph Chamberlain, who had begun political life as the reform leader of the great city of Birmingham, seceded under the name of Liberal Unionists. In effect, they joined the Conservative party, which was often known in the next few decades, so great were the passions aroused in Great Britain by this proposed cutting loose of Ireland, simply as the Unionist party. Gladstone lost the election brought on by the split, and home rule was dropped for the moment.

Agitation continued in Ireland, becoming more bitter when Parnell, involved in a divorce scandal, was dropped by the virtuous Gladstone and by some of his own equally virtuous Irish followers. In 1892, however, Gladstone won a close election on the Irish issue—or, rather, he obtained enough English seats to get a second home rule bill through the Commons with the aid of eighty-one Irish nationalists. The bill was defeated, however, in the Conservative House of Lords, and was dropped once more. The Conservatives, when they came in for their ten-year reign in 1895, sought to "kill home rule by kindness," enacting several land reform bills that furthered the process of making Ireland a land of small peasant proprietors.

But Ireland was now beyond the reach of kindness, and Irish problems were no longer—if ever they had been—largely economic and administrative. Irish nationalism was now a full cult, nourished by a remarkable literary revival in English and in Gaelic which produced writers like W. B. Yeats, John Synge, and Lady Augusta Gregory. Irish men and women everywhere—including Irish-Americans—were keyed to a pitch of emotional excitement. They would be satisfied with nothing less than an independent Irish nation.

The Liberals, back in power after 1905, found they needed the votes of the Irish nationalists to carry through their proposal for ending the veto power of the Lords. After some soul-searching, the Liberals struck the bargain: home rule in return for the Parliament Act of 1911, which destroyed the veto power of the Lords. A home rule bill was placed on the books in 1912 but never went into force, for as home rule seemed about to become a fact, the predominantly Protestant north of Ireland, the province of Ulster, bitterly opposed to separation from Great Britain, threatened to resist by force of arms. The home rule bill as passed carried the rider that it was not to go into effect until the Ulster question was settled. The outbreak of war in 1914 made such a settlement out of the question, and the stage was set for the Irish Revolution of the 1920s.

Issues and Parties in the Early Twentieth Century

As Great Britain approached the twentieth century, still other problems arose to disturb the underlying serenity and assurance of the Victorian age. Irish troubles, the Boer War in South Africa (in which world opinion generally supported the Boers, not the British), the rising international tensions that were leading to World War I, and the difficulties of raising the additional government revenue to finance both the naval armament race with Germany and the measures inaugurating the welfare state—all confronted the British people at the same time. And to top off everything, the long lead Britain had had in the Industrial Revolution was being lost as other nations acquired the technical skills of large-scale production. Germany, the Low Countries, Switzerland, the United States, and in a measure all the West were competing with Britain on the world market.

Under such conditions, it was natural that some Britishers should come to doubt the wisdom of the free trade policies that had won the day in 1846. For the Germans and others were not only underselling the British abroad; they were actually invading the British home market. Why not protect that market by a tariff system? Few Britishers believed that the home islands, already by the 1880s too densely populated to feed themselves and constitute a self-sufficient economy, could surround themselves with a simple tariff wall. But the empire was worldwide, with abundant resources in agricultural lands. Within it the classical mercantilist interchange of manufactures for raw materials could still in theory provide a balanced economic system. Britain could still be, if not the workshop of the world, at least the workshop of the quarter of the world that composed the British Commonwealth and Empire.

The same Joseph Chamberlain who led the secession from the Liberals on the question of home rule for Ireland also led a secession on an issue of even more fundamental importance. He became a protectionist and imperialist. He gave special importance to the establishment of a system of imperial preference through which the whole complex of lands under the crown would be knit together in a tariff union. Many Conservatives, never wholly reconciled to free trade,

David Lloyd George, 1898.

welcomed the issue, and the new Unionist party made protection a major plank in its program. Liberal opposition, however, was still much too strong, and there was opposition also in Conservative ranks. Chamberlain, reversing the aims but imitating the methods of Cobden and the Anti-Corn Law League of the 1840s, organized a Tariff Reform League. In 1903, he made in the cabinet sweeping proposals that would have restored moderate duties on foodstuffs and raw materials (largely to give a basis for negotiating with the dominions, which already had tariff systems of their own) and on foreign manufactured goods. But the Conservative leader, Balfour, did not dare go so far, and Chamberlain resigned with his bill unpassed. Indeed, Chamberlain, who had already split the Liberal party on home rule, now split the Conservatives on tariff reform. Although the new Liberal government after 1905 continued free trade, the rift Chamberlain had made in the old Liberal party was never really repaired.

The Liberals were, however, committed to another policy as contrary to the classical philosophy of laissez faire as was protectionism. This was the welfare state—social security through compulsory insurance managed by the state and in part financed by the state, minimum-wage laws, compulsory free public education, public works and services of all kinds. The dramatic point in the working out of the program was the People's Budget of 1909, introduced by a new figure on the political stage, a Welshman, the Liberal chancellor of the exchequer, Lloyd George (1863–1945). This budget, which frankly proposed to make the rich finance the new welfare measures through progressive taxation on incomes and inheritances, was clearly no ordinary tax measure. It was a means of altering the social and economic structure of Britain; its opponents called it "not a budget, but a revolution." It passed the Commons, but was thrown out by the Lords, even though it was a "money bill." The Liberals went to the country for the second time in 1910 and after an exciting election which altered the makeup of Commons very little, put through the Parliament Act of 1911, which took away from the Lords all power to alter a money bill, and left them with no more than a delaying power of not more than two years over all other legislation. The Liberal program of social legislation was saved. It was saved under conditions strongly reminiscent of 1832, for the new king, George V (1910–1936), had promised Prime Minister Asquith that if necessary he would create enough new peerages—which might have meant several hundred—to put the Parliament Act through the House of Lords. As in 1832 the threat was enough, and the Peers yielded.

But was it a *Liberal* program? The dissenting Liberals who had followed Joseph Chamberlain out of the party in the 1880s thought not, and it was normal enough for Chamberlain's two sons, Austen and Neville, who played an important part in twentieth-century politics, to think of themselves as Conservatives. For what happened in the generation after 1880 was a major change in the political orientation of British parties. The Liberals, who had believed that that government governs best which governs least, and least expensively, had come to believe that the state must interfere in economic life to help the underdog, and had adopted Lloyd George's plan for redistributing the national wealth by social insurance financed by taxation of the rich and well-to-do. And the Conservatives, who in the mid-nineteenth century had stood for factory acts and at least mild forms of the welfare state, were now in large part committed to a laissez faire program against government "intervention," a program astonishingly like that of the Liberals of 1850.

One factor in this change had been the growth of the political wing of the labor movement, which by 1906 held fifty-three seats in Commons, less than 10 percent of the total, twenty-nine under the aegis of the Independent Labour Party and the balance on the left fringe of the Liberal Party. The political ideas that went into the making of the British Labour party antedate by a good deal its formal organization. They derive from the legacy of 1776 and 1789 as modified by the Marxists, by the Christian socialists, and by the rapidly growing trade unions. Labourites wanted the welfare state, and a great many of them also wanted a socialist state in which at least the major industries would be nationalized. Labour had the backing of many upper- and middle-class people who sympathized with the quest for social justice. From their ranks came intellectuals like G. B. Shaw, H. G. Wells, and Sidney and Beatrice Webb, who participated in the influential Fabian Society, formed in the 1880s, which preached the "inevitability of gradualness," the attainment of social democracy through the peaceful parliamentary adaptation of the strategy of advancing one step at a time used by the Roman republican general Fabius to wear down the Carthaginians.

By the early 1900s Fabianism seemed to be working, for the Liberals, who depended on Labour votes to maintain a majority, put through much important legislation in the interest of the workingman: acceptance of peaceful picketing, sanctity of trade union funds, and employer's liability to compensate for accidents (all in 1906); modest state-financed old age pensions (1909); health and unemployment insurance (1911); and minimum wage regulations (1912). Part of the motivation for Liberal social legislation was the desire to forestall Labour. Just as in 1867 the Tories had caught the Whigs bathing and "walked away with the Whigs' clothes" by giving the workers the vote, so in 1909–1911 the Liberals stole Labour's clothes and gave the workers social security. But these tactics worked no better in the twentieth century than they had in the nineteenth, and the workers on the whole stuck by the Labour party. The Liberal party was beginning a long decline, which would be hastened by the upsetting effects of World War I and would drive

its right wing to Toryism and its left wing to Labour.

Not all the motivation of the Liberals in these early years of the new century was, however, mere fear of Labour. In part, their conversion from laissez faire to social security was a positive one, a sincere belief that the logic of their democratic assumptions must drive them to raise the general standard of living in Britain by state action. Something broadly analogous was happening throughout the democratic West—in France, in the smaller democracies, and a few decades later, in the United States. An important part of the bourgeoisie in all these countries swung not to doctrinaire socialism, but to programs of social legislation put through by the usual machinery of change under a democratic franchise. The English Chartists back in the early nineteenth century had been justified in their apparently naïve belief that universal suffrage would eventually pave the way to greater social and economic equality.

III France: Second Empire and Third Republic

A century ago France seemed to many English-speaking critics, as she sometimes still appears, a rather uncertain member of the community of nations ruled by the democratic decencies—that is, government by discussion, peaceful alternation of "ins" and "outs" through the working of the party system, and the usual freedoms of civil rights. The democratic revolution, so optimistically begun in 1848, had by 1852 brought still another Bonaparte to the throne of France in the person of Napoleon III, nephew of the first Napoleon. ("Napoleon II," son of the first Napoleon by Marie Louise, never really ruled, any more than did the son of Louis XVI, the "Louis XVII" who died in prison during the great French Revolution.) As president of the Second Republic, Prince Louis Napoleon had soon quarreled with the new National Assembly elected in 1849, in which monarchist sentiment favoring a restoration of either the Bourbons or the house of Orléans greatly outweighed Bonapartism. The Assembly refused to amend the constitution of 1848 to allow him a second four-year term. Fearful of radicals and socialists, the Assembly also whittled down the universal male suffrage of 1848, depriving about three million Frenchmen of the vote and enabling the prince president to denounce the move and act as the champion of persecuted democracy.

The coup d'état of December 2, 1851, was artfully timed for the sacred Bonapartist day of the coronation of Napoleon I (December 2, 1804) and the greatest Napoleonic victory, Austerlitz (December 2, 1805). Controlling the army and the police, Louis Napoleon and his fellow conspirators arrested seventy-eight noted anti-Bonapartists, including sixteen members of the Assembly. Street fighting in Paris, which broke out on December 3, ended with hundreds of casualties, mainly bystanders fired upon by panicky soldiers. It gave Louis Napoleon the chance to pose as the champion of order against a largely imaginary socialist plot. He strengthened his posture by massive arrests, which ultimately sent twenty thousand Frenchmen to prison or into exile. What Karl Marx called "the eighteenth Brumaire of Louis Napoleon Bonaparte" was destroying the Second Republic.

Toward the end of December 1851 Napoleon restored universal male suffrage for a plebiscite which by 7,500,000 votes to 640,000 gave him the right to draw up a new constitution. The plebiscite was accompanied by skillful propaganda, but it was not crudely a work of force. Though many opponents of Napoleon simply did not vote, it seemed that a substantial majority of Frenchmen over twenty-one really were willing to try another dictator. There were many reasons why men voted yes. Almost all were weary of the struggles of the last three years, and many were frightened by the specter of socialism raised by the June days of 1848. For nearly three decades the full force of fashionable French literature had been at work making the Napoleonic legend and identifying the name of Napoleon with the "pooled self-esteem" of French patriotism. Many a man voted yes, not to Louis Napoleon, nor to any approval of dictatorship in the abstract, but to the music of the *Marseillaise,* the cannon of Austerlitz, to all the glories of France.

The Second Empire: Constitution and Economy

In 1852 yet another plebiscite authorized Louis Napoleon to assume the title of emperor and inaugurate the Second Empire, which he proceeded to do, inevitably, on December 2, 1852. The new constitution sponsored by the two plebiscites set up a lightly veiled dictatorship very much like that of Napoleon I. The emperor, who was responsible only to the nation, governed through ministers, judges, and a whole bureaucracy, in the appointment of which he had the final voice. The popularly elected assembly, the Corps Législatif, was filled with "official" candidates whose success at the polls was assured by the pressure of the emperor's loyal prefects. The assembly had no power to initiate or amend legislation; it had only a veto, which in the first few years it rarely used. Yet Napoleon III insisted that he was no mere tool of the possessing classes, no conservative, but an agent of real reform, an emperor of the masses, a "Saint-Simon on horseback" who would use strong government to realize the great public works and deeper international understanding dreamt of by the early utopian social engineer. Somewhat similar claims have been made by almost all the dictators of the twentieth century; communist, fascist, or merely nationalist, they all claim to be true democrats, protectors of ordinary men who in the classical Western democracies, they insist, are actually victims of capitalist exploitation. Napoleon III has sometimes been seen as the first of these modern dictators, as a protofascist; it must be said that both his methods and his ideology seem

decidedly mild when put next to those of twentieth-century totalitarians.

Napoleon III did carry through a great program of public works, bringing to both the capital and many provincial cities great public markets known as Les Halles, new boulevards and promenades, and other manifestations of urban renewal. Urban France still bears the stamp of the Second Empire, especially in Paris, where the emperor's prefect, Haussmann, cut through the medieval maze of streets those broad straight avenues with their splendid vistas which all the world knows so well—and which could easily be swept by gunfire and made street fighting that much more difficult. The Second Empire also helped with housing and encouraged workers' mutual aid societies, yet the benefits were meager in comparison with those resulting from later social legislation in Germany, Britain, and Scandinavia. The legal code of labor in the France of 1860 was less generous than that of Britain, and the standard of living of the working class in French cities was well below that in Britain, Germany, and the smaller European democracies. Although French labor benefited from the general prosperity of the 1850s, the gains in wages were partly offset by rising prices. Altogether, France lagged as a welfare state.

It was the bourgeoisie that gained most from the Second Empire, greatly assisted by the capital supplied through the government-sponsored Crédit Foncier and Crédit Mobilier, set up to promote investment in real estate and movable property, respectively. Napoleon's government also encouraged improvement in banking facilities, helped the rapid extension of French railways by state guaranties, and in general furthered the rise of industry in the two decades after 1850. Paris grew into a major metropolitan area, and centers such as Lyons and Rouen in textiles, Clermont-Ferrand and St. Etienne in metallurgy, and many other cities came to have genuine industrial economies, with all the accompanying problems. Yet both under the Second Empire and under its successor, the Third Republic, many Frenchmen remained loyal to older methods of doing business, to small firms under family control, to luxury trades in which handicraft skills remained important in spite of the machine. In consequence, the industrial growth of France was slower than that of the leading economic powers, especially in heavy industry. In the 1860s France lost her continental leadership in iron and steel production to the new Germany, and was subsequently far outdistanced by the burgeoning economy of the United States.

The French rate of population growth also lagged, and the exodus to the cities from impoverished rural departments, especially in the mountainous southern half of the country, was beginning under the Second Empire. At the end of the nineteenth century, France was not much more than 50 percent more populous than at the beginning—and this with almost no emigration. Britain, in spite of a large emigration, had about tripled her population, and Germany, too, was growing rapidly. Even Italy, with slender natural resources and less industry than France, was growing in population faster than France despite heavy emigration, and was to outstrip her in our own times. Though the reasons for French demographic weakness are imperfectly understood, a major factor in this country of a great many small proprietors appears to have been a determination to avoid division of modest inheritances among many heirs.

Napoleon III's Foreign Policy

Nevertheless, the France of the Second Empire was still a very great power, and the extent of her comparative decline was by no means clear to contemporaries. Although the French gained little from the Crimean War, they did at least have the satisfaction of playing host to the postwar congress at Paris in 1856. And the Paris Exposition of 1855, a counterpart of the famous London exhibition of 1851, was a great success that showed Napoleon III at the height of his power. He had pledged himself to use that power for peace; but he allowed himself, partly through a romantic interest in "oppressed nationalities," partly from age-old motives of prestige, to join Piedmont in a war against Austria for the liberation of Italy. In this war of 1859, French armies won victories at Magenta and Solferino—names which, incidentally, were soon exploited commercially, as in the new shade called magenta introduced by the fashion trade. Yet the defeated Austrians were not knocked out of the war. In the summer of 1859, sickened by the bloodshed on the battlefields and fearful that Prussia might come to Austria's assistance, Napoleon III suddenly made a separate peace with Austria, which agreed to relinquish Lombardy, but not Venetia, to Piedmont.

In 1860 the Italians took things into their own hands and set about organizing almost the whole peninsula, including papal Rome, into an Italian kingdom. Napoleon depended too much on Catholic support at home to be able to permit the extinction of papal territorial power; moreover, the too great success of Italian nationalism was threatening the European balance of power. He therefore temporized, permitting the union of most of Italy under the house of Savoy, but protecting the pope's temporal power with a French garrison in Rome and leaving Venetia still in Austrian hands. In 1860, as a reward for his services, he received from Piedmont the French-speaking part of Alpine Savoy plus the Mediterranean city of Nice and its hinterland. Napoleon III thus managed to offend most Italians, and liberals everywhere, as well as most of his own Catholic supporters at home.

To make matters worse, in 1861 he used the Mexican government's defaulting on payments of its foreign debt as the pretext for a wild imperialist venture. A French expedition installed the Austrian archduke Maximilian, brother of the emperor Francis Joseph, as emperor of Mexico, and French arms and men continued to assist him. The europeanized Mexican upper classes were in part willing to support this venture, for like most Latin Americans of the nineteenth century, their cultural ideal was France. But from the start the Mexican people resented the foreign intruder, and Maximilian had to rely heavily on French support to penetrate to Mexico City, where he was proclaimed emperor in June 1863. The United States, engaged in the Civil War, could do nothing at the time against what Americans regarded as an infraction of the Monroe Doctrine. But after peace had been restored in the United States, the American government protested strongly. The Mexican republican leader Juárez had no difficulty in prevailing, once American pressure had forced Napoleon to abandon Maximilian and his Mexican supporters. Maximilian fell before a firing squad in 1867.

The Liberal Empire

Louis Napoleon had come to power in 1848 on a platform of order and national unity against the threat of socialist upheaval. But, in spite of his one-sided victories in the presidential election of 1848 and the plebiscites of 1851 and 1852, it became more and more clear that if France had a national unity, it was not of the monolithic, totalitarian sort, but a unity that had to be worked out in the open competition of modern Western political life with parties, parliamentary debate, newspapers—in short, with government by discussion. Napoleon could not in fact be a symbolic head of state, above the struggle, nor even a final umpire. He could not be a republican; he could not be a legitimate monarchist, for much of France, and particularly the conservative France that held authoritarian views, was loyal to the legitimacy of the Bourbons, or the somewhat dubious legitimacy of the Orléanists. He could not even be a good devout Catholic, in spite of the orthodoxy of his wife, the empress Eugénie, for his Bonapartist background was heavily tinged with the anticlericalism of the eighteenth century, and his bungling of the Italian problem had deeply offended clericals. He could only head an "official" party, relying on the manipulative skills of his bureaucrats to work the cumbersome machinery of a parliamentary system designed, like that of Napoleon I, as a disguise for dictatorship.

As the pressure of genuine party differences rose, in reflection of genuine moral, social, and economic group interests, Napoleon slowly abandoned the measures of repression he had begun with and sought to establish himself in something like the position of a constitutional monarch. An act of 1860 gave the Legislative Assembly power to discuss freely a reply to the address from the throne, and throughout the 1860s these powers were extended in the name of the Liberal

Empire. Gradually, political life in France began to assume the pattern of parliamentary government, with parties of the Right, Center, and Left. After the general election of 1869, the government faced a strong legal opposition, thirty of whom were declared republicans. On July 12, 1869, Napoleon granted the Legislative Assembly the right to propose laws, and to criticize and vote the budget. Partial ministerial responsibility to the legislature seemed just around the corner as Napoleon entrusted the government to the head of the moderates, Emile Ollivier. A plebiscite in May 1870 overwhelmingly ratified these changes.

It is possible that the Second Empire might thus have been converted into a constitutional monarchy with full parliamentary government. Yet the changes had been wrung from an ailing and vacillating emperor by popular agitation, which was not just political but also economic in the form of strikes, since the Liberal Empire had relaxed the ban on unions and strikes imposed by the Le Chapelier Law of 1791. Thus, it is also possible that a radical republican groundswell would have submerged the empire in any case. But the Franco-Prussian War, into which Napoleon III was maneuvered by Bismarck in July 1870, put an abrupt end to the experiment of the Liberal Empire. The sluggish mobilization and overconfidence of the French armies gave the Prussians a decisive head start. Within six weeks Napoleon III and a large French army capitulated at Sedan, September 2, 1870. Two days later, rioting Parisians forced the remnant of the Legislative Assembly to decree the fall of the empire, and at the classic center of French republicanism, the Paris City Hall, the Third Republic was proclaimed. Napoleon III went to captivity in Germany and eventually to exile in England, where he died in 1873.

The Birth of the Third Republic

The new republic was too good a child of 1792 to give up the war against the national enemy. A government of national defense tried to continue the struggle, but the miracle of Valmy was not to be repeated. In October, General Bazaine surrendered a second large French force at Metz, and the disorganized elements of other French armies were helpless before the powerful German forces. An exhausted nation, sick of the war, chose in February a National Assembly that met at Bordeaux and sued for peace. The special circumstances of that election, however, placed on the new republic an additional handicap. For meanwhile Paris, besieged by the Germans, had resisted desperately until starvation forced its surrender in January 1871. Even under pressure of the siege, Parisian radicals tried to seize power and revive the old Paris commune, or city government, of 1792. These radicals could not stomach the capitulation for which the rest of the country seemed to be preparing. In the elections to the National Assembly, their intransigence helped to turn the provincial voters toward conservative candidates pledged to make peace—and to restore, not the republic, but the old monarchy.

This new Assembly, on March 1, 1871, voted to accept a peace ceding Alsace and a substantial part of Lorraine to Germany and paying an indemnity of five billion francs (about a billion dollars). Then the Paris National Guard, which had not been disarmed by the Germans, went over to the radicals because the National Assembly had suspended its pay. The Assembly and the provisional government it had set up under the veteran Orléanist politician Thiers sent troops into Paris in a vain attempt to seize National Guard artillery on the heights of Montmartre. Thiers and the Assembly established themselves in Versailles; in Paris the commune was set up, March 18, 1871.

Marxist legend has consecrated the Parisian Commune of 1871 as the first major socialist government. Most of the communards were in fact rather Jacobins, radical anticlericals and highly patriotic republicans who wanted a society of small independent shopkeepers and artisans, not the abolition of private property. Although some communards were affiliated with the First International, most of these were followers of Proudhon rather than of Marx; some other communards were followers of Blanqui, the aged champion of revolutionary violence who was arrested in the provinces before he could get to Paris. Neither Proudhonians nor Blanquists were socialists in any Marxian sense.

In any event, the communards had no chance to introduce sweeping social reforms. But their revolutionary aspect alarmed the rest of France, and their refusal to accept the peace was a challenge the National Assembly had to meet. To the horrors of the first siege by the Germans were added the horrors of a new siege by the government of the National Assembly, which gathered its troops at Versailles and in the Bloody Week of May 21–28 advanced through the barricades to clear the city. Twenty thousand Frenchmen died in the fighting, a total far exceeding that of the June Days of 1848.

The Third Republic, born in the trauma of defeat and civil war, at once came into a heritage of unresolved cleavages. More than half the members of the new National Assembly were monarchists, anxious to undo the formal declaration of a republic made in republican Paris right after Sedan. But now we encounter one of those concrete events that are the despair of those who seek the clue to history in vast impersonal forces beyond the play of human personality. About half the monarchist deputies were pledged to the elder legitimate Bourbon line represented by the count of Chambord, grandson of Charles X and the posthumous son of the duke of Berri who had been assassinated in 1820. The other half supported the younger Orléanist line that had come to the throne in 1830, represented by the count of Paris, grandson of Louis Philippe. Since Chambord was childless, he agreed to designate the count of Paris as the eventual heir to the throne. Chambord might have become in fact what he was to his supporters, King Henry V, had he also been willing to make the slightest concession to Orléanist sentiments and accept the revolutionary blue, white, and red tricolor flag that Louis Philippe had himself accepted as the flag of France. But he insisted on the white flag and gold lilies of Bourbon, which for millions of Frenchmen meant complete repudiation of all that had happened since 1789. Chambord did not, of course, act just for a white flag and against a tricolor one; behind these symbols lay real motives tied up with all of French history. He meant to be not just a Victorian "decorative" monarch, but a real king. No one, however, could be that sort of king in France any more.

In the resulting stalemate, the republican minority was able to maintain itself, and slowly gather strength. Thiers was recognized as "president of the Republic" and carried through the final settlement with Germany. Thiers, however, pushed a little too hard to convince the Orléanists that they should endorse the republic as "the regime that divides us least." In 1873 he lost what amounted to a vote of confidence in the Assembly, and was succeeded by Marshal MacMahon (a descendant of a Catholic British Jacobite who had fled to France after the departure of James II), a soldier and a monarchist who was chosen to hold the government together until the monarchist majority of the Assembly worked out a compromise between its legitimist and Orléanist wings. The compromise was never achieved, as Chambord continued to insist on the white flag. Ultimately, Thiers' strategy worked, and in 1875 enough Orléanists joined the republicans for the Assembly to pass a series of constitutional measures formally establishing the Third Republic.

These laws, known collectively as the Constitution of 1875, provided for a president elected by an absolute majority of Senate and Chamber of Deputies sitting together as a National Assembly. The Chamber of Deputies was directly elected by universal male suffrage; the Senate was chosen, one-third at any given time, by elected members of local governmental bodies. All legislation had to pass both houses, though only the lower could initiate finance bills. The critical point was that of the responsibility of the ministers, which was not spelled out in the laws of 1875. Had the president been able to dismiss them, a new Napoleon III might easily have arisen to destroy the republic. MacMahon attempted to exercise this power when on May 16, 1877, he dismissed the anticlerical premier, Jules Simon, and got the conservative duke of Broglie to form a cabinet. But the Chamber was now really republican—or at least antimonarchist—and voted "no confidence" in Broglie by a big majority. MacMahon dissolved the Chamber and called for a new national election—which he had the constitutional right to do. In the new elections the republicans, though losing some seats, still retained a good majority in the Chamber, and could now force the president to name a republican premier. Disgruntled, MacMahon resigned in 1879 and was succeeded by a conservative republican, Jules Grévy. This crisis of the Seize Mai (May 16) set a precedent for the Third Republic. No president thereafter dared to dissolve the Chamber, and the presidency became a ceremonial office, made fun of in the press and on the stage. But at any rate, nine years after its establishment in name, the Third Republic had at last become a fact.

It was in form a kind of republican transposition of constitutional monarchy, with an ornamental president instead of an ornamental king. The real executive, as in England, was the ministry, in effect a committee responsible to the legislature—indeed to the Chamber of Deputies, which soon became the focus of political action, leaving the Senate little real power. The Chamber, reflecting the political habits of the ideologically divided country, was composed not of two, but of a dozen or more parties, so that any ministry had to be supported by a coalition subject to constant shifting in the play of personalities and principles. The result was a marked instability of ministries, whose average life expectancy was scarcely a year.

Yet such a figure is misleading. A French ministry under the Third Republic did not usually give way to a totally different cabinet with totally different policies. Instead, ministerial personnel was shifted a bit, a compromise or two was made with certain parliamentary groups, and the new ministry behaved much like the old. The same faces kept reappearing: Briand, for instance, the great champion of collective security after World War I, headed ten different cabinets at various times between 1909 and 1926; and Delcassé, the architect of France's entente with England, served as foreign minister continuously through several cabinets and seven years (1898–1905). Moreover, the day-to-day task of governing was carried on by a civil service, by experts in the law courts and in the educational system as well as in the executive branch. This permanent personnel, or bureaucracy, subject only to broad policy control from above, preserved a basic continuity in French political action, especially in foreign policy.

The system was highly democratic, for it could work only by means of constant and subtle compromises. These, the essence of democratic government, were made in France—and in most of the democratic world outside the English-speaking countries—by the several parties in open debate and voting in the legislature *after* an election. In the English-speaking countries, these compromises are made *before* an election, *within* each of the two major parties, often in the privacy of the famous smoke-filled room. Probably the English-speaking method both conceals antagonisms and encourages the habit of willing compromise more effectively than does the continental method. But neither method will work if the underlying antagonisms are really intense and beyond compromise. For example, the American two-party system obviously failed to avert the Civil War.

Boulanger, Panama, and Dreyfus

Bitter antagonisms did in fact threaten the Third Republic between 1879 and 1914, but they did not destroy it. For one thing, the republic's opponents on the right could never get together with the Marxists and anarcho-syndicalists of the Left. On the right, although the legitimists eventually patched up their quarrels with the Orléanists, the monarchists could not recover the strength they had dissipated in the 1870s. Nor could the Bonapartists make serious gains in public opinion, though they survived as a political group into the twentieth century. After the accession of Pope Leo XIII in 1878 the Catholics were gradually encouraged to develop their way of life by frank acceptance of the freedom of worship that the constitution of the republic offered them. Many Catholics, however, feared the anticlericalism of the republicans, particularly after a law of 1882 making education free and compulsory for French children to the age of thirteen and forbidding religious instruction in public schools. Clerical and rightist enemies of the republic often did violence to their own conservative principles by seeking some new man who would win over the malcontents, including those on the Left and among labor, and then set up a dictatorship.

In the 1880s, they hoped that they had found such a man in General Boulanger, an ambitious soldier who had as minister of war catered to French desire for revenge on Germany. But the Boulangist movement was founded on a man of straw. The general cut an impressive figure in public appearances, and in by-elections to fill vacancies caused by deaths or resignations in the Chamber he showed he could command a popular following. But from the point of view of many traditional conservatives he had compromising origins and radical friends, and, as it became clear that Boulanger in power might rush the country into war, his following threatened to desert him. In January 1889 he swept a by-election in Paris, but his nerve failed when he was faced with the need to resort to the classic technique of the coup d'état. Instead of seizing power by force of arms, he sought refuge with his mistress. The government now took courage and threatened to try him for treason; Boulanger fled to Brussels and committed suicide on the grave of his beloved in 1891. The republic had surmounted its first great crisis.

Boulanger's cause had gained strength from a scandal in republican ranks involving President Grévy's son-in-law, who was implicated in the selling of posts in the Legion of Honor. More fuel went on the fire in the early 1890s, when there burst into public view one of those crises of graft and racketeering that seem endemic in modern Western societies. This was the Panama scandal, brought on by the failure of De Lesseps' attempt to duplicate in Panama his success in building the Suez Canal. As in the somewhat comparable Crédit Mobilier scandal in the United States (1873), it was established that ministers and deputies had accepted financial reward for backing the shaky Panama company. Anti-Semitic propagandists made much of the fact that several Jewish financiers were implicated, including the banker Reinach, who either committed suicide or was murdered just before his trial. Bad as it was, the Panama scandal was to pale before the Dreyfus Affair, in which the force of anti-Semitism first attained dramatic intensity and worldwide attention.

Captain Dreyfus, a Jew from a wealthy family that had fled to France when Alsace was lost to Germany, was the almost accidental victim of an espionage intrigue and of the anti-Semitism then prevalent in France, especially in military and Catholic circles. Accused of selling military secrets to the Germans, he was railroaded to trial as a scapegoat because he was the first Jew to serve on the French general staff. He was convicted of treason in 1894. Colonel Picquart, an intelligence officer, became convinced that the document on which Dreyfus had been convicted was a forgery, and that the real traitor was a disreputable adventurer of Hungarian blood but of French birth, Major Esterhazy. Picquart was quietly shipped off to Africa by his superiors, who wished to let sleeping dogs lie. But the Dreyfus family, by independent investigation, arrived at the conclusion that Esterhazy was the traitor, and sought to reopen the case. Esterhazy was tried and acquitted, but the affair was now too public for such silencing. In 1898, the famous novelist Zola brought matters to a crisis by publishing his open letter, *J'Accuse*. Zola accused the military leaders, one by one, of sacrificing an innocent man deliberately in order to save the reputation of the army.

France was now divided into Dreyfusards and Anti-Dreyfusards; the former defended in Dreyfus the republic, the latter attacked it. Almost all the far Left, which had hitherto held aloof from the affair as just one more example of the rottenness of the bourgeois state, now rallied to the Third Republic. Dreyfus was brought back from his prison on Devil's Island in French Guiana and was retried in the midst of a frenzied campaign in the press and on the platform. The military court, faced with new evidence brought out by the suicide of Colonel Henry, the forger of the most incriminating of the original documents used to convict Dreyfus, again found Dreyfus guilty of treason, but with the almost incredible qualification—in a treason case—of "extenuating circumstances." This attempt at face-saving saved nothing. Dreyfus was pardoned by the president of the republic in 1899, and in 1906, after the tensions had abated, he was acquitted and restored to the army with the rank of major.

The Dreyfus Affair presents a remarkably well-documented case study in social psychology. The simple juridical issue—was this man guilty or not guilty of treason—never wholly disappeared in the mass hysteria. Many Frenchmen who did not like Dreyfus or Jews or who did revere the Church, army, and the whole apparatus of the right nonetheless sought to make up their minds solely on the basis of the facts. Colonel Picquart was a case in point. Yet many on both sides worked themselves up to a point where the question of Dreyfus' guilt was wholly submerged in this great confronting of the "two Frances"—the France of the republic, heir to the great revolution and the principles of 1789, on the one hand, and on the other, the France of the monarchy, of throne and altar, and of the army, which had never really reconciled itself to the great revolution. For the unprejudiced person the open admission of forgery by Colonel Henry and his subsequent suicide were enough; he now thought Dreyfus innocent. But for the violent Anti-Dreyfusard, Henry's act made him a hero and a martyr; he had died for his country! A paper was circulated in Paris asking for a memorial to Henry:

> *Colonel Henry's Devotion to his Country.*
>
> Public subscription for a monument to be raised to him.
>
> When an officer is reduced to committing a pretended forgery in order to restore peace to his country and rid it of a traitor, that soldier is to be mourned.
>
> If he pays for his attempt with his life, he is a martyr.
>
> If he voluntarily takes his life,
> HE IS A HERO.*

A More Republican Republic

With the victory of the Dreyfusards, the republic moved to the Left and punished the Church for its support of the army and the Anti-Dreyfusards. The triumphant republicans in a series of measures between 1901 and 1905 destroyed the Concordat of 1801 between Napoleon I and the pope that had established the Roman Catholic Church in a privileged position in the French state. The Catholic teaching orders were forced to dissolve, and some 12,000 Catholic schools, which had been formidable rivals of the state school system, had to close down. The state was no longer to pay the clergy, and private corporations organized by the faithful were to take over the expenses of worship and the ownership and maintenance of the churches. The Catholics refused to accept this settlement, and the churches remained technically government property.

But, though the separation had been carried out amid great bitterness, though the debates had revived the ferocious language of the 1790s, there was no recourse to the violence of the past. Catholicism was not proscribed, and somehow or other worship continued in churches that were not the full legal property of the faithful. Catholic education, while severely handicapped, was not formally persecuted. The separation did not really alter the fundamental social position of the Church in France. The upper classes, and the peasantry of the north, northeast, and west, remained

*F. C. Conybeare, *The Dreyfus Case* (London, 1898), p. 298.

Captain Alfred Dreyfus, 1899.

for the most part loyal Catholics; many of the urban middle and working classes, and many peasants in parts of the south, southwest, and center remained what they had become over the last few centuries, indifferent Catholics or outright and determined secularists.

The indifferent Catholics and the anticlericals formed the backbone of the central supporting party of the republic, the Radical Socialists, who were not socialists at all but petty bourgeois. The French republic of the early twentieth century was a typically bourgeois state. It made certain concessions to demands from the workers for social security and better living conditions, but not nearly so many as the British constitutional monarchy was then making, nor indeed so many as the only partly constitutional German monarchy had made already. A measure initiating the progressive income tax failed of passage on the eve of World War I, although this was widely considered the most equitable way of raising revenue in a free-enterprise democracy and had been accepted by Britain in the budget of 1909, and by the United States in the Sixteenth Amendment, 1913. Trade unions in France were legal, but they had hard sledding against the reluctance of French workers to pay dues and accept union discipline. Moreover, good republicans like

Clemenceau and Briand had no scruples about using force against strikers; when railroad workers went on strike, they were conscripted into the army so that trains could be kept running under military management, even though it was peacetime.

The Third Republic had become more republican without moving very noticeably toward the welfare state. This was hardly surprising in a country that remained what it had been since 1789, a land of small farm-owning peasants, very conservative in their agricultural methods, and of relatively small family-controlled industries, very conservative in their business methods. Although in the early 1900s French steel production was actually growing faster than that of Britain, Germany, and the United States, this was a relatively isolated exception to the rule that France did not welcome large-scale industry. Yet it is worth noting that the French economy, while backward by the standards of ever-advancing industrialization, was well balanced by old-fashioned measures of self-sufficiency.

The Third Republic had weathered the storms of domestic differences because, though some Frenchmen disliked it intensely, and though many Frenchmen felt toward it that distrust of "the government" familiar to Americans, most Frenchmen felt it somehow to be the embodiment of *la patrie,* the fatherland. Differences did arise among them, notably on questions of colonial policy. The Third Republic's great territorial expansion in Africa, Indochina, and Oceania, which made the world empire of France second only to Britain's, was the work of a determined minority. Many Frenchmen viewed their colonies with apathy or with antagonism as improper distractions from the main business of foreign policy, which was revenge for 1870 and recovery of Alsace and Lorraine. Disagreements over foreign policy concerned details of timing and tactics rather than major goals.

Toward those goals the foreign ministry of the Third Republic worked systematically, despite shifts in personnel at the upper level occasioned by the operation of the multiparty system, until France gained enough strength and sufficient allies to make revenge a real possibility. Democracies are sometimes held to be at a disadvantage in the conduct of foreign relations in comparison with states under strong monarchic or dictatorial control. After the war with Prussia, democratic France was isolated, and imperial Germany was the center of a marvelous system of alliances. Yet by 1914 democratic France was firmly allied with a powerful Britain and a Russia powerful at least in appearance; and imperial Germany, save for a weak Austro-Hungarian ally and a dubiously loyal Italian one, was essentially isolated.

IV Italy, 1848–1914
Cavour and Garibaldi

Italian national unity, which seemed almost as remote as ever after Piedmont's two defeats by Austria in 1848–1849, was nevertheless accomplished between 1859 and 1870. The three men who led the Risorgimento in its years of triumph were the romantic nationalist adventurer Garibaldi (1807–1882); Victor Emmanuel II of the house of Savoy, king of Piedmont-Sardinia (and subsequently of a gradually united Italy), 1849–1878; and, above all, Victor Emmanuel's chief minister, Cavour (1810–1861). Though of aristocratic origin and trained for an army career, Cavour enthusiastically supported the economic revolutions and the aspirations of the business classes. He visited France and England as a young man and was deeply influenced by their economic accomplishments and by their economic and political ideas and institutions. Back in Piedmont, he applied the newest agricultural methods to his family estates and promoted the introduction of steamboats, railroads, industries, and banks in order to prepare Piedmont for leadership in unified Italy. Cavour was a good, moderate, mid-nineteenth-century liberal.

Cavour was also a superlatively adept practitioner of the realistic diplomacy often called *Realpolitik.* As the chief minister of Piedmont, he set about cultivating French and English support, bringing Piedmont into the Crimean War on their side against Russia. He got no immediate reward, for England was unwilling to take steps that would offend Austria, possessor of Lombardy and Venetia. But, though bitterly disappointed, he put a good face on his defeat and finally persuaded Napoleon III that the Austrian hold in northern Italy was an anachronistic denial of the principle of nationality. In 1859, France and Piedmont went to war with Austria, and won the not quite decisive battles of Magenta and Solferino in June. Meantime, sympathetic nationalistic risings in Tuscany and the Papal States seemed likely to bring their merger into an expanding Piedmont. Dismayed by this prospect and by that of possible Prussian intervention on Austria's behalf, Napoleon III backed out of the war, as we have already seen. At a conference with Francis Joseph, the Austrian emperor, at Villafranca, July 1859, he arranged a compromise whereby Lombardy was to go to Piedmont, Venetia was to remain Austrian, and the old arrangements were to be restored in the other states. Cavour resigned in bitter protest.

He had, however, already won. The wave of popular agitation rose higher in northern and central Italy; in Parma, Modena, Tuscany, and the Romagna, the most northerly province of the Papal States, there were largely bloodless revolutions and plebiscites demanding annexation to Piedmont. Early in 1860, Cavour returned to office in order to manage the annexations and also to pay off Napoleon III by ceding to France the Piedmontese territories of Savoy and Nice. Next, he turned to the rapidly developing situation in the Papal States and the south. In May 1860 an expedition outfitted in ports under Piedmontese control, but not acknowledged by Cavour's government, set out for Naples and Sicily under the redshirted Garibaldi. A republican

Engraving published in English newspaper, 1860, depicts Garibaldi's entry into Naples.

as well as a nationalist agitator, Garibaldi had served his apprenticeship in Mazzini's Young Italy, then won a reputation as a formidable guerrilla fighter in South America; in 1849, he had fought for a lost cause with distinction when he defended Mazzini's Roman republic against a French siege. Cavour deeply distrusted Garibaldi, who he feared might make Italy a republic and so alarm the powers that they would intervene to undo Cavour's own annexationist achievements. Cavour therefore sought to control Garibaldi's expedition and exploit its success in the interests of his own policy.

Garibaldi and his thousand redshirts had relatively little trouble in overcoming the feeble opposition of the Bourbon Francis II in Sicily. Recruits swarmed to his flag, and popular opinion throughout the West, even in cautious England, was overwhelmingly on his side. Garibaldi, who had announced his loyalty to Victor Emmanuel, now crossed the Straits of Messina to continue his victorious march on the mainland territories of Naples. He had the support of the British prime minister, Palmerston, with the implication that British

naval forces might act to block outside intervention against his movement. Cavour, alarmed lest Garibaldi bring on a new crisis by marching north, taking the city of Rome from the pope and offending France and other Catholic powers, sent Piedmontese troops to occupy all the remaining papal territories except Rome and its environs. King Victor Emmanuel soon joined forces with Garibaldi near Naples and assured the triumph of Cavour's policy. In the autumn of 1860 Sicily, Naples, and the papal domains of Umbria and the Marches voted for union with Piedmont.

The upshot of all these rapidly unrolling developments was the proclamation of the Kingdom of Italy, essentially a much-enlarged Piedmont-Sardinia, with Florence as its capital and Victor Emmanuel as its monarch. This was in March 1861; in June, Cavour died, a grave loss for a struggling new kingdom with many problems. Territorially, however, the work of the Risorgimento was almost complete. Only two more major areas were needed—Austrian Venetia, and the remnant of the Papal states in Rome and its vicinity; both were soon acquired through the play of interna-

"Right Leg in the Boot at Last": English cartoon of 1860 commenting on Garibaldi's retirement after having given Italy to Victor Emmanuel.

tional politics. Venetia came as a reward for Italy's siding with Prussia in the brief war of 1866 in which Prussia defeated Austria; Rome came when the Franco-Prussian War forced Napoleon III to withdraw from papal territory. On October 2, 1870, Rome was annexed to the Kingdom of Italy and became its capital. All the peninsula, save for Trieste and Trent in the North, was now under one rule. These two small bits of Italia Irredenta (Unredeemed Italy) were of no small importance, for Italian nationalists remained unreconciled to Austrian possession of them. Irredentism, as the movement to redeem Trieste and Trent was called, did much to bring Italy into World War I against Austria and Germany.

Assets and Liabilities of United Italy

The new kingdom started out with the asset of favorable public opinion throughout the non-Catholic segments of the Western world. Italian national unity seemed a natural and desirable thing, and it had been achieved without very much bloodshed, with a mixture of Garibaldian romance and Cavourian realism. The enthusiasm that had brought the Risorgimento to fruition was now in the service of united Italy. Italians were a frugal, hardworking people, and in the north they made promising beginnings in the new industry of the machine age.

Yet striking liabilities impeded the new Italy. Italians, too, were divided between Catholics and anticlericals, though perhaps not so sharply as the French were; more Italians were inclined to seek the middle of the road on clerical issues in practice. Nevertheless, ardent

Italian Catholics were deeply embittered by the "Roman question," that is, by the circumstances of the final drive for union and the annexation of the Papal States without the pope's consent. Italy lacked coal and iron; in terms of modern economic competition, she was a "have-not" country, a shocking discovery that the Italians made in the years following unification. Much of mountainous central Italy and all southern Italy were really marginal to nineteenth-century Western civilization, with a poverty-stricken, illiterate peasantry rooted in age-old local ways utterly different from those of modern urban life, and with a small feudalistic aristocracy to whom a man like Cavour was really quite incomprehensible. Neapolitans and Sicilians resented the new political preponderance of north Italians in the unified kingdom, much as American southerners resented Yankee "carpetbaggers" after the Civil War. If one spoke of the "two Italies," the division would be that between the already somewhat industrialized north, especially the thoroughly "modern" Po Valley, and the rural, impoverished south, still "medieval."

Moreover, at least half of Italy lacked experience in self-government. It had no tradition of government by discussion, of law-abidingness, of comfortable middle-class compromise. Italy was not indeed the land of mixed stereotypes—sunny gaiety, dark passions, music, and *banditti*—that northern Europeans and Americans believed it to be. It was a land of deep-seated class antagonisms, profound mistrust of governments, fervent localism, a whole inheritance from the past that made democratic government most difficult. Consequently, united Italy moved very cautiously toward more democracy. Its constitution remained that granted to Piedmont in 1848 by Charles Albert; it put effective checks on the power of the king by making the ministers responsible to the Chamber of Deputies, but it also put severe limitations on the suffrage. After 1881 the property qualification was lowered to the payment of a direct tax of about four dollars a year, so that more than two million Italian men now had the franchise. It was only in 1912 that something close to universal male suffrage was introduced.

As time went on, the Roman question became a chronic rather than a critical one. The pope, who refused to accept the legality of the new kingdom, simply stayed in the Vatican Palace as a "prisoner." The Vatican remained the center of the worldwide organization of the Roman Catholic Church, and in no important sense was the pope impeded in the exercise of his powers over the faithful throughout the world. Within Italy, the Church forbade Catholics to participate in politics and urged a Catholic boycott of the new state. Gradually, in fact, Catholics did take an increasing part in politics, but the Roman question itself remained unsettled until 1929, when Mussolini and Pope Pius XI agreed to set up Vatican City as a sovereign state of 108 acres.

The new kingdom made appreciable economic progress. Railroads, built and managed by the state, were pushed rapidly into the backward south, where some of the seaboard area came by the twentieth century to look deceptively prosperous and modern; a brand-new merchant marine and an army and navy gave Italy some standing as a power. Even the national finances seemed for a time under conservative leadership to be sound. In the political field, the 1880s brought a letdown, the growth of parliamentary corruption, the beginning of a long era of unashamed political opportunism. Meantime, the industrial proletariat was small, labor inadequately organized, and the socialists were both too small and too rent by divisions to constitute a dynamic instrument of opposition and

reform. Moreover, as recent economic historians insist, the very economic progress of the north, made in part at the expense of a south both exploited and neglected, increased regional differentiation and helped build up the social tensions that were to affect twentieth-century Italy very seriously.

Frustrated Empire-Building

Finally, in the 1880s and 1890s Italy launched herself on a career of imperial aspiration that seems a good example of the desire to keep up with the Joneses. Since France—the envied "Latin" sister—and Britain had

Unification of Italy, 1859–1870

Kingdom of Sardinia before 1859
To Kingdom of Sardinia:
1859   1860
To Kingdom of Italy:
1866   1870
Italia Irredenta
Battle site

empires, since a great power had to have an empire, and since Italy's leaders wanted her to be a great power, some way of territorial expansion had to be found. Economic explanations of the imperialist drive hardly make sense for Italy, a nation with no important exportable capital, with no need for colonial markets, and with plenty of domestic difficulties. True, Italy had a rapidly expanding population that found relatively few economic opportunities at home, especially in the south. But, since other countries had such a head start in empire-building, very little was left for the Italians, and the leftovers were not suitable for colonial settlement by Europeans. They were the poorer parts of Africa, hardly worth the difficulty of exploitation; Italy acquired two of them in the late nineteenth century—Eritrea, on the Red Sea, and Somaliland, on the "horn" of Africa where the Indian Ocean meets the Red Sea.

Next, Italy attempted to conquer the larger and more attractive neighbor of her new colonies, the independent highland empire of Ethiopia (then generally termed Abyssinia). The Abyssinian War drained the resources of the Italian government and was abruptly terminated by the disastrous defeat of the Italian expedition by a larger Ethiopian army at Adowa in 1896. This remote battle was a landmark in the history of European colonialism, much publicized by the press of the world; while imperial powers had previously suffered temporary setbacks at the hands of native forces, Adowa was the first decisive native victory. It was not until 1935, under Mussolini, that the Italians took Ethiopia, which they then held for only a few years.

The disaster at Adowa cast a shadow over Italy that has been compared, with some exaggeration, to that cast over France by the Dreyfus case. The shadow was deepened by a bank scandal and by the general depression of the 1890s. Grave bread riots broke out in Milan in May 1898, the *fatti di Maggio* (Deeds of May), and in 1900 King Humbert (who had succeeded Victor Emmanuel II in 1878) was assassinated by an anarchist. The accession of a new king, Victor Emmanuel III, who was believed to have liberal leanings, gave new heart to many, and the years just before the outbreak of World War I were on the whole years of comparative quiet and prosperity, of partial reconciliation with the Church, and of the final establishment of universal suffrage. Parliamentary democracy seemed at last to be sending down solid roots. And in the years 1890–1914 the vast emigration to North and South America—the number of emigrants exceeded half a million in the peak year of 1913—almost canceled out the serious economic difficulties attendant on the high Italian birth rate and lack of new industrial employment.

Yet frustrated Italian imperialism was still seeking an outlet. Italy's leaders, and millions of their followers, could not content themselves with casting their country in the role, say, of a Mediterranean Sweden, quite outside the competition for empire with no pretensions toward the status of a great power. Denied Tunisia by the French occupation of 1881, then forced out of Ethiopia, Italy finally got from the great powers a free hand in poverty-stricken and parched Tripoli, a fragment of the old Ottoman Empire in North Africa, and now known as Libya. In 1911, Italy went to war with Turkey for Libya, thus initiating the cycle of Balkan wars that touched off World War I, which in turn would bring Italian nationalism new expectations—and fresh frustrations.

V   The United States

World War I was also to mark the full participation in the international balance of another relative newcomer to the family of nations. The United States came to be a great power, despite words and even sentiments that placed her outside international competition, in "isolation." Two simple sets of statistics point up this fact. In 1790, the United States comprised 892,000 square miles, and in 1910, 3,754,000 square miles; even more important, the population of the United States was 3,929,000 in 1790, and 91,972,000 in 1910, a total greater than that of either of the most powerful European states, Germany and Great Britain, and second only to that of Russia. And, still more important, the combined industrial and agricultural capacities of America were already greater than those of any other single country.

The Federal Union

The land that had become so powerful in a brief century was in the late 1700s almost empty beyond the Alleghenies, save for a relatively few Indians of Stone Age culture; yet millions of acres were as suited to intensive human use as any in Europe. Most interested observers knew this at the end of the American Revolution, and they expected the central parts of the North American continent to fill up eventually with white men. But most of them, including Americans like Jefferson, did not believe that the process would be as rapid as it in fact was. Moreover, all but the most sanguine felt that the developed and fully peopled continent could not possibly come under one political rule. They felt that it must be divided—as indeed the South American continent came to be—into a number of independent nations on essentially the European model. Some unsympathetic observers did not believe that the thirteen Atlantic seaboard colonies gathered together to fight the British could possibly maintain their own union.

Yet hold together the former colonies did. Though the union was often sorely tested, once in the bloodiest war Americans have yet fought, it is a central fact of history that the United States did not go the way of the Latin American states. Why the United States held together cannot be explained by any single factor. Geography was certainly kinder to her than to the Latin Americans, for the Appalachians were no real barrier at all; the Rockies were not the barrier the Andes are; and the Mississippi Valley, unlike that of the Amazon, was a help rather than a hindrance to settlement and communications. The railroad and the telegraph arrived just in time to enable goods and ideas to move fast and far enough to hold Americans together. The communications and transportation network already developed by 1860 enabled the North to count on the West in the decisive struggle of the Civil War. The sheer size of the new republic after the acquisition of the Mississippi-Missouri Valley by purchase from Napoleon in 1803 seemed historically compatible with a loosely held empire of many tongues and peoples, like those of ancient Persia or Rome, but not with a unified nation-state. The achievements of modern technology in effect reduced sheer size to manageable proportions. After the first transcontinental railway was completed in 1869, Californians could get to the federal capital at Washington more quickly than New Yorkers could in 1801.

Moreover, the resistance to Britain had helped forge a genuine national patriotism. The colonists, in spite of contrasts between seventeenth-century Puritan New England and Cavalier tidewater South, in spite of Dutch and German elements in the middle colonies, recognized one language and one law, one basic culture. Almost all the colonies had "frontiers"—in the new American sense of the word, not a guarded line with custom houses as in Europe, but free areas on their western edges where a lively population was winning new lands from the wilderness. This frontier population was a powerful force for unity, for it had little attachment to the older colonial centers. The frontiersmen had great confidence in their own "manifest destiny" to keep pushing westward with the blessing and patronage of the new federal government but with only remote control by that government.

Americans gained their independence from Britain by a war and a revolution that were rather mild compared with the French Reign of Terror. After the more committed Loyalists had left for Canada or Britain, Americans took up national life without any seriously alienated minorities. They achieved at the Philadelphia convention of 1787, and in the campaign for adoption during the next two years, a federal constitution that set up a central government with the essential attributes of all governments—the ability to tax individuals (not just to ask for monies as contributions from constituent states), to control armed forces, and to conduct all foreign relations. The new constitution, in short, set up a sovereign federal state, not a mere league of sovereign states. On the whole, this result was achieved under conservative groups anxious to preserve their economic and social privileges, afraid that democracy in separate,

quasi-independent states would go too far. But this conclusion to the American Revolution gave the infant federal state a safer start. Finally, the threat that British control of Canada seemed to offer put a limit on domestic divisions. The United States grew up in its critical earliest years aware of the need for union against a possible foreign danger.

The new republic entered the world war of the Napoleonic period in 1812. Neither the French nor the British really tried to observe the freedom of commerce that the United States claimed as the right of a neutral, but the British, who were by 1812 masters of the sea, seemed to be infringing neutral rights more seriously than the French. Moreover, American expansionists, the "war hawks," saw a possible prize in Canada to be wrested from England, and no such prize to be got from France. The American attempt to invade Canada failed, not only from ineptness, but from the determined resistance of the Canadians. In isolated combats on the seas, the United States won victories that made up for her failures on land, and helped bolster national pride. The war on the whole was a stalemate, in which the United States experienced no important gains or losses. A generation later, she acquired an enormous block of territory, from Texas to California, at the expense of Mexico. This came in part as a result of annexing the Republic of Texas (1845), which had been settled by pioneers from the southern states and had broken away from Mexico in 1836. President Polk now resolved to acquire Mexican territories west of Texas by purchase and, when negotiations collapsed, launched the Mexican War of 1846–1848, which ended with Mexico's cession of New Mexico and California.

Civil War and Reconstruction

The great test of the Federal Union was the war that broke out in 1861 after long years of sectional strife within the union between North and South. The Civil War was really an abortive nationalist revolution, the attempt of the Confederate states to set up a separate sovereignty. The South was predominantly agricultural, with a society based on plantation slavery and on cotton and tobacco, much of which was exported abroad. The North was increasingly industrial, with a society based on free labor and on independent farm owners.

To the conflict of economic interest was added a conflict of ideals, of ways of life. That conflict was not so deep-seated, so irreconcilable, as it seemed to be to the generation that went to war in 1861—or the South, like Ireland or Poland, would presumably have tried again to free itself, something it did not even really discuss seriously in the integration crisis of the 1950s and 1960s. The fires of conflict were fanned especially by the question of slavery, which seemed immoral to many in the North and which seemed the order of nature to many in the South. They were fanned also

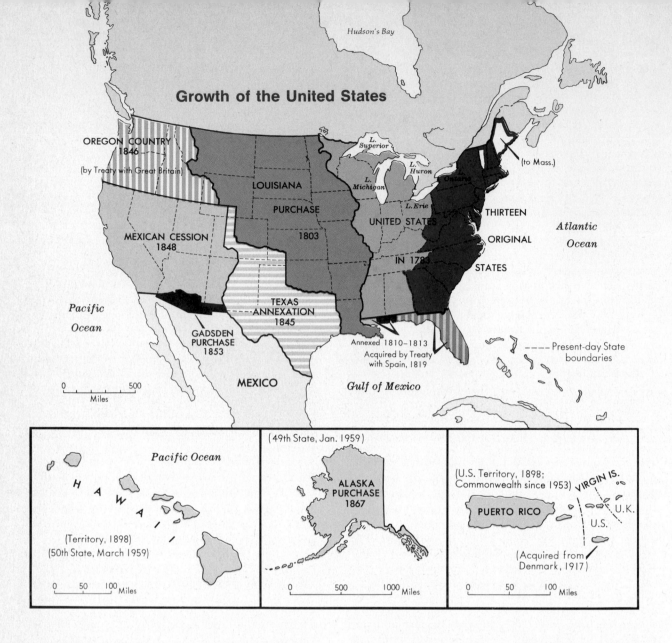

Growth of the United States

OREGON COUNTRY
1846
(by Treaty with Great Britain)

LOUISIANA

PURCHASE

1803

UNITED STATES

IN 1783

THIRTEEN

ORIGINAL

STATES

MEXICAN CESSION
1848

GADSDEN
PURCHASE
1853

TEXAS
ANNEXATION
1845

Annexed 1810-1813
Acquired by Treaty
with Spain, 1819

MEXICO

Pacific
Ocean

Atlantic
Ocean

Gulf of Mexico

Hudson's Bay

L. Superior
L. Huron
L. Michigan
L. Erie
L. Ontario

(to Mass.)

- - - - Present-day State
boundaries

0   500
Miles

Pacific Ocean

H A W A I I

(Territory, 1898)
(50th State, March 1959)

0   50   100 Miles

(49th State, Jan. 1959)

ALASKA
PURCHASE
1867

0   500   1000 Miles

(U.S. Territory, 1898;
Commonwealth since 1953)

VIRGIN IS.

PUERTO RICO

U.K.

U.S.

(Acquired from
Denmark, 1917)

0   50   100 Miles

by writers and preachers on both sides, the northerners thinking of themselves as heirs of the Puritans, the southerners as heirs of the Cavaliers. With the secession of South Carolina and its sister states, antagonism reached the point of open war.

In retrospect, the victory of the North has an air of inevitability, especially since by 1861 the middle and upper Mississippi Valley was bound firmly to the North by economic and cultural ties. In population—especially since the South did not dare use blacks as soldiers—and in industrial resources above all, the North was greatly superior. Yet, aided by a very able corps of officers, by the advantages in morale that accrue to determined underdogs, and by the disastrous early overconfidence of the North, the South won initial victories that gave its cause great momentum. But the North thwarted the efforts of Confederate diplomats to secure British intervention and was able to improvise a naval force that gradually established a blockade,

shutting off the South from importation of necessary war materials. In the long run, northern strength in men and materials wore the southern armies down.

The striking thing about the Civil War is not that the North won it finally in the field, but that the South accepted the verdict of battle as final. The road to reunion after 1865 was not easy, and in the first years of the Reconstruction period after the war it appeared to many to be almost impossible. With the assassination of Lincoln by the fanatical Booth in 1865, the one great moderate who might have lessened the vengefulness of the northern radicals was lost. The South was occupied by northern soldiers, the illiterate blacks were enfranchised, and northern "carpetbaggers" and southern "scalawags"—and many sincere idealists who believed they could bring liberty and equality to a "misguided" South—combined to bring what seemed a reign of terror to old Confederates.

Yet even in these early days the Civil War did not

end, as such wars have often ended, in wholesale re-prisals, executions, and exile. Northerners had sung during the war, "We'll hang Jeff Davis to a sour apple tree"; but after the war Jefferson Davis, president of the Confederacy, was not hanged on a sour apple tree or anywhere else. He was imprisoned for two years, and then lived quietly for another thirty, of course writing a book to justify his career. The fate of Davis measures the miracle of reunion. There were very few political refugees of the kind that often emerge from defeated causes. The soldiers of the South returned, often to devastated homes and lost fortunes, but they returned home under amnesty. Gradually, the crusading fervor of the North subsided, and in a sense it was not renewed until the 1954 decision of the Supreme Court against segregated public schools. Conservative, business-conscious northerners were anxious to get back to normal conditions and quite prepared to compromise with like-minded southerners at the expense of racial equality and other high ideals. By 1876 the southerners, reinforced by some immigrant northerners, had regained control over their states. Slavery, abolished by Lincoln's proclamation of 1863, was never restored, but the blacks were in effect disenfranchised, "white supremacy" was restored, and the racial question in the new South assumed the forms familiar to the twentieth century.

The South of the later nineteenth century was indeed becoming a new South, which is one of the basic reasons why the region came to accept the verdict of what it termed "the war between the states," with due sentimental compensation in wistful feeling for the past. Slowly in the late 1800s, more rapidly thereafter, the South built up its own industries, and began to free itself from cotton monoculture and to integrate its economy and society with the rest of the country. The South long remained a relatively backward area, with its own special problems of poverty, illiteracy, and racial difficulties, but it was not an oppressed nationality eager to revolt.

The end of Reconstruction left the Democratic party in control of what came to be called the "solid South." This was a natural development, for it was the Republican party that had guided the North during the war and that had tried to carry through Reconstruction. This fact worked to strengthen the American two-party system, since with so solid a block secure for the Democrats, the Republicans were forced either to make compromises among themselves to preserve their own party unity, or to lose power; and the northern Democrats were forced to make compromises with their southern wing.

Free Enterprise and Government Regulation
In 1865, the American economy was still in some respects "colonial"—that is, it produced in the main foods and other raw materials to be exchanged abroad for manufactured goods—and, in financial terms, it was

"Emigrants Coming to the 'Land of Promise'": 1902 photo.

dependent on foreign money markets, chiefly London. But in the northern and midwestern states the Industrial Revolution had already entered the take-off stage. By 1914 the United States had been transformed into a great industrial nation, with its agriculture already to a high degree mechanized, and with financial resources so great that after World War I New York was to take over in part the place of London as a world financial center. This transformation could not have taken place, certainly not at the rate it did, without the existence of abundant manpower, of great and still almost untouched natural resources, and of the traditions of individual initiative and freedom of enterprise—which were in some degree a product of the "frontier." Europe played a significant role in American economic growth by furnishing investment capital and, above all, by sending forth a steady flow of emigrants.

This great expansion in national wealth was achieved in a climate of opinion that supported overwhelmingly the view that the federal government should not interfere directly with business enterprise beyond maintaining public order, enforcing contracts, exercising some control over the actual coinage of money—and maintaining a protective tariff. Nor, of course, were the state and local governments supposed to go beyond such appropriate limits. This view, which we have already met in the classical economists, generally accompanied the Industrial Revolution in the West. In the United States, however, a belief in free

Accompanying the demands for economic reform early in the twentieth century was the woman suffrage movement. Here suffragettes march on Fifth Avenue in New York demanding participation in the nation's political life.

enterprise and a minimum of government interference in economic activities maintained itself more firmly in the twentieth century than in the other parts of the Western world.

This belief was reinforced by the Fourteenth Amendment to the Constitution, passed in 1866 and aimed to protect the freed slaves in the South from state action to deprive them of civil rights. The Amendment contained the famous "due process" clause: "nor shall any state deprive any person of life, liberty, or property without due process of law." In the great era of free enterprise that followed the Civil War, the Supreme Court of the United States interpreted the celebrated clause to mean that state governments should not deprive businessmen—including corporations as "persons"—of property by regulating wages, prices, conditions of labor, and the like.

Immigration since the 1890s had brought in mil-

lions of aliens from eastern and southern Europe, men and women ignorant of American ways and readily exploited by unscrupulous or merely insensitive employers. These immigrants were hard to organize in labor unions; moreover, they and their children, uprooted and scorned though they might be, readily absorbed the American belief that no man is a proletarian by nature, that there is always room at the top. Yet even at the height of this Gilded Age or Age of the Robber Barons there was a movement toward the welfare state.

Much the same forces that had produced the Factory Acts in Britain gradually brought to the United States minimum-wage acts, limitation of child labor and women's labor, sanitary regulation, control of hours of labor, and workmen's compensation. Characteristically, and in spite of the Fourteenth Amendment, these measures were taken at the state rather than at the national level, and they varied greatly in the different states. The state of Wisconsin early established a reputation for advanced social legislation, but many of the older northeastern states played an important part in the movement. By the early twentieth century, public opinion was ready for increased participation of the national government in the regulation of economic life.

Theodore Roosevelt, a Republican, president from 1901 to 1909, promised to give labor a "square deal" and to proceed vigorously with trust-busting, attacks on the great trusts or combinations that had come to monopolize important sectors of the American economy. Although Roosevelt did not always fulfill his promises, his administration did assail the trusts in railroads and tobacco and did press regulation of great corporations by the federal government. A federal prosecution of the Standard Oil Company begun in 1906 resulted in 1911 in a Supreme Court decision dissolving the great holding company. Some of the separated parts familiar today, such as Exxon (Standard of New Jersey), Mobil (Standard of New York), and Chevron (Standard of California) are in fact bigger than the parent company of John D. Rockefeller ever was. Yet the work of the radicals of 1900, particularly the "muckrakers" who wrote exposés of questionable business practices for popular magazines, was clearly not in vain. American big business was in the later twentieth century bigger than it had been in the days of Theodore Roosevelt. But, it was also aware of its responsibilities to the public—or at least afraid of what might happen if it followed the advice of one of the great nineteenth-century robber barons, Cornelius Vanderbilt: "The public be damned!" In short, big business in the United States is usually, as in democratic theory it must be, responsible to public opinion.

During the first administration of Woodrow Wilson (1913–1917), a Democrat, the process of regulation gained momentum. The Federal Reserve Act of 1913, for example, gave federal officials more control over banking, credit, and currency. Meantime, the Sixteenth Amendment legalizing a progressive income tax and the Seventeenth, providing for direct election of senators rather than their appointment by state governments, made the federal republic more democratic in practice. Approval of such measures was not, of course, unanimous, since Americans differed loudly and widely about almost everything from metaphysics to sports. To outsiders, and to many native critics, American life in the decades between the Civil War and 1917 often seemed one great brawl, a more-than-Darwinian struggle for wealth and power. Yet this apparently anarchistic society achieved extraordinary material growth that required the cooperation of millions of men and women disciplined to a common task. This paradox of the coexistence in the United States of rugged individualism and social cohesion still disturbs and puzzles many commentators on the American scene.

In spite of the substantial American distrust of "government," government in the United States came to play a larger and larger part in the lives of all. Although this was true of local and state governments too, it held more especially for the federal government. The gradually increasing importance of the federal government, and the gradually decreasing initiative of state governments, were as clear in the period 1789–1917 as was the material growth of the United States in population and wealth.

The Myth of Isolation

Quite as clear, though still the subject of infinite debate among Americans, was the emergence of the United States as a great international power. The United States was never literally "isolated." From the very beginning, this country had a department of state, our senior department, and the proper apparatus of ministers, consuls, and later, ambassadors. The United States was involved in the world war of the Napoleonic era, and by the Monroe Doctrine of the 1820s took the firm position that European powers were not to extend their existing territories in the Western hemisphere. This was no mere negation, but an active extension of American claims to a far wider sphere of influence than the continental United States. Although Americans took no direct part in the complex nineteenth-century balance-of-power politics in Europe, they showed an increasing concern with a balance of power in the Far East, where they had long traded and wanted an "open door" to commerce. After the brief war of 1898 with Spain, which broke out in Cuba, always a concern of the United States because of its proximity to Florida, Americans found themselves involved with the newly annexed territories of the Philippine Islands, Hawaii, and Puerto Rico, and with newly "independent" Cuba, in fact a veiled American protectorate. In short, all this seemed to outsiders and to many Americans to constitute an American empire.

Theodore Roosevelt, who owed his rapid political rise partly to his military leadership of the Rough Riders in the Spanish-American War, was a vigorous imperialist. He pressed the building of the Panama Canal, stretched the Monroe Doctrine to justify American military intervention in Latin American republics, upheld the Far Eastern interests of the United States, and advocated a larger navy. This new "navalism," which also had assertive spokesmen in Britain and Germany, derived many of its doctrines from the writings of an American officer, Captain Alfred T. Mahan. Mahan's book, *The Influence of Sea Power upon History* (1890), and his later works assigned navies a place of preeminent importance in determining power status and found an influential audience both at home and abroad. Furthermore, Americans as individuals had long been active in work for better international organization, and a world court.

Over these many decades of expanding wealth and trade, the United States had come to take full part in international commercial relations. Except when the federal government was blockading the Confederacy, she had stood out firmly for rights to trade even though there was a war on somewhere, stood out for the rights of neutrals. This fact alone would probably have brought the United States into the world war of 1914–1918, as it had brought her previously into the world war of 1792–1815. But in 1917 America was, as she had not been in 1812, an active participant in the world state system, though she had followed the admonition of George Washington's farewell address and avoided "entangling alliances."

Reading Suggestions on the Western Democracies in the Nineteenth Century

General Accounts

F. B. Artz, *Reaction and Revolution, 1814–1832;* W. L. Langer, *Political and Social Upheaval, 1832–1851;* R. C. Binkley, *Realism and Nationalism, 1852–1871;* C. J. Hayes, *A Generation of Materialism, 1871–1900.* (*Torchbooks); O. Hale, *The Great Illusion, 1900–1914* (*Torchbooks). These five volumes in The Rise of Modern Europe series all have fairly up-to-date bibliographies, though some of them were written a generation ago.

P. Gay and R. K. Webb, *Modern Europe since 1815* (*Harper). A recent textbook, with very good bibliographies.

The New Cambridge Modern History, 14 vols. (Cambridge Univ. Press, 1957–1970). Volumes X, XI, and XII of this uneven collaborative work are a handy source of information on the smaller democracies.

Great Britain

E. L. Woodward, *The Age of Reform,* new ed. (Clarendon, 1962), and R. C. K. Ensor, *England, 1870–1914* (Clarendon, 1936). Two very meaty volumes in The Oxford History of England.

A. Briggs, *The Making of Modern England* (*Torchbooks). An excellent survey of the period 1783–1867; originally entitled *The Age of Improvement.*

E. Halévy, *A History of the English People in the Nineteenth Century,* 2nd rev. ed., 6 vols. (P. Smith, 1949–1951). Though incomplete—it covers only the years 1815–1852, 1895–1915—and often outdated, this study by a French scholar ranks as a classic. Halévy also wrote a standard work on the Utilitarians, *The Growth of Philosophic Radicalism* (*Beacon).

G. Kitson Clark, *The Making of Victorian England* (*Atheneum), and G. M. Young, *Victorian England: Portrait of an Age,* 2nd ed. (*Galaxy). Two very good introductions.

E. Longford, *Queen Victoria* (*Pyramid). Recent standard biography.

C. Woodham-Smith, *The Great Hunger* (Hamish Hamilton, 1962) and *The Reason Why* (*Dutton). Dramatic accounts of the Irish famine and of British bungling in the Crimean War, respectively.

E. Cohen, *The Growth of the British Civil Service, 1780–1939,* rev. ed. (Cass, 1965). Enlightening study of the administrative apparatus.

N. Gash, *Politics in the Age of Peel* (Longmans, 1953) and *Reaction and Reconstruction in English Politics, 1832–1852* (Clarendon, 1965). Scholarly studies of an important epoch for reform and political change.

R. Blake, *Disraeli* (Eyre and Spottiswoode, 1966); P. Magnus, *Gladstone* (*Dutton); D. Southgate, *"The Most English Minister. . ."*: *The Policies and Politics of Palmerston* (St. Martin's, 1966). Sound and relatively recent biographies.

G. F. A. Best, *Mid-Victorian Britain, 1851–1875* (Weidenfeld & Nicolson, 1971). Solid account of a quarter-century of reform and resistance to it.

M. Bruce, *The Coming of the Welfare State,* rev. ed. (Schocken, 1966). Good study of the post-Victorian reforms. May be supplemented by C. Cross, *The Liberals in Power, 1905–1914* (Barrie & Rockcliff, 1963), and by studies of two Liberal leaders: M. Gilbert, ed., *Lloyd George* (*Prentice-Hall), and Roy Jenkins, *Asquith* (*Dutton).

France

Gordon Wright, *France in Modern Times* (Rand McNally, 1960); A. Cobban, *History of Modern France,* rev. ed., Vol. 2 (1799–1871) and Vol. 3 (1871–1962) (*Penguin). Enlightening surveys by an American and a British scholar, respectively.

D. W. Brogan, *The French Nation from Napoleon to Pétain* (*Colophon). Brilliant essay of interpretation by a British expert on democracy. Brogan has also written a detailed and perceptive study of the Third Republic, *France under the Republic* (Harper, 1940).

T. Zeldin, *France, 1848–1945,* Vol. 1 (Clarendon, 1973). Initial volume of a study in the Oxford History of Modern Europe series.

A. Guérard, *France: A Modern History,* rev. ed. (Univ. of Michigan Press, 1969). By an American scholar of French background who also wrote sympathetic studies of Louis Napoleon: *Napoleon III* (Harvard Univ. Press, 1943) and a biography with the same title for the series Great Lives in Brief (Knopf, 1955).

J. M. Thompson, *Louis Napoleon and the Second Empire* (*Norton). The standard scholarly synthesis. Other useful up-to-date works on the Second Empire are T. Zeldin, *The Political System of Napoleon III* (St. Martin's, 1958) and *Emile Ollivier and the Liberal Empire of Napoleon III* (Clarendon, 1963); R. Williams, *The World of Napoleon III,* rev. ed. (*Free Press); and B. D. Gooch, *The Reign of Napoleon III* (*Rand McNally).

David Thomson, *Democracy in France since 1870,* 5th ed. (*Oxford Univ. Press). Brilliant essay of interpretation, particularly good on the period 1870–1914.

R. Soltau, *French Political Thought in the Nineteenth Century,* new ed. (Russell & Russell, 1959). An older and still useful work; rather harsh on conservative thinkers.

R. L. Williams, *The French Revolution of 1870–1871* (Norton, 1969). Sound study of the highly controversial period climaxed by the Commune.

G. Chapman, *The Dreyfus Case: A Re-assessment* (Hart-Davis, 1955) and D. Johnson, *France and the Dreyfus Affair* (Blandford, 1966). Scholarly appraisals.

J. H. Jackson, *Clemenceau and the Third Republic* (Hodder & Stoughton, 1946), and G. Bruun, *Clemenceau* (Harvard Univ. Press, 1943). Succinct studies of a formidable politician.

H. Goldberg, *Life of Jean Jaurès* (Univ. of Wisconsin Press, 1962). Sympathetic study of the famous socialist.

Italy

D. Mack Smith, *Italy: A Modern History* (Univ. of Michigan Press, 1959). Standard account by a ranking expert; he has also written other illuminating studies, including *Cavour and Garibaldi, 1860: A Study in Political Conflict* (Cambridge Univ. Press, 1954) and *Garibaldi* (Knopf, 1956).

C. Seton-Watson, *Italy from Liberalism to Fascism, 1870–1925* (Methuen, 1967). Detailed scholarly study.

A. W. Salomone, ed., *Italy from the Risorgimento to Fascism* (*Anchor). An informative survey of the background of totalitarianism.

B. Croce, *A History of Italy, 1871–1915* (Clarendon, 1929). A perceptive analysis by the famous philosopher-historian.

D. Beales, *The Risorgimento and the Unification of Italy* (Barnes & Noble, 1971). Useful recent reappraisal.

The United States

R. Hofstadter et al., *The United States,* 3rd ed., 2 vols. (*Prentice-Hall). A readable scholarly account.

R. B. Morris, ed., *Encyclopedia of American History* (Harper, 1961); *Harvard Guide to American History,* rev. ed. (Harvard Univ. Press, 1974) Standard works of reference.

S. E. Morison, *The Oxford History of the American People,* 3 vols. (*New American Library). Reworking of a popular earlier book, by a distinguished historian.

L. Hartz, *The Liberal Tradition in America* (*Harvest); R. Hofstadter, *The American Political Tradition* (*Vintage); C. Rossiter, *Conservatism in America* (*Vintage). Representative divergent interpretations of American political life.

Tocqueville, *Democracy in America* (*several editions). The famous pioneering study by the great French observer.

C. A. Beard and M. A. Beard, *The Rise of American Civilization* (Macmillan, 1936). An early and influential economic interpretation.

R. W. Fogel and S. L. Engerman, *Time on the Cross,* 2 vols. (Little, Brown, 1974). Based on a detailed statistical analysis and arguing for a revisionist upgrading of the efficiency and humanity of Southern slavery as an institution. Another important recent reappraisal is E. D. Genovese, *Roll, Jordan, Roll: The World the Slaves Made* (Pantheon, 1974).

Historical Fiction

Disraeli, *Coningsby* (*Putnam). A plea to democratize the program of the Tory party; written early in the career of the great Conservative.

Trollope, *The Prime Minister* (*Oxford Univ. Press). Probably the best novel on Victorian politics; written by a Victorian.

Zola, *The Downfall* (Appleton, 1902). Very good novel of the Franco-Prussian War. Arnold Bennett's *Old Wives' Tale* (Grosset and Dunlap, 1911) has a superb account of life in Paris during the siege of 1870–1871.

Anatole France, *Penguin Island* (*Signet). French history satirized at the turn of the century.

R. Martin du Gard, *Jean Barois* (*Bobbs Merrill). Faithful fictional re-creation of the impact of the Dreyfus affair on French life.

William Dean Howells, *The Rise of Silas Lapham* (*several editions) The famous realistic social novel of late nineteenth-century Boston.

Upton Sinclair, *The Jungle* (*several editions). Celebrated exposé of the Chicago meat-packing industry around 1900.

Margaret Mitchell, *Gone with the Wind* (*Pocket Books). The Civil War seen through a mist of Confederate nostalgia.

MacKinlay Kantor, *Andersonville* (*Signet). Grimly faithful account of military prison life in the Civil War.

Otto von Bismarck.

other hostile house, and then repeated the process. He suppressed opposition newspapers in defiance of a constitutional provision that the press should be free. He indicted an opposition deputy, himself a judge and a loyal Prussian, in spite of the constitutional provision that deputies could not be indicted for anything they said on the floor of the house. Yet after four years of this illegal behavior (1862–1866), he got away with everything in the end because of the glittering successes he scored by his unorthodox daring in foreign policy.

Since Bismarck intended to overthrow the German Confederation as it was then constituted, he opposed Austrian efforts to reform it. Austria wished to create an assembly of delegates chosen by the parliaments of the member states, in addition to those named by the princes, and a directorate of six monarchs. Bismarck prevented William I from attending a congress of princes called by Austria to discuss these proposals, and thus wrecked the congress (1862). In 1863, he kept Austria out of the Zollverein, the German customs union. He also consolidated his good relations with Russia during the Polish revolt by concluding the Alvensleben convention, which allowed the Russians to pursue fleeing Poles onto Prussian territory and capture them there. Thus Bismarck wooed the Russians a second time, as he had during the Crimean War.

The Schleswig-Holstein Question, 1863–1865

When the king of Denmark died in late 1863, the celebrated Schleswig-Holstein question gave Bismarck further opportunities. The prime minister of England once remarked that only three men had ever understood this complex problem, and that one was dead and one insane, while he himself, the third, had forgotten all about it. In brief, the duchies of Schleswig and Holstein at the southern base of the Danish peninsula had been ruled by the king of Denmark, but not as part of Denmark. A fifteenth-century guarantee assured

the duchies that they could never be separated from one another. Yet Holstein to the south was a member of the German Confederation; Schleswig to the north was not. Holstein was mostly German in population; Schleswig was mixed German and Danish. In 1852, Prussia had joined the other powers (London Protocol) in agreeing on an heir who would succeed both to the Danish throne and to the duchies, and in recommending that Denmark and the duchies should be united by a constitution. But when the constitutional union of Denmark and the duchies was attempted, the duchies resisted, and the Danes tried to incorporate Schleswig. German patriots objected. The Prussians and Austrians wanted the duchies to have special representation inside the Danish parliament and insisted that Schleswig should *not* be incorporated into Denmark. None the less, the king of Denmark in 1863 followed a policy that supported annexation.

Bismarck now moved to win the duchies for Prussia. He wanted both the prestige that Prussia would gain and the valuable commercial port of Kiel in Holstein. First he maneuvered Prussia and Austria together into a victorious war against Denmark (1864), although Austria had no real interest in the duchies. Then he quarreled with the Austrians over the administration of the duchies. At the Convention of Gastein, 1865, it was decided that Prussia was to administer Schleswig and that Austria was to administer Holstein. But this arrangement provided only a temporary halt in Bismarck's drive against Austria.

War with Austria, 1866

Bismarck kept nagging Vienna about Austrian behavior in Holstein. He tried and failed to tempt France into an alliance. But he did succeed in signing a secret treaty with Italy, whereby the Italians obliged themselves to go to war on the side of Prussia if Prussia fought Austria within three months. This was contrary to the constitution of the German Confederation, which forbade members to ally themselves with a foreign power against other members. So distressed was William I at this illegality that he lied flatly when the Austrian emperor asked him if such a treaty existed. Finally, Bismarck suddenly proposed that the German Confederation be reformed, and that an all-German parliament be elected by universal suffrage, which everybody knew he hated.

Bismarck probably advanced this proposal for universal suffrage in order to make it appear that his quarrel with Austria rested on a less sordid ground than the mere Schleswig-Holstein question. Yet the proposal also reflected his calculation that enfranchisement of all Germans would weaken the Progressive party, heir to the liberalism of 1848, and would produce many conservative and royalist votes from the peasantry. He had seen how Napoleon III had risen to imperial power in France on the strength of universal suffrage. And he had been influenced by conversations with Ferdi-

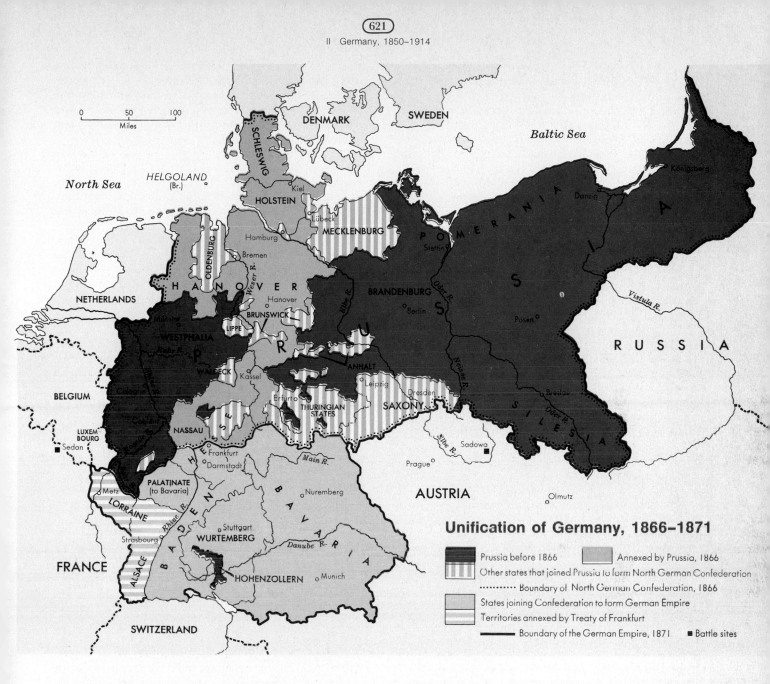

Unification of Germany, 1866–1871

Prussia before 1866   Annexed by Prussia, 1866

Other states that joined Prussia to form North German Confederation

⋯⋯⋯ Boundary of North German Confederation, 1866

States joining Confederation to form German Empire

Territories annexed by Treaty of Frankfurt

──── Boundary of the German Empire, 1871   ■ Battle sites

nand Lassalle, a German socialist, who argued that universal suffrage would weaken the middle classes. Bismarck had hoped that the Austrians might try to throw his plan out, but the other members of the Confederation asked Prussia to propose a full plan of reform. Austria now laid the Schleswig-Holstein question before the Diet of the Confederation. Bismarck ordered Prussian troops into Holstein and declared that Austrian motions in the Diet were unconstitutional. He succeeded in provoking war with Austria. It was an all-German civil war, since Bavaria, Württemberg, Saxony, Hanover (the four other German kingdoms), and most of the lesser German states sided with Austria.

The war lasted seven weeks and was virtually decided in less than three. The Austrians had to commit a substantial part of their forces against Italy. Skillfully

using their railway network, the telegraph, and superior armaments, the Prussians quickly overran northern Germany, invaded Bohemia and defeated the Austrians at Königgrätz (Sadowa), defeated the Bavarians, and entered Frankfurt, seat of the German Confederation. The states of Hanover, Hesse-Cassel, and Nassau were all annexed to Prussia and their dynasties expelled. Schleswig-Holstein and the free city of Frankfurt were also taken over.

Bismarck successfully opposed the generals and even his king, who wished to punish Austria severely. Except for the cession of Venetia to Italy, Austria suffered no territorial losses as a result of the Peace of Prague (1866), but she did pay a small indemnity. Most important from Bismarck's point of view, Austria had to withdraw forever from the German Confederation, which now ceased to exist. Germany north of the Main River was to join a new North German Confederation to be organized by Prussia. However, it was stipulated that the German states south of the Main were to be free to form an independent union of their own. But Bismarck had previously concluded secret treaties of alliance with the most important south German states—Bavaria, Württemberg, and Baden—who promised to put their armies at the disposal of the king of Prussia in case of war. So the proposed South German union could never come into existence. Bismarck thus broke the Peace of Prague even before it had been concluded, a real piece of diplomatic skill. Bismarck's gentle treatment of Austria was not just a matter of generosity. He was convinced that Prussia would need Austrian help in the future. Now that he had expelled Austria from Germany, imposed a "Little German" solution, and elevated Prussia to the position of dominance, he had scored his point.

Now Bismarck was free to turn to the Prussian parliament, with which he had been feuding for four years. He asked for an "indemnity"—that is, a certification that all the revenue he had illegally collected and illegally spent, ever since the parliament had refused to pass the budget in 1861, had in fact been legally collected and legally spent. The deputies were so dazzled by the feats of arms against Denmark and Austria, and by the enormous new acquisitions of power and territory, that they voted the indemnity and awarded Bismarck personally a cash gift of roughly $300,000.

The North German Confederation

An assembly elected by universal manhood suffrage now debated and adopted a constitution for the new North German Confederation, of which the Prussian king was president. The draft that Bismarck submitted is eloquent testimony to his determination to "kill parliamentarism through parliament." The future parliament (*Reichstag*) was to have no power over the budget, and the ministers were not to be responsible to it. Instead, a Federal Council (*Bundesrat*), consisting of delegates from the member states and voting according to instructions from their sovereigns, would reach all key policy decisions in secret and would have veto power over any enactment of the Reichstag. A chancellor would preside over the Bundesrat, but would not have to explain or defend its decisions before the Reichstag. Since Prussia now had not only its own votes in the Bundesrat but also those of the newly annexed states, Bismarck's plan in effect made it possible for the king of Prussia to run Germany.

This plan was only slightly modified so that the future chancellor would have to sign every act undertaken by the king of Prussia as president of the Confederation. But the executive was in no way made "responsible" to the Reichstag. Bismarck's plan also specified that, beginning five years later in 1872, the size of the army would be fixed by law and that the Reichstag would have a vote on the budget. However, Bismarck, who became chancellor, saw to it that the debate on the military budget did not take place every year, but that sums were appropriated for long periods in advance.

Showdown with France

As long as Bismarck needed the benevolent neutrality of Napoleon III, he had hinted that he might not object if Napoleon took Belgium. Now the gullible Napoleon found that Bismarck no longer remembered the matter. Hoping to be compensated for his assistance in making peace between Prussia and Austria, Napoleon III tried to acquire Luxembourg by purchase from the king of Holland. Again he was frustrated by Bismarck. Suddenly confronted with the new Germany, many members of the French public and press hoped to get "revenge for Sadowa," and became strongly anti-German. The German press responded in kind. Napoleon III tried to obtain an alliance with Austria and Italy in order to thwart further Prussian expansion. But the Austrians shied away from a true commitment, and the Italians were unable to reach an agreement with the French because of the Roman question.

When the Spaniards ousted their queen in 1868, one of the candidates for the throne was a Hohenzollern prince, whom Bismarck secretly backed by discreetly bribing influential Spaniards. Because of family dynastic practice, it was necessary to secure the consent of the reluctant king William I of Prussia, and this consent Bismarck finally extracted without hinting that war with France might result. Napoleon III, also deep in Spanish intrigue, feared that a Hohenzollern on the Spanish throne would expose France to a two-front attack. French diplomatic pressure was exerted directly on King William, and the Hohenzollern candidate withdrew. At this moment, Bismarck seemed to be defeated.

But the French, overstimulated by their success, now demanded that William publicly endorse the withdrawal of the candidacy, and promise never to allow it to be renewed. William, who was at Ems, courteously refused, and sent a telegram to Bismarck describing his interchange with the French ambassador. Bismarck then abridged this famous Ems telegram, and released his doctored version to the press and all the European chanceries. He made it seem that William had thoroughly snubbed the French ambassador, and that the ambassador had been "provocative" to the king. Public opinion in Germany was now inflamed, and Bismarck set out to bait the French still further by unleashing a violent campaign against them in the German press and boasting of his prowess in editing the Ems despatch. The French reacted as Bismarck had hoped. They declared war on July 19, 1870.

Within six weeks the Germans had advanced into

France, bottled up one French army inside the fortress of Metz, defeated another at Sedan, and captured Napoleon III himself. The protracted siege of Paris followed, ending in surrender early in 1871. A new French government had to sign the treaty of Frankfurt. Bismarck forced the French to pay a billion-dollar indemnity, to cede the rich province of Alsace and about two-fifths of Lorraine (which the German military wanted as a defense against possible future French attack), and to support German occupying forces until the indemnity had been paid.

The German Empire

Even before this peace had been imposed, King William of Prussia was proclaimed emperor of Germany in the great Hall of Mirrors in Louis XIV's palace at Versailles. Bismarck had to make a few unimportant concessions to the rulers of the south German states to secure their entry into the new empire, but he never had to consult the Reichstag, which simply hastened to send its own deputation begging the king to accept the crown. The proclamation took place in a ceremony of princes and soldiers. When a constitution for the new empire was adopted, it was simply an extension of the constitution of the North German Confederation of 1867.

As chancellor of the German Empire from 1871 to 1890, Bismarck became the leading statesman in all Europe. He felt that Germany had no further need for territory or for war. As a nineteenth-century realist with no dream of world empire, he felt that his limited goals had been attained. As diplomat, he henceforth worked for the preservation of Germany's gains against threats from abroad, especially the threat that haunted him most: foreign coalition against Germany. As politician, he worked for the preservation of the Prussian system against all opposing currents.

Bismarck's chancellorship falls naturally into two periods: (1) a period of free trade, cooperation with the Liberals, and opposition to the Catholics (1871–1878); and (2) a period of protective tariffs, cooperation with the Catholics, and opposition to the socialists (1878–1890).

Domestic Developments, 1871–1878

At home, a multitude of economic and legal questions arose as a result of the creation of the new empire. Working with the moderate Liberal party in the Reichstag, Bismarck put through a common coinage and a central bank, coordinated and unified the railroads and postal systems, and regularized the legal and judicial systems. In 1871, the Reichstag voted to maintain 1 percent of the population under arms for three years. In 1874, Bismarck, simply by threatening to resign, forced the Reichstag to fix the size of the army at 401,000 for a seven-year period, until 1881. In 1880,

a year before the period expired, he forced an increase to 427,000 for another seven years, to 1888. The privileged position of the army made a military career ever more attractive and served as a constant spur to German militarism.

But the great drama of the 1870s in Germany was furnished by Bismarck's attack on the Roman Catholic Church, the *Kulturkampf* ("battle for civilization"). The *Syllabus of Errors* published by the Vatican in 1864 had denounced the toleration of other religions, secular education, and state participation in church affairs. Then in 1870 the Vatican Council, the first general council of the Church to meet since the Council of Trent in the Reformation period, adopted the dogma of papal infallibility. This dogma asserted that the judgments of the pope on faith and morals were infallible. To many non-Catholics, this seemed to say that no state could count on the absolute loyalty of its Catholic citizens.

In Germany, the Catholics were a large minority of the population. They had formed a political party, the Center, that quickly became the second strongest party in the empire. The Center defended papal infallibility, and wished to restore the pope's temporal power, which had been ended by the unification of Italy. The Center not only had many sympathizers in the Catholic Polish provinces of Germany but also sponsored a labor movement of its own, which seemed to pose a social threat. Catholic peasant and workman, priest and nobleman, all opposed the Protestant urban middle-class and the Prussian military predominance in the state. Bismarck identified his clerical opponents with France and Austria, the two nations he had defeated in making the new Germany.

In collaboration with the Liberals, Bismarck put through laws expelling the Jesuits from Germany, forbidding the clergy to criticize the government, and closing the schools of religious orders. In Prussia, civil marriage was now required, appropriations for the Catholic church were stopped, and priests were forced to study at secular universities. The pope declared these laws null and void, and summoned all good Catholics to disobey them. Catholic services stopped in towns and villages, and many Catholics were deprived of their sacraments.

Bismarck never appreciated that the Church thrives on persecution. By declaring that he would not "go to Canossa," he summoned up for Protestant Germans the picture of the German emperor Henry IV humbling himself before the pope in 1077. But Bismarck in the end had to go to Canossa, and repealed in the Eighties most of the anti-Catholic measures he had passed in the Seventies. By then he needed the support of the Center party against his former allies the Liberals, whose demands for power he found exorbitant, and against the growing menace of the Social Democrats. Moreover, the Protestant church itself and many of the conservative Prussian nobility had grown alarmed over the excesses of the anti-Catholic campaign.

Domestic Developments, 1878–1890

Indeed, in 1877 and 1878, Bismarck had begun a gradual shift in policy, dictated in the first place by the need for more revenue. The empire got its money in part from indirect taxes imposed by the Reichstag on tobacco, alcohol, sugar, and the like. The rest came from the individual states, which controlled all direct taxation and made contributions to the imperial budget. As military costs mounted, the government's income became insufficient, and Bismarck did not want to increase the empire's dependence on the states by repeatedly asking them to increase their contributions. He wanted the Reichstag to vote higher indirect taxes, but its Liberal members suspected that if they acceded he might do to them what he had formerly done to the Prussian parliament: govern without them if a dispute arose and depend on the money he would collect from the higher taxes they had granted him. Therefore they wanted some sort of guarantee before they united Bismarck's hands.

Basically, German tariff policy had been one of free trade, with little protection for German goods. But after a financial panic in 1873, the iron and textile industries put pressure on Bismarck to shift to a policy of protection that would help them compete with England. Moreover, an agricultural crisis led conservatives to abandon their previous support of free trade and to demand protection against cheap grain from eastern Europe. In 1879, Bismarck put through a general protective tariff on all imports, a move on which his former allies, the Liberals, were split.

In order to avoid granting the constitutional guarantees demanded by the Liberals, Bismarck gradually abandoned the Kulturkampf. The Catholic Center favored his protectionist policy; moreover, the lessening of the clerical threat in France and the conclusion of a firm German alliance with Austria in 1879 removed the foreign causes for the attack on the Church. Bismarck therefore secured the support of the Center as well as that of the conservatives. Thus he was able to avoid making concessions to the Reichstag, and thus he launched Germany on an era of protection. The protectionist policy spurred still further the rapid and efficient growth of industry, especially heavy industry. Politically, the conservative Protestant agrarian forces now grew stronger, and gained many urban votes. But Bismarck never entirely trusted the Center, and strove successfully to remodel the Liberals into a staunchly conservative industrialist group.

While he was easing the Kulturkampf and swinging to protection in 1878–1879, Bismarck also began to proceed against the Social Democratic party. The Marxists Liebknecht and Bebel had founded this small party in 1869; in 1875, they enlarged it, much to Marx's own disgust, by accepting the followers of Lassalle, an apostle of nonviolence. The German Social Democrats were not nearly so revolutionary as their own Marxist phraseology suggested and had no doubt inherited some of Lassalle's willingness to make a deal with the existing regime. They had many supporters among intellectuals and former liberals, and a substantial trade-union following, polling half a million votes in 1877, about 10 percent of the total electorate. They were prepared to concentrate their efforts on improving working conditions rather than on revolution. But Bismarck always needed an enemy against whom he could unify his supporters; besides, he had been deeply impressed by the Paris Commune of 1871, and believed that something similar might occur in Germany.

Using as a pretext two attempts by alleged Social Democrats to assassinate William I, Bismarck called a general election in 1878, and rammed through the Reichstag a bill making the Social Democratic party illegal, forbidding its meetings, and suppressing its newspapers. Individual socialists could even be expelled from their houses by the police. Abandoning their alleged principles, the Liberals supported this law, but they would not allow Bismarck to make it a permanent statute. He had to apply to the Reichstag for its renewal every two or three years; it was renewed each time, until just before Bismarck's downfall in 1890. Interestingly enough, Social Democrats were still allowed to run for the Reichstag, and their votes increased during the years when they were suffering legal disabilities.

But Bismarck felt that "a remedy cannot be sought merely in repression of Socialist excesses—there must be simultaneously a positive advancement of the welfare of the working classes." As a result, all during the 1880s, the government put forward a series of bills in favor of the workers: in 1882 compulsory insurance against illness and in 1884 against accidents. The sickness insurance funds were raised by contributions from both workers and employers; the accident insurance funds were contributed altogether by the employers. In 1889, old-age and invalidism insurance followed, with employers and employees contributing equally, and with an additional subsidy from the state. The German system of social security as developed initially under Bismarck did not reduce the Social Democratic vote, but it did provide much that the worker desired.

William II

Bismarck's faithful William I died at the age of ninety in 1888, and William's son, Frederick III, already mortally ill, ruled for only about three months. The next emperor was Frederick's son, William II, a young man of twenty-nine whose accession his father had greatly feared because of his immaturity, impulsiveness, and conceit. William I had allowed Bismarck to act for him, but William II was determined to act for himself. This determination underlay the subsequent controversy between him and Bismarck.

On his accession, William loudly proclaimed his

sympathy with the workingman. When the antisocialist law came up for renewal, the emperor supported a modified version that would have taken away the power of the police to expel Social Democrats from their residences. Bismarck opposed the measure, hoping that the Social Democrats would indulge in excesses which would give him the excuse to suppress them by armed force. As a result, there was no antisocialist law after 1890. Other differences arose between the chancellor and the emperor over relations with Russia, and over procedure in reaching policy decisions. Finally, in March 1890, William commanded Bismarck to resign.

Although four chancellors succeeded him during the years before the outbreak of war in 1914, none of them can be compared with Bismarck in ability and influence. The years 1890–1914 are truly the years of William II. Energetic but unsteady, pompous and menacing but without the intention or the courage to back up his threats, emotional and vacillating, William was ill-suited to govern any country, much less the militaristic, highly industrialized imperial Germany with its social tensions and its lack of political balance.

Domestic Tensions, 1890–1914

Party structure reflected the strains in German society. The Liberals, a party of big business, usually had little strength in the Reichstag, although many industrialists were on intimate terms with the emperor personally. The great landowners banded together in protest against a reduction in agricultural duties which was included in a series of trade treaties concluded between Germany and other continental European countries between 1892 and 1894. In 1894, they organized the Agrarian League, which spearheaded all conservative measures and became enormously powerful in German politics. In 1902, they forced a return to protection.

The electoral strength of the Social Democrats increased during William's reign from 1,500,000 to 4,250,000, and embraced a third of the voting population by 1914. Freed from interference by the removal of the antisocialist law, they organized trade unions, circulated newspapers, and successfully brought pressure on the regime for more social legislation. The party had no immediate plan for a revolution, although its radical wing expected, especially after the Russian Revolution of 1905, that a revolution would come. The moderate or "revisionist" wing, which expected no open conflict between capital and labor, hoped that, by allying themselves with the middle class to attain a majority in the Reichstag, the Social Democrats might eventually overthrow the militarist regime. This the radical wing scornfully dismissed as mere temporizing.

As the Social Democrats became more powerful, the government allied itself more closely with the Catholic Center. Between 1895 and 1906, and again between 1909 and 1914, a coalition of conservatives and the Center formed the majority group in the Reichstag. The coalition did not wish to see any increase in the powers of parliament. Yet left-wingers within the Center party occasionally called for a liberalization of the system, and for tactical purposes would even ally themselves with the Social Democrats.

Meanwhile, issues of military, colonial, and foreign policy began to complicate the internal politics of Germany. The size of the army rose from 479,000 in 1892 to 870,000 in 1913. And for the first time Germany sought a big navy, after Admiral Tirpitz became minister of the navy in 1897. The emperor issued a series of warlike and grandiose statements hailing Germany's "future on the water," and he and Tirpitz planned a high-seas fleet to supersede the naval forces that had been designed for coastal defense and for the defense of commerce. The navy boom was at least partly intended to supply a market for the expanding steel industry. A Navy League, ostensibly a private organization but constantly hand in glove with the regime, spread propaganda on behalf of the new fleet. The first rather modest naval law of 1898 provided for a navy that was doubled by the second law of 1900.

But the army and navy were only the most obvious weapons of world power. Bismarck's satisfied country seemed satisfied no longer. The Colonial Society thrived, as Germany seized lands in the Far East and in Africa, despite the drain on the budget (for the colonies were never profitable), and despite scandal after scandal (for the Germans were often brutal colonial administrators). "Pan-Germans" planned the great Berlin-Baghdad railway to the Near East and cried shrilly for more and more adventure and conquest.

William's naval and colonial policies embittered Germany's relations with Great Britain. In 1896, the emperor himself sent the Boer president, Kruger, a telegram congratulating him on having repelled the Jameson Raid and hinting that Germany would have been willing to intervene on the side of the Boers against Britain. Again in 1908, he gave an interview to a London newspaper, the *Daily Telegraph*, in which, with monumental indiscretion, he protested his friendship for Britain, yet at the same time declared that the English had been ungrateful to him in not acknowledging that his own military plans, sent to them in secrecy, had enabled them to win the Boer War. Of course there was nothing in his claim.

The *Daily Telegraph* affair aroused a storm of protest against William in Germany itself, and the emperor had to apologize and promise to do better in the future. This episode illustrates the dangerous instability of the man who was all-powerful in a mighty military state. Moreover, it also reveals the general uneasiness that underlay the apparently smooth and prosperous surface of William's Germany. The protest against the anachronistic system under which Germans lived and labored, and against the external bombast and internal insecurity of the regime, was expressed in the enormous vote of the Social Democrats in 1912.

In 1913–1914, a German army officer in the Alsatian town of Saverne (Zabern) wounded a lame shoe-

William II, center, observing army maneuvers just before the outbreak of World War I.

maker with his sword, and the commanding officer of the German garrison illegally arrested and jailed townspeople who protested. The bitter resentment of the Alsatians was echoed by many Germans who thoroughly disliked the outrageous and unrestrained behavior of their military. By a vote of 293 to 54, the Reichstag passed a resolution of censure against the government. Even more interesting is the sequel, for William decorated the guilty officer, who was acquitted by a court-martial. The Saverne affair proved that the German public was still capable of feeling discomfort over the excesses of their Prussian masters, but it also proved that even a public expression of disapproval had little effect on these masters—the emperor, the Junkers, and the military.

III The Hapsburg Monarchy, 1850–1914
Character of the Empire

The extraordinary empire of the Hapsburgs has been called ramshackle, heterogeneous, and anachronistic. And much scorn has been poured upon it for its incompetence, its smugness, its stupidity, and its failure to keep up with modern times. No doubt these charges are largely justified. But during the past half-century many voices have been raised mourning the empire's disappearance and regretfully echoing a nineteenth-century Czech patriot's celebrated remark that

if the empire did not exist it would be necessary to invent it. These expressions of longing came not only from monarchists and clericals lamenting a past hopelessly beyond recovery but also from many who experienced the far more oppressive nationalist or fascist regimes that governed much former Hapsburg territory in the 1920s and 1930s, or the communist regimes of the period since 1945. By contrast, even the Hapsburgs have seemed preferable.

For sixty-four mortal years, from 1850 to 1914, the emperor Francis Joseph sat on the Hapsburg throne. Simple in his personal life and immensely conscientious, he worked hard at his desk, reading and signing state papers for hours every day. But he was without fire or imagination, uninterested in books dealing with current problems, or even in newspapers, devoted to the rigid court etiquette prescribed for Hapsburgs, inflexibly old-fashioned and conservative. He was intensely pious. He loved to hunt. His mere longevity inspired loyalty, but it must be admitted that he was a dull fellow, in every sense of the term. His decisions usually came too late, and conceded too little. His responsibility for the course of events is large.

Political Experiments, 1850–1867

Hapsburg history between 1850 and 1914 divides naturally into unequal portions at the convenient date 1867, when the Empire became the dual monarchy of Austria-Hungary. After the suppression of the Revolution of 1848, there was a decade of repression usually called the Bach period, from the name of the minister of the interior, ending in 1859 with the war against Piedmont and France. Then came eight years of political experimentation, from 1859 and 1867, punctuated by the war of 1866 with Prussia.

In 1849, all parts of the empire were for the first time unified and directly ruled from Vienna by German-speaking officials. In 1855, the state signed a concordat with the Catholic church, giving clerics a greater influence in education and in other fields than they had enjoyed since the reforms of Joseph II. The repressive domestic policies of the Bach period required expensive armies and policemen. Instead of investing in railroads and industry, Austria went into debt by enforcing the Bach system. These expenditures left it at a disadvantage compared with Prussia. Then, during the Crimean War, instead of repaying Czar Nicholas I for Russia's aid in subduing the Hungarian Revolution, Austria "astonished the world by her ingratitude." Not only did Francis Joseph fail to assist the Russians; he actually kept them in fear of an attack by occupying the Danubian principalities (modern Romania) and so threatening the flank of the Russian armies. In 1857, Austria experienced a severe financial crisis partly as a result of this long mobilization.

The defeat of 1859 at the hands of the French and Italians, and the loss of Lombardy with its great city of Milan, brought about the end of the Bach system.

War continued to threaten, and the nationalities inside the empire, especially the Magyars, could not be kept in a state of smoldering discontent, which would render their troops unreliable. Several solutions were now tried in an effort to create a structure that would withstand the domestic and foreign strains but that would not jeopardize the emperor's position. Francis Joseph made no effort to consult the people. Instead, he listened first to the nobles, who favored a loose federalism, and then to the bureaucrats, who favored a tight centralism.

The October Diploma (1860) set up a central legislature to deal with economic and military problems. To it the provincial assemblies (diets) throughout the empire would send delegates. All other problems were left to the provincial diets, elected by a system that worked to disfranchise the peasants and to benefit the rich and (in Bohemia) the German townspeople rather than the Czech farmers. But the October Diploma did not satisfy the most important non-German province: Hungary. The Magyars continued to press for autonomy, as they had in 1848. Francis Joseph, who really preferred the Bach system, opposed Magyar wishes for special treatment, and hoped that the nobles could stave off further liberalization.

On the other hand, the German liberals and bureaucrats of Austria felt that the October Diploma went too far and gave the Magyars too much. To them it seemed that the empire was being dismembered on behalf of the nobility, who dominated the provincial assemblies. The February Patent of 1861 was actually a new constitution in line with their views. It proclaimed a more centralized scheme. The imperial legislature took over most of the powers the October Diploma had reserved for the provincial assemblies or diets.

Naturally, the Magyars objected to this second solution even more than to the first, and flatly refused to participate. To the applause of the Germans in Vienna, including the liberals, Hungary was returned to authoritarian rule. Czechs and Poles also eventually withdrew from the central parliaments and left only a German rump. Disturbed, the emperor suspended the February Patent; he began to negotiate with the Magyars, who were represented by the intelligent and moderate Francis Deák, but the negotiations were interrupted by the war with Prussia in 1866. The Austrian defeat at Sadowa, the expulsion of Austria from Germany, and the loss of Venetia seemed to threaten the entire Hapsburg system. Francis Joseph resumed negotiations with the Magyars, with the help of the great Magyar noble Andrássy, and of Beust, who had become Austrian foreign minister. In 1867, a formula was found that was to govern and preserve the Hapsburg domains down to the World War of 1914–1918.

The Dual Monarchy, 1867

This formula was the famous *Ausgleich,* or compromise, which created the dual monarchy of Austria-Hungary.

The Hungarian Constitution of 1848 was restored, and the entire empire was reorganized on a strict partnership basis. Austria and Hungary were united in the person of the emperor, who was always to be a Catholic and legitimate Hapsburg and who was to be crowned king of Hungary in a special ceremony in Budapest. For foreign policy, military affairs, and finance, the two states had joint ministers appointed by the emperor. A customs union subject to renewal every ten years also united them. Every ten years the quota of common expenditure to be borne by each partner was to be settled. A unique body, the "delegations," made up of sixty members from the Austrian parliament and sixty members from the Hungarian parliament, meeting alternately in Vienna and in Budapest, was to decide on the common budget. After the budget had been approved, it had to be ratified by the full parliaments of both countries, and signed by the emperor-king. The delegations also had supervisory authority over the three joint ministers, and might summon them to give an account of their activities. In practice, the delegations seldom met, and were almost never consulted on questions of policy. The system favored Hungary, which had 40 percent of the population but never paid more than a third of the expenses. Every ten years, when the quota of expenses and the customs union needed joint consideration, a new crisis arose.

Otherwise, Hungary and Austria were separate states. As king of Hungary, Francis Joseph appointed cabinet ministers, professors, bishops, civil servants, and other officials. He was obliged at least once a year to summon the Hungarian legislature, which had an upper house of hereditary peers and a lower house elected by an elaborate system with more than fifty categories of voters. However, qualifications regarding economic status and nationality made the Hungarian lower house entirely undemocratic; the voters never totaled more than 6 percent of the population. For its part, Austria retained the parliament and the seventeen provincial assemblies provided by the February Patent of 1861. By the new Austrian Constitution of 1867, the authority of the emperor somewhat resembled that of other constitutional monarchs, with the fundamental exception that he could legislate on his own when parliament was not in session. Since he could dissolve parliament at will, he enjoyed a very large discretion, and was potentially a strong personal ruler.

The dual structure of Austria-Hungary was unique in Europe and indeed in history. Because of it, many domestic developments in the two parts of the monarchy may be considered quite separately. Yet one overwhelmingly important and complicated problem remained common to both halves of the monarchy: the problem of the national minorities that had not received their autonomy. Some of these minorities (Czechs, Poles, Ruthenes) were largely in Austria; others (Slovaks, Romanians) were largely in Hungary; the rest (Croats, Serbs, Slovenes—all of them south Slavs) were in both states. These nationalities were at different

Early Prague: the Old Town Square. The town hall (left), with its ancient clock of the seasons, was burned down during the 1945 uprisings.

Moravia, and Austrian Silesia—possessed rights comparable to those that the Magyars had successfully claimed for the lands of the Crown of Saint Stephen (975?–1038). But the Czechs never had the power or the opportunity that the Magyars had to bring pressure on the Austrians, although Czech deputies boycotted the Austrian parliament in the hope that Francis Joseph would consent to become king of Bohemia in Prague as he had become king of Hungary in Budapest.

In 1871, the emperor did indeed offer to be crowned as king of Bohemia. The Bohemian diet, from which all Germans had withdrawn in a fury, drew up proposals that would have produced a triple instead of a dual monarchy. The rage of Austrian and Bohemian Germans, the opposition of Magyar politicians, who predicted chaos, and a Slavic uprising in southern Austria forced Francis Joseph to change his mind. Deeply disappointed, the Czech nationalist leaders returned to passive resistance.

By 1879, when the Czech deputies returned to the Vienna parliament, they were divided into moderate "old Czechs" and radical and impetuous "young Czechs." In the 1880s and 1890s, each time the Czechs won cultural or political gains, the German extremists bitterly opposed them, strengthening the Czech extremists and weakening the moderates. A statute requiring all judges in Czech lands to conduct trials in the language of the petitioner led to the development of an experienced body of Czech civil servants, since many Czechs knew German already, while Germans usually had to learn Czech. In 1890, the government and the old Czechs had tentatively agreed on an administrative division of Bohemia between Germans and Czechs, but the young Czechs rioted in the Bohemian diet, and Prague was put under martial law, which lasted until 1897. When a new law was passed requiring that all civil servants in the Czech lands would have to be bilingual after 1901, the Germans in the Vienna parliament threw inkwells, blew whistles, and forced out the ministry, while Czech extremists began to talk ominously about a future Russian-led Slavic showdown with the Germans. All moderation vanished in the waves of noise and hatred. No Austrian parliament could stay in session, and the government had to be conducted by decree.

Under the stress of prolonged agitation, and influenced by the apparent triumph of constitutionalism in Russia, Francis Joseph finally decided to reform the franchise. In 1907, all male citizens of the Austrian lands were enfranchised and could vote for deputies of their own nationality. Of the 516 deputies in the new parliament, 233 would be German and 107 Czech, a figure almost proportional to the census figures.

Yet in 1913 the Bohemian diet was dissolved by a coup, and in 1914 Czech deputies in the Austrian parliament refused to allow national business to proceed. Thus World War I began with both parliament and the Bohemian diet dissolved and with the emperor and ministers ruling by themselves. Perhaps chief

stages of development and of national self-consciousness. Some of them were subject to pressures from fellow nationals living in states outside the dual monarchy.

The Austrian Constitution of 1867 provided that all nationalities should enjoy equal rights and guaranteed that each might use its own language in education, administration, and public life. Even the Hungarians in 1868 abandoned on paper the fierce Magyar chauvinism of Kossuth and the superpatriots of 1848, and put on the statute books a law that allowed the minorities to conduct local government in their own language, to hold the chief posts in the counties where they predominated, and to have their own schools. But in practice, neither the Austrian nor the Hungarian statute was respected. The nationalities suffered varying degrees of discrimination and even persecution. Since the nationality problem was common to Austria and to Hungary, and since it ruined the entire dual monarchy in the end, after the disastrous defeats of World War I, we must examine it in some detail.

The Czechs

After 1867, many Czechs felt that they were entitled to an Ausgleich on the model which the Magyars had obtained. They argued that the lands of the Crown of Saint Wenceslaus (d. 929)—the provinces of Bohemia, among the many causes for this general parliamentary breakdown was the failure to give the Czech provinces the self-government they had vainly sought since 1867. Most Czechs did not wish to cut loose from the empire and establish a separate state of their own. Amounting to about 23 percent of the Austrian population, the Czechs formed a hard core of discontent.

Yet, from the economic and cultural points of view, the Czechs were by far the most advanced of the Slavic peoples in the dual monarchy. By 1900, the famous Skoda armament works had become the largest in the empire, and the rival of Krupp in Germany. Porcelain and glassware, lace and beer, sugar and the tourist trade made the Czech middle class rich and Czech craftsmen famous. Laboring conditions were bad, however, and the Czech Social Democrats were weakened by their refusal to work with their German opposite numbers.

Czech nationalism was fostered by an active Czech-language press, by patriotic societies, by Czech schools, and by the famous *sokols* ("hawks"), a physical-training society with strong nationalist leanings. At the ancient Prague University, learned Czech scholars taught, of whom Thomas Masaryk, married to an American, became the most famous. Professor of philosophy and student of Slavic culture but a lover of the West, Masaryk deeply influenced generations of students, and upheld democratic ideals in politics. Historians studied the heroic past of the Czechs, and poets, novelists, and musicians glorified it for the popular audience. Deprived of their national autonomy and exposed to German bias though the Czechs were, they can hardly be regarded as a persecuted minority. They had their language and their freedom to develop under Austrian domination.

Poles and Ruthenians

Of all the minorities in Austria, the Poles (18 percent of the population) were the most satisfied, the only contented Poles in Europe. Most of them lived in Galicia, where they formed the landlord class and generally oppressed their peasants, especially the backward Ruthenians (Ukrainians). Like the Czechs, the Galician Poles asked for provincial self-government on the Magyar model and, like the Czechs, they were denied. But they had their own schools, and Polish was the language of administration and the courts. The Poles enjoyed favorable financial arrangements, and after 1871 there was a special ministry for Galicia in Vienna. Since they hated Russia, pan-Slavism never tempted them as it did the Czechs; they were not even very much interested in a future independent Poland.

The contrast between this generous treatment in Austrian Poland and the brutality suffered by the Poles living in Prussian and Russian Poland led Poles everywhere to look to Austrian Galicia as the center of national life and culture. Polish refugees from tyranny elsewhere took refuge in the cities of Cracow and Lem-

berg. Here were splendid Polish universities, noble families living grandly as they always had in Poland, and opportunities to serve the Hapsburg Crown in the provincial administration. The universities trained generations of Poles who were available later for service in independent Poland. Polish literature and the study of Polish history flourished. Though slowly, industrialization began, and a promising petroleum industry was launched. Only the Ruthenians and the Jews suffered discrimination and hardship.

The Poles eliminated Ruthenians from the Galician diet and until 1907 kept them from the imperial parliament. The Ruthenians themselves were divided into an older pro-Russian generation and a younger generation of Ukrainian nationalists, often fanatical, who hated Poles and Russians alike and who hoped for their own autonomous status within the monarchy. In 1908, a Ukrainian assassinated the Polish governor of Galicia after a horrible instance of Polish police brutality.

Other Minorities in Austria

The other minorities in Austria were far less numerous. Less than 3 percent of the population was Italian in 1910; about $4\frac{1}{2}$ percent was Slovene; and less than 3 percent was Serb and Croat. The Italians of the south Tyrol and Istria, where their center was the seaport of Trieste, were far more important than their numbers warranted, however, because of the existence of the Kingdom of Italy across the monarchy's frontier. Almost all of them wanted to belong to Italy, and Italy regarded their lands as *Italia Irredenta*. Of all the Austrian minorities, the Italian proved itself the most anxious to get out of the Hapsburg monarchy altogether.

Among the south Slavs in Austria proper, the Slovenes were the most contented. Scattered in six provinces and often living at odds with their German or Italian neighbors, they usually made only local demands, like that for lecture courses in Slovene at Graz university. The Croats in Austria (mostly in Dalmatia) were fewer and less disaffected than those in Hungary, and the Serbs in Austria were far fewer and less disaffected than the Serbs in Hungary and in the separate province of Bosnia. Yet both Serbs and Croats in Austria were divided: some preferred autonomy within the empire and others hoped one day to join a still hypothetical south Slav state.

Minorities in Hungary: Slovaks, Romanians, South Slavs

In Hungary, minority problems were even more acute. Magyar behavior toward other national groups grew increasingly outrageous as moderate counsels vanished in the face of shortsighted demagoguery. The Slovaks, the Romanians, and the Serbs and Croats living in Hungary proper were the worst victims of a deliberate policy of Magyarization, but even the Croatians of Croatia, whose province had its own constitutional special status, suffered. The Magyar aim was actually to destroy the national identity of the minorities and to transform them into Magyars. The weapon used was language.

It is difficult to appreciate the passionate attachment felt by the peasant peoples of southeastern Europe for their own languages. Deprived of economic opportunity and sometimes of complete religious freedom, these peoples in the nineteenth century found in the languages they talked a living proof of national identity. The Magyars too, who made up only 55 percent of the population of their own country exclusive of Croatia, had a fanatical devotion to their own language, an Asian tongue quite unrelated to the German, Slavic, or Romanian languages of the minorities. They tried to force it upon the subject peoples, particularly in education. All state-supported schools, from kindergartens to universities, had to give instruction in Magyar. The state postal, telegraph, and railroad services used only Magyar.

The Slovaks, numbering about 11 percent of the population of Hungary, were perhaps the most Magyarized. Poor peasants for the most part, the more ambitious of them often became Magyars simply by adopting the Magyar language as their own. As time passed, a few Slovaks came to feel a sense of unity with the closely related but far more advanced Czechs across the border in Austria. The pro-Czechs among the Slovaks were usually liberals and Protestants. Catholic and conservative Slovaks toward the end of the century found their leader in a priest, Father Hlinka, who advocated Slovak autonomy. After Czechoslovakia had been formed in 1918, the Hlinka movement continued to be anti-Czech, and became pro-Hitler in the 1930s.

The Romanians, who lived in Transylvania, amounted in 1910 to 16½ percent of the population of Hungary, and possessed a majority in Transylvania itself. For centuries they had been downtrodden by the Magyars, and had had to fight to achieve recognition of their Orthodox religion. Indeed, largely in the hope of receiving better treatment, many of them had become Uniates, accepting papal supremacy but otherwise preserving their own liturgy. Despite laws designed to eliminate the use of the Romanian language, and a great deal of petty persecution, the Romanians stoutly resisted assimilation. For redress of grievances, many looked to Vienna, which before the Ausgleich had often been a source of assistance against the Magyars, but which was now committed to give the Magyars a free hand. These Romanians hoped that Transylvania might again be made autonomous, as it had been in the past. They pressed for the enforcement of the liberal Hungarian nationalities law of 1868. They wanted their language and their church to have equal standing with other languages and other churches.

But when in 1892 the Romanians petitioned Vienna on these points, their petition was returned unopened and unread. When they circulated the petition widely abroad, their leaders were tried and jailed. It was little wonder that many Transylvanian Romanians ceased to look west to Vienna for help that never came and began to look south and east across the Carpathians to Romania, where their fellow nationals had a kingdom of their own and a strong wish to annex the whole of Transylvania.

Under Magyar rule, some Serbs and Croats lived in Hungary proper and others in Croatia. In 1910, those in Hungary totaled about 600,000, of whom two-thirds were Serbs. Living in a compact mass in the southern and western frontier regions, these were the inhabitants of the old Hapsburg "military frontier" against the Turks. They were transferred to Magyar rule in 1869, and they resented it. The Serbs especially disliked Hungarian administration and looked to the independent kingdom of Serbia to the south. But a far greater menace to Hungarian unity was provided by Croatia proper.

Croatia

The Croats, though connected since the eleventh century with the Crown of Hungary, had become strongly nationalistic under the impact of the Napoleonic occupation and had fought on the side of the monarchy against the Magyar revolutionaries of 1848. Nonetheless, Francis Joseph, as part of the Ausgleich settlement, handed them back to the Magyars. Croatian nationalists were deeply disappointed. Led by the Roman Catholic bishop, Strossmayer, a man of deep intelligence, high culture, and liberal views, they had hoped for an autonomous Croatia and Dalmatia (the coastal strip along the Adriatic, inhabited largely by Croats but governed by Vienna), which would serve as a nucleus to attract all the other southern Slavs. But instead, the Magyar moderates, led by Deák, worked out in 1868 an Ausgleich of their own between Hungary and Croatia.

All military and economic affairs were to be handled in Budapest by a special cabinet minister for Croatian affairs. Representatives from the Croatian parliaments at the Croatian capital of Zagreb would sit in Budapest whenever Croatian affairs were under discussion. Croatian delegates would be part of the Hungarian "delegation" of the dual monarchy. The Croatian language could be spoken by Croat representatives at the sessions of any body they attended, and the language of command in the Croatian territorial army would be Croatian. The Croats would control their own educational system, their church, their courts and police; but all taxes would be voted by Budapest and collected by agents of Budapest. Although the Croats were far better off than any national minority in Hungary, this "compromise" did not satisfy them.

The "Party of the Right," the ancestor of Croat extremism in our own day, wanted a completely autonomous Croatia and scorned as inferior the Serbs and other non-Catholic south Slavs, whom Strossmayer had hoped to attract. Further problems were created in

Catholic Croatia by the existence of a Serb Orthodox minority (more than a quarter of the population), which spoke the same language as the Croats and which was racially indistinguishable from them. But the Serbs worshiped in different churches, and were therefore subject to religious discrimination.

For twenty years at the close of the nineteenth century, the Hungarian-appointed governor cleverly fostered this Serb-Croat antagonism by using the Serbs for local offices. He received the support only of those Croats who had become Magyar-speaking, usually great landowners or government officials.

By 1903, Serbs and Croats were beginning to co-operate against Hungarian rule and to spread pro-Slav propaganda in Dalmatia. In 1905, Croats asked Vienna for Dalmatia and for electoral reforms, but professed that they wanted to observe faithfully the arrangement of 1868 with Hungary. Serbians endorsed these Croatian demands, though some Serbs hoped for union with independent Serbia, and some Croats still hoped for complete independence.

In spite of these hopeful signs, the hopes of the moderates were dashed by the fearfully unpopular Railway Servants Act (1907), which forced all railroad workers to speak Magyar. Croats began to boycott Hungarian-made goods; the Croatian diet refused to collaborate with the new governor, who in 1909 arrested fifty-odd Croats and Serbs and charged them with plotting to unite Croatia and Bosnia with Serbia. The evidence was ridiculously inadequate, and the defendants, though condemned, obtained a reversal of the sentences on appeal to a higher court. But these Zagreb trials gave the Slavic press a splendid opportunity to denounce the policy of the dual monarchy.

In the same year, 1909, a celebrated Austrian historian, Friedjung, charged in the Vienna press that the Croatian and Serbian politicians in Croatia were plotting with Serbians in Serbia. Friedjung was eventually forced to admit that his documentary sources, which in all probability had been fed to him by the Vienna foreign office, were forgeries. The Zagreb trials and the Friedjung case, coming only five years before the assassination of Archduke Francis Ferdinand by a Bosnian Serb and the outbreak of war, demonstrated the incompetence of the dual monarchy in dealing with its own loyal south Slav inhabitants. In 1912, 1913, and 1914, Bosnian students tried to assassinate the Hungarian governor of Croatia. These were ominous rehearsals for the crime of June 28, 1914, which led not merely to internal crisis but to world war.

Bosnia-Herzegovina

In the dual monarchy, the region of Bosnia-Herzegovina had a special status. In the 1870s, these two provinces had been part of the Ottoman Empire for about four centuries. Although solidly south Slavic by race, the population included in 1879 about half a million Muslims, half a million members of the Orthodox

Francis Ferdinand, archduke of Austria, with his wife and children.

church, and perhaps 150,000 Catholics. Under Turkish rule, those who accepted Islam had enjoyed economic advantages. Most of the Orthodox Christian population consisted of peasants working on the estates of Muslim landlords and looking across the frontiers to Serbia in hope of liberation. Some of the Catholics were educated in Strossmayer's seminary and leaned toward eventual absorption in his south-Slav state, but almost nobody wanted to join the Hapsburg monarchy as it was then constituted.

A Herzegovinian uprising in 1875 against the Turks precipitated a general Balkan Slavic attack on the Turks. Russia, too, went to war against the Ottoman Empire, but first the Austrian and Russian foreign ministers reached an agreement on the future status of the two provinces. But they later disagreed on what the agreement had been. At the Congress of Berlin in 1878, the Hapsburgs obtained the right to occupy the provinces, but not to annex them.

From 1878 to 1908, then, the forces of the dual monarchy occupied Bosnia and Herzegovina. The sovereignty of the Ottoman sultan was recognized throughout this period, but in fact the provinces were ruled from Vienna, though not as part of either Austria or Hungary. Instead, they were put under the joint Austro-Hungarian minister of finance.

The discontent of the Orthodox Serbs of Bosnia

was fanned by propaganda from Serbia itself. Patriotic Serbs considered that the first logical step toward creating a greater Serbia would be to incorporate these provinces inside their own frontiers, and they resented the decision of the Congress of Berlin that had allowed Hapsburg occupation. However, so long as the occupation was not turned into annexation, the Serbs preserved the hope that the provinces might some day become theirs and meanwhile flooded them with agents and plotters. The Muslims, though favored by the Hapsburg authorities, never reconciled themselves to the ending of Ottoman rule, and the Catholics hoped to join Croatia.

Thus these provinces perpetually threatened to create an explosion. The more intelligent observers in Vienna pressed for some sort of an all-south-Slav solution, not unlike that of Strossmayer. This would have put Dalmatia, Croatia, and Bosnia-Herzegovina together into a south-Slav kingdom under Francis Joseph, with the same status as Hungary—a triple rather than a dual monarchy. The advocates of this solution, known as "trialists," met with violent Magyar opposition.

However, the Young Turk Revolution of 1908 caused the adventurous Austrian foreign minister Aehrenthal to fear that the status of the provinces might be changed. Fortified by a prior secret agreement with Russia, Aehrenthal simply annexed the two provinces in October 1908 and announced that they would be given a diet of their own. This move precipitated a major European crisis, which threatened world war but which eventually subsided, leaving the Serbs bitterly resentful. Serbian ambition to acquire the provinces now seemed permanently checked. The humiliation of Serbia, the disappointment of Russia, the solidarity of Germany with Austria-Hungary as revealed by the crisis, helped set the stage for the catastrophe of 1914. The discontent of the population of Bosnia, when added to the discontent of the Czechs and Italians in Austria and of the Slovaks, Romanians, Croats, and other south Slavs in Hungary, goes far to account for the wartime weaknesses and postwar disintegration of the dual monarchy.

Yet the minority question, critical though it was, does not provide the entire answer. We must now briefly consider the Austrian-German and Hungarian majorities, both in their separate development and in their critical relationship to each other. Only then can we see that even the two ruling groups were subject to divisive forces that crippled them individually and together.

Austrian Society and Politics, 1867–1914

From the earliest days of the Ausgleich, the Austrian liberals fought the clerical conservatives. The liberals legalized civil marriages, secularized all but religious instruction, canceled the papal Concordat of 1855 after the proclamation of papal infallibility in 1870, and taxed church property (1873). These measures were the Austrian counterpart of the German Kulturkampf, but they were much milder, since Austria was 90 percent Catholic, and did not share the Protestant Prussian suspicion of the Vatican. The liberals were discredited by the financial crash of 1873, during which it was revealed that some of them had accepted bribes in return for voting in favor of charters for shady and unstable new companies. From this period dates the earliest political anti-Semitism in Austria, since some Jewish liberals were involved in the scandals and served as convenient scapegoats. Economic advance during the early years of the monarchy had brought the usual increase in the working class, which after the crash turned toward socialism in both its Marxist and its milder forms.

The Austrian nobles, who often owned great estates which they ruled almost like independent potentates, were on the whole frivolous in their tastes, and took little interest in the problems of the nineteenth and twentieth centuries. They squandered their incomes on high living and gambling. Yet they supplied almost all the political leadership that the nation got. The large size of their estates was one fundamental reason for the small size of the average peasant holding, and made it necessary even for landowning peasants to try to obtain part-time employment on a noble's property. The peasants' standard of living and level of literacy were extremely low, yet the influence of the clergy kept them subservient to their masters, loyal to the dynasty, and almost contented with their lot.

The middle class of town dwellers and men of business, so familiar in western Europe, came later and was smaller in number in Austria. The wealthier tried to imitate the aristocracy's mode of life and to buy their way into the charmed circle. Others joined the professions, which they found overcrowded and badly paid. The unemployment of intellectuals is an extremely dangerous matter politically.

Among the bourgeoisie there were many Jews. Numbering 5 percent of the total population of Austria, the Jews (except for very few) could not be nobles, peasants, members of the clergy, bureaucrats, or army officers. So they were forced to enter trade, the professions, and the arts, where they often prospered and distinguished themselves. What we mean when we refer loosely to prewar "Viennese" life, with its charm and gaiety, its cultivation, its music, its cafés, its newspapers, chocolate cake and whipped cream, its high reputation in medicine and science, is the life of a society very largely Jewish or part-Jewish. Conversion, intermarriage, and assimilation were not uncommon among the upper-middle-class Jews.

Anti-Semitism, fanned by the continued migration of poorer Jews from regions of eastern Europe where oppression had rendered them squalid and uncouth, was general among the non-Jews of Austria. But we must distinguish between the social anti-Semitism of most aristocrats, which was often simply a form of snobbery, and the serious political anti-Semitism of the lower middle classes, often the unsuccessful competitors of the Jews in the world of small shopkeeping. Partly out of religious prejudice, partly out of distaste for the liberal politics usually preferred by the middle-class Jews, the clericals inveighed against them. One response among the Jews to the swelling chorus of anti-Semitism was Zionism (sponsorship of a future Jewish state in Palestine), which originated in the dual monarchy.

The stresses and strains inherent in this social structure, aggravated by the problems of the national minorities, produced in the late nineteenth century two important new political movements among the Germans of Austria: Pan-Germanism and Christian Socialism. In the early 1880s, even moderate Austrian Germans wanted to hand over the Slavic lands of Austria to the Hungarians to rule, and then, stripped to the German core, to unite economically with Germany. The Pan-Germans were more radical and more violent. They opposed the Hapsburg dynasty. They opposed the Catholic church and led a noisy movement called *Los von Rom* ("Away from Rome"). They demanded that Austria become Protestant, and unite politically with Germany. They were furiously anti-Slav and anti-Semitic. They adored Bismarck and Wotan, but Bismarck did not encourage them. Their leader, Schönerer, himself a convert to Protestantism, was elected to the Austrian parliament in 1873 from the same district that later gave birth to Adolf Hitler. But the Pan-Germans never managed to become more than an extreme vocal minority.

The Christian Socialists, on the other hand, became the most important Austrian political party. Strongly Catholic and loyal to the Hapsburgs, they appealed at the same time to the peasant and the small businessman by favoring social legislation and by opposing big business. They too were violently anti-Semitic. At first skeptical of the value of Christian Socialism, the clergy later made the movement its own, and especially in the country prevailed on the people to vote for its candidates. The most famous single Christian Socialist was the perennial mayor of Vienna after 1895, Karl Lueger, the idol of the lower middle classes of the capital. For years he sponsored public ownership of city utilities, parks, playgrounds, free milk for schoolchildren, and other welfare services. Lueger always catered to his followers' hatred of Jews, Marxian socialists, and Magyars. Hitler, who saw Lueger's funeral procession in 1910, hailed him in *Mein Kampf* as the greatest statesman of his time. It is impossible to understand the doctrines of German Nazism in this century without understanding the social and racial structure of the Hapsburg monarchy in which Hitler grew up, and especially the doctrines and the appeal of Pan-Germanism and Christian Socialism.

To the Pan-Germans and the Christian Socialists, the Austrian Social Democrats, founded in 1888, responded with a Marxist program calling for government ownership of the means of production and for political action organized by class rather than by nationality. But the Austrian Social Democrats were not revolutionaries, and set as their goals such political and social gains as universal suffrage, secular education, welfare legislation, and the eight-hour day. They were usually led by intellectuals, many of them Jewish, but they were followed by an ever-increasing number of workers.

On the nationality question, Social Democratic leaders strongly urged a reform in the direction of democratic federalism. Each nationality should have control of its own affairs in its own territory; in mixed territories, minorities should be protected; and a central parliament should decide matters of common interest. Cultural autonomy for the nationalities of a multinational state was by no means an impractical or doctrinaire Marxist idea. Its practicality was later attested by the Soviet Russians, faced as they were with a similar problem and much influenced by the thinking of Austrian Social Democrats on the question. Otto Bauer, a doctrinaire Marxist, tried to explain away national antagonisms in the empire as a manifestation of class warfare. But the program of another Social Democrat, Karl Renner, who lived to be chancellor of the Austrian Republic when it was founded in 1919 and again when it was re-created in 1945, might have averted the necessity for the foundation of any republic at all. A believer in the dual monarchy, Renner advocated treating the nationalities as if they were churches, and allowing each citizen to belong to whatever one he chose. Each of these "national associations" would have its own schools, and disagreements among them would be settled by a high court of arbitration. If these views had been adopted, the monarchy might perhaps have avoided collapse.

Hungarian Society and Politics, 1867–1914

In Hungary, the social structure was somewhat different. The great landed nobility, owning half of Hungary in estates of hundreds of thousands of acres apiece, were a small class numerically. Loyal to the dynasty, sometimes kind to their tenants, and socially contemptuous of all beneath them, they were often intelligent and discriminating, yet more often just as frivolous and empty-headed as their Austrian counterparts. But Hungary had a much larger class of country gentlemen, the squirearchy or gentry, whose holdings were far smaller and whose social position was lower, but whose political influence as a group was even greater. After the emancipation of the serfs in 1848, and during later periods of uncertain agricultural conditions, many members of the gentry became civil servants or entered the professions. The peasantry suffered from small holdings, insufficient education, primitive methods of farming, and a low standard of living.

The Magyars were country folk, and the towns for centuries had been centers for Germans and Jews. But during the nineteenth century, the towns became steadily more Magyar, as members of the gentry and peas-

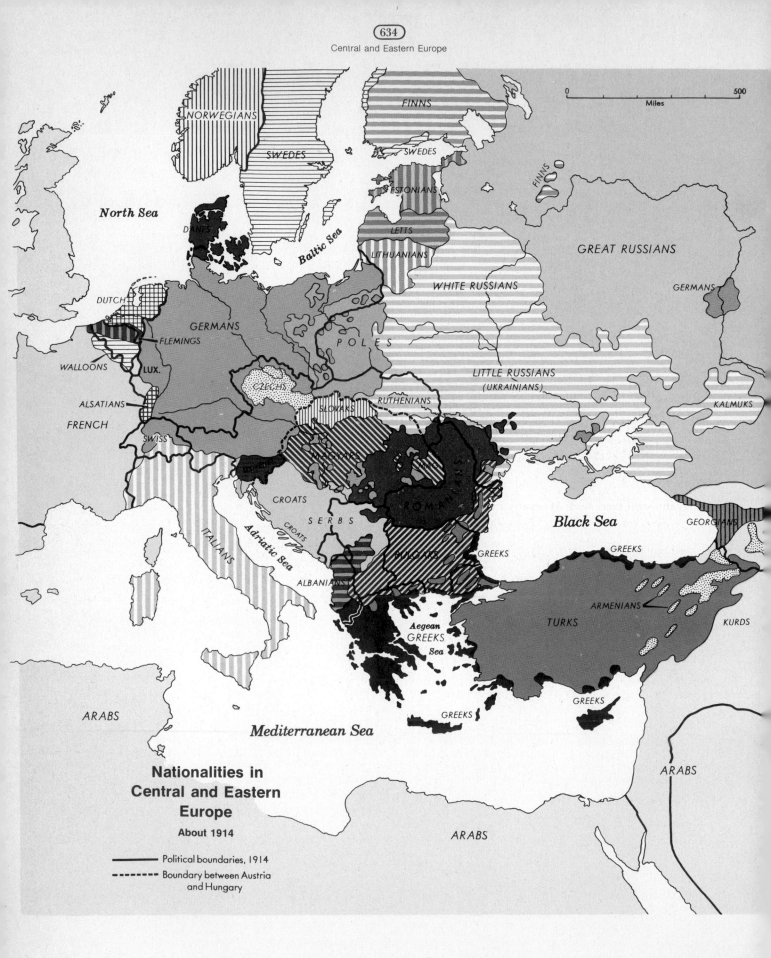

North Sea

NORWEGIANS

SWEDES

Baltic Sea

FINNS

SWEDES

ESTONIANS

LETTS

LITHUANIANS

GREAT RUSSIANS

GERMANS

WHITE RUSSIANS

DANES

DUTCH

GERMANS

POLES

FLEMINGS

WALLOONS

LUX.

ALSATIANS

FRENCH

SWISS

CZECHS

SLOVAKS

RUTHENIANS

LITTLE RUSSIANS
(UKRAINIANS)

KALMUKS

MAGYARS

CROATS

SERBS

CROATS

ROMANIANS

Black Sea

GEORGIANS

ITALIANS

Adriatic Sea

ALBANIANS

BULGARS

GREEKS

GREEKS

ARMENIANS

TURKS

KURDS

Aegean
GREEKS
Sea

GREEKS

ARABS

Mediterranean Sea

GREEKS

GREEKS

ARABS

**Nationalities in
Central and Eastern
Europe**

About 1914

——— Political boundaries, 1914

- - - - Boundary between Austria
and Hungary

0   500
Miles

antry moved into them. The Jewish population grew very fast during the same period, mostly by immigration from the north and east. In Hungary, many Jews were converted and assimilated and became strongly Magyar in sentiment and behavior. When they grew rich enough, they bought land and titles and became gentry. But in Hungary, as in Austria, they were disliked, especially among the poorer city population and in the countryside, where they were associated with moneylending and tavernkeeping, two professions that kept the peasant in their debt. Yet though anti-Semitism existed in Hungary, it never became as important a political movement as in Austria.

At the bottom of the social pyramid was a small class (never more than 20 percent of the population) of industrial workers in the cities, mostly in the textile and flourmilling industries. Wages were low, and living and working conditions were abominable, like those in Russia. Yet more and more welfare measures were passed toward the end of the century. Because of its feebleness this class was never organized into an effective socialist party.

The Catholic church was immensely powerful and rich in Hungary as in Austria, but in Hungary Catholicism was the faith only of about 60 percent instead of 90 percent of the population. Some Hungarian magnate families and many of the gentry had never returned to Catholicism after the Reformation. They remained Calvinists. Several hundred thousand Germans, chiefly in Transylvania, were Lutheran. And in Transylvania also there were Magyar Unitarians. Clericalism could never become in Hungary the dominant force it was in Austria.

Thus, because of its differing social and religious structure, Hungary could not produce strong parties like the Austrian Social Democrats and Christian Socialists. Austria had a relatively liberal franchise before 1907 and universal manhood suffrage thereafter. Hungary, in contrast, never effectively changed its law of 1874, by which only about 6 percent of the population could vote. Moreover, Magyars of all shades were pretty well united in their determination to subjugate the national minorities in Hungary. Internal political or social issues, therefore, did little to determine Hungarian political alignments. The only real issue, and the chief source of Magyar political differences, was the question of Hungary's position in the dual monarchy.

Hungarian opponents of the Ausgleich were in the early days organized into two groups. The Kossuthists favored complete independence; a slightly more moderate party called the Tigers wished to improve the position of Hungary inside the monarchy by securing for the Hungarians control over their own army, their own diplomatic service, and their own finances, and by limiting the tie with Austria to the person of the monarch. When the great Deák passed from public life, one of the Tigers, Coloman Tisza, abandoned his opposition to the Ausgleich, joined the pro-Ausgleich Deákists, and came to power in 1875, to govern as prime minister

for the next fifteen years. Thereafter, this merger of the Tigers and Deákists dominated Hungary except for the period from 1905 to 1910, and stayed in power largely by electoral manipulation. Called Liberals, this group resisted any reform of the franchise and agrarian conditions, or of the treatment of the minorities.

Kossuthists maintained their opposition to the Ausgleich. They wanted Magyar used as the language of command for all Hungarian troops in the army, and agitated against Austria. In 1902, when the government refused their demands, they began to filibuster, and effectively paralyzed the Hungarian parliament. The emperor refused to yield to pressure. Coloman Tisza's son, Stephen, became premier in 1903 and worked through the increasing storm to preserve the Ausgleich. When he tried to limit debate in order to permit the accomplishment of official business, the Kossuthists wrecked the parliament chamber. In 1905, Tisza was defeated by an opposition coalition including the Kossuthists, who now won a majority. When Francis Joseph refused to meet the demands of the new majority and appointed a loyal general as premier, the Kossuthists screamed military dictatorship and urged patriots not to pay taxes or perform military service.

This struggle between the partisans of dualism and those of independence moved only the ruling caste of Magyars and bore no relation to the sentiments and needs of the larger part of the population. To mitigate the struggle, Francis Joseph had only to threaten to decree universal suffrage for Hungary, as he intended to do in Austria. This would open the gates to the discontented minorities and would encourage social and economic change. Under this threat, the opposition coalition eventually yielded (1906) and voted the necessary economic and military measures. They obtained the right to revise the franchise themselves, a task they had every interest in putting off.

In 1910, the younger Tisza won a victory in the elections by the time-honored methods of corruption and intimidation. He dropped the separatists' demands, which had been convulsing the country for more than a decade. Hungary got no bank, no separate army, and no substantial franchise reform. Kossuthists had to be removed by force from parliament, and gag rule had to be imposed. Tisza was kept busy fighting saber duels with the Kossuthist leaders. It was in this deplorable atmosphere that Hungary received the news that Franz Ferdinand, heir to the throne, had been assassinated.

IV Russia,1825–1914
Character of the Empire

The third and largest of the great eastern European empires, Russia, took far longer, as was its way, to catch up with the political and social developments elsewhere in Europe. Thus there was no parliament whatever in Russia until after the Revolution of 1905, and even then the czardom was able to weaken and eventually to dominate the new representative body. Serfdom did not disappear until 1861, and agrarian problems were in some ways intensified by the liberation of the peasants. Each time reform came, in the 1860s and in 1905 and 1906, it came as a direct result of military defeat abroad, which rendered reform absolutely essential. Thus the reforms of Alexander II (1855–1881) were inspired by Russia's defeat in the Crimean War (1854–1856), and the Revolution of 1905 was made possible by Russia's failure in the Russo-Japanese War (1904–1905). During most of the nineteenth and early twentieth centuries, even after the reforms, the Russian czars claimed for themselves the same autocratic rights that Peter the Great and his Muscovite predecessors had exercised. Thus the Russian people experienced long periods of reaction: the entire reign of Nicholas I (1825–1855), and a protracted period from 1866 through 1904, including the last fifteen years of Alexander II's reign (1866–1881), the whole of Alexander III's (1881–1894), and the first ten years of Nicholas II's (1894–1917), the last of the czars.

The failure to adjust willingly to the currents of the times and the attempt to preserve autocratic rule produced unparalleled discontent in Russia. Disillusioned and angry intellectuals in the 1830s and 1840s gave way to proponents of social change in the 1850s and early 1860s, and these in turn to determined revolutionaries and terrorists in the late 1860s and the years that followed. Although Marxist literature was known early in Russia, and Marxist political groupings existed after 1896, the Marxists were by no means either the most numerous or the most effective of Russian revolutionaries. Native non-Marxist revolutionary parties long performed the killings and other acts of violence that convulsed the regime and won the support of large groups of Russians. It was only Lenin's transformation of the Marxist doctrines and his adaptation of Marx to the Russian scene that made it possible for his Bolsheviks to emerge as an important threat. And it was only Lenin's supreme tactical skill and boldness that enabled him to bring his Bolsheviks, still a minority, to power during the Revolution of 1917, a movement that was itself made possible by Russian losses in still another war. There was nothing inevitable about the triumph of the Bolsheviks.

Amid the official attempts to preserve sixteenth-century patterns, Russia experienced the impact of nineteenth- and twentieth-century industrialization. New resources were developed, thousands of miles of railroads were built, and factories sprang up, engaged in both heavy and light industry. A new laboring class thronged the cities, as elsewhere in Europe, but it lived and worked under conditions far worse than those in any other country. The native Russian revolutionaries looked to the peasants, in traditional Russian fashion, to provide them with their base, and they considered peasant problems paramount. The Marxists, on the other hand, true to the teachings of their master, recruited their following among this new proletariat and

focused their attention on its problems. But they deliberately relied for their tightly organized leadership almost exclusively on a little body of intellectuals and theorists.

Despite censorship and an atmosphere of repression, Russia experienced during the nineteenth century an amazing literary flowering. Poets, novelists, and playwrights produced works that rank with the greatest of all time. Like a sudden blossoming of orchids on an iceberg, the Russian literary renaissance cannot easily be explained. The literary talents of the Russian people had long lain dormant and now awoke in an expression of unparalleled vigor and beauty.

Nicholas I (1825–1855)

Coming to the throne amid the disorders of the Decembrist Revolution, Nicholas I (1825–1855) himself personally presided over the investigation of the revolutionaries and prescribed their punishment. He used their confessions as a source of information on the state of Russian opinion. Nicholas I has been more resoundingly damned by liberals, both Russian and foreign, than has any other czar. They have portrayed him as a kind of scarecrow of an autocrat. Reactionary and autocratic though he was, literal-minded and devoted to military pursuits, he was perhaps not such an inflexible tyrant as he has been made out.

Nicholas I worked hard at the business of the state, and firmly believed that the imperial word was sacred. Although he despised all constitutions, he honored the liberal constitution that his elder brother Alexander had granted to the Poles until the Poles themselves revolted. He believed that his own autocratic power had been ordained by God; the autocrat could not, even if he wished, limit his own authority. Naturally such a man loathed the thought of revolution anywhere, and was perfectly prepared to cooperate abroad with the Metternich system. At home, he was prepared to make changes and improvements but not to touch the fundamental institution of the autocracy. Though

"The 'Montagne Russe.'—A very dangerous game."
A view of Nicholas I, April 1834.

he was uneasy over the dangers inherent in serfdom, he was afraid to reform it in any serious way, because he feared that concessions would stimulate revolution among the peasants. Nicholas leaned heavily on the nobility as a class, referring to its members as his "benevolent police chiefs."

So personal was Nicholas' rule that his own chancery or secretariat became the most important organ of Russian government. He enlarged it by creating several sections, including a notorious "third section" for political police activity, which spread rapidly and kept Russian political life under surveillance. This enormous expansion of the czar's own secretariat did not result in the abolition of any of the older organs of government. Consequently, bureaucratic confusion became very great, paperwork was multiplied, and much injustice was done through sheer incompetence. Although the Russian laws were collected under the direction of Speransky, for the first time since 1649, the collection was not a true codification or modernization.

In the field of education, Nicholas favored the improvement of technical schools but was deeply worried about the possibility that subversive foreign ideas might penetrate into the universities. After the revolutions of 1848 in Europe, his reactionary minister of education, Uvarov, abolished the study of philosophy in the University of St. Petersburg because, as he said, the usefulness of the subject had not been proved, and it might do harm. Uvarov formulated Nicholas' policies under the three heads of Autocracy, Orthodoxy, and Nationality: the unlimited power of the monarch, the sanctity of the Russian church, and the adoption of policies in accordance with the "Russian national character." The result was a police state, complete with censorship and terror, yet not nearly so efficient as a twentieth-century despotism.

We have already seen Nicholas putting down the Polish revolution of 1830 and intervening in 1849 to restore Hungary to the Hapsburgs. He believed in dynastic friendships, and counted on the alliance with Prussia and Austria without realizing that conflicting national interests were more important than friendships between monarchs. Thus he failed to see that Prussia would combat his own efforts to thwart the unification of Germany, and that Austria's interests conflicted with his own in southeastern Europe. It was partly Nicholas' failure to see the weaknesses of his own system of alliances that led him into the disastrous Crimean War.

The Crimean War

Like other Russian rulers before him, Nicholas confidently expected the collapse of the Ottoman Empire. Russia wished to protect the Orthodox subjects of the sultan, and also had important economic interests at stake. The great Russian wheat-producing areas in the south were being developed in earnest, and Odessa on the Black Sea had become a great commercial port for the grain trade. Nicholas hoped to establish a Russian sphere of influence in the Balkans, and even to take possession of Istanbul itself. We have already witnessed his intervention in the Greek War of the late 1820s. When the governor of Egypt, Mohammed Ali, revolted against the Ottoman sultan in 1832 and threatened Istanbul, Nicholas landed a Russian army and got credit for saving the sultan's capital.

In 1833, the Turks paid the bill for these services. But by now, Russian policy had undergone an important change. Instead of wishing to annex large sections of the Ottoman Empire, the czar, under the influence of a well-argued memorandum from his foreign minister, Nesselrode, preferred to maintain a weak and friendly Ottoman Empire that would serve as a buffer between Russia and the Hapsburg Empire, which was naturally nervous whenever the Russians seemed about to expand into the Balkan region. So, in the Treaty of Unkiar Skelessi with Russia, Nicholas took the Ottoman Empire under his protection, and the Turks agreed to close the Straits (the Bosporus and Dardanelles) to the warships of any nation.

Alarmed at the preponderance that the treaty gave to Russia in an area of the world vital to British imperial and commercial interests, British diplomacy turned its efforts to undoing it. The next time Mohammed Ali revolted, in 1839, the British were able to put him down with their fleet before he came within distance of a Russian land force. In 1841, all the other important powers joined Russia in guaranteeing the integrity of Turkey, thus putting an end to the exclusive position obtained by Russia at Unkiar Skelessi.

During the next twelve years (1841–1853), Nicholas tried to reach an agreement with Britain on what should be done with Ottoman territory if Turkey collapsed. The British did not believe that such collapse was imminent, and they hoped to prevent Russia from doing anything to hasten it. The two parties misunderstood each other. By 1853, the czar mistakenly believed that Britain was not opposed to Russian domination of Turkey, and Britain mistakenly believed that the czar would not act in Turkey without consulting her.

Then a dispute arose over whether the Roman Catholics, backed by Napoleon III, or the Orthodox clergy, backed by the czar, should have the right to perform certain functions in the Christian Holy Places in Palestine, which was still part of the Ottoman dominions. This trivial dispute was the immediate cause of the Crimean War. But the underlying cause was the czar's wish to reestablish the exclusive Russian position of the Treaty of Unkiar Skelessi, and the British unwillingness to permit him to do so. Nicholas coupled a demand for this exclusive position with the demand that the Turks settle the dispute over the Holy Places amicably. The latter demand was possible; the former was not. When Nicholas occupied the Danubian principalities to enforce his demands, the situation became even tenser. And so, after many months of elaborate diplomatic negotiations in which all the powers strove

A camp of the 5th Dragon Guards during the Crimean War.

to work out a suitable formula to avoid war, the drift toward war proved too strong to be checked. England, France, and eventually the Italian kingdom of Sardinia fought the Russians to protect the Turks.

Famous as the occasion of the charge of the Light Brigade and of Florence Nightingale's pioneer efforts to save the lives of sick and wounded soldiers, the Crimean War consisted mostly of the English and French siege of the great Russian naval base at Sebastopol in the Crimea. Military operations on both sides were inefficiently conducted, but eventually the Russians were compelled to surrender. In the Peace of Paris of 1856, Russia was forbidden to fortify the Black Sea coast or to maintain a fleet there. This made it impossible for the Russians to defend their own shores or to conduct their shipping in security. It now became the paramount object of Russian foreign policy to alter the Black Sea clauses of the treaty. Not only had Russia lost the war, but Prussia had not helped her, and Austria had been positively hostile. Nicholas did not live to see the total failure of his policy. He died during the war and was succeeded by his son Alexander II (1855–1881).

Alexander II and Reform
By this time a very substantial segment of Russian public opinion favored reforms, in reaction to the long period of repression at home and failure abroad. Moreover, the economic developments of the early nine-

teenth century had rendered the system of serfdom less and less profitable. In the south, where land was fertile and crops were produced for sale as well as for use, the serf tilled his master's land usually three days a week, but sometimes more. In the north, where the land was less fertile and could not produce a surplus, the serfs often had a special arrangement with their masters called quit-rent. This meant that the serf paid the master annually in cash instead of in work, and usually had to labor at home as a craftsman or go to a nearby town and work as a factory hand or small shopkeeper to raise the money. It is probable that about a quarter of the serfs of all Russia paid quit-rent by 1855. Neither in the south nor in the north was serfdom efficient in agriculture. As industries grew, it became clearer and clearer to factory owners who experimented with both serf and free labor that serf labor was not productive. Yet free labor was scarce, and the growing population needed to be fed. Many estates were mortgaged to state credit institutions because of inefficient management and the extravagance of the landlords. Serfdom had become uneconomic.

But this fact was not widely realized among Russian landowners, who knew only that something had gone wrong somewhere. They wished to keep things as they were, and they did not as a class feel that emancipation was the answer. Yet the serfs showed increasing unrest, and cases of revolt rose in number. Abolitionist sentiment had now spread widely among intellectuals. Conscious of the unrest, Alexander II, though almost as conservative as his father, determined to embark on reforms, preferring, as he put it, that the abolition of serfdom come from above rather than from below. Through a cumbersome arrangement in which local commissions made studies and reported their findings to members of the government, an emancipation law was eventually formulated and proclaimed early in 1861.

A general statute declared that the serfs were now free, laid down the principles of the new administrative organization of the peasantry, and prescribed the rules for the purchase of land. A whole series of local statutes governed the particular procedure to be followed in the different provinces. All peasants, crown and private, were freed, and each peasant household received its homestead and a certain amount of land, usually the amount the peasant family had cultivated for its own use in the past. The land usually became the property of the village commune, which had the power to redistribute it periodically among the households. The government bought the land from the proprietors, but the peasants had to redeem it by payments extending over a period of forty-nine years. The proprietor retained only the portion of his estate that had been farmed for his own purposes.

This statute, liberating more than forty million human beings, has been called the greatest single legislative act in history. There can be no doubt that it acted as an immense moral stimulus to peasant self-respect. Yet there were grave difficulties. The peasant had to accept the allotment, and since his household became collectively responsible for the taxes and redemption payments, his mobility was not greatly increased. The commune took the place of the proprietor, and differing local conditions caused great difficulty in administering the law. Moreover, the peasants in general got too little land, and had to pay too much for it. They did not get important forest and pasture lands. The settlement, however, was on the whole surprisingly liberal, despite the problems it failed to solve and despite the agrarian crises that developed in part as a result of its inadequacies.

The end of the landlords' rights of justice and police on their estates made it necessary to reform the entire local administration. By statute, in 1864, provincial and district assemblies, or *zemstvos,* were created. Chosen by an elaborate electoral system that divided the voters into categories by class, the assemblies nonetheless gave substantial representation to the peasants. The assemblies dealt with local finances, education, medical care, scientific agriculture, maintenance of the roads, and similar economic and social questions. Starting from scratch in many cases, the zemstvos made great advances in the founding of primary schools and the improvement of public health. They brought together peasant and proprietor to work out local problems. They served as schools of citizenship for all classes, and led tens of thousands of Russians to hope that this progressive step would be crowned by the creation of

a central parliament, or *duma.* Despite the pressure that such men tried to bring on the government, the duma was not granted, partly because after the first attempt on the life of the czar in 1866 the regime swung away from reform and toward reaction.

But before this happened, other advances had been made. The populations of the cities were given municipal assemblies, with duties much like those of the zemstvos in the countryside. The Russian judicial system and legal procedure, which were riddled with inequities, were reformed. For the first time, juries were introduced, cases were argued publicly and orally, all classes were made equal before the law, and the system of courts was completely overhauled. Censorship was relaxed, new schools were encouraged, the universities were freed from the restraints that Nicholas had imposed on them, and the antiquated and often brutal system of military service was modernized and rendered less severe.

Yet, despite all these remarkable advances accomplished in a relatively few years, Alexander II became the target for revolutionaries in 1866, and terrorist activity continued throughout the Seventies until the assassins finally killed the czar in 1881. It is impossible to understand these developments without taking a brief look at Russian intellectual life under Nicholas and Alexander.

Russian Intellectual Life

Early in Nicholas' reign, Russian professors and students, influenced by German philosophers, were devoting themselves to passionate discussions on art, philosophy, and religion. Many intellectuals outside the universities followed suit. These were the first groups known as the intelligentsia, a peculiarly Russian class. By the 1830s, they were beginning to discuss Russia's place in the world, and especially its true historical relationship to the West and the proper course for it to follow in the future. Out of their debates there arose

Cartoon by Gustave Doré showing Russian nobles betting their serfs in a card game.

two important opposing schools of thought: the "Westerners" and the "Slavophiles" (friends of the Slavs).

The Westerners stated their case in a famous document called the *Philosophical Letter,* published in 1836, though written earlier. Its author, Chaadaev, lamented the damaging effect of Byzantine Christianity and the Tatar invasions upon Russian development, and declared that Russia had made no contribution to the world. He hailed Peter the Great's efforts at westernizing Russia as a step in the right direction. He regarded the Roman church as the source of much that was fruitful in the West of which Russia had been deprived. Nicholas I had Chaadaev certified as insane and commanded that he be put under house arrest with a physician visiting him every day. Yet, despite scorn and censorship, the Westerners could not be silenced. They continued to declare that Russia was a society fundamentally like the West, but that history had delayed its full development. Russia should now catch up. The implication was that the time had come for Russia to emerge from a period of absolutism and to enter upon the paths of parliamentary government and constitutional monarchy already trodden by the West.

In response, the opponents of the Westerners, the Slavophiles, vigorously argued that Russia had its own national spirit, like the Volksgeist that Herder had discovered in the Germans. Russia was, they maintained, essentially different from the West. The Orthodox religion of the Slavs was not legalistic, rationalistic, and narrow like the Roman Catholicism of the West, but substantial, emotional, and broad. The Slavophiles violently attacked Peter the Great for embarking Russia on a false course. The West ought not to be imitated but opposed. The Russian upper classes should turn away from their Europeanized manners, and look for inspiration to the simple Russian peasant who lived in the truly Russian institution of the village commune. Western Europe was urban and bourgeois; Russia was rural and agrarian. Western Europe was materialistic; Russia was deeply spiritual. Like the Westerners, the Slavophiles attached fundamental importance to the national religion, and made it the center of their arguments; but they praised where the Westerners damned. The Westerners' views had democratic and constitutional political implications; the Slavophiles' views had anticonstitutional and antidemocratic implications.

It is very important, however, to realize that this does not mean that the Slavophiles embraced the "nationality" doctrine of Nicholas I or that they approved of his regime. These were not the chauvinist nationalists who appeared later. They opposed the tyranny and the bureaucratic machine of Nicholas I as bitterly as did the Westerners. But they wanted a patriarchal, benevolent monarchy of the kind they fancied had existed before Peter the Great, instead of a constitutional regime on the Western pattern. Instead of a central parliament, they looked back with longing to the feudal Muscovite assembly, to the zemski sobor, and to other

institutions of the czardom before Peter. Extremists among them went about the streets dressed in the old boyars' robes that Peter had made illegal. Many intellectuals shifted back and forth between the hotly debating camps, and few ever adopted in full the ideas of either side.

Alexander Herzen (1812–1870), for example, began his intellectual career as a Westerner and a devotee of French culture. The illegitimate son of a nobleman, brought up in his father's house, he was charming, engaging, and highly intelligent. Like most Russians, he was not a reliable interpreter of Western society, however, and was deeply fascinated with the thought that its structure might be rotten and doomed. The failure of the Paris revolution of 1848, which he saw as an eyewitness, convinced him that this was true, and he now became a revolutionary socialist. At the same time, he became convinced that the Westerners' thesis must be wrong. How could Russia in a short time pass through the stages of development that the West had taken centuries to experience but that Russia had missed? So Herzen became a Slavophile. As a revolutionary, he preached the destruction of existing institutions and, as a Slavophile, he looked to Russia, with its peculiar institution of the peasant commune, the *mir,* to provide an inspiration for all Europe. Herzen became an influential publicist and issued a Russian-language paper in London, which was widely read by Russian intellectuals. His memoirs provide perhaps the best picture preserved to us of the intellectual ferment of the age of Nicholas.

Michael Bakunin (1814–1876) reached roughly the same conclusions as Herzen at roughly the same time. But he was a practical anarchist tactician who loved violence, not a peaceful man of letters. He enjoyed participating in revolutions, and had a long career in and out of jail in most of the countries of Europe. He looked forward to a great revolution spreading perhaps from Prague to Moscow and thence to the rest of Europe, followed by a tight dictatorship; beyond this he was entirely vague about the future. Atheism was a fundamental part of his program—not a casual part, as it always was to the Marxists. In his long career, Bakunin was to exert from abroad a considerable influence on Russian radicals.

Nihilism, Populism, Terrorism

In the 1860s, and especially after the emancipation in Russia, the Russian intelligentsia, like intellectuals elsewhere in Europe, reacted against the romanticism of their predecessors. Suspecting idealism, religion, and metaphysics, they turned now to a narrowly utilitarian view of art and society. As one of these young men said, a pair of shoes to him was worth more than all the madonnas of a great Renaissance painter. All art must have a social purpose, and the bonds holding the individual tightly to society must be smashed. Away with parental authority, with the marriage tie, with the tyr-

Police in St. Petersburg discovering a nihilist press, 1887.

anny of custom. For these people the name "nihilist" (a man who believes in nothing) quickly became fashionable. The portrait of a nihilist was drawn by the great novelist Turgenev in Bazarov, the hero of his novel *Fathers and Sons*. Rude and scornful, obstinate and arrogant, Bazarov was actually accepted as a model by intellectual leaders of youth in revolt against established ways of behavior. Yet nihilism as such was not a political movement. The nihilists enjoyed shocking their parents by calling for an end to the old moral system, advocating, for instance, the extermination of everybody in Russia over the age of twenty-five.

In the 1860s, many of these young Russian intellectuals went to Switzerland, where the proper Swiss bourgeoisie were scandalized at the men with their hair cut long and the girls with their hair cut short, at their loud voices and insolent behavior. The standard cartoonist's picture of a Russian revolutionary dates from the first startled glimpse that the Swiss had of the nihilists, who at the time had not even begun to be interested in political revolution. Herzen himself was shocked by their behavior. He died in 1870, his intellectual leadership forfeit. But Bakunin understood them and influenced many of them during their stay in Switzerland. Bakunin urged them to go back to Russia and preach an immediate revolution to the peasants.

Also present in Switzerland were two other important Russian revolutionary thinkers: Lavrov and Tkachev. Lavrov (1823–1900) taught his followers that as intellectuals they owed a great debt to the Russian peasant, whose labor for many generations had enabled their ancestors to enjoy leisure and had made their own education possible. More gradual in his approach and more realistic in his estimates of the Russian peasant than Bakunin, Lavrov advised the nihilist students first to complete their education and then to return to Russia and go among the peasants, educating them and spreading among them propaganda for an eventual, not an immediate, revolution of the masses. On the other hand, Tkachev (1844–1886) taught that no revolution could ever be expected from the peasant masses but that it would have to come from a tightly controlled small revolutionary elite, a little knot of conspirators who would seize power. Though not very influential at the time, Tkachev was important in Lenin's later thinking.

Under the impact of these teachers, especially Bakunin and Lavrov, Russian nihilists turned to a new kind of movement, which is called populism. Young men and women, swept by idealistic fervor, decided to return to Russia and live among the peasants. When a government decree in 1872 actually summoned them back, they found that a parallel movement had already begun at home. About three thousand young people now took posts as teachers, innkeepers, or store managers in the villages. Some tried to spread revolutionary ideas, others simply to render social service. Their romantic views of the peasantry were soon dispelled. The young populists did not know how to dress like peasants or how to talk to peasants. Suspicious of their talk, the peasants often betrayed them. The populists became conspicuous, and were easily traced by the police, who arrested them in droves. Two famous mass trials were held in the 1870s, at which the general public for the first time learned about the populist movement. After the trials, the populists who remained at large decided that they needed a determined revolutionary organization. With the formation of the Land and Liberty Society in 1876, the childhood of the Russian revolutionary movement was over.

The revolutionaries had been stimulated by Alexander II's grant of reforms. So great had the discontent become that it is doubtful whether any Russian government could have proceeded fast enough to suit the radicals, who had come to believe in violent overturn of the regime, and were not satisfied with piecemeal and gradual reform. Stemming from John Stuart Mill and from Western Utopian socialists like Fourier and Robert Owen, Russian socialism was not yet greatly influenced by Marx. In some ways it was almost Slavophile, not urban but rural, not evolutionary but revolutionary, not a mass political party but a conspiracy. Its members lived underground, and developed a conspiratorial psychology. They proposed to overthrow a bourgeois society in Russia before one ever got started. The movement became more and more radical, and in 1879 those who believed in the use of terror as a weapon separated from the others and founded the group called the People's Will; the antiterrorists called themselves the Black Partition.

The members of the People's Will now went on a hunt for Czar Alexander II himself. They shot at him and missed. They mined the track on which his train was traveling, and blew up the wrong train. They put dynamite under the dining room of the palace and exploded it. But the czar was late for dinner that night, and eleven servants were killed instead. They rented a cheese shop on one of the streets along which he drove and tunneled under it. Finally they killed him (March 1881) with a crude handmade grenade, which blew up the assassin too. The supreme irony was that Alexander II had that day signed a document designed to summon a consultative assembly, which everybody expected to lead to further constitutional reform. His successor, the reactionary Alexander III (1881–1894), refused to confirm the document, and Russia was left to stagnate in a renewed repression. The terrorists were rounded up and punished, and their organization was smashed. Despite their occasional high-flown claims to enormous popular support, they had never numbered more than a mere handful of people, and their movement had been a failure.

Foreign Policy under Alexander II

In foreign policy, Alexander II made an uneven record. In Europe, the Russians successfully repressed the Polish uprising of 1863. They seized the opportunity provided by the Franco-Prussian War of 1870, and simply tore up the Black Sea provisions of the Treaty of Paris, declaring unilaterally that they would no longer be bound by them. This was an illegal act, to which the powers later reluctantly gave their assent. It was another illustration of the immorality in international affairs that Bismarck had made fashionable.

In 1877, the Russians went to war against Turkey on behalf of the rebellious Balkan Christians of Bosnia, Herzegovina, and Bulgaria. By the peace of San Stefano, dictated early in 1878 to the defeated Turks, Russia obtained, contrary to her previous agreements, a large independent Bulgarian state, which Russian policymakers hoped to turn into a useful Balkan satellite. But the powers at the Congress of Berlin later in the same year reversed the judgment of San Stefano. They permitted only about a third of the planned Bulgaria to come into existence as an autonomous state, while another third obtained autonomy separately, and the rest went back to Turkey. Russian public opinion resented the powers' depriving Russia of the gains scored in the Russo-Turkish War. Bitterness ran particularly high among those who hoped to unite all Slavs in a kind of federation, the Pan-Slavs (not to be confused with the Slavophiles).

Meanwhile, in Asia, encroachments begun under Nicholas I against the Chinese territory in the Amur River valley were regularized by treaty in 1860. Russian settlements in the "maritime province" on the Pacific Ocean continued to flourish. In central Asia, a series of campaigns conquered the native Turkish khanates and added much productive land to the Crown. Here, however, the advance toward the northwest frontier of India seemed to threaten British interests and aroused public opinion in Britain against Russia.

The Reaction, 1881–1904

The reign of Alexander III and the first ten years of the reign of his son, Nicholas II, formed a quarter-century of consistent policies (1881–1904). Both czars loathed liberalism as expressed in the earlier reforms, and were determined that there would never be any more of it. Yet a peasant bank set up under Alexander III made the redemption payments easier for the peasants to pay. And a few pieces of labor legislation, enacted under the influence of Bismarck's example, made working conditions a bit more tolerable—for example, hours were shortened for women workers. Offsetting these measures were the establishment of a special bank that extended credit to the impoverished nobility, the reinstitution of rigorous censorship, and the institution in the countryside of so-called rural leaders or land captains in place of the elected justices of the peace of Alexander II. Election procedure for the zemstvos and for the city assemblies was made far less democratic. Now there began a vigorous persecution of the minority nationalities, a policy called Russification and quite in line with the "nationality" of Nicholas I's formula. The

The assassination of Alexander II, March 13, 1881.

Finns, Poles, Ukrainians, Armenians, and Jews all suffered discrimination, varying from loss of their own institutions, which the Finns had enjoyed, to outright government-sponsored massacres in the case of the Jews. On his accession in 1894, Nicholas II referred to all hopes for a change as "senseless dreams."

These years were notable also for the steady growth of the Russian railroad network, largely built and owned by the state. The Donets coal basin was exploited for the first time; the Baku oilfields came into production; steel and cotton output soared. In 1892, there came to the Ministry of Finance a self-made railroad man, Witte, who for the next twelve years was personally responsible for the ever-mounting economic progress. Witte began the trans-Siberian railroad, put Russia on the gold standard, attracted much foreign capital, especially French, for investment, and balanced the budget, in part through the government monopoly of the sale of vodka. The railroad network doubled in length between 1894 and 1904, and the need for rails stimulated the steel industry. Correspondingly, the number of urban workers multiplied, and strikes called in protest against wretched working conditions

mounted in number. In 1897, the working day was fixed by the state at eleven hours for adults, and other provisions were adopted to improve and regularize conditions. These laws, however, were difficult to enforce.

Under the circumstances, many of the young generation of revolutionaries now turned to Marxist "scientific" socialism, preaching the class struggle and predicting the inevitable downfall of capitalism. A small clandestine group of intelligentsia, formed in 1894–1895 at St. Petersburg, proposed to overthrow the regime, working with all opponents of the class system. The members of the group included Lenin, a vigorous young intellectual of upper-middle-class origin, whose brother had been executed for an attempt on the life of Alexander III. In 1898, this group and others formed the Social Democratic party, which in 1900 began to publish its own newspaper. Within party ranks, grave dissension sprang up over the question of organization. Should the party operate under a strongly centralized directorate, or should each local group of Social Democrats be free to agitate for its own ends? In the tradition of Bakunin and Tkachev, Lenin insisted on the tightly knit little group of directors at the center. At the party congress of Brussels and London in 1903, the majority voted with him. Lenin's faction thereafter was called by the name *Bolshevik,* meaning majority, as against the *Menshevik* (minority) group, which favored a loose democratic organization for the party. Both groups remained Social Democrats, or SD's, as they were often called.

Meanwhile, the non-Marxist revolutionaries, who were the direct heirs of the People's Will tradition, also organized a political party. They were the Social Revolutionaries, or SR's, with their own clandestine newspaper. Whereas the SD's as Marxists were interested almost exclusively in the urban workers, the SR's as populists were interested in the peasantry. Their chief aim was to redistribute the land, but they continued in their terrorist ways. They assassinated several cabinet ministers, using as their slogan the cry "We don't want reforms, we want reform."

A third political grouping was that of the moderates and liberals, not SD or SR in orientation, but mostly veterans of the zemstvos, and intellectuals indignant over the government's policies of repression, who favored nothing more radical than compulsory free private education and agrarian reform. The regime stupidly made no distinction between these men and the diehard terrorists or the rabid Marxists. Thus the moderates also gradually organized and had their own clandestine paper favoring a constitution and a national parliament for Russia. In 1905, they took the name "Constitutional Democrats" and were thereafter usually referred to as Kadets, from the Russian initials KD. Faced by this political activity among its radical and moderate opponents, the government only tightened the reins and by 1904 had adopted the view that a short victorious war was all that would be necessary to unite the country.

The Russo-Japanese War

Trans-Siberian railway construction made it desirable for the Russians to obtain a right of way across Chinese

Russian peasant women pulling a raft in prerevolutionary Russia (1910).

territory in Manchuria. They took the initiative in preventing Japan from establishing herself on the Chinese mainland after her defeat of China in 1895, and then required the Chinese in exchange to allow the building of the new railroad. In 1897, they seized Port Arthur, the very port they had earlier kept out of Japanese hands. Further friction with the Japanese took place in Korea, where both powers had interests. Then, after the Boxer Rebellion of 1900 in China, the Russians kept their troops in Manchuria after the other nations had withdrawn theirs. Although the Russians promised to withdraw their forces by stages, they failed to do so, largely because Russian foreign policy fell into the hands of shady adventurers, some of whom had a lumber concession in Korea and wanted war with Japan. After it became apparent that the war party had got control in Russia, the Japanese without warning attacked units of the Russian fleet anchored at Port Arthur in February 1904. The Russo-Japanese War had begun.

Far from their bases and taken by surprise, the Russians nonetheless stabilized a front on land. But their fleet, which had steamed all the way around Europe and across the Indian Ocean into the Pacific, was decisively defeated by the Japanese in the battle of Tsushima (May 27, 1904). To the Russian people, the war was a mysterious, distant political adventure of which they wanted no part. Many intellectuals opposed it, and the SR's and SD's openly hoped for a Russian defeat, which they expected would shake the government's position. Alarmed at the growing unrest at home, the Russian government was persuaded by President Theodore Roosevelt to accept his mediation, which the Japanese also actively wished.

Witte, the go-getting businessman who had opposed the war from the first, was sent to Portsmouth, New Hampshire, as Russian representative. Here he not only secured excellent terms for Russia but also won a favorable verdict from American public opinion, which had previously been strongly pro-Japanese and had thought of Russians as either brutal aristocrats or bomb-throwing revolutionaries. By the Treaty of Portsmouth (1905), Russia recognized the Japanese protectorate over Korea, ceded Port Arthur and the southern half of Sakhalin Island, together with fishing rights in the North Pacific, and promised to evacuate Manchuria. Russian prestige as a Far Eastern power was not deeply wounded or permanently impaired by the defeat or by the treaty. Yet the effect of the defeat in Asia was to transfer Russian attention back to Europe, where a world crisis had already begun.

The Revolution of 1905

The most important immediate result of the Russo-Japanese War was its impact on Russian domestic developments. While it was still going on, Plehve, the reactionary minister of the interior, was assassinated by an SR bomb in July 1904. His successor was a moder-

A demonstration in Moscow, October 1905.

ate. The zemstvo liberals, the future Kadets, were encouraged, and held banquets throughout Russia to adopt a series of resolutions for presentation to a kind of national congress of zemstvo representatives. Although the congress was not allowed to meet publicly, its program—a constitution, basic civil liberties, class and minority equality, and extension of zemstvo responsibilities—became widely known and approved. The czar temporized, issued so vague a statement that all hope for change was dimmed, and took measures to limit free discussion.

Ironically, it was a police agent of the government itself who struck the fatal spark. He had been planted in the St. Petersburg factories to combat SD efforts to organize the workers, and to substitute his own union. He organized a parade of workers to demonstrate peacefully and to petition the czar directly for an eight-hour day, a national assembly, civil liberties, the right to strike, and a number of other moderate demands. When the workers tried to deliver the petition, Nicholas left town and ordered the troops to fire on the peaceful demonstrators, some of whom were carrying his portrait to demonstrate their loyalty. About a thousand workers were killed on "Bloody Sunday" (January 22, 1905). The massacre made revolutionaries out of the urban workers. Strikes multiplied, the moderate opposition joined with the radical opposition, and university students and professors demanded the same reforms as wild-eyed bomb hurlers.

Amid mounting excitement, the government at first seemed to favor the calling of a zemski sobor, consultative, not legislative, in the old Russian pattern rather than the Western parliamentary one, but still a national assembly of sorts. But then even this project was whittled away, as the timid, vacillating, and unintelligent Nicholas II listened to his reactionary advisers. Under the impact of delays and disappointments, demonstrations and outbreaks occurred during the summer of 1905. In October, the printers struck. No newspapers appeared, and the printers, with SD aid, formed the first *soviet* or workers' council. When the railroad workers joined the strike, communications were cut off between Moscow and St. Petersburg. Soviets now multiplied. Of the one formed in St. Petersburg, Lenin declared that it was "not a workers' parliament, nor an organization of proletarian autonomy, but a combat organization pursuing definite ends."

This reflects the Bolsheviks' view of the soviet as an instrument for the pursuit of their program of armed revolt, for the establishment of a provisional government, for the proclamation of a democratic republic, and for the summoning of a constituent assembly. This program, put forth by the most "extreme" of the revolutionaries of 1905, differed relatively little from the program of the most moderate liberals, who would, however, have kept the monarchy and striven to obtain their ends by persuasion and pressure rather than by violence. At the time, and for years to come, the

Bolsheviks, like other Marxists, accepted the view that it was necessary for Russia to pass through a stage of bourgeois democracy before the time for the proletarian revolution could come. They were therefore eager to help along the bourgeois revolution.

Nicholas was faced, as Witte told him, with the alternatives of imposing a military dictatorship and putting down the opposition by force, or of summoning a truly legislative assembly with veto power over the laws. The czar finally chose the latter course, and in October 1905 issued a manifesto that promised full civil liberties at once, and a legislative assembly or duma to be elected by universal suffrage. In effect, this famous October Manifesto put an end to the autocracy, since the duma was to be superior to the czar in legislation.

Yet the issuance of the October Manifesto did not meet with universal approval or even end the revolution at once. On the right, a government-sponsored party called the Union of the Russian People demonstrated against the manifesto, proclaimed its undying loyalty to the autocrat, and organized its own storm troops, or Black Hundreds, which killed more than 3,000 Jews in the first week after the issuance of the manifesto. The armies returned from the Far East, and proved to be still loyal to the government. Thus the soviets of 1905, unlike those of 1917, included only workers, and no soldiers. On the Left, the dissatisfied Bolsheviks and SR's made several attempts to launch their violent revolution, but failed, and the government was able to arrest their leaders and eventually to put them down after several days of street fighting in Moscow in December 1905. In the Center, one group of liberals, pleased with the manifesto, urged that it be used as a rallying point for a moderate program. These were the Octobrists, so called after the month in which the manifesto had been issued. The other group, the Kadets, wished to continue to agitate by legal means for further immediate reforms. But the real fires of revolution had burned out by the opening of the year 1906.

The Dumas, 1906–1914

Suffrage for the Duma was universal, but voters chose an electoral college which then selected the 412 deputies. Although SR's and SD's boycotted the elections out of discontent over the indirect election system, many of their number were elected. The Kadets were the strongest single party. Quite against the expectation of the government, the peasants' vote was not conservative, but highly liberal. But even before the first Duma had met, Witte was able to reduce its powers. He secured a large French loan, which made the government financially independent of the Duma, and issued a set of "fundamental laws," which the Duma was not to be competent to alter. The Crown was to continue to control war and foreign policy; the minister of finance was to control loans and currency. The czar's council of state was transformed by adding members

from the clergy, nobility, the zemstvos, the universities, and chambers of commerce. It became a kind of upper house, which had equal legislative rights with the Duma, and could therefore submit a rival budget, for example, which the government could then adopt in preference to that of the Duma. Finally, the czar could dissolve the Duma at will, provided he set a date for new elections. When it was not in session he could legislate by himself, although his enactments had later to be approved by the Duma.

The first Duma, the "Duma of Popular Indignation," met between May and July 1906. It addressed a list of grievances to the czar, asking for a radical land reform that would give the peasants all state and church land, and part of the land still in private hands. The government flatly refused to accept this attack on property, and after some parliamentary skirmishing the Duma was dissolved. The Kadet membership, maintaining incorrectly that the dissolution was unconstitutional, crossed the frontier into Finland, and there issued a manifesto urging the Russian people not to pay taxes or report for military service unless the Duma was recalled. Its authors were soon tried and declared ineligible for office; so future Dumas were deprived of the services of this capable Kadet group of moderates.

With the dissolution of the first Duma there came to power as chief minister the highly intelligent and conservative Peter Stolypin, who stayed in office until 1911, when he was assassinated. Together with Witte, he was the leading statesman of the last period of czarist Russia. Stolypin put through a series of agricultural laws which enabled the peasants to free themselves from the commune. A peasant wishing to detach his property could demand that he be given a single tract, which meant that the scattered strips assigned to other families would also be consolidated so that each would obtain a single plot. This program Stolypin called the "wager on the strong and sober"; he was encouraging the initiative and enterprise of individual Russian peasants who had the will to operate on their own as successful small farmers. His program accomplished much of what he hoped for. It is estimated that about a quarter of the peasant households of European Russia (almost 9,000,000) emancipated themselves from the communes during the years between 1906 and 1917. Only war and revolution kept the process from going still further. Lenin and others who hoped for revolution were deeply suspicious and afraid of Stolypin's agrarian reforms. They rightly feared that the peasant grievances would be removed, and understood that no revolution in Russia could succeed without the peasants.

Simultaneously with his agrarian program, Stolypin carried on unremitting war against terrorists and other revolutionaries. He showed no hesitation in acting in the most unconstitutional fashion when it suited him. He did everything he could to interfere with the elections to the second Duma, but the SR's and SD's were well represented, and the Duma itself (March–June 1907) would not work with the government. It was dissolved because it refused to suspend the parliamentary immunity of the SD deputies, whom Stolypin wanted to arrest.

After the dissolution of the second Duma, the government quite illegally altered the election laws, cutting the number of delegates from the peasants and national minorities, and increasing the number from the gentry. By this means the government got a majority, and the third Duma (1907–1912) and the fourth (1912–1917) lived out their constitutional lives of five years apiece. Unrepresentative and limited in their powers though they were, they were still national assemblies. In their sessions the left-wingers could be heard, and could question ministers like any other members. The Dumas improved the conditions of peasant and worker and helped strengthen national defense as the World War drew closer. Their commissions, working with individual ministers, proved extremely useful in increasing the efficiency of government departments. The period of the third Duma, however, was also notable for the continuation of Russification, and the Finns in particular lost their remaining rights (1910).

Under the fourth Duma, the government, with Stolypin dead, tended more toward reaction. The leftists organized busily for another revolution, working in unions, cooperatives, evening classes for workmen, and a whole network of other labor organizations. A vast web of police spies challenged them at every turn. Meanwhile, the imperial family drifted into a very dangerous situation, as the fanatically religious and autocratically minded empress fell more and more under the sway of a half-mad, wholly evil, dirty, ignorant, and power-hungry monk from Siberia. This man, Rasputin—actually a nickname meaning "the dissolute one"—had the mysterious ability, possibly hypnotic, to stop the bleeding of the young heir to the throne, who suffered from hemophilia. Since the empress had enormous influence on her beloved husband, Nicholas II, Rasputin became in a real sense the ruler of Russia, much to the horror of a great many loyal supporters of the imperial house, and greatly to the detriment of the rational conduct of affairs in an enormous twentieth-century state. At the moment when the World War began, Russia was in the throes of a major crisis precipitated by the government's reactionary policies, the scandal of Rasputin's influence, and the indignation of the loyal Duma. There was a threat of revolution, then, even before 1917.

V Conclusion

Parliamentary government was, as we have seen, a comparative stranger to the three eastern European empires. The king of Prussia, with Bismarck's help, used his extraordinary military system to conquer and unify Germany. He imposed on all non-Austrian Germans the Prussian system of autocracy almost undiluted by a weak and subservient parliament, and backed by the army and the Junkers. The Hapsburg emperor, though faced after 1907 with an Austrian parliament elected by universal suffrage, in 1914 still made virtually all policy decisions by himself. The Hungarian parliament was never genuinely representative, and the emperor, as king of Hungary, successfully used universal suffrage as a threat to quell Magyar separatism. The czars, forced at last by defeat in wars to grant a modified constitution in 1905, were still able to hamstring their own central legislative body, and to wield a preponderant personal influence in politics.

In all three countries, nonetheless, for the first time in their history, modern political parties during this period coalesced around principles. As in the West, the governments collaborated with parties or coalitions of parties, but always faced an opposition. What a party stood for was determined largely by the peculiar circumstances of the country that gave it birth. Yet certain parallels reached across national boundaries. Although no group in Russia can be compared with the German Catholic Center, the Austrian Christian Socialists do resemble it in many ways. No group in either Germany or Austria is comparable with the Russian populists (Social Revolutionaries). Yet German Liberals, Austrian Liberals, and Russian Kadets or Octobrists can perhaps be roughly equated. So can the Pan-Germans with the Pan-Slavs. The Social Democrats were Marxist in all three countries, but increasingly less revolutionary in Germany and Austria-Hungary, and increasingly more so in Russia.

All three countries during this period experienced an economic boom and an occasional depression; the Industrial Revolution struck them late, but with terrific impact. By the turn of the twentieth century, Germany had made such advances that its steel production surpassed that of England, and was second in the world only to that of the United States. Though far behind Germany both in resources and in technology, Austria-Hungary too was becoming rapidly industrialized. In Russia, transport and industry boomed.

Yet in all three countries, the landed nobility continued to exercise political influence quite out of proportion to their numbers. Everywhere the existence of a new and underprivileged class of urban workers stimulated intellectual leaders to form Marxist political groups, to preach the class struggle, and, except in Russia, to strive for immediate improvements in conditions rather than for the violent overthrow of the regime. Last of all the European countries, Russia emancipated her serfs in 1861 and began a new era of agrarian experiment and unrest. In Germany, protection became the great agrarian issue after the late 1870s. In Austria-Hungary, the peasants suffered with docility.

All three countries had minority problems of varying seriousness. Germany persecuted the Poles and, after 1871 and less severely, she persecuted the Alsatians and Lorrainers. More and more, Russia persecuted the Finns, Poles, Ukrainians, and Armenians. In Austria-

Hungary alone, however, the minority problem proved fatal. German anti-Slav sentiment in Austria, and Magyar mistreatment of all non-Magyars in Hungary, alienated potentially loyal subjects, and finally helped explode the state from inside. In all three countries, the Jews created a special problem and suffered different degrees of discrimination and persecution.

In Germany, a combination of circumstances led first to an assault by the government on the Catholic church, and then to an alliance between the government and the Catholic political party. In the Hapsburg monarchy, a milder anticlericalism had its day, but the Church retained its hold on the population, and continued to exercise enormous political influence. In Rus-

sia, the Orthodox church played almost no role in the cultural development of the people. But one group of influential intellectuals attacked it as the source of Russia's troubles, while another group hailed it as the true source of Russia's strength and the fountainhead of national virtue.

So it was that the main currents of the time flowed with uneven force over the Germans, Austrians, and Russians. Nationalism, materialism, militarism, imperialism, clericalism, constitutionalism, landlordism, and socialism were all experienced to a varying degree by all the countries. What determined each country's answer to social pressure, however, was its own peculiar past and its own peculiar character.

Reading Suggestions on Central and Eastern Europe

General Accounts

William L. Langer, *Political and Social Upheaval, 1832–1852* (Harper, 1969). Sensitive and brilliant synthetic treatment of a most difficult period.

R. C. Binkley, *Realism and Nationalism, 1852–1871* (Harper, 1935). Though this volume develops a somewhat implausible thesis about the possibilities of "federative polity," it provides an often illuminating discussion of the period.

C. J. H. Hayes, *A Generation of Materialism, 1871–1900* (Harper, 1941). Penetrating probing beneath the surface of an apparently successful era.

A. J. P. Taylor, *The Struggle for Mastery in Europe, 1848–1919* (Clarendon, 1954). A volume in "The Oxford History of Modern Europe"; crisp and provocative.

Special Studies: Germany

R. Flenley, *Modern German History* (Dutton, 1953), and K. S. Pinson, *Modern Germany: Its History and Civilization* (Macmillan, 1954). Two textbooks, of which Pinson's is the longer and Flenley's perhaps the more useful.

A. J. P. Taylor, *The Course of German History* (Coward-McCann, 1946). A lively essay on the period since 1815, with strong anti-German overtones.

F. Meinecke, *The German Catastrophe* (Harvard Univ. Press, 1950). A useful antidote to Taylor, by a very great German historian.

T. Veblen, *Imperial Germany and the Industrial Revolution,* new ed. (Viking, 1954). An old, brilliant, and still very important analysis by a great American sociologist.

F. Darmstaedter, *Bismarck and the Creation of the Second Reich* (Methuen, 1948). A valuable study.

O. Pflanze, *Bismarck and the Development of Germany* (Princeton, 1963). Coming down only to 1871, this useful study sets the man in his time and digests the vast controversial literature about him.

E. Eyck, *Bismarck and the German Empire* (Allen and Unwin, 1950). Translation and condensation of a large standard work in German.

A. J. P. Taylor, *Bismarck: The Man and the Statesman* (Knopf, 1955). A provocative and often hostile reevaluation.

H. von Treitschke, *History of Germany in the 19th Century,* 7 vols. (Humanities Press, 1915–1919), and *Origins of Prussianism,* ed E. and C. Paul (Humanities Press, 1942). Emphasizing the period before 1870; strongly Prussian in tone.

Special Studies: The Hapsburg Monarchy

A. J. May, *The Hapsburg Monarchy, 1867–1914* (Harvard Univ. Press, 1951). Concise general account.

A. J. P. Taylor, *The Habsburg Monarchy, 1809–1918,* 2nd ed. (Hamish Hamilton, 1948). A spirited brief treatment.

R. A. Kann, *The Multinational Empire,* 2 vols. (Columbia Univ. Press, 1950). A monograph, arranged nationality by nationality, and discussing national sentiments and the government's efforts to deal with them.

O. Jászi, *The Dissolution of the Habsburg Monarchy* (Univ. of Chicago Press, 1929). From a rare point of view, that of the liberal Magyar.

R. W. Seton-Watson, *German, Slav, and Magyar* (Williams and Norgate, 1916). By the greatest British authority on southeast Europe.

E. Wiskemann, *Czechs and Germans* (Oxford Univ. Press, 1938). A good case history of national antagonisms.

Special Studies: Russia

H. Seton-Watson, *The Decline of Imperial Russia, 1855–1914* (Praeger, 1952). The only sound work in English covering virtually all the period dealt with in this chapter.

G. T. Robinson, *Rural Russia under the Old Regime,* 2nd ed. (*California). A splendid monograph on the peasant question.

A. Herzen, *My Past and Thoughts,* 6 vols. (Chatto and Windus, 1924–1927). The classic picture of nineteenth-century Russia, by its most distinguished rebel.

Martin Malia, *Alexander Herzen and the Birth of Russian Socialism* (*Grosset and Dunlap, Universal Library, 1965). Excellent monograph on Herzen's life and thought, considered in the framework of contemporary European ideas.

N. V. Riasanovsky, *Russia and the West in the Teaching of the*

Slavophiles (Harvard Univ. Press, 1953) and *Nicholas I and Official Nationality in Russia, 1825–1855* (*California). Useful studies.

Sidney Monas, *The Third Section: Police and Society in Russia under Nicholas I* (Harvard Univ. Press, 1961). Pioneering study of the repressive machinery.

D. Footman, *Red Prelude* (Yale Univ. Press, 1945). A good biography of Zhelyabov, populist and terrorist.

Peter Kropotkin, *Memoirs of a Revolutionist,* ed. James A. Rogers (*Anchor, 1962). A delightful anarchist's story of his own life and times.

James Joll, *The Anarchists* (*Grosset and Dunlap, Universal Library, 1964). Excellent chapters on Bakunin and Kropotkin, and a fine study of the movement.

B. Pares, *The Fall of the Russian Monarchy* (Jonathan Cape, 1939). An excellent study of the period 1905–1917; by an authority who was frequently on the spot.

S. Witte, *Memoirs* (Doubleday, 1921). The somewhat apologetic memoirs of the man who did most to industrialize imperial Russia.

B. D. Wolfe, *Three Who Made a Revolution* (Dial Press, 1948; *Beacon). A fine triple study of Lenin, Trotsky, and Stalin; with emphasis on the period before 1914.

A. Lobanov-Rostovsky, *Russia and Asia*, rev. ed. (G. Wahr, 1951). A useful introductory survey.

B. H. Sumner, *Russia and the Balkans, 1870–1880* (Clarendon, 1937). A monograph including a helpful discussion of Panslavism.

Historical Fiction

T. Mann, *Buddenbrooks* (*Pocket Books). Novel of a family in imperial Germany.

G. Hauptmann, *The Weavers, Hannele, The Beaver Coat* (*Rinehart, 1951). Three plays that convey some of the flavor of nineteenth-century Germany.

R. Musil, *The Man without Qualities* (Coward-McCann, 1953). A novel steeped in the atmosphere of pre-1914 Vienna.

M. Jókai, *Eyes like the Sea* (Putnam, 1901). Fictionalized autobiography of a romantic Hungarian novelist whose works give insights into Magyar nationalism.

N. Gogol, *The Inspector General* (many editions) and *Dead Souls,* trans. George Reavey (Oxford Univ. Press, 1957). Brilliant satirical play and novel.

I. Turgenev, *Fathers and Sons* (sometimes called *Fathers and Children*—many editions), and *Smoke* (Dutton, 1949; *Everyman). Superb contemporary realistic fiction reflecting Russian intellectual and political life.

F. Dostoevsky, *The Brothers Karamazov* and *Crime and Punishment* (*Modern Library). Famous novels depicting the turbulent life of Russian intellectuals in the mid-nineteenth century; more romantic in tone than Turgenev's works.

The Portable Chekhov (*Viking, 1947). A selection from the short stories and plays of A. Chekhov, a skillful portraitist of the upper classes in czarist Russia.

L. Tolstoy, *Anna Karenina* (*Modern Library). A celebrated novel set in late nineteenth-century St. Petersburg and the countryside.

23

The Intellectual Revolution of the Nineteenth Century

Introduction: An Age of Science

The nineteenth century could well be called an age of science. In the early years of the century, in the face of the romantic revival of religion and philosophy, science lost some of the prestige and popularity it had enjoyed in the days of Newton and of the Enlightenment. But after 1840 it recovered rapidly, greatly helped by repeated demonstrations of its practical utility. The London exhibition of 1851, the Paris expositions of 1855 and 1867, and all their international successors in the last third of the century dramatized the great accomplishments of engineering. The telegraph, the submarine cable, the telephone, the great railroad bridges and tunnels, and the high-speed printing press all radically improved communications and stepped up the pace of life. University courses in science multiplied, partly eclipsing those in philosophy that had dominated the curriculum in the early 1800s.

Most important of all, new scientific discoveries were made and fresh scientific theories advanced that not only had valuable practical applications but also deeply affected men's attitudes toward religion, politics, the arts, and other realms seemingly remote from science. The sum total of these changes constituted a new intellectual revolution that in part confirmed, and in part challenged and modified, the earlier intellectual revolution which had reached its culmination in the Enlightenment. In the seventeenth and eighteenth centuries mathematics and astronomy had been in the vanguard of progress. While they continued to advance in the nineteenth century, leadership passed to physics, chemistry, and, above all, biology, where Darwin's hypothesis about the evolution of species through natural selection sent a shock wave through the intellectual and ecclesiastical worlds.

Before examining Darwinism in more detail, we may note other hypotheses emanating from physics that had revolutionary implications for man's under-

standing of the universe. These were the laws of thermodynamics and the contrasting theories of a universe of continuity, based on waves, and a universe of atomicity, subdivided into an infinitesimal quantity of particles. The study of thermodynamics was fostered by the steam engine, which used heat to create power and led physicists to the idea of the conservation of energy. According to this first law of thermodynamics, energy was in a sense immortal, transforming itself from heat into power and then back again into heat. Scientists from France, Britain, Germany, and Denmark all contributed to the formulation of the law in the mid-nineteenth century—one of many instances of fruitful international scientific collaboration. But it was also characteristic of nineteenth-century scientific caution that learned societies and their journals were slow to accept the new law and sponsor its publication.

Another law of thermodynamics, also the work of experts from many nations, soon modified the first. This was the law of the dissipation or degradation of energy: it stated that, though the total amount of energy in the universe remains constant, the amount of energy useful to human beings is being steadily dissipated. Although scientists could contemplate with equanimity the possibility that the sun would gradually lose its heat and the earth would get colder and colder, many laymen could not. The pessimistic American intellectual Henry Adams (1838–1918), for instance, was obsessed with the likelihood that the universe was in the process of running down toward a kind of scientific final cataclysm or Day of Judgment.

Meantime, a very different view of the universe was emerging from studies of electricity and magnetism made by the Dane Oersted, the Frenchman Ampère, the German Ohm, and the Britishers Faraday and Clerk-Maxwell. They noted so many similarities between the two sets of phenomena that they fused them into the single category of electromagnetism, which appeared to function in the manner of continuous waves. The idea of waves was also being applied to light. Since light waves must move through some medium, and not just empty space, it was supposed that space was filled with a conductor, a substance called the ether. Although the ether hypothesis created many difficulties, the wave theory of light convinced many physicists that they should abandon the Newtonian concept of light as made up of minute particles. To them mankind lived in a world of waves and therefore of continuity.

Yet to other physicists and also to chemists, biologists, and physicians, mankind continued to live in a world of particles, a world therefore of atomicity. Atoms of one chemical element combined with those of another to form molecules of some familiar substance, as in the case of hydrogen, oxygen, and water. But the process of combination raised some important questions. For example, the volume of hydrogen in water was twice that of oxygen, as indicated by the familiar formula H_2O; but experiments showed that the weight of the oxygen was eight times that of the hydrogen. It seemed evident, therefore, that an atom of oxygen must weigh sixteen times more than an atom of hydrogen. To establish a standard table of atomic weights, an international congress of experts met in 1860 at Karlsruhe in Germany and devised a table based on the calculations of two Italians, Avogadro and Cannizzaro.

The biological counterpart of the atomic theory was the cell theory, the idea that all plant and animal structures were composed of living units known as cells. The medical counterpart was the theory of germs (today further refined into bacilli, viruses, and the like), a great advance over the older belief that disease was in effect a phenomenon of spontaneous corruption, as evidenced by the term "consumption" for tuberculosis. The German microbiologist Koch discovered the organisms causing tuberculosis and cholera; the American doctor Walter Reed found that the virus responsible for yellow fever was transmitted by a mosquito, with the result that careful mosquito control greatly reduced the incidence of disease among the force building the Panama Canal. In Britain, the Quaker physician Lister, who demonstrated that germs were responsible for the infection of wounds, greatly reduced the mortality rate of surgical and battlefield patients by the application of rigorous antiseptic measures. In France, the chemist Pasteur became a scientific hero by developing a vaccine for inoculating victims of rabies, until then invariably fatal, and by devising the process of sterilizing milk that we call by his name. These great advances and dozens of others almost equally great brought Western medicine, surgery, and public health to the "take-off" point for impressive growth by 1900. In the twentieth century the average life expectancy in North America and many European countries was to increase by twenty to thirty years.

Louis Pasteur in his laboratory.

II Darwinism
"The Origin of Species"

In 1859 there was published in London a volume on natural history that began with the true scientist's caution:

When on board H.M.S. "Beagle," as naturalist, I was much struck with certain facts in the distribution of the organic beings inhabiting South America, and in the geological relations of the present to the past inhabitants of that continent. These facts . . . seemed to throw some light on the origin of species—that mystery of mysteries, as it has been called by one of our greatest philosophers. On my return home, it occurred to me, in 1837, that something might perhaps be made out on this question by patiently accumulating and reflecting on all sorts of facts which could possibly have any bearing on it. After five years' work I allowed myself to speculate on the subject, and drew up some short notes; these I enlarged in 1844 into a sketch of the conclusions, which then seemed to me probable: from that period to the present day I have steadily pursued the same object. I hope that I may be excused for entering on these personal details, as I give them to show that I have not been hasty in coming to a decision.*

Darwin's *On the Origin of Species by Means of Natural*

*Charles Darwin, *The Origin of Species*, Modern Library ed. (New York, n.d.), p. 11.

Comment by political cartoonist Thomas Nast on the controversy over Darwin's theories (1871).

Selection, thus modestly introduced to the public, is one of the seminal books in intellectual history. Like all important revolutions, the Darwinian was no bolt from the blue. Into Darwin's work had gone long years of preparation, not merely his own extended field work in the 1830s as the *Beagle* made a leisurely voyage around South America, but those of his predecessors and colleagues in the study of what was then called natural history. Before him was the long record of the hundreds of thousands of years of organic life on earth. Already well established by geologists and paleontologists, this record told of the rise, the development, and sometimes the disappearance of thousands of different forms of plant and animal organisms, or species. The record contradicted the biblical Book of Genesis, which described all forms of life as begun in the space of a single week by a Creator about 6,000 years ago. And it stated explicitly that all existing men and animals were descended from single pairs of each species preserved in Noah's ark during a great universal flood that took place some time thereafter.

Now Darwin was by no means the first to find a discrepancy between the historical and scientific record and the accepted biblical explanation. The men of the Enlightenment had already given up the biblical explanation as inadequate, and some of them had conjectured that there must have been a very long evolutionary process in which no personal, Christian God had a hand, but only the impersonal forces of Nature or the deist's "watchmaker God." But they had arrived at no satisfactory explanation of how Nature or the watchmaker God had done the job; they had no satisfactory theory of how organisms had evolved. This Darwin gave the world.

Darwin found one clue in Malthus' *Essay on Population,* which maintained that organisms—including man—tended to multiply to a point where there was not sufficient food for them all. In the intense competition for food, some of these organisms did not get enough, and died. This was the germ of the conception Darwin phrased as the *struggle for existence.* He next asked himself what determined that certain individuals would survive and that others would die. Obviously the surviving ones got more food, better shelter, better living conditions of all sorts. If they were all identical organisms, the only explanation—apart from the intervention of a supernatural being or force—would have to be accidental variations in their environment. But it was clear from observation that individual organisms of a given species are not identical. Variations appear even at birth. Thus in a single litter of pigs there may be sturdy, aggressive piglets and a runt, who is likely to get shoved aside in suckling by his sturdier siblings, and starve. In the struggle for existence, the runt is proved "unfit."

Here is the second of Darwin's key phrases, the *survival of the fittest.* The organism best endowed in its variations to get food and shelter lives to procreate young that will tend to inherit these favorable variations. The variations are slight indeed, but over generation after generation they are cumulative; finally an organism so different from the long-distant ancestor is produced that we can speak of a new species. This new species has *evolved.* It has evolved by the working of *natural selection.* Man as a plant and animal breeder has long made use of this process and has hastened and indeed directed it for his own purposes by artificial selection, by breeding only the most desirable strains. But man has been doing this with domesticated plants and animals for but a tiny period of geological time, and with but few species. Over the eons, natural selection has been the working force; and for man himself, according to the Darwinian system, natural selection alone has been at work, since man has yet to breed his own kind as he breeds his domestic plants and animals.

Darwin held that the variations in individuals of the same species at birth are accidental, and that they are generally transmitted through inheritance. Those biologists who developed his doctrine, notably the German Weismann, did not believe that the evidence showed that variations produced in an individual organism in the course of its life could be transmitted to its offspring. Thus, orthodox Darwinism denies the inheritance of acquired characteristics. Obviously, a man with an amputated leg will not produce one-legged children. Experimenters have docked the tails of generations of laboratory rats, but their offspring are still born with long tails. The actual mechanism of heredity we know much better than Darwin did, thanks to the Austrian monk Gregor Mendel (1822–1884), whose experiments with crossbreeding garden peas laid the basis of modern genetics, and its study of genes and chromosomes.

Darwin's theory has undergone later modification as scientists have found that variations of importance in the evolutionary process are probably not so much the numerous tiny ones Darwin emphasized, but rather bigger and much rarer ones now known as mutations. Scientists have begun to study the effect of various forms of radiation on such mutations. A still much-disputed geological theory holds that catastrophic movements of the earth's crust in the past have so radically altered environment as to wipe out whole species and speed up the evolution of others. Emphasis on mutations or on extensive crustal movements tends also to be emphasis on the sudden and violent rather than on the gradual—an attitude more in tune with our own century than with the nineteenth.

"The Warfare of Science with Theology"

The first edition of *The Origin of Species* was sold out the day of its publication. The book that Darwin himself considered of interest only to students of natural history became a bestseller, reviewed in newspapers and magazines all over the world. The major reason for this attention was almost certainly the challenge that orthodox Christians found in the book. Darwinism was a phase of what President Andrew D. White of Cornell University called "the warfare of science with theology." Yet Darwin's book was no new denial of the fundamentalists' belief in the accuracy of the account of Creation in the Book of Genesis. Natural scientists had for over a century been publishing work that flatly denied the possibility that the earth could be only 6,000 years old. The doctrine of God's special creation of each species had also been challenged before Darwin.

Darwin got attention because he seemed to provide for the secularist a process (evolution) and a causal agent (natural selection) where before there had been only vague "materialistic" notions. He also seemed to have struck a final blow against the argument, still very popular in Victorian times, that the organic world was full of incontrovertible evidence of God the great designer. The human eye, for instance, the theologians said, was inconceivable except as the design of a God; and now Darwin said it is the result of millions of years of natural selection working on certain nerve ends "accidentally" more sensitive to light than others. Finally, Darwin gained notoriety because of the frequent, though unfair, accusation that he made the monkey man's brother. Later, in *The Descent of Man* (1871), Darwin carefully pointed out that *Homo sapiens* is descended not from any existing ape or monkey, but from a very remote common primate ancestor.

The Origin of Species stirred up a most heated theological controversy. Fundamentalists, both Protestant and Catholic, simply stuck by Genesis and damned Darwin and all his work. But the Catholic Church and many Protestant bodies eventually took at least a neutral attitude toward Darwinism, which they viewed as a scientific biological hypothesis neither necessarily correct nor necessarily incorrect. The great majority of Christians tacitly or openly accepted sufficient modification of Genesis to accommodate themselves to the scientist's time scale, and adjusted the classic theological arguments from first cause, design, and the like to a God who worked his will in accordance with organic evolution. Moreover, it was quite clear to reflective men that nothing Darwin or any other scientist or scholar could produce would give ultimate answers to the kind of problem set by the existence of God. It was quite clear to them that since God's eye is now on the sparrow, it must once have been on the dinosaur. Christians can be Darwinians: millions of them are. But Darwinism, if taken over completely into a philosophy of life, denies any supernatural intervention in the planning and running of the universe.

Social Darwinism

This theological conflict had pretty well run its course by the beginning of the twentieth century. More important in the long run was the use men made of some of Darwin's basic concepts—or at least of his more smoothly coined phrases—in debates on matters moral, economic, and political. The blanket term Social Darwinism covers all these transfers of ideas from biology to the social sciences and human relations. Although Darwin himself was a biologist, not a social scientist, in a free and literate society ideas produced by scientists invariably spread to many people not trained in science and underwent substantial modification in the process.

The central idea that social and political thinkers took over from Darwin was that of competition among individuals and groups. This was of course a conception already implicit in their thinking, and Darwin buttressed it with the prestige of the natural sciences. The majority of these late nineteenth-century thinkers interpreted the human struggle for existence as a struggle for the means of livelihood. The variations that counted here were those bringing success in economic, political, and cultural competition—the variations that produced inventors, business moguls, statesmen, leaders in the professions and, perhaps, even the arts. Darwin's work in natural history confirmed the classical economists' doctrine of laissez faire and the liberals' doctrine of individual freedom for a man to do what his capacities permitted.

Here was scientific validation of the middle-class conviction that the universe was designed to reward hard work, thrift, intelligence, and self-help and to punish laziness, waste, stupidity, and reliance on charity. Above all, Darwin seemed to vindicate the notion that the poor were poor because they were unfit, badly designed for living, and the complementary notion that efforts by private charity or by state action to take from

the well-to-do and give to the poor were useless attempts to reverse the course of evolution. If a man
cannot earn enough to feed himself, it was argued, he
had better die; lowlier organisms too incompetent to
feed themselves certainly die off, to the greater good
of the species. Herbert Spencer (1820–1903), an ardent
British evolutionist, summed it up neatly:

> Of man, as of all inferior creatures, the law by conformity
> to which the species is preserved, is that among adults the
> individuals best adapted to the conditions of their existence
> shall prosper most, and the individuals least adapted to the
> conditions of their existence shall prosper least. . . . Per-
> vading all Nature we may see at work a stern discipline
> which is often a little cruel that it may be very kind. . . .
> The ultimate result of shielding men from folly is to fill the
> world with fools.*

Spencer himself, if it came to that, could not have
stood by while the unemployed and their families
starved to death, for he was a kindly man. Yet he had
an almost maniacal hatred of the state, of local government as well as national; he held out even against laws
requiring houseowners to connect their houses with
sewers in cities. Even Spencer could not transfer to the
struggle for existence among human beings the ruthless
freedom of the jungle, of what Tennyson called "Nature
red in tooth and claw." He was against all forms of
government provision for what we now call social security. But what government may not do he believed the
ethically sound individual will do as charity. The well-
to-do will take care of the poor voluntarily—not
enough to spoil them, not enough to frustrate the designs of evolution by letting them prosper and prop-
agate their kind, but enough to prevent their starving
or freezing to death.

Spencer later decided that the softer emotions promoted by Christianity and the other higher religions—
kindness, dislike of cruelty, love—were also in accord
with the intentions of the laws of the universe as
summed up in evolution. Mutual extermination might
be the law for tigers, but not for human beings. Indeed,
Spencer and many other Social Darwinists held that
the altruistic moral sentiments that impel us toward
charity are the highest achievement of the evolutionary
process, and that a society with many altruists is
thereby shown to be the fittest for survival.

The Social Darwinists were, then, faced with this
primary difficulty. Darwin seemed to have shown that
the unmitigated struggle for life within a given species,
and among rival species, was the law of the universe;
but human history, and human feelings, showed that
men could not look on with indifference while their
fellows starved to death. One way out of the dilemma
was that recommended by Spencer, a sort of humanized
and mitigated struggle in which the incompetent were
shelved but not destroyed. Many who held this view

*H. Spencer, *Principles of Ethics* (London, 1879–1893), sec. 257; *Social Statics*
(London, 1851), p. 149; *Autobiography* (London, 1904), 2:5.

accompanied it with a faith in what came to be called
eugenics.

Eugenicists sought to encourage child-bearing by
the fit and to discourage it by the unfit. Darwin had
begun his *Origin of Species* with a consideration of the
extraordinary success men had had with artificial selection in the breeding of plants and animals. Why not
do the same thing with human beings? Since, according
to strict Darwinian theory, acquired characteristics were
not transmitted by heredity, no amount of manipulation of the social environment, no amount of wise
planning of institutions, would alter human beings.
Therefore, the only way to secure permanent improvement of the race was by deliberate mating of the fit
with the fit.

The eugenicists, however, ran at once against the
fact that man, though he domesticates plants and animals, is still himself in this respect a "wild" animal.
The individual human being in choosing a mate is no
doubt influenced by a great variety of motives, but no
master human breeder decides who shall mate with
whom. So far, the eugenicists have had little success
with the positive side of their program. On the negative
side, they have urged that the obviously unfit, the
feeble-minded, the insane, the pathologically criminal,
be prevented, if necessary by compulsory sterilization,
from having children. Only a tiny handful of human
beings, not enough to affect in the slightest the general
course of human physical evolution, have undergone
such treatment. A greater effect may possibly result
from recent advances in testing human fetuses in the
early stages of pregnancy and the aborting of those
destined to have serious birth defects because the parents are carriers of congenital diseases.

Racism

By far the commonest way out of the dilemma facing
the Social Darwinists lay in the obvious notion that
it is not so much among individual human beings that
the struggle for existence really goes on, as it is among
human beings organized in groups, as tribes, "races,"
or national states. What counts is not the struggle, say,
among individual Englishmen to survive, but that between Great Britain and her rivals. The struggle for
existence is now lifted from the biology of the individual to the politics of the group. And for the nineteenth
century the group meant the nation-state, perhaps kin-
dred nation-states that could be formed into a single
bloc, such as the Nordic, Latin, Slavic, or at the very
widest, the Caucasian or white peoples in competition
with the colored peoples, yellow, brown, or black. This
struggle had an ultimate form: war. The group that
defeated another group in war had thereby shown itself
to be fitter than the beaten group. It had a right—
indeed, in evolutionary terms, which usually have
moral overtones, a duty—to eliminate the beaten
group, seize its lands, and people them with its own
fitter human beings. The English imperialist Cecil

Rhodes held that a world wholly and exclusively peopled with Anglo-Saxons would be the best possible world.

The idea of a Chosen People was not new in Darwin's time. But there is no doubt that Darwin's work, however little he may have meant it to be, became a most important element in the competition among organized states in the latter half of the nineteenth century, and right on to our own day. Although Darwinism came too late to do more than prop up the philosophy of laissez faire in economics, it came at just the right time to intensify the international political struggle.

The particular groups or states that were to benefit as the elect of evolution in this special political sense varied with the aims, sympathies, and actual citizenship of the individual who was seeking to promote an ultimate evolutionary victory. Britain, Germany, the United States, the Latins, the Slavs, all were defended as the true elect of evolution. Most of the writers who preached this kind of political evolution proceeded from the assumption that at bottom the men of a given group had certain physical and therefore intellectual and spiritual traits in common, traits that gave them their superiority, and that could not possibly be transmitted to men of another group. Most of these writers, in short, were racists who believed that *Homo sapiens* had already evolved into what were really separate species. A black skin, for instance, was for them a sign of innate inferiority, and the blacks would simply have to go the way of the dinosaurs, into extinction. Evolution had spoken. Few of these writers quite dared to preach what has in our own day been christened genocide, the wholesale murder of those held to be of inferior race. Most of them were willing to see the inferiors duly subjected to the superiors, to have the less fit peoples serve as hewers of wood and drawers of water for their masters.

Some Social Darwinists applied their theories to a new form of caste organization, which came to be known as elitism. The fit were not limited to any one race, but they were still marked out by the rigid hand of biological inheritance. They were the master group, the elite, the "supermen"; and they should everywhere band together against the dull average men, and dutifully exploit them. The German Friedrich Nietzsche (1844–1900), who gave currency to the term "superman," was a subtle and difficult thinker, one who disliked Darwin as a grubbing Englishman and who was certainly no racist, no Social Darwinian. Still Nietzsche's influence among the half-educated who admired him in the late nineteenth and early twentieth centuries was to further racist and elitist causes.

Theories of the evolution-guided superiority of certain groups were not limited to Europe. In the United States, the innate, unchangeable superiority of whites to blacks was an article of faith among many whites in the North and almost universally in the South. This faith was greatly bolstered by Darwinian anthropologists and biologists. The notion that the degree of blondness and other readily visible traits, such as longheadedness and tallness, measured suitableness for citizenship in a great democracy helped dictate the American immigration act of 1924, which encouraged immigrants from northwestern Europe and almost excluded those from southern and eastern Europe. The American Madison Grant, in his *The Passing of the Great Race,* published in 1916, asserted that the Nordics were "a race of soldiers, sailors, adventurers and explorers, but above all, of rulers, organizers and aristocrats." Grant continued:

> Before leaving this interesting subject of the correlation of spiritual and moral traits with physical characters we may note that these influences are so deeply rooted in everyday consciousness that the modern novelist or playwright does not fail to make his hero a tall, blond, honest and somewhat stupid youth and his villain a small, dark and exceptionally intelligent individual of warped moral character.*

The title of Madison Grant's book betrays an anxiety that is never far from the surface even in the most confident of these Social Darwinists. Grant feared that his "great race," gifted summit of evolution though it was, was not going to survive. The lower races were breeding faster; democratic equalitarianism was lopping off the best and encouraging the worst. Somehow evolution was going wrong, producing degeneration, not progress. Like those other "scientific" determinists, the Marxists, the Social Darwinists believed that men of good will had to set to work with pen and tongue to help along the predetermined process and keep it on the right track.

A New Historical Determinism

Darwinian science no more than Newtonian science answered the great questions about good and evil, about the ends of human life, that men have been asking and trying to answer ever since we have had historical records. Darwinian science, and the physics, chemistry, and other sciences that flourished in the nineteenth century, recast for many the whole frame of reference in which these questions were asked. Traditional Christianity, as well as other transcendental and supernatural faiths, survived Darwin as they had survived Newton. Many men continued to believe in a God or powers not bound by the laws men discovered in laboratory experiments and, further, to believe that such a God guided their steps and gave meaning to their lives in this world and in the other world after death. But with the spread of popular education, especially in the West, great numbers came to believe that no such God or powers existed, that the material universe of science and common sense went on its regular ways in accordance with laws which men might even-

*M. Grant, *The Passing of the Great Race,* 4th rev. ed. (New York, 1921), p. 229.

tually understand completely, and which they were already beginning to understand quite well.

Darwin's work and that of many other scientists, in combination with the work of historians and philosophers and men of letters, worked a major change in the way men looked at their universe. It is a permissible oversimplification to say that the Newtonian universe was static, the Darwinian dynamic. The Enlightenment was certainly feeling its way toward a view of the universe as developing, progressing, evolving; but it did not have a good explanation of the way change came about. This explanation Darwin provided for natural history, and the romantic historians and their fellow workers in other fields provided it for human history.

Today many still believe in what has been labeled historicism—that is, in the doctrine that the course of history in the widest sense shows a regular, if bewildering, unfolding that has "determined" everything now existing and that will determine everything in the future. The wildest believer in this doctrine has had to admit that since he cannot in fact know the whole process in the past, he cannot wholly understand the present or predict the future. Nevertheless, the clue for him has lain in the past, out of which the present has developed.

The Christian and Hebraic calendar made the earth 6,000 years old, but the Darwinian calendar envisaged millions of years for organic life alone. It might seem, therefore, that historicism, especially when reinforced by the emphasis Darwin put on the immense reaches of time, would confirm conservative opposition to rapid change, or at least encourage in men a certain resignation in the face of the slow-moving process of evolution on this earth. And so it did for some men. Darwin's grandson, Sir Charles Galton Darwin, published in 1953 a book entitled *The Next Million Years.* He concluded that, since it is now held that it takes about a million years for a new species to evolve, it will be a million years before evolution produces a creature any better adapted than man; and that therefore for the next million years we shall have a history much like that of the last few thousand.

But historicism in the nineteenth and twentieth centuries has had for most others a quite different consequence. It has served to convince impatient and hopeful men that they have really mastered the secrets of the universe, that they have understood, as their misguided predecessors did not understand, just where the forces of history are leading. They could, then, help the process instead of hindering it, perhaps even hasten it. Marxism is the classic example of this faith in historical determinism, but nationalism, racism, and a host of others all have drawn nourishment from it. The extraordinary acceleration of technological improvements that produced the Industrial Revolution lent strength to this view that moral and political improvement could also be speeded up. The doctrine of evolution, then, though logically one can argue that it should have lessened the force of utopian faiths, did in fact

increase it. People thought of the sureness of evolution and forgot its slowness.

III Literature and the Arts

The scientific and industrial revolutions, occurring almost simultaneously as they did, made a major impact not only on the human view of history, past and future, but also on the whole cultural life of the West. They helped to stimulate an explosion of creativity and experiment that had revolutionary consequences and produced what we think of as modern and contemporary, as opposed to traditional, culture. This explosive force transformed the novel, the drama and the fine arts.

The Victorian Age

In literature the later nineteenth century may well be called the Victorian Age. Because the label is applied here not only to Britain but also to the United States and to Germany, France, and other continental nations, we cannot expect the age to have the unified style to be found in Periclean Athens, for example, or Renaissance Italy or Elizabethan England. We can evoke a Victorian drawing room, where Maud or Mélanie in ringlets and crinolines, surrounded by whatnots, bric-a-brac, plush hangings, and Landseer engravings of noble animals, reads Tennyson, Longfellow, or Heine, or plays Liszt on the pianoforte. But so much went on outside that drawing room!—not only in the lives of peasants, workers, country gentlemen, and businessmen, but even in art and letters. Maud or Mélanie might have been reading Dickens or Balzac, but these writers hardly fitted the drawing room. Nor would Thoreau and Melville, Zola and Dostoevsky. It is quite certain that the girls would not have been reading Marx.

The gap between genteel writing and the cruder and more vigorous forms was widening because so much important work was now, more clearly than ever before in Western history, produced and cultivated by men and women in conscious revolt against the tastes of the politically and economically dominant class of their time—that is, the middle class. Unless Maud and Mélanie were very advanced young women, they did not like much of what a hundred years later we single out as important in Victorian art and literature. They probably read sentimental novels now forgotten save by the social historian, and they lived in a culture to which the derogatory overtones of the word "Victorian" may still be applied.

Their fathers and brothers were often so concerned with industry and trade that they had no time for literature and the arts, which they tended to leave to their womanfolk. Or if they did have wider concerns, these were with political and social problems, with the material betterment of their own class, and of the working class, too. But these middle-class men felt that the most that could be done for the workers was to raise their standard of living slowly under existing laissez faire capitalism. They held that church and state should join to restrain by law and by religion of an essentially puritanical cast the lack of self-restraint these middle-class men found among their "inferiors." With these Victorians, laissez faire liberalism was a strictly economic matter; in morals they believed firmly that organized institutions should interfere to restrain the populace from the drunkenness, idleness, and loose living they were supposedly inclined to. Libertarians in economics, the educated, middle-class Victorians were most certainly authoritarians in morals.

Realistic and Naturalistic Fiction

In literature, the last two-thirds of the nineteenth century proved to be a great period for fiction, for the novel of realism in contrast with the romanticism of the century's earlier decades. Yet the realists were also children of the romantics. The romantic of 1830, fleeing this ugly world for the idealized Middle Ages, when knighthood was in flower and there were no sooty factories, or writing of the idyllic Indian tribes of America, can look very different from the realist of 1860, analyzing with fascination and disgust the men and women of the mill towns, the slums of the great cities, the unidyllic countryside of peasant labor. Yet both romantics and realists were individualists, and both were revolting against middle-class respectability. Both denied the older classical ideals of aristocratic moderation, of a natural law of decency and decorum. Both were obsessed with the analysis of human souls.

The English novelists, Dickens (1812–1870) and Thackeray (1811–1863), the French Balzac (1799–1850), and the Russian Dostoevsky (1821–1881) all have qualities that we label romantic. They reveled in exaggeration and sermonizing and poured out undisciplined torrents of words, writing at such a rapid rate, often against the repeated deadlines of serial publication, that they had little time to revise or polish. Yet they were thoroughly immersed in the world of their time and were in many ways realists. Dostoevsky wrote about the Russia and the Russians he knew; but his was a dark Russia, and the Russians of his novels, such as *The Possessed* and *Crime and Punishment,* were tortured, driven, unhappy seekers, no children of the Age of Reason. Many of Dickens' novels, though hardly comparable to Dostoevsky's in intensity and gloom, explored serious social problems and presented in unvarnished fashion the exploitation of children, the interminable delays in the courts of law, and the dehumanizing effects of industry. Dickens seemed to specialize in exposing the fatal flaws of character in a series of young men who, in romantic novels, would have turned out to be heroes. Thackeray subtitled his masterpiece, *Vanity Fair,* "A novel without a hero," and the title itself, taken from Bunyan's *Pilgrim's Progress,* is an implicit condemnation of the false values of a money-mad, power-hungry society, as exemplified by Thackeray's heroine (perhaps "antiheroine" would be more exact), Becky Sharp. The novels that constituted what Balzac called "the human comedy"—*Père Goriot, Eugénie Grandet, Cousin Bette* and many others—were a savage exposé of the crassness and corruption of bourgeois society under the July Monarchy. There is something of the romantic in the way he piles fraud upon fraud, villainy upon villainy, victim upon victim.

And there is also something of the romantic in the leading French realist of the next generation, Flaubert (1821–1880), who wrote one of his novels, *Salammbô,* about ancient Carthage, which he was unable to make very real, despite his careful research. Flaubert, who had the scientist's obsession with accuracy, wrote very slowly and devoted much time to the search for *le mot juste,* the precisely right word to express his meaning. He is said to have enlisted the help of a friend in a provincial town when he wanted to describe where the shadows fell on a certain café there at the end of the afternoon in spring. In Flaubert's masterpiece, *Madame Bovary,* which analyzes the romantic longings of a small-town doctor's wife, he displayed a most ambivalent attitude toward his heroine, and once declared, "I am Madame Bovary." In any case, Flaubert hated the bourgeois world he wrote about quite as much as the escapist writers of an earlier generation had hated theirs.

Some modern critics call these middle and late nineteenth-century writers "romantic realists," who eschewed the remote, the Gothic, the fantastic, and chose subjects close to their own time and place. But there were also more conventional—or at least more subdued—realists. Representative of these last were the Englishman Trollope, the Russian Turgenev, and the American Howells. Trollope (1815–1882) wrote dozens of novels about Victorian clergymen, politicians, and country gentlemen, carefully observing the English decencies, never raising his voice or his style, but imparting understanding, sympathy, and a suitable, modest irony, not to mention specific information about the annual income that enabled his characters to live as they did, waited upon by many servants. Turgenev (1818–1883), who wrote about his fellows with classic restraint, skirting delicately the depths of the Slavic soul, also had a taste for irony. In *Fathers and Sons,* his novel about the generation gap in the mid-century Russian gentry, he sketched a portrait of the nihilist Bazarov's old-fashioned mother—pious, superstitious, emotional, utterly devoted to her doctor husband and to her son—and then remarked: "Such women are not common nowadays. God knows whether we ought to rejoice!" William Dean Howells (1837–1920), editor of the *Atlantic Monthly* at the peak of its prestige, sought to apply realism to the American scene, notably in *The Rise of Silas Lapham,* chronicling the newly rich and socially ambitious in Boston, who knew it was time to leave the South End for fashionable Back Bay when a neighbor was seen sitting on his front stoop in his shirt-

Ivan Turgenev.

sleeves on a warm summer day. Howells was so restrained that today he is often pigeonholed as a follower of the "genteel tradition."

As the twentieth century drew near, the realists were confronted with a rebel generation that found them not realistic enough. This school rose first in France, where it took the name naturalism, often defined as "realism with an ideology" and criticized for "calling a spade not a spade but a bloody shovel." The leading naturalist author, Emile Zola (1840–1902), showed clearly the influence of the scientific revolution inspired by Darwin (and, ironically, was to die by asphyxiation in his own residence as a result of a technological defect, a faulty gas line). Zola was not content with the realist's aim to reflect the life around him with simple accuracy; he sought to arrive at laws of human development, much as the biologist seeks for laws of organic development. He would show what men are like, but he would also show how they came to be what they are, and even what they were going to be. He called his twenty volumes about a family under the Second Empire the "natural history" of a family. Each novel focused on some problem—*La Terre* (*The Earth*) on the land and the peasantry; *L'Assommoir* (*The Killer*) on alcoholism; *Germinal* (named for the month of sprouting in the revolutionary calendar) on strikes in a coal mine and radical agitators; and *La Débâcle* on the trauma of the war of 1870.

The Literature of Pessimism and Protest

Zola's work points up one of the tendencies not only of the novel, in those days the spearhead of literature,

but of other forms of writing in the late Victorian age as well. Literature was becoming what it was to be in the twentieth century, overwhelmingly a literature of discontent and protest. From the days of the ancient Greek philosophers and Hebrew prophets, many great thinkers have held that their own times were peculiarly out of joint. Yet there have been periods when intellectuals have been relatively well disposed to the existing government and society—the Augustan Age in Rome, the Elizabethan in England, the great century of Louis XIV. And there have also been periods when intellectuals, though bitterly opposed to the existing regime, have written with hope and confidence of what was to come—as in the Enlightenment. The succeeding romantic generations exhibited a pessimistic strain, which deepened in the later nineteenth century and has continued ever since.

The pessimists reacted against the eighteenth-century doctrine of the natural goodness of man. Certainly "nature" and "natural" as they figure in the work of a Zola carry connotations very different from the optimistic ones they had had in the eighteenth century. By the close of the Victorian age nature apparently made most men greedy, selfish, combative, not very bright, and addicted to sexual irregularities that brought out to the full their other bad traits. Some writers, like the English novelist Thomas Hardy (1840–1928), built this pessimism from a series of incidents in private lives into a grand cosmic irony not without its consoling side; his characters are so often the victims of coincidence, accident, and other unforeseen circumstances. But for the most part, these writers were concerned directly with the cruelties, stupidities, and aberrations of real people.

In France, Maupassant (1850–1893), a master of the short story, wrote sparely and simply, after the manner of his master Flaubert, about the tragedies and comedies of ordinary life; but the tragedies, or at least the ironies, prevail. In Russia, Chekhov (1860–1904), a medical man by training, used the prose drama and the short story to show how life harasses us all. Ibsen (1828–1906) in Norway, Brieux (1858–1932) in France, and George Bernard Shaw (1856–1950) in England all helped to develop the characteristically late nineteenth-century form of the drama, the problem play. The problem was sometimes one of wide moral and political concern, as in Ibsen's *Enemy of the People* or Shaw's *Man and Superman*, but it was very often concerned mainly with the stupid tangles of men's private lives. Ibsen shocked his contemporaries in *A Doll's House* by having his play begin at the point where the usual nineteenth-century drama ended and by permitting his heroine to rebel against the doll-house atmosphere her husband had created for her. Ibsen's *Ghosts* and Brieux's *Damaged Goods* scandalized the public by bringing to the stage the problem of venereal disease.

The problem play, the problem novel, the problem short story spread throughout Western literature. In the United States, by the end of the nineteenth century the "genteel tradition" was already scorned by the bright young men, and the novelists Stephen Crane (1871–1900) and Theodore Dreiser (1871–1945) were bringing out the harsh realities of war, business, and love; but it was not until almost our own day, and then of all places in the South of magnolia and roses, that William Faulkner, Erskine Caldwell, and others really plumbed the depths of human perversities behind the four-letter words they used so freely.

Most of this realistic or naturalistic writing, even when it is by no means of Marxist inspiration, is hostile to the middle classes. The bourgeois is no longer just the Philistine whom the romantic disliked, the puritanical conformist. He is still that, but he is also the rapacious titan of industry, the jingoistic nationalist, the authoritarian browbeater of his children, the tasteless addict of "conspicuous consumption" (a phrase of the American economist Thorstein Veblen), and the hypocritical practitioner of a "double standard" of sexual morality. In England, Samuel Butler (1835–1902) in *The Way of All Flesh* set the pattern for the kind of novel in which the writer-son blames all on the tyrannical male parent. Shaw found a simple phrase to sum up what was wrong—"middle-class morality." Ibsen's *Enemy of the People* is ironically named; the real enemy of the people is the people themselves, not the misunderstood leader who would bring them better things.

Even when writers are not embittered, the middle class does not often come out well. Bourgeois values are mocked or criticized by English novelists like H. G. Wells, Galsworthy, and Arnold Bennett, French novelists like Anatole France, and most writers of czarist Russia. An epitome of this attack is afforded by an American who wrote in the 1920s, chronologically rather later than the period with which we are here concerned but quite in its style. Sinclair Lewis' *Main Street* and *Babbitt* are realistic rather than naturalistic novels, and George Babbitt is almost a hero without ironic quotation marks. Still, Babbitt came to sum up for thousands of American intellectuals what was wrong with naïve materialistic civilization. The novels of Sinclair Lewis sold by the hundreds of thousands, so that the George Babbitts of real life and their families must have read these satires on their way of life. Since most of these writers were able to sell their works in a mass market, one may conclude that a good portion of the middle classes in the West were in revolt against their own shortcomings.

Not all that was written between 1850 and the outbreak of war in 1914 was a literature of scorn or protest. The daughters of the Maud or Mélanie with whom we began could read the standard conventional fare, historical novels, novels of escape, and novels of true love. They could even find in writers like Kipling men who, if not exactly convinced that this was the best of all possible worlds, were at least convinced that the English middle and upper classes were the least bad of the lot. They could, in short, read for enjoyment and go on with the serious business of life.

Poetry

In England Tennyson, in America Longfellow and his New England colleagues, in France Victor Hugo wrote the staple poetry the late nineteenth century liked and read a great deal. These poets deserve the tag "household words." In form, their work differs little from the norms set by the earlier romantic movement, and their subjects are love, death, nature, patriotism, faith, doubt, and longing, the eternal lyric repertory. They sometimes came down into the arena to deal with politics, as in Whittier's antislavery poems and in James Russell Lowell's "Biglow Papers," poems in Yankee dialect on the crisis of the Civil War. The spiritual crisis brought on by loss of Christian faith in a scientific age is evident in many poems of Matthew Arnold and Arthur Hugh Clough, as well as Tennyson.

The horrors of the Industrial Revolution also caused poetic protests, the most famous of which was prompted by a London news report of the arrest of a seamstress for pawning articles belonging to her employer. Paid by the piece, she could earn at the maximum seven shillings ($1.75) a week, on which she was expected to support herself and two young children. Thomas Hood summed up the indignant public reaction in *The Song of the Shirt*, published in the Christmas number of *Punch* for 1843; the third, fourth, and final stanzas read:

> "Work—work—work
> Till the brain begins to swim;
> Work—work—work
> Till the eyes are heavy and dim!
> Seam, and gusset, and band,
> Band, and gusset, and seam,
> Till over the buttons I fall asleep,
> And sew them on in a dream!

> "O! Men, with Sisters dear!
> O! Men! with Mothers and Wives!
> It is not linen you're wearing out,
> But human creatures' lives!
> Stitch—stitch—stitch,
> In poverty, hunger, and dirt,
> Sewing at once, with a double thread
> A Shroud as well as a Shirt."

> . . .

> With fingers weary and worn,
> With eyelids heavy and red,
> A Woman sate in unwomanly rags,
> Plying her needle and thread—
> Stitch! stitch! stitch!
> In poverty, hunger, and dirt,
> And still with a voice of dolorous pitch,
> Would that its tone could reach the Rich!
> She sang this "Song of the Shirt"!

On a higher poetic level the American Walt Whitman exalted democracy and the common man, employing free verse (which has no regular patterns of rhyme and meter). Whitman was no radical innovator, however, and the common man he celebrated had no trouble understanding his poems.

Yet in these same years poetry was beginning to move along the road that brought it to our own times, when the serious poet usually writes difficult private verse not for a mass audience but for a handful of initiates. Romantic poetry reflected the poet's inner world, but the romantic wanted to be read. In the second half of the nineteenth century, the French Parnassians deliberately sought the seclusion of perfect form, of polished verse fit for but few, or "art for art's sake." Symbolists like Mallarmé went on to very difficult verse, in which the meaning had to be wrung with effort from symbols nested one within another, in which the harmonies, like those of modern music, were by no means at once apparent to the untrained listener. Significantly, when twentieth-century poets went back for precedents to their literary teachers, they did not go to Tennyson, Hugo, Longfellow, or Kipling, but to late Victorian poets hardly known to their contemporaries, like the American Emily Dickinson and the English Catholic convert Gerard Manley Hopkins.

Painting, Academic and Realistic

In Victorian literature, there was a popular and conventional, but not vulgar, level of writing represented by men like Hugo and Tennyson. In painting, there was a similar level, represented by the Fontainebleau school in France; Watts, Burne-Jones, and Rossetti in England; George Inness, and later Winslow Homer and John Singer Sargent in the United States; animal painters like Rosa Bonheur (*The Horse Fair*) and Sir Edwin Landseer (*The Stag*); and many, many others throughout the West. The avant garde, the rebels and innovators in art, gave the paintings of these men the derogatory label "academic." Actually, the academic painters were technically very skillful, for they had the advantage of the long tradition of Western painting since the Renaissance. They could often mirror man and nature more faithfully then their great rival for the patronage of the many, the camera. They were sometimes realists, but they were not naturalists in Zola's sense. They rather avoided the shambles of the Industrial Revolution, and to their avant garde opponents they seemed too much concerned with the pretty in nature and with the aristocratic or striking in portraiture.

The rebellion against academic painting, begun in the romantic generation by Delacroix, continued in the mid-nineteenth century with the Frenchmen Daumier (1808–1879) and Courbet (1819–1877), who also protested against the values of laissez-faire capitalism. Daumier exploited to the full the new technological developments that made it possible to mass-produce inexpensive copies of his lithographs. With a moral indignation and savage bite worthy of Voltaire or Hogarth, Daumier exposed the evils of French society, especially under the July Monarchy. He attacked its zeal for law and order in defense of class interests, and the selfishness and repressiveness of its judges and politicians, including Louis-Philippe himself, whose pear-shaped figure and inevitable umbrella afforded superb opportunities for caricature. Courbet upset the academic painters by taking commonplace subjects—wrestlers, stonecutters, nudes who bore no resemblance to classical nymphs—and portraying them as they were, with no attempt to prettify them. The hostility of the academics reached a peak in 1863 when canvases by followers of Courbet were refused showing in the annual Paris salon. The rejected artists countered by organizing their own "salon des réfusés," which gained the backing of Napoleon III.

Among the paintings by the "réfusés" was *Déjeuner sur l'Herbe* (*Picnic Lunch*) by Edouard Manet (1832–1883), depicting two fully-dressed young men with nude female companions. Manet defended himself against hostile comment by observing that a good realist simply painted what he saw. What Manet saw—or more exactly, the ways in which he saw things—did not necessarily correspond to the image recorded by the camera. His version of the execution of the hapless emperor in Mexico demonstrates the distortions so characteristic of modern art, and so disturbing to unprepared viewers. *The Death of Maximilian* destroys the Renaissance idea of perspective, placing the firing squad almost on top of its victim, and abandons factual accuracy by making the executioners French soldiers rather than the Mexicans they actually were. Manet used real objects and events for his own artistic purposes, as occasions for effects of color and composition that he felt to be truer and more real than what the camera records. This feeling that the artist sees more and sees it more profoundly than any mechanical device or any layman with conventional scientific training underlies the revolt of modern art against mere "representational" painting.

Impressionism and Post-Impressionism

That science might encourage, as well as impede, artistic revolution was evident in the case of the Impressionists, whose name was invented by hostile critics after viewing a painting entitled *Impression: Sunrise* by the leader of the school, Claude Monet (1840–1926). The Impressionists learned from physics that light was a complex phenomenon put together by the human eye from the prismatic reflections of nature. They proposed to break both light and shadow into their component colors and then allow the viewer's eye to reassemble them. They painted landscapes and seascapes for the most part, using thousands of little dabs of pure color for their trees, flowers, buildings, rocks, skies, and water. The result, when seen from close on, is hardly more

Manet's "The Death of Maximilian."

than a formless mesh of color, but when viewed from a proper distance is magically transformed into a recognizable scene flooded with light.

The nature of light and color had interested painters before the Impressionists, like the Romantic Constable, with his luminous landscapes, and his fellow Englishman Turner (1775–1851). Turner has been termed the great precursor of impressionism because his marine paintings led him to more and more daring experiments in the depiction of light and mist. Monet put experiment on a sustained scientific basis, painting the same subject again and again—the cathedral at Rouen, the lily pond in his own garden—to show how greatly its appearance varied at differing times of day and under changing conditions of light.

Two other qualities augmented the revolutionary impact of Impressionist painting. One was the abandonment of traditional conventions of symmetry in favor of an arrangement which put the principal figure well to one side, sometimes even partially cut off. This technique, borrowed from the Japanese print, was employed with telling effect by the Frenchman Degas (1834–1917) and the American Whistler (1834–1903), who made misty London scenes look quite Japanese and who was, incidentally, quite ashamed of having been born in Lowell, Massachusetts. The other new

departure was the concentration on subjects evoking everyday life rather than the artificial world of the studio. Milliners, prostitutes, cardplayers or solitary drinkers in a café, cabaret and circus performers, ballerinas in rehearsal populate the canvases of Degas, Toulouse-Lautrec, Renoir, Van Gogh, Cézanne, and other masters of the late nineteenth century.

Most of these men are cataloged by historians of art as post-Impressionists, because they were going on from impressionism to further experiments. Cézanne (1839–1906), in particular, thought that impressionism was too obsessed with light at the expense of the geometrical and architectural qualities also to be found in the world of nature. He proposed to restore these qualities, not with the classic, flowing perspective inherited by the academics from the Italians, but with blocks or chunks of color. Much of twentieth-century painting stems from Cézanne. Cubism, which is the exaggeration of his insistence on three-dimensionality, is most in his debt, but so too are abstractionism and even surrealism.

The Other Arts

In contrast to painting, sculpture did not flourish exuberantly in the nineteenth century. An age that had mastered the industrial arts so well produced monu-

Cézanne's "The Card Players."

mental statues aplenty, of which the most famous is Liberty in New York harbor, the work of the French sculptor Bartholdi, a gift from the Third French Republic to the American Republic. But the statues of statesmen and warriors that adorn public places everywhere in the West are so conventionally realistic that we hardly accept them as human beings. Sculpture would appear to be an aristocratic art, designed for the palace and the formal garden. Its nineteenth-century civic use seems at its best—or least bad—in Paris, in the decoration of the great Arc de Triomphe, a delayed memorial to the Grand Army of Napoleon I, and in the new Opéra and many other buildings. Toward the end of the century, the French sculptors Rodin and Maillot began to simplify, strengthen, and, to a degree, exaggerate the contours of their men and women, treating their subjects with less academic convention and more power. It should be noted that inexpensive, small-scale copies of the great sculpture of antiquity and the Renaissance now became common, and many a Victorian drawing room boasted a plaster Venus or a bronze Mercury. Museums in various parts of the world could all afford large plaster casts of classical works, so some exposure to the great artistic achievements of the past was now possible for a very wide general public.

In consequence, the nineteenth century knew almost too much of the past of the arts and became too eclectic and derivative in its tastes. This eclecticism weighed heavily on architecture: banks, seeking an impression of appropriate dignity and permanence, favored Greek or Roman temples, at least for the façade; universities and churches, both with lofty aspirations, preferred the Gothic. The medieval predecessor of Gothic, the Romanesque, with its rounded arches and air of solidity, was revived by the talented American architect Richardson, and used for structures as diverse as Trinity Church on Boston's Copley Square, Sever Hall housing classrooms in Harvard Yard, and a series of stations along the Boston and Albany Railroad.

Two styles were particularly popular in the late nineteenth century. The architecture for public buildings was basically derived from the Renaissance, embellished with pediments and balconies and sometimes with domes or friezes, the particular adaptations varying somewhat from country to country. French public structures, much under the influence of the Ecole des Beaux Arts (the school of fine arts in Paris), looked vaguely like a château in Touraine; German buildings kept a touch of the huddled Middle Ages; and British buildings, much imitated in Boston, New York, and

Philadelphia, were simpler, more in the manner of Palladio, the neoclassical master of the Renaissance. The other style, for private homes, was represented in Europe by the "villa," and in America by the "mansion" that the successful businessman built for himself on Elm Street. In the United States this style was at its most flaunting in the mansions of the 1870s, the "era of General Grant." These were big houses, for families were large, domestic servants were plentiful and cheap, and building costs were relatively low. They ran to high ceilings, for the bourgeois wanted nothing to remind him of the low rooms of his past. They looked too tall for their width, and their lines were broken by little towers, porches, scrollwork, and other sorts of decorative devices. But they had the latest comforts, if they were in a town large enough—gas light, bathrooms, and central heating, though western Europeans came rather slowly to this last innovation.

In architecture, as in painting and sculpture, true innovation began toward the end of the century. In structural steel, men now had a way of emancipating themselves from the limitations that had so taxed the Gothic builders; they could now go almost as high as they pleased. They began to do so in the United States, where the first "skyscrapers" were put up in Chicago in the 1880s. Although some later skyscrapers ended up in Gothic towers, abundantly decorated, the general tendency imposed by the materials was toward simplicity of line. This taste for simplicity began to spread, and with the twentieth century the way was open for modern "functional" architecture. Mention of structural steel may serve as a reminder that some of the finest examples of the late 1800s were designed by engineers. Great bridges, like the Brooklyn Bridge or the railroad span across the Firth of Forth in Scotland, are still handsome today as well as impressive and useful.

To sample the minor arts of furniture and household decoration, we return once more to the drawing room of Maud and Mélanie. It was incredibly heavy and incredibly dark. The height of the windows was canceled by the dark carpets, upholstery, hangings, and pillows, and by the mahogany or walnut furniture. Everywhere there was a clutter of objets d'art. The movement for simplification of decoration, however, began in Victorian England with William Morris (1834–1896), designer of the easy chair that bears his name, who wanted to go back to more austere medieval styles. And it was in full swing in the 1890s, particularly with art nouveau in France, which relied on botanical motifs and sought to give structures the look of living organisms.

Music

Perhaps music exists in more of an ivory tower than the other arts; in any case, it responded more slowly to the rapidly changing social and intellectual environment of the 1800s. It recorded many major achievements in the Victorian decades—the foundation of

Rodin's "The Thinker."

The Home Insurance Company Building, Chicago, designed by Louis H. Sullivan, one of the pioneers of modern architecture.

Wagner in 1868.

tively undramatic passages of recitative, Wagner sought to combine music and action in a realistic entity. His characteristic device was the *Leitmotiv,* a recurring melodic theme associated with a given character or symbolizing an element in the drama. He made a bold innovation by employing musical dissonance as a theatrical device and a second departure by writing his own librettos. Apart from the comic and *gemütlich Die Meistersinger,* celebrating Hans Sachs and the master singers of Nuremberg in the early sixteenth century, he chose epic subjects: *Parsifal,* on the theme of the Holy Grail; *Tristan and Isolde,* a drama of fated love and death taken from the Arthurian legends; and the four operas comprising the *Ring of the Nibelung* cycle, based on the heroic epic of early medieval Germany.

Twentieth-century psychologists find in Wagner's choice of subjects an awareness of the human need for archetypes and myths, the demigods and supermen of the past who still haunt us. Political critics deplore Wagner's bombastic nationalism, which made him so popular with Hitler and the Nazis, though it is only fair to note that Wagner considered himself a left-wing liberal and was exiled to Switzerland for thirteen years after taking part in an abortive rebellion against the king of Saxony in 1848. His reputation has also suffered because of his Victorian heaviness and the inordinate length and the great noise of his works. Nietzsche once remarked that Wagner's music "sweats."

Wagner's Russian contemporary, Moussorgsky (1839–1881), was even more daring when he composed the opera *Boris Godunov,* based on Pushkin's account of the sordid and bloody Time of Troubles around 1600. He employed harsh dissonances again and again, for the barbaric splendor of Boris' coronation as czar and for a drunken brawl in a rustic tavern. Since Moussorgsky's score was considered too strong for a conventional audience, it was tamed down for actual productions by Rimsky-Korsakov (1844–1908). Rimsky, a Russian naval engineer who traveled extensively in Asia, was fascinated by Eastern music, echoes of which can be heard in his *Scheherazade* and in his less well known operatic works.

Both Russian and Asian influences helped to qualify the Frenchman Debussy (1862–1918) for the title of founder of modern music conferred upon him by many musicologists. He was greatly impressed by Moussorgsky's *Boris* and by the strange Far Eastern instruments, and the still stranger sounds they made, at the Paris exhibition of 1889 (the one for which the Eiffel Tower was built). Debussy developed new rhythms, harmonies, and dissonances that were a radical change from conventional composition. In reaction against Wagnerian gigantism, he employed them to convey the subtle sensuous moods of *The Afternoon of a Faun,* a setting for Mallarmé's symbolist poem. Debussy's style is often called impressionistic, for he sought to convey the sounds of a transitory moment as the impressionist painters sought to capture its light and its color.

many of the great symphony orchestras and opera companies, and the composition of many standard items in their repertoires, such as the symphonies of Tchaikovsky and Brahms, Bizet's *Carmen,* Gounod's *Faust,* and half a dozen hardy perennials by Verdi. Although most of them differed little from the masterpieces of the romantic generation, the success of *Carmen,* with its seductive plebeian heroine, precipitated a spate of operas with characters from the workaday world— Leoncavallo's *I Pagliacci,* Puccini's *La Bohême,* Charpentier's *Louise*—or with plots hardly suitable for proper Victorians—Richard Strauss' *Electra* and Saint-Saëns' *Samson and Delilah,* which was actually banned from production on the British stage for a whole generation after its completion in 1877.

The most ambitious composer of the age did attempt a greater break with tradition. Richard Wagner (1813–1883) was stage-struck and regarded the theater as a "demon world" excitingly different from humdrum reality. He rechristened opera "music drama" and set out to make it the supreme synthesis of the arts, with drama, music, costumes, and scenery all fused in one great transcendence of the conventional world. Giving up the traditional alternation between aria and rela-

IV Philosophy and Political Thought

Comte and Positivism

The culture of the later nineteenth century, and its literature in particular, furnish samples of almost the full range of human attitudes toward the world. The formal philosophy and the less formal view of life taken by educated people varied quite as widely, and we can find as many different schools in metaphysics and ethics as we can find in literature. Even before Darwin published his *Origin of Species* a major attempt was undertaken to make the new discoveries of science the basis for a comprehensive program to secure the intellectual, political, and economic improvement of mankind.

The program was called "positivism" by its author, Auguste Comte (1798–1857), who had served his intellectual apprenticeship with Saint-Simon, the great champion of industry and spinner of projects for greater international harmony. Though Comte later broke with his mentor, his own recommendations for bettering the human conditions retained some of the utopian and messianic qualities of Saint-Simonian teachings. Comte applied the term "positivist" to the third stage of man's attitude toward the world around him. First, in the infant period of human history, man was in the theological age, when he stood in awe and fear of nature and sought to placate the gods that controlled it. Second, in the adolescence of human history, metaphysical concepts replaced divinities as the controlling forces of the world. Finally, science would enable man to understand nature without recourse to theological or metaphysical intermediaries so that he might take positive action to manipulate the world to his advantage. The epoch of maturity, the positivist age, was at hand.

Comte also ranked according to maturity the sciences that enabled humanity to emancipate itself from theological and metaphysical supports. He gave seniority to mathematics and astronomy, put chemistry and physics next, then biology and psychology, and last, and youngest, the science of society, or sociology. It was sociology, Comte believed, that would give man the key to the positive age.

In many ways, Comte was simply restating the Enlightenment's optimistic faith in the miracle-working potential of science; he was a belated philosophe, another would-be "Newton of the social sciences." Yet he also realized that the French revolutionary attempt to build a new society from the blueprints of eighteenth-century intellectuals had ended in terror and dictatorship. Accordingly, Comte concluded, utopia must be achieved peacefully through the teaching of dedicated men, who would enable the mass of their fellows to free themselves from their old dependency on theology and metaphysics. Comte envisaged these liberators as preachers of a new "religion of humanity," but his critics argued that they were a new set of priests, propagandists of a new positivist dogma that might be more intolerant than old religious dogmas. The undemocratic implications of doctrines of leadership by a new elite continued to concern Western thinkers, we shall find,

long after the transient popularity of Comte's teachings had passed. Comte's ultimate failure to base everything on science, his recourse to a "religion of humanity" to wean men away from traditional faiths, foreshadowed the uncertainties and perplexities that science engendered in the intellectual life of the Victorian age.

Idealism and Realism

The polar antithesis between idealism and realism that runs through the Western philosophical tradition persisted during the nineteenth century. The philosophical school of idealism was born in its modern form in the Germany of Kant and Hegel. In the Victorian decades it continued to thrive in the land of its birth; it made converts in the Oxford School of T. H. Green, Bradley, and Bosanquet, and in the American philosopher Josiah Royce; and it even penetrated into the Latin countries. Modern philosophical realism, the opposite of idealism, was at least as widespread. Although the realists attempted to answer the questions the scientist does not try to answer so far as he is a scientist, they had their roots in the same soil as modern science and the scientific rationalism of the eighteenth-century philosophes. Auguste Comte doubtless thought of himself as a realist.

The American philosopher William James (1842–1910) summed up this antithesis of idealism and realism by arguing that men are by disposition either "tender-minded" or "tough-minded." They are either tough-mindedly convinced that the world of sense experience is the real world or tender-mindedly convinced that the world of sense-experience is somehow an illusion, or at any rate a flawed copy, if not a kind of caricature, of the real world which is in our minds imperfectly, and perfectly in God's mind.

One might conclude that, since the later nineteenth century was a period of great material progress, deeply concerned with this world of the senses, then the tough-minded would prevail over the tender-minded. Yet this was by no means true in philosophy, where the tender-minded were quite numerous and articulate. Perhaps the unreflective man, at least in our Western civilization, leans toward the tough-minded side, if only because common sense urges upon him the presence of the world of matter. But there are no reliable statistics on this point, and to the extent that Christianity forms an inescapable underpinning for the world view of Western men, not even tough common sense can altogether dispose of the world of the tender-minded, of concepts like value judgments, soul, spirit, ideal, and otherworld.

Darwinism left its mark on the philosophy of the later nineteenth century. The thought of the period had a dynamic historical and evolutionary cast that not even the tender-minded could avoid. The idealist, following Hegel, believed that above the whirl and change of this world of the senses there was an unchanging, perfect world of the Absolute. But he also believed that this imperfect world was being slowly drawn toward that other world, developing by ways he could only incompletely understand, but growing, evolving. On the other hand, the nineteenth-century realist no longer held that his reason could give him a neat, static, mathematical formula for the good life; he too thought that everything grows, that even what is made according to human plans must take account of nature's mysterious ways of growth.

A second and related note in the thought of the period is an emphasis on will, often capitalized into Will, on doing, on the life force that makes the "struggle for existence." The word appears everywhere, even as a title—Schopenhauer's *World as Will and Idea*, Nietzsche's *Will to Power*, William James' *Will to Believe*. It appears but slightly disguised in the French philosopher Henri Bergson's "creative evolution" and *"élan vital"* and in Bernard Shaw's "life-force." It appears in the work of the Italian idealist philosopher Benedetto Croce, as an insistence that knowing is not a passive registering but a creative doing. It lies behind the use of the word "myth" by the French anarcho-syndicalist Georges Sorel, and the German Hans Vaihinger's phrase "the philosophy of the as-if." For both these latter thinkers, the great ideas, the great abstractions of Right and Wrong, are not mere attempts of the mind to understand the world; indeed they are quite false if taken as analytically descriptive of this world. But they are, rather, the guides our desires, our wills, set up for our action. They are fictions, myths, "as-if," but all the more real for being such.

The pragmatism of William James, somewhat unfairly described by its critics as the philosophy that nothing succeeds like success, is one of these philosophies of the will. To James, himself tough-minded, reality is no absolute as in the idealist tradition; indeed, reality is nothing fixed and certain. Reality is what works for us human beings; truth is what we want to believe. James thought he had saved himself from the obvious danger of this line of thought—that is, making reality and truth purely subjective, purely a matter of the individual's judgment or faith—by granting that not everything we want is practical, that not all our desires "work." If my will to believe tells me I can make a broad jump of three hundred feet, experience, the "pragmatic" test, will prove that I cannot. But to many of James' critics, he had by no means saved himself from subjectivism. Pragmatism remained to these critics a doctrine dangerously erosive of traditional values, leading either to an exaltation of mere vulgar success, or to "fideism," a silly faith in believing for the sake of believing.

The Revolt against Reason Intensifies

The cult of the will brings us to a major current in the broad stream of later nineteenth-century thought, a current more evident among intellectuals and creative artists than among average educated men and women. This was an intensification of the revolt against reason already initiated by the romantics earlier in the century; it may be called anti-intellectualism, irrationalism, or more exactly, antirationalism. This antirationalism is one of the "roots" of twentieth-century totalitarianism, but it is by no means a simple synonym for totalitarianism or fascism. It is a much broader and more inclusive term. It is quite possible to have been influenced by antirational currents and remain a good, if not altogether orthodox, democrat and individualist. It is quite possible to be a Marxist totalitarian and reject a great deal, especially in its psychological core, of modern antirationalism. The conventional Marxist retains some of the naïve optimism of the eighteenth-century rationalist: Get the economy to work perfectly, he says, and men will behave themselves perfectly.

The basic position of antirationalism, and one for which it is heavily indebted to the romantic movement, is a rejection of the Enlightenment's belief that the typical human being is naturally reasonable. To the extent that it rejects the Enlightenment, antirationalism is a negation, as the "anti" implies. But it has its positive side—the belief that if men can accept their true nature as human beings they can lead richer lives than any rationalist ever planned for them; what they must accept is the radical limitation of the potential of their thinking mind, or brain, to which so much of their experience never penetrates.

Broadly speaking, there are two kinds of antirationalism, which shade into one another: the moderate and the extreme. Moderate antirationalism at bottom is trying to salvage as much as possible of the eighteenth-century belief in human rationality. Such on the whole is the attitude of modern psychology, beginning with William James and Sigmund Freud. This psychology seeks to aid human reason by pointing out the difficulties under which it must work. Reason, these thinkers maintain, is limited by men's instincts or "drives," by their biological inheritance of animality, so much emphasized by the evolutionists, and by their sociological inheritance of custom and tradition so much emphasized by historians and by the school of Edmund Burke.

To use a metaphor from John Locke (which he in turn derived from the slogan of the Cambridge Platonists, "the mind of man is the light of God"), moderate antirationalists regard human reason as a flickering candle, not as the great white universal light it appeared to be to philosophes like Condorcet. Far from wishing to extinguish this candle, they want to keep it alive, to nurse it along into greater and greater brightness. This process, in keeping again with the views of the evolutionist, they regard as inevitably long and slow, likely to be hindered rather than helped by ambitious plans to hasten it. These moderate thinkers are perhaps not so much antirationalists as they are chastened rationalists.

By contrast, the extreme antirationalists would

actually put out the candle of human reason, which they regard as not only feeble but downright bad. For them, reason is, so to speak, a mistake evolution has made—a wrong turning from which the human race must somehow retrace its steps to a sounder life of pure unsullied instinct, emotion, and faith. Thomas Hardy, the English novelist, remarked: "Thought is a disease of the flesh." There was to be a strong dose of anti-rationalism in the Nazi movement. Hitler himself distrusted reason as a degenerate French invention and hoped that good Germans would come to think with their blood, with their German folk inheritance.

The Reaction against Democracy

Many of the extreme antirationalists turned violently against democracy, which seemed to them to rest on an altogether false estimate of what human beings were really like. The democrat believes at bottom that every man can be freed from the weight of erroneous traditions, habits, and prejudices. Once he has the real facts before him, he can attain by free discussion among his fellows a series of decisions that will be incorporated in acts and institutions under which all men can live more happily. But if you hold that most, or even many, men are by nature incapable of fair, dispassionate thinking and discussion, if you hold that men are by nature hopelessly irrational, you will at least have to revise drastically your notions of democracy.

The German philosopher Nietzsche, who did most of his work in the 1880s, will serve as a sample of such political thinkers. Nietzsche wrote mostly in short aphoristic passages, which are hard to systematize and often quite contradictory. But the central line of his thinking led to the concept of a new aristocracy, to the "superman." Nietzsche's followers, who were numerous throughout the West in the two decades before 1914, insisted that he meant a new *spiritual* aristocracy. The supermen would be above the petty materialism and national patriotism of the middle classes. Nietzsche's opponents, who were also many, held that he was just another preacher of Nordic superiority, that his supermen were, as he put it in one of his famous passages, "the blond beasts" who had so often terrorized Europe. Certainly some of his German followers held that he meant the real live Germans to be his supermen.

At any rate, Nietzsche was clearly an enemy of democracy, which he held to be second only to its child, socialism, as a society in which the weak unjustly and unnaturally ruled the strong. Here are some of his aphorisms, from which the reader can judge for himself:

Democracy represents the disbelief in all great men and in all élite societies: everybody is everybody else's equal. "At bottom we are all herd and mob."

I am opposed to Socialism because it dreams ingenuously of "goodness, truth, beauty, and equal rights" (anarchy pursues the same ideal, but in a more brutal fashion).

I am opposed to parliamentary government and the power of the press, because they are the means whereby cattle become masters.*

Nietzsche may have hoped that the herd, the slaves, the masses would, in spite of their crass materialism, somehow recognize the true masters, the new enlightened despots; or he may have thought of himself as the prophet of a vast moral and religious revolution which would, in his own phrase, achieve a "transvaluation of all values," a new world for a new species of man.

Even the defenders of the democratic values attacked by Nietzsche were also influenced by the doubts raised by the romantics and the antirationalists. They were not at all sure about the reasonableness and the natural goodness of the average man and woman, about the beneficent workings of a free market and the "invisible hand" of laissez faire economics, and about many other established doctrines of liberalism. John Stuart Mill in the mid-century had worried over the "tyranny of the majority." Walter Bagehot, a good English liberal much influenced by Darwin, pointed out in his *Physics and Politics* (1872—Biology and Politics would have been a better title) how strong was the accumulated force of habit and tradition, which he called the "cake of custom," how hard it was to persuade men to break the cake of custom and take rational action. By the end of the century, liberals throughout the West were facing the problem of revising their attitudes toward life to conform with the new emphasis on the tough network of habit, custom, and prejudice.

Elitism

Already by 1914 the broad lines of the social attitudes of our own time were being laid out. One line went toward some kind of revolutionary elitism, toward the seizure of power by a minority that believes itself to have the formula whereby the gifted few can put order into a society threatened with chaos because of attempts to make decisions democratically by counting heads, no matter what is inside them. The variety of these specific formulas was great. Some made race the mark of the elite, and went so far as to preach world rule for their chosen race. Others made class the mark of the elite, and sought to achieve the "dictatorship of the proletariat." Indeed, as Lenin developed Marxian socialism, its elitist implications came out in the doctrine often called the Leninist corollary—that the enlightened minority must seize power and rule dictatorially in the name of and in the "true" interest of the proletarian masses. Others dreamed of a brand-new elite, such as Nietzsche's supermen, to be created by a kind of new religion. Still others looked to eugenics to make possible the breeding of such a new elite.

A second line went toward a more flexible form

*F. Nietzsche, *The Will to Power*, trans. A. M. Ludovici (London, 1910), 2:206.

of elitism, one that tried to conserve as much as possible of democratic values. On the whole, English Fabianism and continental revisionist socialism deserve this classification. The leaders of these movements wanted no violent overturns, no seizure of power. They believed in gradualness, even in the basic democratic counting of heads. But there was in all of them a strong touch of doubt as to the political capacity of the average man. They were not for the extension of New England town-meeting democracy to the millions of the modern state. They hoped they could persuade the millions to elect legislators who would listen to the wise planners who had studied the social sciences and could devise the new institutions that would make human life so much better. Above all, the planners themselves would by no means disdain what the antirationalists had taught them about human irrationality; they would use for good ends what they could learn from the politician, the advertising man, the skilled professional manipulator of human beings; they would be Machiavellians, but Machiavellians on the side of the angels.

A third line sought to preserve and protect an existing elite from democratic drives toward equality, especially in the form of state intervention in economic and social life to promote security for all. This was substantially the line followed by men like the American sociologist William Graham Sumner, by the English philosopher Herbert Spencer, and by many others throughout the West. They are not unfairly labeled conservatives, for they sought to preserve in its broad lines an established order. But they were not simply routine, unphilosophical conservatives who opposed any changes at all. They had a definite philosophy, strongly influenced by antirationalism. Their basic position was a distrust of the instrument of thought applied unsparingly to human society, and in this they go back to Burke and to philosophical conservatives throughout the Western tradition.

They were clearly children of their age, above all in their dread of "socialism," in which they included such mildly liberal reforms as those proposed by J. S. Mill. Most of them believed in progress, and most of them prized material plenty, peace, industrial society. They held, however, that the existing middle classes, the leaders of the business world, and the network of Victorian habits and morals were the best insurance that progress would continue. Above all, they feared planners and planning, at least in political positions. They distrusted the state, for they were good Darwinians, who believed that the evolutionary process depended on the struggle for life among competing individuals fettered as little as possible by attempts to "rig" the struggle. They believed that social evolution could not be hastened, and that attempts to hasten it, no matter how well meant, would in fact retard it by limiting actual human variation and initiative. They are by no means altogether without sympathizers today, but it must be admitted that theirs has not, so

far, been the wave of the future. The Herbert Spencer who thought compulsory sewage disposal in cities was an interference with the right of the individual to conduct his own private struggle against typhoid fever would be even more uncomfortable in the late twentieth century than he was in the late nineteenth.

"The Century of Hope"

It would be a mistake to dismiss the whole nineteenth century as something altogether outlived. We are all still living with the achievements as well as the problems it bequeathed to us. The achievements are obvious, and we have noted them in the last few chapters. They add up to an impressive command over natural forces, attained by the collaboration, often the chance collaboration, of pure scientists, applied scientists and engineers, businessmen, bureaucrats, and politicians, and on down to clerks and laborers.

The problems are also evident. Above all, there was the widespread feeling, particularly among intellectuals, that "something was wrong," that the new and better world promised by 1776 and 1789 had proved illusory. It is easy to point out how many nineteenth-century writers—the youthful Marx, Flaubert, Nietzsche—were alienated from the ways of their world. It is even easier to find how many more can be labeled pessimistic, if not alienated—genteel Victorians like Matthew Arnold or John Ruskin, worried liberals like Mill and Tocqueville, deeply concerned critics of their national culture like the great Russian novelists. Even the Americans were not always optimistic children of the Enlightenment—think of James Fenimore Cooper, the bitter critic of American democracy, of Mark Twain despairing of the "damned human race," and of Thoreau who believed that even in gentle Concord men led lives of quiet desperation.

Yet, despite all this the nineteenth century has been entitled "the century of hope." The title can be reconciled with the record of the century's intellectual history in part by insisting that, while many thinkers inclined toward pessimism, the great majority of Europeans and Americans, especially the dominant middle class, were cheerful believers in progress. The bulk of newspaper and magazine writing, the testimony of informal letters, and much other evidence can support the social historian in contending that Victorian nonintellectuals, in contrast to intellectuals, were on the whole contented and hopeful, if a bit self-righteous. Even among the intellectuals there was an attitude, hard to pin down, that it was the century of hope. Few of them, no matter how bitter and indignant about their times or skeptical about human nature, displayed a cosmic despair. Almost all of them shared with their grandfathers of the eighteenth century a kind of energy and gusto, a conviction that what they wrote and said would have results, a belief in the future and in ultimate progress.

Reading Suggestions on the Intellectual Revolution of the Nineteenth Century

General Accounts

W. H. Coates and H. V. White, *The Ordeal of Liberal Humanism* (*McGraw-Hill). A compact and useful survey of intellectual history since 1789.

C. Brinton, *The Shaping of Modern Thought* (*Prentice-Hall). A more rapid survey.

R. W. Stromberg, *European Intellectual History since 1789* (*Appleton). Another helpful textbook.

W. L. Langer, *Political and Social Upheaval, 1832–1852;* R. C. Binkley, *Realism and Nationalism, 1852–1871;* C. J. H. Hayes, *A Generation of Materialism, 1871–1900;* O. J. Hale, *The Great Illusion, 1900–1914* (*Torchbooks). These four volumes in the series The Rise of Modern Europe have substantial sections on the topics covered in this chapter and full bibliographical listings.

F. S. Marvin, *The Century of Hope,* 2nd ed. (Oxford Univ. Press, 1927). A bird's-eye view of cultural history, rather old-fashioned in point of view. May be contrasted with Morse Peckham, *Beyond the Tragic Vision* (*Braziller), written from the standpoint of modern psychology.

Science

R. Taton, ed., *Science in the Nineteenth Century* (Thames and Hudson, 1965). An encyclopedic account by various French experts; Volume 3 of A General History of Science.

W. P. D. Wightman, *The Growth of Scientific Ideas* (Yale Univ. Press, 1951). A most enlightening interpretation.

C. C. Gillispie, *The Edge of Objectivity* (*Princeton Univ. Press). Darwin and other nineteenth-century scientific innovators appraised. Gillispie has also written *Genesis and Geology* (*Torchbooks), a study of the tension between science and religion prior to Darwin.

L. Eisely, *Darwin's Century* (*Anchor). Instructive study of the doctrine of evolution and of the men who formulated it.

Charles Darwin, *Autobiography* (*Norton); *Voyage of the Beagle* (*Bantam); *On the Origin of Species* (*several editions). Three key works for understanding the development of Darwin's ideas. His writings may be sampled in *The Darwin Reader,* ed. M. Bates and P. S. Humphrey (*Scribner's).

G. Himmelfarb, *Darwin and the Darwinian Revolution* (*Norton). Excellent critical introduction. For a rather different assessment consult M. T. Ghiselin, *The Triumph of the Darwinian Method* (*Univ. of California Press).

W. Irvine, *Apes, Angels and Victorians* (*World). A lively study of the social ramifications of Darwinism.

J. C. Greene, *The Death of Adam* (*Iowa State Univ. Press). Assessment of the impact of evolution on Western thought.

A. D. White, *A History of the Warfare of Science with Theology in Christendom* (*Free Press). By the first president of Cornell University, an American champion of Darwin's ideas.

Herbert Spencer, *Man versus the State* (*Penguin). Representative work by a wholehearted English Social Darwinist.

M. R. Davie, *William Graham Sumner* (*T. Y. Crowell). A good introduction to a leading American Social Darwinist. See also R. Hofstadter *Social Darwinism in American Thought* (*Beacon), an admirable study by a highly respected historian.

Jacques Barzun, *Darwin, Marx and Wagner,* rev. ed. (*Anchor).

Suggestive study stressing the common denominators among three contemporaneous innovators usually cataloged as very different from one another.

Literature

G. M. Young, *Victorian England: Portrait of an Age* (*Anchor), and W. E. Houghton, *The Victorian Frame of Mind, 1830–1870* (*Yale Univ. Press). Informative introductions to the English literary scene.

C. M. Cipolla, *Literacy and Development in the West* (Penguin, 1969). On the expansion of the reading public.

J. Hillis Miller, *The Disappearance of God* (Belknap, 1963). A sensitive study of five nineteenth-century writers.

E. Wilson, *Axel's Castle* (*Scribner's). Stimulating study of imaginative literature in the late 1800s and early 1900s.

H. House, *The Dickens World,* 2nd ed. (Oxford Univ. Press, 1960). Excellent brief introduction.

F. Steegmuller, *Flaubert and Madame Bovary* (*Noonday). Illuminating portraits of the great French realist and his famous heroine.

H. Levin, *The Gates of Horn: A Study of Five French Realists* (Oxford Univ. Press, 1963). Scholarly assessments of Stendhal, Balzac, Flaubert, Zola, and Proust.

F. W. Hemmings, *Emile Zola* (*Oxford Univ. Press). Enlightening study of the man and his ideology.

C. Graña, *Modernity and Its Discontents* (*Torchbooks). The original title of this study—*Bohemian versus Bourgeois*—was more revealing; samples of bohemian abuse of the bourgeoisie are included.

H. Muchnic, *An Introduction to Russian Literature,* rev. ed. (Dutton, 1964). Helpful survey.

The Arts

G. H. Hamilton, *19th and 20th Century Art* (Abrams; Prentice-Hall, 1972). Encyclopaedic, copiously illustrated survey.

F. Novotny, *Painting and Sculpture in Europe, 1780–1880* (Penguin, 1960); H.-R. Hitchcock, *Architecture: The Nineteenth and Twentieth Centuries* (Penguin, 1958). Detailed and informative volumes in "The Pelican History of Art."

E. P. Richardson, *The Way of Western Art, 1776–1914* (Cooper Square, 1969). Helpful general survey.

J. Leymaire, *French Painting: The Nineteenth Century* (Skira, 1962). Well-illustrated survey down to the mid-1880s.

P. Courthion, *Impressionism* (Abrams). Well-illustrated introduction to the painters of light and color.

J. C. Sloane, *French Painting between Past and Present* (Princeton Univ. Press, 1951). Stressing the years 1818 to 1870, which marked "the birth of modern painting."

P. Schneider, *The World of Manet* (Time-Life Books, 1968); R. W. Murphy, *The World of Cézanne* (Time-Life Books, 1968). Very informative volumes relating key artists to the world around them.

Music

H. D. McKinney and W. R. Anderson, *Music in History,* 3rd ed. (American Book, 1966). Crisp and informative survey.

D. J. Grout, *A History of Western Music* (Norton, 1960). Another valuable introduction.

K. B. Klaus, *The Romantic Period in Music* (Allyn & Bacon, 1970). Organized by topic (melody, harmony, counterpoint, chamber music, vocal music) and goes down through the early 1900s.

Philosophy and Political Thought

W. L. Burn, *The Age of Equipoise* (*Norton). Stimulating study of the mid-Victorian intellectual climate.

W. M. Simon, *European Positivism in the Nineteenth Century* (Cornell Univ. Press, 1963). Scholarly assessment of Comte and his disciples.

F. E. Manuel, *The Prophets of Paris* (Harvard Univ. Press, 1962). Comte is the last of the five men treated in this informative study.

F. Meinecke, *Historism: The Rise of a New Historical Outlook* (Routledge, 1972). Translation of an important German study of historicism written in the 1930s.

G. Masur, *Prophets of Yesterday: Studies in European Culture, 1890–1914* (Macmillan, 1961), and H. S. Hughes, *Consciousness and Society: The Reorientation of European Social Thought, 1890–1930* (*Vintage). Two very suggestive studies of the twilight of the nineteenth century.

K. Löwith, *From Hegel to Nietzsche* (*Anchor). Analysis of the revolution in nineteenth-century thought, especially in Germany.

W. Kaufmann, *Nietzsche: Philosopher, Psychologist, Antichrist* (*Vintage). Widely considered the best book on the controversial German.

G. D. Charlton, *Secular Religions in France, 1815–1870* (Oxford Univ. Press, 1963). Interesting scholarly survey of surrogate religions.

H. D. Aiken, ed., *The Age of Ideology* (Mentor). Selections from nineteenth-century philosophers, with helpful introductory comments.

E. Bellamy, *Looking Backward, 2000–1887* (*several editions); H. G. Wells, *A Modern Utopia* (Scribner's, 1905); and W. Morris, *News from Nowhere* (Longmans, 1901). Three contrasting visions of utopia in the light of science and industrialism.

Novels and Dramas

Dickens, *Bleak House, Hard Times, Oliver Twist* (all *several editions).

Thackeray, *Vanity Fair* (*several editions).

Trollope, *Barchester Towers* (*several editions), *The Eustace Diamonds* (*Oxford Univ. Press), *The Way We Live Now* (*Bobbs Merrill).

Balzac, *Cousin Bette* (*Penguin), *Père Goriot & Eugénie Grandet* (*Modern Library).

Flaubert, *Madame Bovary* (*several editions).

Zola, *Germinal* (*Signet) and *L'Assommoir* (*Penguin).

Best Short Stories of Guy de Maupassant (*Airmont)

Ibsen, *Six Plays: A Doll's House, Ghosts, An Enemy of the People, Rosmersholm, Hedda Gabler, The Master Builder* (*Modern Library).

E. Brieux, *Damaged Goods,* preface by G. B. Shaw (Fifield, 1914).

G. B. Shaw, *Back to Methuselah, Man and Superman, Major Barbara, Heartbreak House* (all *Penguin).

24

Nineteenth-Century Imperialism

Introduction

New Elements in Imperialism

In the *Oxford English Dictionary,* which tries to find the earliest possible example of the use of a word, the editors can go no further back than 1881 for "imperialism: the principle of the spirit of empire; advocacy of what are held to be imperial interests." The word is relatively new; what it stands for is in part very old indeed—as old as human war and conquest. Yet there were some important new elements in the imperialism of Western peoples in the nineteenth century (again, the historian's century, 1815–1914). Imperialism was in almost every country a major part of political life, with goals, methods, and advocates known to all who were concerned with politics. And since by 1900 almost all of western and central Europe, the United States, and indeed all the outposts of European culture enjoyed high literacy and widespread public discussion, imperialism took its place with liberalism, conservatism, nationalism, socialism, and a host of other isms as a subject of universal debate. Today, less than a century after the heyday of this imperialism, none of the other great isms of the nineteenth century seems quite so outdated. "Imperialism" and its twentieth-century synonym, "colonialism," are scarcely ever employed except pejoratively.

Carefully defined, another element, the economic, may be said to distinguish the imperialism of the nineteenth century from earlier forms. The material, acquisitive motive runs through all forms of territorial expansion from prehistoric times to the present. It is clear in the earliest days of Spanish and Portuguese expansion in the quest for gold, silver, and profits. But, as the nineteenth century wore on, imperialist nations were responding to economic pressures in a new form. Liberal, and especially Marxist, economists and sociologists no doubt exaggerated this new element, but there is a basis of truth in their arguments.

According to these economic critics of imperialism, capitalists and industrialists in the older countries began to discover that they were unable to market at home all they could produce. But, being capitalists, they could not bring themselves to solve their difficulty by paying proportionately *less* of the total product of society in interest, dividends, and other payments to their own kind of people, the upper classes, and paying *more* in wages, pensions, bonuses, and the like to their workmen. Instead of sharing the wealth and creating at home the mass purchasing power and the mass market they needed, they preferred to turn to the non-Western world, to markets abroad, to the exploitation of dependent peoples. This attempt to bolster the capitalist system meant competition among the great Western industrial powers for land and peoples to exploit. In 1917 Lenin modified the left-wing argument in his *Imperialism, the Highest Stage of Capitalism* ("Imperialism as the Latest Stage of Capitalism" is an alternative translation of the title). Lenin stressed the capitalists' need to use the finance capital that was rapidly accumulating, rather than the need for markets. The great bankers, according to him, drove the willing politicians into the search for dependencies in which this available capital could be profitably invested, a search that marked what he termed the inevitable "last stage of capitalism."

A non-Marxist would of course call attention to the fact that the nineteenth-century colonial world produced raw materials and little else; the exchange of these for European and American manufactured goods was easy, "natural," and not yet held to be wicked or unfair to the colonial areas. Furthermore, as we have already seen, leading industrial powers in both America and Europe were experiencing an increasing demand for higher tariffs by the late 1800s. In the United States and Germany, and even in free-trading Britain, industrialists wanted protection against foreign competitors. This was an era of neomercantilism, reviving and streamlining the older mercantilist doctrines of Colbert and others. Colonies as well as tariffs entered into the strategy of the neomercantilists, as they had done in the case of the old.

The Powers and Areas Involved

The year 1870 is a convenient dividing line between the more active age of imperialism that was to come and the less active age that had preceded. The period from 1815 to 1870 saw a partial decline in imperialist fortunes, as most of Spain's American colonies gained their independence, and as Britain took the first steps leading to the virtual independence of Canada. In this same period, however, the French established themselves in Algeria, and the British extended their rule in India. The dividing line of 1870 does not mark a sharp break in the history of imperialism, but rather the acceleration of a movement that had never ceased.

The successful competitors in nineteenth-century imperialism, those who brought new lands under their flags, were Great Britain, which already in 1815 had a great empire, France, Germany, Italy, and the United States. Even little Belgium, itself a "new" nation in 1830, acquired a tremendous piece of tropical Africa, the Congo, 900,000 square miles in area in comparison to the homeland's 11,775 square miles. Russia did not expand overseas, and indeed parted with her vast but thinly inhabited possession in North America when the czarist government sold Alaska to the United States in 1867. But she began the effective settlement of the great areas east of the Urals and began to push into the borderlands of the Middle and Far East, toward Persia, India, and China. During the reign of Alexander II, for example, the Russians incorporated the formerly independent Turkish principalities in central Asia.

In the process of expansion, the expanding nations inevitably rubbed up against one another in all sorts of competition, from the economic to actual shooting war. Almost every great international conflict of the nineteenth century, save for the mid-century duels between Prussia and Austria and between Prussia and France, had a direct concern with imperialist rivalries outside Europe. Imperial competition is a complicated story, then, woven into the whole fabric of international relations in the nineteenth century. Before turning to the high points in the growth of the major empires over the century, we should note briefly the major areas of inter-European rivalries.

The Americas and the lands of the British Empire were, on the whole, outside the scramble. The Monroe Doctrine, toward which European nations were increasingly respectful as the strength of the United States increased, helped to keep both American continents free from further actual annexation by outside powers. So, too, did the British navy, for British policy was there to support the status quo. Toward the fateful year 1914, the competition between Britain and Germany for markets and for fields of investment in South America intensified and was one of the many factors that brought these powers to war. Since no state was strong enough to take from Britain her older colonies, throughout the nineteenth century British problems in both colonies of settlement and colonies of exploitation were essentially internal problems of the British system itself.

A major field of imperialist rivalry and penetration was the Near or Middle East, essentially the widespread territories under varying degrees of Turkish control, plus Persia. In earlier chapters we saw how the Balkans and the Straits became major issues in nineteenth-century diplomatic history. The whole Eastern Question, as it used to be called, revolved around the problem of what was to be done with these old territories, which were peopled principally by Muslims. They were backward regions by nineteenth-century Western standards, farmlands exhausted by centuries of primitive agriculture, mostly with poor rainfall, and with ancient irrigation systems often in disrepair. They were poor also in natural resources, for their great wealth in petroleum was not really known or very important until the twentieth century. England, France, Austria, and Russia were in active competition over the Near East early in the nineteenth century, and they were later joined by Italy and Germany.

Africa was the scene of the most spectacular imperial rivalry. In 1815, except for the nominally Turkish lands of North Africa, the little Dutch settlement at the Cape of Good Hope (taken over by the British in 1815), and a string of Portuguese, Spanish, French, and British "factories" or trading posts along the coasts, Africa was untenanted by Europeans and, in the interior, almost unexplored. It was inhabited by black peoples, long subjected to the horrors of the slave trade and often living at the level of primitive tribesmen. The slave trade was almost abolished in many areas by mid-century, and exploration was well under way. Then in the latter half of the century the great powers—Britain, France, and Germany—with Portugal, Italy, and Belgium tagging along, succeeded in blocking out in territorial units under their respective flags almost the whole of the continent. The only exceptions were the small Republic of Liberia, which had been set up by American antislavery groups as a land for emancipated black American slaves (though very few of them went there), and the mountainous and backward inland state of Abyssinia (now known as Ethiopia). Abyssinia, coveted by Italy, had a very narrow escape. In 1896, the Abyssinians, under their emperor Menelek and with French help, defeated an Italian army at Adowa and maintained their independence until the Italians tried again under Mussolini in 1935.

The Far East, too, was a major scene of imperialist rivalries. European powers strengthened their hold on older colonies and acquired new ones in Southeast Asia—the mainland areas of Burma, Indochina, and Malaya, and the island groups of Melanesia and Polynesia. But the ancient, thickly populated, highly civilized Chinese Empire was never subjected, as was Africa, to actual partition and direct annexation. China was, however, not well enough organized politically or industrially to stand up against European penetration and was by the end of the century subjected to a rough, de facto partitioning among Britain, France, Germany, and Russia. Each power, operating from certain "treaty ports" as centers, was able to exercise a degree of control—basically economic—over considerable areas, "spheres of influence" as they were called. Rivalry among these European powers, and the rising power of the United States, which was exercised in favor of the Open Door policy of permitting as much free trade in China as was possible and of preserving Chinese sovereignty, served to counterbalance Chinese weakness and kept China throughout this period on the list of independent nations.

Finally, Japan kept herself isolated from the rest of the world for two centuries, from the mid-seventeenth to the mid-nineteenth. This compact island empire was closed to foreigners during the period when the European powers slowly strengthened their small holds in China. Then in 1853 the American naval officer Perry induced Japan to open her ports to outside trade. By adopting some Western ways, particularly economic ways, Japan was able not merely to preserve her real independence during the late nineteenth century but actually to begin her own imperial expansion on the mainland of Asia after winning a brief war with China in 1894–1895. Japan was thus the first modern nation-state in the Far East.

II   The British Empire

We may now move on through the imperial record, country by country. Nineteenth-century Britain retained and, with the help of emigrants from the mother country, developed the great areas that were suitable to white colonization—Canada, Australia and New Zealand, and South Africa. This section focuses on Britain's imperial possessions in Africa and Asia. The development of self-government in Canada, Australia, and New Zealand will come more appropriately at the close of this chapter, in our survey of the results of nineteenth-century imperialism.

South Africa

In 1815, Britain had just acquired Cape Colony at the southern tip of Africa from the Netherlands. Cape Colony was inhabited by a few Dutch and French Huguenot colonists and was suited, in spite of a relatively low rainfall, to European living. As Britishers moved in, the older colonists, known in their own Dutch vernacular as Boers, grew more and more discontented. The adoption of English as the sole official language, the abolition of slavery throughout the empire in 1834, the attempts of the government at London

to protect the native blacks, and other measures of Victorian liberalism went against the grain of the patriarchal Boers, who were fundamentalist Christians for whom slavery was ordained of God and for whom liberalism was the work of the devil. Between 1835 and 1837, some ten thousand Boers moved north overland into country sparsely settled by primitive black tribes in the Great Trek, a heroic folk migration that bulks even larger in South African nationalist feeling than do the comparable sagas of covered-wagon days in American tradition. After some confused three-cornered fighting among Boers, British, and native Zulus, the Boers established two virtually independent states—the Transvaal and the Orange Free State. Well inland, on territory suitable for grazing but not for intensive agriculture, these thinly populated states lived on for a time hardly noticed by the outside world.

The British in South Africa noticed them, of course, and many of the British wished to add these lands directly to the empire. They settled from the sea another British province to the east, along the Indian Ocean side, known as Natal. In the course of the century, Cape Colony and Natal, which together had a black population heavily outnumbering the British and remaining Boers combined, acquired the self-governing rights that British colonies of settlement in Canada, Australia, and New Zealand were also acquiring. British South African leaders for the most part wanted to bring the Boer republics under the British flag. But as the London home government swung between Tory and Liberal domination, it also swung between a policy of imperialist expansion and the "Little Englander" policy of leaving the Trekkers alone. In 1852, by the Sand River Convention, the British under a Liberal cabinet acknowledged the independence of Transvaal; soon thereafter they also acknowledged that of Orange Free State. But in 1877 under Disraeli and the Conservatives they reversed themselves and annexed Transvaal as a step toward the federation of all South Africa under the British crown. The Boers revolted in 1880 and the Liberal Gladstone, then in power, lived up to his principles by making at Pretoria in 1881 a treaty with the Boers which reestablished Transvaal as independent, though under the "suzerainty" of Great Britain.

The British were already filtering up through the semidesert country to the west of the Boer republics when the discovery of gold and the development of the diamond industry in these republics undid Gladstone's work. The Transvaal was no longer just a poor and isolated grazing country; it offered a great source of wealth that tempted quite different kinds of settlers. The region about Johannesburg, the famous Rand, filled up with adventurers and entrepreneurs of a dozen nations, all looking to Britain to protect them from the conservative Boers, to whom they were undesirable *Uitlanders* ("outlanders," "foreigners").

The inevitable conflict came to a head with the Jameson Raid of December 29, 1895—midsummer in South Africa. The British in South Africa were now

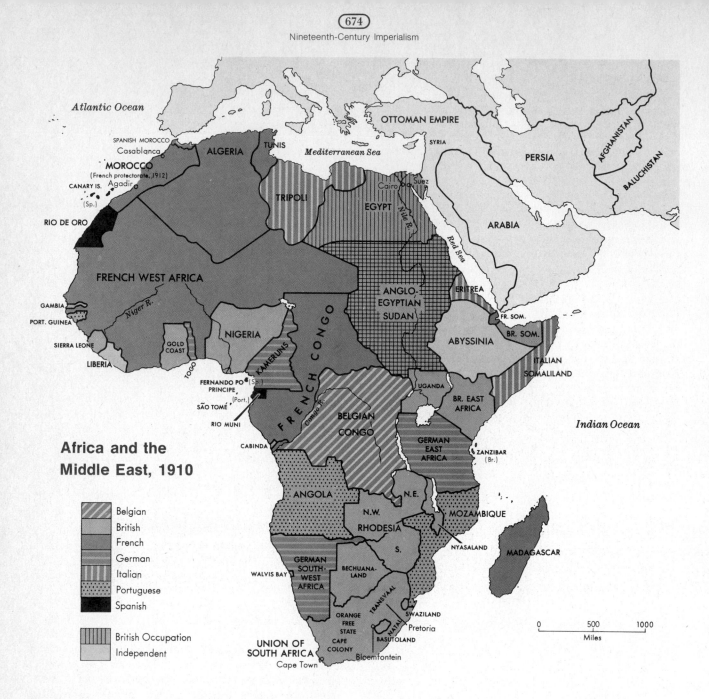

Africa and the Middle East, 1910

Belgian
British
French
German
Italian
Portuguese
Spanish

British Occupation
Independent

under the leadership of Cecil Rhodes, prime minister of Cape Colony, a determined and articulate imperialist who had made a quick fortune consolidating the chaotic diamond industry. The raid itself, under a follower of Rhodes, Dr. Jameson, was an invasion of Transvaal from British territory to the west, and was planned to coincide with a rising of Uitlanders in Johannesburg. But the rising did not take place, and the president of Transvaal, Kruger, had no trouble in defeating Jameson's handful of invaders. The famous "Kruger telegram," in which the German kaiser congratulated the Boer president, was one of the critical steps in sharpening the Anglo-German rivalry that helped lead to world war in 1914. Its immediate effect in South Africa was to harden Boer resistance and bring about

open war between Britain and the two Boer republics in 1899.

The war, following the pattern of British wars in modern times, went badly at first for the British. They did not have enough troops immediately available to put down determined men who were fighting on their own ground and were accustomed to the rigors of outdoor life. Western opinion, including opinion in the United States, generally sided with the underdog Boers, and in Britain itself many Liberals and Labourites strongly opposed the war as rank imperialism. But in the long run the overwhelming strength of the British prevailed. By the middle of 1900 the British had won in the field, but they needed another eighteen months to subdue the desperate guerrilla bands into which Boer opposition dissolved. In 1902, by the Treaty of Vereeniging, the Boers accepted British rule, with the promise of ultimate self-government. This promise the British fulfilled speedily. In 1910 there came into being a Union of South Africa, linking Cape Colony, Transvaal, Orange Free State, and Natal. The seat of the legislature was in the first, at Capetown; that of the executive in the second, at Pretoria; and that of the judiciary in the third, at Bloemfontein. In the new state the central government was stronger than the provinces; English and Afrikaans, as the South African Dutch dialect had come to be called, were set up as equally official languages.

On the eve of World War I, South Africa was among the self-governing British dominions. British and Boer seemed to be well on the way to composing their long quarrel and to be ready to collaborate in developing an increasingly important outpost of the West. But there were ominous signs even then. The Boers had by no means been anglicized, and they were still fundamentally opposed to their partners in empire. And the two European elements together were in a minority of one to four as compared with the non-Europeans—the native blacks, the East Indians (who had come in numbers as immigrants, especially to Natal), and the "colored" peoples of mixed blood. The seeds of the later troubles in South Africa were clearly present even in the hopeful days immediately after the establishment of the Union.

Egypt

At the opposite end of Africa, Britain during the second half of the nineteenth century excluded the French from control of Egypt, a semi-independent province of the crumbling Ottoman Empire. French influence had continued there, even after the collapse of Napoleon's venture and the setback suffered in 1840 by Muhammad Ali, the ambitious viceroy of Egypt and protégé of France. In the third quarter of the nineteenth century, French prospects in Egypt seemed particularly bright. Between 1859 and 1869 a private French company headed by Ferdinand de Lesseps built the Suez Canal, which united the Mediterranean with the Red Sea and shortened the sea trip from Europe to India and the Far East by thousands of miles. The British had bitterly opposed the building of this canal under French patronage; but now that it was finished, the canal came to be considered an essential part of the lifeline of the British Empire.

The British secured a partial hold over this lifeline in 1875, when Disraeli arranged the purchase of 176,000 shares of stock in the canal company from the financially desperate khedive Ismail (1863–1879), the grandson of Muhammad Ali. The shares gave Britain a very large minority interest in the company, though not a controlling one. Despite the sale of the stock, Ismail's fiscal difficulties soon increased, for he was a heavy spender, partly on useful public improvements

Cecil Rhodes.

and partly on vainglorious items like the new title of khedive (Persian for "prince"), which the Ottoman emperor granted for a stiff price. In 1876, with Ismail's bankruptcy threatening, the European powers from whose private banks Ismail had borrowed large sums at high interest obliged Egypt to accept the financial guidance of a debt commission that they set up.

Two years later, he had to sacrifice still more sovereignty when he was obliged to appoint an Englishman as his minister of finance and a Frenchman as minister of public works to ensure that his foreign creditors had first claim to his government's revenues. In 1879 Ismail himself was sacrificed when his creditors prevailed on the Ottoman emperor to depose him. Egyptian nationalists, led by army officers whose pay had been drastically cut as an economy move, now revolted both against foreign control and against the government that had made this control possible. Both Britain and France threatened to intervene with force, but when

President Theodore Roosevelt on a steam shovel in Panama during the construction of the canal.

"Moses in Egypt": a Tenniel cartoon of 1875 commenting on Disraeli's purchase of Ismail's interest in the Suez Canal. The title is borrowed from that of Rossini's opera.

an antiforeign riot in Alexandria claimed some European lives in the summer of 1882, the French held back because of a cabinet crisis at home and also because they were involved in establishing themselves in Tunisia, occupied the year before.

These events constituted one of those "fits of absence of mind" through which Britain enlarged her empire. By the eve of World War I she exercised virtual sovereignty over Egypt. Legally Egypt was still part of the Ottoman Empire, and the khedive and his government remained. But a British Resident was always at hand to exercise quiet but firm control, and each ministry was guided by a British expert. For a quarter of a century this British protectorate was in the hands of the famous imperial proconsul, Lord Cromer, Resident in Cairo from 1883 to 1907. Under Cromer and his successors the enormous government debt was systematically paid off and a beginning made at modernizing Egypt, symbolized by the completion of the first dam on the Nile at Aswan, which increased the amount of water for irrigation and thus the potential agricultural output. But nationalist critics complained that this was too small a beginning, that too little was being spent on education and public health, and that British policy was designed to keep Egypt in a colonial economic status, exporting long-staple cotton and procuring manufactured goods not from home industries but from Britain. Egyptian nationalists were also offended by British tentativeness in permitting experiments in representative government and by British policy toward the Sudan.

This vast region, south of Egypt, today the largest of African states in area, had been partially conquered by Muhammad Ali and Ismail, then lost in the 1880s as a result of a revolt by an Islamic leader who called himself the mahdi (messiah). Fears that France or some other power might gain control over the Nile headwaters vital to Egypt decided Britain to reconquer the Sudan. The reconquest was completed in 1898, just in time for the British commander, Kitchener, to march south from Khartoum, the Sudanese capital, and confront a French expedition that had traveled from the Atlantic coast of Africa and reached Fashoda on the upper Nile. Again the French could not press their claim, this time because the uproar over Dreyfus was at its peak, and the British made the Sudan an Anglo-Egyptian condominium, an enterprise in which they clearly intended to function as the senior partner. Egyptian nationalists feared that Egypt had lost a province, while Britain had gained one more possession and a vital link in their dream of an "all-red route" from Cairo to the Cape.

Other British Colonies and Spheres of Influence

In between the Cape and Cairo the British pieced out their African possessions throughout the century. At its end, they had the lion's share of the continent. They had only four million square miles out of over eleven million, but they controlled sixty-one million poeple out of some one hundred million. A mere listing of these holdings would be a dull and unenlightening catalog. They can be found, usually colored red, in any good atlas of the turn of the century and, also with British possessions colored in red, on a famous Canadian postage stamp of 1898. A good sample of these colonies is Nigeria, in which the great administrator Sir Frederick (later Lord) Lugard worked out the characteristic British method of colonial government in tropical Africa that was known as indirect rule.

The colony and protectorate of Nigeria, centering around the great river Niger, was formally put together from earlier west African colonies in 1914. Northern Nigeria was ruled by Muslim emirs of the Fulani people whose culture was superior to that of the subject and exploited blacks; southern Nigeria was inhabited by numerous heathen tribes that had long been harassed by slave raids. The British had first to subject the Fulani by force, a process that was completed late in the nineteenth century.

They then applied, as a French statesman put it, "with method but not with system," what came to be called indirect rule. Emirs and tribal chieftains were confirmed in their separate rules, subject to the banning of internal warfare, the abolition of slavery, and similar measures imposed from above. A British Resident supervised the rule of the leading chiefs, with district residents (later commissioners) to supplement the work in the local subdivisions. But native law, native religion, and native traditions, insofar as they did not conflict violently with Western standards, were carefully maintained. The British staff was never large; Lugard complained that in 1903 he had only one British administrator on the average for every 400,000 natives. But somehow the handful of imperial officials were able to ensure the peace. Slowly, much too slowly for impatient idealists, railroads, roads, improved agriculture, commerce, and education—the externals at least of Western civilization—were extended to Nigeria. Early in this century the first black African students began to appear in British universities.

Ideally, this method of rule would eventually bring the great material and spiritual benefits of Western civilization to the natives without destroying their own centuries-long development, without trying to make them over into Europeans. In practice, although material progress had been marked by 1914, the transition from primitive to modern ways of life had been but spottily achieved. A black elite had been developed far beyond the capacity of the great mass of the natives to follow them. But Lugard's achievements were great. The following passages from his book, *The Dual Mandate in British Tropical Africa*, show the spirit with which he approached his work, and notably his defense against the charge of Christian missionaries who held that he unduly restricted their activities:

Bishop Tugwell, whose long and faithful service in West

Africa has chiefly lain in the coast area and its immediate hinterland, writes: '"Indirect rule" is direct rule by indirect means. The Emir's position and salary are secure. His sway, backed by British authority, is rendered absolute, while his people become his serfs, or those of the British Government. Their life is thus robbed of all initiative or desire for progress—intellectual, social, moral, religious, or political.' The Emir, he adds, who is appointed by the Government, is the instrument of the Resident, and 'the name of Christ must not be proclaimed lest this blighting system should be overturned.' . . . Bishop Tugwell, unconsciously perhaps, gives imperfect expression to an aspect of the matter on which I have already touched. It was naturally a cause for anxiety and misgiving that the British Government, by supporting native rule, and the authority of the native courts, should accept some measure of responsibility for evils which its meagre staff of British officials was unable to control adequately. . . . To overthrow an organisation, however faulty, which has the sanction of long usage, and is acquiesced in by the people, before any system could be created to take its place—before, indeed, we had any precise knowledge of Moslem methods or of native law and custom—would have been an act of folly which no sane administrator could attempt. The very necessity for avoiding precipitate action, and the knowledge that reform could only be effective, and enlist native cooperation, if it was gradual, made the responsibility all the more onerous. To infer that it was not realised, or was lightly regarded, is to do a great injustice to the administrative staff of the early Government of Northern Nigeria. . . .

. . . .

The object of substituting for British rule, in which the chiefs are mere agents of the Government, a system of native rule under the guidance and control of the British staff, whether among advanced or backward communities, is primarily educative. Among backward tribes the chiefs have to learn how to exert and maintain authority, and establish a chain of responsibility reaching down to the village head. Among the more advanced their interest is directed to education, forestry, sanitation, prevention of disease, and public works. In all alike the endeavour is to prevent denationalisation, to develop along indigenous lines, to inculcate the principle that the function of the ruler is to promote the welfare of his people and not to exploit them for his own pleasure, and to afford both to rulers and people the stimulus of progress and interest in life.*

In the Americas, Britain maintained her colonial dependencies in the Caribbean, in Bermuda and the Bahamas, and on the mainland, in British Honduras and British Guiana. Limited self-government of the seventeenth-century kind, which some of them had lost in the mid-nineteenth century, was only gradually granted them in the twentieth. These were all tropical or semitropical lands, with a relatively small planter class and with large black or mixed lower classes. They suffered gradual impoverishment as a result of economic developments, notably the great competition

*F. D. Lugard, *The Dual Mandate in British Tropical Africa* (Edinburgh and London, 1923), pp. 223–224, 228–229.

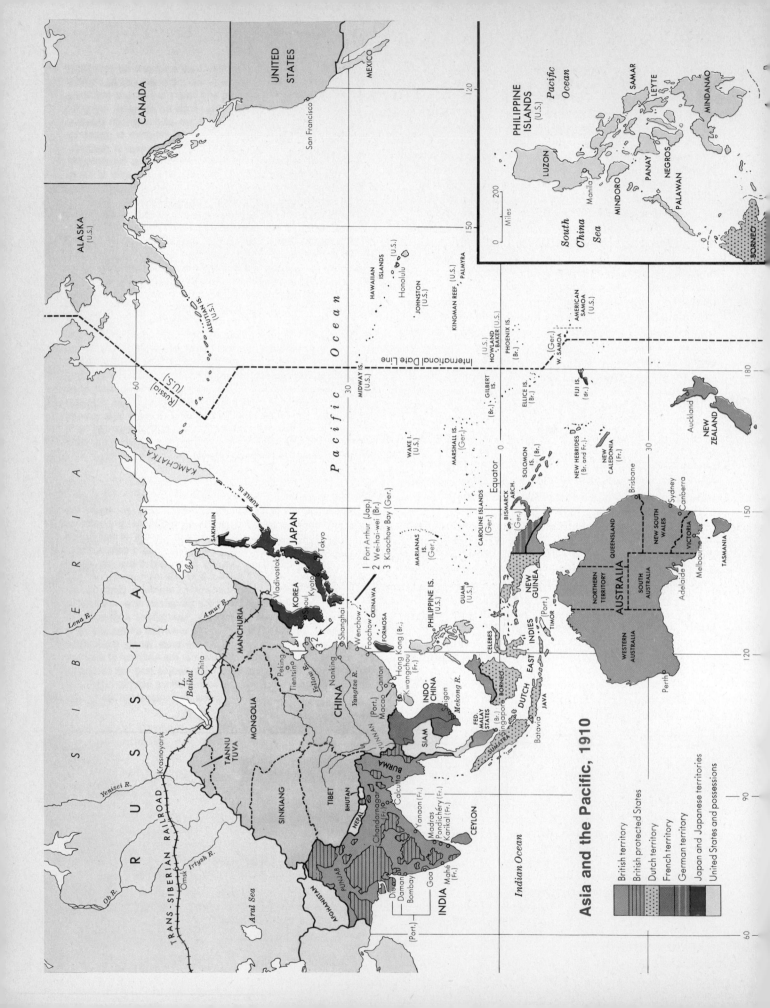

Asia and the Pacific, 1910

British territory
British protected States
Dutch territory
French territory
German territory
Japan and Japanese territories
United States and possessions

CANADA

UNITED STATES

MEXICO

120

ALASKA
(U.S.)

ALEUTIAN IS.
(U.S.)

60

(Russia)
(U.S.)

150

San Francisco

Pacific Ocean

HAWAIIAN ISLANDS
(U.S.)

Honolulu

JOHNSTON
(U.S.)

KINGMAN REEF (U.S.)   PALMYRA

30

MIDWAY IS.
(U.S.)

WAKE I.
(U.S.)

MARSHALL IS.
(Ger.)

HOWLAND
BAKER (U.S.)

PHOENIX IS.
(Br.)

AMERICAN
SAMOA
(U.S.)

(Ger.)
W. SAMOA

International Date Line

GILBERT
IS. (Br.)

ELLICE IS.
(Br.)

FIJI IS.
(Br.)

180

S I B E R I A

KAMCHATKA

KURILE IS.

Lena R.

Amur R.

L. Baikal

Chita

R U S S I A

Yenisei R.

Ob R.

Irtysh R.

Omsk

Krasnoyarsk

TRANS-SIBERIAN RAILROAD

Aral Sea

AFGHANISTAN

SINKIANG

TANNU
TUVA

MONGOLIA

TIBET

BHUTAN

NEPAL

INDIA

[Port.]
Diu
Daman
Goa
Bombay
Mahé (Fr.)

Madras
Pondichéry (Fr.)
Karikal (Fr.)
Yanaon (Fr.)
Chandannagar (Fr.)
Calcutta

PUNJAB

CEYLON

CHINA

Peking
Tientsin
Yellow R.
Nanking
Yangtze R.

MANCHURIA

Vladivostok

KOREA
Seoul
Kyoto
Tokyo

JAPAN

SAKHALIN

1 Port Arthur (Jap.)
2 Wei-hai-wei (Br.)
3 Kiaochow Bay (Ger.)

1
2
3

Shanghai

Wenchow

Foochow
OKINAWA
FORMOSA

Hong Kong (Br.)
Kwangchou (Fr.)
Canton
Macao (Port.)
YUNNAN

INDO-CHINA

Saigon
Mekong R.

SIAM

BURMA

FED.
MALAY
STATES

Singapore (Br.)

SUMATRA

DUTCH EAST INDIES

Batavia
JAVA
BORNEO
(Br.)

CELEBES

TIMOR
(Port.)

MARIANAS
IS. (Ger.)

GUAM
(U.S.)

PHILIPPINE IS.
(U.S.)

CAROLINE ISLANDS
(Ger.)

Equator
0

SOLOMON
IS. (Br.)

BISMARCK
ARCH.
(Ger.)

**NEW
GUINEA**

NEW HEBRIDES
(Br. and Fr.)

NEW
CALEDONIA
(Fr.)

30

Pacific Ocean

Brisbane

Sydney
Canberra
VICTORIA
Melbourne

AUSTRALIA

QUEENSLAND

NEW SOUTH
WALES

NORTHERN
TERRITORY

SOUTH
AUSTRALIA

WESTERN
AUSTRALIA

Perth

Adelaide

TASMANIA

Auckland

**NEW
ZEALAND**

Indian Ocean

150

120

90

60

Inset map

Pacific Ocean

**PHILIPPINE
ISLANDS**
(U.S.)

LUZON

Manila

MINDORO

PANAY

NEGROS

PALAWAN

MINDANAO

SAMAR

LEYTE

South China Sea

BORNEO

0   200
Miles

120

offered to the staple cane sugar of the region by the growth in temperate climates of the beet-sugar industry, together with an increase in population beyond the limited resources of the region. By 1914, the British West Indies had already become an impoverished "problem area."

In the Pacific and in Southeast Asia, Britain in the nineteenth century added some red dots on the map of her empire, and especially in Malaya she developed the great rubber plantations and tin mines that were to be major factors in her economy after World War I. She took an important part in the process of opening China to Western trade by means of treaty-port concessions and spheres of influence. Indeed, Britain took one of the great steps in countering Chinese attempts to keep off the foreigner, for in 1841 she waged what has come to be called invidiously but not unjustly the Opium War. This war was brought on by a Chinese attempt to control the opium trade in which British merchants had an important stake. By the Treaty of Nanking in 1842, Britain acquired Hong Kong and secured the opening of five ports, including Canton and Shanghai.

India

In China, however, Britain was but one, though the most important, of the great powers scrambling for empire in that densely peopled land. In India her victory over France in 1763, confirmed by her victory in 1815, left her in sole control over a subcontinent of Asia. The remnants of French and Portuguese possessions there hardly counted, and the island of Ceylon off the southern tip of India passed from Dutch to British control as a result of the French Revolutionary and Napoleonic wars. India was the richest of Britain's overseas possessions, the center and symbol of empire, as the imaginative Disraeli realized when in 1876 he had Queen Victoria proclaimed empress of India.

In 1763, India was already a great and well-peopled land, but not, in the Western sense, a single *nation*. It was a vast congeries of races and religions, ranging from the most cultivated and philosophic Brahmins to the most primitive tribesmen, still in the Stone Age. As the nineteenth century began, the two main methods of British control had already become clear. The richest and most densely populated regions, centering on the cities of Calcutta, Madras, and Bombay and on the Punjab, were maintained under direct British control. The British government did not originally annex these lands; they were first administered as the property, so to speak, of the English East India Company, a chartered enterprise surviving from the great days of mercantilism in the seventeenth and eighteenth centuries. The company in its heyday, led by empire makers like Clive and Warren Hastings, had taken on enormous territories and made treaties like a sovereign power. Hastings was prosecuted for "high crimes and misdemeanors" in a famous trial of the late

British and Sikh leaders at the Lahore Durbar meeting, December 1846, which led to the British annexation of the Punjab: contemporary Sikh gouache.

eighteenth century. But what he acquired the British kept.

In the nineteenth century, the company was regarded by most economists and political thinkers as a shocking anomaly, and the India Office of the central government in London gradually took over the real control and administration of British India. The trading monopoly of the company had long since been undermined. In 1857, the company's native army of Sepoys rebelled. As usual in such major uprisings, the rebellion was brought on by a number of causes, fed by rumors that bullets issued to soldiers were coated with grease made from beef fat, repugnant to Hindus, or from pork fat, repugnant to Muslims. But the basic cause was that all the soldiers had come to fear that British ways were being imposed on them to the destruction of their own ways. The Sepoy Rebellion was put down, but not before several massacres of Europeans had occurred, and not without a serious military effort by the British. The mutiny meant the end of the English East India Company. In 1858, the British crown took over the company's lands and obligations, announcing that no further annexations were sought in India.

The rest of India—roughly a third of its area and a fourth or a fifth of its population—came to be known as the "feudal" or "native" states. These were left nominally under the rule of their own princes, who might be the fabulously rich sultan of Hyderabad or the gaekwar of Baroda, or merely a kind of local chieftain. The "native" states were actually governed by a system of British Residents somewhat like the system we have just seen in Nigeria. The India Office never hesitated to interfere with the succession, or to disallow acts of princes, who were frequently irresponsible and extravagant, or even to assume direct rule for a time when it was thought necessary. The "native" states add many picturesque notes to a detailed history of India, but in the long run the distinction between direct and indirect rule in India did not mean very much in practice.

The years between 1763 and 1919 in India are a fascinating record of what Arnold Toynbee, the philosopher of history, calls "contacts between civilizations." Indeed, anyone who wants to understand the great contemporary problem of relations between the West and the rest of the world—to use clear terms, between white peoples and yellow, brown, or black peoples—will do well to learn all he can of this great meeting of East and West in the subcontinent of India.

In material terms, many phases of the British rule in India are readily measurable. In 1864, the British *Statesman's Year Book* gave the population of India as about 136,000,000 and in 1904 close to 300,000,000. Although the latter figure includes additional territories, in Burma and elsewhere, it is clear that nineteenth-century India experienced a significant increase in total population. In 1901, one male out of ten could read and write, a low rate of literacy by Western standards, but already a high one by contemporary Asian standards. It is characteristic of Indian society that the comparable figures for women in the same census of 1901 show that only one out of one hundred and fifty could read and write.

Such statistics are plentiful, and what they show is an India on the eve of World War I with thousands of miles of railroads, telegraph lines, universities (teaching in English), hospitals, factories, and great and busy seaports. But, in proportion to the total population, India did not have these advantages to anything like the extent that even the poorest of European countries had them. Statistics show a native ruling class sometimes fantastically rich, and an immense peasant class for the most part living as their ancestors had lived, on the edge of starvation. A middle class was just beginning to form, and like all the middle classes formed in non-European lands under European penetration, it had proportionately far more aspirants to genteel white-collar posts in law, medicine, and other liberal professions than to posts in commerce, engineering, and industry, to say nothing of scientific research.

The total wealth of India certainly increased under British rule in this century and a half, and in 1914 it was spread more widely among the Indian populations, save for the most primitive areas, than it had been in 1763. Proportionately less and less wealth went directly from an "exploited" India to an "exploiting" Britain. The familiar Englishman of the seventeenth and eighteenth centuries, the "nabob" who made a fortune in India and retired with it to comfort, and perhaps to a peerage, in England almost ceased to exist as the nineteenth century wore on. Anglo-Indian economic relations took on more and more the form of trade between a developed industrial and financial society in Britain and a society geared to the production of raw materials—we should now call it an "underdeveloped" society—in India. In this trade, native Indians took an increasing part if only as middlemen, and toward the

end of the century native industries, notably textile manufacturing, financed for the most part with British capital, began to arise in India.

Throughout the century, of course, a large number of British—small in proportion to the total population, but numbering in the thousands—were basically supported by the Indian economy; they "lived off India." Some of them were private businessmen, but the greater number were military and civilian workers, the latter the celebrated Indian civil service who "ran" India. Yet natives were gradually working their way into positions of greater responsibility, into both private and public posts at the policy-making level.

Of this British ruling class in India one very important fact is now plain. It did not, like the English and Scots who went to Ireland in early modern times, really take root in India. Britain—one must be careful not to say "England," for the Scots played a conspicuous role in India as they did throughout the empire—was always home, always the place where one hoped to end one's days. Though son not infrequently followed father in the Indian army or civil service, or even in business, these "sahibs" as a whole never became fully adjusted to life in India. The spiritual climate was perhaps an even greater barrier than the physical climate. Here is a letter from an Englishwoman in Madras in 1837:

> It is wonderful how little interested most of the English ladies seem by all the strange habits and ways of the natives; and it is not merely that they have grown used to it all, but that, by their own accounts, they never cared more about what goes on around them than they do now. I can only suppose they have forgotten their first impressions. But this makes me wish to try and see everything that I can while the bloom of my Orientalism is fresh upon me, and before this apathy and listlessness have laid hold on me, as no doubt they will.

> I asked one lady what she had seen of the country and the natives since she had been in India. 'Oh, nothing!' said she: 'thank goodness, I know nothing at all about them, nor I don't wish to: really I think the less one sees and knows of them the better!'

The natives, too, often found the gap between East and West too great to be bridged. Another Englishwoman writes in 1913:

> Coming home we saw a native cooking his dinner on a little charcoal fire, and as I passed he threw the contents of the pot away. Surprised, I asked why. "Because," I was told, "your shadow fell on it and defiled it!"*

Yet the work of raising the economic basis of Indian life was in large part the work of the British. They were often overbearing, insensitive, white men at their worst in their dealings with the natives. But they were, more often than the doctrinaire anti-imperialist will admit, men devoted to the task of bettering the lot of

*H. Brown, ed., *The Sahibs* (London, 1948), pp. 225, 230.

their charges, men who made a real effort to understand them. Some of them applied Western scholarly methods to the study of Indian culture and society, thus laying the foundations on which Indian scholars now build.

III   The Other Empires

The French

The British victory in the "Second Hundred Year's War," capped by their defeat of Napoleon in 1815, had stripped France of all but insignificant remnants of her former empire. Yet during the nineteenth century France succeeded in building up a new colonial empire second in area only to that of the British. France, despite her frequent revolutionary changes in government, maintained an imperialist policy that added in the century before 1914 close to three and a half million square miles to the lands under the French flag, and some fifty million people, almost all non-European. The figures for area are somewhat misleading, for a million and a half square miles represent the virtually uninhabited Sahara Desert.

Little of this second French colonial empire was suitable for settlement by Europeans. The great exception was French North Africa, including Tunisia, Algeria, and Morocco. As the provinces of Africa and Mauretania, these lands were once flourishing parts of the Roman Empire; after France took them over, they reached a greater degree of material prosperity than they had enjoyed for nearly eighteen centuries. These lands, which have a typically Mediterranean climate, were inhabited chiefly by Berber and Arab peoples of Muslim faith. Though the total native population increased greatly under French rule, something over a million European colonists moved in. In majority French, but with sizable groups of Italians and Spaniards, these *colons* took some land from the natives, though they added to the total arable acreage by initiating irrigation projects and other improvements. They remained, however, an alien group.

The French got a toehold in North Africa in 1830 through an expedition against the Algerian pirates, with whose Tripolitan counterparts, incidentally, the United States had fought in 1801. The French stayed on, and it took them forty years to pacify the hinterland of Algiers in the face of stubborn native resistance. They added protectorates over Tunisia to the east (1881) and over Morocco to the west (1912). In 1904 Britain gave the French a free hand in Morocco as compensation for their exclusion from Egypt.

Especially in Algeria and Tunisia, the French promoted European settlement while trying not to antagonize the natives. They called their policy one of "assimilation," in contrast with the British policy of hands off and indirect rule. They hoped, they explained, to assimilate Africans into French civilization, making them ultimately into good children of the eighteenth-century Enlightenment, good citizens of the republic founded on the principles of 1789. They hoped to create an empire of "100,000,000 Frenchmen," more than half of them overseas, and to draw on abundant native manpower to fill up the ranks of the republic's armies.

In the military sense, the policy of assimilation worked out somewhat as the French had hoped, and black troops from Senegal and *goums* from North Africa gained a reputation as tough fighters. In the main, however, assimilation proved difficult and was only partially successful. The French, always desirous of spreading their culture, did assimilate part of the native ruling classes. Under the Third Republic they made Algeria politically a part of France itself, organizing it into three departments and giving them representatives to the Chamber of Deputies, with a franchise open to the relatively small group of europeanized natives as well as to colons. In Morocco, the French took a somewhat different tack. They sought, in part successfully, to open this backward land to French business and to the international tourist trade. Their urban center of Casablanca became a great modern city. And, without quite admitting the fact, they really abandoned assimilation for something close to the British policy of indirect rule. In 1912, the very able colonial administrator Marshal Lyautey began to organize turbulent Morocco, applying the "splash of oil" policy—that is, he pacified certain key centers by establishing firm working relations with the natives and then let pacification spread over the surface of Morocco like a splash of oil on water. The sultan and his feudal subordinates were maintained in Morocco, relatively free to carry on many of their age-old ways but stripped of real power. Tunisia, like Morocco, was formally a protectorate (technically, a regency). Because Tunisia was small and easily pacified, assimilation worked more successfully there than it did in other French possessions, thereby giving the Tunisians a head start in modernization when France relinquished her North African empire.

In 1815, the British had left France her small posts in West Africa at the mouth of the Senegal River, together with the slight foothold France had obtained in the seventeenth century on the great island of Madagascar off the East African coast. By 1914, the French had been very successful in the partition of Africa, perhaps because the British preferred French to German aggrandizement, especially after 1870. Today, the former colonies of French West Africa comprise eight separate independent states, those of the French Congo, four.

By 1914 France numbered in Africa alone nearly as many inhabitants as in her home territories (about thirty-nine million). Yet outside of North Africa, these people were almost all blacks of primitive material culture, and although some of them had accepted Christianity or Islam, their orthodoxy was often diluted by pagan survivals. Except in certain coastal towns, where their administration and business enterprises were concentrated, the French had not by 1914 achieved very much toward assimilating or westernizing these vast districts. Most of their attempts to hasten the economic development of their African lands by organized joint-stock companies failed miserably.

It is quite possible that France spent more on these African colonies than she gained from them. Indeed, one of the stock arguments of nineteenth-century anti-imperialists was that colonies did not "pay" the mother country, and the French African colonies were one of their favorite exhibits. One economist—an Englishman, to be sure, and presumably unmoved by much that moves Frenchmen—concluded that in 1892 French gains from colonial trade were 16,000,000 francs, whereas net government expenditures for the colonies were 174,000,000 francs. For 1915, he made an even more discouraging estimate.* Such figures, however, seem not to have discouraged any of the great powers in their imperialist efforts. Obviously the simplest form of the economic interpretation of history, the notion that political entities are moved by simple bookkeeping concepts of governmental economic profit and loss, does not hold true for nineteenth-century imperialism. Furthermore, note that such statistics apply solely to government expenditures; many French private businessmen undoubtedly made money out of their colonial ventures.

Again, though French colonies in tropical Africa had by no means been modernized even in material conditions by 1914, everywhere a beginning had been made. Everywhere the tricolor went, there also went the beginnings of medicine and hygiene, modern methods of communication, industry, and agriculture, and formal education for at least a few natives. In justifying the policy of assimilation, the French claimed for themselves, in contrast with the British, a lack of race prejudice, a willingness to accept the blacks as equals. This contrast is underlined by the English economist whose figures we have just quoted:

> Of course, it is true that the French also attempt to understand the native and in the main to give him freedom to produce as he pleases. The Frenchman actually tends much more to be a "good fellow" with the natives than does the Briton, who is much more aloof. But this greater democracy does not seem to inspire a greater degree of confidence. Somehow, the Briton is more apt to succeed in instilling in the native confidence in the results of producing by the system that he recommends.†

Although there is some truth in the claim for greater French toleration, the deed is not quite up to the word. The French in Africa did not often marry blacks; but intermarriage is in this real world an unreal test of racial equality. Blacks very rarely commanded white Frenchmen in military or civilian activity. Both at home and in Africa, on the other hand, once the blacks seemed firmly under control, the French went

a long way toward encouraging black arts and folkways, in keeping with a policy very close to the ideal delineated by Lugard for Nigeria. The British, however, especially in the twentieth century, edged toward some kind of assimilation; black African undergraduates in British universities took on a lot more of Britishness than just their fine standard English accent. The contrast between British and French African policies was far from complete—there were many similarities.

In Asia, the French took over in the nineteenth century lands that came to be called French Indochina. These lands included two rich rice-growing deltas (around Hanoi in the north and Saigon in the south), inhabited by peoples culturally and in part racially related to the Chinese. They also included Cambodia, culturally related to India, and the primitive mountain peoples of Laos. French experience here on the whole ran parallel to imperialist experience elsewhere in Southeast Asia, though the Anglo-Saxon fondness for nagging the French has tended to create the impression that the French did far worse in Indochina than did the Dutch in Java or the British in Malaya. Slow but real material progress was made, though the basic problem of poverty among the masses remained unsolved. Native nationalist movements, nourished by educated natives with jobs of less dignity and authority than they believed should be theirs, rose in strength as the years went on. France also took part, from her base in Indochina, in the struggle for control of China proper. The French sphere of influence was southern China, in particular the province of Yunnan adjoining Indochina, and in the year 1898 the French got a lease on a port in Kwangchou Bay on the South China Sea.

The Germans

We can be brief in listing the colonial acquisitions of the other powers. Germany and Italy came late to the imperial scramble, as they came late to national unity. Nevertheless, Germany was clearly a great power, and Italy aspired to be one; hence, both sought to acquire the token colonies, at least, that seemed necessary to that dignified status—the familiar policy of keeping up with the Joneses. Germany in 1914 had three really large pieces of tropical and subtropical Africa—the Kameruns (Cameroons), German Southwest Africa, and German East Africa—and the smaller Togoland, close to a million square miles in all, nearly four times the size of Texas. These were not rich or well-developed areas, and their total contribution to the German economy was almost negligible. The German achievement on the whole was not greatly different from that of other European powers in Africa; it was neither morally nor economically much better or much worse. In the Pacific, the Germans picked up some small islands, and a large, primitive territory on the island of New Guinea. Germany took part in the attempted partition of China; her ninety-nine-year lease was on Kiaochow Bay, on the north China coast.

*C. Southworth, *The French Colonial Venture* (London, 1931), p. 122.
†Ibid., p. 193.

The French capture of Sontay (Indochina) in 1883: contemporary French engraving.

The German drive for colonies was efficiently organized by pressure groups with all the fixings of modern propaganda. Bismarck himself, who thought colonies were more trouble than they were worth, was obliged to give way and consent to African ventures. His successors went further, and William II helped Germany to enter one of the most confused and dangerous fields of imperialist expansion, the Near East. On the eve of World War I, the German "Berlin to Baghdad" push was well under way, and the Germans had supplanted the British as patrons of the Turks.

The Italians and Belgians

Italy, condemned to the role of weakest of the great powers, got very little even out of the partition of Africa. Tunis, which she coveted, went instead to France. Italy's major effort centered on the African lands at the southern end of the Red Sea, but after her defeat by the Abyssinians under Menelek in 1896 she had to content herself with a few thousand square miles, most of it desert, in Eritrea and Somaliland. Italian efforts to add to this inadequate empire by taking Tripoli from its nominal Turkish suzerain succeeded in 1912, and they also secured Rhodes and other islands off the southwestern corner of Anatolia known collectively as the Dodecanese ("the twelve"). These acquisitions were the fruit of the Italo-Turkish War of 1911–1912.

Little Belgium, largely through the enterprise of her shrewd and ruthless king Leopold II (1865–1909), managed to acquire a large piece of equatorial Africa.

This project began as the Congo Free State, with all sorts of noble ideals of cooperative European civilizing missions in Africa; but it ended up in 1908 as simply the Belgian Congo. Nineteenth-century scandal about forced labor and native exploitation in the Congo called Leopold's experiment to the attention of the world and provided anti-imperialists with fresh arguments. The Belgians soon moderated Leopold's policies and developed the Congo into one of the most profitable of colonies, thanks to its copper, rubber, and other riches. They made no move to groom the Congolese for eventual self-government, however.

The Americans

To the horror and indignation of many Americans, to the delight of others, the United States at the very end of the century joined the great powers and acquired overseas lands. In 1898, the United States waged a brief and successful war with Spain, for which the immediate cause was the still mysterious sinking of the American battleship *Maine* in the harbor of Havana, Cuba. The Spanish-American War left the United States in control of the remnants of the Spanish Empire in America (the Caribbean islands of Cuba and Puerto Rico) and the large archipelago of the Philippines (about the size of Montana) off the coast of Asia. Meantime, the United States also acquired Hawaii (1898) and part of the Samoan Islands in the Pacific (1899). In 1903 American support of a revolution in Panama, then a part of Colombia, assured the independence of a new republic

The opening of the Suez Canal in 1869.

and direct American control of the zone of the projected Panama Canal.

The Americans withdrew from Cuba, leaving her as an independent republic, though subject under the Platt Amendment of 1901 to what in foreign eyes always seemed American "protection." The Platt Amendment, named from its proposer, Senator Orville Platt of Connecticut, limited Cuban control of its foreign policy and its national debt and gave the United States the formal right to intervene to preserve Cuban independence. It was resented bitterly by Cuban patriots as an infringement of Cuban sovereignty and was given up by the United States in 1934. The rest of her acquisitions the United States kept for the time, though in the Phillippines she had to put down an armed rising by Filipinos who wanted immediate independence. American anti-imperialists attempted to upset the somewhat anomalous arrangement under which their government kept lands without strict authorization from the American Constitution. But a Supreme Court decision in the so-called Insular Cases (1901) held that territory might be subject to American jurisdiction without being incorporated constitutionally in the United States of America. Under this decision, Americans began the process of training the Filipinos for eventual independence. Meanwhile, the United States, too, had an empire, which on the maps was duly colored as an American "possession."

The Japanese

One more empire was being formed during the decades before World War I, the only empire to be created by a people of non-European stock—the Japanese. Even during their long self-imposed isolation the Japanese had maintained an interest in Western developments through the trading station that the Dutch were allowed at Nagasaki. When Japan was opened to the world in 1853, its basic political and economic structure had long needed overhauling. An oligarchy of the feudal type ruled, but its ineffective government made it widely unpopular. Discontent was growing, especially among two important social classes. One was the urban middle class of merchants and craftsmen. Although the Industrial Revolution had not yet reached Japan, the country already had populous cities, notably Tokyo (then called Yedo or Edo). The urban middle class, somewhat like the French bourgeoisie on the eve of 1789, wanted political rights to match their increasing economic power. The other discontented class may be compared roughly with the poorer gentry and lesser nobility of Europe under the Old Regime. These were the samurai or feudal retainers, a military caste now threatened with impoverishment and political eclipse. The samurai dreaded the growth of cities and the subsequent threat to the traditional preponderance of agriculture and the landlords; many of them also resented the fact that they were largely excluded from positions

Theodore Roosevelt: "The World's Constable": a cartoon by Dalrymple.

of power by the prevailing oligarchical regime. These social pressures, more than any outside Western influence, forced the modernization of Japan.

Economically, the transformation proceeded rapidly. By 1914, much of Japan resembled an advanced Western country. She, too, had railroads, fleets of merchant vessels, a large textile industry, big cities, and big business firms. The industrialization of Japan was the more remarkable in view of her meager supplies of many essential raw materials. But she had many important assets. As a glance at the map will show, her geographical position with respect to Asia is very like that of the British Isles with respect to Europe. Japan, too, found markets for her exports on the continent nearby and used the income to pay for imports. The ambitious Japanese middle class, supplemented by recruits from the samurai, furnished aggressive business leadership. A great reservoir of cheap labor existed in the peasantry, a large and submissive class. The peasants, who needed to find jobs away from the overcrowded farms, were inured to a very low standard of living and were ready to work long and hard in factories for what seemed by Western standards indecently low wages.

Politically, Japan appeared to undergo a major revolution in the late nineteenth century and to remodel her government along Western lines. Actually, however, the change was by no means so great as it seemed. A revolution did indeed occur, beginning in

The American commodore Perry, who "opened" Japan: Japanese woodblock print, 1853.

1868 when the old feudal oligarchy crumbled under the pressure of the discontented elements. Authority and prestige were restored to the position of mikado (emperor), who had for many years been only a figurehead. In 1889, the emperor bestowed a constitution on his subjects, with a bicameral diet composed of a noble House of Peers and an elected House of Representatives.

The architects of these changes, however, were not democrats. They were aristocrats, ambitious young samurai, supported by allies from the business world and determined to make Japan over from above as they wished. The result was to substitute a new oligarchy for the old; a small group of aristocrats dominated the emperor and the state. The Constitution of 1889, rather like that of the German Empire, provided only the outward appearances of liberal parliamentary government. The ministry was responsible not to the Diet but to the emperor, and hence to the dominant ruling class. The Diet itself was scarcely representative; the right to vote for members of its lower house was limited to a narrow electorate, including the middle class but excluding the peasants and industrial workers. As Sir George Sansom, a British expert on Japan, observed, she had no trouble in accepting Western "things" but a great deal in handling Western "ideas."

Japan began her expansion by taking from China, after a brief war in 1894–1895, the island of Formosa, which she annexed, and the piece of Asiatic mainland closest to Japan, the peninsula of Korea, whose independence China was forced to recognize as a preliminary to eventual Japanese annexation. But Russia, too, had designs on Korea; the results of this rivalry were the Russo-Japanese War of 1904–1905 and a second great Japanese victory. Japan now secured unchallenged preponderance in Korea, which she annexed in 1910, special concessions in the Chinese province of Manchuria, and the cession by Russia of the southern half of the island of Sakhalin, to the north of the main Japanese islands. She had expanded in the classic European way by collecting an empire.

IV   Some Consequences of Imperialism

Two particularly important consequences of nineteenth-century imperialism were the debate over its propriety within the colonizing countries themselves and the promising precedent set as Britain gave her colonies of white settlement self-government with dominion status. All the Western countries, even monarchical states like Germany, had a wide range of free public opinion and some kind of government by discussion. The kind of expansion we call imperialism, therefore, had to be defended articulately, since it was attacked articulately. The defense and attack are both important parts of modern intellectual history.

The Debate over Imperialism: The Defense

One central argument for the defense borrowed heavily from the Social Darwinists. Europeans both in Europe and in their colonies, so ran the argument, were able to beat non-Europeans in war and thus demonstrated that, in terms of evolution, they were fitter to survive than were the non-Europeans. Eternal competition is the price of survival and the best always survive—or *ought* to survive, for these theorists of imperialism had already begun to worry a bit. White men, this argument insisted, are simply better specimens of *Homo sapiens* than are colored men, and Anglo-Saxons—or Germans, or Slavs, or Latins, depending on the writer's allegiance—are superior to all other white men.

An imperialist like Cecil Rhodes, to judge from much that he wrote and said, very likely dreamed of a world which in the fullness of time and evolution would be peopled entirely by Anglo-Saxons. Their breed would actually be improved over their ancestors of 1900, after the inferior peoples had died out—or had been killed off. But these were very distant views indeed. The prospect of ruddy Kentish farmers actually established in freeholds along the Congo simply was unrealistic. More fashionable imperialistic doctrine held that throughout the tropical world, the superior white men would put order and prosperity into the lives of colored men, would as trustees of civilization give up the comforts of Europe to rule in discomfort in the hot countries. Some imperialists thought that this benevolent rule of white men in the tropics would last indefinitely, since in their opinion nonwhites were totally unable to assume the tasks demanded by responsible leadership.

Other European imperialists, however, took the attitude that, though the nonwhites could not run their own affairs then, they could ultimately learn to do so. For the present and for a good many years to come, whites would have to educate them on the spot; someday—the length of time judged necessary varied with the temperament of the judge—the nonwhites would have matured sufficiently to take over responsibilities now confined to whites. The whites would not be owners, merely trustees. Kipling put the case comfortably enough—for white men—in his famous poem:

Take up the White Man's Burden—
   Send forth the best ye breed—
Go bind your sons to exile
   To serve your captives' need;
To wait in heavy harness,
   On fluttered folk and wild—
Your new-caught, sullen peoples,
   Half-devil and half-child.*

*By permission of Mrs. George Bambridge and Macmillan of London & Basingstoke.

This argument of trusteeship was by all odds the most popular defense of imperialism, particularly among Anglo-Saxon peoples.

Yet the historian, aware of the complexities of human nature, will be wary of the notion that the ethical arguments of the imperialists were insincere. Many a European both in and out of the colonies of exploitation really believed in the trusteeship theory, and really did his best to live up to it. The Christian missionary was a major factor in the nineteenth-century expansion of the West. Kenneth Latourette's long and thorough history of the expansion of Christianity has a volume entitled *The Great Century* for the nineteenth. More converts to Christianity were made all over the world in this century, so often labeled the century of materialism, than ever before.

The reality of the conversion of the colored peoples presents a difficult problem. In areas of primitive culture, whole tribes nominally accepted Christianity but continued many of the immemorial ways of their heathen past. In India, China, and Japan, old civilized countries with deep-rooted religious faiths of their own, Christianity did not win over anything like a majority of the people. Nevertheless, the missions did succeed in the course of the century in building up devoted native followers, of whom the most intelligent or most enterprising were often sent to Europe or to the United States for higher education.

Finally, the imperialist philosophy of 1900 was by no means based on an unworried sense of white supremacy. Western civilization is one of the most worrying of all civilizations. Many publicists regarded imperialism as essentially defensive. The whites, outnumbered in a harsh world, had to find a weapon that would hold the nonwhites at bay. Alarm over the swarming population of China and other Asian countries led to talk of the "yellow peril" and of possible "race suicide" by the whites. The writings and speeches of such apparently confident imperialists as Rhodes, Kipling, the German emperor William II, and Theodore Roosevelt sounded this curious note of fear and uncertainty. We are the best, but really we are a little too good for this world; we cannot breed fast enough.

Another variant of the defensive argument hinged on the necessity of securing naval bases and coaling stations, the latter particularly important at a time when vessels had to refuel relatively frequently because of their dependence on coal. Here the British took the lead, with their enormous navy and merchant marine, and the sun never set on the bases strung along their imperial lifeline, from Gibraltar and Malta in the Mediterranean on east of Suez to Aden, at the southwestern tip of the Arabian peninsula, and to Singapore, off the southern end of Malaya. Other powers also raced to acquire bases and stations, notably along the Yellow Sea between China and Korea, where Wei-hai-wei was British, Kiaochow Bay German, and Port Arthur first Russian and then, after 1905, Japanese.

A caricature of Rudyard Kipling, "with Britannia, 'is girl," by Max Beerbohm.

The Debate over Imperialism: The Attack

Against imperialism, opponents marshaled a great many arguments. To the Social Darwinists the anti-imperialists replied by denying that the struggle for existence applied to human groups in the way it applied to plants and animals. It is precisely by sublimating the crude conflict of kill-or-be-killed into the higher rivalry for cultural excellence, they argued, that human societies transcend the struggle for life. Each group, each race, has something to contribute to the total of civilization, and the deliberate destruction or suppression of any group lames and lessens the others, prevents the true working out of evolution—that is, *cultural* evolution—among human beings as contrasted with mere animals. The anti-imperialists also brought forward very prominently the economic argument we have already noted. They worked hard to show that in fact, especially in Africa, colonies did not "pay," that the imperialist appeal to self-interest in the homeland was a delusion, was the dishonest work of propagandists for the privileged minority in the homeland and in the colonies who *did* profit personally from imperialist ventures.

From this point the anti-imperialists went on to maintain that support at home for colonial expansion rested therefore on the ordinary man's vicarious satisfactions from national achievements. The ordinary man liked to see his country figure in the world atlas as an imperial power. He liked to think of Britain's empire on which the sun never set; or, if he was a Frenchman, of the tangible evidence that France was still a great power, still carrying on her *mission civilisatrice;* or, if he was an Italian, that at last Italy too was a nation, and behaving as nations should, not to mention as the heirs of ancient Rome should, too. The anti-imperialists were on the whole not very successful in their attempts to use ridicule and irony against behavior that they found irrational. But their conviction that human action ought to be rational and devoted to the greatest good of the greatest number placed them firmly in the liberal tradition.

So strong was the anti-imperialists' belief that they were right—in spite of the growth of empires all about them—that in Britain the school of Little Englanders, much influenced by laissez faire economics, came to the comforting assurance that imperialism was impossible. The colonies, they held, must inevitably drop away from the mother country—to use their favorite stereotype—like ripe fruit from a tree. Why not then avoid getting into the futile process further by *not* taking any more of Africa or China? Why not hasten the inevitable by giving up the empire? In fairness, we must add that much liberal opposition to imperialism was motivated by humanitarian sympathy for the colored peoples under imperial rule.

Not all the anti-imperialists were liberals or idealists. In France some of the most vehement were the extreme nationalists who wanted *revanche* (revenge) on Prussia for the French defeat in the war of 1870. These *revanchards* were not sorry for the blacks; they opposed French colonialism because it distracted French energies from what they thought was the sole proper national business—getting ready to beat the Germans. Bismarck's encouragement of French colonial expansion could easily be interpreted as a Machiavellian maneuver to increase friction between France and the other imperial powers, especially Britain.

What sank into the mind and feelings of the ordinary Westerner as a result of the anti-imperialist arguments was an uneasy awareness that somehow the practice of imperial expansion did not square with the best avowed intentions of democracy. Particularly in the United States, the feeling grew that imperialism and colonialism were contrary to the ideas of liberty and equality, even if the imperialists honestly claimed to be following the "trusteeship" principle. America took over an empire in 1898, but not without vigorous protests from numerous groups of anti-imperialists, and not without specific promises from the government that it would "free" dependents the moment they were capable of self-rule. This opposition of Americans to colonialism, especially when practiced by themselves, became an important element in the foreign policy of the United States.

The Colonies of White Settlement

The United States itself was a product of an earlier age of imperialism that had brought Englishmen, Scotch-Irish, Germans, and other Europeans to the thirteen colonies of settlement. This serves as a reminder that our account of the nineteenth-century expansion of Europe so far has been limited largely to the "colonies of exploitation," the protectorates, and the spheres of influence held by Europeans. No such account is at all complete, for the most striking thing about this expansion was that it involved an actual transplantation of Europeans to "colonies of settlement" on a scale incomparably greater than in the previous three centuries since Henry the Navigator and Columbus.

The colonies of settlement were originally very thinly inhabited lands. Australia was almost empty; and the whole native Indian population of America north of the Rio Grande was almost certainly in 1800 not over a million, perhaps less. The European settlers simply overwhelmed these primitive peoples. In Tasmania, a large island to the south of the Australian mainland, the aborigines were totally wiped out, and in Australia the "blackfellows" came close to meeting the same fate. On the north island of New Zealand the less primitive Maoris, who were Polynesians, fought two guerrilla wars (in the 1840s and 1860s) in a vain attempt to exclude white settlers from their lands. Their numbers, estimated to have shrunk from 200,000 to 40,000 in the course of the nineteenth century, have fully recovered in the twentieth as they benefited from special protective legislation. In the United States the Indians were eliminated to the point that many an American grew up in the later nineteenth century without ever so much as seeing one except perhaps in a Wild West show.

In most of Latin America, however, the native Indian stock, far from being wiped out, persisted; the upper class, politically and economically, was drawn from European "creole" stock; and a great many people of mixed European and Indian and Negro blood filled the lower social ranks. In the far south of the continent, in the Argentine, Uruguay, and Chile, conditions resembled more nearly those in the United States, and these twentieth-century nations are now almost wholly European in stock, largely from the Iberian peninsula and Italy.

The expansion of Europe into the Americas was also an expansion of Africa. By 1850 the leading European powers had pretty generally got the slave trade under control; but the nucleus of blacks brought into both North and South America by the trade in the earlier centuries continued to grow. Despite handicaps of race barriers, strongest in the United States, the blacks multiplied; by 1900, for example, there were some nine million of them in the United States.

Apart from the extraordinary growth of the United States, the most important phase of the movement of

The Nineteenth and Twentieth Centuries

During the past hundred and fifty years an aesthetic revolution has created a modern art that leaves literal representation to the photographer and experiments with new ways of expressing the fundamentals beneath surface appearances. In painting, a high point of the revolution was reached in the 1870s and 1880s with the French impressionists, who took their name from a canvas by their leader, Claude Monet (*Impression: Sunrise*). In a sustained scientific experiment Monet painted the same subjects over and over in varying lights—Rouen Cathedral, the lilies in his own garden pond—applying many little dabs of pure color and leaving it to the eye of the viewer to fuse and focus them into a recognizable scene.

The impressionists were by no means the only revolutionaries. Earlier, the leading French painter of the romantic era, Delacroix, who claimed that the purpose of art was "not to imitate nature but to strike the imagination," employed raw colors, such as the reds, blues, and greens in *The Abduction of Rebecca*, which illustrates an episode in Scott's romantic novel, *Ivanhoe*. A French contemporary of Monet, Edouard Manet, made another departure from the realism of the camera with portraits of boldly outlined individuals against an indistinct background, as in *Torero Saluting*. Manet was influenced by pictures he saw in Madrid, among them

works by Goya, the most original genius of the romantic era, who often chose subjects from the lower depths or the disreputable fringes of Spanish society, as in his *Majas*. Whistler, an American contemporary of Monet, converted a rowdy London resort, *Cremorne Gardens*, into a dreamlike vision.

The color plates illustrate works by other ranking artistic revolutionaries. Cézanne restored to landscapes the basic architecture of nature, which he thought the impressionists' obsession with color had neglected. Matisse captured the fundamentals of life by reducing colors and figures to a minimum in a joyous though frenzied series of paintings, *The Dance*. Picasso moved from the expressionism of his early "blue period," in which the dominant color underscores the mood of the subject (*The Blind Man's Meal*), to the more radical experiments discussed in Chapter 33. After World War II the abstract expressionists sought to convey a mood nonrepresentationally, by color and design alone; the American Jackson Pollock hurled paint on huge canvases with his "spatter" painting. Finally, in the 1960s, pop art, reacting against the alleged social irrelevance of abstractionism, employed a mixture of painting and other media to illustrate what it termed the "everyday crap" of our standardized machine-dominated society, as in Marisol's *Women and a Dog*.

Water-Lilies, by Claude Monet.
Formerly in the Museum of Modern Art, New York. Robert S. Crandall from the Granger Collection.

Majas on a Balcony, by Francisco de Goya.

The Abduction of Rebecca, by Eugene Delacroix.
The Metropolitan Museum of Art, Wolfe Fund, 1903

Torero Saluting, by Edouard Manet.

The Gulf of Marseilles Seen from L'Estaque, by Paul Cezanne.

The Metropolitan Museum of Art, bequest of Mrs. H. O. Havemeyer, 1929.
The H. O. Havemeyer Collection.

Cremorne Gardens, No. 2, by J. A. M. Whistler.

The Metropolitan Museum of Art, Kennedy Fund. 1912.

Blind Man's Meal, by Pablo Picasso.
Robert S. Crandall from the Granger Collection.

Dance, by Henri Matisse.
Oil on canvas, 1909. 102⅝ x 153½ inches. Collection The Museum of Modern Art, New York,
gift of Governor Nelson A. Rockefeller in honor of Alfred H. Barr, Jr.

Autumn Rhythm, by Jackson Pollock.
The Metropolitan Museum of Art, George A. Hearn Fund, 1942.

Women and Dog, by Marisol.
Wood, plaster, synthetic, polymer paint, and miscellaneous items, 1964. 72 x 82 x 16 inches.
Gift of the Friends of the Whitney Museum of American Art.
Collection Whitney Museum of American Art, New York.

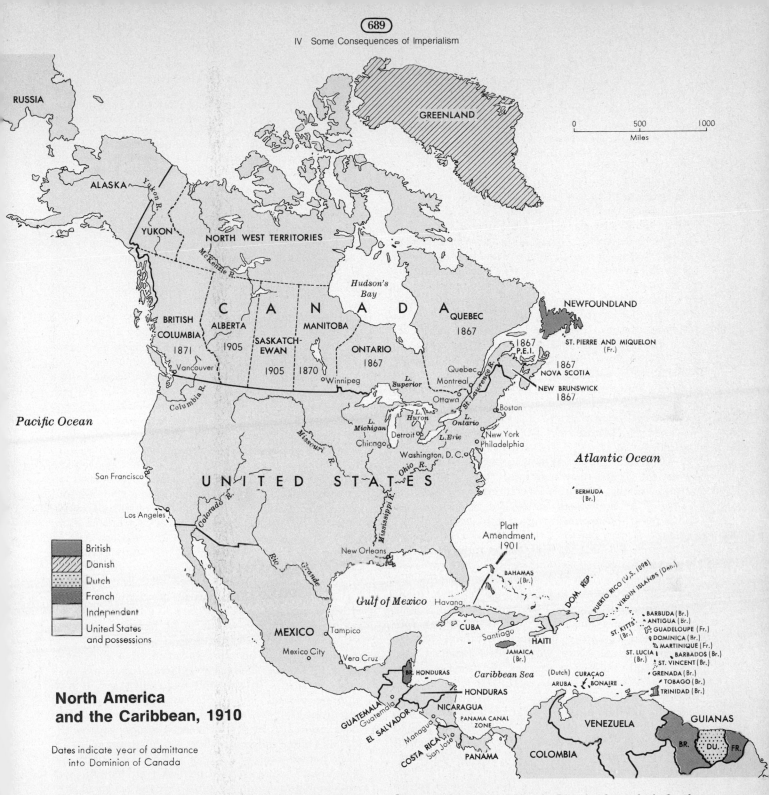

RUSSIA

GREENLAND

0   500   1000
Miles

ALASKA

YUKON

NORTH WEST TERRITORIES

McKenzie R.

Hudson's
Bay

NEWFOUNDLAND

C   A   N   A   D   A

BRITISH
COLUMBIA

ALBERTA

SASKATCH-
EWAN

MANITOBA

ONTARIO

QUEBEC

ST. PIERRE AND MIQUELON
(Fr.)

1871   1905   1905   1870   1867   1867

P.E.I.

NOVA SCOTIA
1867

NEW BRUNSWICK
1867

Vancouver

Columbia R.

Quebec
Montreal
Ottawa

St. Lawrence R.

Winnipeg

L. Superior

L. Huron

L. Ontario

Boston

Pacific Ocean

Missouri R.

L. Michigan

Detroit

L. Erie

New York
Philadelphia

Chicago

Washington, D.C.

Ohio R.

Atlantic Ocean

San Francisco

UNITED STATES

BERMUDA
(Br.)

Los Angeles

Colorado R.

Platt
Amendment,
1901

New Orleans

Rio Grande

Gulf of Mexico

Havana

BAHAMAS
(Br.)

DOM. REP.

PUERTO RICO (U.S. 1898)

VIRGIN ISLANDS (Dan.)

British
Danish
Dutch
French
Independent
United States
and possessions

MEXICO

Tampico

CUBA

Santiago

HAITI

JAMAICA
(Br.)

ST. KITTS
(Br.)

ST. LUCIA
(Br.)

BARBUDA (Br.)
ANTIGUA (Br.)
GUADELOUPE (Fr.)
DOMINICA (Br.)
MARTINIQUE (Fr.)
BARBADOS (Br.)
ST. VINCENT (Br.)
GRENADA (Br.)
TOBAGO (Br.)
TRINIDAD (Br.)

Mexico City

Vera Cruz

Caribbean Sea

(Dutch) CURAÇAO
ARUBA   BONAIRE

**North America
and the Caribbean, 1910**

BR. HONDURAS

HONDURAS

GUATEMALA
Guatemala

NICARAGUA

Dates indicate year of admittance
into Dominion of Canada

EL SALVADOR

Managua

PANAMA CANAL
ZONE

VENEZUELA

GUIANAS

COSTA RICA
San José

PANAMA

COLOMBIA

BR. DU. FR.

Europeans overseas in the 1800s was the transformation of Britain's major colonies of white settlement into self-governing dominions. Doubtless it is an oversimplification to claim that the British learned their lesson from the American Revolution, and that consequently in Canada, Australia, New Zealand, and South Africa they were wise enough to abandon the policies of

George III and Lord North. But the formula is fundamentally sound. The first laboratory for this experiment in a new kind of colonialism was Canada.

The rebellious thirteen colonies of North America had wanted to add a fourteenth, and had tried hard to win Canada. But a complex of causes all contributed to leaving Canada in British hands at the peace in 1783.

The Catholic French Canadians in Quebec distrusted the new Protestant power growing up to the south; the American rebels had grave difficulties keeping up an army to cope with the British on their own soil without risking on invasion of Canada; America's French ally did not wish the new country to be too strong. Later, the United States failed in the War of 1812 to reverse the verdict of 1783.

Upper Canada (Ontario), which was mainly British in stock, and Lower Canada (Quebec), which was mainly French, and the Maritime Provinces of Nova Scotia, New Brunswick, and Prince Edward Island were at first quite separate colonies, as the American thirteen had once been. Each had an apparatus quite like the old American one—a royal governor appointed by the crown, a council appointed by the governor, and an elected assembly based on a more or less popular franchise. But just as in the thirteen colonies during the preceding century, the arrangement bred conflicts between the assemblies and the royal government. In 1837, revolts broke out in both Upper and Lower Canada, with popular leaders like Mackenzie and Papineau arrayed against the governor and his followers, and with essentially the same kind of constitutional and financial grievances that the thirteen colonies had had sixty years before.

The revolt of 1837 was a military fiasco, and it is probable that public opinion in both provinces was against the rebels; there was a fear that too close an imitation of the American Revolution would lead to absorption by the United States. But the British government was alarmed and sent out as governor-in-chief of all the British North American provinces the earl of Durham, a young lord of Whig antecedents and Utilitarian leanings. Durham, feeling that he was not properly supported from London, resigned after less than a year in Canada. But the famous report he made to the British Parliament on his return in 1839 became the cornerstone of the new British imperial structure of dominions, a constitutional document that Durham's admirers have sometimes ranked with Magna Carta.

The Durham Report proposed the union of Upper and Lower Canada and the establishment of responsible government—that is, a popularly elected legislature with ultimate authority—for both the union and each of the separate provinces. The report is still of great interest. Durham had all the average Englishman's insensitivity to things French, and it is an understatement to say that he never understood the Québecois of Lower Canada. But he was true to his principles—even these French Canadian Catholics must have their own responsible government. As he wrote, with prescience:

The maintenance of an absolute form of government on any part of the North American Continent can never continue for any long time, without exciting a general feeling in the United States against a power of which the existence is secured by means so odious to the people; and as I rate the preservation of the present general sympathy of the

United States with the policy of our Government in Lower Canada as a matter of the greatest importance, I should be sorry that the feeling should be changed for one which, if prevalent among the people, must extend over the surrounding Provinces. The influence of such an opinion would not only act very strongly on the entire French population, and keep up among them a sense of injury and a determination of resistance to the Government, but would lead to just as great discontent among the English. . . .*

The actual realization of Durham's recommendations was achieved with due British slowness. The first step, passed by the British Parliament in 1840, the Union Act though uniting both Upper and Lower Canada, was unspecific on the critical point of responsibility—that is, on whether an administration defeated in the legislature had to resign or not. Nearly a decade later, under the governorship of Lord Elgin, the principle was quietly established in practice, never to be withdrawn. Nor was the next step unduly hurried. The British North America Act of 1867 achieved in principle the union of all the British provinces in North America, except Newfoundland, oldest of all, whose separatist tendencies were so strong that it did not join Canada until 1949. The act of 1867, itself basically due to formal Canadian initiative at a meeting of the Fathers of Confederation at Charlottetown, set up the Dominion of Canada by the union of Ontario, Quebec, and the Maritime Provinces, with provision for the admission of territories in the west as provinces on something like the pattern for admission of the western states in the United States. There were still many survivals of the former colonial status of Canada, from the bestowal of titles, especially knighthood with its unrepublican and undemocratic "Sir," to the possibility of judicial appeal from Canadian courts to the Privy Council in Westminster. Above all, the relation of Canada to Britain in terms of international affairs, armed forces, right of secession, and much else was not yet spelled out, nor was it to be formally until the Statute of Westminster in 1931.

Dominion status soon spread to other colonies of white settlement. The six provinces of Australia had common British origins and relatively short lives as separate colonies—the oldest, New South Wales, dating only from 1788. Nevertheless, they soon developed their local differences and separateness, symbolized by the fact that three different gauges were used on railroads. They gained the essentials of self-government in the Australian Colonies Government Act of 1850, but federal union and dominion status were not achieved until New South Wales, Queensland, Victoria, South Australia, Western Australia, and Tasmania were linked as the Commonwealth of Australia in 1901. The influence of the American example is clear in the constitution of the Commonwealth, which provides for a senate with equal membership for each of the six states, a house

*Sir Reginald Coupland, *The Durham Report* (Oxford, 1954), pp. 155–156.

of representatives apportioned on the basis of population, and a supreme court with something close to the American power of judicial review. But in Australia as in the other British dominions, the parliamentary system of an executive (prime minister and cabinet) dismissible by vote of the legislative body was retained; the American presidential system was deliberately rejected.

Australia, like Canada, was essentially an empty country in 1800, and like Canada it filled gradually with immigrants, mostly from Britain. Perhaps the head start of the United States, with its great attraction for British and European immigration, slowed down the growth of these British dominions. But the process, though slow, was steady, and by 1914 all the dominions, including the quiet islands of New Zealand, traditionally most "English" of them all, were prosperous, democratic societies just settling down from the last of the pioneer stage. It is worth noting that Australia, well before it became a dominion, pioneered in the secret printed ballot; that New Zealand (in 1893) and South Australia (in 1894) extended the suffrage to women; and that South Australia also pioneered in legislating compulsory arbitration of industrial disputes. In a textbook like this it is impossible to examine other aspects of the dominions' separate histories or to investigate the fascinating and illuminating subject—insufficiently pursued—of the likenesses and unlikenesses of the corporate personalities of these new countries and the United States, all offsprings of the frontier.

In the nineteenth century, Americans pushing west and Russians pushing east added millions of square miles to their respective lands as colonies of settlement. Although in both, and especially in America, this process of the "frontier" had important effects on their national character, it did not create great immediate problems concerning the independence of the settlers. The British, however, went thousands of miles overseas for their colonies of settlement. They found very soon that these colonies could not be treated as the long tradition since Columbus prescribed—that is, as mere outposts of the motherland with no political self-rule, held in strict mercantilist economic leading strings. Nor could they be, if only because of the separating seas, simply added as a territorial continuation of the motherland as they filled up, as Siberia was added to Russia and the territories of the American West to the federal Union. By 1914, the British at home and the citizens of their overseas colonies of settlement had worked out something new in political configurations, unprecedented in man's brief history.

Canada, Australia, New Zealand, and South Africa were by 1914 wholly self-governing. They could and did even levy customs dues on imports from Britain. They had the beginnings of military forces of their own, and of course complete control of that clear attribute of "sovereignty"—their own internal police. Men were even beginning to speculate about whether they were not in possession of that other clear attribute of sovereignty—the right to conduct foreign relations, both diplomatic and military. For example, could Canada be at peace with a country with which Great Britain was at war?

The first test came in 1914. All the dominions went to war against Germany and her allies. Even the dubiously loyal Union of South Africa went to war against the sender of the Kruger telegram; we are bound to record that the always land-hungry Boers had their eyes on the German colonies in Africa, and especially on the big empty colony of German Southwest Africa, directly adjacent to the Union. The government of each dominion, however, went through the formal process of declaring war, just as sovereign countries do. Yet the relation between Canada, for instance, and Great Britain was something different from the relation between two such sovereign countries as the Argentine and Spain. The dominions had not quite set up wholly for themselves, nor, to revert to the favorite cliché of the nineteenth-century Little Englander, had they dropped off like ripe fruit. The nature of the tie between the dominions and Britain was not clear then, and it must be admitted it is not fully clear even now, though it has obviously weakened since World War II.

The Results Reviewed

The broad general results of this long phase of European expansion down to 1914 may now be summarized.

First, in the nineteenth century almost the whole planet was affected by the process. The white man was almost everywhere by 1914, and white explorers not infrequently found that the tin can, that ubiquitous symbol of the West, had got there ahead of them.

Second, the expansion of Europe was accompanied by a numerical expansion of the whole human race. Between 1800 and 1900, the population of the world just about doubled, from some 800,000,000 in 1800 to some 1,600,000,000 in 1900. European white stock accounted for the most spectacular part of the rise, but nonwhites in Asia and elsewhere also increased. We do not sufficiently understand human population growth to say flatly that the expansion of Europe *caused* the growth of population among non-European peoples in the nineteenth century. But it did bring to many areas of the world some increase of law and order, some increase in material production and improvements in transportation and distribution, health and sanitation—factors that probably contributed to population growth. And, with such exceptions as some Australian aborigines and some North American Indians, European expansion did not usually mean the physical extermination of non-European peoples.

Third, we may say with no reservations whatsoever that by 1914 it was quite clear that "natives" were beginning to reject the claims of white supremacy. Among the more civilized and long-established peoples in the Middle East and Asia, the educated classes were already developing a sense of nationalism. They took over from the West that particular form of group consciousness that is attached to a territorial political unit and that is shared, in principle at least, by all who live within the unit. This nationalism was a new thing outside Europe, and a very important one for us today, for it has gone on increasing and developing. In the early twentieth century, it was most evident in Japan and, to some extent, China, and in advanced "colonial" nations like Egypt and India, though there were signs of it almost everywhere.

This new phenomenon was not the same thing as simple hostility to whites, or to particular nations among the whites. It was an organized political faith—in short, modern "patriotism." Naturally, Egyptian, Indian, and Chinese patriots were first of all concerned with getting rid of their European imperial masters; their attitudes were those of oppressed nationalistic groups everywhere, even in Europe itself. After all, the most striking and most successful rebellion of early twentieth-century nationalist movements against an imperial "master" was that of very European and very white Ireland against the British. These "colonial" peoples were touchy, addicted to nursing grievances imaginary as well as real, eager to seize on any national trait that could be glorified, admiring, hating and envying their masters. Above all, they were organized on a new principle taken from the West, a principle that is ultimately perhaps more destructive of their own traditional cultures than anything else that has come to them from the West. This is the equalitarian and leveling, if not democratic, spirit inherent in the secular religion of nationalism. In theory at least nationality transcends the dividing lines of profession, social class, and even caste. The fellah, the Egyptian peasant whose ancestry reaches back more than fifty centuries, could claim to be as good an Egyptian as the aristocratic pasha—indeed a better one, since he was uncorrupted by European culture. People began to talk and write of "Arab" nationalism; yet the "Arabs" were not exactly a race, nor a people, nor any specific political-territorial entity—at most, "Arab" referred to a language, a culture, and to some of those who held the Muslim faith, and even then a significant minority of Arabs was Christian.

Fourth, and in spite of the gloomy economic conclusions of anti-imperialists, there seems no doubt that over the century the homelands of Europe gained in total wealth from their expansion overseas. Indeed, raw materials from overseas were necessary to maintain the standard of living in thickly populated countries like Britain, Germany, Belgium, and the Netherlands. Theoretically, these raw materials could have come into European lands in free trade with free countries overseas; actually they came in part from imperial expansion. In purely empirical terms, the imperialism of the nineteenth century does seem to confirm Professor Walter Webb's contention that the vast new lands of the frontier proved to be a decisive windfall to Western civilization.

Finally, imperialist rivalries, especially after 1870, exacerbated the normal rivalries among the European great powers and were thus a major factor in the complex of causes that brought on general war in 1914. This is particularly true of the Anglo-German rivalry, which, unlike that of France and England or of Austria and Russia, had no long historical background. This Anglo-German rivalry was everywhere by 1900—among commercial travelers of both nations, trying to sell machinery in Peru; among missionaries trying to convert the heathen in Africa; among army officers, naval officers, editors, organizers, all seeking to make German influence more important than British somewhere or to keep British influence more important than German. The rivalry extended even to the academic world and to that world in the United States. There were those who regarded the Rhodes Scholarships for study at Oxford (1904) as a British attempt to counterbalance the great prestige that the German universities, and especially their degree of Ph.D., had acquired in America during the later nineteenth century.

Reading Suggestions on Nineteenth-Century Imperialism
Imperialism in General

D. K. Fieldhouse, *The Colonial Empires* (*Dell). An authoritative survey from the eighteenth century on.

R. Koebner and H. D. Schmidt, *Imperialism: The Story and Significance of a Political Word* (*Cambridge Univ. Press, 1964). An enlightening monograph.

A. P. Thornton, *Doctrines of Imperialism* (*Wiley), and T. Kemp, *Theories of Imperialism* (Dobson, 1968). Useful analyses of the ideological background.

H. Gollwitzer, *Europe in the Age of Imperialism, 1880–1914* (*Harcourt). Informative general survey.

W. L. Langer, *The Diplomacy of Imperialism, 1890–1902,* 2nd ed. (Knopf, 1951). Detailed case histories from a particularly hectic period in the scramble for empire.

J. A. Schumpeter, *Imperialism and Social Classes* (*Meridian). A valuable essay by a distinguished economist.

J. A. Hobson, *Imperialism: A Study* (*Ann Arbor). The mild title masks a celebrated hostile critique.

Grover Clark, *A Place in the Sun* (Macmillan, 1936). Lucid evaluation of the extent to which colonies were a paying proposition.

Lenin, *Imperialism: The Highest Stage of Capitalism* (*International). The classic communist critique.

B. Kidd, *The Control of the Tropics* (Macmillan, 1898). A characteristic defense of imperialism.

O. Mannoni, *Prospero and Caliban* (Methuen, 1964). Enlightening analysis of the psychology of colonization by an Italian expert.

P. Mason, *Patterns of Dominance* (Oxford, 1970). Examples of the varieties of colonial rule.

T. Geiger, *The Conflicted Relationship* (*McGraw-Hill). The awkward title refers to the role of the West in the transformation of Asia, Africa, and Latin America.

K. S. Latourette, *A History of the Expansion of Christianity,* 7 vols. (Harper, 1937–1945). Volumes 5 and 6 treat its expansion into the non-European world.

Africa

P. Duignan and L. H. Gann, *Colonialism in Africa.* Vol. I: *The History and Politics of Colonialism* (Cambridge Univ. Press, 1969). A comprehensive survey. The same authors have also published *Burden of Empire* (*Hoover Institution), a moderate defense of the contribution of the colonial powers to the development of sub-Saharan Africa.

R. Robinson and J. Gallagher, *Africa and the Victorians* (*Anchor). Excellent study of the climactic years of imperialism.

R. F. Betts, ed., *The Scramble for Africa* (*Heath). Excerpts from varying opinions on the causes and dimensions of the competition.

James Duffy, *Portugal in Africa* (*Penguin). The best study of an important and often neglected colonial enterprise.

C. Hollis, *Italy in Africa* (Hamish Hamilton, 1941). Good analysis of a late starter.

H. R. Rudin, *Germans in the Cameroons, 1884–1914* (Yale Univ. Press, 1938). Valuable case study of an imperialist venture.

P. Gifford and W. R. Lewis, eds., *Britain and Germany in Africa* (Yale Univ. Press, 1967). Materials on their rivalry and their respective institutions of colonial rule.

F. D. Lugard, *The Dual Mandate in British Tropical Africa,* 3rd ed. (Blackwood, 1926). Significant detailed account of British policy in Nigeria.

D. S. Landes, *Bankers and Pashas* (*Torchbooks). Illuminating account of French economic imperialism in Egypt during the mid-nineteenth century.

R. L. Tignor, *Modernization and British Colonial Rule in Egypt, 1882–1914* (Princeton Univ. Press, 1966). Full and balanced appraisal of the British record.

L. de Lichtervelde, *Leopold of the Belgians* (Century, 1929), and L. Bauer, *Leopold the Unloved, King of the Belgians and of Wealth* (Little, Brown, 1935). Vindicating and denouncing, respectively, the great exploiter of the Congo.

C. W. de Kiewiet, *A History of South Africa, Social and Economic* (*Oxford Univ. Press), and E. A. Walker, *A History of South Africa,* 2nd ed. (Longmans, 1940). Two very good surveys by scholars who lived in South Africa.

F. Gross, *Rhodes of Africa* (Cassell, 1956). A standard study of the famous empire-builder. Good older accounts are B. Williams, *Cecil Rhodes* (Constable, 1921) and G. S. Millin, *Cecil Rhodes* (Harper, 1933).

Asia

M. Edwardes, *The West in Asia, 1815–1914* (*Putnam). Good introduction to the increasing involvement of the imperialist powers.

K. S. Latourette, *China* (*Prentice-Hall). Enlightening introduction by an expert.

J. K. Fairbank, *The United States and China,* rev. ed. (*Harvard Univ. Press). By a leading scholar, with greater stress on Chinese history and culture than the title might suggest.

J. T. Pratt, *The Expansion of Europe into the Far East* (Sylvan Press, 1947). Excellent introductory account.

G. Sansom, *The Western World and Japan, a Study in the Interaction of European and Asiatic Cultures* (*Vintage). By a distinguished British scholar, the author of many other important works on Japan.

E. O. Reischauer, *Japan Past and Present,* 4th ed. (*Knopf). Admirable introduction by another distinguished scholar.

R. Coupland, *Britain and India, 1600–1941* (Longmans, 1941). Brief introduction by an authority on imperial questions. For fuller discussions consult M. Edwardes, *British India, 1772–1947* (Taplinger, 1968); H. Brown, ed., *The Sahibs: The Life and Ways of the British in India as Recorded by Themselves* (Hodge, 1948); and A. Seal, *The Emergence of Indian Nationalism* (*Cambridge Univ. Press).

B. H. Sumner, *Tsardom and Imperialism in the Far East and Middle East, 1880–1914* (British Academy, 1944). Good short account.

J. F. Cady, *The Roots of French Imperialism in Eastern Asia,* rev. ed. (Cornell Univ. Press, 1967). Lucid scholarly study.

The Middle East

B. Lewis, *The Emergence of Modern Turkey,* rev. ed. (*Oxford Univ. Press). The best study of the Ottoman Empire in the nineteenth century.

R. H. Davison, *Turkey* (*Prentice-Hall). Clear and concise introduction.

A. Hourani, *Arabic Thought in the Liberal Age, 1798–1939* (*Oxford Univ. Press). Informative study, with considerable stress on Western influences.

The British Empire and Commonwealth

M. Beloff, *Imperial Sunset.* Vol. I: *Britain's Liberal Empire, 1897–1921* (Knopf, 1970). Recent study by a prolific scholar.

P. Knaplund, *The British Empire, 1815–1939* (Harper, 1941). An authoritative account.

C. J. Lowe, *The Reluctant Imperialists,* 2 vols. (Routledge, 1967). One volume analyzing British policy, and a second of documents.

C. E. Carrington, *The British Overseas: Exploits of a Nation of Shopkeepers,* rev. ed. (*Cambridge Univ. Press). Detailed study, very British in point of view.

The Cambridge History of the British Empire, 7 vols. (Macmillan, 1929–1940). With separate volumes on India, Canada, and Australia and New Zealand together.

G. M. Craig, *The United States and Canada* (Harvard Univ. Press, 1968). Sound scholarly study with more stress on Canadian developments than the title might suggest.

D. G. Creighton, *History of Canada: Dominion of the North* (Houghton, 1958); C. Glazebrook, *Canada: A Short History* (Oxford Univ. Press, 1950). Two good general accounts.

R. Coupland, ed., *The Durham Report* (Clarendon, 1946). The famous document that in a sense marks the beginning of the development of the British Commonwealth.

G. Greenwood, ed., *Australia: A Social and Political History* (Praeger, 1955). Good collaborative work, with bibliographies. A readable brief survey is in M. Barnard, *A History of Australia* (Praeger, 1963).

H. Belshaw, ed., *New Zealand* (Univ. of California Press, 1947). An informative volume.

J. B. Condliffe, *New Zealand in the Making* and *The Welfare State in New Zealand* (both Macmillan, 1959). These books constitute a good history from 1792 to 1957.

Other Empires

H. Brunschwig, *French Colonialism: Myths and Realities, 1871–1914* (Praeger, 1966). Perceptive study by a Frenchman.

S. H. Roberts, *History of French Colonial Policy* (Archon, 1963). Reissue of a valuable detailed older work by an Australian scholar.

M. E. Townsend, *The Rise and Fall of Germany's Colonial Empire, 1884–1918* (Macmillan, 1930). The standard account; may be supplemented by W. O. Henderson, *Studies in German Colonial History* (Quadrangle, 1963).

E. R. May, *Imperial Democracy* (*Torch books) and *American Imperialism: A Speculative Essay* (Atheneum, 1968). By a ranking scholarly expert on America's emergence as a world power.

J. W. Pratt, *America's Colonial Experiment* (Prentice-Hall, 1950). Good survey.

D. Perkins, *A History of the Monroe Doctrine,* rev. ed. (*Little, Brown). Popular account by a leading specialist.

Historical Fiction

R. Kipling, *Kim* (*many editions) and *Soldiers Three* (many editions). Famous works by the even more famous champion of imperialism.

S. Cloete, *The Turning Wheels* (Houghton, 1937). A novel about nineteenth-century Boers.

A. Gide, *The Immoralist* (*Vintage). European hero corrupted by North Africa.

E. M. Forster, *A Passage to India* (*many editions). Classic novel on the gap between East and West.

L. Hémon, *Maria Chapdelaine* (Macmillan, 1940). The best-known novel about rural French Canada.

Hugh McLennan, *The Precipice* (Duell, Sloan, 1948). Instructive study of relations between English-speaking and French-speaking Canadians.

H. H. Richardson, *The Fortunes of Richard Mahony* (Readers Club, 1941). A series of novels about modern Australia by an Australian.

D. H. Lawrence, *Kangaroo* (*Compass). Novel set against a background of Australian politics.

H. Rider Haggard, *King Solomon's Mines* (*Dell). A splendid example of the rousing novel of imperialist adventure.

25

The First World War

Introduction

On June 28, 1914, the Hapsburg archduke Francis Ferdinand, heir to the throne of Austria-Hungary, and his wife were assassinated in the streets of Sarajevo, capital of the recently annexed provinces of Bosnia and Herzegovina, which had been occupied by Austria-Hungary since 1878. The assassin, Princip, was a Serbian nationalist, and Bosnia had long been coveted by the Serbs. The Austro-Hungarian government, alarmed by the ambitions of Serbian nationalists, took the occasion of the assassination to send a severe ultimatum to Serbia. The Serbian government's refusal to accept the ultimatum in its entirety led to an Austrian declaration of war on Serbia, on July 28. Within the week, the great states of Europe were engaged in a general war—the Central Powers (Austria-Hungary and Germany) against the Allies (Serbia, Russia, France, and Britain). Princip's revolver shot was eventually to kill some ten million men.

This was the first general war, the first war to involve most of the members of the world state system, since the wars of the French Revolution and Napoleon a century earlier. There had been wars enough, foreign and civil, in the century between. They had been, however, save for relatively minor wars like the Crimean War of 1853, wars between two parties, like the Franco-Prussian War of 1870, the American war between North and South in 1861–1865, and a whole series of colonial wars against rebellious natives.

In 1914 a great many people in Europe and America felt that this sort of general war was all but impossible. These people, predominantly liberal intellectuals, had been alarmed by the series of crises we shall shortly describe, crises that showed how close a general war might be. But they had followed hopefully the movements for international peace and cooperation—the Red Cross, the international labor movements, and the

Hague conferences of 1899 and 1907, which, though they failed to achieve their avowed purpose of limiting armaments, did set up a tribunal for the arbitration of international disputes, the World Court. And many intellectuals simply refused to believe that a world war, should it break out, could last more than a few months. The cost of such a war, they maintained, would be so great that it would bankrupt any government. Such was the thesis of a bestseller, Norman Angell's *The Great Illusion* (1910).

World War I was long, bloody, and destructive. The shock of its outbreak, vastly increased by the strains of the war itself, and above all by the failure of the postwar peace settlement, brought on in the 1920s a most extraordinary discussion of the causes of the war. This discussion was by no means limited to professional historians. It was carried on in the press and on the platforms by all the agencies that touched public opinion. Most of it was designed to "revise" the verdict of the Versailles Treaty of 1919, in which the victorious Allies declared Germany and Austria-Hungary solely responsible for precipitating the war of 1914. The beaten Germans, penalized in the peace, had obvious reasons for trying to prove themselves innocent of war guilt. But important currents in public opinion in Great Britain, the United States, and even in France also flowed into this "revisionist" movement. So far did revisionism go in the 1920s that some American historians parceled out varying portions of the guilt among the victors and the vanquished alike, with the confidence of schoolmasters handing out merits and demerits.

We cannot be so confident today. From our further perspective, the question of war guilt in 1914 fades out into the question of historical causation, and into the fact of historical tragedy. We can say with the English writer Geoffrey Meredith:

In tragic life, God wot,
No villain need be! Passions spin the plot.
*We are betrayed by what is false within.** *

No one power or group of powers "caused" the war of 1914. Its causes lie deep in the history of the state system of Western civilization, and, more particularly, in its history since 1870. They lie deep also in that fundamental form of group consciousness we call nationalism and in the very structure of the modern nation-state. The dramatic date of the assassination of Francis Ferdinand, June 28, 1914, serves as a dividing line between the long-term and the short-term factors involved.

II Causes of the War
The Shift in the Balance of Power

In the long term, an obvious factor that made war more likely was the unification of Germany and Italy. The creation of these two new major states in the 1860s and 1870s altered the always delicate balance of power in the European state system. The efforts of statesmen during the next forty years to adjust the system and to take account of the two new powers and their claims proved ultimately unsuccessful. The older established powers were by no means willing to give up their own claims. We have seen that ever since the modern West-

*G. Meredith, "Modern Love," XLIII, *Poems* (New York, 1907), p. 45.

Aerial combat in World War I.

ern state system developed out of medieval fragmentation, its separate states have tried to grow in wealth, in prestige and, most conspicuously of all, in territory. In the second half of the nineteenth century, with the principle of national sovereignty well established, even the smaller western European states like Switzerland and Sweden were no longer regarded as suitable victims, so that there was little territory available in Europe for making adjustments. Unification had closed off Germany and Italy, which as recently as 1815 had been classic areas for "compensation." Only southeastern Europe, the Balkan lands of the obviously weakening Turkish Empire, remained in the late nineteenth century as possible pickings for ambitious powers. Even there, the growth of national feeling in states like Romania, Serbia, Bulgaria, and Greece made sheer annexation difficult. Nevertheless, Russia and Austria-Hungary both had ambitions in the Balkans; behind them, aiming rather at domination of Turkey and the Near East, came Germany and Great Britain. Finally, as the last chapter noted, amid intense rivalry, much of Africa, Asia, and the Pacific islands underwent a partitioning that it always seemed possible to revise.

Meantime, influenced by their rivalries in Europe and abroad, the great powers were also choosing sides in a series of alliances and agreements. By the early years of the twentieth century two camps existed—the Triple Alliance of Germany, Austria-Hungary, and Italy, and the Triple Entente of France, Britain, and Russia. The system, as many people at the time saw clearly, had grown so tightly organized that there was almost no free play left, and with the wisdom of hindsight we can now see that after 1900 almost any crisis might have led to war. Sarajevo was the one that did.

This state of international politics was christened by an English liberal, Lowes Dickinson, "the international anarchy." It was, however, no chaos, but a highly organized rivalry, "anarchical" only in the sense that there was no higher authority to put a stop to the rivalry. In concrete instances, two or more powers wanted the same piece of land, as a territorial addition or as a sphere of influence. France and Great Britain both wanted Egypt; France and Germany both wanted Morocco; Russia and Austria-Hungary both wanted control over the Balkans; Russia and Japan both wanted Manchuria; and so on around the map. Compromises were made, lands and spheres of influence were shared, but in the long run there simply wasn't enough to go around.

The Role of Public Opinion

In this outline we have used the shorthand of names like Great Britain or Germany. But these are mere symbols, as colored blobs on a map are symbols, for millions of human beings whose desires prompted the actions of states and helped to bring on the war of 1914. In no state were the millions all in agreement. There were Germans who wanted no bit of Africa or any other

Gavrilo Princip, immediately after his assassination of Archduke Ferdinand at Sarajevo.

"Peace": Daumier's view of the European situation after 1871.

piece of land. There were Englishmen who, far from being content with Britain's place in the world, wanted more, wanted Britain to be for the whole round world what Rome had been for the Mediterranean world in the first centuries of the Christian era, who hoped eventually to eliminate all but Englishmen (and perhaps Scotsmen) in a fine Darwinian struggle. There were everywhere in Europe at least a few absolute pacifists, men who were determined under any conditions to refuse to fight, men who once war broke out became conscientious objectors. Thus, the war and the events that led up to it were not simply the work of a few men at the top in each nation, the professional soldiers, the villainous diplomats in frock coats and striped trousers. In all the countries, there was a spectrum that ran from militarist to pacifist, through all opinions in between.

But the outbreak of the war saw in each belligerent nation a broad national public opinion in support of the government. In 1914, a good many men marched to war convinced that war was a beneficial thing; the bands played, the crowds shouted, and war, perhaps for the last time, seemed romantic as well as necessary. Here is the account of a young German on the last train out of Switzerland before the outbreak of war:

An elderly gentleman was sitting in our compartment. He began to talk to us at once, as if we were intimate acquaintances. On the back of his hotel bill he had added up the numerical strength of the European armies and balanced them against each other. He compared the two totals and assured my mother that the spiritual qualities of the German troops compensated for the numerical superiority of the Russians. For in this war spiritual qualities alone would decide the day, and Germany's spiritual qualities were the best in Europe. As a university professor he knew that our youth were ready for the fray, and full of ideals. At last the hour had come when our people could enter on its great world mission. . . .*

The Germans were led by their kaiser, William II, who had come to the throne in 1888. The "revisionist" historians have been able to show that in the hectic five weeks after the assassination at Sarajevo the kaiser, contrary to world opinion at the time, did not work steadily for war, and as July 1914 wore on, he tried to avoid a general war. But he cannot be even partially absolved for the long-term causes of the war. In the decisive years between 1888 and 1914 he was the posturing, aggressive leader of patriotic expansion, the "White Knight" leading his people to glory. He was perhaps more of a figurehead, less of an actual maker of policy, than the world took him to be, but still a willing and effective figurehead for expansionists and violent nationalists.

German ambitions and German fears produced an intense hatred of Britain, a hatred mixed with envy and a sense of inferiority, a hatred that focused on the English upper classes, perfectly tailored, serene in effortless superiority, the favorite children of fortune. Many a German tourist, perhaps quite accidentally given an Italian hotel room inferior to that given a traveling Englishman, would come home burning with indignation at this personal evidence that Germany was being denied its place in the sun. In the German navy, in the years just before the war, there was a simple toast in the officers' mess: *Der Tag* (The Day). Everyone knew that this was the day of the declaration of war between Germany and Britain. These feelings are all condensed in the famous "Hymn of Hate" of the German poet Ernst Lissauer:

We will never forego our hate,
Hate by water and hate by land,
Hate of the head and hate of the hand,
Hate of the hammer and hate of the Crown,
Hate of the seventy millions choking down.
We love as one, we hate as one,
We have one foe and one alone:

England!†

Few Englishmen returned this hate; the English were still on top. Yet as the years wore on, the expensive race between Britain and Germany in naval armaments continued; in incident after incident German and British diplomats took opposite sides; and—this seemed

especially important to the hard-headed—German wares of all sorts undersold British wares in Europe, in North and South America, and in Asia. Englishmen began to think that someone ought to teach these ill-mannered Germans a lesson. Moreover, they had begun to worry about their own position of prosperity and leadership. In India, the greatest possession of the English, it was clear already that great concessions toward self-government would have to be made to the natives. Close at home the Irish crisis was in one of its most acute phases, with Protestant Ulster in arms against the proposed home rule and British officers stationed there guilty of planning actual mutiny. Englishmen were worried about their obsolescent industrial plants, their apparent inability to produce goods as cheaply and as efficiently as the Germans; they were self-critical about their failures as salesmen abroad, their stodgy self-satisfaction.

A great many Britishers thought of themselves as good liberals and good internationalists, anxious to preserve the peace and the decencies of international life. Many were radicals and Labour party men committed to pacifism. The coming of war in 1914 was to show how thoroughly almost all these men identified Great Britain and righteousness. As for the bulk of the conservatives, they were as nationalist as in any other great country. In Britain, their nationalism attached itself to the empire, to the White Man's Burden, to a whole set of symbols that the Germans found intolerable.

In democratic France as in democratic England there was a wide spread of opinion on international politics. A numerous socialist Left was committed to pacifism and to the concept of an international general strike of workers at the threat of actual war. A more moderate group also opposed conventional patriotic aggressiveness toward the foreigner. Both among the men who conducted French foreign relations and among the general public, however, there remained right down to the eve of the Great War the embittered patriotism of the beaten. Frenchmen wanted *revanche*, revenge for the defeat of 1870. They wanted Alsace-Lorraine back. For all these years, the statue representing Strasbourg among the cities of France in the Place de la Concorde in Paris was draped in black. With the warmest patriots, the organizers of patriotic societies, the editors of patriotic journals, this feeling for revenge was an obsession. By the opening decade of the 1900s many observers thought that the new generation was losing its desire for revenge, that Frenchmen had at last decided to accept the verdict of 1870. But French diplomats continued to preserve and strengthen the system of alliances against Germany, and in the excited weeks of July 1914 it was clear that Frenchmen were ready for war.

Among the other major belligerents, too, the ultimate decisions of governments won much popular support. Russians were filled with the "pooled self-esteem" of nationalism, were convinced that God and the right

*E. Glaeser, *Class of 1902*, trans. W. and E. Muir (London, 1929), pp. 171–172.
†E. Lissauer, "A Chant of Hate Against England," trans. Barbara Henderson, in Burton E. Stevenson, comp., *The Home Book of Verse*, 3rd ed. (New York, 1918), 2:2549–2550.

were on their side. Italians saw in war the chance to get Italia Irredenta (Trent, Trieste, and their surrounding lands) and still more territory from the Hapsburg monarchy. In the dual monarchy, as we have seen, the loyalty of subject nationalities could scarcely be counted on; but the dominant Germans of Austria and Magyars of Hungary welcomed the opportunity to put the troublesome Slavs in their place for good and all.

Triple Alliance and Triple Entente

The road to Sarajevo starts in 1871, when France was obliged to cede Alsace and Lorraine to the new German Empire. It was no straight road, but one of many twists and turnings, and few historians would now maintain that 1871 made 1914 inevitable. For some twenty years Bismarck was its chief engineer. In fairness to the Iron Chancellor, it must be said that during his last two decades in office he sought peace, and indeed obtained it. Powerful elements in the new empire made it impossible for him to grant to France the same kind of generous peace he had given Austria in 1866. Yet Bismarck did try to salve the wounds he knew France had suffered; he encouraged her to expand her empire in North Africa by the acquisition of Tunisia in 1881, even though this offended the Italians, who also coveted Tunisia. But he feared a French attempt at revenge and sought to isolate her diplomatically by building a series of alliances from which she was excluded. Germany, he insisted, was now a "saturated" power, and wanted nothing more in Europe; and in a famous phrase he insisted that all the Balkans were not worth "the bones of a single Pomeranian grenadier." Above all, he sought to keep on good terms with *both* Austria and Russia, and, what was much more difficult, to keep both these powers on good terms with each other. Since both wanted predominance in the Balkans, Bismarck's task was formidable.

He laid the cornerstone of his diplomatic system by a defensive alliance with Austria-Hungary in 1879, an alliance that held right down to 1918. And he was able to bring about the so-called League of the Three Emperors, which bound Germany, Russia, and Austria together. The three powers agreed to act together in dealings with Turkey and to maintain friendly neutrality should any one of them be at war with a fourth power other than Turkey. Next, working skillfully on Italian annoyance over the French expansion in Tunis and on Italian fears that France might join an international effort to restore Rome to papal sovereignty, Bismarck secured an alliance among Germany, Austria-Hungary, and Italy, directed chiefly against France. This was the famous Triple Alliance of 1882, often renewed, which still existed on paper in 1914.

On this series of tightropes Bismarck maintained a precarious balance through the 1880s. Chief in his mind was the danger that the Russians, always fearful of Austrian schemes in the Balkans, would desert him and ally themselves with France, still a great power and

anxious to escape from the isolation that Bismarck had designed for her. In 1887, Russia did refuse to renew the League of the Three Emperors, but Bismarck was able to repair the breach for the moment by a secret Russo-German agreement known as the Reinsurance Treaty. The two promised each other neutrality in case either was involved in a war against a third power; but this neutrality was not to hold if Germany made an "aggressive" war against France or if Russia made an "aggressive" war against Austria. Since Russian nationalist agitation continued against both Austria and Germany, Bismarck in 1888 made public as a warning to Russia the terms of the Austro-German alliance and allowed the main terms of the Triple Alliance to be known informally.

Then in 1890 the young emperor William II dismissed Bismarck. The emperor's advisers, headed by Baron von Holstein, persuaded him not to renew the Reinsurance Treaty with Russia in spite of the Russian wish to continue it. Shortly afterward, what Bismarck had worked so hard to prevent came about. After lengthy negotiations, Russia and France in 1894 made an alliance that ended French isolation. It was a defensive agreement, by which each was to come to the other's aid in the event that Germany or Austria made "aggressive" war against either ally. It was supplemented by military agreements between the two general staffs. Against the Triple Alliance there now stood the Dual Alliance of republican France and absolutist Russia.

Great Britain still remained technically uninvolved by any formal treaty with a European ally and indeed never entered a full legal commitment, even with France. Yet the next great development in the tightening network of alliance was to align Great Britain against the Triple Alliance, at least by informal agreement. In the two decades after the accession of William II, Britain made a formal alliance with Japan and informal "understandings" (ententes) with France and Russia. What chiefly drove Britain to these actions was the naval race with Germany and the rapid worsening of Anglo-German relations, a worsening even more evident perhaps in public opinion than at the level of formal diplomacy.

A concrete instance of this rising hostility is the Kruger telegram of 1896, in which the kaiser congratulated President Kruger of the Boer Republic of Transvaal on the defeat of the Jameson raid. It may be that the kaiser and his circle hoped that this gesture would be taken by the English government as a kind of polite and permissible diplomatic blackmail, an evidence of how great a nuisance the German government could be to the British if it were not on their side. But the British press took the telegram as an unbearable insult, and the German press replied angrily to British anger.

It was fear of Russia rather than fear of Germany, however, that inspired Britain to make the first break with formal isolationism, the alliance with Japan in

1902. The outbreak of war between Russia and Japan hastened negotiations between Britain and France; both wanted to improve their mutual relations, which were threatened by the hostilities between their respective allies. In the Entente Cordiale of 1904, France gave England a free hand in Egypt, England gave France a free hand in Morocco, and various outstanding difficulties between the two in other parts of the world were ironed out. More important, the base was laid for further collaboration, particularly in advance planning for military and naval cooperation in case of war. Only six years previously, in 1898, there had been a grave flareup of the traditional colonial rivalry between France and England when a French column was met by a British column at Fashoda in the disputed Sudan territory of the upper Nile Valley. Fashoda caused quite as big an outbreak of fury in the French and the British press as the Kruger telegram only two years before had caused in the German and the British press. Yet Fashoda left wounds much less deep than the Kruger telegram; the press is not always a faithful guide to the climate of public opinion, let alone to that of professional diplomacy.

The final stage in aligning the two camps came in 1907 when Russia, chastened by her defeat at the hands of Japan and encouraged by the French, came to an understanding with Great Britain. Both countries made concessions in regions where they had been imperialist rivals—Persia, Afghanistan, Tibet—and the British at last made some concessions to Russia's desire to open up the Straits (Bosporus and Dardanelles) for her warships. The agreement was scarcely based on any genuine sympathy between the two peoples, for the British had been Russophobic for well over a century. Nevertheless, it did round out the Triple Entente against the Triple Alliance.

A Decade of Crises, 1905–1914

The last decade before 1914 was a series of crises and local wars, any one of which might have spread into a world war. First came a deliberately theatrical gesture from the kaiser, when in 1905 he made a ceremonial visit to Tangier in Morocco as a way of telling the world that the Germans would not accept the Anglo-French assignment of Morocco to France. The net effect of this blustering was to tighten the entente between France and Britain, for the British indicated clearly to the French that they would support them. Moreover, the British and the French now began the informal military and naval conferences that the French, at least, believed committed Britain to armed support if the Germans attacked. The Germans did succeed in a campaign to force out of office the French foreign minister, Delcassé, who believed they were bluffing about Morocco. This partial victory did the Germans no real good, for French public opinion was infuriated by this intervention in their domestic politics. In the end, a general international conference at Algeciras in Spain (1906)

backed up the French, who went ahead with their plans for a protectorate in Morocco. At Algeciras American diplomatic influence was used on the side of France; the United States, too, was beginning to emerge from isolation.

A second Moroccan crisis in 1911 heightened tensions and brought the possibility of a general war home to most Frenchmen. The kaiser sent a German gunboat, the *Panther*, to the Moroccan port of Agadir as a protest against French occupation of the old city of Fez. In ensuing negotiations, well publicized in the press, the Germans finally agreed to leave the French a free hand in Morocco, but only at a price the French considered blackmail: part of the French Congo was ceded to Germany.

In the Balkans, a decisive turn of the road toward Sarajevo came in 1908. Austria formally proclaimed the annexation of the Turkish provinces of Bosnia-Herzegovina, which she had occupied since 1878. Austria's action infuriated the Serbs, who wanted to annex Bosnia. It also infuriated the Russians, all the more since few Russians knew that their diplomat Izvolski had in fact made an informal agreement with the Austrian minister Aehrenthal, in September 1908, to accept the annexation of Bosnia-Herzegovina in return for Austrian support of an agreement permitting Russian warships to use the Straits. Austria did the annexing, but Russia did not get her use of the Straits. This wound to Russian pride was profound.

Meantime, a situation was developing that might give Russia a chance to salve her wounds. What prompted the Austrian annexation of Bosnia-Herzegovina was the successful rising against the Ottoman sultan in the summer of 1908 by the Young Turks, who were chiefly army officers. The Young Turks wanted the modern industrial achievements of the West, they wanted its political apparatus of representative government, and they wanted above all to have Turks respected, admired, and feared as members of a thoroughly modern nation. Some of their intellectuals followed the nineteenth-century romantic pattern back into the past, glorifying their nomadic Turanian ancestors from the steppes of central Asia. A Pan-Turanian movement, instigated largely by Turks from central Asia, whose independent principalities had been extinguished by Russian expansion during the reign of Alexander II and who were now undergoing forced Russification, sought to group the Turkish peoples of central Asia with the Ottoman Turks and the Magyars of Hungary, who were only distantly related to each other, as children of a common destiny. No wonder the Hapsburgs were alarmed! It began to look as if those who hoped to divide up the Ottoman Empire had better hurry while the dividing was good.

In the hurry, the world was swept into World War I, the immediate forerunners of which were the Italian war with Turkey for Tripoli, 1911–1912, and the subsequent Balkan Wars. In the first Balkan War (1912), an alliance of Bulgaria, Serbia, and Greece, backed by

Russia, defeated the Turks and started the process of dividing up European Turkey. But here Austria imposed an absolute veto on granting Serbia territories that would give her access to the Adriatic Sea. Meanwhile, the victors quarreled among themselves, and in the Second Balkan War (1913) the Bulgarians were readily defeated by the Greeks and Serbs, joined by the Romanians and the all-but-beaten Turks, who recovered some territory in Europe. Thus the Balkans were in a state of flux when Francis Ferdinand was assassinated; Bulgaria in particular was ready to side with Austria and Germany against her own former allies.

The Final Crisis, July–August 1914

There are millions of words in print about the immediate causes of World War I in the six weeks between the assassination on June 28 and the general spread of war on August 4, when Britain came in against Germany. Thanks to the end of Hohenzollern, Hapsburg, and Romanov rule as a result of the war, the secret archives were thrown open much sooner than would be usual. And in the pressure of debate in the 1920s over the question of war guilt, even the victorious countries, Britain, France, and the United States, opened their archives to a surprising extent. These are weeks for which documents, often telegrams, can be dated by the hour and minute. These are weeks during which messages swirled back and forth between national capitals, confusing things hopelessly. Professional diplomatists and statesmen, egged on by an excited—and it must be said often irresponsible—press, nevertheless tried for the most part to master the crisis without recourse to war.

The diplomats and statesmen were drawn into war because almost all of them believed that they faced an alternative worse than war, a defeat or loss of face for their nation. Austria believed correctly, though without positive proof, that the Serbian government had some foreknowledge or at least suspicion of Princip's plot and should therefore have given her warning. For this reason, and also because she wished to check the Serb agitation that had long been unsettling the Yugoslav peoples living in the dual monarchy, Austria-Hungary decided to make stiff demands on Serbia after the assassination of Francis Ferdinand. Before doing so, however, she consulted her German ally, who promised to support whatever policy Austria might adopt toward Serbia. This German response has become famous as a diplomatic "blank check," duly signed by Germany in advance with the precise amount to be filled in later by Austria.

Thus encouraged, the Austrian government, on July 23, sent Serbia an ultimatum to be answered within forty-eight hours. The ultimatum made many separate demands, which added up to an insistence that Serbia and Serb propagandists keep their hands off Hapsburg territories and populations, now and in the future. Most of the demands the Serbs accepted, at least

in principle; but they refused to accept two of them, which would have permitted Austrian police or military men to take, on Serbian soil, an actual part in a Serbian investigation of Princip's plot. Probably Serbia had some assurance that Russia would assist her if the partial refusal of the ultimatum led to war. The Serbian reply, therefore, was a little less virtuously honest than it seemed to be to most of the world in July 1914. Still, the Austrian ultimatum was couched in terms deliberately unacceptable to the Serbs, and the Serb reply was intended to provide a base for more consideration than it got from the Austrians. Because the Serbs had not accepted the whole of the ultimatum, Austria declared war on July 28, after turning down as inconsistent with national honor a European conference proposed by the British foreign minister, Sir Edward Grey, on July 26.

Thereafter, the German diplomatists, backed by William II and actually resisting the German military men, tried to hold back their Austrian ally. It is impossible to clear William from responsibility for the German blank check, which had emboldened Austria and had perhaps been designed by Germany to do just that. Now, however, the Germans certainly tried to revoke the check and made a last effort to stop the spread of the war. Since Russia was beginning the full mobilization of her armies, the kaiser, on July 29, told Czar Nicholas II in a personal telegram of the German attempt to get the Austrians to compromise. Apparently this telegram served to get full Russian mobilization modified into partial mobilization and to get direct Austro-Russian talks resumed on July 30. For a brief moment it looked as if the crisis might be overcome.

But mobilization was not easy in Russia, a country of long distances, poor communications, and bureaucratic red tape; and the Russian military feared that their enemies would get the jump on them. In perhaps the most crucial decision of that hectic last week, the Russian government, probably against the deeper inclinations of the czar himself, decided to renew general mobilization. Germany at once insisted that all Russian mobilization cease, and, when it continued, ordered her own at 4:00 P.M. on August 1, and declared war on Russia at 7:00 P.M. the same day. France, meantime, had determined to stand by her Russian ally, now evidently about to be attacked, and also mobilized at 3:55 P.M. on August 1. Germany declared war on France on August 3.

Britain was still wavering. Although her entente with France did not legally bind the two nations together, it had led to the very close coordination of defense plans by the French and British military and naval staffs. Perhaps, then, Britain would have come into the war anyway. What made her entry certain was the German violation of the neutrality of Belgium, which both Britain and Prussia had joined with other powers to guarantee in 1839, thirty years before German unification. The German military were determined

TOGETHER WE WIN

UNITED STATES SHIPPING BOARD EMERGENCY FLEET CORPORATION

An American recruiting poster by James Montgomery Flagg.

The Entry of Other Powers

By August 6, when Austria declared war on Russia, all the members of the Triple Alliance and the Triple Entente had come to blows, with the exception of Italy, which, however, had never really been a good ally of Austria because of the Irredentist issue. Italy, refusing to consider herself bound by the Triple Alliance, declared her neutrality. The Central Powers of Germany and Austria-Hungary, then, stood against the Allies—Russia, France, Britain, and Serbia. Japan came in on the side of the Allies late in August, and Turkey came in on the Austro-German side in November 1914. After competing territorial offers from both Allies and Central Powers, Italy finally joined the Allies in May 1915. Bulgaria came in on the side of the Central Powers in 1915, Romania on the side of the Allies in 1916.

As the war turned into a stalemate, on both western and eastern fronts in the winter of 1916–1917, the Germans made the desperate decision to try to get at Great Britain by using their submarines to cut off the food and raw materials that came to the British Isles from overseas, and without which their peoples would have starved. This unrestricted submarine warfare meant sinking American ships that Americans held were quite legally bringing such supplies, *not* contraband of war, to England and France. After much hesitation, on April 6, 1917, the United States completed the roster of great powers involved in the conflict by declaring war on Germany. Lesser powers all over the world joined in, so that all told there were 53 declarations of war before the end of 1918.

Dissident Americans, then and since, have declared that the United States was enticed into the war by the wicked few—by sentimental lovers of England or France; by bankers who had lent money to the Allies and wanted to protect their investments; by silly idealists who agreed with President Wilson in wishing to "make the world safe for democracy"; and, of course, by scheming Allied diplomatists, corrupt Europeans who held a strange fascination over American "babes in the wood." Deep-seated sentiments among many Americans in 1916–1917 rebelled against jeopardizing American ideals by involving the country in what seemed to them an evil European struggle for power. Yet it is worth noting that ever since King William's War (in Europe, the War of the League of Augsburg, 1688–1697), the colonists and then the citizens of the United States had been drawn sooner or later into every major general war in the Western state system. Thus it may be argued, first, that the normal expectation is for the United States to enter any world war, and second, if more debatably, that in the Western state system a general or world war never breaks out unless there is an aggressor nation whose activities appear to threaten the independence of other nations. The United States, in this view, went to war in 1917 for a very deep-seated reason. The possible victory of Germany threatened the very existence of the United States as

to take decisive action in the West and to knock France out of the war before the Russians could get their vast but slow-moving armies into action. Accordingly, German plans called for a sweep through a corner of Belgium to avoid the heavily fortified and hilly terrain in northeastern France. On August 2, the Germans had notified Belgium that they intended to march through her territory, though they promised to respect her territorial integrity in the peace to come.

Belgium rejected this demand and appealed to the other guaranteeing powers. Sir Edward Grey, though opposed by some members of the British cabinet who did not believe defense of the neutrality of Belgium worth a war, seized firmly on this ground of action. On August 4 Britain declared war on Germany. The German chancellor, Bethmann-Hollweg, informed of this action, let slip the phrase that Britain had gone to war just for a "scrap of paper"—the treaty of 1839 that established Belgium neutrality. This unhappy phrase, seized upon by the press of the world, not only solidified British opinion in favor of the war but was responsible more than any other single factor for the charge of war guilt that was laid against Germany.

an independent, but committed and cooperating, participant in an international order.

More specifically, in 1917 the United States insisted that the existing international order gave Americans the right to travel and to trade freely with neutrals and, in dealings with belligerents, to be limited only by well-known principles of international law forbidding actual transport of munitions or other direct forms of aid to belligerents. This is the doctrine of freedom of the seas, which would have allowed Germans to search American vessels, but which quite clearly did not permit German submarines to sink American vessels on sight and without notice. The German decision to undertake unrestricted submarine warfare was in Western historical precedent a complete justification of the declaration of war by the United States. But, we must repeat, behind this reason lay a widespread though by no means universal feeling among many Americans, especially those most concerned with foreign relations, that a German victory would mean a world order where the kind of America in which they wanted to live could not be secure.

Jefferson had delayed, but not prevented, American entry into the Napoleonic wars by abandoning the doctrine of freedom of the seas. The Embargo Act of 1807 had simply forbidden American vessels to trade either with the French or the British side. In 1917, the United States would have had to put an embargo on all American shipping to most foreign ports, or else put up with German torpedoing of American ships and the drowning of American citizens. Neither course would seem to have been acceptable then to a majority of Americans. After more than two years of strenuous efforts to keep the United States out of the war, President Woodrow Wilson found that he had no choice but to go in.

III The Course of the War
Resources of the Belligerents

As the opposing nations lined up before the American entry, the Allies (British, French, Russians, and others) had an overwhelming superiority in total population and resources. The Central Powers (Germany, Austria-Hungary, and Turkey) had in their own continental lands not over 150,000,000 people; Britain, France, Russia, and Italy in their own continental lands had at least 125,000,000 more people than their enemies. Moreover, in their overseas possessions, which included the 315,000,000 people of India, the Allies had many millions more. As for material resources, the Central Powers had, especially in Germany, admirably organized industries and enough coal and iron to fight a long war. But here too the statistics were overwhelmingly in favor of the Allies. Moreover, though German submarines and, in the early days, surface raiders were able to interrupt seriously Allied lines of communica-

tion overseas, on the whole the Allies were still able to get from these overseas sources indispensable food and other supplies. And when in 1917 a beaten Russia, in the throes of a revolution, ceased to be of aid, the Allies gained the great resources of the United States.

In the long run, the side with the most men and materials wore down its enemies and won the war, but it was by no means the uneven struggle that the statistics of total population and material resources would indicate. The weaker side had initially important advantages, won great victories, and seemed at critical moments on the point of final victory. Geography gave Germany and Austria the advantages of being side by side, and of having interior lines of communication, which enabled them to make rapid transfers of troops from one threatened front to another. Though the Germans and Austrians did not always see eye to eye, they did speak the same language and had for long been firmly allied. Most important of all, Germany in particular was more ready for war than were her enemies. She had an efficiently organized military machine and a good stock of munitions, her industry could be readily geared to war, her plans were complete, her people were united in support of the war, and they enjoyed the great psychological advantage of being on the offensive, of carrying the war to the enemy. Indeed, no important part of the war was ever fought on German soil; it ended, with important results for later history, with the German army still in being, and the German Fatherland still uninvaded.

By contrast, geography separated the Western Allies from Russia. German control of the Baltic and Turkish control of the Straits proved throughout the war a serious obstacle to communication between Russia and her allies, who had to take roundabout and difficult routes through Archangel in Arctic waters and even through Vladivostok on the Pacific at the end of the long, slow, single-track Trans-Siberian railway. For the Allies, transfer of troops between eastern and western fronts was militarily almost impossible, even had it been politically possible. It was not, however, politically possible, and here was one of the greatest weaknesses of the Allies.

Russia, Britain, and France had only recently come together, as "friendly" powers and not as close allies. Each of them was a strongly marked nationality, having many sources of conflict with the others. They had no long tradition of mutual cooperation, no common language. France and England were democracies, and though the peoples of both rallied firmly to the national cause in 1914, they were of recent years unused to the kind of firm, centralized political and military control that is necessary in war. As for unified military planning and administration, it was never achieved between Russia and the Western Allies. Even among Britain, France, and the United States on the western front, it was not achieved until the French general Foch was appointed commander in chief in 1918, and then only imperfectly, without full merging of staffs.

Finally, of the three great Allied powers in 1914, only France was ready with a good big land force, and France, with only 39 million people against Germany's 65 million, was the weakest of the Allies in manpower. Britain was well prepared on the sea, and her navy was an invaluable asset; but it could not be of direct use against the German army. Russia had universal military service and an army great in numbers. But she had vast distances to overcome, an inadequate railway system, a relatively undeveloped heavy industry, an army whose morale had been shaken by its recent defeat at the hands of Japan, a people whose morale had been shaken by the recent abortive revolution, and whose military and political organizations were riddled with inefficiency and corruption.

The Western Front: German Offensive

The Germans had a plan, the so-called Schlieffen plan, which they immediately put into execution. It called for a holding operation on the left, with a strong right wing that was to advance swiftly through Belgium, take Paris, and then fall on the rear of the French armies. While this great enveloping movement in the west swiftly eliminated France, relatively weaker German forces, it was planned, would hold down the slow-moving Russians. With France beaten, the Germans could turn their full force against the Russians and beat them. Then only the British would remain.

The German plan almost succeeded. It failed for two reasons, to which a great number of separate tactical factors contributed. In the first place, the German chief of staff, Moltke, had seriously modified the Schlieffen plan by weakening the critical right wing, partly in order to send divisions to the east, which, ironically, arrived there too late to participate in the defeat of the Russians. By the time the German right wing neared Paris, it had too few divisions to take the capital and then roll up the French army to the eastward. In the second place, the French, though at first they rashly developed the offensive eastward, shifted their armies northward and westward to meet the invading Germans. With the help of the British they exploited a gap that developed between the German First and Second armies. The Germans lost this first great test, known as the battle of the Marne (September 5–12, 1914).

The German advance, which had been almost continuous since August 2, had been stopped. In the next few weeks the opposing forces engaged in what came to be called the "race for the Channel," with the Germans trying to outflank the Allies and get the Channel ports, thus shutting the short sea passage to future British reinforcements. They failed here, too, and throughout the war the ports of Calais and Boulogne, and indeed a small southwestern corner of Belgium, were to remain in Allied hands.

By the autumn of 1914 the western front was thus stabilized. For over three hundred airline miles between the Channel and the Swiss border of Alsace near Basel, hundreds of thousands of soldiers faced each other in a continuous line that was full of bends called "salients." Both sides dug in and made rough fortifications, the central feature of which was a series of parallel trenches deep enough to conceal a man standing upright. As time went on, these trenches were greatly improved; they were supplied with parapets, machine-gun nests, and an elaborate network of approach trenches and strong points, until the whole front became one immense fortification. Thousands of local actions in the four years of trench warfare shifted the lines here and there, and a series of partial breakthroughs occurred on both sides. But on the whole the lines held, and the actual fighting in the west was confined to an extraordinarily narrow, though very long, field.

On this western front the ultimate decision was reached; but there were many other fronts, sometimes disparaged as "sideshows" by those who advocated concentrating on the west. In perspective we can see that they all played a part in determining the final result. Since, over the long pull, the Germans had fewer men and resources, the dispersal of energies that these "sideshows" called for, and the continuous need to bolster their Austrian, Turkish, and Bulgarian allies, were major factors in their defeat. For the sake of clarity, we shall here take up these other fronts separately and briefly, but the reader must never forget that for the belligerents the war was a whole; its wide-flung theaters were mutually dependent, with each one influencing the others.

The Eastern Front

The eastern front, where the Russians faced both the Germans and the Austrians, was certainly no mere sideshow. Millions of men were involved on both sides, and had the Russians not held out, as they did, until the end of 1917, the Allies in the West could hardly have withstood the reinforcements that the Germans and Austrians would have been able to send to France and Italy. The war in the east was more a war of movement than the war in the west. But even in the east there were long periods of stalemate, especially during the winters, when the opposing armies faced each other in improvised fortifications resembling the trenches of the west.

The Russians began well. Against the exposed Austrian salient of Galicia (Austria's share of the eighteenth-century partitions of Poland), the Russians threw in vast masses of men. They took the Galician capital of Lemberg (later the Polish Lwów, now the Soviet Lvov), and by the end of September 1914 they had reached the northern ends of some of the passes leading into Hungary through the Carpathian Mountains.

Russian and German soldiers fraternizing after the December 5, 1917,
armistice between Russia and the Central Powers.

Against the Germans, who also had to defend in East
Prussia a salient surrounded on the east and south by
Russian territory, the Russians won the battle of Gum-
binnen, in August 1914, and so alarmed the German
general staff that it reorganized the eastern command.
General von Ludendorff, under the nominal command
of his senior, von Hindenburg, and aided by a brilliant
junior, von Hoffmann, turned successfully against the
two Russian armies, which were attempting a pincers
movement. Late in August, at Tannenberg, the Germans decisively defeated a Russian army under Sam-
sonov, who committed suicide. And early in September
they again won decisively at the Masurian lakes, thus
clearing the Russians from East Prussia.

The Germans' hard-pressed Austrian allies to the
south were by now clamoring for help, and the western
front was still demanding men. Hindenburg and his
aides had to do their best with what they had. In a
series of hard-fought battles in Poland, they succeeded
in relieving the pressure on the Austrians. The end of
the year 1914 found the Austrians still hanging on in
Galicia and the Germans in a good position to push
eastward from East Prussian and Polish bases. In two
great joint offensives in May and July 1915 the Central
Powers won substantial successes, inflicting on the Russians severe losses from which they never really recovered. At the end of the year 1915 the battle line ran

roughly from near Riga, deep in the Baltic provinces
of Russia, to the eastern edge of Galicia at Tarnopol
and Czernowitz.

In 1916, the Russians, with a new commander,
General Brusilov, undertook a great new offensive
against the Austrians in the south. The Russian need
to bolster their failing morale would probably have
made some action necessary, but the Russians were also
being pressed by the Western Allies to do something
to help the Italians, who were threatened by the Austrians in the region of Trent. The Brusilov offensive was
begun too soon, without adequate preparation, although it scored a striking success at first, in places
driving the Austrians back some eighty miles, and taking large numbers of prisoners. Once more the Germans
came to the rescue; with fresh troops transferred from
the West, they halted Brusilov before he had won a
decisive success.

It was from the backwash of this defeat that the
Russian Revolution, which began early in March 1917,
was born. In the moderate phase of that uprising, before
the Bolshevik revolution of November 1917, Brusilov
undertook one last desperate offensive. But he was soon
checked, and the way was open for the Bolsheviks to
carry out their promise to make peace. By the end of
1917, Russia was out of the war. She was forced by
the Central Powers to sign the extraordinarily punitive

Peace of Brest-Litovsk (March 1918), by which she lost her Polish territories, her Baltic provinces, the entire Ukraine, Finland, and some lands in the Caucasus. The Caucasian lands went to Turkey; most of the others came under what proved to be the temporary domination of Austria and Germany.

The Italian Front

In April 1915 Italy concluded with Britain, France, and Russia the secret Treaty of London, which promised the Italians their long-sought Trent and Trieste and other lands at Austro-Hungarian and Turkish expense, notably the Dalmatian coast. In May, the Italians formally declared war on Austria-Hungary (they did not declare war on Germany until August 1916), and a new front was added along the Austro-Italian frontier at the head of the Adriatic. Since much of this front was mountainous, action was largely confined to some sixty miles along the Isonzo River, where for two years there was a series of bloody but indecisive engagements that pinned down several hundred thousand Austrian troops. Then in the late autumn of 1917, with Russia already beaten, came the blow that very nearly knocked Italy out. Once again the Germans supplied the propulsive force, as Ludendorff, now in supreme command, sent six German divisions to the Isonzo. The Germans and Austrians broke through at Caporetto and sent the Italians into a retreat across the Venetian plains, a retreat that was really a rout. French and British reinforcements were hastily rushed across the Alps, but what did most to stop the Austro-Germans was probably the grave difficulty, under modern conditions of warfare, of supplying their own mass armies of infantry in rapid advance. The Italians were finally able to hold along the line of the Piave River, almost at the Po.

The Dardanelles and the Balkans

One of the most important of the "sideshows," the Dardanelles campaign of 1915, not only proved in its failure to be a bad blow to the morale of the Allies, but was to have important repercussions in World War II. With the entry of Turkey into the war on the side of the Central Powers in November 1914, and with the western front capable for the moment of being held against the Germans by the French alone, a group of British leaders advanced the idea that British strength should be put into amphibious operations somewhere in the Aegean area. A steady drive could also be made overland toward Vienna and Berlin through territory where the Central Powers were not expecting an attack in force. The great exponent of this Eastern Plan was Winston Churchill, first lord of the admiralty. The point of attack chosen was the Dardanelles, the more westerly of the two straits that separate the Black Sea from the Aegean. The action is sometimes known as the Gallipoli campaign from the long narrow peninsula on the European side of the

Dardanelles that was a key to the whole action. Here Allied victory would have had the additional advantage of opening communication with Russia via the Black Sea.

In March 1915 the British and French fleets tried to force the Straits, but they abandoned the attempt somewhat prematurely when several ships struck mines. Later landings of British, Australian, New Zealand, and French troops at various points on both the Asian and European shores of the Dardanelles were poorly coordinated and badly backed up. They met with fierce and effective resistance from the Turks—their ranking officer at Gallipoli, Mustafa Kemal, greatly distinguishing himself—and in the end they had to pull out. Russia remained sealed in by the Straits all during the war. But Churchill continued to believe that the Dardanelles plan had failed not because it was faulty, but because it had not been carried out with determination. And in World War II, against American military opinion, he was to revive it with proposals to strike at the "soft underbelly" of the Axis.

Serbia's part in the crisis that produced the war meant that from the start there would be a Balkan front. In the end there were several such fronts, and no Balkan state remained uninvolved. The Austrians failed here also, and although they managed to take the Serbian capital, Belgrade (December 1914), they were driven out again. Bulgaria, wooed by both sides, finally came in with the Central Powers in the autumn of 1915. The Germans sent troops and a general, von Mackensen, under whom the Serbs were finally beaten. The remnant of their armies was driven to take refuge on the island of Corfu in neutral Greece.

To counter this blow in the Balkans, the Allies had already landed a few divisions in the Greek city of Salonika and had established a front in Macedonia. The Greeks themselves were divided into two groups. One was headed by King Constantine, who sympathized with the Central Powers, but who for the moment was seeking only to maintain Greek neutrality. The other was a pro-Ally group headed by the able old politician Venizelos. Although the Allies rode roughshod over formal notions of Greek neutrality, Venizelos did not get firmly into the saddle until June 1917, when Allied pressure compelled King Constantine to abdicate in favor of his second son, Alexander.

Meanwhile Romania, which the Russians had been trying to lure into the war, finally yielded to promises of great territorial gains at the expense of Austria-Hungary and came in on the Allied side late in August 1916, at a time most inopportune for the Romanians. Stiffened by German help, the Austrians swept through Romania and by January 1917 held most of the country. When the Russians made the separate Peace of Brest-Litovsk with the Germans in March 1918, the Romanians were obliged to yield some territory to Bulgaria, and to grant a lease of oil lands to Germany.

In spite of the formal accession of Greece to the Allied side in June 1917, the Macedonian front re-

Europe, 1914–1918

NORWAY
SWEDEN
GREAT BRITAIN
IRELAND
North Sea
DENMARK
Battle of Jutland
Baltic Sea
St. Petersburg
Volga R.
Riga
Moscow
Königsberg
Smolensk
London
NETH.
Ostend
Elbe R.
Berlin
E. PRUSSIA
Masurian Lakes
Tannenberg
Niemen R.
RUSSIA
BELG.
Rhine R.
GERMANY
Warsaw
Brest-Litovsk
Kiev
Dnieper R.
Seine R.
Paris
Verdun
LUX.
Oder R.
POLAND
Vistula R.
Cracow
Lemberg
FRANCE
Belfort
Danube R.
Prague
GALICIA
Tarnopol
Czernowitz
Dniester R.
SWITZ.
Vienna
AUSTRIA-HUNGARY
Budapest
TRANSYL-VANIA
Loire R.
Isonzo R.
Locarno
Caporetto
Milan
Piave R.
Bordeaux
Rhône R.
Genoa
Rapallo
ROMANIA
Bucharest
Black Sea
PORTUGAL
Madrid
Ebro R.
Leghorn
BOSNIA
Sarajevo
Belgrade
Danube R.
Tagus R.
SPAIN
DALMATIA
SERBIA
MONTENEGRO
BULGARIA
Sofia
ITALY
Rome
Constantinople
Bosporus
CORSICA (Fr.)
ALBANIA
Gibraltar (Br.)
SARDINIA
MACEDONIA
Salonika
Gallipoli
BALEARIC IS.
GREECE
Dardanelles
OTTOMAN EMPIRE
SPANISH MOROCCO
CORFU
Athens
DODECANESE (It.)
RHODES
MOROCCO
ALGERIA
SICILY
MALTA (Br.)
CRETE
CYPRUS (Br.)
Mediterranean Sea
TUNISIA

Allied and Associated Powers
Central Powers and their Allies
Neutrals
— Political boundaries, 1914
–·– Boundary between Austria and Hungary
▪▪▪ Greatest advance by Central Powers
•••• Greatest advance by Allies
■ Battle site

0   500
Miles

LIBYA
EGYPT
Cairo
Suez Canal
Nile R.

The Middle East, 1914-18

Black Sea
Trebizond
Caspian Sea
Tigris R.
Euphrates R.
Baghdad
Mediterranean Sea
Damascus
Nile R.
Jerusalem
Basra
Cairo
Persian Gulf

▨ Area of military action, 1914-18

Asia and the Pacific, 1914-15

Tsingtau
JAPAN
CHINA
FORMOSA
Pacific Ocean
INDIA
Madras
PHILIPPINE IS.
YAP
PENANG I.
CAROLINE IS.
Indian Ocean
Rabaul
AUSTRALIA

■ Battles and other military actions, 1914-15

mained in a stalemate until the summer of 1918, when, with American troops pouring rapidly into France, the Allied military leaders decided they could afford to build up their forces in Salonika. The investment paid well, for under the leadership of the French general Franchet d'Esperey the Allied armies on this front were the first to break the enemy completely. The French, British, Serbs, and Greeks began a great advance on September 15, 1918, all along the line from the Adriatic to the Bulgarian frontier. They forced the Bulgarians to conclude an armistice on September 30, and by early November they had crossed the Danube in several places. The armistice in the west on November 11 found the tricolor of France, with the flags of many allies, well on its way to Vienna. This victory, reminiscent of Napoleon, helped inspire in the French a somewhat unfounded confidence that they were once more the dominant nation on the continent of Europe.

The Near East and the Colonies

Another series of fronts developed in the outlying parts of the Turkish Empire and in the German colonies.

T.E. Lawrence.

The Turks, trained and in part officered by German experts, often resisted effectively. In Mesopotamia in April 1916, in a blow to British prestige as bad as the Dardanelles defeat, they forced the surrender of the British general Townshend, who had landed as Basra from India in 1915 and had marched up the Tigris-Euphrates Valley. Later the British marched north again and took Baghdad.

Elsewhere in the Near East, the Turks were never able to advance very far into Russian Armenia or to take the Suez Canal. Moreover, the British exploited the Arabs' dislike for their Turkish suzerains with the particular assistance of the romantic Colonel T. E. Lawrence, who knew the Arabs intimately and played a leading part in coordinating an Arab revolt with a British expedition from Egypt under Allenby. By the end of 1917, the British held Jerusalem. In September 1918, a great British offensive in Syria was so successful that on October 30 the Turks concluded an armistice which took them out of the war.

From these campaigns in the lands that had been the cradles of Western civilization there later emerged not only the independent Arab states but also the Jewish national state of Israel, to which they are so hostile. In November 1917, in the Balfour Declaration, the British promised "the establishment in Palestine of a national home for the Jewish people." This promise bore fruit in the mandate of 1922 from the League of Nations, by which such a home was set up under British protection.

In their overseas colonies the Germans, though cut off from the homeland by the British navy, fought well. In East Africa they actually managed to hold out in a series of skillful campaigns, so that they still had forces in the field on Armistice Day, November 11, 1918. But elsewhere they were fighting from inadequate bases and with inadequate forces, so that by the end of 1914 the British, Australians, South Africans, French, and Japanese had pretty well taken over the German overseas possessions. The Allies had won the "colonial war." Only years later, however, did the most important result of that war become clear. The subject races had learned that their rulers were by no means invulnerable.

The War at Sea

This brings us to a most important front—the war at sea. In the long pull, British seapower, reinforced by the French and later by the Italian and the American navies, once more proved decisive. The Allied command of the sea made it possible to draw on the resources of the rest of the world, and in particular to transfer with surprisingly few losses large numbers of British and American troops to the crucial western front. Quite as important, seapower enabled the Allies to shut Germany and her allies off from overseas resources. The Allied blockade slowly but surely constricted Germany, limiting not merely military supplies for her armies, but food supplies for her civilian population. At the end of 1918, many Germans were suffering from malnutrition, an important factor in the German willingness to surrender without fighting to the bitter end.

Yet the war at sea was not easy for the Allies. The submarine proved every bit as dangerous as British alarmists before the war had feared. When the Germans launched their unrestricted submarine warfare, they made dangerous inroads on the merchant ships that were essential to the very life of Britain. By the end of 1917, some eight million tons of shipping had been sunk by the Germans, most of it by submarines. And at one point in 1917, the British had barely enough food reserves to last a month. The submarine menace was eventually overcome by a series of measures coordinated between the Allies and the Americans—extensive use of the convoy system, attacks on submarines by depth bombs, constant antisubmarine patrols, and development of small, fast subchasers. But we might wonder what would have happened in 1916–1917 (and again in 1942–1943) if the Germans had contented themselves with holding actions on land and had put all their productive and fighting energies into the submarine. This they did not do in either world war. Temptation for quick and obvious success on land proved to be too great in both cases.

The navy of surface vessels that the Germans had built up since the 1890s and that had proved to be so important in the growth of Anglo-German hostility never played a really decisive part in the war itself. German surface raiders caused severe damage in the first year, but they were finally swept off the seas. Once, however, the main German fleet threw a bad scare into the British. This was the famous battle of Jutland, which has been refought over and over again by naval historians. This running battle, fought in the North Sea on May 31 and June 1, 1916, resulted in the sinking of twice as much British as German tonnage, and showed how good the German navy was. But the German admiral, Scheer, was forced to run into port before the British capital ships, for which he was no match. Although Jutland was a tactical victory for the Germans, the strategic victory remained with the British; the German surface navy never again seriously threatened Britain's command of the sea in European waters. At the war's end the German high command attempted to get the fleet out in a heroic last stand. It was the German sailors' refusal to take the ships out—their mutiny, in fact—that gave a critical push to the German revolution which led to the Armistice of 1918.

The Western Front: Allied Victory

This war also saw the beginnings of air warfare. German dirigibles known as Zeppelins raided London many times in 1916–1917, and both sides made airplane bombing raids on nearby towns. But the total damage was relatively light and had no decisive effect on the final result. The airplane was of more impor-

tance in scouting, and especially in spotting for artillery; in spite of its short range in those days, it also proved useful as a means of locating submarines. The fighter plane was greatly improved during the war, and the base was laid for the development of the air forces we now know. Indeed, the airplane made greater technical strides in these four years of war than it had made since the Wrights first flew at Kitty Hawk in 1903.

Although the great new invention of the airplane did not itself alter traditional warfare, a new type of warfare was developed, especially on the great western front, the warfare of the trenches. The machine gun, the repeating rifle, and fast-firing artillery, with the guidance of spotter planes, could pour in such deadly fire that it was almost impossible for either side to break through the opposing trench systems on a wide front. Both sides tried to break through in the two years after the Marne, and both sides suffered losses of a magnitude that had never been suffered before.

Two new weapons almost broke the deadlock. The first was poison gas, which was first used by the Germans in shells in October 1914, with disappointing results. Then in April 1915 the Germans used chlorine gas discharged from cylinders. The overwhelmed French broke in a line five miles wide, leaving the line completely undefended. But the Germans had not prepared to follow through, and the gap was closed once the gas had dispersed. Meanwhile the experts developed a simple countermeasure, the gas mask, which became part of the equipment of every soldier on both sides. The age-old balance of attack and defense was once again reestablished.

The second new weapon came much nearer to producing decisive success. This was the tank, a sort of armored land battleship for which plans had been made back in the Renaissance by the fertile Leonardo da Vinci. But Leonardo's tank remained a mere sketch for lack of propulsive power. In the second decade of the twentieth century, however, the internal-combustion engine was ready to do what horses could not do. The tank was a British invention that had been nursed along in its infancy by the always adventurous Winston Churchill; it acquired its improbable name when early models were shipped under tarpaulins, which the curious were told covered water tanks. But the new weapon was used too soon, in inadequate numbers and before sufficient mechanical tests had been made, in the British Somme offensive of 1916. Even so, nine tanks led or accompanied the infantry triumphantly through the German lines. Had the tanks been withheld for a few more months and been introduced after careful planning, they might have broken the German lines on a wide front. The Germans, however, were soon producing tanks of their own.

The Germans also developed a spectacular new weapon that struck the imagination of the world, though it had no effect on the outcome of the war. Big Bertha was a gun of incredibly long range, which began throwing occasional shells into Paris from the nearest point in the German lines, some seventy-five miles away. The Parisians were astounded, since no hostile planes had appeared. But Big Bertha could fire only a few shells before it needed repair and proved to be of no more than nuisance value.

Techniques of attack gradually developed over the years and in the end broke the defensive stalemate in the west. Long and massive discharge of artillery, known as a barrage, literally flattened out a section of the enemy defenses and the no-man's land in front of them and forced the enemy to retire to rear trenches. Then, accompanied or preceded by tanks, the infantry edged in while the artillery barrage was lifted and focused on the next enemy line. It was a slow and costly process that did not work on a wide scale until 1918. Then the Germans, with the Russians out of the fight, made a last and almost successful effort to break through, trying to separate the British from the French where their lines joined near Amiens. With the failure of this last German push in the summer, Foch ordered a general attack. French, British, and American armies had all broken the German lines by early autumn and were just gaining freedom of action in the open country when the Germans surrendered. The Germans later maintained that they were not beaten decisively in the field. Most experts, however, now think that had the war gone on the Germans could not have stopped an Allied invasion of Germany in 1919.

Morale on the Fighting Fronts

The long, narrow battle lines of the four-year trench war were the scene of a concentrated destruction hardly

Trench warfare.

equaled in the war of 1939–1945, except by the atomic bomb at Hiroshima; at some points in France the top-soil was blown completely away by shellfire, producing a desert that is still visible today. The war itself was not unique or unprecedented, as many an excited publicist at the time declared. It produced military heroes and military scapegoats, great generals and generals who failed. As with the Confederacy in the American Civil War, the defeated Germans seem to have had the most praised generals, the Ludendorffs, the Mackensens, the Hoffmanns. The old traditional chivalrous warfare, the warfare of athletic heroes, was continued and even heightened in the air, where the "aces" of the highly individualistic duels between planes were the Rolands of a machine age. And in many of the fronts on land, and in the war at sea, the age-old and for many males not altogether unhappy melodrama of war lost none of its reality. Lawrence in Arabia was no disgrace to the tradition of Sir Walter Scott or even, in the eyes of good patriotic Englishmen, to the tradition of Homer.

Yet especially on the western front, this war seemed to many of its participants an unheroic nightmare of blood and filth. Sensitive young intellectuals, who in earlier times would never have had to fight, survived to write bitterly about their experiences—in war novels like *Under Fire* by the Frenchman Barbusse, or *All Quiet on the Western Front* by the German Remarque, and in war poems like those of Siegfried Sassoon and Wilfred Owen. But this literature cannot be trusted fully as an accurate reflection of what the millions of common soldiers who were not intellectuals felt about the war. We know simply that for four years they bore up under it in stints in the front lines separated by rest leaves. For most of them the dullness, the discomforts, and the brief terror of battle must have tested their patriotism and worn out their sense of adventure.

Here is a passage not by one of the most bitterly radical of the intellectuals, or about the western front. John Masefield, the British poet, is writing about Gallipoli, where he took part in the Dardanelles campaign:

Let the reader imagine himself to be facing three miles of any very rough broken sloping ground known to him. . . . Let him say to himself that he and an army of his friends are about to advance up the slope towards the top and that as they will be advancing in a line, along the whole length of the three miles, he will only see the advance of those comparatively near to him, since folds or dips in the ground will hide the others. Let him, before he advances, look earnestly along the line of the hill, as it shows up clear, in blazing sunlight only a mile from him, to see his tactical objective, one little clump of pines, three hundred yards away, across what seem to be fields. Let him see in the whole length of the hill no single human being, nothing but scrub, earth, a few scattered buildings. . . . Let him imagine himself to be more weary than he has ever been in his life before, and dirtier than he has ever believed it possible to be, and parched with thirst, nervous, wild-eyed and rather lousy. Let him think that he has not slept for more than a few minutes together for eleven days and nights, and that in all his waking hours he has been fighting for his life, often hand to hand in the dark with a fierce enemy, and that after each fight he has had to dig himself a hole in the ground, often with his hands, and then walk three or four roadless miles to bring up heavy boxes under fire. Let him think, too, that in all those eleven days he has never for an instant been out of the thunder of cannon, that waking or sleeping their devastating crash has been blasting the air across within a mile or two, and this from an artillery so terrible that each discharge beats as it were a wedge of shock between the skull-bone and the brain. Let him think too that never, for an instant, in all that time, has he been free or even partly free from the peril of death in its most sudden and savage forms, and that hourly in all that time he has seen his friends blown to pieces at his side, or dismembered, or drowned, or driven mad, or stabbed, or sniped by some unseen stalker, or bombed in the dark sap with a handful of dynamite in a beef-tin, till their blood is caked upon his clothes and thick upon his face, and that he knows, as he stares at the hill, that in a few moments, more of that dwindling band, already too few, God knows how many too few, for the task to be done, will be gone the same way, and that he himself may reckon that he has done with life, tasted and spoken and loved his last, and that in a few minutes more may be blasted dead, or lying bleeding in the scrub, with perhaps his face gone and a leg and an arm broken, unable to move but still alive, unable to drive away the flies or screen the ever-dropping rain, in a place where none will find him, or be able to help him, a place where he will die and rot and shrivel, till nothing is left of him but a few rags and a few remnants and a little identification-disc flapping on his bones in the wind.*

The Home Fronts

These soldiers and sailors were, for the most part, not professionals; they were civilians, drafted from civilian families unused to the ways of the military. Behind the front, on the production lines, subject to the unheroic but harassing strains of rationing and all sorts of limitations in daily living, subject also to the constant prodding of war propaganda, the families too were part of this great "total war." They too bore up under it, though in France in 1917, after the bloody failure of a great offensive under General Nivelle, civilian and military discontent, fanned by politicians, came almost to the point of breaking French morale. And in Germany, the collapse that resulted in the armistice of November 11, 1918, though it obviously had many complex causes, looks like a general failure of morale, a psychological collapse under intolerable spiritual and material pressures.

For the Germans, still influenced by nineteenth-century ideas about the rights of the individual and laissez faire economics, were slow to organize their society for total war. They failed notably to ensure the proper and equitable distribution of food supplies, so that as 1918 wore on whole sectors of the urban population began to suffer from malnutrition. Nor were

finances and war production managed with that perfection of techniques that most of the world had already come to expect of the Germans. Rationing, strict control of production, price control, systematic use of the resources of conquered countries, these and many other measures were employed by the Germans, but not with the care, decisiveness, and long preparation that were to characterize them in the conflict of 1939–1945.

All countries engaged in the war, the democratic Western Allies as well as the autocratic Central Powers, sooner or later felt obliged to introduce drastic wartime economic planning, which anticipated in some sense the more collectivistic economy of today. Everywhere there was compulsory military service. Even in Britain, proud of its long devotion to the rights of the individual, the famous Defense of the Realm Act—known with wry affection as DORA—clamped down severely on the Englishman's sacred right to say and do what he liked, even if he did not seem to be giving aid and comfort to the enemy. In the United States, all sorts of men, including the famous "dollar-a-year men," business executives who were working for the government for the first time, flocked to Washington and helped build up an enormous new central government, which regulated the economy as it had never been regulated before. And of course all the belligerents engaged in the war of propaganda or, as it came to be called in the next great war, psychological warfare.

The Allies won the battle of the production lines, in which the United States played a major part, though not the decisive one it was to play in World War II. Allied production was slow in getting started, with mistakes, bottlenecks, and overhasty experiments like that with the first tanks. At the beginning the Allies were often at cross purposes in production as they were in military strategy. Nevertheless, the Allies eventually were able to realize to the full their potential superiority over the Central Powers in material resources, and by the end of 1917 their military machine was adequately, and in some ways wastefully, supplied.

Propaganda and Politics

The Allies also won the most critical phase of the war of propaganda. They sought to convince the neutral world, especially the neutrals of Western civilization, the United States, Latin America, and the Swiss, Dutch, Scandinavians, and Spaniards, that the Allies were fighting for the right and the Central Powers for the wrong. It was not a complete victory, for important groups in all these countries remained pro-German to the end, and Spain on the whole was probably throughout the war pro-German, or at least anti-French and anti-English. Still, a majority of the neutral West was early convinced that the cause of the Allies was just, a conviction strengthened by the traditional liberalism of France and Britain in contrast with the traditional autocracy of the German and the Austrian empires, though the presence of the autocratic Russian

*J. Masefield, *Gallipoli* (New York, 1916), pp. 96–99.

Women working in a U.S. factory to help the war effort.

Empire on the Allied side somewhat handicapped Allied propagandists. In the early days of the crisis of 1914, the intransigence of the Austrians toward the Serbs, and in particular the blundering phrase of Bethmann-Hollweg, that Britain had gone to war for a mere "scrap of paper," got the Central Powers off to a bad start in world opinion.

Allied propaganda was often one-sided and unfair, notably in accusing the Germans of frightful atrocities in Belgium. The Germans imposed rigorous military controls on conquered populations, but little in their record was worse than is usual, and perhaps inevitable, in all warfare. Allied propaganda also simplified and falsified the complex chain of causation that produced the war, making it appear that the Germans and Austrians were wholly responsible for the outbreak of the war, that the "predatory Potsdam gang" had planned the whole thing from the beginning, and that Serbs, French, Russians, and British had been wholly innocent of deed or word that might have brought on the war. This propaganda backfired shortly after the war; revulsion against its unfairness had much to do with the widespread acceptance of the extreme revisionist thesis that on the whole Germany, in particular, had been quite guiltless of starting the war.

Except in Russia, the four years of war saw no major changes in political structure. The Central Powers retained until their collapse their incompletely responsible parliamentary governments, and the parliaments on the whole were reasonably submissive. And in spite of the inevitable strengthening of the executive in wartime, France, Britain, and the United States carried on their democratic institutions. In the United States the critical presidential election of 1916 came just

before American entrance into the war, and resulted by a narrow margin in the return of the incumbent, Woodrow Wilson. In Britain and France the democratic process brought to power in the midst of wartime crisis two strong men—Lloyd George and Clemenceau—who carried through with great vigor the prosecution of the war, and who, though their fame was dimmed in the troubled years after the war, remain in historic memory as great national heroes of their respective countries.

In Britain the skillful but indecisive Liberal leader Asquith proved unable to master events, even though he widened his government into a coalition in May 1915. In December of that year he was succeeded by another Liberal, Lloyd George, the architect of Britain's social insurance system, who had also proved himself an admirable organizer of war production. Under Lloyd George the coalition really worked, and his position as war leader was to remain unchallenged. We shall meet him again at the peace negotiations, as we shall meet his French counterpart, Clemenceau. The Tiger, as Clemenceau was known to his friends and enemies alike, came to power at the end of 1917, at a time when defeatism threatened both the military and the civilian strength of France. Clemenceau took firm command of the war effort and disposed summarily of the disaffected politicians with the decisiveness—and disregard for the peacetime "rights of man"—of an old Jacobin.

IV The Peace Settlements

As in Westphalia in 1648, at Utrecht in 1713, and at Vienna in 1815, the warring powers gathered in a great meeting to make the peace settlement. This time they met at Paris—or, rather, in suburban Paris. They met at Versailles to settle with the Germans, and at other suburban châteaux to settle with the rest. Peace congresses almost never meet in a world that is really at peace. There is always an aftermath of local war, crises, and disturbances; in 1918–1919 they were so numerous and acute that they conditioned the whole work of the peace congresses. We must examine this aftermath of the 1914–1918 war before considering the actual settlements.

The Aftermath of World War I

The sorest spot was Russia, in 1919 in the throes of civil war and foreign invasion. No sooner had the Germans been forced to withdraw from the regions they had gained at Brest-Litovsk than the Allies sent detachments to various points along the rim of Russia—on the Black Sea, on the White Sea in the far north, and on the Pacific. The Allies still hoped to restore in Russia, if not the monarchy, at least a moderate democratic republic. Their dread of final Bolshevik success ("Bolshevism," not "communism," was the term almost universally used during this period) and of the possible spread of Bolshevism westward added to the tensions at Versailles and confirmed the conservative position that both Clemenceau and Lloyd George were taking.

Bolshevism was certainly spreading westward. The German revolution of November 1918 had been carried out under socialist auspices. But all through the winter of 1918–1919 there were communist riots and uprisings, and in Bavaria in April a soviet republic was proclaimed. The government of the new republic of Germany put these communist uprisings down, but only by an appeal to the remnants of the old army and to officers thoroughly hostile to any form of republic. In the breakup of the Austro-Hungarian monarchy in the autumn of 1918, the successor states—Czechoslovakia, Austria, Hungary, Yugoslavia, Romania—which had been formed in whole or in part out of the former Hapsburg lands, were disturbed by all sorts of social and economic troubles. In Hungary, Bela Kun, who had worked with Lenin in Moscow, won power by means of a socialist-communist coalition, and then elbowed out his socialist colleagues and set up a Bolshevik dictatorship. In August 1919, a Romanian army that had invaded Hungary forced Bela Kun to flee. Finally, all through the Germanies groups of ex-soldiers, the Freikorps ("free corps") were stirring up trouble and threatening the overthrow of the German Republic.

In the Near East the Allies had even worse troubles to face. Greece, which had been so hard to drag into the war, was now in full cry against the Turks. Her nationalists had revived the old hope of a restored Byzantine Empire, with the Greeks once more in command of the Straits. Her armies, not without Allied encouragement, landed at Smyrna in Asia Minor in the spring of 1919 and marched off in the track of Alexander the Great. The French and the British, to whom

control over different parts of the former Turkish Empire had been assigned, began at once having trouble with their new Arab wards. The Jews were already pressing for the establishment of a national home in Palestine in accordance with the Balfour Declaration, and the Arabs were already opposing them.

In India the aftermath of war was particularly bad. The universal epidemic of influenza in 1918 (which most public-health experts believed killed more people than were killed in battle) had been especially disastrous in India. Indians had fought well as professional soldiers during the war on the Allied side; educated Indians thought their country was ripe for much more self-rule. The disorders of 1918–1919 culminated in the Amritsar massacre of April 1919, in which a British general, reverting to old-time methods, ordered his soldiers to fire on an unarmed crowd, killing or wounding some sixteen hundred people. Amritsar shocked world opinion, added to the odium the Allies were already acquiring among liberals everywhere, and knitted India more closely together in opposition to the British.

The situation in China was even shakier. There, as a later chapter will detail, a revolution in 1911–1912 had ended the rule of the Manchu dynasty and inaugurated a precarious republican regime. The internal distractions of the Chinese and the weakening of Russia led the Japanese to renew their ambitious plans in north China. The American troops sent to Vladivostok in Siberia were there less to oppose the Bolsheviks than to oppose the Japanese.

Problems, Promises, and Expectations

So the world was in turmoil and disorder when the Allies, great, small, and middle-sized, assembled in and near Paris to make the peace. The problems that faced the peacemakers were worldwide, complex, and often insoluble in the sense that no decision on a given problem, say the disposition of the Adriatic port of Fiume, which was claimed by Italians and Yugoslavs, could possibly satisfy all the major groups concerned, to say nothing of the minorities. Yet the world hoped, and expected, from the peacemakers more than it had in any previous settlement. Public opinion in the eighteenth and nineteenth centuries had built up a tremendous faith in the possibility of a peaceful, just, and happy world. This war had been a war to "make the world safe for democracy," a "war to end war." It had produced in the American president Wilson a man who could phrase skillfully the hopes of men, and who as he journeyed to Paris after the Armistice appeared to be the heroic savior and hope of mankind.

All men were not Wilsonians. There were, as always, the selfish, the disillusioned, the narrow, the jingoists, and the professionals who had made promises to the Italians and the Romanians, who had planned all sorts of compensations and adjustments. There were the average men and women who wanted peace and security but who also wanted national glory and the

The Big Four in Paris, December 1918. Seated from left to right: Orlando, Lloyd George, Clemenceau, and Wilson.

punishment of the wicked Germans, who, they believed, had put them through those four years of hell. There were, in short, thousands of conflicting hopes and fears, all of them embodied in living human flesh, not just the abstractions they must seem to be on the printed page.

The more generous of these hopes were in 1918 clearly embodied in one man and in one text. Woodrow Wilson, on January 8, 1918, in an address to the American Congress, had announced the famous Fourteen Points, which were widely accepted by people in Allied countries and even in Germany and Austria as a platform for the peace to come, but were also widely misunderstood and subject to the most divergent interpretations. Here is the whole of this important document:

I. Open covenants of peace, openly arrived at, after which there shall be no private international understandings of any kind but diplomacy shall proceed always frankly and in the public view.

II. Absolute freedom of navigation upon the seas, outside territorial waters, alike in peace and in war, except as the seas may be closed in whole or in part by international action for the enforcement of international covenants.

III. The removal, so far as possible, of all economic barriers

and the establishment of an equality of trade conditions among all the nations consenting to the peace and associating themselves for its maintenance.

IV. Adequate guarantees given and taken that national armaments will be reduced to the lowest point consistent with domestic safety.

V. A free, open-minded, and absolutely impartial adjustment of all colonial claims, based upon a strict observance of the principle that in determining all such questions of sovereignty the interests of the populations concerned must have equal weight with the equitable claims of the government whose title is to be determined.

VI. The evacuation of all Russian territory and such a settlement of all questions affecting Russia as will secure the best and freest co-operation of the other nations of the world in obtaining for her an unhampered and unembarrassed opportunity for the independent determination of her own political development and national policy and assure her of a sincere welcome into the society of free nations under institutions of her own choosing and, more than a welcome, assistance also of every kind that she may need and may herself desire. The treatment accorded Russia by her sister nations in the months to come will be the acid test of their good will, of their comprehension of her needs as distinguished from their own interests, and of their intelligent and unselfish sympathy.

VII. Belgium, the whole world will agree, must be evacuated and restored, without any attempt to limit the sovereignty which she enjoys in common with all other free nations. No other single act will serve as this will serve to restore confidence among the nations in the laws which they have themselves set and determined for the government of their relations with one another. Without this healing act the whole structure and validity of international law is forever impaired.

VIII. All French territory should be freed and the invaded portions restored, and the wrong done to France by Prussia in 1871 in the matter of Alsace-Lorraine, which has unsettled the peace of the world for nearly fifty years, should be righted, in order that peace may once more be made secure in the interest of all.

IX. A readjustment of the frontiers of Italy should be effected along clearly recognizable lines of nationality.

X. The peoples of Austria-Hungary, whose place among the nations we wish to see safeguarded and assured, should be accorded the freest opportunity of autonomous development.

XI. Rumania, Serbia, and Montenegro should be evacuated; occupied territories restored; Serbia accorded free and secure access to the sea; and the relations of the several Balkan states to one another determined by friendly counsel along historically established lines of allegiance and nationality; and international guarantees of the political and economic independence and territorial integrity of the several Balkan states should be entered into.

XII. The Turkish portions of the present Ottoman Empire should be assured a secure sovereignty, but the other nationalities which are now under Turkish rule should be assured an undoubted security of life and an absolutely unmolested opportunity of autonomous development, and the Dardanelles should be permanently opened as a free passage to the ships and commerce of all nations under international guarantees.

XIII. An independent Polish state should be erected which should include the territories inhabited by indisputably Polish populations, which should be assured a free and secure access to the sea, and whose political and economic independence and territorial integrity should be guaranteed by international covenant.

XIV. A general association of nations must be formed under specific covenants for the purpose of affording mutual guarantees of political independence and territorial integrity to great and small states alike.*

The fourteenth point, the germ of the League of Nations, was especially dear to Wilson.

The hopes and promises that opposed and contradicted the Fourteen Points were not neatly embodied in a single document. We may classify them roughly in three categories: the previous diplomatic commitments made by the Allies; the immediate and widespread popular hopes fanned by Allied propaganda and confirmed at the last moment by some Allied statesmen; and—much more difficult to pin down—the long-established habits and traditions that had become

*W. Wilson, *War and Peace: Presidential Messages, Addresses, and Public Papers*, eds. R. S. Baker and W. E. Dodd (New York, 1927), 1:159–161.

part of the dominant policies and trends of each nation, big and little.

In the first category, the most difficult of the diplomatic commitments was the contradictory set of promises made to both Italy and Serbia by the original Entente, including Russia, about the disposal of Hapsburg lands. And there were other commitments, especially in the Balkans, that were very difficult to sort out. In the second category were the promises, widely believed by the British and French peoples, that Germany would be made to suffer to the full for her war guilt. She would have to pay the whole cost of the war in reparations, her war criminals would be punished, she would be rendered incapable ever again of assuming the role of the aggressor. In some vague way, everything would shortly be much better for everybody. Britain, for example, would be "a land fit for heroes."

Finally, in the third category were the deeply rooted drives of the various nations—French drives for revenge against Germany, for restoration of French hegemony in Europe, and, no doubt inconsistently but very humanly, for security; the Italian Irredentist drive; the British longing for a Victorian serenity and economic leadership well armored against German commercial competition; and the nationalist aspirations of the new states of central Europe, released at last from long frustration. And by no means the least important was the old and firmly held American tradition of isolationism, the desire to be free from European alliances and entanglements.

The Process of Peacemaking

The peace conference first met formally on January 18, 1919. Nearly thirty nations involved in the war against the Central Powers sent delegates. Russia was not represented. None of the victorious great powers—Britain, France, the United States—was in a mood to invite the Bolsheviks, now in power in Moscow, to the peace table; and no Russian government-in-exile seemed to the Allies suitable for an invitation. The defeated nations took no part in the deliberations; they were simply notified of the final terms and asked to sign. The Germans, in particular, were given but the slightest chance to comment on or criticize the terms offered them. Very soon the German publicists coined a term for the treaty—Diktat, the imposed, the dictated peace. The Germans' anger over this failure of the Allies to negotiate with their new and virtuous republic was to play a large part in the ultimate rise of Hitler.

Although a few Western liberals were from the first disillusioned by the exclusion of Communist Russia and the Central Powers from the peace conference, the conference did get off to a good start. Wilson's reception in Europe had been extremely enthusiastic. People everywhere were still rejoicing over the end of the nightmare. The Fourteen Points seemed already a realized peace; and for the future, it was held, the proposed association of nations, working together in the freedom of parliamentary discussion, would soon eliminate the costly burdens of armament. Wilson's hopeful phrases sounded in press and pulpit, and none more loudly than his "open covenants openly arrived at." To many a liberal these words meant that the peace would be made in a sort of big, idealized New England town meeting, in which the representatives of all the powers, big and little, would have their free say in public, in which decisions would ultimately be taken by majority vote, in which the caucus, the smoke-filled room, the backstairs intrigues would all be missing.

These liberals were almost at once disillusioned, for the conference soon relapsed into a familiar pattern. The small nations were excluded from the real negotiations; the business of the conference was carried on in private among the political chiefs of the victorious great powers—the Big Four of Wilson, Lloyd George, Clemenceau, and Orlando (it was really a Big Three, for Italy was by far the weakest of the quartet, and Orlando was a much less striking personality than his colleagues). Decisions were made in the traditional way of diplomacy, with only indirect consultation of public opinion and with all the pressures, chicanery, intrigue, compromises, and horse-trading that go on when leaders get together in private.

The hopeful members of the general public were by no means the only ones who grew disillusioned as the Paris conference went the way of the Vienna Congress a hundred years before. The professional diplomats of the little and middle-sized powers had probably never really expected that they would be treated on equal terms, but the completeness of their exclusion from the real work of the conference annoyed them and angered their people back home. More important, all the major powers had brought with them large staffs of experts—economists, political scientists, historians, career men in many fields. These bright young men were sure they knew better than their elders how to solve the problems of human relations, were confident that they would do the real work and make the really important decisions. They drew up report after report, some of which went up through devious channels to Clemenceau or Lloyd George or Wilson. But they did not make policy. The disillusionment of the young experts was great and long-lived, and since many of them were quite articulate they did much to discredit the work of the conference, especially among liberal intellectuals everywhere. The most celebrated of these experts was the economist John Maynard Keynes, then in his thirties, who represented the British Treasury at Versailles until he quit in disgust and wrote the highly critical analysis, *The Economic Consequences of the Peace.*

Wilson and his experts were gradually badgered into accepting harsher peace terms. The reparations bill against Germany was lengthened; Poland, Italy, and Japan made claims to lands that clearly could never be justified on the basis of self-determination by the peoples concerned; the victors more and more openly showed that they proposed to behave as victors in war

habitually have behaved. Wilson gave way or compromised on a dozen points and then chose to stand fast against the weakest of the Allies. He would not let the Italians have Fiume, which had once been the sole seaport of Hungary. They might have neighboring Trieste and their coveted Trentino, where they could rule over German or Slavic-speaking minorities (indeed, in some areas, majorities), but Fiume they might not have. Fiume was Italian-speaking and historically was linked with the great past of Venice; but it had never been part of modern Italy, and it had not been promised to Italy in the secret treaties of 1915. The Italian delegation left the conference in anger, but Wilson was immovable. The fate of Fiume was not settled at the conference; only in 1924, by treaty with Yugoslavia, did the city go to Italy in return for Susak, a port right next door that served the Yugoslavs quite adequately for the next two decades.

But Wilson did get his new international organization; the covenant of the League of Nations was an integral part of the Treaty of Versailles. The League was no true supranational state, but a kind of permanent consultative system composed of the victors and a few neutrals. The way was left open for the Germans and the Russians to join the League, as they later did. But in 1919–1920, Wilson's League looked to many liberals a lot like Metternich's and Castlereagh's old congress system of 1815, by no means worth the sacrifices Wilson had made to obtain it. The League had an assembly in which each member state had one vote, and a council in which the five great powers (Britain, France, Italy, the United States, and Japan) had permanent seats, and to which four other member states were chosen by the assembly for specific terms. A permanent secretariat, to be located at Geneva, was charged with administering the affairs of the League. In its working out, as we shall see, the League never fulfilled the hopes it had aroused. It did not achieve disarmament, nor did its machinery of peacemaking prove capable of preventing aggression. The great powers simply went on their usual ways, using the League only as their policymakers—their heads of state rather than their diplomats—saw fit.

The Territorial Settlement

Central to all the work in Paris was the problem of territorial changes. The peacemakers were confronted not merely with the claims of the victorious Allies but also with those of the new nations that had sprung up from the disintegrating Austrian, Russian, and Turkish empires. They had to try to satisfy the eternal land hunger of those who run nations, without violating too obviously the great Wilsonian principle of "self-determination of peoples." This principle was hard to apply in much of central Europe, where peoples of different language and national self-consciousness were mixed together in an incredible mosaic of unassimilated minorities. The result was to multiply the number of

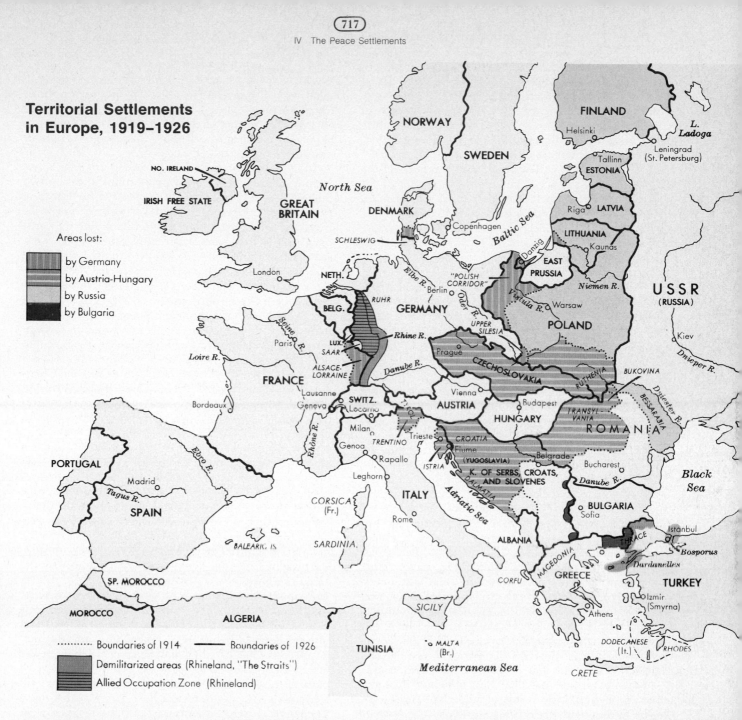

Territorial Settlements in Europe, 1919–1926

Areas lost:

- by Germany
- by Austria-Hungary
- by Russia
- by Bulgaria

········· Boundaries of 1914   ——— Boundaries of 1926

Demilitarized areas (Rhineland, "The Straits")

Allied Occupation Zone (Rhineland)

"sovereign" nations in this world. Nationalism, which some hopeful people had thought was on the wane, was now fanned to intense new life in a dozen states.

France received Alsace-Lorraine back from Germany. Clemenceau also hoped both to annex the small but coal-rich Saar Basin of Germany as compensation for French coal mines destroyed by the Germans during the war and to detach from Germany the territory on the left (or west) bank of the Rhine, thereby strengthening French security and setting up a Rhineland republic that might become a French satellite. Both French hopes, opposed by Wilson and Lloyd George, went unrealized. The Saar was to be separated from Germany for fifteen years as an international ward

supervised by the League of Nations. During that period its coal output would go to France, and at its close a plebiscite would determine its political future. The Rhineland remained part of the German Republic, though it was to be demilitarized and occupied for a time by Allied soldiers.

Belgium was given some small towns on her German border. After a plebiscite provided for in the Treaty of Versailles, Denmark recovered the northern part of Schleswig, which the Danish crown had lost to Prussia in 1864. Italy redeemed her Irredenta of Trent and Trieste in generous measure, for thousands of German and Slavic-speaking peoples were included within her new boundaries. Poland, erased from the map as an independent state in 1795, was now restored and given lands that she had had before the partitions of the eighteenth century and that contained important minorities of Germans and other non-Polish peoples. The old Hapsburg Empire was entirely dismembered. The heart of its German-speaking area was constituted as the truncated Republic of Austria, which was forbidden to join itself to Germany, and the heart of its Magyar-speaking area became a diminished Kingdom of Hungary. The Czech-inhabited lands of Bohemia and Moravia were joined with Slovakia and the Ruthenian lands of the Carpatho-Ukraine further east in the brand-new "succession state" of Czechoslovakia. This new state faced the problem of a large and discontented Sudeten German minority.

Another "succession state" was Yugoslavia, then officially the Kingdom of Serbs, Croats, and Slovenes, a union between prewar Serbia and the south Slav territories of the Hapsburgs. Romania, which received the former Hungarian province of Transylvania, was also rewarded with Bessarabia, a Russian province that the Bolsheviks could not defend. Romania thus emerged with doubled territory and some restive non-Romanian minorities. In the southern Balkan peninsula, Greece received all of Thrace, at the expense of Turkey and Bulgaria.

Out of the former czarist domains held at the end of the war by the Germans there were set up, in addition to Poland, the Baltic republics of Estonia, Latvia, and Lithuania. Once Europe had settled down, plebiscites determined certain other territorial adjustments, notably whether certain parts of East Prussia and Silesia should go to Poland or remain German. The new Polish state had been granted access to the Baltic Sea through the so-called Polish Corridor, a narrow strip of land that had once been Polish and that terminated in the almost wholly German city and port of Danzig. The Poles wanted Danzig, but the Allies compromised by setting up a Free City of Danzig and by giving the Poles free trade with the city. Even so, the Polish Corridor now separated East Prussia from the rest of Germany, and Germans had to cross it in sealed trains.

Outside Europe, the Near East presented the most acute problems. By the Treaty of Sèvres the Turks were left in Europe with only Constantinople and a small area of land around it, and in Asia with Anatolia. Mesopotamia and Palestine were given as mandates—a term we shall shortly explain—to Britain, while Syria and Lebanon were given as mandates to France. The Greeks were to hold Smyrna and nearby regions in Asia Minor for five years and then submit to a plebiscite. But the Treaty of Sèvres never went into effect, though it was duly signed by the sultan. In Anatolia a group of army officers headed by Mustafa Kemal led a popular revolt against the government at Constantinople and galvanized the Turkish people into a new national life. The Turks drove the Greek army out of their country and set up a republic with its capital not at Istanbul (the Turkish name for Constantinople)

but at Ankara in the heart of Anatolia. With this new government the Allies were finally obliged to conclude the Treaty of Lausanne in 1923. The new peace transferred the area of Izmir (Turkish for Smyrna) and eastern Thrace from Greek to Turkish control and was in general much more advantageous to the Turks than the Treaty of Sèvres had been.

The Lausanne settlement included a radical innovation: a formal transfer of populations affecting two million people. Greeks in Turkey, except for Istanbul, were moved to Greece, and Turks in Greece, except for western Thrace, were moved to Turkey. Each government was to take care of the transferred populations, and though much hardship resulted, on the whole the plan worked. No such exchange occurred on Cyprus, the British-controlled island in the eastern Mediterranean, where Greeks outnumbered Turks 4 to 1 and the two peoples were intermingled in the main towns and many villages, so that an exchange would have been extremely difficult. Nor were any measures taken to satisfy the national aspirations of two other minorities—the Muslim Kurds of eastern Anatolia, and the Christian Armenians, many of whom had perished during the war when the Turks forced them to march from their home provinces in northeastern Anatolia to northern Syria.

In the rest of the world the old straightforward policy of annexing overseas territories of defeated powers, as practiced in 1713, 1763, and 1815, seemed no longer possible in 1919. Liberal opinion both in Europe and in America had already been offended to the bursting point, and Wilson himself would never have permitted outright annexations. The consequence was the mandate system, whereby control over a given territory was assigned to a particular mandatory power by the League of Nations, which undertook periodic inspections to see that the terms of the mandate were being fulfilled. This system was designed by its proponents as a means of educating colonial peoples, leading them into the ways of democratic self-government, and preparing them for eventual independence. Under it the former German overseas territories and the non-Turkish parts of the Ottoman Empire were now distributed. Of Germany's African possessions East Africa (rechristened Tanganyika) went to Britain; Southwest Africa went to the Union of South Africa; and both the Cameroons and Togoland were divided between Britain and France. In the Pacific, the German portion of New Guinea was given to Australia, western Samoa to New Zealand, and the Caroline, Marshall, and Mariana island groups to Japan. In the Near East, as we have seen, France secured Syria and Lebanon, while Britain took Palestine, Transjordan, and Iraq (the new Arabic designation for Mesopotamia).

The mandate system may seem to have been a way of disguising annexation. And so to a man like Clemenceau it probably was. The Japanese quite openly annexed and fortified their new Pacific islands in defiance of the terms of their mandate. But to many of the men who put through the idea of mandates the system really was what it professed to be, a nursery for eventual nationhood. Apart from Japan, the mandatory powers at least made a show of treating mandated territories in a way that would prepare them for eventual freedom, and most of them achieved it.

The Punishment of Germany

After land transfers, the most important business of the peace conference was reparations, which were imposed on Austria, Hungary, Bulgaria, and Turkey as well as on Germany. It was, however, the German reparations that so long disturbed the peace and the economy of the world. The Germans were made to promise to pay for all the damage done to civilian property during the war, and to pay at the rate of five billion dollars a year until 1921, when the final bill would be presented to them. They would then be given thirty years in which to pay the full amount. The amount was left indefinite at Versailles, for the Allies could not agree on a figure. But the totals suggested were astronomical. It was clear from the first that the payments would ultimately have to be in goods—German goods in competition with the goods of the Allies. A Germany prosperous enough to pay reparations could not be the weak and divided nation that men like Clemenceau really wanted. Thus from the very start the "realists" at Versailles—Lloyd George and Clemenceau—cherished quite inconsistent hopes for the future.

The Versailles settlement also required Germany to hand over many of her merchant ships to the Allies and to make large deliveries of coal to France, Italy, and Belgium for a ten-year period. Furthermore, a whole miscellany of articles in the treaty was directed toward the disarmament of Germany on land, on sea, and in the air. The German army was to be limited in size to 100,000 men, and the western frontier zone, extending to a line 50 kilometers (about 30 miles) east of the Rhine, was to be completely "demilitarized"— that is, to contain neither fortifications nor soldiers. In addition, the Allies could maintain armies of occupation on the left bank of the Rhine for fifteen years, and perhaps longer. The treaty forbade Germany to have either submarines or military planes and severely limited the number and size of surface vessels in her navy.

Last, and by no means least important, Article 231 of the Treaty of Versailles obliged Germany to admit that the Central Powers bore sole responsibility for starting the war in 1914. Here is the article that was to cause so much history to be written—and made:

The Allied and Associated Governments affirm, and Germany accepts, the responsibility of Germany and her allies for causing all the loss and damage to which the Allied and Associated Governments and their nationals have been subjected as a consequence of the war imposed upon them by the aggression of Germany and her allies.

The Settlement Evaluated

To the Germans, Versailles was of course a cruel and humiliating peace, the Diktat, the great national grievance on which Hitler was to play so skillfully. To liberals of the time and later it seemed an unsound, vengeful peace, above all disastrous in its unrealistic reparations policy. In the era of cold and hot wars, following World War II, Versailles almost aroused nostalgia. It was at least a settlement, and one that in the later 1920s seemed a basis for slow improvement in international relations.

The League it set up was potentially a means by which a new generation of international administrators might mitigate the old rivalries of nations. The reparations could be, and were, scaled down to something more reasonable. The new succession states were based on a modern popular national consciousness that had been developing for at least a hundred years. Though the theorist might protest at the "balkanization of Europe," the fact remains that it would have been impossible to deny national independence, or at least autonomy, to the Czechs, the Poles, the Baltic peoples, and the south Slavs. Germany, though she certainly was not treated generously, was at least not wiped off the map, as Poland had been in the eighteenth century. She was not even actually demoted to a second-rate position in the world. She remained, as she was shortly to prove, a first-rate power. In the long series of settlements under our modern Western state system, which goes back to the Italian wars of the Renaissance, Versailles looks nowadays like neither the worst nor the best, but like a typical compromise peace.

It was, however, too much for the American people, who were not used to the harsh needs of international compromise. But it is an oversimplification to argue that this was solely a matter of American idealism turning away in disgust from a settlement that was all too spotted with unpleasant realities. The final American refusal to ratify the Treaty of Versailles, like all great collective decisions, was the result of many forces. Domestic politics certainly played an important part, for the Republicans had won control of both the Senate and the House of Representatives in the congressional elections of November 1918. The president was still Wilson, a Democrat, and Wilson made no concessions to the Republicans either by taking a bipartisan delegation of Democrats and Republicans to Paris with him or by accepting modifications in the treaty that would have satisfied some of his Republican opponents. The Senate thereupon refused to ratify the treaty.

It is extremely unlikely that even a much more pliable and diplomatic American president than Wilson could have secured from the Senate ratification of another important treaty involved in the proposed settlement. This was the project of a defensive alliance among France, Britain, and the United States into which Wilson had been pushed as part of the price of getting France to give up her proposals for a separate

The Balkans and the Middle East 1878

Rhineland republic and for annexation of the Saar. With the United States out, Britain refused a mere dual alliance with France against a German attack. France, still seeking to bolster her security, patched up a series of alliances with the new nations to the east and south of Germany—Poland, and the Little Entente of Yugoslavia, Czechoslovakia, and Romania, a wholly unsatisfactory substitute for Britain and the United States as allies.

The peace thus left France with an uneasy hegemony in Europe, a hegemony dependent on the continued disarmament and economic weakening of Germany, on the continued isolation of Russia, and on the uncertain support of her new allies. Moreover, France had been disastrously weakened by the human and material losses of the war, and her posture of leadership, though it alarmed the British with their long memories

of French rivalry in the past, was unreal. In reality, Germany was the strongest nation in Europe, and the Great War had checked, but not halted, her attempt to dominate the Continent and the whole world. The next German attempt was to bring both Britain and America out of the isolation into which they had attempted to withdraw after the collapse of the system planned at Paris in 1919.

A most important matter was not directly touched by the Versailles settlement: Russia, or the Union of Soviet Socialist Republics (USSR), the formal name of the new communist state, did not figure in the great treaties. Yet in many senses the most important result of World War I was the emergence of this new-old Russia, her strength and capabilities before long greatly increased by the stimulus of successful revolution.

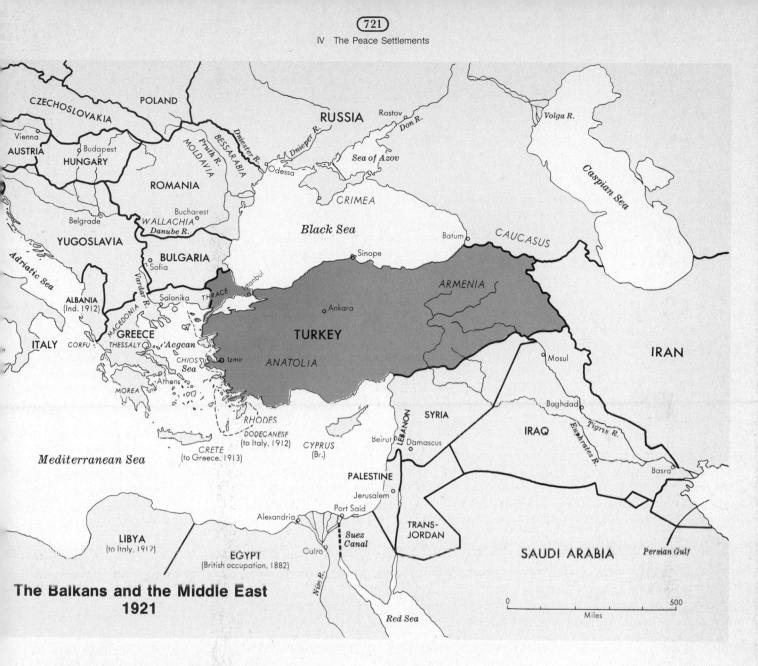

**The Balkans and the Middle East
1921**

Reading Suggestions on the First World War

The Background

A. J. P. Taylor, *The Struggle for the Mastery of Europe, 1848–1914* (Clarendon, 1954). A crisp and suggestive survey.

O. J. Hale, *The Great Illusion, 1900–1914* (*Torchbooks). Stressing the economic and cultural background; with full bibliographies.

B. Schmitt, *The Coming of the War, 1914,* 2 vols. (Scribner's, 1930). Compare with the more revisionist S. B. Fay, *Origins of the World War,* 2 vols. (*Free Press).

L. Lafore, *The Long Fuse* (*Lippincott), and J. Remak, *Origins of World War I* (*Holt). Illuminating studies incorporating recent scholarship.

Barbara Tuchman, *The Proud Tower* (Macmillan, 1966). Instructive and very readable account of the European society that produced the great war.

W. L. Langer, *European Alliances and Alignments, 1871–1890,* 2nd ed. (*Vintage) and *The Diplomacy of Imperialism, 1890–1902,* 2nd ed. (Knopf, 1951). Detailed scholarly analyses, with valuable bibliographies.

G. Ritter, *The Sword and the Scepter: The Problem of Militarism in Germany* (Univ. of Miami Press, 1970). Volume II deals with the European powers and William II's Germany, 1890–1914.

R. J. Sontag, *Germany and England: Background of Conflict, 1848–1894* (*Norton); R. J. S. Hoffman, *Great Britain and the German Trade Rivalry, 1875–1914* (Univ. of Pennsylvania Press, 1933); E. L. Woodward, *Great Britain and the German Navy* (Clarendon, 1935). Excellent studies of Anglo-German tension.

C. Andrew, *Théophile Delcassé and the Making of the Entente Cordiale* (St. Martin's, 1938), and S. R. Williamson, *The Politics of Grand Strategy* (Harvard Univ. Press, 1969). Assessments of the Anglo-French rapprochement before 1914.

G. Monger, *The End of Isolation* (T. Nelson, 1963). British foreign policy reviewed. For Anglo-American relations, it may be supplemented by Bradford Perkins, *The Great Rapprochement* (Atheneum, 1968).

W. Laqueur, *Russia and Germany: A Century of Conflict* (*Little, Brown). Yet another factor in the background scrutinized.

E. N. Anderson, *The First Moroccan Crisis, 1904–1906* (Univ. of Chicago Press, 1930), and Ima C. Barlow, *The Agadir Crisis* (Univ. of North Carolina Press, 1940). Two useful monographs on the Moroccan issue.

J. B. Wolf, *Diplomatic History of the Bagdad Railroad* (Univ. of Missouri Press, 1936). Review of another major issue in prewar diplomacy.

Outbreak of the World War: German Documents Collected by Karl Kautsky (Oxford Univ. Press, 1924) and *German Diplomatic Documents, 1871–1914* (Methuen, 1928–1931). English translations of some of the vast flood of documents released by the German republican government at the end of the war. May be compared with *British Documents on the Origins of the War, 1898–1914* (H. M. Stationery Office, 1926–1938).

The War

A. J. P. Taylor, *History of the First World War* (*Medallion); B. H. Liddell Hart, *The Real War* (*Little, Brown). Lively and rather opinionated surveys.

C. R. M. Cruttwell, *History of the Great War*. 2nd ed. (Oxford Univ. Press, 1936); C. Falls, *The Great War* (*Capricorn); Hanson Baldwin, *World War One* (*Evergreen). Three sober and reliable accounts.

W. S. Churchill, *The World Crisis*, 6 vols. (Scribner's 1923–1931). Detailed and often fascinating narrative; not always objective.

Barbara Tuchman, *The Guns of August* (*Dell). Well-written narrative of the first critical month of the war and the crisis preceding it.

G. Ritter, *The Schlieffen Plan* (Dufour, 1969). Scholarly reassessment.

Alan Moorehead, *Gallipoli* (Harper, 1956), and A. Horne, *The Price of Glory: Verdun, 1916* (*Colophon). Excellent accounts of particular campaigns.

R. M. Watt, *Dare Call It Treason* (*Simon and Schuster). The story of the most concerted French attempt to break the deadlock of trench warfare and of the mutiny that resulted in 1917.

E. R. May, *World War and American Isolation, 1914–1917* (*Quadrangle) and *The Coming of War, 1917* (*Rand McNally). The most reliable and balanced treatment of the events that made the United States a belligerent.

F. Fischer, *Germany's Aims in the First World War* (*Norton). A revisionist estimate of German policy that has caused considerable debate.

Z. Zeman, *The Gentlemen Negotiators* (Macmillan, 1971). Study of diplomacy during the war.

E. Monroe, *Britain's Moment in the Middle East 1914–1956* (Johns Hopkins Univ. Press, 1963). Persuasive explanation of the contradictions in Britain's policy toward Arabs and Jews, particularly during World War I and the ensuing peace negotiations.

T. E. Lawrence, *Seven Pillars of Wisdom* (*Dell). Colorful but untrustworthy account of the Arab revolt by a major participant.

F. P. Chambers, *The War behind the War* (Harcourt, 1939). On the "home front."

Economic and Social History of the World War: Outline of Plan, European Series (Carnegie Endowment for International Peace, 1924). Guide to an enormous series of monographs on home-front developments in all the major belligerent powers.

The Peace

P. Birdsall, *Versailles Twenty Years After* (Reynal and Hitchcock, 1941). Excellent appraisal by an American scholar.

H. Nicolson, *Peacemaking 1919* (*Universal Library). Informative study by a British expert on diplomacy.

T. A. Bailey, *Woodrow Wilson and the Lost Peace* and *Woodrow Wilson and the Great Betrayal* (*Quadrangle). Stressing the setbacks his program suffered in Paris and in Washington, respectively.

A. J. Mayer, *The Political Origins of the New Diplomacy, 1917–1918* and *The Politics and Diplomacy of Peacemaking* (both *Vintage). Studies stressing the role played by the fear of Bolshevism. For another interpretation, see J. M. Thompson, *Russia, Bolshevism and the Versailles Peace* (Princeton Univ. Press, 1966).

J. M. Keynes, *The Economic Consequences of the Peace* (*Torchbooks), and E. Mantoux, *The Carthaginian Peace; or, the Economic Consequences of Mr. Keynes* (Scribner's 1952). Respectively, the most famous attack on the Versailles settlement and a thoughtful study of the results of that attack.

Historical Fiction

J. Romains, *Verdun* (Knopf, 1939). Excellent and balanced novel about French troops on the western front, 1914–1916.

H. Barbusse, *Under Fire* (Dutton, 1917), and E. M. Remarque, *All Quiet on the Western Front* (*Crest). Two famous novels, by a Frenchman and a German respectively, reflect the horror aroused in intellectuals by trench warfare.

J. Dos Passos, *Three Soldiers* (*Sentry), and E. Hemingway, *A Farewell to Arms* (*Scribner's). Two American novels reflecting postwar disillusionment.

e. e. cummings, *The Enormous Room* (*Liveright), and A. Zweig, *The Case of Sergeant Grischa* (Viking). Respectively, on prisoners of war and the eastern front.

C. S. Forester, *The General* (Little, Brown, 1947). A careerist dissected.

John Buchan, *Greenmantle* (Nelson, n.d.), and W. Somerset Maugham, *Ashenden* (*Avon). Tales of espionage and high adventure.

26

Communist Russia
1917-1941

Introduction

On June 22, 1941, Adolf Hitler's German armies poured over the frontier of his Russian ally and began a rapid advance toward Moscow, toward the major Russian industrial centers, and toward the most productive Russian agricultural regions. The Russia Hitler invaded was no longer the Russia into which Napoleon had sent the Grande Armée a hundred and twenty-nine years before, or the Russia whose millions of embattled soldiers had perished in the First World War against the Germany of William II and his Hapsburg allies. It was no longer the Russia of the czars. Since 1917 it had been the Russia of the Bolsheviks. Yet it was still Russia.

Along with the czars, the nobility and the bourgeoisie had gone down to ruin after the communist revolution of 1917, and the clergy as a class had suffered almost as much. A small, tightly knit, conspiratorial group of fanatical Marxist revolutionaries had seized power and for the next twenty-four years had striven to make Russia over. Drawn mostly from the peculiarly Russian class of the intelligentsia, and declaring themselves to be the representatives of the industrial proletariat, the Bolsheviks had worked gigantic changes, especially in the years after 1928. Industry, proceeding under forced draft, had expanded enormously, and the proportion of the population employed in industry had risen to almost 50 percent; the proportion engaged in agriculture had fallen correspondingly.

The peasant had been a victim of serfdom until 1861, had been subject to the initiative-destroying domination of the commune until 1906, and had then been encouraged by Stolypin to make himself a free farmer. Now, under the Bolsheviks, he found himself subjected to new and grievous pressure. Agriculture had been collectivized, and the age-old longing of the peasant for private property in land had been ruthlessly suppressed.

These staggering social and economic changes had not been accomplished without internal friction. Inside the government, personal rivalries, plots, counterplots, fake plots, and charges of plots had produced repeated purges extending down through the ranks of the population. The choking conspiratorial atmosphere which the Bolshevik rulers had breathed during their long years of underground preparation for a seizure of power now enveloped the citadels of power. Personal rivalries for domination of the machinery of state were cloaked beneath the Byzantine theological language of doctrinal controversy over fine points in the sacred writings of Marx and Lenin. Yet the controversies had immediate significance in the formulation and choice of government policies. The Communist party, the secret police, and the army had become the interlocking agencies which ran the state at the bidding of the dictator. The dictator himself, Stalin, had made his own career possible chiefly through the ruthless use of his position as Secretary of the Communist party.

The foreign policy of the communist state had after 1917 passed through a brief period in which ideological considerations had seemed occasionally to outweigh national interest in the old sense. It had then returned to the pursuit of traditional Russian ends, coupled with the objective of promoting eventual world revolution. But in furthering Russian aims abroad, the Bolshevik leaders were now in possession of an instrument more flexible than any the czars had ever commanded. This was the Communist International, or Comintern, a federation of the Communist parties in the individual countries of the world. These parties could often be used as promoters of purely Russian ends rather than strictly communist ends. With the shifting stresses and strains of international politics during the late 1920s and 1930s, the "line" of the Comintern shifted often and bewilderingly, but always in accordance with the aims of the Soviet foreign office. Usually

A postrevolutionary Soviet Propaganda poster.

its heresies, its places of pilgrimage, its doctrinal quarrels. Thus the old Russian orthodoxy had by 1941 not been replaced but rather modified. Russian nationalism, too, asserted itself ever more insistently and crudely, until finally, in the war that Hitler began, the government encouraged the cult of traditional heroes of earlier times and even glorified Ivan the Terrible himself, a symbol no longer of "feudal" domination but of the Russian national spirit. The early revolutionary departures from accepted standards in Russian marriage, family life, and education, had by 1941 all been abandoned in favor of a return to conventional bourgeois behavior. This chapter will trace in some detail the series of vast changes here summarized and will attempt to demonstrate the continued survival of the old Russia beneath the veneer of the new.

II   The Russian Revolution of 1917

The Immediate Background

Ridden by domestic crisis though Russia was in 1914, the country greeted the outbreak of World War I with demonstrations of national patriotism. The Duma supported the war and did yeoman service in organizing Red Cross activities. The left-wing parties—the radical agrarian SR's (Social Revolutionaries) and the Marxist SD's (Social Democrats)—abstained from voting war credits but offered to assist the national defense. Yet it was the war and the regime's failure to deal with the crises it provoked that in the end was the decisive factor in precipitating a revolution.

Russia was very nearly isolated from the outside world and the munitions and supplies that would otherwise have come from the Allies. Only Vladivostok, thousands of miles away from European Russia, on the Siberian Pacific coast, and Archangel, on the White Sea, were available as seaports, and for the first three years of the war Archangel was still not connected with the interior by rail. Despite the great resources of the country in agriculture and industry, transport was inadequate from the beginning, and when trains had to move troops, food shortages developed in the cities although there was enough food in the countryside to feed the urban population. Moreover, the imperial government was not only inefficient in mobilizing the resources of Russia for war, but was reluctant to give the existing public bodies—Duma, zemstvos, city governments—the opportunity to exercise authority, sure that such powers, once delegated, would never be recovered.

By 1917, more than 15,000,000 Russians had been drafted into the armies. Losses in battle were staggering from the first; the Russians suffered more than 3,800,000 casualties during the first year of war. On the home front, criticism was aroused by the inadequate handling of the supply of munitions and by mid-1915 the center and left groups in the Duma were urging moderate reforms, such as the end of discrimination against minority nationalities and an increase in the

the majority of communists elsewhere in the world fell meekly into position and when necessary proclaimed the opposite of what they had proclaimed the day before.

Yet the changes during the first twenty-four years of the Soviet period, vast though they were, could not conceal the continuities between the new Russian system and the old. The dictator of 1941, the revered leader of his people for whom his followers made increasingly grandiose claims, was not unlike the czar of 1917 in his assumption of autocratic power. The individual Russian of 1941, despite his sufferings under the new system, had remained deeply patriotic, ready to sacrifice himself for his country, even under a government he hated. The peasant of 1941 still yearned hopelessly for his land; the worker struggled for economic advancement and social security. Bureaucrats, managers, intellectuals, and artists, all in the service of the state, formed in 1941 a new elite which replaced but did not differ greatly from the old privileged class. A police force superior in efficiency to those of Ivan the Terrible, Peter the Great, and Nicholas I, but not different in kind, in 1941 exercised thought control over all citizens and terrorized prominent members of the system itself.

More and more, Stalinist communism had taken on the trappings of a religion, with its sacred books, powers of the zemstvos. The empress Alexandra—a devoutly mystical enemy of all parliamentary government—took the lead in opposing all such measures and kept urging her weak husband, Czar Nicholas II, to act more autocratically. In the autumn of 1915, in answer to a demand by this "progressive" bloc for a Cabinet that would be responsible to it, and not to the Czar, Nicholas dismissed (prorogued) the Duma, and himself took personal command of the armies in the field. This made the empress and her favorite, the unscrupulous adventurer Rasputin (see above, p. 647) virtually supreme on the home front.

With the empress and Rasputin in control, a gang of shady adventurers, blackmailers, and profiteers bought and sold offices, speculated in military supplies, put in their own puppets as ministers, and created a series of shocking scandals. Confusion, strikes, and defeatism mounted at home during 1916, while the armies slowly bled to death at the front. Even the conservatives began to denounce Rasputin publicly, and in December 1916 he was poisoned, shot several times, and ultimately drowned, all in one nightmare evening, by a group of conspirators closely related to the imperial family. Despite repeated warnings from moderates in the Duma that the government itself was preparing a revolution by its failure to create a responsible ministry and to clean up the mess, the Czar remained apathetic. Relatives of the imperial family and members of the Duma began independently to plot for his abdication. In the early months of 1917, all conditions favored a revolution, but the revolutionaries were not prepared.

The March Revolution

On March 8, strikes and bread riots broke out in the capital, and four days later Romanov rule, which had governed Russia since 1613, was doomed. Yet this revolution of March 1917 has been well called leaderless, spontaneous, and anonymous. SR's and both the Bolshevik and the Menshevik factions of SD's were genuinely surprised at what happened. Indeed, the Bolshevik leaders were either abroad in exile or under arrest in Siberia. The determining faction in the overthrow of the Czar was the disloyalty of the garrison of Petrograd (the new Russian name given to St. Petersburg during the war). Inefficiency had led to a food shortage in the capital, though actual starvation had not set in. When the Czar ordered other troops to fire on the rioters, only a few obeyed, and on March 12, in revulsion against the order, the troops joined the dissidents, broke into the arsenals, and began to hunt the police, who quickly disappeared from the scene. On March 12, the progressive bloc in the Duma formed a provisional government to keep order until there could be a constituent assembly. By March 14, when the Czar had finally decided to appoint a responsible ministry, it was too late. On March 15, he abdicated in favor of a younger brother, Michael, and on March 15 Michael in turn abdicated in favor of the provisional government.

On March 12, the same day that the provisional government was formed, leftists, released from prison by the mobs, formed a soviet of workers and soldiers, modeled on the 1905 soviet. Its "Army Order No. 1," setting up within every unit of the army a committee of soldiers which should control weapons, dealt a body blow to military discipline and organization. The Soviet also proceeded to create a food-supply commission and to issue newspapers. Its fifteen-man executive committee of SR's and Mensheviks became the policymakers of the revolution. The Soviet located its headquarters across the corridor in the same building as the Duma, which did not obey the czar's order to dissolve, but remained in session.

The Marxists among the Soviet leaders—mainly Mensheviks—believed in the necessity of a preliminary bourgeois revolution and did not yet regard the Soviet itself as an organ of power. Therefore, though they would not participate in the provisional government, they offered it their limited support. Despite their widely differing social and economic aims, both agreed to grant political liberties immediately and to summon a constituent assembly, which was to establish the future form of government by giving Russia a constitution. The provisional government was composed mainly of Kadets (Constitutional Democrats) and other moderates and was headed by the liberal Prince Lvov, chairman of the union of zemstvos and of the Red Cross. It included also one member of the Soviet, the moderate SR Alexander Kerensky, minister of justice, a clever lawyer, and a member of the Duma. Nicholas II and Alexandra were arrested. On March 20, the Duma had thus accepted the mandate given it by the revolutionaries.

The Provisional Government

The provisional government—which held office during the turbulent months between mid-March and early November 1917—is usually regarded as having been a total failure. Measured by the final results, such a view is perhaps justified. But one must remember the dreadful difficulties it faced. These were not only immediate and specific but general and underlying. Russian moderates had had no experience of authority. They were separated by a great cultural gulf from the lower classes. Their opportunity to rule now came to them in the midst of a fearful war, which they felt they had to pursue while reconstructing and democratizing the enormous and unwieldy Russian Empire.

Moreover, the Soviet possessed many of the instruments of power, yet refused to accept any responsibility. Workers and soldiers in the capital supported the Soviet, while in the provinces the new governors appointed by the provisional government had no weapon except persuasion to employ against the local peasant-elected soviets, which multiplied rapidly. Present-day critics of the provisional government often denounce its failure to suppress its revolutionary opponents, but

The first session of the Duma of the provisional government, March 1917.
The empty frame behind the speaker's platform formerly held the czar's portrait.

they overlook the fact that the provisional government did not possess the tools of suppression. The Petrograd garrison, for instance, by agreement with the Soviet, could not be removed or disarmed. The support given by the Soviet to the provisional government has been vividly compared to the kind of support that is given by a hangman's noose.

The two great specific issues facing the provisional government were agrarian discontent and the continuation of the war. The peasants wanted land, and they wanted it immediately. The provisional government, however, believed in acting with deliberation and according to law. It refused to sanction peasant seizure of land despite increasing disorder in the countryside. Instead, it appointed a commission to collect material on which future agrarian legislation was to be based—an act totally inadequate to the emergency.

As to the war, the members of the government felt in honor bound to their allies not to make a separate peace. Moreover, most of them still unrealistically hoped that Russia might win and gain the territories which the Allies had promised. But the Soviet subverted discipline in the armies at the front by issuing a "decla-ration of the rights of soldiers," which virtually put an end to the authority of officers over enlisted men. Although the Soviet made it as hard as possible for the government to pursue the war, it did not sponsor a separate peace. Even the Bolshevik members of the Soviet, who now began to return from exile, demanded only that Russia participate in general peace negotiations, which, they urged, should begin at once.

Lenin and Bolshevism

The most important of the returning Bolshevik exiles was Lenin. His real name was Vladimir Ilyich Ulianov, but in his writings he used the pen name Lenin, to which he sometimes prefixed the initial N., a Russian abbreviation for "nobody," in order to tell his readers that he was using a pseudonym. This "N." has given rise to the mistaken but still widely held idea that Lenin's first name was Nikolai (Nicholas). Son of a provincial official and intellectual, Lenin became a revolutionary in the 1880s and, as we have seen, took a chief role in the early years of the SD's as the leader of the party's Bolshevik wing. He had returned to

Russia from abroad for the Revolution of 1905, but he left Russia once more in 1908, and stayed abroad. He joined a small group of socialists in wholly opposing the war, and in urging that it be transformed into a class war: a position that most socialists repudiated, voting for war credits in each of their countries, more patriots than revolutionaries. Poor, and with few followers, Lenin was in Switzerland when the March Revolution broke out in Russia.

Though he had for a time despaired of living to see a true socialist revolution, he was desperately anxious now to get back to Russia. The German general staff, which knew all about him, thought his return to Russia would help disrupt the Russian war effort, so the German military transported Lenin across Germany from Switzerland to the Baltic in the famous sealed railroad car. He arrived at the Finland Station in Petrograd on April 16, 1917, a little more than a month after the March Revolution.

Most Russian Social Democrats had long regarded a bourgeois parliamentary republic as a necessary preliminary to an eventual socialist revolution and socialist society. For this reason, they were prepared to help in transforming Russia into a capitalist society, though not without grave doubts that the bourgeois capitalists might be as bad as the czar and the landlords or that the masses might be "deluded" into accepting the new system. They favored the creation of a democratic republic, at the same time believing that complete political freedom was absolutely essential for their own future rise to power. Despite the Marxist emphasis upon the industrial laboring class as the only proper vehicle for revolution, Lenin early realized that in Russia, where the "proletariat" embraced only about 1 percent of the population, the SD's must seek other allies. At the time of the Revolution of 1905, he began to preach the need for limited alliances for tactical purposes between the Bolsheviks and the SR's, who commanded the support of the peasantry. When the alliance had served its purpose, the SD's were to turn on their allies and destroy them. Then would come the socialist triumph.

Instead of a preliminary bourgeois democratic republic, Lenin called in 1905 and later for an immediate "revolutionary-democratic dictatorship of the proletariat and the peasantry," a concept that seems to us self-contradictory and is surely vague. Lenin's view, however, was not adopted even by most Bolsheviks. Together with the Mensheviks, they continued to believe and urge that a bourgeois revolution and a parliamentary democracy were necessary first steps.

Because Lenin did not trust the masses to make a revolution (by themselves, he felt, they were capable only of "trade-union consciousness"), he favored a dictatorship of the Bolshevik party over the working class. Because he did not trust the rank and file of Bolshevik party workers, he favored a dictatorship of a small elite over the Bolshevik party. And, in the end, because he really trusted nobody's views but his own, he favored,

though never explicitly, his own dictatorship over this elite. Another future Russian leader, the brilliant intellectual Leon Trotsky, early warned that in Lenin's views one-man dictatorship was implicit.

Trotsky, for his part, voiced an opinion of his own, held by neither Mensheviks nor Bolsheviks. The bourgeoisie in Russia, he argued, was so weak that the working class could telescope the bourgeois and socialist revolutions into one continuous movement. After the proletariat had helped the bourgeoisie achieve its revolution, he believed that the workers could move immediately to power. They could nationalize industry and collectivize agriculture, and, although foreign intervention and civil war were doubtless to be expected, the Russian proletariat would soon be joined by the proletariats of other countries, which would make their own revolutions. Except for this last point, Trotsky's analysis accurately forecast the course of events. Between 1905 and 1917, Lenin himself accepted Trotsky's view from time to time, but warned that it endangered political democracy.

Lenin had been deeply depressed by the failure of 1905 and by the threat posed by Stolypin's agrarian reforms. He almost despaired when the socialist parties of Europe went along with their governments in 1914 and supported the war. To him this meant the end of the second socialist International, for the Social Democrats had failed to recognize the war as the "bourgeois-imperialist" venture that it appeared to Lenin to be. He preached defeatism as the only possible view for a Russian SD to follow.

Lenin's greatest talent was not as an original thinker but as a skillful tactician. He often seemed able to judge with accuracy just what was politically possible in a given situation, and he was not afraid to gamble. Thus, even before he returned to Russia in April 1917, he had assessed some of the difficulties facing the provisional government and decided that the masses could take over at once. Immediately upon his arrival, he hailed the worldwide revolution, proclaiming that the end of imperialism, "the last stage of capitalism," was at hand. Ignoring the positions previously taken by Bolsheviks and Mensheviks alike, he demanded now that all power immediately be given to the soviets. His speeches sounded even to his fellow SD's themselves like the ravings of a madman.

Almost nobody but Lenin felt that the loosely organized soviets could govern the country or that the war would bring down the capitalist world in chaos. In April 1917 Lenin called not only for the abandonment of the provisional government and the establishment of a republic of soviets but for the confiscation of estates, the nationalization of land, and the abolition of the army, of government officials, and of the police. He was offering land at once to the impatient peasants, peace at once to the war-weary populace. This program fitted the mood of the people far better than the cautious and well-meant efforts of the provisional govern-

Pro-Bolshevik soldiers, red flags fixed to their bayonets, patrolling the streets of Petrograd in March 1917.

ment to bring about reform by legal means. Dogmatic, furiously impatient of compromise, and entirely convinced that he alone had the truth, Lenin galvanized the Bolsheviks into a truly revolutionary group waiting only for the moment to seize power. He also had millions of German marks at his disposal to pay for the party newspaper, *Pravda* (*Truth*), for antiwar propaganda, and for armed "Red Guard" contingents.

The Coming of the November Revolution

The months from March to November 1917, before the Bolsheviks came to power, can be divided into a period between March and July, during which revolution deepened, a feeble reaction from July to September, and a new quickening of the revolutionary current from September to the final uprising in November. In the first period, the government faced a crisis, because the Kadet ministers wished to maintain the Russian war aim of annexing the Straits, while the Soviet wanted a peace "without annexations or indemnities." Out of the crisis Kerensky, now war minister, emerged as the dominant leader. He failed to realize that it was no longer possible to restore the morale of the armies, which were dissolving under the impact of Bolshevik propaganda. A new offensive ordered on July 1 collapsed, as soldiers refused to obey orders, deserted their

units, and rushed home to their native villages, eager to seize the land. Ukrainian separatism also plagued the officials of the government. The soviets became gradually more and more Bolshevik, as Lenin and Trotsky worked at recruitment and organization. Although the June congress of soviets in Petrograd was less than 10 percent Bolshevik in make-up, the Bolshevik slogans of peace, bread, and freedom won overwhelming support.

Yet an armed outbreak by troops who had accepted the Bolshevik slogans found the Petrograd Soviet unwilling and unable to assume power. While the mob roared outside, the Soviet voted to discuss the matter two weeks later and meanwhile to keep the provisional government in power. A regiment loyal to the Soviet protected it against the working class! The government declared (truly) that Lenin was a German agent and, as his supporters wavered, raided the newspaper offices of *Pravda*. Lenin had to go into hiding in Finland to avoid arrest. This episode of mid-July is what is known among Bolsheviks as "playing at insurrection." Though shots had been exchanged and overt action had been embarked upon, there had been no revolutionary follow-through. Power had not been seized, probably because Lenin felt that the Bolsheviks did not have enough support in the provinces.

Now Kerensky became premier. The government

hardened its attitude toward the Ukrainians but could not come to a popular decision on either land or peace. General Kornilov, chosen by Kerensky as the new commander in chief of the armies, quickly became the hope of all conservative groups and in August plotted a coup, intended to disperse the Soviet. His attitude toward the provisional government was less clear, but had he succeeded he would probably have demanded a purge of its more radical elements. Tension between Kornilov and his superior, Kerensky, mounted. The Soviet backed Kerensky, fearing Kornilov's attack. When Kornilov refused to accept his dismissal as war minister and seemed about to march on Petrograd, the Bolsheviks, adopting the slogan, "We will fight against Kornilov, but will not support Kerensky," threw themselves into preparations for a defense which proved unnecessary. Kornilov's troop movements were sabotaged, and by September 14 he had been arrested, and the affair ended without bloodshed. The threat from the right helped the Bolsheviks greatly, and sentiment in the Petrograd and Moscow Soviets now for the first time became predominantly Bolshevik. Kerensky was gravely weakened.

The Kornilov affair turned the army mutiny into a widespread revolt. Instances of violence multiplied. No longer satisfied with merely disobeying their officers, more and more soldiers murdered them instead. No longer satisfied with merely refusing to pay their rent or pasturing their animals on their landlords' land, more and more peasants burned the manor house and killed the owner. It was true that the nobility owned only a quarter as much land as the peasants, but the peasants no longer listened to statistics or to arguments that rash action retarded progress. As disorder mounted in the countryside, the Bolsheviks tightened their hold over the soviets in the cities.

Lenin returned to Petrograd on October 20. Trotsky kept warning that Kerensky was planning to surrender Petrograd to the Germans. This was untrue, but it enabled Trotsky to get control over a "Military Revolutionary Committee" to help defend Petrograd and to transform it into a general staff for the revolution. Beginning on November 4, huge demonstrations and mass meetings were addressed by Trotsky, and on November 7 the insurrection broke out. All along Trotsky intended that it should; all along he confused his opponents by contradictory statements; all along he accused them of planning the violence that he was planning himself.

In Petrograd, the revolution had been well prepared and proceeded with little bloodshed. Kerensky escaped in a car belonging to the American Embassy. The Military Revolutionary Committee, as an organ of the Petrograd Soviet, simply took over. A long-awaited Congress of Soviets, representing less than half of the soviets in Russia, opened on November 7. Both Lenin and Trotsky appeared. When the Mensheviks and right-wing SR's walked out, Trotsky called them refuse that would be swept into the garbage can of

history. Cooperating with the left-wing SR's and adopting their land program, Lenin abolished all property rights of landlords and of the crown and transferred the land thus affected to local land committees and soviets of peasant deputies. Though Lenin did not in the least approve of the system of individual small holdings which this decree put into effect, he recognized the psychological advantage of appearing to accept what was happening in the countryside in any case. He also urged an immediate peace without annexations or indemnities and appealed to the workers of Germany, France, and England to support him in this demand. Finally, a new cabinet, called a Council of People's Commissars, was chosen, with Lenin as president and Trotsky as foreign commissar.

As commissar of nationalities the Bolsheviks installed a younger man, a Georgian named Joseph Djugashvili, who had been a successful organizer of bank robberies in the days when the party treasury was filled in this way, but whose role had otherwise been relatively obscure. He had taken the name Stalin, which suggests a steel-like hardness. Under Lenin's coaching, Stalin had also become the party authority on questions of minority nationalities and had published a pamphlet on the subject in 1913.

Outside Petrograd, the revolution moved more slowly. In Moscow there was a week of street-fighting between Bolshevik Reds and Whites, as anti-Bolshevik forces were already known. Elsewhere in factory towns, the Bolsheviks usually won speedily; in nonindustrial centers it took them longer. Most of Siberia and central Asia came over, but Tiflis, the capital of Georgia, went Menshevik and passed resolutions calling for a constituent assembly and the continuation of the war. The reason for the rapid and smooth success of the Bolsheviks was that the provincial garrisons opposed the war and willingly allied themselves with the workers. Local military revolutionary committees were created in most places and held elections for new local soviets. Naturally there was much confusion at first but surprisingly little resistance to the consolidation of the authority of the new regime. Gradually the town of Rostov-on-Don, near the Sea of Azov, became the main center of resistance, as Kornilov and other generals, together with a number of the leading politicians of the Duma, made their way there.

This initial triumph of the revolution did not mean that the population of Russia had been converted to Bolshevism. By cleverly sensing the mood of the people, Lenin had opportunistically given the Bolsheviks a set of slogans around which the people could rally, although some of the slogans did not at all correspond with the true Bolshevik views. As we shall shortly see, the Russian people were in fact strongly anti-Bolshevik. But the Bolsheviks had triumphed, and the democratic hopes for freedom of the press and other freedoms were now doomed to disappointment.

Deprived of competent civil servants, the new regime worried along through an atmosphere of con-

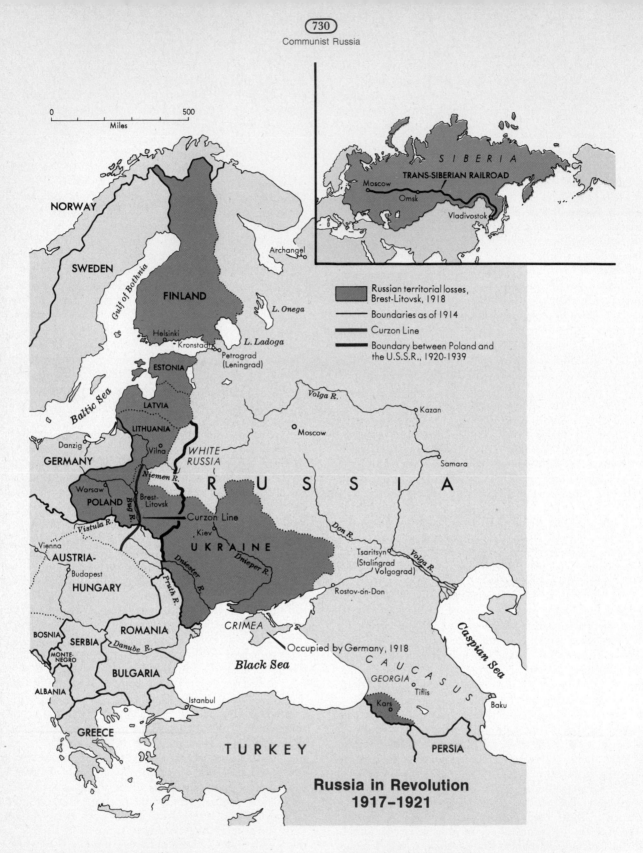

Russia in Revolution
1917–1921

0   500
Miles

Russian territorial losses,
Brest-Litovsk, 1918
Boundaries as of 1914
Curzon Line
Boundary between Poland and
the U.S.S.R., 1920-1939

tinued crisis. Late in November 1917, an agreement was reached with the left-wing SR's, three of whom entered the government, and peace negotiations were begun with the Germans. The revolution proper was over. Lenin was in power.

The Constituent Assembly

It is of great interest to record that the Bolsheviks now permitted elections for a constituent assembly. Lenin had no use for this sort of democratically chosen parliament, which he considered "inferior" to the Soviet. Yet, probably because he had so long taunted the provisional government with delaying the elections, he seems to have felt compelled to hold them. The Russian people for the first and last time in their entire history had a completely free election, under universal suffrage. Lenin himself accepted as accurate figures showing that the Bolsheviks polled about a quarter of the vote. The other socialist parties, chiefly the SR's, polled 62 percent. As was to be expected, the Bolshevik vote was heaviest in the cities, especially Moscow and Petrograd, while the SR vote was largely rural.

Disregarding the majority cast for his opponents, Lenin maintained that "the most advanced" elements had voted for him. It was of course only his opinion that made those who had voted Bolshevik more "advanced" than those who had voted SR or Kadet. The constituent assembly met only once, on January 18, 1918. Lenin dissolved it the next day by decree and sent guards with rifles to prevent its ever meeting again. The anti-Bolshevik majority was naturally deeply indignant at this act pure of force against the popular will, but there was no public outburst and the delegates disbanded. In part, this was because the Bolsheviks had already taken action on the things that interested the people most—peace and land—and in part because of the lack of a democratic parliamentary tradition among the masses of the Russian people.

In spite of the many years of agitation by intellectuals and liberals for just such a popular assembly, Russia did not have the large middle class, the widespread literacy, the tradition of debate, and the respect for the rights of the individual which seem to be an essential part of constitutionalism. Yet it is surely hasty to decide that there was no chance for constitutional government in Russia in 1917–1918. Was the constituent assembly "an attempt to transplant an alien concept of government to a soil where it could never flourish"? Or was it "a noble experiment incorporating a sound principle but doomed by the crisis into which it was born"? The fact that Lenin had the rifles to prevent the constituent assembly from fulfilling the function that the popular will had assigned to it does not answer the question either way.

III War Communism and NEP, 1917–1928
War Communism
The first period of Soviet history, which runs from the end of 1917 to the end of 1920, is usually called the period of war communism, or military communism. The term itself of course implies that the main features of the period were determined by military events. Civil war raged, and foreign powers intervened on Russian soil. But the term is also somewhat misleading. This was a period of militant as well as military communism, symbolized early in 1918 by the change of the party's name from Bolshevik to Communist. At the same time, the capital was shifted from Petrograd, with its exposed location on the western fringe of Russia, to the greater security of Moscow, in the heart of the country.

Flushed with victory in Russia, the Bolsheviks firmly believed that world revolution was about to begin, probably first in Germany, but surely spreading to Britain and even to the United States. This view led the Bolsheviks to hasten the construction of a socialist state in Russia and to take a casual attitude toward their international affairs, since they expected that relations with capitalist states would be very temporary. Although the actions of the Russian government during this period were later described almost apologetically as emergency measures, this is only partly true. Many of the decisions that were taken in part under the spur of military pressure were also regarded as leading to a new society.

Nine political parties were liquidated (Kadets) or persecuted (SR's and Mensheviks). A supreme economic council directed the gradual nationalization of industry. Sugar and petroleum came first, and then in June 1918 a large group including mines, metallurgy, and textiles. By 1920, the state had taken over all enterprises employing more than ten workers (more than five, if motor power was used). Labor was compulsory and strikes were outlawed. The state organized a system of barter, which replaced the free market. Internal trade was illegal; only the government food commissary could buy and sell; money disappeared as the state took over distribution as well as production. It expropriated the banks, repudiated the czarist foreign debt, and in effect wiped out savings. Church and state were separated by decree, and judges were removed from office and replaced by appointees of the local soviets.

The government subjected the peasantry to ever more arbitrary and severe requisitioning. It mobilized the poorer peasants against those who were better off, called *kulaks* (from the word meaning "fist" and used to apply to usurers, as if to say "hardfisted"). By calling for a union of the hungry against the well-fed, the regime deliberately, and not for the last time, sowed class hatred in the villages and stimulated civil war in the countryside. It should be remembered that by western European standards even a Russian kulak was often wretchedly poor. The decree forming the first secret police, the Cheka (from the initials of the words meaning "extraordinary commission"), was issued in December 1917, only a few weeks after the revolution and long before any intervention from abroad. Terror became a weapon in the civil war. Protesting peasants, SR's, even dissident communists resisted.

Before the communist government could function at all, peace was necessary, as the army had virtually ceased to exist. Negotiations between the Russians and the Germans and Austro-Hungarians at Brest-Litovsk dragged on into 1918, the Russians hoping that revolution would break out in Germany, and the Germans demanding enormous territorial cessions, stepping up their demands as the Russians delayed. Finally, on March 3, 1918, the Russians signed the Peace of Brest-

Russian soldiers returning from the front, 1917. Many men simply left the war and went home.

Litovsk, which deprived them of the entire Ukraine, the Baltic provinces, Finland, and some Caucasian lands. It cost Russia a third of its population, 80 percent of its iron, and 90 percent of its coal. Many communists resigned rather than accept the peace, and the left SR's quit the government. The Germans overran the Ukraine and the Crimea and installed a highly authoritarian regime, against which the communists continued to agitate. The Whites, with German help, put down the Reds in Finland.

Civil War

During the months following Brest-Litovsk, disorder in the countryside as a result of requisitioning and class warfare was swelled by the outbreak of open civil strife. During the war, a brigade had been formed inside Russia of Czechs resident in the country and of deserters from the Hapsburg armies. When Russia withdrew from the war, it was decided to send the Czech brigade around the world: east across Siberia by rail, and next by ship across the Pacific, through the Panama Canal, and finally across the Atlantic to France, to fight the Germans there. On the rail trip across Siberia, the Czechs got into a brawl with a trainload of Hungarian prisoners, and one of the Hungarians was killed. This obscure quarrel on a Siberian railway siding between members of the unfriendly races of the Hapsburg Empire touched off civil war in Russia. When the Soviet government tried to take reprisals against the Czechs, who numbered fewer than 35,000 men, the Czechs seized a number of towns in western Siberia. The local soviets were unprepared, and the SR's were sympathetic to the Czechs. Local anti-Bolshevik armies came into being. It was under threat from one of them,

in July 1918, that a local soviet decided to execute the czar and his entire family rather than lose possession of them. All were murdered.

By late June 1918 the Allies had decided to intervene in Russia on behalf of the opponents of Bolshevism. The withdrawal of Russia from the war had been a heavy blow to them, and they now hoped to protect the vast amounts of war supplies still at Vladivostok and Archangel, which had never reached the imperial Russian armies, and to create a new second front against the Germans in the East. The idea of a capitalist "crusade" against Bolshevism, later popularized by Soviet and pro-Soviet historians as the sole motive for the intervention, was in fact much less significant. Yet the Allies had been at war a long time, and their populations were war-weary. So it is true that they were apprehensive at the communist efforts to stimulate revolution in all the capitalist nations of the world.

Out at the eastern end of the Trans-Siberian Railroad in Vladivostok, the Czechs overthrew the local soviet in June 1918, and by early August British, French, Japanese, and American forces had landed. The assignment of the Americans was to occupy Vladivostok and to safeguard railroad communications in the rear of the Czechs. Of the Allies, only the Japanese had long-range territorial ambitions in the area. In effect, the Bolshevik regime had now been displaced in Siberia. The SR's disbanded the soviets and reestablished the zemstvos, calling for "all power to the constituent assembly." There were three anti-Red governments of varying complexions in three different Siberian centers. In August 1918, a small British and American force landed at Archangel. An SR assassin killed the chief of the Petrograd Cheka, and Lenin himself was wounded.

The regime now sped its military preparations. As minister of war, Trotsky imposed conscription, and, by a mixture of cajolery and threats of reprisals against their families, secured the services of about 50,000 czarist officers. The Red Army, which was Trotsky's creation, grew to over 3,000,000 strong by 1920. Its recapture of Kazan and Samara on the Volga in the autumn of 1918 temporarily turned the tide in the crisis that seemed about to engulf the Soviet state.

The German collapse on the western front in November 1918 permitted the Bolsheviks to repudiate the Treaty of Brest-Litovsk and to move back into parts of the Ukraine, where they faced the opposition of a variety of local forces. Elsewhere, the opposition consisted of three main armies. General Denikin led an army of Whites, which moved from Rostov-on-Don south across the Caucasus, and received French and British aid. Admiral Kolchak's forces in western Siberia overthrew the SR regime in Omsk, and Kolchak became a virtual dictator. General Yudenich's army, including many former members of the German forces, operated in the Baltic region and threatened Petrograd from the west. Allied unwillingness to negotiate with the Bolsheviks was heightened by a successful Red coup

The first mobilization of Moscow workers in the spring of 1918.

of Bela Kun in Hungary, which seemed to foreshadow the further spread of revolution.

In the spring of 1919, the Reds defeated Kolchak, and by winter took Omsk. In 1920, the Admiral was arrested and executed. Though the Reds also reconquered the Ukraine, mutinies in their own forces prevented them from consolidating their victories and from moving, as they had hoped to do, across the Russian frontiers and linking up with Bela Kun in Hungary. In the summer of 1919, Denikin took Kiev and struck north, advancing to within two hundred and fifty miles of Moscow itself. But his position was weakened by the repressive character of the regime he brought with him and by his recognition of Kolchak as his superior officer, together with the poor discipline of his troops and his own rivalry with one of his generals, Baron Wrangel. Yudenich advanced to the suburbs of Petrograd, but the Reds by the end of 1919 were able to defeat the White threat everywhere, though Wrangel retained an army in the Crimea. Trotsky now called for the militarization of labor to reconstruct the ravaged country;

labor battalions were formed, but recovery was long delayed.

Even after the defeat of the Whites, the Reds in 1920 had to face a new war with the Poles, who hoped to keep Russia weak, and to create an independent Ukraine. After an initial retreat, the Red armies nearly took Warsaw, failing only because the French chief of staff, General Weygand, assisted the Poles. The Reds, eager to finish off the Whites and persuaded that there was after all no hope for the establishment of a communist regime in Poland, concluded peace in October 1920. The Poles obtained a large area of territory in White Russia and the western Ukraine. This area was not inhabited by Poles but had been controlled by Poland down to the eighteenth-century partitions. It lay far to the east of the "Curzon line," the ethnic frontier earlier proposed by the British foreign minister, Lord Curzon. The Reds then turned on Wrangel, who had marched northward from the Crimea and had established a moderate regime in the territory he occupied. He was forced to evacuate, assisted by a French fleet, in November 1920. The White movement had virtually come to an end.

Why the Reds Won

Many factors accounted for the Whites' failure and the Reds' victory. The Whites could not get together on any political program beyond the mere overthrow of the Reds. They adopted a policy of "nonanticipation," which meant that some future constituent assembly would settle the governmental structure of Russia. Their numbers included everybody from czarists to SR's, and they disagreed so violently on the proper course for Russia to follow that they could agree only to postpone discussion of these critical problems.

Moreover, their movement was located on the geographical periphery of Russia—in Siberia, in the Crimea, in the Ukraine, in the Caucasus, and in the Baltic. But the Whites never reached an understanding with the non-Russian minorities who lived in these regions. Thus they ignored the highly developed separatist sentiments of the Ukrainians and others, to which the Bolsheviks, by contrast, were temporarily willing to cater.

Furthermore, the Whites could not command the support of the peasantry. Instead of guaranteeing the results of the land division already carried out with Bolshevik sanction, the Whites often restored the landlords in areas they temporarily controlled, and undid the land division. During the civil war, the peasantry on the whole grew sick of both sides. Atrocities were frequent on both sides. And peasant anarchist ("green") bands committed many of their own. Moreover, the Whites simply did not command as much military strength as the Reds, who outnumbered them in manpower and who had inherited much of the equipment manufactured for the czarist armies. Holding the central position, the Reds had a unified and skillful command, which could use the railroad network to shift troops rapidly. The Whites, moving in from the periphery, were divided into at least four main groups and were denied effective use of the railroads. Finally, the intervention of the Allies on the side of the Whites was ineffectual and amateurish. It may even have harmed the White cause, since the Reds could pose as the national defenders of the country and could portray the Whites as the hirelings of foreigners.

NEP ("The New Economic Policy")

Since 1914, Russia had been deeply involved in fighting and turmoil. By early 1921, with the end of the civil war, famine was raging and sanitation had broken down. The American Relief Administration, under the direction of Herbert Hoover—later President of the United States—saved millions of lives, but family ties were disrupted, human beings brutalized, and class hatreds released on an unparalleled scale. Industry was producing at a level of about an eighth of its prewar output, and agricultural output had decreased by at least 30 percent. Distribution approached a breakdown. The communist regime appeared to be facing its most serious trial of all: the loss of support in Russia.

A large-scale anarchist peasant revolt broke out in early 1921 and lasted until mid-1922. Lenin remarked that this revolt frightened him more than all the Whites' resistance. But the decisive factor in bringing about a change in policy was the mutiny at the Kronstadt naval base near Petrograd in March 1921. Formerly a stronghold of Bolshevism, Kronstadt now produced a movement of rebellious anarchists who called for "soviets without communists" to be chosen by universal suffrage and secret ballot, for free speech and free assembly, for the liberation of political prisoners, and for the abolition of requisitioning. Except for the last item and for the phraseology of the first, the program was ironically similar to that of all liberals and socialists in czarist Russia. The Kronstadt movement seems to have expressed the sentiments of most Russian workers and peasants. Had the government been conciliatory, there might have been no bloodshed; but Trotsky went to war against the rebels, and defeated them after a bloody fight.

This episode led directly to the adoption of the New Economic Policy, always referred to by its initials as NEP. But the underlying reason for the shift was the need for reconstruction, which seemed attainable only if militant communism were at least temporarily abandoned. Lenin himself referred to "premature" attempts at socialization. It was also necessary to appease the peasants and to ward off any further major uprisings. Finally, the expected world revolution had not taken place, and the resources of capitalist states were badly needed to assist Russian reconstruction. The adoption of NEP coincided with the conclusion of an Anglo-Russian trade treaty. Abroad, NEP was hailed as the beginning of a Russian "Thermidor," a return to normality like that following the end of the Terror in the French Revolution.

Under NEP the government stopped requisitioning the whole of the peasant's crop above a minimum necessary for subsistence. The peasant had still to pay a very heavy tax in kind, but he was allowed to sell the remainder of his crop: to the state if he wished, but to a private purchaser if he preferred. Peasant agriculture became in essence capitalist once more, and the profit motive had reappeared. Lenin imitated Stolypin by guaranteeing the peasant permanency of tenure. The whole system tended to help the rich peasant grow richer and to transform the poor peasant into a hired, landless laborer.

Elsewhere in the economy, under NEP the state retained what Lenin called "the commanding heights"—heavy industry, banking, transportation, and foreign trade. In domestic trade and in light industry, however, private enterprise was once more permitted. This was the so-called "private capital sector" of the economy, in which workers could be paid according to their output, and factory managers could swap some of their products in return for raw materials.

Lenin himself described NEP as a partial return to capitalism, and urged the communists to become good businessmen. Yet NEP was never intended as more than a temporary expedient. Lenin believed that it would take a couple of decades before the Russian peasant could be convinced that cooperative agriculture would be the most efficient. He also argued that a temporary relaxation of government intervention would increase industrial production and give the Russians a useful lesson in entrepreneurship.

Economic recovery was indeed obtained. By 1928, industrial and agricultural production were back at prewar levels. But NEP was bitterly disliked by leading communists, who were shocked at the reversal of all the doctrines they believed in. By 1924, private business accounted for 40 percent of Russian domestic trade, but thereafter the figure fell off. Those who took advantage of the opportunities presented by the NEP were known as NEPmen. They were often persecuted in a petty way by hostile officials, who tried to limit their profits, tax them heavily, and drag them into court on charges of speculation. The kulak had essentially the same experience. Thus the government often seemed to be encouraging private enterprise for economic reasons and simultaneously to be discouraging it for political reasons.

Within the Communist party, one group favored the increase of the private sector and the extension of NEP, as a new road toward the socialist goal. These were the so-called right deviationists. Their opponents favored the ending of concessions, the liquidation of NEPmen and kulaks, and a return to Marxist principles at home and the fostering of world revolution abroad—in short, the pressing of the "socialist offensive." These were the "left deviationists," who included Trotsky. In the center stood men who attacked both deviations: the right as an abandonment of communism, the left as likely to lead to a disruption of the worker-peasant alliance.

The Struggle for Power: Stalin against Trotsky

But NEP was not the only question to agitate the communist leaders in the early twenties. Lenin suffered two strokes in 1922 and another in 1923, and finally died in January 1924. During the last two years of his life, he played an ever-lessening role. Involved in the controversy over NEP and the other controversies was the question of the successor to Lenin. Thus an individual communist's answer to the question of how to organize industry, what role to give organized labor, and what relations to maintain with the capitalist world depended not only upon his estimate of the actual situation but also upon his guess as to what answer was likely to be politically advantageous. From this maneuvering the secretary of the Communist party, Joseph Stalin, was to emerge victorious by 1928.

The years between 1922 and 1928, especially after Lenin's death, were years of a desperate struggle for power between Stalin and Trotsky. Lenin foresaw this struggle with great anxiety. He felt that Trotsky was abler, but feared that he was overconfident and inclined to make decisions on his own. He felt that Stalin had concentrated enormous power in his hands, in his role as party secretary, and feared that he did not know how to use it. When he learned that Stalin had disobeyed his orders in smashing the Menshevik Republic of Georgia instead of reaching an accommodation with its leaders, he wrote angrily in his testament that Stalin was too rude and that he should be removed from his post as general secretary. At the moment of his death, Lenin had published a scathing attack on Stalin, had broken off relations with him, and was about to try to relegate him to the scrapheap. Trotsky's suggestion that Stalin poisoned Lenin is not based on any evidence, but it is clear that Lenin's death rescued Stalin's career, and that, far from being the chosen heir, as he later claimed, he did not enjoy Lenin's confidence at the end.

During these years, Trotsky argued for a more highly trained managerial force in industry and for economic planning as an instrument that the state could use to control and direct social change. He favored the mechanization of agriculture and the weakening of peasant individualism by encouraging rural cooperatives, with even a hint of the collective farms where groups of peasants, in theory, would own everything collectively, rather than individually. As Trotsky progressively lost power, he championed the right of

Lenin and Stalin in 1923.

individual communists to criticize the regime. He referred to the policies of Stalin and his other increasingly powerful enemies as "bureaucratic degeneration" and came to the conclusion that only through the outbreak of revolutions in other countries could the Russian socialist revolution be carried to its proper conclusion. Only if the industrial output and technical skills of the advanced Western countries could be put at the disposal of communism could Russia hope to achieve its own socialist revolution. This is the famous theory that socialism could not succeed within the boundaries of one country. Either world revolution must break out; or Russian socialism was doomed to inevitable failure.

The opponents of Trotsky's "left deviation" found their chief spokesman in Nikolai Bukharin. A man who never held such responsible administrative posts as Lenin or Trotsky or Stalin and who had often shifted his position on major questions, Bukharin nonetheless took a consistent line during these years; as editor of *Pravda,* he was extremely influential. A strong defender of NEP, Bukharin softened the rigorous Marxist doctrine of the class struggle by arguing that, since the proletarian state controlled the commanding heights of big capital, socialism was sure of success. This view is not unlike the "gradualist" position taken by western European Social Democrats. Bukharin did not believe in an ambitious program of rapid industrialization; he favored cooperatives, but opposed collectives. In foreign affairs he was eager to cooperate abroad with noncommunist groups who might be useful to Russia. Thus he sponsored Soviet collaboration with Chiang Kai-shek in China and with the German Social Democrats.

In his rise to power, Stalin used Bukharin's arguments to discredit Trotsky and to eliminate him. Then, partly because Bukharin's policies were failing, Stalin adopted many of Trotsky's policies, and eliminated Bukharin. Original Stalinist ideas, however, developed during this process. Stalin was not basically an intellectual or a theoretician; he was a party organization stalwart. He adopted theoretical positions partly because they seemed to him the ones most likely to work, and partly because he was charting his own course to supreme power. He came to favor rapid industrialization and to understand that this meant an unprecedentedly heavy capital investment. At the end of 1927, he suddenly shifted from his previous position on the peasantry and openly sponsored collectivization. This shift arose because of his concern that agricultural production was not keeping pace with industry. He declared that the balance could be redressed only if agriculture, like industry, was transformed into a series of large-scale unified enterprises.

In answer to Trotsky's argument that socialism in one country was impossible, Stalin maintained that an independent socialist state could exist. This view did not at all imply the abandonment of the goal of world revolution, as has often been thought. Stalin always maintained that the socialist state (Russia) should be the center of inspiration and assistance to communist movements everywhere; Russia would help them and they would help Russia. But, in his view, during the interim period before the communists had won elsewhere, it was perfectly possible for Russia to exist as the only socialist state and indeed to grow more socialist all the time. In international relations, this doctrine of Stalin made it possible for the Soviet Union to pursue either a policy of "peaceful coexistence" with capitalist states, when that seemed most profitable, or a policy of militant support of communist revolution everywhere, when that seemed most profitable. Stalin's "socialism in one country" also struck a responsive chord in the rank and file of Russian communists, who were disappointed in the failure of revolutions elsewhere. It also meant that Russia, not the West, was to be the center of the new society. Stalin's doctrine reflected his own Russian nationalism rather than the more cosmopolitan and more Western views of Trotsky.

The Struggle for Power: Stalin's Victory

Analysis of the rival theories competing for acceptance in Russia in the twenties helps explain the alternatives before the communist leadership. It does not explain how Stalin won. To understand this, we must move from the realm of theory and political platforms to the realm of practice and political power. At the end of the civil war, as we have seen, Stalin was commissar of nationalities. In this post, he dealt with the affairs of 65,000,000 of the 140,000,000 inhabitants of the new Russian Soviet Republic. He managed the destiny of the Asians, whom he, as one of them, understood. Their local Bolshevik leaders became his men; where they did not, as in his native Georgia, he ruthlessly crushed them. Though a Georgian, he identified himself with Russian nationalism in the interests of a centralized Bolshevik state.

It was Stalin who took charge of creating the new Asian "republics," which enjoyed the appearance of local self-government, programs of economic and educational improvement, and a chance to use their local languages and develop their own cultural affairs, so long as these were entirely communist-managed. It was he who in 1922 proposed and guided the adoption of a new Union of Socialist Soviet Republics as a substitute for the existing federation of republics. In the USSR, Moscow would control war, foreign policy, trade, and transport, and would coordinate finance, economy, food, and labor. And on paper it would leave to the republics home affairs, justice, education, and agriculture. A Council of Nationalities, with an equal number of delegates from each ethnic group, would join the Supreme Soviet as a second chamber, thus forming the Central Executive Committee, which would appoint the Council of People's Commissars—the government. Stalin regarded this administrative transformation as an achievement equal to Trotsky's creation of the Red Army.

Stalin was also commissar of the Workers' and Peasants' Inspectorate. Here his duties were to eliminate inefficiency and corruption from every branch of the civil service and to train a new corps of civil servants. His teams moved freely through all the offices of the government, observing and recommending changes, inspecting and criticizing. In creating this post, Lenin had hoped to clean house, but the ignorance and the lack of tradition that rendered the czarist and Bolshevik civil service incompetent and corrupt operated in Stalin's Inspectorate as well. Although the Inspectorate could not do what it was established to do, it did perform another role. It gave Stalin control over thousands of bureaucrats, and so over the machinery of government. Lenin attacked Stalin's work in the Inspectorate just before he died, but by then it was too late.

Stalin was also a member of the Politbureau—the tight little group of party bosses elected by the Central Committee, which included only five men throughout the civil war. Here his job was day-to-day management of the party. He was the only permanent liaison officer between the Politbureau and the Orgbureau, which allocated party personnel to their various duties, in factory, office, or army units. In addition to these posts, Stalin became general secretary of the party's Central Committee in 1922. Here he prepared the agenda for Politbureau meetings, supplied the documentation for points under debate, and passed the decisions down to the lower levels. He controlled party patronage—that is to say, all party appointments, promotions, and demotions. He saw to it that local trade unions, cooperatives, and army units were put under communist bosses responsible to him. He had files on the loyalty and achievement of all managers of industry and other party members. In 1921, a Central Control Commission, which could expel party members for unsatisfactory conduct, was created; Stalin, as liaison between this commission and the Central Committee, now virtually controlled the purges, which were designed to keep the party pure.

In a centralized one-party state, a man of Stalin's ambitions who held so many key positions had an enormous advantage in the struggle for power. Yet the state was so new, the positions were so much less conspicuous and so much more humdrum than the ministry of war, for instance, held by Trotsky, and Stalin's manner was in those days so often conciliatory, that the likelihood of Stalin's success did not become evident until it was too late to stop him. Inside the Politbureau he formed a three-man team with two other prominent Bolshevik leaders, the demagogue Zinoviev and the expert on doctrine Kamenev. Zinoviev was chairman of the Petrograd Soviet and boss of the Communist International; Kamenev was Lenin's deputy and president of the Moscow Soviet. All three were old Bolsheviks, in contrast to Trotsky, who had been a Menshevik and an independent member of the intelligentsia.

The combination of Stalin, Zinoviev, and Kamenev proved unbeatable. The three put down all

real and imagined plots against them by the use of the secret police. They resisted Trotsky's demands for "reform," which would have democratized the party to some degree and would have strengthened his position while weakening Stalin's. They initiated the cult of Lenin immediately before his death and kept it burning fiercely thereafter, so that any suggestion for change coming from Trotsky seemed almost an act of impiety. They dispersed Trotsky's followers by sending them to posts abroad. They prevented the publication of Lenin's "testament," so that the rank and file of the party would not know about Lenin's doubts concerning Stalin. They publicized all Trotsky's earlier statements in opposition to Lenin and did not hesitate to "revise" history in order to belittle Trotsky. They were confident, and rightly, that Trotsky was too good a communist to rally around him such anti-Bolshevik groups as old Mensheviks, SR's, and NEPmen.

Early in 1925, Stalin and his allies were able to force the resignation of Trotsky as minister of war. Soon thereafter the three-man team dissolved; Stalin moved into alliance with Bukharin and other right-wing members of the Politbureau, to which he began to appoint some of his own followers. Using all his accumulated power, he beat his former allies on all questions of policy and in 1926 they moved into a new but powerless alliance with Trotsky. Stalin now (1926) deposed Zinoviev from the Politbureau, charging him with intriguing in the army. Trotsky was the next one to be expelled from the Politbureau, and Zinoviev was ousted as president of the Comintern. In December 1927 a Communist party congress expelled Trotsky from the party itself. Stalin had won.

IV   Stalin's Supremacy:
Russian Internal Affairs, 1928–1941

The Communist party congress also brought NEP to an end and proclaimed that the new "socialist offensive" would begin in 1928. The thirteen years between 1928 and 1941 were to see almost incredible changes in the domestic life of Russia—collectivized agriculture, speedy industrialization, forced labor, the great purges and the extermination of all political opposition, the building of an authoritarian state apparatus, and a "retreat" to bourgeois standards in almost every department of social and intellectual life.

Collectivized Agriculture

In 1928, the failure of the peasants to deliver to the cities as much grain as had been required seemed to underline the dangers inherent in the land divisions of 1917 and in the concessions of NEP. Farm productivity on the small individual holdings was not high enough to feed the city population. Food prices for the workers were high, yet the kulaks wanted further concessions. Grain was hoarded. Stalin had often inveighed against

Russian peasants carrying banners bearing Stalin's 1929 slogan "Liquidation of the kulaks as a class."

"fanning the class struggle in the countryside," and had denied the intention of collectivizing agriculture rapidly or on a mass scale. The government economic plan issued during 1928 set a figure of 20 percent of Russian farms as the maximum to be collectivized by 1933. Yet during 1929, Stalin embarked on immediate full-scale collectivization, declared war on the kulaks, and virtually put an end to individual farming in Russia.

The government did not have the money or the credit to import food. Furthermore, no governmental machinery is adequate to force peasants to disgorge crops that they are hiding. Therefore, the government enlisted on its side the small peasants; in exchange for their assistance in locating and turning over the kulaks' crops, the peasants were promised a place on a collective farm, to be made up of the kulaks' land and equipped with the kulaks' implements. Some of the subsistence farmers (about 20 percent of the number of private farms, possibly 5,000,000 households) more or less welcomed this opportunity. Initial encouraging reports led Stalin to go full speed ahead. The kulaks, he declared in late 1929, were to be liquidated as a class. There were about 2,000,000 households of them, perhaps as many as 10,000,000 people in all. They were now to be totally expropriated, and at the same time barred from the new collectives. Since no provision was

made for them, this move turned collectivization into a nightmare.

Peasants now were machine-gunned into submission; kulaks were deported to forced labor camps or to desolate regions in Siberia. In desperate revolt, the peasants burned crops, broke plows, killed and ate their cattle rather than turn them over to the state, and fled to the cities. More than half the horses in all Russia, 45 percent of the cattle, and two-thirds of the sheep and goats were slaughtered. Russian livestock has never since caught up with the losses it suffered because of the excesses of collectivization. Land lay uncultivated, and over the next few years famine took a toll of millions of lives. As early as March 1930 Stalin showed that he was aware of the ghastly mistakes he had made. In a famous statement on "dizziness with success," he put the blame on local officials who had been too eager to rush through the program. By contradicting his own orders of a few months before, he managed to escape some of the hatred that would otherwise have been directed at him. As usual, many Russian peasants disliked the man they could see, the local official, and were willing to exculpate the "little father" in the capital.

Fifty percent of Russian farms had been hastily thrown together into collectives during this frightful year. Only an additional 10 percent were added during the next three years, so that by 1933 60 percent in all had been collectivized. The number rose again later in the 1930s, until by 1939 more than 96 percent of Russian farms were collectivized. In 1941, there were 250,000 collectives, 900,000,000 acres in extent, supporting 19,000,000 families. Yet the excesses of the early "dizziness with success" were never repeated.

The 1930s also brought a modification of the original rules governing collectives. Originally, collectives had been of two main types: the *sovkhoz*, or soviet farm, not strictly a collective at all but a state-owned enterprise, operated by the government and worked by hired laborers who were government employees; and the *kolkhoz*, or collective farm proper. The sovkhozes were designed as centers of government research and development in agriculture and were often very large in size. But they were mostly brought to an end by Stalin in the 1930s when he ordered some forty million acres originally allotted to them to be distributed among the kolkhozes. As of 1941, the sovkhozes occupied no significant area of land.

The kolkhoz itself was also originally of two types: the commune, in which all the resources of the members without exception were owned together, and the *artel*, or cooperative, in which a certain amount of private property was permitted to the members. After Stalin's modifications of the system in the thirties, the artel became the overwhelmingly predominant form of collective farm. In an artel, each family owned its homestead, some livestock, and minor implements; these could be left by will to the owner's descendants. But most of the work was done on the collectively cultivated land. Each collective had its own managing board, responsible to the government, which supervised the work of the peasants, who were organized in brigades, each under a brigadier. Like factory laborers paid on a piece-work basis, peasants were remunerated according to their output, which was measured by the artificial unit of the labor-day. One day's work in managing a farm might be, for example, assessed at three labor-days, while one day's work weeding a vegetable patch might be assessed at only half a labor-day.

Each kolkhoz turned over to the government a fixed amount of produce at fixed rates and the total of all these amounts was designed to guarantee the feeding of the urban population, especially workers in heavy industry and members of the Red Army. In addition, the kolkhoz paid further taxes to cover government expenses for local construction and education. Any surplus might be sold by the peasant directly to the consumer, without the participation of any middleman. Private resale was regarded as speculation and was subject to punishment. After 1934, the government obtained at least two-thirds of its revenue by the resale on the market at a large profit of farm produce bought at low fixed prices from the kolkhoz. This government profit was known as the turnover tax.

The government assisted and controlled the kolkhoz through the supply of mechanical equipment furnished by the Machine Tractor Stations. The collectives could not own their own tractors, but rented them from the stations, paying in exchange a fee ranging up to perhaps 20 percent of the crop. The stations became important centers for political surveillance. By the decision when and to whom to allot tractors and how many tractors to allot, administrators of the Machine Tractor Stations could directly affect the success of a collective; so their good will was of utmost importance to the management.

Industrialization

Intimately related to the drive in agriculture was the drive in industry. Here, too, Stalin originally had viewed with scorn the grandiose plans of the "super-industrializers" and as late as 1927 had proposed an annual increase rate in industrial production of only 15 percent. But just as he shifted to the frantic pace of collectivizing agriculture, so he first gradually, then suddenly, shifted to forced draft in industry also.

In 1928 began the era of the five-year plans, each setting ambitious goals for production over the next five years. In 1929 and 1930, Stalin appropriated ever higher sums for capital investment, and in June 1930 he declared that industrial production must rise by 50 percent in the current year, a fantastic and impossible figure. Under the first five-year plan, adopted in 1928, annual pig-iron production was scheduled to rise from 3,500,000 tons to 10,000,000 tons by 1932, but in that year Stalin demanded 17,000,000 tons instead. It was not forthcoming, of course, but Stalin's demand for it was symptomatic of the pace at which he was striving to transform Russia from an agricultural to an industrial country.

Part of the reason for this rapid pace lay precisely in the collectivization drive itself. Large-scale farming, to which Stalin was committing Russia, must be mechanized farming. Yet there were only 7,000 tractors in all Russia at the end of 1928. Stalin secured 30,000 more during 1929, but this was nowhere near a beginning. Industry had to produce millions of machines, and the gasoline to run them. Since the countryside had to be electrified, power stations were needed by the thousands. And literally millions and millions of peasants had to be taught how to handle machinery. But there was nobody to teach them and no factories to produce the machinery. The output of raw materials was inadequate and the plants to process them were not there.

Another part of the reason for the drive to industrialize lay in the tenets of Marxism itself. Russia had defied all Marx's predictions by staging a proletarian revolution in a country almost without a proletariat. Yet despite the communists' initial political successes, Stalin felt that "capitalism had a firmer basis than communism in Russia, so long as it remained a country of small peasants." The communists felt that the world proletariat expected them to industrialize Russia, but even more they were determined to create as a support for themselves the massive Russian proletariat which as yet did not exist. Furthermore, Stalin was determined to make Russia as nearly self-sufficient as possible, in line with his theory of socialism in one country. Underlying this was a motive at least as intense as any dictated by Marxist doctrine—Russian nationalism.

The strength of this motive is revealed in a speech that Stalin made in 1931:

> To slacken the pace means to lag behind, and those who lag behind are beaten. We do not want to be beaten. No, we don't want to. . . . Old Russia . . . was ceaselessly beaten for her backwardness. She was beaten by the Mongol Khans, she was beaten by Turkish Beys, she was beaten by Swedish feudal lords, she was beaten by Polish-Lithuanian gentry, she was beaten by Anglo-French capitalists, she was beaten by Japanese barons; she was beaten by all—for her backwardness. For military backwardness, for cultural backwardness, for political backwardness, for industrial backwardness, for agricultural backwardness. She was beaten because to beat her was profitable and went unpunished. . . . We are fifty or a hundred years behind the advanced countries. We must make good this lag in ten years. Either we do it or they crush us.*

Whatever one may think of this quotation as history (and it omits all Russia's *victorious* wars), it reveals that Russian national self-interest as interpreted by Stalin required the most rapid possible industrialization. And it is of interest that ten years afterward the Germans did attack, something Stalin could of course not have predicted so accurately, but something that he seems to have sensed.

Stalin seems also to have felt that he had only to keep a fierce pressure on the management of industry and the desired commodities and finished goods would be forthcoming in the desired quantities. The goals of the first five-year plan were not attained, although fulfillment was announced in 1932. Immediately, the second plan, prepared by the state planning commission, went into effect, and ran until 1937; the third was interrupted only by Hitler's invasion. Each time the emphasis was on the elements of heavy industry—steel, electric power, cement, coal, oil. Between 1928 and 1940, steel production was multiplied by four and one-half, electric power by eight, cement by more than two, coal by four, and oil by almost three. Similar developments took place in chemicals and in machine production. Railroad construction was greatly increased, and the volume of freight carried quadrupled with the production of new rolling stock.

By 1940, Russian output was approaching that of Germany, although Russian efficiency and the Russian standard of living were far lower. What the rest of Europe had done in about seventy-five years Russia had done in about twelve. Enthusiasm was artificially whipped up by wide publicizing of the high output of

*Quoted in Isaac Deutscher, *Stalin* (New York, 1950), p. 328.

individual workers called Stakhanovites, after a coal miner who had set production records. "Stakhanovites" and "heroes of labor" were richly rewarded, and the others were urged to imitate them in "socialist competition."

All this was achieved at the expense of dreadful hardships, yet eyewitnesses report that many of the workers were as enthusiastic as if they had been soldiers in battle, as indeed in a sense they were. Valuable machinery was often damaged or destroyed by inexperienced workers right off the farm. The problems of repair, of replacement, of achieving balance between the output and consumption of raw materials, of housing workers in the new centers, of moving entire industries thousands of miles into the Ural region and Siberia, were unending and cost untold numbers of lives. An American eyewitness estimates that Russia's "battle of ferrous metallurgy alone involved more casualties than the battle of the Marne."

Administratively, the Russian economy was directly run by the state. The Gosplan, or state planning commission, drew up the five-year plans and supervised their fulfillment at the management level. The Gosbank, or state bank, regulated the investment of capital. An economic council administered the work of various agencies. Its major divisions were metallurgy and chemistry (iron and steel, nonferrous metals, chemicals, rubber, alcohol); defense (aviation, armaments, munitions, tanks, ships); machinery (heavy machines, medium machines, machine tools, electrical industry); fuel and power (coal, oil, electric power); agriculture and procurement; and consumer goods (grain, meat and dairy products, fisheries, textiles, light industry). Under iron and steel, for example, there functioned the production trusts controlling their own mines as well as blast furnaces and rolling mills. These were the so-called *combinats,* or great production complexes like that at Magnitogorsk in the Urals. In each plant, as in each collective, the manager was responsible for producing the quota set for him within the maximum cost allowed him. He was consulted on production targets, and had considerable leeway in selecting his staff and allocating labor and raw materials. He was bound to render a rigid accounting to the government, which of course fixed the price he must pay for his raw materials.

The Social Impact

The social effects of the economic program were dramatic. Urban population rose from about 18 percent in 1926 to about 33 percent in 1940. The number of cities with a population between 50,000 and 100,000 doubled, and the number of cities with a population exceeding 100,000 more than quadrupled. The largest cities, Moscow and Leningrad (the new name for Petersburg-Petrograd after the death of Lenin), almost doubled in size, and among smaller cities, to take just one example, Alma Ata in Siberia grew from 45,000 to 230,000 between 1928 and 1939. The entire social picture was radically altered.

The relative freedom to choose one's job which had characterized the NEP period disappeared. Individual industrial enterprises signed labor contracts with the kolkhozes by which the kolkhoz was obliged to send a given number of farm workers to the factories, often against their will. Peasants who had resisted collectivization were drafted into labor camps. In the factories, the trade unions became simply another organ of the state. The chief role of the unions was to achieve maximum production and efficiency, to discourage absenteeism and poor work. Trade unions might not strike or engage in conflict with management. All they could do was administer the social insurance laws and seek improvements in workers' living conditions by negotiation.

Thus in the USSR the old privileged class of noble landlords, already weak at the time of the revolution, ceased to exist. The industrial, commercial, and financial bourgeoisie, which was just coming into its own at the time of the revolution, was destroyed after 1928, despite the temporary reprieve it had experienced under NEP. Most of the old intelligentsia, who had favored a revolution, could not in the end stomach Stalin's dictatorship, and many of them emigrated. Of the million and a half émigrés from Russia after the revolution, only a very small number (contrary to the general view in the West) were cousins of the czar. Those of the old intelligentsia who remained were forced into line with the new Soviet intelligentsia, which Stalin felt to be a very important class. All were compelled to accept the new Stalinist dogma and to drop their interest in the outside world. The new intelligentsia were expected to concentrate on technical advance, and on new administrative devices for speeding up the transformation of the country.

Although the effect of these social changes would presumably have been to level all ranks, Stalin set himself against the old Bolshevik principles of equality. The Marxist slogan "From each according to his capacity, to each according to his needs" was shelved in favor of a new one, "From each according to his capacity, to each according to his work." Where Lenin had allowed none of the members of the government to earn more than a skilled laborer, Stalin set up a new system of incentives. A small minority of bureaucrats and skilled laborers, factory managers, and successful kolkhoz bosses earned vastly more than the great majority of unskilled laborers and peasants. Together with the writers, artists, musicians, and entertainers who were willing to lend their talents to the services of the regime, these men became a new elite, separated by a wide economic and social gulf from the toiling masses. They had a vested interest in furthering a regime to which they owed everything, and without which they would be nothing.

Soviet propagandists declared that this was a temporary situation. They described the present society in the Soviet Union as "socialist," while regarding "communism," not yet achieved, as the goal toward which the USSR was still moving. Yet, just as the "withering away" of the state, which the Marxists predicted, was instead replaced under Stalin by the enormous swelling of state power and state machinery, so the equality predicted by the Marxists was replaced by a new caste system. The means of production were publicly owned in the Soviet Union, as the Marxists had urged. But the power of the state, the birth of a new elite, the brutalization of millions of human beings, and the ruthless use of force after the revolution had been achieved were all the contributions of Stalin.

The Purge Trials

Stalin's program was not achieved without opposition. The crisis of 1931 and 1932, when industrial goals were not being met and starvation swept the countryside, created discontent inside the regime as well as outside. A small number of officials circulated memoranda advocating Stalin's deposition as general secretary, an act which the party had every right to perform. Stalin jailed them for conspiracy, and one leading Bolshevik committed suicide. It is widely believed that Stalin's own wife reproached him at this time with the ravages that the terror was working, and that she too committed suicide. At one moment, but only at one, we are told, Stalin's self-confidence wavered and he offered to resign, but nobody in the Politbureau dared accept the offer, and the moment quickly passed. A preliminary purge in 1932 swept one-third of the party from membership. And in 1934 began the full-scale terror, continuing at intervals until 1938.

These purges remain the most mysterious episode in Soviet history. They are often compared with the Jacobin Terror of the French Revolution, when the revolution "devoured its children." But, in contrast to the rapid appearance of the Terror in France, the purges did not begin for seventeen years after the Russian Revolution. Members of the opposition had been demoted, expelled from the party, and even exiled, as in the case of Trotsky, but nobody had been executed. There is an entirely credible story that the Bolshevik leaders had agreed among themselves early in their career never to start guillotining each other. Yet, when the terror began in Russia, it was even more drastic than it had been in France. Moreover, unlike Robespierre, Stalin managed the entire affair and survived it, more firmly in power than ever.

From exile, Trotsky continued to attack Stalin in a journal called *The Bulletin of the Opposition.* Clever as always, he scored telling points against Stalin, and his words were carefully read by Soviet officials. Yet the older generation of communists, though they may have hated Stalin, made no move against him. A younger group, however, seemingly more restless and convinced that Stalin had abandoned Lenin's program, found the model for conspiracy in the heroes of the terrorist movement who had assassinated Alexander II. They were apparently prepared to use terrorism against Stalin and his henchmen. Even within the Politbureau men loyal to Stalin grew restless at his ruthlessness, and urged him to relax the pressure; Sergei Kirov, boss of Leningrad, took the lead.

Stalin at times seemed to yield to this urging, as when he ordered more gentle treatment for rebellious kulaks in June 1932 and limited the powers of the political police. But at other times he seemed to be taking the opposite course, as when he issued a decree making an entire family responsible for the treason of any of its members. On the whole, however, tension relaxed during 1932–1934. Kirov proclaimed a new era of lenience at a party conference, and former leaders of the opposition, including Bukharin, were appointed to help draft a new and liberal constitution.

Then on December 1, 1934, Kirov was assassinated. The story that Stalin himself had plotted the assassination cannot be confirmed, but he used it as a pretext. The assassin was executed. Accused of complicity, Zinoviev and Kamenev were jailed and forced to admit that they had plotted to restore capitalism. Yet the drafting of the new "democratic" constitution went on. Stalin became ever more withdrawn, ever more autocratic, ever more resolved to destroy the old Bolsheviks, as Ivan the Terrible had destroyed the old nobility. After an interlude during 1935 and early 1936, during which Stalin said that "life had become more joyous," the purges proper began.

The official story was that Trotskyite agitation abroad was linked with the murder of Kirov and with the alleged plans for the murder of Stalin. A series of public political trials took place. In the first (1936), Zinoviev, Kamenev, and fourteen others admitted these charges and were executed. In the second (1937), seventeen other leading Bolsheviks declared that they had knowledge of a conspiracy between Trotsky and the German and Japanese intelligence services, by which Russian territory was to be transferred to Germany and Japan. All were executed. Then (June 1937) came the secret liquidation of the top commanders in the Red Army, who were accused of conspiring with "an unfriendly foreign power" (Germany) with a view to sabotage. All were executed after an announcement that they had confessed. The last of the public trials took place in March 1938, as twenty-one leading Bolsheviks, including Bukharin, confessed to similar charges and were executed.

But these public trials and the secret trial of the generals give only a faint idea of the extent of the purge. Every member of Lenin's Politbureau except Stalin and Trotsky was either killed or committed suicide to avoid execution. Two vice-commissars of foreign affairs and most of the ambassadors of the diplomatic corps, fifty of the seventy-one members of the Central Committee of the Communist party, almost all the military judges who had sat in judgment and had condemned the generals, two successive heads of the secret police, themselves the leaders in the previous purges, the prime ministers and chief officials of all the non-Russian Soviet Republics—all were killed or vanished. A list of those who disappeared reads like a "who's who" of high officialdom in state and party throughout the twenties and thirties. Literally thousands were executed or disappeared without a trace. The public trials probably included only those who were willing to confess, whether guilty or not. The rest were condemned privately and quite without due process of law.

Although some of those who were executed opposed Stalin, the charges against them were certainly not true. Had they been true, the great conspiracy involving almost everybody but Stalin himself would surely have accomplished more than the assassination of Kirov. It is altogether unlikely that any of the top communists conspired with Hitler, little though they may have loved Stalin. Some who confessed may have felt so great a loyalty to the cause of communism, however perverted, that they sacrificed themselves for Stalin's soviet state. Some doubtless hoped to save their families, or even themselves, and a few leaders were spared the death penalty to encourage confessions from the others. Many may have hoped that the confessions were so ridiculous that nobody could believe them.

What Stalin apparently wanted was to destroy utterly all possibility of future conspiracies. So he trumped up charges against anybody who conceivably could become a member of a regime that might replace his own. Despite the enormous upheaval of the purges, no breakdown took place in the state. New bureaucrats were found to take the places of the old. The new Stalin-trained officials now manned all top-level positions. And terror had been enthroned as a principle of government, keeping every official in constant fear for his life—let alone his job. In the end, perhaps lest all talent and initiative vanish into the clouds of fear, the purgers too were finally purged, used as scapegoats by Stalin for the ghastly things they had done at his command.

The Authoritarian State

In the midst of the purges, in 1936, Stalin proclaimed the new constitution, the "most democratic in the world." By its provisions nobody was disfranchised, as priests and members of the former nobility and bourgeoisie had previously been. Civil liberties were extended, but even on paper these were never more than a sham, since the constitution provided that they could be modified in the "interest of the toilers." The fact that the USSR was a one-party state prevented elections from being anything but an expression of unanimity. The right to nominate candidates for the Supreme Soviet belonged to Communist party organizations, trade unions, cooperatives, youth groups, and cultural societies; but all were completely dominated by the party. The party picked the candidates, and no more than one for each post was ever presented to the voters. The party controlled the soviets, and the party hierarchy and government hierarchy overlapped and interlocked.

Every citizen was eligible for membership in the party on application to a local branch, which voted on his application after a year of trial. Communist children's organizations fed the youth groups, which in turn fed the party. The party was organized both territorially and functionally in pyramidal form, with organizations at the bottom level in factory, farm, and government office. These were grouped together by rural or urban local units and these in turn by regional and territorial conferences and congresses. The party organizations elected the All-Union party congress, which selected the Central Committee of the party and which was in theory the highest policy-making organ, though actually no party congress was held between 1939 and 1954. The Central Committee selected the Politbureau. At each level of the party pyramid there were organizations for agitation and propaganda, for organization and instruction, for military and political training. The party exercised full control over the government, which simply enacted formally what the party had decided upon. The five-year plans, for example, were party programs that went into effect even before they were formally adopted by the government.

The highest organ of the government was the Supreme Soviet, made up of two houses—a Soviet of the Union, based on population, and a Soviet of Nationalities, elected according to national administrative divisions. In theory, the Supreme Soviet was elected for a term of four years. The Supreme Soviet itself did little; it appointed a presidium which issued the decrees and carried on the work of the Supreme Soviet between sessions. It also appointed the Council of Ministers (long called the Council of People's Commissars). This cabinet, rather than the Supreme Soviet or its presidium, enacted most of the legislation and was thus the legislative as well as the executive organ of the Russian state. The chairmanship of the Council of People's Commissars, the chairmanship of the Politbureau, and the general secretariat of the Communist party were all posts held by Stalin, who in addition served as commissar of defense, chief of the State Defense Council, which ran the country during wartime, and generalissimo. Similar overlapping of party and government posts was the regular practice.

In 1924, Stalin's constitutional reform had created the new Union of Soviet Socialist Republics, including the enormously large Russian Federative Republic, the Ukraine, White Russia, Georgia, Armenia, and Azerbaidjan, and three central Asian Soviet Socialist republics: Uzbekistan, Turkmenistan, and Tadjikistan. In 1936, Kazakh and Kirghiz republics were added, making a total of eleven. As a result of the annexations of the Baltic states and of Finnish and Romanian territory in 1940, five more republics were created: Lithuania, Latvia, Estonia, Karelia, and Moldavia. These sixteen "Union" republics differed widely in population. Within the huge Russian republic were sixteen "autonomous" republics, and numerous other subdivisions, all called "autonomous." The larger SSR's had similar subdivisions.

Each of the Union republics and autonomous republics had a government patterned exactly on that of the Soviet Union, except that the supreme soviet of each republic was unicameral and not bicameral, since it lacked a chamber of nationalities. Many complaints have been heard in recent years about the way in which "Great-Russian chauvinism" has permeated official policy toward the individual minority republics. Although this soviet descendant of czarist russification policy has always been a menace, it is widely believed that in the years before World War II, the chief objective was not to try to russify the nationalities but to communize them. With this end in view, the party permitted and encouraged local nationalities to revive their culture, study their past traditions, and use their own language. Like every other cultural manifestation permitted in the USSR, these national cultural achievements were "managed." Not only was it impossible for anti-Soviet or anti-Communist material to appear in print or in any of the plastic arts, but, as everywhere, all artistic effort was closely supervised and had to serve the regime positively. The value of "cultural autonomy" under these circumstances is of course highly debatable.

Although the Stalin constitution specifically gave each republic the right to secede, this provision was pure window-dressing. The central government was overpoweringly stronger than the government of any one republic, which in any case was often not even made up of natives. Although each of the sixteen republics was in 1944 given its own foreign office by an amendment to the constitution, this amendment was never intended to give them autonomy in this critically important field. Actually it seems simply to have been a device for securing representation of the Ukraine and White Russia in the United Nations. The representatives of these two republics to the United Nations have never been anything but extra Soviet delegates; the first Ukrainian delegate to the UN was not even a Ukrainian, but a Russian who was once Soviet ambassador to the independent Ukraine of the revolutionary era.

The Russian Thermidor

The period between 1934 and 1941, notable for the purges and for the constitutional development of Stalin's one-party state, is also called by many shrewd observers of revolutions the true Russian Thermidor, as distinct from NEP. The term "Thermidor" has come to mean a period in which a revolution has burnt itself out, and the prevailing mood shifts from messianic enthusiasm to one of desire for normality. In revolutionary France, the shift was signalized by the fall of Robespierre and the Jacobin regime and the advent of the Directory, a different government with different objectives, policies, and personnel, which was in turn succeeded by Napoleon's dictatorship. In the USSR, the striking fact was that Stalin stayed in office throughout. He was in effect the Russian Robespierre, Directory, and Napoleon all rolled into one. If we accept the parallel, the Russian Thermidor was a managed and manipulated Thermidor, involving no real liberalization of the regime or relaxation of controls.

In any case, the period of the late 1930s saw a wholesale retreat from many ideas of the revolution. Simultaneously with the purges and the new constitution, the bread ration was raised; the kolkhoz was reformed to permit the individual farmer to own his homestead; new medals and titles were awarded to leading workers in plants, and to scientists, engineers, and military men. In the Red Army, the traditional czarist distinctions between officers and men were restored and marshals were named for the first time. Thus, without relaxing political control, Stalin introduced an element of relaxation into the daily life of the rank and file, at the very height of his Terror. The standard of living went up as the production of consumer goods was encouraged and as workers were invited to spend their earnings on little luxuries previously unavailable.

Simultaneously, the state rediscovered Russia's great past. The standard communist teaching had been that proletarians have no fatherland; the very name of Russia had almost been abandoned. Now, in contrast, officially controlled organs of opinion editorialized that one should love one's own country and hailed the heroes of the czarist era. Alexander Nevsky, who had defeated the Teutonic Knights; Dmitri Donskoi, who had defeated the Tatars; Peter the Great; Kutuzov, who had defeated Napoleon; even Ivan the Terrible—all were praised to the skies. The reputations of the great literary figures of the nineteenth century underwent a similar rehabilitation. This retreat to Russian nationalism reached its climax during World War II, when the Marxist *Internationale* itself was dropped as the national anthem.

The old Bolsheviks had attacked the family as the backbone of the old order, had made marriage difficult and divorce easy, had drawn no distinction between legitimate and illegitimate children, and had encouraged promiscuity and abortions. Stalin's state now rehabilitated the sanctity of marriage, denounced the seducer, made divorces very hard to get, declared the family essential to the state, and encouraged children to obey their parents. Doubtless the shift came in part as a result of the falling birthrate and increasing juvenile delinquency.

The early Bolsheviks had destroyed the old school system, abolished homework and examinations, and allowed children to administer the schools collectively with their teachers. Attendance fell off, the schools became revolutionary clubs of youngsters, and the training of teachers was neglected. The universities deteriorated, since anybody aged sixteen could enroll in them. Degrees were abolished, and technical training was stressed to the exclusion of other subjects. Under NEP, this chaotic situation was modified and the basic problem of increasing literacy was seriously tackled. But the subjects of ordinary school curricula were replaced by the so-called "project" system, with heavy emphasis on labor problems and Marxist theory. The teachers had little to do except memorize texts and quiz the children to test their mastery of them. The Communist party itself took over the universities, purged the faculties, and compelled the students to spend one week in three at work in factories—a system that helped neither the student nor the university, and cannot have increased industrial production by very much.

The thermidorean reaction, as might have been expected, changed this system drastically. Training of teachers improved, their salaries were raised, and regular ranks in the civil service were established for them. The old prerevolutionary system of admissions and degrees in the universities was restored, as was the prerevolutionary school curriculum. Examinations and homework reappeared; discipline was enforced on school children. The emphasis on political education was reduced, and coeducation was abandoned. Fees for tuition were restored for secondary schools, the Russian counterpart of the American high school or the French lycée. These tuition fees made higher education difficult to obtain except for children of the new elite or unusually talented students who were able to win state scholarships. Literacy rose to about 90 percent, if we may believe Soviet figures.

The educational reforms certainly made books, theaters, museums, and libraries available to many more Russians than ever before. Newspapers and periodicals multiplied, and the regime's respect for science and learning was genuine. But the regime's attitude was narrowly utilitarian and thoroughly intolerant. All cultural activities were measured by their positive contribution to the state. Education became indoctrination. Systems of ideas that might rival communism were not allowed to compete, since the government could always silence those who might be their spokesmen. In this respect the Soviet regime was even more authoritarian than that of a ruler like Czar Nicholas I.

Under Nicholas I, censorship prevented the writer from saying certain things, but it did not positively prescribe what he must say. It was a negative, not a positive censorship, and it left a margin of personal freedom that permitted some of the greatest works of all literature to be written in Russia. The Soviet censorship, on the other hand, was positive and required of all artists that they constantly praise the new system and devote their talents to publicizing its merits. The party line extended into all cultural fields, even music, where talented composers had to apologize abjectly for failing to produce communist symphonies, whatever they may be. The creative artist, the scientist, the scholar did not know from day to day whether his efforts would win him a Stalin prize or a sentence to a Siberian labor camp.

The Russian Thermidor came last of all, and doubtless very reluctantly, to modify the traditional communist position on religion. Here militant atheism had been the policy of the early Bolsheviks. They jailed and sometimes executed bishops and priests; they sponsored an atheist society and a museum of antireligious propaganda. Behind this attitude lay more than the standard Marxist feeling that religion was the opium of the masses; in Russia, the Orthodox church had always been a pillar of czarism. Many years of attacks on religion, however, failed to eradicate Orthodoxy from among the people. When in 1937 Hitler built a Russian church in Berlin and took every occasion to speak kindly of the Orthodox church, Stalin moved in the religious field also. Declaring that Christianity had contributed to past Russian progress, the government called off its antireligious propaganda and enlisted its own atheist society to rehabilitate the Church. Churchgoing became respectable once more, although members of the party were not encouraged to profess religion. As a result, when war came, the leading church dignitaries supported the regime enthusiastically, although Hitler won a number of Ukrainian clerics to his side. In 1943, Stalin received high churchmen; the government lowered taxes on church property, lifted the curfew for Easter, and appointed a new patriarch, on whose subservience the regime could count.

Viewed together, the changes of the Thermidor period seem to have had a double purpose. They were designed in part to retain popular loyalty during a period when the party itself was being disrupted by the purges. But they were also designed in part to strengthen the country to meet an expected attack from Germany. However far the return to old and popular forms and ideas was carried, it was always the regime that took the lead. And never at any moment did Stalin relax his firm control over all departments of national life, both public and private.

V Soviet Foreign Policy, 1918–1941
Foreign Office and Comintern, 1918–1928

During the period of "war communism," the Bolsheviks had a chance to reflect upon their previously firm conviction that the world revolution was to be expected in the immediate future. The communist states in Bavaria and in Hungary proved to be short-lived; everywhere the moderates triumphed. As the civil war drew to a close, Lenin and his followers realized that to rebuild a shattered Russia it would be necessary to deal with the capitalist world. In the Foreign Office they

Early postrevolutionary education: adults learning to read and write.

had two competent men: Chicherin, a learned aristocrat turned Bolshevik, and Litvinov, his shrewd and able chief assistant. These two and their staff now became diplomats in the service of the Soviet state, like diplomats in the service of other states.

But the idea of world revolution was of course not abandoned. Lenin in 1919 founded the Third International, known thereafter as the Comintern. It issued what amounted almost to a new Communist Manifesto, summoning communists all over the world to unite against the "bourgeois cannibals" of capitalism. Zinoviev was put in charge, and his chief assistants were also Russians. Labor, socialist, and anarchist parties in Bulgaria, Norway, Italy, and Spain began to adhere to the new organization, although many withdrew in disgust when it became clear that the Bolsheviks were establishing a dictatorship in Russia with secret police and an army. Yet the Comintern continued to operate side by side with the Foreign Office, and during the next few years often in seeming contradiction to it. This duality gave Russian foreign policy a unique aspect. The maintenance of the Comintern aroused suspicion abroad and made capitalist states reluctant even to recognize the new Russia.

The Foreign Office concluded a trade treaty with England in 1921, at the beginning of the NEP period, which bound Russia not to stir up the peoples of the British Empire by any means, and reopened trade between the two countries. Similar treaties were concluded between Russia and Poland, the Baltic states, Scandinavia, Germany, and Italy. A truce had been arranged between the communist and capitalist worlds. In 1922, the Russians were invited to an international economic conference at Genoa. The British and French were convinced that NEP meant a return to capitalism and had worked out a scheme for investment in Russia as part of a program for the postwar economic reconstruction of Europe. Not only did the Russians reject this plan, but they signed with defeated Germany the Treaty of Rapallo (April 1922), which provided for the renunciation of all claims for reparations, and implied a German willingness to recognize Bolshevik nationalizations. This recognition the other powers, especially France, were unwilling to grant because of the large amounts of capital they had invested in Russia before the revolution. Rapallo relieved Russian isolation and brought German technical knowledge to the service of the Bolsheviks. They permitted the Germans to build and operate armament and aircraft factories on Russian soil in defiance of the Treaty of Versailles.

In 1923, at Lausanne, Russia lost a dispute with Britain over international regulation of the Straits, and further friction with Britain arose over Afghanistan. But Britain recognized the Soviet regime in 1924, despite Trotsky's description of the mild Labourite Ramsay MacDonald as a "Christian Menshevik" whose country was full of cockroaches—a comment whose characteristic vituperative tone illustrates some of Russia's difficulty in getting along with the rest of the world. Later in the same year, 1924, the so-called Zinoviev letter was published in England. It purported to instruct the British Communist party in the techniques of revolution, and it was almost certainly a forgery. But the "Zinoviev letter" influenced the British voters to elect a Conservative government, which denounced the treaties with Russia. In 1927, a raid on the offices of a Russian firm doing business in London produced further evidence of communist agitation in England, and the British government now broke relations with Russia altogether. The Anglo-Russian council of trade unions set up by the communists collapsed when the Russians criticized British moderation in the general strike of 1926. Meantime, the United States had no diplomatic relations with the Soviet regime and did not recognize it until 1933.

During the years 1918–1927, the Comintern compiled a record of failure. First, the Russians failed to keep in line the leaders of the Italian left in a conference at Leghorn in 1921 and thus contributed handsomely to the success of Mussolini in the next year. Next, they failed in Bulgaria to collaborate with a liberal agrarian regime and allowed the triumph of a right-wing group in 1923. Most important, they failed in Germany, where a revolution actually threatened during 1923 as a result of French occupation of the Ruhr. After Lenin's death, the feud between Stalin and Trotsky was reflected in the Communist parties of other countries and cost the Comintern heavily.

The Russians failed in Poland, where they helped Pilsudski to dictatorial power in 1926, after which he turned against them. They failed in the Muslim and colonial world. But their greatest failure came in China, where in 1923 the Chinese nationalist revolutionary leader, Sun Yat-sen, agreed to take communist advice and received one of the Comintern's best men, Borodin. Borodin helped Sun reorganize his political party, the Kuomintang, and admitted communists to it, although this alienated the right-wing supporters of the national party. In March 1926, Sun having died, his brother-in-law Chiang Kai-shek led a coup against the government, and began to arrest communists. It is often argued that, had Stalin at that moment broken with Chiang and proceeded to sponsor a Chinese communist revolution, he might well have won China. Indeed, Trotsky analyzed the situation that way at the time. But Stalin in his own analysis fell back on a theory that the Bolsheviks had not espoused since Lenin's return to Russia in April 1917: the theory that a bourgeois revolution must precede a socialist revolution and that all the communists could and should do in China was to help Chiang achieve this first revolution. The eventual result was a series of massacres of Chinese communists by Chiang, and a loss of prestige for Stalin and for Russia. It seems probable that neither then nor later did Stalin actually *want* the Chinese communists in power, in view of the enormous difficulty of maintaining Russian control there.

Indeed, Stalin had apparently never really believed in the effectiveness of the Comintern as an instrument of world revolution. When he came to sole power, he could not abandon it, however, because of the criticism he would have aroused, and because he sought to dilute and eventually to eradicate the largely Trotskyite sentiments of communists in other countries. He therefore applied to the Comintern the same techniques he had used against the party at home and established full control over it through use of the Russian delegation. This delegation was responsible to the Politbureau, and as the representative of the only successful revolutionary country it enjoyed great prestige. Successively, the Comintern was influenced to denounce the enemies of Stalin: Trotsky and the Left in 1924, Bukharin and the Right in 1928. Thereafter there was no divergence between the Comintern and the Foreign Office.

Stalin and the West, 1928–1939

Simultaneously with the adoption of the "new socialist offensive" at home, Stalin swung the Comintern leftward into a new period of militant revolutionary activity. The Social Democrats of Western countries were denounced now as "social fascists" and as the most dangerous enemies of communism. The communists were going to bring about revolutions by themselves. Yet Stalin's personal belief in the possibility of revolution elsewhere seems to have been small. "One Soviet tractor is worth more than ten good foreign communists" is a remark quoted as typical of the views of Stalin's entourage in the days of the first five-year plan; it reflects his real contempt for the rest of the world and his deep-rooted Russian nationalism.

This lack of real interest in the behavior of communists abroad and the failure to understand the true play of forces inside other countries led directly to the triumph of Hitler in Germany in 1933. The communists in Germany, who had been instructed by the Comintern that the Social Democrats and not the Nazis were their worst enemies, fought the Nazis in the streets, but allied themselves with them in the Reichstag. They believed that a Nazi triumph would very soon be followed by a communist revolution. Thus even after Hitler came to power, the Russians renewed their nonaggression pact with Germany.

Yet the shock of realization that Hitler had meant precisely what he said about liquidating communists, and the fear that the USSR itself might be in danger, soon led Stalin to modify Russian policy in the direction of collective security. After Hitler had refused to guarantee the Baltic states jointly with Stalin, Russia entered the League of Nations in September 1934. The Soviet delegate, Litvinov, now became the most elo-

quent defender of universal disarmament and of punishment for aggressors. Soon afterward, the Russians began to negotiate for an "eastern Locarno" security pact to balance the agreement reached by the western European nations at Locarno in 1925. Although no such structure could be created because of Polish and German hostility to the USSR, Russia did sign pacts with France and Czechoslovakia in 1935 providing for consultation, under the terms of the League, in the event of aggression, and for mutual aid, if the League certified that aggression had occurred. Soviet aid to Czechoslovakia, if the Czechs became victims of aggression, was to be delivered only if the French, who were bound to the Czechs by a long-standing alliance, honored their obligations first.

In view of the shift in Soviet foreign policy, the Comintern also shifted its line. In 1935, their recent deadly enemies, the Social Democrats and bourgeois liberals of the West, were suddenly embraced as allies against the fascist menace. Communists were to take the lead in forming "popular fronts" against fascism and might properly welcome anybody, no matter how conservative in other ways, who would stand together with them on this principle. Revolutionary propaganda and anticapitalist agitation were to be soft-pedaled. The communists in all the countries of the world led the fight for the defense budgets that they had previously sabotaged. Georgi Dimitrov, the Bulgarian communist, hero of the Reichstag fire trial (to be discussed), and a symbol of antifascist courage and wit, was made boss of the Comintern. Inside the Soviet Union, the adoption of the "popular front" strategy was probably not unrelated to the purges, since the "right deviationists" were anxious to reach an accommodation with the fascist states and the "left deviationists" insisted on the steady pursuit of world revolution.

This was the period when popular front governments came to power in France and Spain and when some people in the West naïvely accepted the communists as their true brothers in arms against the menace of Hitler. However effective the "popular front" may have been as a tactic with Western individuals, the purges inside Russia disillusioned Western governments. A state that had to exterminate its top civil and military personnel for the crime of collaborating with the enemy did not make an attractive ally. If one believed the purge charges, one regarded a Soviet alliance as of doubtful value; if one did not believe them, how could one trust Stalin? On Stalin's side, Western appeasement of Hitler and Mussolini doubtless increased his disillusionment with the West.

Russia and the western European bloc each assumed that the chief purpose of the other was to turn the full force of Hitler's forthcoming attack away from itself and in the opposite direction. That Hitler intended to attack, nobody could doubt. On September 12, 1936, in a speech at Nuremberg, he specifically declared once more that

If I had the Ural mountains with their incalculable store of treasures in raw materials, Siberia with its vast forests, and the Ukraine with its tremendous wheatfields, Germany under National Socialist leadership would swim in plenty.*

There was, then, much reason for the West to hope that the attack would be directed against the USSR; this Stalin was determined to avert.

Soviet intervention in the Spanish Civil War is an interesting demonstration of Stalin's real position. General Francisco Franco, who led an army revolt against the republican government of Spain in 1936, soon obtained aid from Mussolini and Hitler. The Russians, though reluctant to intervene in Spain at all because of their anxiety to prove their respectability to the Western powers, realized that a failure to help the Spanish republic would cost them support all over the world. But their aid was too little and came too late and consisted largely of police agents who devoted themselves to fighting Spanish anarchists and Trotsky-ites. The Russians hoped that the Western powers would intervene also, feeling that if they did so they would be irrevocably committed to continue the fight against Hitler on other battlefields. But the fact of

*A. Hitler, *My New Order,* ed. R. de Sales (New York, 1941), p. 400

Western neutrality in Spain helped convince Stalin that a Western alliance could not be counted upon.

A still more important factor here was the Western appeasement of Hitler, which reached its climax in the Munich agreement among Britain, France, Germany, and Italy in September 1938. From the Russian point of view, the Munich cession of Czech lands to Hitler, and the French failure to support Czechoslovakia and thus make operative the Russo-Czech alliance, could have only one purpose—to drive Hitler east. Stalin was apparently ready to support the Czechs if the French did too; when they did not, he seems to have decided that he had better sound out Hitler for an understanding. Thus a truly effective alliance between Stalin and the West proved impossible between 1935 and 1939.

When the British and French realized that appeasement had failed to stop Hitler, they sought reluctantly for a firmer alliance with the USSR. From March to August 1939, Stalin kept open both his negotiations with the West and his slowly ripening negotiations with the Germans, which at first seemed to be concerned only with a trade agreement. The British and French mission, when it finally arrived in Moscow, was not composed of sufficiently highranking men to inspire Russian confidence. Moreover, the Western powers nat-

"Rendezvous": Low cartoon comment on the Hitler-Stalin pact.

urally could not agree to turn over to Stalin the territories that he wanted as a bulwark against Germany—Finland and the Baltic republics of Estonia, Latvia, and Lithuania.

The growing eagerness of the Germans to secure a nonaggression pact gave Stalin the opportunity he sought to divert the war from Russia. In May 1939 Litvinov was dismissed as foreign minister because he was Jewish and could therefore not negotiate with the Germans; he was replaced by Molotov. In the pact that Molotov eventually reached with Hitler late in August 1939, each power undertook to remain neutral toward the other in the event of war. A secret additional protocol provided for a division between Germany and Russia of Poland, which Hitler was about to attack. At worst, this put Russia's frontier farther west in the event of a subsequent German attack. The Russians lived up to the economic clauses of the agreement to the letter, although the Germans did not. The publication of the Hitler-Stalin pact necessitated an abrupt shift in the world communist line, which had remained staunchly "popular front." Now it was once more necessary for puzzled communists to denounce liberals and Social Democrats as enemies. They had to call the war that Hitler launched against Poland within a few days an "imperialist war," in which there was no difference between the two sides and in which communists should not get involved.

Stalin and the Second World War

Stalin overrated the military power of the Poles to resist Hitler and thus miscalculated the course of the first weeks of war. Faced with the complete collapse of Poland, he marched into the eastern portion. Disturbed by the lull ("the phony war") on the western fronts, he probably feared that Hitler would turn against him at once. This might well have happened had Hitler been able to secure peace with France and England, as he strove to do. During the lull, in December 1939, came Stalin's attack on Finland, which, unlike the Baltic states, had refused to grant him strategic bases. The attack on the Finns by Stalin aroused a storm of anti-Russian sentiment in the West. Both Britain and France supported the recruitment of armies of volunteers, and considered air raids against Russian targets in support of the Finns. The League of Nations expelled Russia. Despite severe setbacks to the Russian troops, the war against the Finns was won by the spring of 1940, before the Western allies had been able to give them effective aid.

And in the spring of 1940, Stalin's second major calculation went awry. Like many observers, he apparently expected France to hold out a long time, and believed that, even if Hitler eventually defeated the French, Germany would be greatly weakened. Now instead came the lightning German operations in the West, and the war on the Continent seemed to be over. Only the British held out. Preoccupied with the security of his western frontiers, Stalin simply seized the three Baltic republics, and staged rigged plebiscites in which the Latvians, Estonians, and Lithuanians asked to be included in the Soviet Union. He demanded of Romania in June 1940 the province of Bessarabia, whose loss after World War I the USSR had never recognized, and also northern Bukovina, which had formerly been Austrian, not Russian, territory, but which had a large Ukrainian population and was strategically valuable. Parts of these territories were annexed to existing SSR's and parts were incorporated into the new Moldavian SSR. The Germans had expected Russian seizure of Bessarabia, but not of northern Bukovina; they permitted the seizure, however, telling the Romanians that they could expect no help from Hitler. But that was as far as Hitler's cooperation with Stalin in eastern Europe went. The reannexation of Bessarabia had given the USSR the mouth of the Danube, controlling an important artery. The Russians seemed to be moving into southeast Europe, a region in which the Germans were not prepared to let them operate alone.

Only a few weeks after the Russian seizure of Romanian territory, Hitler asserted his own southeastern interests by forcing the Romanians to cede territory to Hungary (August 1940) and then guaranteeing the new Romanian frontiers, a guarantee that could apply only against the USSR. Soon afterward, German troops appeared in Finland "to reinforce the German armies in Norway," Hitler explained. And in the autumn of 1940, German troops entered Romania proper "to guard the Romanian oilfields against British sabotage." These maneuvers on his new frontiers deeply disquieted Stalin, as well they might have.

In October 1940 Italy attacked Greece, and open war had spread to the Balkans. In November, when Molotov went to Berlin, Hitler tried to dazzle him with grandiose offers of an enormous future Soviet sphere of influence extending through Persia to the Persian Gulf and Indian Ocean, and including India, after the British Empire was destroyed. Each time this luscious bait was held out, Molotov tried to bring the discussion back to southeast Europe and Finland and to establish Russia's sole rights in this sphere. This the Germans would not allow. After the failure of the conversations, Hitler ordered preparations for an attack on the USSR.

In the spring of 1941, the Germans had to rescue the Italians from the Greek campaign, which had bogged down in Albania. This rescue was preceded by the movement of German troops into Bulgaria, which the USSR regarded as essential to its own defense. Then came an unsuccessful German effort to win Yugoslavia without war, and swift victorious German campaigns in Yugoslavia and Greece (March–May 1941). Germany alone ruled supreme in the Balkan region, and, though the Yugoslav and Greek resistance had delayed the German timetable, Hitler was able to launch the invasion of the USSR on June 22, 1941. Stalin must have known it was coming; indeed, the Western powers had warned him. But he seems to have hoped against hope to the end. A few weeks before it came, Stalin, proudly calling himself an Asiatic, had secured a neutrality pact with Japan, Hitler's ally. The Japanese, deeply engaged in China and intending to go to war with the United States, wished as much as did the Russians for insurance against a war on two fronts.

VI Conclusion

Karl Marx, who scorned and disliked Russia, would have been utterly dumfounded had he lived to see that backward agricultural land, almost without a proletariat, produce the only successful European communist revolution. Although much ink has been spilled in an effort to discover why a Marxist revolution took place in the country where, in theory, the conditions were least favorable, the problem is not really so difficult. Two possible general solutions suggest themselves. Either Marx was wrong, or what happened in Russia was not a Marxist revolution at all. Or perhaps both these answers are partly right. It seems clear that Marx did not correctly estimate the revolutionary force latent in the Russian peasantry; since Marx died in 1883, he could not foresee the full inadequacy of the czarist regime, the extent of the tensions created by World War I, or the feebleness of the provisional government of 1917. But it also seems clear that to bring the Bolsheviks to power it took Lenin's appreciation of the importance of the peasantry, his grasp of the immediate situation,

his willingness to risk everything, and his luck at being in the right place at the right time with the right weapons.

On the other hand, the revolution was not wholly Marxist. Once the Bolsheviks were in power, of course, it was inevitable that the succession of real situations they faced should modify their Marxist-Leninist theories. Thus civil war and foreign intervention brought chaos, from which NEP provided a necessary respite. And in Stalin there came to power an amalgam of Marxist, Russian nationalist, and power-hungry politicians such as nobody could have foreseen. Moved by a combination of motives, Stalin proceeded hastily and brutally to make over Russia in a decade. Although he fell short of his goal, his program had created an industrial state not totally unprepared for the blows that Hitler was to deal it. Slaves of the state though they were, collectivized by force, industrialized by force, purged, terrorized, and struggling by the million to exist in forced labor camps, the Russians in World War II succeeded, with much help from the United States, in defeating Hitler and his allies.

How much the loyalty of Russians to Stalin was due to the failure of the German invaders to treat them well, and how far Hitler with a different policy might have won their support are questions with which we cannot deal here. The Russians were facing a coalition of fascist states—Germany, Hungary, Romania, and others grouped together in an alliance called "the Axis powers" (from the German-Italian "Axis"), a coalition pledged to the utter destruction of communism. We turn now to the history of these powers.

Reading Suggestions on Communist Russia, 1917–1941
General Accounts
E. H. Carr, *A History of Soviet Russia.* Eleven volumes of this work, still in progress, have so far appeared (Macmillan, 1950–1971). The only attempt at a complete history of the Soviet Union from original sources, it has only reached the year 1929. Carr is a somewhat uncritical admirer of Lenin, and his work must be used with care.

B. Moore, Jr., *Soviet Politics: The Dilemma of Power* (*Torchbooks). An illuminating analysis of the relationship between the communist ideology and Soviet practice.

R. N. Carew Hunt, *The Theory and Practice of Communism* (Macmillan, 1951). An excellent introduction to the subject.

M. Fainsod, *How Russia Is Ruled,* 2nd ed. (Harvard Univ. Press, 1963). An analysis of the Soviet system in 1963, firmly rooted in the historical background.

Robert V. Daniels, *The Nature of Communism* (*Vintage). A valuable study of totalitarianism.

Special Studies
W. H. Chamberlin, *The Russian Revolution, 1917–1921,* 2 vols. (*Grosset's Universal Library). Still the standard work on the subject.

L. Trotsky, *The History of the Russian Revolution,* 3 vols. (Simon and Schuster, 1932). A brilliant but biased study by one of the leading participants.

Robert V. Daniels, ed., *The Russian Revolution* (*Spectrum). A well-chosen and well-discussed selection of sources.

B. D. Wolfe, *Three Who Made a Revolution* (*Beacon). Excellent triple study of the careers of Lenin, Trotsky, and Stalin down to 1914.

D. Shub, *Lenin* (Doubleday, 1948; *Mentor abridgment). A good biography of Lenin.

Adam B. Ulam, *The Bolsheviks: The Intellectual and Political History of the Triumph of Communism in Russia* (Macmillan, 1965); and *Stalin: The Man and His Era* (Viking, 1973). Excellent detailed accounts.

I. Deutscher, *The Prophet Armed, The Prophet Unarmed, The Prophet Outcast* (Oxford Univ. Press, 1954, 1959, 1963; *Vintage). Biography of Trotsky, written by an admirer.

J. Maynard, *Russia in Flux* (Macmillan, 1948). Enlightening though sometimes farfetched attempts to show basic continuities between the old and new regimes in Russia, written by a British civil servant stationed in India who made the study of Russia his avocation.

C. Brinton, *The Anatomy of Revolution,* 2nd ed. (*Vintage). Comparison of the Russian Revolution with the French Revolution of 1789 and the English seventeenth-century Revolution.

M. Fainsod, *Smolensk Under Soviet Rule* (*Vintage). A uniquely important study, based on a huge collection of captured documents, of the actual workings of the communist system in Smolensk in the 1930s.

R. C. Tucker and S. F. Cohen, eds. *The Great Purge Trial* (*Grosset's Universal Library, rev. 1965). Transcript of the 1938 purge trial with excellent notes.

H. Schwartz, *Russia's Soviet Economy,* 2nd ed. (Prentice-Hall, 1954). Good introduction to the subject.

N. Timasheff, *The Great Retreat* (Dutton, 1946). An account of the "Russian Thermidor."

R. Pipes, *The Formation of the Soviet Union,* 2nd ed. (Harvard Univ. Press, 1964). Excellent monograph on the question of national minorities in Russia, 1917–1923.

Adam B. Ulam, *Expansion and Coexistence: The History of Soviet Foreign Policy, 1917–1967* (Praeger, 1968). The first six chapters of this excellent analytical work deal with the period to 1941.

R. H. Crossman, ed., *The God That Failed* (Harper, 1959). Brief statements by Arthur Koestler, Stephen Spender, Ignazio Silone, and other intellectuals recording their disenchantment with communism.

Svetlana Alliluyeva, *Twenty Letters to a Friend,* trans. P. J. McMillan (Harper, 1967). Memoirs of Stalin's own daughter, perhaps the most prominent of the many Soviet citizens who have escaped to the West.

Historical Fiction

A. Koestler, *Darkness at Noon* (Modern Library, 1956; *New American Library). A famous novel, presenting in fictional form a keen analysis of the attitudes of the Old Bolsheviks whom Stalin purged.

V. Serge, *The Case of Comrade Tulayev* (Doubleday, 1950). Another excellent novel of the purges.

G. Blunden, *The Room on the Route* (Lippincott, 1947). Perhaps the most vivid fictional portrayal of the impact of terror on the ordinary person.

A. Tolstoy, *Road to Calvary* (Knopf, 1946). Translation of a Stalin Prize Novel about the revolution and civil war.

The Rise of Facism
1918-1939

Introduction

In this chapter we shall deal with the rise of fascism in Europe in the period between the two great wars. By 1939 authoritarian governments of the right had taken firm control of Italy, Germany, Spain, and all the countries of eastern and southeastern Europe except Russia. The process by which these regimes came to power differed widely from country to country, as did some of the external features of the regimes. At first glance, fascism is more complex and more difficult to understand than communism, whose development as a doctrine can be traced from Marx through Lenin before its followers were able to put it, or something like it, into practice in Russia. Unlike communism, fascism has no such line of theoretical development. Its proponents often seem to have acted first and worried about doctrine later, devising theories to meet the needs of the moment.

Fascism has been called the revolution of the classes of order. Political parties on the Continent have often represented the interests of the various social classes. When those interests have seemed to be about evenly balanced in a parliamentary state, a long and indecisive political tug-of-war has often ensued. For example, let us assume that a revolution from the left threatens or can be made to seem to threaten. Then the middle classes, so the theory runs, seize power and take refuge in their own form of extremism—fascism, that is, nationalism tricked out with a few radical phrases to win mass support, and draped in mystical garments. This formula can be applied to Mussolini's rise to power in Italy in 1922, to Hitler's rise to power in Germany in 1933, to Franco's rise to power in Spain in 1936–1939, and to many of the eastern European dictators. The formula, like most such efforts, suffers from over-simplification. Fascism was far more than the extremism of the middle classes. Its theorists often agreed with the Marxists that existing institutions were

the mere instruments of a ruling class, but substituted for a Marxist working-class revolution a take-over by the dictatorial rule of "the nation as a whole." When democratic institutions seem not to be working, when efforts at socialism fail, disillusionment sets in, and disillusioned activists embrace some form of radical right-wing activity: fascism. Only a study of the different circumstances in each of the countries can give body and meaning to the formula.

Economic depressions played a role in the rise of almost every dictator—in Italy the postwar depression, and elsewhere the worldwide depression of 1929 and later. We notice, moreover, a certain similarity in the externals of fascism everywhere—colored shirts, private armies, mass hypnotism, special salutes, special war cries and ceremonies, mystical glorification of the nation, and a vast program of conquest. The dictator justified his program by references to "have" and "have-not" nations; his own nation was always a "have-not," always oppressed.

Fascism was just as violent in its hatred of democracy, liberalism, and parliamentary institutions as in its professed dislike of communism. Indeed fascism shared communism's abhorrence of constitutional procedure, its disregard of the individual human being, and its insistence that the state is supreme. Fascism persecuted its enemies, both real and fancied, with the same ruthlessness we have observed in Stalin's Russia. Censorship, political police, concentration camps, the rule of the bludgeon, the end of legal protection—all these practices were common to both fascism and communism.

When Mussolini ruled in Rome, public buildings everywhere carried the admonition to loyal Italians *"Credere, combattere, obbedire"* ("Believe, fight, obey"). Presumably this was intended to be inspiring. All it really means is: Believe (what Mussolini tells you), fight (for Mussolini and his backers), obey (Mussolini).

When put this way, the formula is seen to subvert all religion and all human decency. Yet under the stress of the unbearable pressures on individuals generated by the tension of the years between the wars, many an idealist was taken in, surrendering his right to think and to make his own decisions.

II Italy and Fascism
The Setting

Although Italy was a member of the victorious Allied coalition, she finished the First World War with a sense of defeat. Six hundred and fifty thousand Italians had been killed and a million wounded. Industry slumped immediately after the war and within a few months 10 percent of the industrial workers were unemployed. Prices rose rapidly and wages failed to keep up. The promised pensions for wounded veterans and families of the killed were long delayed. Strikes and disorders became frequent. Many of the young men released from the armies with no trade but war and no job to go to drifted restlessly and discontentedly, fit prey for leaders with glittering promises.

Perhaps most important, the Italian government itself, hoping to influence the peace negotiations, began to spread propaganda among the Italian people to the effect that their wartime allies were robbing them of, across the Adriatic, Dalmatia, populated by Slavs, and

promised to Italy by the secret Treaty of London (1915) in exchange for Italy's entrance into the war. This arrangement the United States had never agreed to and now would not accept. Although the Allied leaders at the Paris Peace Conference remained unaffected by the storms of protest arising from Italy, the Italian people did come to believe that they had shed their blood in vain. Popular sentiment in Italy, especially in the army, swung toward extremists.

Some Italians hysterically supported Gabriele d'Annunzio, a short, bald nationalist poet and romantic novelist, who formed a band of volunteers. They seized the city of Fiume, the Adriatic seaport over which Croatians and Hungarians had long disagreed. Referring to "the stench of peace" and denouncing Woodrow Wilson, d'Annunzio declared that the time for heroic individual action was at hand. Fiume had actually not been awarded to Italy even by the Treaty of London, but d'Annunzio felt that Italy must have it, and that was enough. He ran his own government in Fiume until the end of 1920.

D'Annunzio patterned his regime there upon that of an imaginary medieval commune in a poem by Italy's Romantic poet Carducci (1835–1907). Modeling himself consciously upon the governor of the commune in the poem, d'Annunzio would appear on the balcony of the city hall, address an inspirational harangue to the crowd, and ask for its unanimous consent for whatever he wished to do. This his listeners would grant,

Hitler and Mussolini in Venice, 1933.

raising their right hands high, as the imaginary citizens of Carducci's commune had done. Some of d'Annunzio's followers wore black shirts. When d'Annunzio asked them to whom Fiume belonged they would shout *"a noi"*—"to us"—and when he asked them to whom Italy belonged, they would give the same answer. Indeed, he planned to lead his followers from Fiume to Rome and thence out into the world to conquer it, presumably with daggers, which he preferred to mechanized weapons. He drafted the Statutes of Fiume, a constitution in which he made a conscious attempt to organize society along the lines he imagined to have existed in the guilds and artisans' corporations of the Middle Ages.

In November 1920, the Italian government signed the Treaty of Rapallo with Yugoslavia, by which Fiume was to become a free city. Italian forces drove d'Annunzio out, and into retirement in a villa on the Italian lakes. But the techniques of force, the haranguing of the mob from the balcony, the straight-arm salute, the black shirts, the rhythmic cries, the plans for conquest, and the "corporative" scheme of the Statutes of Fiume served as precedent and inspiration for Benito Mussolini, founder of Italian fascism.

In the first four years after the end of the war, Mussolini created and brought to power a new political force in Italy. In October 1922 he was summoned to office by King Victor Emmanuel III (1900–1947); from then on he gradually created a totalitarian state of which he was the sole, undisputed ruler. Suppressing all opposition at home and threatening the peace abroad, the fascist state in Italy served in some degree as model for the Nazis in Germany, for the Falangists in Spain, and for totalitarian regimes in virtually all the European successor states of the Hapsburg and Ottoman empires. Eventually Mussolini was forced, largely by his own propaganda, into an alliance with Hitler. In 1940, this alliance took Italy into World War II, and in 1945 it brought Mussolini himself to an ignominious death, upside down on a communist partisan gallows, with his mistress beside him.

Mussolini's Early Career

Mussolini was born in 1883, in the Romagna, a province of central Italy famous for its political extremists and for the violence with which they express themselves. His father was an ardent socialist who had begun his career as an anarchist under the influence of Bakunin. Trained as an elementary-school teacher, Mussolini was already a passionate socialist by the time he was eighteen. He spent some time as an agitator among Italian emigrant laborers in Switzerland (1902–1904) and in Austria (1909), but was expelled by the police. Back in Italy, he was imprisoned for opposing the war against Turkey over Tripoli (1911). In 1912, he became editor of the most important Italian socialist newspaper, *Avanti* (*Forward*).

When World War I began, Mussolini at first vigorously opposed Italy's entry. But then, during 1914, he changed his mind. First he favored "relative neutrality," meaning that socialists should leave themselves free to support Italian entry if such a course seemed likely to prove favorable to them. When the Italian Socialist party refused to follow this idea, he resigned as editor of *Avanti*. Soon afterward (November 1914), he founded his own newspaper, *Il Popolo d'Italia* (*The People of Italy*), in Milan, and began to advocate an immediate Italian declaration of war on the side of the Allies. For this the Socialist party expelled him.

But these bare bones of a biography reveal only the externals. As a socialist, Mussolini before 1914 was a passionate left-winger. He was an apostle of violent social revolution and a bitter opponent of milder evolutionary and reformist doctrine. He urged that a small, well-knit armed minority should seize power and establish a dictatorship. He loathed militarism, was himself a draft-dodger, and urged soldiers to desert the army. He hated monarchy and savagely attacked in his writings all the crowned heads of Europe, especially the Italian House of Savoy. He was a vigorous atheist, urged workers to stay away from church, and scorned the teachings of Christ. As an international revolutionary, he opposed nationalism, and even referred to the Italian flag as "a rag to be planted on a dunghill."

Yet he was to repudiate almost all these positions, and as fascist chieftain to substitute almost the exact opposites. As a fascist, he attacked Bolshevism and all left-wing movements; he made his peace with the monarchy and the Church; he became a militant nationalist, a mystic patriot, and a rabid militarist. The repudiation of the views he had held so long and advocated so skillfully is not nearly so astonishing as it seems at first. Mussolini did not much care for programs; what he wanted was to rule.

A complete opportunist, he could shift his line on any question at a moment's notice if it seemed advantageous. For example, after the war, though he was now a fascist, he at first supported a radical program of social change, indistinguishable from the program he would have advocated had he still been a socialist. He favored the action of the Italian workers in the fall of 1920 when they occupied the factories in a kind of sit-down strike. Yet, within a year, he was using the fears which this strike had aroused in the middle classes to argue that he was the only possible bulwark against "Bolshevism." About certain matters, however, he was consistent. He always hated parliaments and loved violence.

Mussolini's switch from isolationism to interventionism in the war in 1914 was the first of his important shifts. After his expulsion from the Socialist party, he agitated furiously for war, speaking to groups of similarly minded young men called *fasci* (the image is of a bundle of rods, a symbol of office in the Roman Republic of antiquity). Soon after Italy did enter the war in 1915, Mussolini was conscripted and sent to the front. He was wounded in 1917 by an Italian mortar shell that exploded during practice. When he got out of the hospital, he continued to edit his newspaper, spewing forth a mixture of extreme revolutionary and extreme nationalist propaganda.

Mussolini's Rise to Power

In March 1919 Mussolini founded the first *fasci di combattimento* ("groups for combat"). There was no sign as yet to indicate that by October 1922 the leader of this small movement would become the most powerful man in Italy. In 1919, he called for every kind of revolutionary violence—seizure of the land, attacks on the factories, shooting of storekeepers who charged high prices, expropriation of mines and transports, and war by the vanquished "proletarian" nations against the victorious capitalists who had kept Italy from annexing Dalmatia. He now maintained that socialism was too conservative; his movement, far from setting itself against a revolution, was in the vanguard of those who were crying for one.

Yet in Italy a revolution along Bolshevik patterns was most unlikely, if not impossible. The peasants were not very revolutionary, for they already held much of the land except in the extreme south. And the industrial workers, though often discontented, knew that a revolution could be starved out because the country needed to import most of its raw materials. The Socialist party was overwhelmingly in the hands of moderates, and in 1919 Catholics founded the Popular party (*Partito Popularе Italiano*), designed to compete with the socialists for the votes of the lower classes, who now had universal suffrage.

In the postwar disorders, the peasants seized without consent of the landowners less than a tenth of a percent of the arable land in Italy. The leaders of the Socialist party and the General Confederation of Labor voted down the proposals of anarchist and communist extremists to turn the workers' occupation of the factories into a revolution. The government waited for the workers to grow tired. This they did in less than a month (September 1920); then they left the occupied factories and went home.

Yet, although the danger of revolution was small, the fear of revolution was great. During 1920 and 1921, the industrialists and landowners, squeezed by taxation and inflation, became bitter. Shopkeepers and tradesmen wanted street disorders to end, food prices to be regulated, and the cooperative food stores of the Socialist and Catholic parties to be put out of business as competitors. Professional men and others with fixed incomes suffered as prices and wages went up and salaries lagged behind. The police grew tired of suppressing local disorders and of being repaid with insults. Ex-servicemen, insulted by anarchists and communists for their war records, naturally grew more patriotic.

All these groups identified the forces they did not like as Bolshevik and accepted as an article of faith the myth of an impending Bolshevik revolution. After a series of fascist-socialist street fights and riots, these "anti-Bolsheviks" began to look to Mussolini's fascist bands as the defenders of their interests. D'Annunzio's defeat left Mussolini as his natural heir. The left opposition to Mussolini was weakened when the communists split off from the Socialist party in 1921. The fascisti grew enormously, from 30,000 in May 1920 to 100,000 in February 1921 to more than 300,000 at the time of the "March on Rome" in October 1922. No longer were they merely squads of discontented and idle youths with vaguely revolutionary and nationalist ideas. Now, says one fascist of the period, "the sons and hangers-on of the bigwigs" poured into the organization.

> They had come into the Fascio for their own ends. . . . If they met men in working clothes, they fell on them and began beating them. Their mentality was on a par with that of the Communists, who had beaten and murdered anybody who was decently dressed. One saw . . . the well-known surly and rapacious faces of war profiteers . . . and we were obliged to accept their money because we needed it to stifle an evil worse than they.*

The liberal parliamentary leaders of Italy felt that the fascist bands were teaching the left a useful lesson. They encouraged the commanding officers of the army to issue rifles and army trucks and gasoline to the fascists and even assigned army officers to command their operations. The police were encouraged to look the other way during disorders started by the fascists, and local judges were urged to help by releasing arrested fascists. Mussolini's newspaper was circulated free to the soldiers in the army as a "patriotic" sheet.

A campaign of terror now began against the socialists and Christian Democrats, as the fascist squadrons cruised around Italy in trucks, burning down labor-union offices, newspaper offices, and local Socialist party headquarters, and beating up and sometimes murdering labor leaders or local antifascist politicians. The fascisti forced duly elected officials to resign. The torch, the cudgel, and the famous castor-oil treatment were all characteristic weapons. It is estimated that 2,000 people, antifascist and fascist, policemen and innocent bystanders, died by violence between October 1920 and October 1922.

The "March" on Rome

In the elections of May 1921 Mussolini and thirty-four other fascists were elected to Parliament, along with ten Nationalists, their political allies. The momentum of the fascist movement was now too great to be slowed down. Mussolini abandoned his anti-monarchical views, and fascism became a political party (November 1921) as a necessary step in the drive for power. Too late, the government became alarmed and tried to take measures against the fascists, but the squads were too

---

*Umberto Banchelli, *Memorie di un Fascista*, quoted by G. Salvemini in *The Fascist Dictatorship* (New York, 1927), pp. 67–68.

Mussolini (left center) and some of his followers at the time of the "March on Rome."

strong, the police too accustomed to collaborating with them, and the politicians themselves as yet unaware that a tightly directed armed mob could really take over the state. Inside the royal family, the king's cousin, the duke of Aosta, had become a fascist sympathizer, as had many army generals, the entire Nationalist party, and the leading industrialists.

In the fall of 1922, it was clear that the army would not resist a fascist coup in Rome itself. When a decree of martial law was presented to the king, he refused to sign it, probably influenced by his knowledge that the army would not fight the fascists and that the duke of Aosta would gladly take his crown. The refusal of the king to declare martial law greatly heartened the fascists. Now, as the fascists "marched" on Rome, mostly by storming railroad trains and stealing free rides, the king (October 29, 1922) telegraphed Mussolini in Milan to come to Rome and form a cabinet. Mussolini arrived by sleeping-car the next morning.

Fascism, which had begun as a patriotic anti-Bolshevik movement, and had then turned into an antilabor movement in the service of the industrialists and landowners, had finally come to power as a conspiracy against parliamentary government in the service of a military clique. Just before taking office, Mussolini announced:

Our program is simple: we wish to govern Italy. They ask us for programs, but there are already too many. It is not programs that are wanting for the salvation of Italy but men and will-power.*

The Fascist Dictatorship

Mussolini now moved gradually to turn his premiership into a dictatorship. A month after coming to office, he obtained dictatorial powers that were to last only until the end of 1923. Although the constitution theoretically remained in force, Mussolini proceeded to take over the administration. He created a fascist militia almost 200,000 strong, which owed complete allegiance to him. He enlarged the regular army and required its members to take an oath of personal loyalty to him. Before his dictatorial powers expired, he secured from Parliament by pressure a new electoral law. This law provided that the political party that received the largest number of votes in a general election, if that number amounted to at least one-quarter of the vote, should automatically receive two-thirds of the seats in Parliament. The rest of the seats would be divided proportionately. This law made certain the fascists' domination of future parliaments. Indeed, in the election of April 1924, the fascists actually polled 65 percent of the vote cast; but this figure reflects a widespread use of intimidation and terrorism at the polls. The first all-fascist cabinet was now appointed. Meanwhile, local administration was

*Quoted by H. Finer, *Mussolini's Italy* (New York, 1935), p. 152.

made secure by the appointment of fascist prefects and subprefects in the provinces; these officials pursued the enemies of fascism with the same weapons of murder and mayhem that had been used before Mussolini's March on Rome.

Early in 1924, the leader of the opposition to Mussolini, the socialist Giacomo Matteotti, published a book called *The Fascists Exposed,* in which he detailed many of the outrages the fascists had committed on their way to power. It seemed probable that further revelations were in store, exposing some of Mussolini's cabinet members as corrupt. On June 10, 1924, Matteotti was "taken for a ride" in true gangster style and murdered. The crime was traced to members of Mussolini's immediate circle. This scandal rocked Italy, and for a moment it even seemed possible that Mussolini would fall. But he dismissed from office those who were involved and pledged himself to restore law and order. Actually, he delayed trying the guilty men until March 1926 and even then they all got off lightly.

What really helped Mussolini over the crisis, ironically enough, was the departure of most of the opposition deputies from Parliament. They declared that they would not return until the Matteotti murder had been solved and the government had been shown to be innocent. Far from making things harder for Mussolini, as they had intended, their departure actually made things easier. Mussolini denied his own guilt, imposed a rigid press censorship, and forbade the opposition to meet. Most of the deputies never did return to Parliament, and in 1926 their seats were declared forfeit.

Next, a series of laws called the "most fascist laws" (*legge fascistissime*) tightened control over the press, abolished secret societies like the Freemasons, whom Mussolini had loathed ever since his socialist youth, and replaced all elected local officials by men appointed from Rome. Opponents of the regime were arrested and exiled to desolate islands off the Italian coast. Early in 1926, Mussolini was empowered to govern by decree. Three attempts on his life led to a new law providing the death penalty for action against the king, the queen, or Mussolini. All opposition political parties were abolished in the same year, and the Fascist party was left as the only legal political party in Italy.

More and more the Italian state and the Fascist party were brought into coordination. Mussolini was both the *duce* (leader) of the facists and the *capo di governo,* the chief of state. At one moment he also held eight cabinet posts simultaneously. The members of the Fascist Grand Council, a "politbureau" numbering roughly twenty of the highest party functionaries, all appointed by Mussolini, held all the important posts in the administration not held by Mussolini himself. In 1928, the Grand Council was given important constitutional duties: preparing the lists of candidates for election to the Chamber, advising Mussolini, and proposing changes in the constitution or the succession to the throne. The Grand Council thus became a kind of third house, above the other two houses of Parliament, the Senate and the Chamber.

The Corporative State

Mussolini believed that the interests of labor and capital could and must be made to harmonize with the overriding interests of the state. Instead of a political system as we understand it, he accepted the idea that representation should be based on economic interests organized in "syndicates." Such an idea was not new: the French syndicalist Georges Sorel had already argued in this vein. But Sorel believed in class warfare, and in government by syndicates of workers only. Mussolini, following the Italian nationalist syndicalist Rossoni, believed in capitalism, class collaboration, and producers' syndicates as well as workers' syndicates.

In 1925, fascist labor unions were recognized by employers as having the sole right to negotiate labor contracts. Then, in April 1926, the state officially recognized producers' and workers' syndicates in each of six areas—industry, agriculture, commerce, sea and air transport, land and inland waterway transport, and banking—plus a syndicate of intellectuals, making thirteen syndicates in all. Each syndicate could bargain and reach contracts and could assess dues upon everyone engaged in its own economic field, irrespective of membership in the syndicate. Strikes and lockouts were both forbidden. When labor conditions did not improve, a "charter of labor," promising insurance and other benefits, was issued in 1927. In 1926, the syndicates were put under the control of a special Ministry of Corporations; Mussolini was the minister.

In 1928, the system of parliamentary representation was changed in accordance with fascist syndicalism. A new electoral law provided for a new Chamber of Deputies (400 instead of 560 members). The national councils of the thirteen syndicates could nominate a total of 800 candidates. Each syndicate had a quota, half to be selected by the employers and half by the employees. Cultural and charitable foundations could nominate 200 more candidates. When the total list of 1,000 was completed, the Fascist Grand Council could either select 400 of them, or strike out names and add names of its own, or even substitute an entirely new list. The voters would then vote in answer to the question: "Do you approve of the list of deputies selected by the Fascist Grand Council?" They could vote yes or no on the entire list, but they could not choose from among the candidates. If a majority voted yes, the list was elected; if not, the procedure was to be repeated. Despite the highly touted role of the syndicate, all the power obviously lay with the Fascist Grand Council. Universal suffrage was abolished even for this very limited form of election. Payment of a minimum tax or dues to a syndicate was required of each voter; women could not vote. In 1929, the elections under this system produced a yes vote of 8,519,559 and a no vote of 137,761.

Between 1930 and 1938, several constitutional steps were taken which seemed to move the syndicates into the center of the stage. Representatives from the syndicates and the government were now formed into a Council of Corporations, which was to act as a coordinating committee, settle disputes between syndicates, assist production, and establish the fascist corporations themselves, which had not yet been created. The Council was divided into seven sections corresponding to the seven syndicate areas, and in 1931 each of these sections of the Council was simply declared to be a corporation. In 1933, it was announced that the whole corporate system would be revised, and in 1934 the new elections (which of course returned the Fascist Grand Council's list of candidates) produced a "suicide" Chamber of Deputies, which was expected eventually to put an end to its own existence. Its replacement was to be a new "revolutionary assembly," which Mussolini called into existence in the fall of 1934. The assembly, also called the Central Committee of Corporations, contained 824 members, representing twenty-two newly created corporations. The Fascist party, as well as employers and employees, was represented on each corporation.

Finally, in 1938 the "suicide chamber" replaced itself with the Central Committee of Corporations, now called the Chamber of Fasces and Corporations. Nothing remained of the old parliamentary constitution that had been set up by Cavour except the Senate, nominally appointed by the king but actually subservient to Mussolini, who on one occasion had the king appoint forty fascist senators all at once. This new structure, the corporative state, was influenced by d'Annunzio's strange medieval ideas, and by Mussolini's own wish to produce new political and economic forms. But in spite of much oratory by fascist sympathizers about the corporative state and its virtues, it does not appear that the new bodies ever had very much to do with running the economic or political life of Italy, which remained firmly under the direction of the fascist bureaucracy.

Other Fascist Domestic Policies

During the thirties, the fascist version of the planned economy made its appearance in Italy. The government issued or withheld permits for factory construction. In agriculture, a concerted effort was launched to make Italy more nearly self-sufficient. This effort was dramatized with the "Battle of Wheat," in which the Italians were treated to contests, prizes, and personal appearances by Mussolini. In 1932, official figures reported that wheat production had risen to a point where it could supply 92 percent of the nation's normal needs, and the drive was enlarged to include other cereal products. The government subsidized steamship and air lines, encouraged the tourist trade, and protected Ital-

ian industries by means of high tariffs on foreign products. Marshes were drained and land was reclaimed; the incidence of malaria was reduced. Enormous sums were spent on public works, and great strides were made in the development of hydroelectric power. The trains, at least so thousands of tourists reported, ran on time; many argued that "there must be something in this man Mussolini." Yet Italy's weakness in essential raw materials proved to be insuperable.

The state reached into the life of the individual at almost every point. Though Italy was overpopulated, and had for decades relieved the situation only by mass emigration, Mussolini made emigration a crime. He encouraged people to marry and have the largest possible families. He reduced their taxes, extended special loans, taxed bachelors, and extended legal equality to illegitimate children. He hoped in this way to swell the ranks of his armies and to strengthen his claim that Italy must expand abroad. Children, the future party members, were enrolled in a series of youth movements, beginning at the age of six. The textbooks in the schools, the books in the libraries, the professors in the universities, the plays on the stage, and the movies on the screen were all made vehicles of fascist propaganda. The secret police, OVRA (from the initials of the Italian words for "Vigilance Organization against Anti-Fascist Crimes"), endeavored to discover and suppress all opposition movements.

In 1929, Mussolini settled the Roman question— that of the annexation of the Papal States without the pope's consent—by entering into the Lateran Treaty with the papacy. This treaty recognized the independent state of Vatican City and thus restored the temporal power of the pope, though on a greatly reduced scale. Mussolini also recognized Catholicism as the state religion and promised to halt antipapal propaganda. He gave up the right to tax contributions to the Church or the salaries of the clergy and paid $105,000,000 to compensate the papacy for the Italian occupation of papal territories since 1870. A further concordat legalized religious marriages and extended religious instruction in the schools. The Church agreed not to engage in politics in its newspapers and periodicals.

Yet, despite the fact that many church officials viewed the fascist movement sympathetically, difficulties arose after these agreements had been concluded. In an encyclical, Pope Pius XI (1922–1939) indicated his disapproval of Mussolini's "relentless" economic policies and of the corporations as "serving special political aims rather than contributing to the initiation of a better social order." Mussolini now charged that the Church's "Catholic Action" clubs were engaged in politics and dissolved them. The pope denied the charges and denounced the Fascist party's practice of monopolizing the time and education of the young. In 1931, however, a further agreement was reached, and the clubs were reopened.

Fascist Foreign Policy and Its Consequences

Since Mussolini's foreign policies form an integral part of the international relations leading up to World War II, we shall discuss them more fully in a later chapter. Here we may simply point out that his extreme nationalism, his love of panoply and parades, and his militarism were the logical extensions of his domestic ideas and accomplishments. Mussolini's wish to re-create the glories of ancient Rome impelled him to undertake a policy of adventure in the Mediterranean, which he called *Mare Nostrum* (Latin for "our sea") as a sign that he was the heir to the Caesars. This policy began in 1923, when five Italians working for the League of Nations were assassinated as they marked out the new frontier between Albania and Greece. Mussolini bombarded and occupied the Greek island of Corfu and refused to recognize the League's right to intervene. Only British pressure led to a settlement of the matter.

Later, Mussolini's policy of adventure led him to military aggression in Ethiopia, in Spain, and in Albania (which he dominated during the 1920's and occupied in April 1939). It drove him into an alliance with his fellow fascist, Hitler, and led him to voice loud claims against the French for Corsica, Tunisia, Nice, and Savoy. And it alienated Italy from her natural allies, France and Britain. Thus, Mussolini's grandiose fascist ideology first spurred Italy to win self-sufficiency, to rebuild her seaports, and to create a merchant fleet and navy. But the same ideology ultimately separated her from the only powers who might have saved her from the disaster toward which Mussolini was driving.

The German alliance was also responsible for a striking new departure in fascist domestic policy. This was the official adoption of anti-Semitism, which took place in 1938. With only 70,000 Jews, most of whom had long been resident, Italy had no "Jewish problem." Italian Jews were entirely Italian in their language and sentiments, and could be distinguished from other Italians only by their religion. Many of them were prominent in the fascist movement, and many were anti-fascist. There was no widespread sympathy in Italy for the government's adoption of Hitler's racial policies. Yet Hitler's dominating influence led Mussolini to expel Jews from the Fascist party and to forbid them to teach or attend school, to intermarry with non-Jews, and to obtain new licenses to conduct businesses.

In summing up Mussolini's career, we may turn to a quotation from an article that he himself wrote in 1920 to denounce Lenin. In reading it, substitute Italy for Russia and Mussolini for Lenin, and you will have a clear idea of fascism:

> Russia is a state . . . composed of men who exercise power, imposing an iron discipline upon individuals and groups and practicing "reaction" whenever necessary. . . . In the Russia of Lenin there is only one authority: his authority. There is only one liberty: his liberty. There is only one opinion: his opinion. There is only one law: his law. One might either submit or perish. . . . Russia . . . swallows

up and crushes the individual and governs his entire life. . . . Whoever says state necessarily says the army, the police, the judiciary, and the bureaucracy. The Russian state is the state *par excellence*. . . . It has *statized* economic life . . . and formed a huge army of bureaucrats. At the base of the pyramid, . . . there is the proletariat which, as in the old bourgeois regimes, obeys, works, and eats little or allows itself to be massacred. . . .*

III Germany and the Weimar Republic, 1918–1933

Whereas Mussolini took over in Italy less than four years after World War I ended, the Germans experimented with democracy for fifteen years before succumbing to Adolf Hitler. Two days before the armistice of November 11, 1918, the German Social Democrats proclaimed a republic. On July 31, 1919, this republic adopted a constitution drawn up by a national assembly at Weimar; it is therefore known as the Weimar Republic. The Weimar Constitution was never formally abandoned, but after Hitler became chancellor on January 30, 1933, Germany was in fact a dictatorship.

The history of the Weimar Republic divides itself naturally into three periods: a period of political threats from left and right and of mounting economic chaos, from 1918 to the end of 1923; a period of political stability, fulfillment of the Versailles Treaty requirements, and seeming economic prosperity, from 1924 to late 1929; and a period of economic depression and mounting right-wing power, from late 1929 to January 1933.

The Impact of Defeat

For the overwhelming majority of the German people, defeat in 1918 came as a great shock. The military authorities who ran the German Empire during the last years of the war had failed to report to the public German reverses on the battlefield. No fighting had ever taken place on German soil, and the Germans had got used to thinking of their armies as in firm possession of the foreign territories they had overrun. Now these armies came home. It is often argued that the Allies committed a grave blunder by their failure to march to Berlin and demonstrate to the German people that they had actually been defeated. Schooled in reverence for their military forces, the Germans could not grasp the fact that their armies had lost the war. Moreover, the Allies, under the leadership of Wilson, simply refused to deal with the Supreme Command of the German armies. Field Marshal von Hindenburg, as supreme commander, was never required to hand over his sword to Marshal Foch, or to sign the armistice. Rather, it was the civilian politicians who had to bear

*Mussolini on Lenin in 1920, quoted by G. Megaro, *Mussolini in the Making* (Boston, 1938), pp. 325–326.

the odium. In this way, the Allies unintentionally did the German military caste a great favor.

Before the ink was dry on the armistice agreement, the generals, led by Hindenburg himself, were explaining that the German armies had never really been defeated. This was exactly what the public wanted to believe, and the harsh facts—that Ludendorff and Hindenburg had insisted on surrender because the armies could no longer fight—were never effectively publicized. So the legend that Germany had somehow been "stabbed in the back" by civilians, by liberals, socialists, communists, and Jews, took deep root, and became almost an article of faith among many Germans. This legend was widely disseminated by politicians, especially by those who had a stake in the old Prussian system—the monarchists, agrarians, industrialists, and militarists. All through the period of the Weimar Republic, these groups remained hostile toward it; their hostility ranged from political opposition to conspiracies to overthrow the government.

The Allies added another error by including the celebrated "war-guilt" clause in the Treaty of Versailles. The German signatories were obliged to acknowledge what none of them believed and what subsequent historians would disprove: that Germany alone had been responsible for the outbreak of the war. The war-guilt clause made it harder for the German public to acknowledge defeat and the evils of the past system, to sweep away the militarists, and to bend to the task of creating a virile republic. Instead, it led many Germans to dissipate their energies in denying war guilt, in hating the enemies who had saddled them with the charge, in bewailing the sell-out of their generals, and in waiting for a chance to show by force that they had been right all the time.

Postwar Political Alignments and Activities

Threats to stability from the left further strengthened the antirepublican forces of the right. Responsibility for launching the republic and for preventing disorder fell upon the "majority socialists," made up of Social Democrats and right-wing Independent Socialists, and led by a Social Democrat, Ebert. The Social Democrats were a moderate group. They made no attack on agrarian property, and they allowed the Junkers to maintain intact their estates and the social and political position that went with them. True to their reformist tradition, the Social Democrats concluded with the industrialists collective bargaining agreements that guaranteed the eight-hour day, rather than trying to launch a serious movement for nationalizing German industry.

But to the left of the Social Democrats, the left wing of the Independent Socialists and the communist "Spartacists" (named for Spartacus, the leader of a slave revolt in ancient Rome) agitated for a proletarian revolution on the Russian pattern. Unable to operate effectively through soviets, the left tried to stage a revolution in the winter of 1918–1919, but Ebert called in the army to stop it. The generals used not only regular units but also newly formed volunteer units, or "Free Corps," made up mostly of professional soldiers, who were embittered by Germany's recent military defeat and were violently opposed to democracy.

Now the right wing of the Independent Socialists withdrew from the government and sole responsibility thenceforth rested with the Social Democrats, who put their man, Noske, into the war ministry. As the civil strife continued, the communists attempted a coup, which Ebert, Noske, and the troops put down. Cavalry officers murdered the two chief leaders of the communists after peace had been restored at the cost of more than a thousand casualties. Meanwhile, in Catholic Bavaria, disorders led to the brief emergence of a Soviet republic, which was liquidated in May, leaving Bavaria the home of a permanent red-scare. The Bavarian local authorities, throughout the entire life of the Weimar Republic, encouraged the intrigues of monarchists, militarists, and nationalists. It was in Bavaria that Free Corps assassinations were planned, and it was there that Hitler got his start.

In these ways the forces of the German right, ostensibly crushed by the war, were given a powerful new lease on life. Meantime, Germany still had an army, the Reichswehr, limited in size to 100,000 men, consisting chiefly of officer cadres, magnificently trained and able to take over the command of far larger numbers if and when troops became available.

The political constellation of the new Germany did not consist solely of Social Democrats and extremists of right and left. The old parties of imperial Germany reappeared, often with new labels. The right wing of the old Liberals now emerged as the People's party, including the more moderate industrialists, with a platform of private property and opposition to socialism. Its leader was Gustav Stresemann. Former progressives and left-wing Liberals now formed the new Democratic party, a genuine middle-class republican and democratic group, including many of Germany's most distinguished intellectuals. The Catholic Center party reemerged with its name and program unchanged. It accepted the republic, rejected socialism, and—under pressure from its left wing of trade-union members—favored social legislation, but—under pressure from its right wing of aristocrats and industrialists—opposed far-reaching reform. The Social Democrats, the Democrats, the Center, and the People's party represented those groups, which, though not all enthusiastic, were willing to try to make the new state work. On the right, the former Conservatives reemerged as the National People's party or Nationalists, dominated by the Junkers as before. The Nationalists had the support of some great industrialists, of most of the bureaucrats, and of a substantial section of the lower middle class, which hoped to return to the good old days of the monarchy. The Nationalists did not accept the republic.

The Weimar Constitution, 1919

When the Germans voted for a national constituent assembly in January 1919, the parties supporting the republic won more than 75 percent of the seats, with the Social Democrats alone obtaining nearly 40 percent. The assembly met in Weimar, elected Ebert president of Germany, and formed a government that reluctantly signed the Treaty of Versailles after a delay of some months. The assembly then adopted the new constitution. The new Germany was still a federative state, but the central government had great authority to legislate for the entire country. The president might use armed force to coerce any of the states that failed to obey the constitution or national laws. The cabinet was responsible to the lower house, or Reichstag, which was to be chosen by universal suffrage of all citizens (including women) over twenty.

The president, who was to be elected every seven years by the entire people, was given considerable authority. He was empowered to make treaties, appoint and remove the cabinet, command the armed forces and appoint or remove all officers, dissolve the Reichstag, and call new elections. Furthermore, he could take any measure he deemed necessary to restore order when it was threatened and might temporarily suspend the civil liberties that the constitution granted. Yet the Reichstag could order such measures repealed. Inside the cabinet, the chancellor was a real prime minister, with responsibility for planning policy. The constitution also provided for popular initiative. One-tenth of the electorate could bring in a bill or propose an amendment to the constitution. On the economic side, the constitution provided that the government might socialize suitable enterprises, but it guaranteed both private property and the right of inheritance.

Several other contradictions reflected the conflict of interest between the Social Democrats and the middle-class parties. But the powers of the president and the introduction of proportional representation were perhaps the two chief weaknesses. The powers of the president made dictatorship a real possibility. Proportional representation required that votes be cast for entire party lists of candidates, and thus prevented independent voters from "splitting the ticket," and independent politicians from obtaining office. This system encouraged small splinter parties to multiply.

Right and Left Extremism, 1920–1922

In 1920, pressure from the right loomed as the most serious threat to the Republic. In March 1920 a coup (in German, *putsch*) drove the government from Berlin for several days. The commander of the Berlin military district, supported by Ludendorff and the Free Corps leaders, hoped to bring to power an East Prussian reactionary official named Kapp. Ebert managed to defeat this "Kapp putsch" by calling a general strike that paralyzed Germany. Because the prewar monarchical judicial system still existed, the men arrested and tried for the Kapp putsch all got off with extremely light sentences, whereas left-wingers brought before the courts were very harshly punished.

As an immediate outgrowth of the strike called by the government, a communist revolt took place in the Ruhr. In pursuit of the communists, German troops entered the area, which had been demilitarized by the Versailles Treaty; this action in turn led to French military intervention and a brief occupation of the Ruhr and Frankfurt (April–May 1920). In the elections of June 1920, the electorate began to support the extremists of the right and left. The Democrats and Social Democrats lost strength.

In April 1921, when the Allies presented the bill for reparations, which totaled 132 billion gold marks, the politicians of the right favored simple rejection of the terms, while the Weimar parties realistically decided that the threat of invasion made this course impossible. Again, the moderates had to take responsibility for a necessary decision that was sure to prove unpopular, and that they themselves did not approve. The minister for reconstruction, Walter Rathenau, a Democrat and a successful industrialist, hoped that a policy of "fulfillment" might convince the Allies that Germany was acting in good faith and might in the long run lead to concessions. An intensely patriotic German, Rathenau was also a Jew and drew the particular venom of the anti-Semitic nationalist orators.

The secret terrorist groups of the right began a campaign of assassination. They began (August 1921) by murdering Matthias Erzberger, the Catholic Center politician who had signed the armistice, and a leading moderate. His assassins escaped through Bavaria. When one of them was caught, the courts acquitted him. When the League of Nations awarded to Poland a substantial area of the rich province of Upper Silesia, containing many German inhabitants, the right grew still angrier. Rathenau was killed in June 1922 by men who believed in the "stab-in-the-back" theory and who thought that by murdering a Jew they could avenge the "betrayal" of the German army.

Hitler's Early Career

During the months between the assassinations of Erzberger and Rathenau, a new and ominous element had emerged among the welter of right-wing organizations in Bavaria. This was the National Socialist Party of the German Workers (called "Nazi" as an abbreviation of the word *National*) led by Adolf Hitler, the son of an obscure, illegitimate Austrian customs official, whose real name had been Schicklgruber. Born in 1889, Hitler early quarreled with his father, and seems always to have felt bitter and frustrated. In 1907 he was rejected by the Vienna Academy of Fine Arts, where he wished to study painting. He became an odd-job man, selling an occasional watercolor, but al-

Nazi party membership card No. 1, held by Hitler.

ways hovering on the edge of starvation. It was during these years that his hatred of the Jews began. Lower-middle-class Vienna at the time was deeply devoted to its anti-Semitic Mayor Lueger, whom Hitler admired. Because Karl Marx himself had been of Jewish origin and because many Viennese Jews were socialists, Hitler associated socialism with the Jews and lumped both together as somehow responsible for his own personal troubles and for the ills of the world.

Hitler drew support for his anti-Semitism from several nineteenth-century theorists. The French count Joseph Arthur de Gobineau (1816–1882) had laid the pseudoscientific foundation for modern theories of "Nordic" and "Aryan" supremacy. One of Gobineau's most influential readers was the great German composer Richard Wagner. Wagner's son-in-law, the Englishman Houston Stewart Chamberlain (1855–1927), wrote a long and turgid book called *The Foundations of the Nineteenth Century*, which glorified the Germans and assailed the Jews; one section was devoted to a "demonstration" that Christ had not been of Jewish origin. Chamberlain furiously opposed democratic government and, interestingly enough, capitalism. Thus he provided Hitler with a congenial mixture of racism, nationalism, antidemocratic thought, and radicalism.

Hitler came to hate Vienna as a cosmopolitan and

Jewish community and moved to Munich in 1913. In 1914, he enlisted in the German army, and fought through the war as a corporal. He won the iron cross for bravery, but was regarded by his commanding officer as too "hysterical" to deserve a commission. After the war, he went back to Munich, where, as might have been expected, he loathed the new republic and the "Bolsheviks," admired the Free Corps, and decided to become a politician.

Ludendorff had moved to Munich, and had become the center of the reaction. Hitler was employed as a political education officer for the troops. While engaged in this work, he discovered a small political group that called itself the German Workers' party. This group combined nationalism and militarism with a generous amount of radicalism. Hitler joined the party in 1919 and soon proved himself to be a far abler politician than any of his colleagues. He urged intensive propaganda for the union of all Germans in a greater Germany, the elimination of all Jews from political life, a state guarantee of full employment, the confiscation of war profits, the nationalization of trusts, the encouragement of small business, and a land grant to the peasantry. The seemingly radical character of his program caused many Germans otherwise sympathetic to hesitate before giving Hitler money. As early as 1920, he began to reassure them by saying he opposed not "industrial capital" but only "Jewish international loan capital."

Hitler was an extremely successful orator, with almost hypnotic gifts of capturing a crowd. By 1921 he had made himself the absolute leader, the *Führer* (compare with *duce*), of the Nazi party, and in the same year he strengthened himself by founding the SA (*Sturmabteilung,* or storm troops), brown-shirted units largely recruited from the Free Corps. The storm troopers wore arm bands with the swastika emblem, patrolled mass party meetings, and performed other services for the leader. Their commander was a well-known homosexual, Captain Roehm, who was also political adviser to the commander of the infantry stationed in Bavaria. So the Nazis, like the Italian Fascists, could use their sympathizers in the army to obtain illegal access to government supplies of arms.

Besides Roehm, Hitler's closest collaborators included Hermann Goering, a wartime aviator who had shot down twenty Allied planes, but who found himself restless in peacetime and took on the job of giving the SA a military polish; Rudolf Hess, Egyptian-born private secretary to Hitler; and Alfred Rosenberg, a Baltic German distinguished for fanatical hatred of Jews and Bolsheviks, and the first editor of the party newspaper.

Hitler and his Nazis were still a very minor politi-cal force in 1922 when the middle-of-the-road parties attempted to strengthen the republic. After the assassination of Rathenau, Stresemann's People's party moved away from the Nationalists, who were now tainted by murder, and entered into a collaboration with Center and Democrats. So tense was the political situation that the scheduled presidential elections were postponed to 1925.

The Inflation, 1922–1923

Political maneuvers to meet the increasing threat from the right, however, were largely nullified by the increasing economic problem posed by steadily growing inflation, which in 1922 and 1923 reached unheard-of extremes. Inflation is a complicated economic phenomenon and no mere list or description of its causes can really tell the full story. But the single chief cause for the runaway inflation in Germany after 1921 was probably the failure of the German government to levy taxes with which to pay the expenses of the war. The imperial regime had expected to win and to make the losers pay Germany's expenses by imposing huge indemnities. So it paid for only about 4 percent of the war costs by means of taxation. As defeat neared, the government borrowed more and more money from the banks. When the loans came due, the government re-

Berliners selling discarded tin cans to a sidewalk scrap merchant during the inflation of 1923.

German Elections to the Weimar Assembly and Reichstag, 1919–1933

(*Number of seats obtained by the major parties, arranged with the Left at the top, the Right at the bottom.*)

	Jan. 1919	June 1920	May 1924	Dec. 1924	May 1928	Sept. 1930	July 1932	Nov. 1932	Mar. 1933
Communists	—[a]	2	62	45	54	77	89	100	81
Independent Socialists	22	81	—[b]						
Social Democrats	163	112	100	131	152	143	133	121	125
Democrats	74	45	28	32	25	14	4	2	5
Center	71	68	65	69	61	68	75	70	74
People's party	22	62	44	51	45	30	7	11	2
Nationalists	42	66	96	103	78	41	40	51	52
Nazis			38	20	12	107	230	196	288

[a] The Communist party boycotted the elections to the Weimar constituent assembly.
[b] In these and succeeding elections the Independent Socialists had merged with the Social Democrats.

paid them with paper money that was not backed by gold. Each time this happened, more paper money was put into circulation, and prices rose; each rise in prices naturally led to a demand for a rise in wages, which had to be paid with more paper money. The inflationary spiral was under way. Instead of cutting purchasing power by imposing heavy taxes, the government permitted buyers to compete with each other for goods in short supply, thus causing prices to shoot up and speeding up the whole process of inflation.

Many other forces helped inflation along. For several reasons, Germany lacked gold to back its currency. Germany had to pay in gold for goods bought abroad during the war; the rich sent great sums out of Germany for fear that the government would attach them to pay reparations. Raw materials were in short supply; industry was disorganized; and credit was curtailed. The armies of occupation had to be maintained at German expense, and reparation payments had to be made. Nationalist Germans maintained that these expenses, especially reparations, were the cause of inflation; but, though reparations certainly helped the process, they were by no means solely responsible for it. The total sums involved in reparations were never great enough to affect the German currency until long after the inflation was under way. Indeed, the inflation was partly due to the industrialists' wish to avoid paying reparations and to clear their own indebtedness by letting the currency become worthless.

The following timetable shows how bad the situation had become by the end of 1922. When the war was over, the mark, normally valued at 4.2 to a dollar, had fallen to 8.4. In January 1921 it was 45; by December, 160. By September 1922 it was 1,303, and at the end of the year it was 7,000. In these months, the government begged for a moratorium on reparations payments and for a foreign loan. But the French were unwilling. They had already paid billions for the rebuilding of those parts of France that the Germans had devastated during the war, and they wanted the Germans to pay the bill. As a guarantee, the French demanded the vitally important German industrial region of the Ruhr. Despite British opposition, the French occupied the Ruhr in January 1923, after the Germans

had defaulted on their reparations payments. The French intended to run the mines and factories for their own benefit and thus make up for the German failure to pay reparations.

The Germans could not resist with force, but they declared the occupation of the Ruhr illegal and ordered the inhabitants to embark on passive resistance—to refuse to work the mines and factories or to deliver goods to the French. This order the people of the Ruhr obeyed. Local tension in the occupied area became serious when the French took measures against German police and workers, and when German Free Corps members undertook guerrilla operations against the French.

But the most dramatic result of the French occupation of the Ruhr was its effect upon the already desperate German economy. Not only was the rest of Germany cut off from badly needed goods from the occupied area, but the Ruhr inhabitants were idle at the order of the German government and had to be supported at government expense. The printing press struck off ever-increasing amounts of ever-more-worthless marks. Now the exchange rate went from thousands of marks to the dollar to millions, to billions, and, by December 1923, well up into the trillions.

The Consequences of Inflation

Such astronomical statistics become meaningful only when one realizes their personal and social consequences. A student set off one afternoon for the university with his father's check in his pocket to cover a year's tuition, room, board, and entertainment. When he arrived the next morning after an overnight journey, he discovered that the money he got for the check would pay for one short streetcar ride! Lifetime savings were rendered valueless; people trundled wheelbarrows full of marks through the street in an effort to buy a loaf of bread. Those who lived on fixed incomes were utterly ruined, and the savings of the investing middle classes were wiped out. Real property took on fantastic value. The story is told of two brothers, one frugal and the other spendthrift, who had shared equally in a fortune inherited from their father. The frugal one had invested his money; the spendthrift had bought a fine wine cellar, which he had proceeded to drink up. When inflation came, all the frugal brother's investments would not buy him a haircut, but the spendthrift found that the empty bottles in his cellar were worth billions on billions of marks apiece, and that he was rich again. Under such circumstances, speculation in real estate flourished and speculators made fortunes.

For the German worker, inflation did not mean the liquidation of his savings, because he usually had none. It did mean a great drop in the purchasing power of his wages, so great that he could no longer afford the necessities of life. His family suffered from hunger and cold. Since the financial position of the labor unions was destroyed, they were no longer able to help the workers, who gave up their membership in droves. The great industrialists, however, gained from the inflation, in part just because it did cripple the labor unions, but still more because it wiped out their own indebtedness, and enabled them to absorb small competitors and build giant business combines.

Politically, inflation greatly strengthened the extremists of both right and left. The middle classes, although pushed down to the economic level of the proletariat, still possessed the middle-class psychology. In status-conscious Germany, they would not adhere to the working-class parties of Social Democrats or Communists. Disillusioned, they would not adhere to the moderate parties that supported the Republic—the People's party, the Center, and the Democrats. So the Nationalists, and Hitler's Nazis above all, reaped a rich harvest. The hardships of the working class led many workers to turn away from the Social Democrats to the Communists. But Soviet Russian restraint on the leaders of the German Communist party prevented any concerted revolutionary drive until the fall of 1923, by which time poor organization and strong governmental repressive measures had doomed their efforts.

With the country seething in crisis, Stresemann as chancellor in the fall of 1923 proclaimed that because of the economic dislocation Germany could not keep up passive resistance in the Ruhr. He ordered work to be resumed and reparations to be delivered once again. Political troubles multiplied when the right refused to accept the new policy. At the height of the agitation in Bavaria, Hitler in early November 1923 broke into a right-wing political meeting in a Munich beerhall and announced that the "national revolution" had begun. At gun point he tried to get other local leaders to support him in a march on Berlin. They agreed, but let him down when they learned that the national government was prepared to put down the Nazis. Although Ludendorff himself joined the Nazi demonstration in Munich, as he had joined the Kapp putsch of 1920, troops broke up the demonstration with only a few casualties.

The trials of Ludendorff and Hitler have become famous as the most striking example of the Weimar judicial system's partiality for men of the right. Luden-dorff was respectfully acquitted. Hitler was allowed to use the dock as a propaganda platform for his ideas and was sentenced to the minimum term for high treason: five years. He actually spent eight months in comfortable confinement, during which time he wrote large portions of *Mein Kampf* (*My Battle*), the famous bible of the Nazis.

The End of Inflation, 1923–1924

Communist disorders and the Nazi beerhall putsch marked the last phase of the inflation period. A couple of weeks before Hitler's effort, the government had given extraordinary financial powers to Hans Luther, minister of finance, and Hjalmar Schacht, banker and fiscal expert. All printing of the old currency was stopped. A new bank was opened to issue new marks, which were simply assigned the value of the prewar mark (4.2 to the dollar). The new currency was backed not by gold but by an imaginary "mortgage" on all Germany's agricultural and industrial wealth, a psychological gesture that won public confidence. It took one trillion of the old marks to equal one of the new. Simultaneously, rigorous economy was put into effect in every branch of the government, and taxes were increased. The public protested loudly, but the measures remained in force until they had accomplished the intended effect. The cure for inflation produced serious hardships too. Prices fell, and over-expanded businesses collapsed. Unemployment rose sharply, wages stayed low, and workers labored long hours.

During 1924, the Allies contributed to the ending of the crisis in Germany by formulating the Dawes Plan, named for Charles G. Dawes, the American financier and later vice-president under Calvin Coolidge. The plan recommended the evacuation of the Ruhr by the French, the establishment of a special bank to receive reparations payments, gradually rising annual payments for the first five years, and an international loan to finance the German deliveries in the first year. The Nationalists violently attacked the proposals as a sinister scheme to enslave Germany to foreign masters. In the Reichstag elections of May 1924 the Nationalists scored impressive gains, as did the Nazis and the communists, while the moderate parties all suffered. But a coalition managed to win acceptance of the Dawes Plan in August 1924 by the device of promising the Nationalists representation in the cabinet. When new elections were held in December, the Nazis and communists suffered losses and the Social Democrats and moderates gained. Early in 1925 a Center-People's party-Nationalist coalition took office and governed Germany. One wing of the Nationalists, however, led by the enormously rich industrial press and film magnate, Alfred Hugenberg, who had made a fortune during the inflation, opposed all cooperation with the republic. Though Germany had moved appreciably to the right, foreign policy remained in the conciliatory hands of Stresemann, who remained foreign minister through all governments between November 1923 and his death in October 1929.

Recovery at Home, 1924–1929

During these less-troubled middle years of the Weimar Republic, economic recovery proceeded steadily, until, in 1929, German industrial output exceeded that of 1913. First-rate German equipment, coupled with superb technical skill and a systematic adoption of American methods of mass production, created a highly efficient industrial machine. This "rationalization" of industry increased production, but brought with it overborrowing and some unemployment. "Vertical trusts," which brought together in one great corporation all the parts of an industrial process from coal- and iron-mining to the output of the finished product; and cartels, associations of independent enterprises that controlled sales and prices for their own benefit, were characteristic of the German system. The emphasis was always on heavy industry, which meant that continued prosperity would depend upon a big armaments program.

All through this period, reparations were paid faithfully, with no damage to the German economy. Indeed, more money flowed into Germany from foreign, especially American, investment than flowed out from reparations. Dependence on foreign capital, however, which would cease to flow in time of depression, made German prosperity artificial.

In 1925, after President Ebert died, a presidential election was held in which three candidates competed. The Catholic Center, the Democrats, and the Social Democrats supported the Center leader, Wilhelm Marx. The Nationalists, People's party, and other right-wingers joined in support of Field Marshal Hindenburg, then seventy-seven years old. The communists ran their own candidate and thus contributed to the election of Hindenburg, who won by a small plurality. Abroad, the choice of a man so intimately connected with imperial militarist Germany created dismay; but until 1930 Hindenburg acted entirely in accordance with the constitution, to the distress of most of the nationalist groups. The domestic issues of this period all aroused great heat, but were settled by democratic process. In the elections of 1928, the Social Democrats were returned to power and the Nationalists and Nazis were hard hit. All in all, prosperity encouraged moderation and a return to support of the republic.

"Fulfillment" Abroad, 1925–1930

In foreign affairs, this middle period of the Weimar Republic was one of gradually increasing German participation in the system of collective security. Thus in 1925 Germany signed the Locarno treaties, which took the French armies out of the Rhineland, substituted a neutral zone and a frontier guaranteed by Britain and Italy, and set up machinery for the arbitration of dis-

putes between Germany and her neighbors. These treaties did not, however, guarantee to Poland and Czechoslovakia the eastern frontiers of Germany. In 1926, Germany was admitted to the League of Nations, with a permanent seat on the League's Council. In 1929, Germany accepted the Kellogg-Briand Pact, which outlawed aggressive war.

In 1929, a new reparations plan named after the American Owen D. Young, chairman of the committee that drew it up, substantially reduced the total originally demanded by the Allies. The Young Plan also established lower rates of payments than those under the Dawes Plan and allowed the Germans a greater part in their collection. Before June 1930, the Rhineland was evacuated by the Allies, four years ahead of the date set by the Treaty of Versailles. Many of these gains for Germany were accomplished only with so much preliminary difficulty that they were robbed of their sweetness, and the German Nationalists, Nazis, and Communists thoroughly opposed them all. Yet German foreign policy was generally calculated to reassure the rest of the world.

The Impact of the Depression, 1929–1931

But even before the last achievements of this "period of fulfillment," the depression had begun to knock the foundations out from under prosperity and moderation. Unemployment rose during 1929. After the American stock-market crash in October, foreign credits, on which prosperity had so largely depended, were no longer available to Germany. Short-term loans were not renewed, or else were recalled. Tariff barriers were hurting foreign trade. Hunger reappeared.

Although unemployment insurance cushioned the first shock for the workers, the lower middle classes, painfully recovering from the inflation, had no such barrier between them and destitution. Their desperation helped Hitler, whose fortunes during the years of fulfillment had fallen very low, although he had attracted a number of new followers who were later to be important in his movement.

Paul Joseph Goebbels, publicist and journalist, proved to be a master of mob psychology and an effective orator. Heinrich Himmler, a mild-mannered but ruthless chicken farmer, took charge of the elite black-shirted SS (*Schutzstaffel,* or defense corps), which was formed as a special guard of honor. The SS, with a higher standing than the SA, and with special membership requirements of "racial purity," was later to become the nucleus for the Gestapo, or secret police. Hitler also recruited Joachim von Ribbentrop, champagne salesman and Nazi party ambassador to the German upper classes.

The government fell in 1930 over a disagreement on a question of unemployment insurance benefits. Hindenburg appointed to the chancellorship Heinrich Bruening, a member of the Catholic Center party. Bruening would have liked to support parliamentary institutions and to continue Stresemann's policies of fulfillment, but he was to find it impossible to do either. President Hindenburg, now eighty-two, had fallen more and more under the influence of General Kurt von Schleicher, an ambitious political soldier who had intrigued himself into the president's favor.

Hindenburg was now itching to rule by decree, as the constitution authorized him to do in an emergency. By failing to pass Bruening's economic program, the Reichstag gave Hindenburg the opportunity he wanted. Bruening agreed, partly because he felt that a genuine emergency existed, but partly because he was determined to keep his bitter political rivals, the Social Democrats, from replacing him in office.

A presidential decree proclaimed the new budget. When the Reichstag protested, Hindenburg dissolved it and called new elections (September 1930). Nazis and communists fought in the streets, but both gained greatly at the expense of the moderates. The Nazis' Reichstag representation rose from 12 to 107 and the communists' from 54 to 77. Bruening had to carry on against the wishes of the electorate; supported only by Hindenburg, he too now turned authoritarian.

In order to avoid a new government in which Nazis would participate, the Social Democrats decided to support Bruening. When the Reichstag met, Nazis and communists created disorder on the floor, but voted together in opposition to government measures. These measures passed only because the Social Democrats voted for them. In 1931, Bruening made an effort to arrange an Austro-German customs union which would coordinate the tariff policies of the two countries and help them both fight the depression without affecting their political sovereignty. Whether such an arrangement between two countries that were both suffering from unemployment would actually have succeeded cannot be decided; nor can we be sure whether the impulse for Germany and Austria to unite politically might not have proved overpoweringly strong. At any rate, the whole project raised in the minds of the Allies, especially the French, the specter of a "greater Germany," and the scheme was vetoed by the World Court.

The collapse of the great Austrian bank, the Kredit-Anstalt, further deepened the depression, despite a British loan to Austria in 1931, and despite the one-year moratorium on reparations payments procured for Germany by the American president Herbert Hoover.

The Republic in Danger, 1931–1932

Now Nazis, Nationalists, the veterans organization of the Steel Helmets (*Stahlhelm*), the Junkers' Agrarian League, industrialists, and representatives of the former princely houses formed a coalition against Bruening. This coalition had great financial resources and a mass backing, chiefly Nazi. It had its private armies in the SA, in the Stahlhelm, and in other semimilitary organizations. Because the left was split and the communists

in effect acted as political allies of the right, nothing stood between this new right-wing coalition and a political victory except the person of Hindenburg, who controlled the army, and by virtue of the Weimar Constitution was able to keep Bruening in office. Early in 1932, the great industrialist Fritz Thyssen invited Hitler to address a meeting of coal and steel magnates. Hitler won their financial support by convincing them that if he came to power he would be their man. Though some of Hitler's followers were now impatient for a new putsch, he curbed them, believing that the Nazis could come to power legally.

In the presidential elections of March 1932, Hitler ran as the candidate of the Nazis, and Hindenburg as the candidate of the Center, Social Democrats, and other moderate parties. The Nationalists nominated a Stahlhelm man, and the communists of course ran their own candidate. Hitler polled 11,338,571 votes, and Hindenburg polled 18,661,736, only four-tenths of a percent short of the required majority. In the run-off election, the Nationalists backed Hitler, whose total rose to 13,400,000 as against Hindenburg's 19,360,000. The eighty-four-year-old marshal reelected as the candidate of the moderates was, however, no longer a moderate himself, but the tool of the Junkers and the military.

Although the government now ordered the Nazi SA and SS disbanded, the decree was not enforced. In April 1932 the Nazis scored impressive victories in local elections, especially in all-important Prussia. Bruening was unble to procure in time either an Allied promise to extend the moratorium on reparations payments or permission for Germany to have equality in armaments with France. Schleicher, who was now deeply involved in intrigue against Bruening, worked on Hindenburg to demand Bruening's resignation. This Hindenburg did on May 29, 1932, the first time a president had dismissed a chancellor simply because he had lost personal confidence in him. Bruening's successor was Franz von Papen, a rich Catholic nobleman and a member of the extreme right wing of the center, who installed a cabinet composed of nobles. Papen was Schleicher's man—or so Schleicher thought.

The Center disavowed Papen, who had the real support of no political party or group, but whom the Nazis temporarily tolerated because he agreed to remove the ban on the SA and SS. In foreign policy, Papen succeeded where Bruening had failed, for the Allies scrapped the Young Plan and required Germany to pay only three billion gold marks into a fund earmarked for general European reconstruction. Instead of being bound for many decades to pay reparations, Germany was now freed from all such obligations.

On July 31, 1932, new elections for the Reichstag took place, called by Papen on the theory that the Nazis had passed their peak, that their vote would decrease, and that they would then be chastened and would cooperate in the government. But the Nazis won 230 seats and became the biggest single party in the Reichstag; the communists gained also, chiefly at the expense of the Social Democrats. The Democrats and the People's party almost disappeared, while the Nationalists suffered, and the Center scored a slight gain. Papen had failed. He now wanted to take some Nazis into the government, but the Nazis demanded the chancellorship, which Hindenburg was determined not to hand over to Hitler. Papen now planned to dissolve the Reichstag and to call new elections. By repeating this process, he hoped to wear down Hitler's strength each time, until he brought Hitler to support him and accept a subordinate place. As Papen put pressure on the industrialists who had been supporting Hitler, the Nazi funds began to dry up, leaving Hitler seriously embarrassed. The elections of November 6, 1932, bore out Papen's expectations. The Nazis fell off from 230 seats to 196; and, although the communists gained substantially and ominously, Papen too won some support. Now the Nazis were really desperate. Goebbels wrote in his diary:

> Received a report on the financial situation of the Berlin organization. It is hopeless. Nothing but debts and obligations, together with the complete impossibility of obtaining any reasonable sum of money after this defeat.[*]

Hitler's Rise to Power, 1932–1933

Had Papen been permitted to continue his tactics, it is possible that Hitler might have been kept from power. But Papen resigned as a matter of form because he could not count on majority support in the Reichstag. Angry with Schleicher and sorry to lose Papen, Hindenburg forced Schleicher himself to take the office on December 3, 1932. Now the backstairs general was chancellor, but he had no political support whatever, and had alienated even Hindenburg. He lasted in office only about eight weeks before Hitler was appointed chancellor.

Schleicher did score a great diplomatic success by winning a five-power declaration that recognized in principle Germany's right to parity in armaments. At home, he made every effort to appeal to all shades of opinion except the extreme left. But this attempt in itself alienated the implacably antilabor industrialists and the Junkers. The tortuous Papen, eager for revenge, intrigued with these enemies of Schleicher. Early in January 1933 Papen met Hitler at the house of the Cologne banker Baron Kurt von Schroeder. The industrialists, who had temporarily abandoned Hitler, now agreed to pay the Nazis' debts. Hitler, in turn, no longer insisted on the chancellorship. He thus led Papen to hope that he would come back into office with Hitler's backing. Hindenburg, too, was enlisted. When the president refused to give Schleicher the authority to dissolve the Reichstag at its first new session, which would surely have voted him down, Schleicher had no choice; he was forced to resign (January 28, 1933).

But Hitler had now raised the ante, and demanded

the chancellorship for himself. Papen consented, provided Hitler undertook to govern in strict accordance with parliamentary procedure. Papen was to be vice-chancellor, and still thought he could dominate the government, since only three of its eleven ministers would be Nazis. He therefore persuaded Hindenburg to accept Hitler as chancellor. But Papen underestimated Hitler. Though Hitler swore to Hindenburg that he would maintain the constitution, he had no intention of keeping his oath. The Weimar Republic was doomed from the moment Hitler came to the chancellor's office on January 30, 1933.

IV Germany under Hitler, 1933–1939
The Nazi Dictatorship

Hitler's first weeks in power were devoted to transforming his chancellorship into a dictatorship. He dissolved the Reichstag and called for new elections. During the campaign, opponents of the Nazis were intimidated by violence and threats, and were denied radio time and free use of the press. Yet a Nazi victory in the election still did not seem sure. On February 27, 1933, fire opportunely broke out in the Reichstag building. Hitler pointed to it as a sample of the disorders that the communists were likely to instigate. Hindenburg issued emergency decrees suspending free speech and the free press, and thus made it even easier for the storm troops to use terror against their political opponents. It is now generally supposed that the Nazis themselves set the Reichstag fire, but they convicted and condemned to death a Dutch communist named Vanderlubbe, who apparently was mentally deficient.

Despite their campaign, the Nazis won only 44 percent of the votes, which gave them 288 seats in the Reichstag. Using the SA as a constant threat, Hitler bullied the Reichstag. Except for 94 Social Democrats (the communists were denied their seats), all members voted for the famous Enabling Act (March 23, 1933). This act conferred dictatorial powers upon the government, and suspended the constitution. The act was renewed in 1937 by a subservient Reichstag, and again in 1943.

Now Hitler could act as he chose, unimpeded by the laws. He instituted a ministry of propaganda under Goebbels. He stripped the state governments of the powers they had had under Weimar and made Germany a strongly centralized state (April 1933) by appointing governors from Berlin who had the power to override the state legislatures. When President Hindenburg died in August 1934, at the age of eighty-seven, Hitler assumed the office of president as well as that of chancellor, but he preferred to use the title *Der Führer* (the leader) to describe himself. This new move was approved by a plebiscite in which Hitler obtained 88 percent of the votes cast.

Political parties which opposed Hitler were forced to dissolve. The government banned communists and

*Quoted by S. William Halperin, *Germany Tried Democracy* (New York, 1946), pp. 511–512.

Socialists (May 1933); the Nationalists dissolved themselves (June 1933); the government put an end to the Catholic parties (July 1933) and all monarchist groups (February 1934). The Stahlhelm was incorporated into the Nazi party (June 1933) and was deprived of its identity (November 1935). As early as July 1933 the Nazis were declared to be the only legal political party in Germany.

The appeal of the Nazis to the German people lay in part in their denunciation and repudiation of the "disorderly" parliamentary system. A strong man who got things done struck a responsive chord in the public. In the last elections, November 1933, there were no opposition candidates, 92 percent of the electorate voted Nazi, and there were only two non-Nazi deputies in the chamber of 661. As in fascist Italy and communist Russia, youth groups fed the party, which soon had a powerful regional organization all over Germany and among Germans abroad.

With the Nazi party itself, however, a difficult situation was created by those who had believed Hitler's more radical pronouncements on social and economic questions. Many of these Nazis were concentrated in the SA, whose members, most of them from the lower classes, were also distressed by the way in which Hitler had treated their organization. The SA had made possible his rise to power, but now it was rather an embarrassment to him, no longer quite respectable, and certainly not in favor, as were the SS and especially the army.

On June 30, 1934, Hitler ordered and personally participated in the celebrated "blood purge," or, as he himself called it, "the night of the long knives." Roehm himself, founder and leader of the SA, was shot, and so were, by Hitler's own admission, seventy-three others, including Schleicher and his wife. Other estimates of the casualties run as high as 1,000. In any case, after June 1934 there was no further opposition to Hitler.

Racism and Political Theory

Within a few days after the passage of the enabling law, Hitler struck the first of his many blows against the Jews, whom he had so long denounced. In a country of approximately 60,000,000 people, the Jews counted less than 1 percent of the population (something under 600,000), not including part-Jewish Germans. The Jews had become leading members of the professions and the arts, and had made outstanding contributions to German culture. Since most Jews were assimilated and patriotic Germans, many of them would probably have become Nazis if they had been permitted to. They would have supported Hitler in everything but anti-Semitism. Instead, anti-Semitic doctrines required their ruthless elimination.

The businesses and professions of the Jews were boycotted; they were forbidden to hold office (April 1933), although a temporary exception was made for veterans of World War I. In the "Nuremberg laws"

of September 15, 1935, a Jew was defined as any person with one Jewish grandparent. All such persons were deprived of German citizenship. Intermarriage between Jews and non-Jews was forbidden as "racial pollution." Jews might not fly the national flag, write or publish, act on stage or screen, teach in any educational institution, work in a bank, exhibit paintings or give concerts, work in a hospital, enter any of the government's labor or professional bodies, or sell books or antiques. They were not eligible for unemployment insurance or charity, and the names of Jews who had died for Germany in World War I were erased from war memorials. Many towns and villages, under the spur of government-sponsored propaganda, refused to permit Jews to live inside their precincts.

In November 1938 a Jewish boy of seventeen, driven to desperation by the persecution of his parents, shot and killed a secretary of the German embassy in Paris. Two days later, organized German mobs looted and pillaged Jewish shops all over Germany, burned and dynamited synagogues, and invaded Jewish homes to beat up the occupants and steal their possessions. The state then compelled the Jews to restore the damaged properties and to pay an enormous fine. Jews were forced to take special names, to wear yellow Stars of David, and to belong to a Reich "Union of Jews." Although some Jews managed to leave Germany, it was usually at the cost of abandoning all their possessions; yet they were the lucky ones. All these measures and many others (for example, "cows purchased from Jews may not be serviced by the communal bull") designed to drive the Jews into ghettos and starvation were but the prelude to the physical extermination in gas ovens to which they were to be subjected by the Nazis during World War II. What distressed many horrified Western observers almost more than the actions themselves was the failure of any substantial number of highly educated and "civilized" non-Jewish Germans to register any form of protest.

Enthusiasm for "racial purity" had its positive as well as its negative side. The blond, blue-eyed ideal "Nordic types" were urged to mate with each other early and to have many children. German motherhood was made the object of paeans of praise. And, to keep the race pure, sterilization was introduced, supposedly for the prevention of the inheritance of disease. The functioning of such a law depended upon the condition of the medical and legal professions, which soon fell into the hands of charlatans. Medical experimentation of horrifying cruelty and of no conceivable scientific value was practiced during the war on human beings of "inferior" races—Jews, Poles and other Slavs, and gypsies. These practices were the direct outcome of Nazi pseudoscientific "eugenic" legislation.

The Bases of Foreign Policy

In the field of foreign affairs, German racism justified the incorporation of all territory inhabited by Germans, including Austria, the western borderlands (Sudetenland) of Czechoslovakia, Danzig, the Polish corridor, and other less important places. And the doctrine of *Lebensraum* ("living space") justified the incorporation of non-German areas—the rest of Czechoslovakia, Poland, and all southeastern Europe, as well as large areas of Russia. Hitler felt that what the Germans needed, they were entitled to take, since they were a superior people.

Some German intellectuals looked back with longing upon the Holy Roman Empire of the Middle Ages, the first Reich. Now that the war had ended the second Reich of William II, they hoped to behold a third one, incorporating the old territories, no matter who now lived in them. This is the meaning of Hitler's use of the term "Third Reich" to describe the Nazi state, which he proclaimed would last a thousand years. A "scientific" basis for the Lebensraum theory was supplied by the teachers of "geopolitics," chief among whom was Karl Haushofer, professor of geography, retired major-general, and teacher of Hitler's close friend Rudolf Hess. Haushofer declared that Britain and France were decadent, that small powers must disappear (except for Switzerland and the Vatican City), that Germany, preserving its master race pure, must possess the will to power, and expand ruthlessly, occupying the "heartland" of Eurasia, from which the world could be dominated.

Another school of thought in Germany argued that Germany's future lay in an alliance with Russia in which Russia's inexhaustible manpower would be joined with Germany's industrial output and military techniques for purposes of conquest. This notion had been strong in German army circles in czarist days and continued to exist after the Bolshevik Revolution, especially after the Treaty of Rapallo concluded between Germany and the Soviet Union in 1922. Outside the army, other German nationalists, who were just as antiliberal and antiparliamentarian as Stalin, retained the Bismarckian attitudes of hostility to the West and to Poland and of friendship toward Russia, whatever the color of her regime. Moreover, many German Marxists were highly nationalistic. Indeed, Hitler's "national socialism" succeeded in part because he knew how to use old Marxist clichés in presenting an essentially nationalist program.

Legal and Economic Policies

Hitler entirely revamped the judicial system of Germany, abandoning traditional legal principles and substituting "folk" justice, which, Hitler said, subordinated the individual totally to the people (*volk*). In practice, so mystic a doctrine meant that whatever Hitler wanted was German law. People's Courts were established (May 1934) to try all cases of treason, a crime that was now extended to include a wide variety of lesser offenses, such as circulating banned newspapers. Hitler appointed all the judges of the People's Courts. Concentration camps were established for enemies of the regime, who could be immured or executed by the headsman's axe without appeal. In fact, they could not even have defense counsel of their choice, but had to accept counsel approved by the courts. The Gestapo (*Geheime Staatspolizei*, Secret State Police) was established in April 1933 in Prussia and a year later was extended to all of Germany. It had a free hand in opening private correspondence, tapping wires, and spying on individual citizens.

All economic life was brought under the regime. In agriculture, the Nazis aimed at the largest possible measure of self-sufficiency, and, of course, at political control over the peasantry. The Junkers were protected and no effort was made to divide their vast estates. In 1933, a special law protected farms of less than 312 acres against forced sale and attachment for debt, an act that won the small farmer to Hitler. But the government determined the production required of farms, and fixed farm prices and wages, and fees for distributing farm products. Unused land was put under cultivation and private citizens were required to grow vegetables in greenhouses. This was part of Hitler's preparation for war. By 1937, Germany was 83 percent self-sufficient in agriculture, a rise of 8 percent since the Nazis had come to power. Fats and coffee were perhaps the two most important deficiencies remaining.

In industry, taking a leaf out of Stalin's book, Hitler proclaimed a Four-Year Plan in 1933 and a second one in 1936. The first was aimed chiefly at economic recovery and at ending unemployment. Labor camps for men and women helped decrease unemployment, as did rearmament and a program of public works. By 1936, unemployment had dropped from about 7,000,000 to less than 1,500,000. The second plan was designed to prepare for war, and especially to make Germany blockade-proof. Output of raw materials was increased and the materials were distributed first and foremost to armament and other war industries; labor was allocated with similar ends in view; and prices and foreign exchange were controlled. Goering was made boss of the plan.

Under his direction fell the new Goering Iron Works, designed to make up for the loss of the rich iron resources of Alsace-Lorraine, which had yielded three quarters of Germany's supply. To this end, low-content ores were worked, and the government absorbed the higher costs. Output went up in two years more than 50 percent. Germany's gifted scientists were enlisted to make up for other deficiencies by devising successful but expensive synthetic products. Important in this field were the distillation of motor fuel from coal, and the production of synthetic rubber. The state also built strategic highways, the Autobahnen, excellent modern expressways.

The Nazis abolished all labor unions in 1933, and employers' associations in 1934. To replace them, a "Labor Front" was established under Dr. Robert Ley, including all wage earners, salaried persons, professionals, and employers. Strikes and lockouts had been forbidden. Workers were assured of jobs as long as they quietly accepted the entire system. The Labor Front in one of its aspects was a huge spy organization constantly on the alert for anti-Nazis in the factories; it could reduce their pay, fire them, or put them in jail. An adjunct to the Labor Front was the "Strength through Joy" organization, which provided paid vacation trips for German workers to resorts or tourist centers, and which sponsored concerts and other entertainments.

As the second Four-Year Plan went into effect, the worker found himself increasingly immobile. He had a work book detailing his past training and positions held, and he could not get a new job unless the state decided it would be more suitable for him. All graduates of secondary schools had to register with the employment authorities. Men and women of working age were liable to conscription for labor. Just before the war, all agricultural and mining and certain industrial workers were frozen in their jobs. On the side of capital, the big cartel became the all-pervasive feature of German industrial organization—a system of profitable monopoly under state control. The interlocking directorate made the system even tighter than it looked. Six industrialists, for example, held among them one hundred and twenty-seven directorates in the largest corporations, were presidents of thirty-two, and all held government posts besides. The minister of economics sat at the top of the economic pyramid, authorizing plant expansion, controlling imports and exports, fixing prices and establishing costs, and allocating raw materials.

Religion and Culture

The Christian churches, both Protestant and Catholic, posed a problem for the Nazis. Extremists among Hitler's followers had always been in favor of a return to paganism and the old German gods celebrated by Wagner's operas. Hitler himself, born a Catholic, had once declared that Germany was his only god. Yet office brought sobering second thoughts, since Germany was after all nominally a Christian country. In the hope of avoiding state domination, the Lutheran ministry in 1933 organized a national synod, which the Nazis almost immediately took over by appointing their own bishop. The efforts of extreme Nazis to purge the Bible and to abandon the crucifix led to discontent. The dissidents, led by pastor Martin Niemoeller, objected to Nazi theology and efforts at control. But Niemoeller also pledged his loyalty to Hitler, made no objections to Nazi racism, and went to a concentration camp solely out of determination to resist dictation over the Lutheran church. The "confessional" movement he led probably did not extend beyond about 15 percent of the Protestant clergy.

In July 1933 Hitler and the German Catholics reached a concordat guaranteeing freedom of worship and permitting religious instruction in the schools. Catholics were to be allowed to form youth groups and to appoint professors of theology. But the Nazis did not live up to these terms. They interfered with the circulation of Catholic magazines, persecuted the youth groups, and insulted Catholic priests in their press as members of the "black international." On the other hand, the Catholic church found much to oppose in the teachings to which Catholic children were exposed in the Hitler youth groups. Cardinal Faulhaber of Munich denounced the Nazi violation of the concordat in 1933, but his action only intensified the struggle. Not that millions of Catholics, both clerical and lay, did not support the regime wholeheartedly, persecutions of the Jews and all. They did; and no voice was raised from among the clergy of either major Christian sect to protest against Nazi racism or militarism.

The Nazi process of *Gleichschaltung* (coordination) was applied in every area of the national life, including education and the arts. One of the leading Nazi officials once remarked, "When I hear the word culture, I reach for my revolver," a revealing and not untypical reflection of the extreme Nazi attitude. Hitler's own artistic views were simple in the extreme. He preferred nudes, the more luscious and Germanic the better, and this taste he strove to impose on the nation, denouncing most modern and experimental trends in art as non-Aryan. The school curriculum, especially history, could no longer be taught with that "objectivity" which was a "fallacy of liberalism," but had to be presented to the student in accordance with the Nazi doctrine of "blood and soil." Nazi racial doctrines, the great past achievements of Germany, the military spirit, and physical culture these were the cornerstones of the new education.

V The Failure of Parliamentarianism in Spain and Eastern Europe, 1918–1939

In the troubled years between the wars, nondemocratic authoritarian governments emerged not only in Italy and Germany but also in Spain, in the successor states to the Hapsburg Empire (except Czechoslovakia), and in the other states of eastern and southeastern Europe.

Spain: The Background

Spain differs widely from the other European countries, and one can understand Franco's triumph only in terms of the special Spanish social, economic, cultural, and political conditions. In Spain, local affection—for the language and traditions of a single province—has usually moved most men more than love of the country as a whole. Catalonians and Basques often have striven to create separate states of their own. Although Spain approaches economic self-sufficiency in both agriculture and industrial raw materials, the soil is poor, the system of farming backward, and the rural areas are heavily

Hitler and the Nazi high command at the opera.

overpopulated. Poverty is endemic; discontent is everywhere.

Religion united Spaniards against the Muslims in the Middle Ages and against the Protestants in the sixteenth and seventeenth centuries. But early in the nineteenth century, the Catholic church in Spain decided to lead against liberalism the same kind of struggle it had led against its earlier enemies. So in most parts of Spain the Church became identified with the landowners. Loss of faith became very widespread. Catholic sources report that by the 1930s only minute fractions of the population attended Mass. With the same devotion and passion they had once shown for the Church, the lower classes in Spain adopted one or another of the modern revolutionary doctrines.

When the Spaniards turned to revolutionary doctrine, it was chiefly in Bakunin's anarchist beliefs and later in Sorel's syndicalism that they found ideas they could cling to. Anarchism (and anarchosyndicalism) really took hold in Spain, and in Spain alone. The industrial workers of Catalonia and the miserable peasants of Andalusia were anarchist; they wanted to destroy the state utterly rather than conquer and use it. Despite a long history in Spain, anarchism, which at its peak numbered a million to a million and a half adherents, could only harass governments but could not overthrow them, and its positive achievements were limited to securing by means of strikes an occasional increase in wages. It was deeply puritanical in tone, and fanatically anti-Catholic. Shrewd observers have likened it to a Christian heresy that took all too literally the social teachings of the New Testament. Its adherents turned against the Church with all the fanaticism with which they had once supported it, because they felt that the Church had let them down. The burning of churches and the killing of priests, by which Spanish revolutions have always been marked, have been the work chiefly of anarchists.

But in the 1930s, Spain also had an increasingly substantial Marxist Socialist party, with its own federation of trade unions parallel to that of the anarchists. The socialists drew their first strength from the urban workers of Castile and from the mining and steel-producing centers of the north. When Spain became a republic in 1931 (see below), the socialists added many rural supporters, and the party numbered a million and a quarter in 1934. The socialists were moderates, who had refused to adhere to the Comintern in 1920, but who had joined the revived Second International a few years later. Dissidents founded a small Communist party, from which there were soon Trotskyite deviations. Catalonians had their own socialist formation, and the Church itself supported labor unions of its own in the north, where it had not become identified with the landlords. The socialist doctrine that each should be rewarded according to his needs sustained the traditional Spanish contempt for success and property. In fact, Spain had never accepted the capitalist system or the industrial revolution any more than it had accepted the Protestant Reformation.

Carlism, the doctrine of the extreme right, is another vivid illustration of Spanish maladjustment to the outside contemporary world. Founded in the nineteenth century as a movement supporting Don Carlos, a pretender to the throne, Carlism called for the restoration of the Inquisition, regarded the railroad and the telegraph literally as inventions of the devil, and rejected the Copernican theory of the universe. Carlism had its lower-class devotees, too, especially among the rebellious farmers of Navarre in the north.

Birth of the Spanish Republic

King Alfonso XIII, a constitutional monarch strongly ambitious for absolute power, ruled over Spain until 1923. In his governments—based on electoral corruption and intimidation—"liberals" and "conservatives" took orderly turns at office, and the real power rested with the local political bosses. Not having participated in World War I, Spain was spared much of the ensuing anguish. Yet wartime trade with the combatants had built up Spanish industry and, by making war profiteers, had increased the tension between rich and poor.

In 1923, General Primo de Rivera, acting with the approval of Alfonso, proclaimed martial law, imposed censorship, and persecuted political opponents. His dictatorship lasted until 1930, but lost its popularity after 1926. He spent too much on public works and was caught in the depression. Moreover, he did not fulfill the promises for a constituent assembly and political reform. He got the socialists to participate in his

regime and put through appropriate labor legislation in the hope of weakening the anarchists. But, since he depended on the army and the landowners, he could not institute agrarian reform. He also alienated the Catalonians, and his repressive measures deprived him of middle-class support.

After Primo de Rivera's resignation and death in 1930, King Alfonso soon restored the constitution. Municipal elections (April 1931) resulted in a victory for the republicans, representing the lower middle classes of the towns, small tradesmen, intellectuals, teachers, and journalists. The king left the country without abdicating. Elections to a constituent assembly in June 1931 brought in a republican-socialist majority, and in November the assembly forbade the king's return and confiscated his property. Spain was a republic. The monarchy, having stood only for clergy, army, and aristocracy, had failed.

The assembly went ahead to adopt a new constitution in December. This provided for a responsible ministry, a single-chamber parliament, and a president to be chosen by an electoral college consisting of parliament and an equal number of electors chosen by popular vote. It was clear that the army would rise against the republic whenever the opportunity was presented and that the army would have the support of the Church and the large landowners. Moreover, although the republic temporarily had socialist support, it did not have the support of the anarchists. Danger threatened from both the right and the left.

Crisis of the Spanish Republic, 1933–1936

The first crisis arose over a new constitutional statute defining the position of the Church. The assembly rejected a moderate proposal which would have preserved the Church as a special corporation with its own schools and which might have proved acceptable to most Catholics, even though the cardinal-primate of Spain had already denounced the republic. Instead, the assembly's law was far more extreme: it closed church schools and ended state grants to the Church after two years. This hurt education badly and lost the republicans many supporters, especially among the lower clergy itself. Although the republic secured much Catalan support by a grant of autonomy, it failed to act decisively on agrarian reform.

The anarchists expressed their dissatisfaction by major risings (1933), which the government put down by force. The jails were full, and unemployment was as high as ever. Repression of the anarchists lost the republic much left support, but failed to gain it that of the right, which came back strongly in the elections of November 1933 as the largest party in parliament. Now the government helplessly swung to the right, and much of its previous legislation, especially laws affecting the Church and the working classes, remained a dead letter. The Church and monarchists put forward a young man named Gil Robles, a staunch fascist and admirer of the Austrian chancellor Dollfuss (see below).

On the left, the socialists no longer collaborated with the government. Grown more revolutionary, they now engaged in strenuous competition with the anarchists for the loyalty of the Spanish workers. Strikes and disorders multiplied. In October 1934 the socialists called a general strike in protest against the inclusion of three of Robles' followers in the government. Catalonia declared itself an independent republic and was deprived of its autonomy. The coal miners of the Asturias in the north staged a revolt, joined in by both anarchists and socialists, which was put down with the loss of more than 3,000 lives. The government's use of Moors (Muslims from North Africa) against Spaniards was deeply resented; the Moors had been dispatched by the new minister of war, Francisco Franco.

Thus the right in turn lost its public support; and now the left, under the impact of the Asturias uprising and influenced by the line of the Comintern, united in a "Popular Front" for the elections of February 1936. For the first time, anarchosyndicalists went to the polls and voted for a common list with republicans, socialists, and communists. The left won a considerable victory, perhaps largely because it promised an amnesty for men involved in past outbreaks. Catalan autonomy, land reform, and anticlerical measures were of course the first order of business. The moderate republican Azaña was elected president.

But moderation had gone out of fashion on the left. The Popular Front was a coalition for election purposes only. Instead of entering Azaña's cabinet, Largo Caballero, leader of the left wing of the socialists, now "played at insurrection." He acted as if he intended to seize power. *Pravda* hailed him as a new Lenin. Yet he had no forces of his own. The route to power for left-wing revolutionaries could open up only if the right attempted a military coup, if the government then armed the workers to fight it, and if the workers then won.

On the left also, and for the first time, the Spanish Communist party in 1936 emerged as a considerable element. Under Primo de Rivera's dictatorship, the communists had been so insignificant that he had not even taken the trouble to suppress their newspaper. But their participation in the Asturias uprising and the Popular Front gained them political strength despite their numerical weakness (3,000 members). Oddly enough, they were more moderate in their immediate aims than the socialists, because they felt the need for a long preliminary period of Popular Front cooperation to increase their own power, and because this was Stalin's "respectable" period.

Simultaneously in 1936, on the right, there emerged, also for the first time, the *Falange* (phalanx), a party founded in 1932 by the son of Primo de Rivera, a fascist on the Italian pattern ("harmony of all classes and professions in one destiny") who did not oppose agrarian reform or other socialist programs. The Falange had its symbol, a bunch of arrows and a yoke, and its slogan, "Arriba España" ("Upward, Spain"); its program called for national expansion in Africa, the annexation of Portugal, the building of an empire in South America; it established youth groups and a private army. Although the Falange polled relatively few votes in the election of 1936, most of Gil Robles' right-wing support went over to it after the Popular Front victory. Through the spring of 1936, the Falange worked with army, monarchist, clerical, and Carlist groups for a counterrevolution. Everybody knew a military coup against the government was in the offing. In July it came, under the military leadership of General Franco.

The Spanish Civil War, 1936–1939

The Spanish Civil War (1936–1939) was the first act in the conflict that was to ripen into World War II. Decisively aided by Germany and Italy, Franco's forces pushed on to eventual victory, with the capture of the republican strongholds of Madrid and Barcelona in 1939. During the war, the functions of the weak republican government were usurped by a series of workers' committees, and then a Popular Front regime under Largo Caballero came to office in September 1936. In government territory terror reigned, at first the work of anarchists, and, after their suppression, of the communists, who, with Russia behind them, ruthlessly worked against their rival leftist parties in the regime. The rebels made Franco chief of staff in November 1936. In their territory terror also took its toll, as men of all sorts connected with the republic were killed. After the Franco triumph, the prisons were filled and the executioner was kept busy.

With all its fascist trappings, the Franco regime, the only fascist regime to survive World War II, still depended after the war upon the same classes that had supported the Spanish monarchy—the landowners, the army, and the Church. It was presumably opposed by the poor in city and country alike. But the fear of a new civil war, which lay heavily on all classes, prevented open opposition.

Eastern Europe

The triumph of the right in one form or another in eastern Europe is explained partly by the lack of a firm parliamentary tradition; partly by the failure to solve grievous economic problems, especially after the great worldwide depression of 1929; and partly by a popular fear of Bolshevism, sometimes quite out of proportion to any serious threat, but skillfully played upon by unscrupulous leaders. Perhaps as important as all the other factors put together was the initial impression created by the successes of Mussolini and Hitler. The way to get ahead in the world, at least after 1935, seemed to be to put on a uniform, proclaim a doctrine of extreme nationalism, and launch a war of nerves against your neighbors by loudly voicing your claims

A soldier in the Spanish Civil War, caught at the very moment of death by Pulitzer Prize winning photographer, Frank Capa (1936).

and by threatening to make them good by violence.

After the depression, the economic pressures exerted by Germany, whose industrial economy complemented the agrarian economy of these states, enabled her to dominate their foreign trade, especially in the Balkan area. To examine these factors, let us look at three case histories—Austria, Hungary, and Yugoslavia.

Austria

The Austria that was left at the end of World War I had an almost purely German population of about 8,000,000, about 2,000,000 of whom lived in the former imperial capital of Vienna. Long the great market for an enormous hinterland and the supplier of industrial finished goods to the agricultural provinces, Vienna was now cut off from its former territories by political boundaries and tariff walls. Between 1922 and 1925, Austrian finances were under direct League of Nations supervision; a League loan and reconstruction policies brought a measure of recovery. But what might have represented one road to economic salvation—union of Austria with Germany—though voted by the assembly of the new Austrian republic in March 1919, was forbidden on political grounds by the Allies in the Treaty of St. Germain (September 1919). These two problems, economic survival and union with Germany, were complicated by the continuation in even more violent form of the basic political struggle of imperial Austria: Social

Democrats against Christian Socialists. The Social Democrats were a gradual-reformist, but Marxist, party with strong urban support, especially in Vienna itself. The Christian Socialists were a conservative clerical party with a mass following in the countryside and among the urban lower middle classes, and counted many priests among their leaders.

In the mid-twenties, the two hostile parties, usually almost evenly balanced in the Parliament, organized private armies: the Christian Socialists, the Heimwehr (home guard), and the Social Democrats, the Schutzbund (defense league). The Social Democrats governed Vienna, introducing measures for relief and for workers' housing, paid for by taxes on the rich: a program the Christian Socialists opposed. After 1930, when a treaty was signed with Italy, Mussolini more or less overtly supported the Christian Socialists, who grew more and more fascistic in their outlook. The failure of Bruening's plan for a customs union with Germany and the related collapse of the Vienna Kredit-Anstalt bank increased tension in 1931, and in September 1931 the Heimwehr tried its first fascist coup, which failed. Efforts in 1932 to organize a Danubian economic cooperation scheme— an alternative to Austrian union with Germany, and favored by France—were rendered futile by Italian and German opposition. After Hitler came to power in early 1933, many Christian Socialists became openly Nazi.

The Christian Socialist chancellor, Engelbert

Dollfuss, however, strove to curb the Nazis. To this end he suspended parliamentary government in March 1933, and in effect ended parliamentary democracy. He forbade the wearing of uniforms by political groups and tried to expel Nazi agitators. In retaliation, Hitler made it prohibitively expensive for German tourists to visit Austria and thus destroyed one of the most lucrative sources of Austrian income. In the face of Nazi-inspired disorder, Dollfuss banned the Nazi party (June 1933). But, instead of burying the hatchet and uniting with the Social Democrats against Hitler, Dollfuss pursued them too. He banned all parties except his own "Fatherland Front," a union of all right-wing groups except the Nazis, and raided Social Democratic headquarters, precipitating a workers' riot. The government then bombarded with artillery the workers' new apartment houses, in which the Social Democratic leaders had taken refuge (February 1934), breaking the Social Democratic party, but alienating the workmen of Vienna, and uniting them in opposition to the regime. Dollfuss had to depend more and more upon Italy to support him against the threat from Hitler. He established himself as a fascist dictator (April 30, 1934), but the Nazis assassinated him in July. Only Italian troop concentrations on the frontier prevented Hitler from taking Austria.

Dollfuss' successor, Schuschnigg, was committed to the same policies. But Mussolini now needed Hitler's support for Italian aggression in the Mediterranean. Schuschnigg made plans looking toward a Hapsburg restoration, tried to concentrate armed power in his own hands rather than those of the Heimwehr, and strove to come to an understanding with France and her allies to replace the one with Italy. But he failed in the face of German aggression. In February and March 1938 Hitler increased the pressure on Schuschnigg, who was subjected to the first of the famous series of grim interviews between Hitler and statesmen of smaller countries. The Führer demanded and obtained privileges for the Nazis in Austria. When Nazi disorders broke out, Schuschnigg desperately tried to win working-class support, but it was too late.

When Schuschnigg announced that he intended to hold a plebiscite on the question of Austrian independence, Hitler marched in, installed a Nazi chancellor, put Schuschnigg in jail, and began the extension of the Nazi system to Austria. In April 1938 he held a plebiscite on the question of Austrian union with Germany and obtained a 99.75 percent yes vote. Mussolini had to bow in 1938 to what he had prevented in 1934, and Austria, increasingly fascist since 1930, became a mere province of Nazi Germany.

Hungary

On October 31, 1918, eleven days before the armistice, Count Michael Karolyi became prime minister of Hungary, after the country had already severed its ties with Austria. One of the richest of the great magnates,

Karolyi was also a democrat, and imbued with Wilsonian ideas. He proved his own sincerity as a social reformer by handing over the 50,000 acres of his own estate to be divided among the peasants, and by preparing a land-reform law. He made every effort to reach a compromise with the national minorities, but understandably enough they would no longer trust any Magyar. The French commander of the Allied armies did not assist Karolyi and demanded that the Hungarians withdraw from Slovakia. In March 1919 Karolyi resigned, in protest over the loss of Transylvania.

Thwarted nationalism now combined with a growing radicalism, stimulated by the news of Bolshevik activities in Russia brought by returning Hungarian prisoners of war. A left-wing government took over, more and more dominated by Bela Kun, Lenin's agent, a Hungarian-born Jew. He put through revolutionary nationalization decrees and installed a soviet political system by bloody-handed terrorist methods, especially in the countryside, where the peasants resented the delay in giving them the land. The Allies could not tolerate a Bolshevik regime in Hungary. The Romanians invaded and drove Kun out; during 1919 and part of 1920 they occupied the country, and stripped it of everything they could move. Meanwhile, under French protection, a counterrevolutionary government was formed, and returned to Budapest, where Admiral Horthy, a member of the gentry, became regent and chief of state (March 1, 1920). Hungary was now a kingdom without a king, Horthy an admiral without a fleet. Twice the Hapsburg king Charles tried to regain the throne, but was frustrated largely because Hungary's neighbors objected. The new counterrevolution gave free rein to a "White Terror" directed largely against the Jews but also against Magyar workers and peasants.

The Treaty of Trianon (June 1920) confirmed Hungary's losses: a small strip of land to Austria, Transylvania to Romania, Slovakia to Czechoslovakia, and Croatia and other Serb and Croat territories to Yugoslavia. Thereafter in Hungary the most important political issue for the ruling groups was "revisionism," the effort to revise the treaty and get these lands back. No tourist who visited Budapest could escape the huge statue of Hungary mourning the lost provinces, north, east, south, and west, or the great map laid out in flowerbeds in the public park showing in different-colored blossoms the far-flung territories relinquished but still claimed by the Magyars. The national motto was now "Nem, nem, soha" ("No, no, never").

The rank and file of Hungarians, however, who had never cared much about the nationalist questions that had agitated the upper classes, cared relatively little about revisionism. Hungary had no land reform; the great estates remained intact; and magnates and gentry retained their dominant position. Behind a thin screen of parliamentary government, an authoritarian dictatorship governed the country on behalf of the old ruling groups. It was helped by a swollen bureaucracy, and it became more and more fascist in character as the years went by.

For ten years (1921–1931), Count Bethlen as prime minister ran the country as if nothing had changed since 1914. The peasants were effectively disfranchised as they had always been; the Social Democrats were tolerated as a trade-union party; and the upper house of magnates was reestablished. The League of Nations helped economic recovery by a loan and a reconstruction plan (1923–1926), and in 1927 a treaty with Italy began an intimate relationship between Hungary and Mussolini. The depression and the financial crisis of 1931 drove Bethlen from office. His successor, the strongly nationalist and fascist-minded Gömbös, was pro-German as well as pro-Italian, and permitted the first Nazi-like organizations to form. Of these the Arrow Cross was the strongest, but it remained on the fringes of power almost until the end of World War II, largely because Hitler got what he wanted in Hungary without it.

After Gömbös died in 1936, his successors were all men of the same stripe. The Italians supplied arms to the Hungarians; Hitler favored their revisionism along with his own. After Austria had fallen to Hitler, he had Hungary in his pocket, and, when he broke up Czechoslovakia in March 1939, the Hungarians seized the extreme eastern portion, Ruthenia, and a small part of Slovakia. To pursue revisionism, the Hungarians had to follow Hitler, since he alone offered the opportunity to redraw the map as they felt it should be drawn. So, before war broke out, they had withdrawn from the League, and had enacted anti-Semitic laws in the Nazi pattern. But because Hitler needed Romania too, he would not give the Magyars all of Transylvania. Ironically enough, the price they paid for espousal of revisionism between the wars was the Soviet-dominated regime installed in Hungary after World War II.

Yugoslavia

In the new "Kingdom of the Serbs, Croats, and Slovenes," proclaimed in December 1918, there came together for the first time in one state the former south-Slav subjects of Austria and Hungary and those of the former independent Kingdom of Serbia. This was in most respects a satisfied state from the territorial point of view; revisionism therefore was not an issue. But, as the name of the new state shows, it faced the serious problem of creating a governmental system that would satisfy the aspirations of each of its nationality groups. Over this problem democracy broke down and a dictatorship was established. The dictatorship was not of the fascist type, although, as German power waxed, important politicians in the country became convinced that the future lay in Hitler's hands and responded accordingly. The rank and file of the population, by and large, were peasants deeply devoted to freedom, although unskilled in Western forms of parlia-

mentarianism. They opposed fascism, and, when they got the chance, ousted the politicians who sought to align them with it.

Serbian political ambitions had helped to start the war. The Serbs were more numerous than Croats and Slovenes together (approximately six million to three and a quarter million Croats and a few over one million Slovenes in 1931). Many Serbs felt that the new kingdom, which their Serbian king ruled from his Serbian capital of Belgrade, should be that "greater Serbia" of which they had so long dreamed. Orthodox in religion, using the Cyrillic alphabet, and having experienced and overthrown Ottoman domination, many Serbs tended to look upon the Croats as effete subjects of the Hapsburgs who were lucky to get the chance to live in the same state with them. Roman Catholic in religion, using the Latin alphabet, and having opposed Germans and Magyars for centuries, many Croats felt that the Serbs were crude Easterners who ought to give them a full measure of autonomy within the new state. Thus the issue was posed; Serb-sponsored centralism against Croat-sponsored federalism. The Slovenes, more conciliatory and less numerous, sometimes acted as a balance wheel to keep the political machinery moving. But the Serbs forced the acceptance of their answer to the constitutional question. This brought about dictatorship, alienated large numbers of Croats, bred extremism among them, and contributed greatly to the benefit of the country's enemies and to its own sufferings during the second war.

The Croats, under their peasant leader Radich, boycotted the constituent assembly of 1920, and the Serbs put through a constitution providing for a strongly centralized state. In the 1920s, both sides generally refused to compromise, although occasionally temporary understandings were reached. When a Serb deputy shot Radich dead on the floor of parliament in June 1928, a crisis arose that terminated only when King Alexander proclaimed a dictatorship in January 1929. Alexander made every effort to settle the problem by wiping out all vestiges of old provincial loyalties. There was to be no more Serbia or Croatia, but new artificially created administrative units named after the chief rivers that ran through them. The whole country was renamed Yugoslavia, as a sign that there were to be no more Serbs and Croats. But it was still a Serbian government, and the Croats could not be made to forget it. Elections were rigged by the government, and all political parties were dissolved. Croat leaders spent much time in jails, which, like most Balkan jails, were highly uncomfortable. This dictatorship of King Alexander passed no racial laws, elevated no one political party to exclusive power, and had no colored shirts, special songs, or other fascist paraphernalia. But it was unmistakably authoritarian and antidemocratic.

One result was the strengthening of Croat extremists, who had wanted an independent Croatia in the days of the Hapsburgs and who now combined this program with terrorism, supported from abroad by the

The assassination of King Alexander I of Yugoslavia at Marseilles, October 9, 1934.

enemies of Yugoslavia—Italy and Hungary. The Croat extremists were called *Ustashi* (rebels), and their leader, Ante Pavelich, was subsidized by Mussolini. He was deeply involved in the assassination of Alexander at Marseilles in October 1934. Under the regency of Prince Paul (Alexander's cousin), the dictatorship continued. As German economic power in the Balkans grew, leading politicians grew enamored of Germany, and some efforts were made to bring Yugoslav policies into line with those of the Axis. But these policies met with such unconcealed popular opposition that they were never pursued very far. In the summer of 1939, on the very eve of war in Europe, an agreement was finally reached with the Croats that established an autonomous Croatia. But by then it was too late, since the Croats were not satisfied with the boundaries of their new province.

Though the Yugoslavs in 1941 bravely resisted German invasion, they did not have the military power to hold Hitler's armies back. When the conquering Germans and Italians split the country up, they turned Croatia over to the extremist Croat Pavelich, head of the Ustashi, who carried out horrifying massacres of Serbs and Jews. The innocent men, women, and children suffering death and torture at the hands of Pavelich's forces owed some of their anguish to the short-sightedness of Serbian politicians who had failed to solve the problem of Croat autonomy within a peaceful Yugoslavia and who had thus stimulated the extremists.

Other Authoritarian Regimes

The case histories we have been considering are unique in detail, yet they furnish interesting parallels to developments elsewhere in eastern Europe. Thus in Poland, Pilsudski led a military coup against the democratic government in 1926 and exercised a military dictatorship that became ever more authoritarian especially after the depression. This coup was made possible largely because of the government's failure to grant concessions to Lithuanians and other national minorities and to deal with the economic problems left by the years of war and occupation. Tension was heightened when Germany denounced a trade treaty and precipitated a crisis in the Polish coal industry. The violent hatreds that divided the political parties made it even easier. Once he had won power, Pilsudski turned to the great landowners and big industrialists and built his government on their support and on that of his military clique.

In Romania, it was the deep entrenchment of corruption in political life that initially jeopardized the parliamentary system, as the party in power usually rigged elections without shame. In addition, there was widespread anti-Semitism, which was adopted as the chief program of the "Iron Guard," a Romanian Nazi party. Greenshirted and wearing bags of Romanian soil around their necks, the Guard began a program of assassinating moderate politicians early in the 1930s. Economic dislocation and peasant misery brought about by the worldwide agricultural depression strengthened the Guard and other fascist groups. To head off a Guardist coup, King Carol of Romania installed his own fascist dictatorship in 1938. Although the Guardist leaders were "shot while trying to escape," Romania could not avoid German pressure. After Hitler had acceded to Russian seizure of Bessarabia and Northern Bukovina and had given Hungary northern Transylvania (August 1940), Carol had to leave the country, and Hitler's man, Marshal Antonescu, took over with Iron Guard support.

In Bulgaria, always a strongly pro-Russian country, the genuine threat of communism was a serious problem. Moreover, Bulgaria, like Hungary, was revisionist because of her failure to gain the Macedonian territory given by the peace treaties to Yugoslavia and Greece. The issue was exacerbated by the presence in the country of thousands of Macedonian refugees, who tended to join revolutionary terrorist societies. Bulgaria, an egalitarian country with no minorities problem, no rich landowners, no aristocracy, and no great industries, none the less produced political hostilities even more violent than those in countries where economic inequality prevailed. Unparalleled ferocity has marked its political life. In the early twenties, a peasant politician, Stambolisky, gave the country a period (1920–1923) of reasonably popular government. But even he curbed the press as he fought both Macedonian terrorists and communists. His imposition of high income taxes alienated the bourgeoisie, and his conciliatory policies toward Yugoslavia infuriated the army. In 1923, right-wingers murdered him and installed a strongly authoritarian regime. From then on, communist plots and bomb outrages and Macedonian terrorist strife racked the country. After 1930, the Italian marriage of King Boris led to a rapprochement with Mussolini. In 1934, a military coup brought a group of army officers to power; they dissolved the political parties and tried their hands at a dictatorship of their own. But this development was successfully countered in 1936 by King Boris himself, who, like Alexander of Yugoslavia and Carol of Romania, imposed a royal dictatorship, which lasted from then until his mysterious death during World War II.

In Greece between the wars, the main issues were whether the country should be a monarchy or a republic and how to overcome the economic difficulties consequent on the transfer of 1,250,000 Greeks from Turkey. On the constitutional question, the population wavered, voting for a monarchy in 1920, for a republic in 1924, and for a monarchy again in 1935, always by enormous majorities. Economic dislocation brought strength to communism among the refugees and in labor groups. The political exuberance for which Greece is celebrated made the regular conduct of parliamentary government impossible. The interwar period was punctuated by a whole series of coups by generals, some republican, some monarchist, all more or less authoritarian, but most of them ineffective and none especially bloodthirsty. The last of these was the most fascist, General John Metaxas, who became dictator in August 1936. Metaxas abolished political parties, instituted censorship and political persecution of his opponents, launched a program of public works, and imitated the Nazis in other ways. But when the Italian invasion came from Albania in October 1940, Metaxas ordered resistance, which was the beginning of Greece's heroic showing in World War II.

Fascism in Review

None of these regimes in eastern Europe was fascist in the full sense of the term. In Italy and Germany the regimes rested, at least initially, upon the popular support of a substantial proportion of the people, even though that support was kept alive by the technique of artificial stimulation. In eastern Europe, on the other hand, the dictatorships rested on the police, the bureaucracy, and the army, and not on the support of the peasant masses. To an eastern European politician of almost any complexion, an election was an occasion for bribery, intimidation, and making promises that he had no intention of trying to fulfill. The hope placed by some Western liberals in peasant parties proved in the end illusory.

Thus the growth of antidemocratic governments of the right in Europe during the period between the wars strikingly reveals the difficulties in the way of moderate parliamentary regimes in countries without parliamentary traditions. This does not mean that the Western liberal tradition cannot be exported. But a liberal constitution on paper and a liberal franchise are in themselves no guarantee that a regime on Western models can be stabilized. The postwar economic agony had scarcely disappeared before the depression of the late twenties and early thirties struck. Under these circumstances, men turned to extremists of the left and right. But the fear of communism, combined with the seductive nationalist propaganda of the right, brought about fascist victories in Italy and Germany. Musso-lini's and Hitler's successes helped to tip the scale: the triumph of the right elsewhere was assured, and a new world war proved inevitable.

Reading Suggestions on the Rise of Fascism

The Roots of Fascism

A. Cobban, *Dictatorship: Its History and Theory* (Scribner's, 1939). Highly suggestive survey, reaching well back into history.

P. Viereck, *Metapolitics: From the Romantics to Hitler* (*Capricorn). A survey of the background in German political thought.

George Mosse, *The Crisis of German Ideology: Intellectual Origins of the Third Reich* (*Universal Library Grosset and Dunlap), and Fritz Stern, *The Politics of Cultural Despair* (*Anchor). Contrasting yet solid studies of Hitler's forerunners.

C. J. Hayes, *A Generation of Materialism, 1871–1900* (Harper, 1941). Contains a concise and corrosive section on the seedtime of fascism.

H. Rogger and E. Webber, eds., *The European Right: A Historical Profile* (*University of California Press). A learned and stimulating collection of essays on right-wing movements in the various countries of Europe. Good bibliographies.

Note: The titles listed above present differing views on the origins of fascism, a subject still much debated by historians. Further titles bearing on the subject may be found in the reading suggestions for the chapter "The Intellectual Revolution."

Italy

G. Magaro, *Mussolini in the Making* (Houghton Mifflin, 1938). An unequaled study of Mussolini's early career.

H. Finer, *Mussolini's Italy* (*Universal), and H. A. Steiner, *Government in Fascist Italy* (McGraw-Hill, 1938). Two very solid studies by expert political scientists.

G. A. Borgese, *Goliath: The March of Fascism* (Viking, 1938), and G. Salvemini, *Under the Axe of Fascism* (Viking, 1936). Lively works by important antifascist Italians.

G. Salvemini, *Prelude to World War II* (Doubleday, 1954). A survey of Mussolini's foreign policy, by one of his most implacable enemies.

Germany

A. Hitler, *Mein Kampf* (*Sentry). A complete English translation of the Nazi bible, the basic work to be read for an understanding of the movement.

A. Hitler, *My New Order,* ed. R. de Sales (Reynal and Hitchcock, 1941). Speeches after the Führer's coming to power.

A. L. C. Bullock, *Hitler: A Study in Tyranny* (*Torchbooks). The best biography.

S. W. Halperin, *Germany Tried Democracy* (*Norton). A reliable history of the Weimar Republic, 1918–1933.

R. G. L. Waite, *Vanguard of Nazism* (Harvard Univ. Press, 1952). A good study of the "Free Corps" movement.

J. W. Wheeler-Bennett, *Wooden Titan* (Morrow, 1936) and *Nemesis of Power* (St. Martin's Press, 1954). Two first-rate studies, the first dealing with Hindenburg, the second with the role of the German army in politics from 1918 to 1945.

K. D. Bracher, *The German Dictatorship* (Praeger, 1970). Excellent comprehensive study by a German scholar.

F. L. Neumann, *Behemoth: The Structure and Practice of National Socialism* (*Torchbooks). A good analytical description.

F. von Papen, *Memoirs* (Dutton, 1953). An apologetic autobiography by the right-wing politician.

Albert Speer, *Inside the Third Reich: Memoirs,* trans. Richard and Clara Winston (Macmillan, 1970). Memoirs of Hitler's own city planner and architect: an invaluable picture of life among the Nazis.

E. Wiskemann, *The Rome-Berlin Axis* (Oxford Univ. Press, 1949). A study of the formation and history of the Hitler-Mussolini partnership.

R. Fischer, *Stalin and German Communism* (Harvard Univ. Press, 1948). A study of the role played by the communist movement in the history of Germany between the wars.

Note: Some of the titles listed under the reading suggestions for the chapter that follows deal with international relations during the interwar period and will illuminate Nazi foreign policy.

Other Countries

G. Brenan, *The Spanish Labyrinth* (Macmillan, 1943). A useful study of the Spanish Civil War against its historical and economic background.

S. G. Payne, *Falange* (Stanford, 1961). Good study of the Falangist movement.

C. Bowers, *My Mission to Spain* (Simon & Schuster, 1954); C. J. Hayes, *Wartime Mission to Spain, 1942–1945* (Macmillan, 1945); and Lord Templewood (Sir Samuel Hoare), *Complacent Dictator* (Knopf, 1947). Three differing views of Franco and the Spanish problem, by three ambassadors, the first two American, the last British.

Hugh Thomas, *The Spanish Civil War* (*Colophon). The best single work on the subject.

G. E. R. Gedye, *Betrayal in Central Europe* (Harper, 1939). A careful journalist's account of Austria and Czechoslovakia.

H. Seton-Watson, *Eastern Europe between the Wars, 1918–1941* (*Torchbooks). A useful account dealing with all the eastern European countries except Greece and Albania.

R. L. Buell, *Poland: Key to Europe* (Knopf, 1939). A helpful survey.

R. West, *Black Lamb and Grey Falcon* (Viking, 1941). A highly subjective account of Yugoslavia, loaded with political bias, but fascinating and informative reading.

Historical Fiction

I. Silone, *Bread and Wine* (*Penguin, *New American Library) and *Fontamara* (Smith and Haas, 1934). Two good novels on rural Italy under fascism; by a distinguished antifascist writer.

C. Levi, *Christ Stopped at Eboli* (Farrar, Straus, 1947; *Universal Library). An antifascist Italian doctor and painter writes movingly of his exile in a remote and poverty-stricken southern Italian village.

V   The Failure of Parliamentarianism in Spain and Eastern Europe, 1918–1939

H. Fallada, *Little Man What Now?* (Simon & Schuster, 1933; *Ungar), and E. Remarque, *Three Comrades* (Little, Brown, 1937; *Popular Library). Two touching novels of depression-ridden Germany.

E. von Salomon, *"Der Fragebogen"* (*The Questionnaire*) (Doubleday, 1955). One of the plotters against Rathenau, a strong sympathizer with authoritarian movements, tells his life story satirically, against the background of American military government in post-1945 Germany.

E. Hemingway, *For Whom the Bell Tolls* (Scribner's, 1940). A characteristic Hemingway novel, set in the Spain of the Civil War.

The Democracies
and the Non-Western World
Domestic and Imperial Problems, 1919–1939

I Introduction:
A World Unsafe for Democracy

The central fact—and irony—of politics between the two world wars is that the war "to make the world safe for democracy" seemed to make it a very difficult and very dangerous place for democracy. Idealists like President Wilson had expected that the collapse of the old Romanov, Hapsburg, and Hohenzollern empires would automatically ensure an increase in the number of democratic states. But instead, much of Europe came under regimes that were hostile to liberal democracy. Even Italy, which had appeared to be evolving toward a democratic constitutional monarchy, turned fascist. In the 1920s and 1930s the core of democracy remained in the great North Atlantic powers—Britain, France, and the United States—and in the smaller states of Scandinavia, the Low Countries, and Switzerland.

And this core of democratic states faced a world of nations at the opposite ends of the political spectrum. In the 1920s their efforts to bring the world back to peaceful habits seemed to hold real promise for the future. But in the 1930s the great depression, the entrenched position of the communists in Russia and their mounting strength elsewhere, the advent of Hitler, and the aggressions of fascist states in the West and of an expansionist Japan in the Far East rapidly darkened the international scene. With the outbreak of another general war in 1939, it was clear that the two preceding decades had been at best a twenty years' truce, a truce broken with increasing frequency by international troublemakers.

Certainly the totalitarian aggressors bore the major responsibility for the unleashing of a second world war. Yet a far from minor factor in the deterioration of the twenty years' truce was the failure of the peaceful democracies to present a unified front against those who threatened world peace. In the 1920s Britain, France,

and the United States became preoccupied with their own domestic problems. In the early 1930s their preoccupation increased as a result of the urgent crisis of the depression. But this was the very time when international problems demanded equally urgent attention. International trade was steadily shrinking in the face of the great depression and of mounting tariff barriers; the prospects for peace were steadily fading before the saber-rattling and actual saber-wielding of the enemies of democracy. Faced with two sets of problems, the democracies turned first to the domestic ones, only to discover that the international situation was rapidly moving toward war.

Nor was this all. During the twenty years' truce the democracies faced a third set of problems, not as yet so urgent as the other two, but of very great potential importance. This third set involved imperial issues—the relationship between the great democracies and the non-Western peoples, many of whom were still under colonial rule or some other form of control by democratic mother countries. Particularly in Asia and the Middle East, the non-Western peoples were beginning to assert their nationalism and to demand the loosening of old imperial ties. This formidable political movement did not reach full intensity until the years following World War II, when a long procession of former colonies, protectorates, and mandates began to join the ranks of independent states. But the nationalist movements that were to bring these newcomers into the family of nations after 1945 grew steadily in the 1920s and 1930s.

The three sets of problems—domestic, foreign, and imperial—faced by the democracies during the twenty years' truce were interconnected and interrelated in countless ways. We shall underline some of these interrelations, as we have shown the links between the internal and external policies of the communist and fascist states. But, in order to point up the main issues, we shall also separate national, international, and colonial problems in a way that must oversimplify the complexities of real life. The present chapter emphasizes first the chief domestic problems of the democracies in the interwar years and then considers the growing conflict between their colonialism and the nationalism of the non-Western world. The following chapter examines their foreign policies, as distinguished from their imperial policies. We begin here with an examination of the crisis confronting Britain on the home front after November 1918.

II Great Britain
The Postwar Economic Crisis

Save for trifling losses from German Zeppelin raids and coastal bombardments, the British Isles suffered no direct material damage in World War I. But the British armed forces lost about seven hundred and fifty thousand men killed in action, and about a million and a half wounded. The casualties of the empire and the commonwealth as a whole came to nearly a million killed and over two million wounded.

In addition to these irreplaceable human losses, the economic losses of the mother country were also grave—the almost incalculable difference between the actual cost of destructive war and what might otherwise have been productive effort. The national debt after the war was ten times that of 1914. Many British investments abroad, returns on which had been a major factor in Victorian prosperity, had had to be liquidated to get purchasing power for food and war materials. Forty percent of the great British merchant fleet, the income from which had helped to balance Britain's international accounts and pay for her imports, had been destroyed by enemy action. The whole fabric of international trade on which Britain depended was torn in a thousand places in 1918 and could not be rapidly restored in the unsettled conditions that prevailed in the postwar world. And, finally, to supplement the war production of Britain and France, the industrial plants of the United States, of Canada, and even of India had been called on, and had received a stimulus that made them in peacetime more effective competitors of the British. In the 1920s, the industrial plant of the Germans, nourished in part by loans from America, once more took up the rivalry that had so alarmed the British before the war.

In short, victorious Britain faced in an aggravated form the basic economic difficulty analyzed in an earlier chapter. The country that had been in Victorian days the "workshop of the world" had now lost its head start and could no longer give full employment to its millions of workers. Those workers were in no mood to accept a lower standard of living, for they had made great gains in social security before the war and they had fought the war in the hope of still better things to come. They had been promised that the defeated enemy would through reparations pay the costs of the war and thereby give Britain a new start.

This hope was very early disappointed. No substantial reparations came through; the return to peace caused a sudden boom in production to meet the postwar demand for goods, accompanied by a sharp rise in prices, and quickly followed by the collapse of the boom, leaving Britain in a severe postwar depression. By the summer of 1921 there were over two million people out of work, more than one-fifth of the labor force. In that same year the British government, faced with the rising cost of living, increased the very meager unemployment payments. These payments, soon given the derogatory name of the dole, were strictly speaking not old-fashioned poor relief, but payments on unemployment insurance policies that had been part of Lloyd George's social legislation of prewar days. However, large-scale unemployment continued—it did not drop below one million until World War II—and some young workers never acquired employment status. Unemployment insurance could not be maintained on a sound actuarial basis, and the payments became in fact a form of poor relief.

While the Great Britain of the 1920s experienced no equivalent of the "Coolidge prosperity" that the United States was to enjoy, we must not exaggerate: The British economic decline was not catastrophic. London, Manchester, and Liverpool did not become ghost cities, though some of the gravely depressed areas, like the coal-mining regions of South Wales, did begin to show real signs of permanent decay. What happened was rather a relative decline, the slowing down of an economy geared to dynamic growth, with a working population conditioned psychologically to a gradually rising standard of living and a middle class similarly conditioned to traditional comforts. Moreover, this was the twentieth century, the century of the tabloid newspaper (first developed in Britain), the movie, and the radio. The British were well aware, for instance, that Americans enjoyed automobiles, radios, electric refrigerators, and a lot else that they also wanted to enjoy.

Britain was suffering from ills characteristic of economic old age, well illustrated in the coal industry. There was still a lot of coal in Britain; but much of it was costly to mine, since the most easily and cheaply worked seams were being exhausted. The industry was badly organized, with many small and inefficient mines running at a loss, and with machinery and methods that were antiquated in comparison with American and the best continental standards. Productivity per man-hour over the whole industry was low. Worst of all, perhaps, the 1920s saw the rapid rise all over the industrialized world of major competitors of coal—oil, and electricity based on water power—and the consequent decline of British coal exports. Since the British Isles had no petroleum (the discovery of the oil fields under the North Sea lay in the future), and no very great potential in hydroelectric power, coal, the historic basis of British industrial power, simply had to be mined.

The workers were unionized and were in no mood to accept cuts in wages; the owners did not want to run their businesses at a loss. A strike in March 1921, after the government had rejected Labour party proposals for making permanent the wartime nationalization of the industry, focused national attention on this critical problem. The strike was settled in July, but only by the government's consenting to pay subsidies to cover increased wages.

The Conservative and Labour Programs

Against the background of economic depression, British domestic politics during the twenty years' truce displayed a fairly clear class basis. The Conservatives, still often called Tories, tended to get the support of aristocrats and of middle-class people who wanted to attack new problems with traditional methods and with a minimum of government intervention. The Labour party tended to get the support of trade unionists and of intellectuals from all classes who demanded that the government intervene more vigorously in the economic field. While not every worker or reformer necessarily voted Labour nor every stand-patter Tory, economic issues did sharpen the differences between the two major British parties.

The first casualty in the struggle between Labour and the Conservatives was the old Liberal party, which was ground to a mere husk between the two contending groups. The Conservatives, who had won the lion's share of seats in the "khaki election" of 1918, held immediately after the armistice, decided in 1922 to withdraw their support from the coalition government headed by the immensely popular Liberal Lloyd George. In the ensuing elections the Conservatives won, and the Liberals lost heavily, split as they were between the followers of Lloyd George and those of the more cautious and less theatrical Asquith. Labour won 142 seats—more than the Liberals did—and became for the first time His Majesty's Opposition.

Both Conservatives and Labour realized the underlying difficulties of Britain's position. Both were fully aware that twentieth-century Britain had to sell enough goods and services abroad—enough manufactured goods and shipping, insurance, banking, and tourist services—so that the income from them would buy food for her people and much of the raw materials for her factories. But the parties were not agreed on how to achieve this necessary task. Broadly speaking, the Conservatives wanted to retain private industry, with government and other technical experts helping to make it efficient. But they were thwarted by high tariffs in the United States and elsewhere, by the drive to economic self-sufficiency all over the world, and by the difficulties of trade with communist Russia.

The state of world trade drove the Conservatives more and more to the solution the maverick Liberal Joseph Chamberlain had advocated at the turn of the century—protective tariffs against competing foreign goods, and the knitting of the empire and commonwealth, with their vast variety of resources, into a largely self-sufficient trade area by "imperial preference" agreements. Such agreements would give raw materials from the colonies and dominions preferred treatment in the British market in return for preferred treatment of British manufactures in the colonial and dominion markets. In theory, at least, the scheme could have worked, for the commonwealth and empire of the nineteen-twenties—one-quarter of the world's land and people—had the requisite natural resources and offered a potential market capable of supporting the British Isles in the style to which they were accustomed. In practice the great snag was the evident unwillingness of the constituent parts of the empire and commonwealth to accept for themselves the role of producers of raw materials in exchange for British manufactured goods and British services. The self-governing dominions, loyal though they had been during the war, were in no mood to assume a role essentially like that of colonies in the old mercantilistic days. They were looking toward independent nationhood, and they wanted what seemed to go with nationhood in the modern world—their own industries. This was also true of what was potentially the richest unit of the empire, India.

The Labour solution was nationalization—that is, government purchase and operation of key industries with just compensation to their private owners, rather than seizure without compensation as in Soviet Russia. The key industries were transportation, utilities, coal, steel, perhaps even textiles, cutlery, pottery, machine tools—all the industries that seem to thrive best on large-scale organization. A good many Labourites wanted nationalization simply because, as socialists, they believed that profits, rent, and interest paid to private owners were forms of "capitalist" exploitation of the workers, which would cease under nationalization. But many of their leaders knew that even nationalized industries would still face the fundamental problem of selling enough goods abroad to keep the economy going. They argued, therefore, that nationalization would enable British industries to produce more cheaply and efficiently. It would do away with wasteful competition and with the inefficient firms so conspicuous in the coal industry, for instance. It would, they romantically believed, force into productive work both unnecessary managerial and selling staffs, and stockholders and other investors who lived without working.

Moreover, Labour supporters believed that, once nationalization had been achieved, the British workmen would take a new attitude toward their work. Knowing that they were now the *real* owners of their own industries, they would put their hearts into their work, abstain from featherbedding, absenteeism, and other costly and unproductive practices, and raise output to a point where the goods of Britain could undersell those of her capitalist rivals in world markets. This belief was reinforced by the somewhat paradoxical faith in free trade that the Labour party had inherited from the Liberals, and by its high hopes for improving international relations. Consequently, Labour was hostile to the Conservative policies of protective tariffs and imperial preference.

Politics between the Wars

During the twenty years' truce, neither the Conservatives nor the Labourites were able to carry out their full platforms. The Conservatives, by no means unanimous on the degree of economic self-sufficiency they wanted for the empire, were decisively held up by the refusal of the commonwealth countries to go much further than to accept certain limited imperial preferences. Labour itself came to power for two brief spans—with Ramsay MacDonald, an intellectual and not a worker, as prime minister—for ten months in 1924 and again from 1929 to 1931. In both instances, while Labour won more seats in the Commons than did any other party it did not have an absolute majority. The Labour governments, obliged to rely on the Liberals for parliamentary support, were too shaky to introduce measures as controversial as the nationalization of any industry.

Despite the wider cleavage between the two parties, British politics still retained many of the amenities of Victorian parliamentary life. The House of Commons, even though it now included workingmen and others who by no means spoke with an upperclass Oxford accent, was still one of the best clubs in the world. For a few weeks in 1926 some two and a half million trade-union members attempted a general strike in support of the coal miners, who were striking in protest against a cut in their wages. The general strike failed, but during its brief course fundamental British attitudes were revealed. Thousands of men from the middle and upper classes volunteered to keep essential services operating, and in Plymouth a soccer team of strikers played a team of police. Britain, despite mounting tensions, remained a land of general law-abidingness, where the class struggle that the Marxists talked so much about seemed to have come thoroughly under the control of the parliamentary decencies.

Meantime, two of the last steps were taken toward the political democratization of Britain that had begun in 1832. In 1918, in preparation for the "khaki election," the government had put through a reform bill that eliminated all the old exceptions to universal male suffrage and gave the vote to all men over twenty-one. Culminating a long and spectacular campaign in which suffragettes had demonstrated, marched, orated, and even chained themselves to lampposts, destroyed property, and gone to jail in behalf of women's rights, the bill also gave the vote to women. But, with almost a caricature of British caution, it set the voting age for women at thirty years, thus ensuring that there would always be more male than female voters. The distinction was too irrational to stand up, especially after

experience had demonstrated—as it also did in the United States—that women divide politically about the way men do. In 1928, a measure known as the "bill for flapper suffrage" gave women the vote at twenty-one.

Although the dole, depressed industries, and other signs of economic ill health persisted, Britain did experience a measure of recovery in the late 1920s. But then the great depression, the signal for which was given by the New York stock-market crash in October 1929, began its spread around the world. Britain, already weakened, was one of the first to be engulfed; in eighteen months the number of unemployed jumped from a little over one million to two and a half million. Faced by a serious government deficit and unwilling to try to meet it by cutting the dole and other social services, the second Labour government of Ramsay MacDonald resigned in August 1931.

It gave way to a coalition of Conservatives, Liberals, and right-wing Labourites headed by the same MacDonald. Many Labourites, both in the leadership and in the rank and file, were dismayed by what seemed to them MacDonald's traitorous surrender to the forces of capitalism, and the deep split within the party crippled its effectiveness throughout the 1930s. The "national government," as the coalition cabinet was called, put through reductions in the dole and the social services. Late in 1931, it took the decisive step, a hard one in view of Britain's traditional financial leadership and devotion to the gold standard, of going off the gold standard and letting the pound fall in value. In 1932, it made the first move away from free trade by enacting protective tariffs, and in the same year Britain ceased payment on her war debts to the United States, except for a few token payments. These measures did little to help the unemployed or to get at the roots of British economic troubles. Nevertheless, because of Labour's disarray, two general elections, in October 1931 and in 1935, returned a majority supporting the national government.

The coalition government was in fact dominated by Conservatives, and after the 1935 election the Conservative leader, Stanley Baldwin, took over the post of prime minister. Gradually the British economy pulled out of the worst of the depression, although—some economic theorists might say *because*—Baldwin did nothing beyond keeping the budget in balance. By 1936, however, Mussolini's and Hitler's aggressions were beginning to demand British attention. The economic question and the social question, by no means solved, faded before the threat of another war.

For a few months in 1936 the great issue confronting Baldwin's cabinet appeared to be not social or diplomatic but constitutional, as the cabinet forced the abdication of King Edward VIII in the year of his accession to the throne. Edward had had a long and successful career as prince of Wales, appearing indefatigably and effectively in public all over the world. He fell in love with an American divorcee, Mrs. Wallis

Warfield Simpson, and wanted to marry her. His own family, the cabinet, and most of the British people opposed him, and he abdicated (with the title of duke of Windsor), allowing his brother to become King George VI. Some of the opposition to Edward's marriage stemmed from dislike for America, but much more of it came from a strong feeling against having a divorcee on the throne and a vaguer feeling that Mrs. Simpson's background as a member of what was then called "café society" disqualified her for ceremonial functions. The episode—for it deserves no stronger name—attracted worldwide attention at the time but left little mark on British history.

The Irish Question

The years between the wars were of great importance for Ireland. Although the outbreak of war in 1914 put off the threatened revolt against home rule in Protestant Ulster, the Irish were hardly reliable partners in the war. In 1916, the faction furthest removed from the Ulster rebels, the Irish nationalists, got some German help in guns and ammunition and staged an armed rising in Dublin. The British put down this "Easter rebellion," but not before they had created a fresh and effective set of Irish political martyrs. The British government did not dare extend conscription to Ireland until April 1918, and the attempt made then led the Irish nationalists to boycott the British Parliament and to cease attending its sessions.

By 1919, home rule as decreed in 1914 was not enough for the nationalists of Ireland. The home rulers of prewar days had yielded to more extreme rebels, the Sinn Fein (meaning, in Gaelic, "ourselves alone"), who wanted complete independence. The years 1919–1921 were filled with violence, ambushes, arson, and guerrilla warfare, as the Irish, who now had their own illegal parliament, the Dail Eireann, moved into full revolution. The British, tired from four years of world war, were not in a state of mind to use force effectively; the Irish, on the other hand, were admirably organized and full of fight.

Yet the immediate upshot of the violent phase of the revolution was a compromise, for the Sinn Fein split in two. A moderate wing, led by Arthur Griffith and Michael Collins, was willing to accept a compromise in which Protestant Ulster would remain under direct British rule and the Catholic counties would be given dominion status. A radical wing, led by Eamon De Valera—exceedingly Irish in spite of his Spanish surname—insisted that the whole island achieve complete independence as a unified republic.

The moderates negotiated with the British, and in 1921 obtained for the twenty-six counties of southern Ireland dominion status under the name of the Irish Free State. The Free State had its own parliament, the Dail, and was completely self-governing with its own army and its own diplomatic services; it merely accepted the British crown as symbolic head. The six Protestant counties of Ulster maintained their old relationship with Britain, including the right to send members to the Parliament at Westminster, but they also acquired their own parliament at Belfast and considerable local autonomy. Henceforth Britain was officially styled the United Kingdom of Great Britain and Northern Ireland.

This settlement was unacceptable to De Valera and the more extreme revolutionaries, and the Irish revolution now became a civil war between partisans of the Free State and partisans of a republic, with the old round of burning, ambush, and murder. But the Irish, too, were beginning to tire of violence. When the moderate leader Michael Collins, a man much closer to earth than De Valera, was assassinated by a republican, public opinion turned away from the extremists. Meantime the Free State was gradually settling down. De Valera, after refusing to sit in the Dail because he would have had to take an oath of loyalty to the king, changed his mind and decided to bring his fellow republicans into the national parliament in 1927.

From then on, almost in the manner of illogical and compromise-loving England, the Irish Free State gradually and peacefully got what the extremists had been killing and burning to obtain. De Valera's party won a plurality in the Dail in 1932, and a majority in 1933; thereupon it proceeded to abolish the oath of loyalty to the crown and to cut most of the slender threads that still tied the Free State to England. In 1939, Catholic Ireland was so free from British domination that she could declare and maintain her neutrality throughout World War II. In 1949, the final step was taken when Britain recognized her as the fully independent Republic of Eire (Gaelic for "Ireland").

The Commonwealth

No such secession took place elsewhere among the British possessions in the years between the two world wars. On the contrary, definite constitutional recognition of the essential independence of the dominions seemed to make them more loyal, though at the cost of any central British authority over their economic policies, and, at least in law, over their foreign policies. The capstone of a long process that had begun with the Durham Report nearly a century before was the Statute of Westminster of 1931. This spelled out the new relations between the dominions and the mother country that had been negotiated in an imperial conference five years earlier. The preparatory report of 1926 anticipated the gist of the Statute of Westminster by declaring that Britain and the dominions

are autonomous communities within the British Empire, equal in status, in no way subordinate one to another in any aspect of their domestic or external affairs, though united by a common allegiance to the crown and freely associated as members of the British Commonwealth of Nations.

That phrase "freely associated" meant also "able freely to choose to be dis-associated." In other words, the right of a state to secede (which Americans fought a great civil war to decide was not a part of the United States Constitution) became a part of the constitution of the commonwealth. And the twenty-six counties of Southern Ireland in effect took advantage of this right to set up their republic quite outside the commonwealth. South Africa dis-associated itself in 1961 and became an independent republic, and in 1965 the Rhodesian government made a unilateral declaration of independence.

The new status acquired by the dominions in 1931 was symbolized by a change in terminology. Henceforward they were no longer to be considered parts of the British Empire but free members of the British Commonwealth of Nations (a title abbreviated to plain Commonwealth after World War II in deference to the many new non-Western members, who did not have the emotional ties binding some of the dominions to the Crown). In this new relationship, Britain would have to negotiate with Canada or Australia about tariffs, trade conditions, immigration, and the like, just as if they were foreign countries. Although Britain was unable to build a self-sufficient economic unity out of her dominions, still in 1939, as in 1914, the dominions all came into the war on Britain's side. They made this decision even though they had the legal right to follow the example of Ireland and remain neutral.

III France
The Impact of the War

In France, both World War I and the postwar difficulties caused even more serious dislocation than they did in Britain. In the war itself, France lost proportionately more in human lives and in material damage than did any other major belligerent. Two million Frenchmen in the prime of life were either killed or so seriously mutilated as to be incapable of normal living. In a land of only thirty-nine million, and with an already low birth rate, it is likely that this human loss impaired the French potentiality for achievement in all phases of civilization. Many of the men who would have been statesmen, industrialists, scientists, and artists in the 1930s were killed off in 1914–1918. Three hundred thousand houses and twenty thousand factories or shops were destroyed. In a land of conservative economic organization, where work was done slowly and for the most part without large-scale automatic machinery, this material setback would be long felt. Psychologically, the feeling of victory by no means compensated for the traumatic losses of the four years of struggle.

France set as her goal the laming of her recent enemy, Germany, in every possible way. She tried to extract reparations to the last possible sum, undeterred by the arguments of economic theorists that Germany could not pay. But she insisted even more on keeping Germany down, isolated in international relations, and without the physical means of fighting. In a pinch, most Frenchmen would probably have been willing to forego reparations in order to deprive Germany of the economic plant necessary for modern war. They would have preferred this to collecting reparations from a rich and productive Germany.

In the postwar years, French statesmen attempted to follow both policies simultaneously and of course failed. The culmination came in January 1923, under the premiership of the conservative Raymond Poincaré, when French and Belgian troops occupied the great German industrial region of the Ruhr in an effort to make Germany pay full reparations. The Germans replied by passive resistance, as we have already seen. The occupation of the Ruhr brought France no gains, only the censure of international opinion. The elections of 1924 resulted in a victory for the Cartel des Gauches, a coalition of mildly left-wing parties headed by the Radical Socialists. The French withdrew their last troops from the Ruhr in 1925.

Meanwhile, France was experiencing an inflation that resulted in part from the cost of rebuilding the devastated areas—a cost that drained government finances and that was only partly covered by German payments. It resulted also from the high cost of maintaining armed forces (for the French dared not disarm), from the general disorder of international trade, and from the staggering debts piled up during the war by the French government, which, like the imperial German government, had preferred loans to taxes. By the mid-1920s, the franc had slipped from its prewar value of 20 cents to a dangerous low of about 2 cents. In the crisis, Poincaré was recalled to power to "save the franc." In 1926, he initiated new taxes and stern measures of economy which, together with the gradual restoration of normal international trade after the French withdrawal from the Ruhr, stemmed the decline of the franc. In 1928, it was officially revalued at 3.92 cents.

The French inflation, though mild compared with the German, nevertheless caused economic and social dislocation. Frenchmen who had lent their government francs worth 20 cents now found themselves deprived of four-fifths of their loans. This very considerable repudiation fell with particular severity on the middle class, especially the lower middle class, the petite bourgeoisie. The greatest sufferers were those living on their savings or on relatively fixed incomes—on pensions, for example, or on the return from bonds, or even on the contents of the wool sock in which the suspicious French peasant traditionally hoarded his cash. Bourgeois people naturally fear pauperization, fear being pushed down into the ranks of the proletariat, and the French were no exception. Inflation thus weakened a social class that had long been a mainstay of republicanism in France and added to the social tensions that form the central theme of French domestic history in the period between the two world wars.

Social and Political Tensions

During World War I, the French had temporarily put aside the great political and social conflict they had inherited from 1789. After the war, the "sacred union" of political parties that had carried France through the struggle soon dissolved, and the traditional conflict was resumed. This is sometimes termed the conflict between the "two Frances"—the republican France of the left, and the royalist or authoritarian France of the right. The conflict was not quite a simple Marxian class struggle between rich and poor, capitalist and proletarian, though it was certainly in part such a struggle. On the right were the wealthier classes, many of them openly hostile to the very existence of the parliamentary state. They were reinforced by conservative peasants and by small businessmen and investors, many of them petit bourgeois, who were not hostile to the Third Republic as such but who were determined to resist any attempt to extend the social services of the welfare state. As a result of this right-wing resistance, France lagged behind Britain, Germany, Sweden, and other European states in providing measures of social security.

On the left were the champions of the welfare state, the socialists and the communists, backed by the more radical workers, by many white-collar people, especially in the government service, and by some intellectuals. The effectiveness of the left was hampered by the postwar split between the communists, who followed the Moscow line, and the socialists, who did not, and by a comparable schism within the major trade-union organization, the CGT (Confédération Générale du Travail—General Confederation of Labor). Still nominally part of the left, but actually in the political middle and not anxious to go far toward the welfare state, was the misleadingly named Radical Socialist party, long the political bulwark of the Third Republic. The Radicals were strong among the peasants of southern France, and among white-collar workers and professional men.

Religious difficulties further embittered French politics. The widely held but unproved assumption that women would vote as the priests told them to delayed women's suffrage until after World War II. The traditional anticlericals in France were the leftists, including the Radicals. After World War I they rashly attempted to introduce anticlerical measures into strongly Catholic Alsace, where the separation of church and state carried through in France after the Dreyfus crisis had not been applied because Alsace was at the time part of the German Empire. In the long run, the government was obliged to make compromises on the Alsatian question and on other clerical issues. After bitter public debate, it finally decided in the mid-1920s to resume diplomatic relations with the Vatican—relations that had been broken off at the time of the separation.

In the late 1920s, the years of increased prosperity that coincided with the revaluation of the franc, the Third Republic seemed to be getting the better of its internal difficulties. Indeed, the world economic crisis that began in 1929 was late in striking France, and for a while in 1930 it looked as though the French economy, less devoted to large-scale industry than that of the United States, Britain, or Germany, might weather the crisis much more easily. But France, too, depended on international trade, particularly on the export of perfumes, wines and brandies, Paris gowns, and other luxuries. By 1932, the depression had struck, and the government was in serious economic and political difficulties.

The Stavisky Case and the Popular Front

The political crisis came to a head in February 1934 as a result of the Stavisky case, a financial scandal reminiscent of the Panama scandal of the 1890s. Stavisky was a shady promoter and swindler who long managed to stay clear of the law because of his influential connections, particularly in Radical Socialist circles. He was caught at last in a fraudulent bond issue of the municipal pawnshop of Bayonne in December 1933, and committed suicide—or, as many Frenchmen believed, was "suicided" by the police lest he implicate important politicians in his activities. France was rocked by the event, and also by the mysterious death of a judge who had been investigating the case. On the extreme right, royalists, enjoying the freedom of a democratic society, had long been organized, notably in a pressure group known as the Action Française, and were gaining recruits among upper-class youth. The Camelots du Roi (The King's Henchmen), strong-arm squads of the Action Française, went about beating up communists, who in turn responded with violence. Less fascist in character, yet also supporting the right was a veterans' organization, the Croix de Feu (Cross of Fire—the reference is to war), organized by Colonel de La Rocque. During the agitation following the Stavisky case, the Camelots du Roi, the Croix de Feu, and other right-wing groups took part in riots against the government that broke out in Paris in February 1934. The left countered with a brief general strike; France seemed to be on the eve of revolution.

Once more, however, as in the time of Dreyfus, the republican forces rallied to meet the threat, and once more after the crisis had been surmounted France moved to the left. The February crisis itself was overcome by a coalition of all parties save royalists, socialists, and communists, and the formation of a national government including all living former premiers. But the franc was again falling in value. In 1935 a ministry in which the dominant figure was Pierre Laval, a former socialist turned conservative, attempted to cut back government expenditures by measures similar to those that had worked a decade earlier under Poincaré; this time they did not work. The forces of the left responded by forming the Popular Front, which for the first time linked together the Radical Socialist, Socialist, and Communist parties. It also had the backing of the CGT, which had temporarily healed the schism between communist and noncommunist unions. In the elections of 1936 the Popular Front won a great victory, with the socialists at the top. The premiership was accordingly offered for the first time to a socialist, the highly cultivated Jewish intellectual Léon Blum, who had been roughed up by the Camelots du Roi in the backwash of the Stavisky affair.

The Popular Front came to power with a mandate from voters who wanted a kind of French equivalent of the American New Deal. They wanted more equal distribution of wealth by government action. Convinced that the classical formulas of economic retrenchment were not the remedy for the ills of France, they wanted a direct attack on the stronghold of retrenchment, the Bank of France, still a private institution dominated by the "two hundred families" alleged to control the French economy. Other factors entered into the victory of the Popular Front. Mussolini had begun his Ethiopian adventure, and Hitler his rearmament; many a Frenchman in 1936 voted left as a protest against the compromises that French politicians had been making with the dictators. Finally, these were the years when Russia, just admitted to the League of Nations, seemed to be pursuing a course of collaboration with the West against the threat of Nazi Germany. Moscow therefore urged the French communists to give up their old policy of constant opposition and to cooperate with their hated enemies, the socialists.

On taking office in June 1936, the Blum government rapidly introduced an ambitious program of reform. Labor gained a ceiling of 40 hours on the work week, higher wages, vacations with pay, and provision for compulsory arbitration of labor disputes. The Bank of France, the railroads, and the munitions industry were all subjected to partial nationalization. Strongarm fascistic groups like the Camelots du Roi and Croix de Feu were ordered to disband.

Impressive as this program was on paper, everything conspired to block its successful implementation. The communists did not really cooperate, for they refused to participate in the Blum cabinet and sniped at it from the sidelines in the Chamber and in the press. Businessmen took fright at the mushrooming membership of the CGT and at the effectiveness of the "sitdown" or "stay-in" strikes of French industrial workers in June 1936—the first widespread use of this formidable economic weapon, through which struck plants were occupied by the striking workers. The nation was soon bitterly divided between partisans and enemies of the Popular Front; business and farming classes were traditionally reluctant to pay income taxes, which would have to be raised to meet the costs of social services; the economy was not geared to labor-saving devices. It was in almost every way a bad time for a French New Deal. As the antidemocratic regimes in Germany, Italy, and Spain went on to new victories, France was

driven to expensive rearmament. Capital, however, was rapidly leaving the country to be invested or deposited abroad, and the monied class would not subscribe to the huge defense loans that were essential if the French armed forces were to be put in shape for the war that began to seem inevitable. Faced by mounting opposition from economically conservative Radicals in the cabinet and in the Chamber, Blum was obliged to call a halt in March 1937, and later in the year stepped down as premier in favor of a Radical. With the socialists joining the Communists in opposition, the Popular Front now disintegrated, and the CGT lost millions of its newly recruited members and suffered a new schism between communists and anticommunists.

Divided France

The morale of the French sagged badly after the collapse of the Popular Front. Under the mounting tensions of 1938 and 1939, the Radical Socialist premier, Daladier, kept France on the side of Britain in somewhat wavering opposition to the Rome-Berlin axis, and various measures of retrenchment—including virtual abandonment of the 40-hour week—kept the French economy from collapse. But the workers took very badly the failure of the Popular Front, and as late as November 1938 a general strike almost came off. It was combated by putting the railway workers under military orders. The "have" classes, on the other hand, were outraged by the fact that Blum's experiment had been made at all; many of them were convinced that their salvation lay in a French totalitarian state—"better Hitler than Blum," as their despairing slogan went, with its anti-Semitic echo from the days of the Dreyfus affair. The France that was confronted with war in 1939 was not only inadequately prepared in terms of materials; it was psychologically and spiritually divided, uncertain of what it was fighting for.

Many Frenchmen before 1940 relied on their great empire to restore the flagging morale and material capabilities of the mother country. Colonial troops, particularly from Senegal and North Africa, had helped to replenish the diminished ranks of the army during World War I. Enthusiasts spoke of France as a nation not of just the forty million at home but of one hundred million Frenchmen, which included the population of the colonial territories. But this was stretching the facts too far. Economically, the empire as a whole did advance in the 1920s and 1930s, yet only small native elite groups—only a relative handful of Indochinese or Senegalese or Algerian Arabs, for instance—were assimilated as Frenchmen or desired such assimilation. What the colonial populations were beginning to desire was some sort of home rule or independence. Although some leaders of the French left urged concessions to native aspirations, little was in fact conceded, except in a half-hearted fashion to the new mandates of Syria and Lebanon. The Cartel des Gauches government in the mid-1920s gave the Syrians and Lebanese constitutions, which were, however, subsequently often suspended in the face of nationalist unrest. In 1936 the Popular Front government negotiated treaties with Syria and Lebanon granting them independence, with many strings attached to safeguard the primacy of French interests. But even this moderate compromise was too much for the Chamber of Deputies, which refused to approve the treaties. Perhaps no policy pursued in the interwar years could have averted the disintegration of the French Empire that occurred after World War II, but the old-fashioned policy that prevailed did nothing to reconcile native nationalists to their French overlords.

IV   The United States

Neither the human nor the material losses of the United States in World War I were at all comparable with those of Britain and France. American casualties were 115,000 dead and 206,000 wounded; the comparable French figures were 1,385,000 dead and 3,044,000 wounded in a population one-third as large. Moreover, in purely material terms, the United States probably gained from the war. Heavy industries were greatly stimulated by Allied war orders, in turn made possible by American loans to the Allies; the war put the growing financial center of New York at least on equal terms with that of London; the dollar had begun to dethrone the monarch of the nineteenth century, the pound sterling. The Allies had borrowed from the American government, but these loans helped to stimulate American industry and, until 1933, some interest was paid on them. The United States came out of the war almost unscathed, victorious, and prosperous.

Yet in some ways the American revulsion against the war in 1919 and the years following was as marked as that of Britain, France, and defeated Germany. On the level of party politics, it helped to unseat the Democrats, who under President Wilson had controlled the federal government since 1913. The Republicans won the presidential elections of 1920, 1924, and 1928, and three successive Republicans occupied the White House—Harding (1921–1923), Coolidge (1923–1929), and Herbert Hoover (1929–1933). Although the elections were not very close, the campaign of 1928 was notable for the bitterness aroused in many quarters by the unsuccessful candidacy of the Democrat Alfred E. Smith. Smith, who had a progressive record as governor of New York, was a Roman Catholic, with an accent clearly indicating that he had been born in the tenements of the lower East Side of New York City. Many informed observers felt that Al Smith's religion had been largely instrumental in his defeat, and they concluded that the American people simply would not elect a Roman Catholic or any non-Protestant to the highest office of state. Smith was also a "wet," committed to repeal of the Eighteenth Amendment (1919) outlawing,

at least on paper, the sale of alcoholic beverages, while "dry" sentiment was still strong in the Protestant "bible belt" of the South and Midwest. No such controversy, incidentally, was engendered by the Nineteenth Amendment (1920), granting women the vote.

Isolationism—and Internationalism

On the level of policy and public attitudes, American revulsion against war took the form of isolationism, the desire to withdraw from international politics. This isolationism was by no means universal, although some historians feel that the instincts and attitudes of millions of Americans had already made it certain in 1919. Others feel that a slight shift in the words and deeds of men in high places could have changed the final decision and could at least have brought America into the League of Nations. If, as we have already seen, the Democratic president Wilson had been willing to meet Republican opposition in the Senate by a few concessions, then perhaps the Treaty of Versailles, League of Nations and all, might have achieved the two-thirds majority in the Senate the Constitution requires for treaties. Or if someone on the Republican side, with skill and prestige, had been able to put through the notion of a bipartisan foreign policy, then with patience and good will the United States might have been brought into the League. Public opinion, say those who take this view, was not against our carrying on the task we had begun in 1917; only a noisy minority in the country as a whole, and the little group of obstinate senators at the top, wanted us to withdraw.

Yet those who remember the years right after 1918 find it hard to deny that the country was swept by a wave of desire to get back to "normalcy," as President Harding phrased it in a malapropism that largely replaced the correct "normality." A great many Americans felt that they had done all they needed to do in beating the Germans and that further direct participation in the complexities of European politics would simply involve American innocence and virtue that much more disastrously in European sophistication and vice. The not uncommon American reaction against its strong presidents took the form of repudiating all of Wilson's work at Paris as un-American. Furthermore, as the months of negotiation went on with no final decisions reached, Americans, always an impatient people, began to feel that sheer withdrawal was about the only effective action they could take.

The Treaty of Versailles, containing at Wilson's insistence the League of Nations, was finally rejected in the Senate on March 19, 1920. The United States remained technically at war with Germany until July 1921, when a resolution making a separate peace was passed by Congress and signed under the presidency of Harding. American isolationism was expressed in these years in other concrete measures. The Fordney-McCumber Tariff of 1922 and the Smoot-Hawley Tariff of 1930 set successively higher duties on foreign goods and emphasized America's belief that her high wage scales needed to be protected from cheap foreign labor.

Yet the United States continued all through the 1920s to insist that the debts owed to her by the Allied powers be repaid. It is true that these were refunded in a series of agreements, and that in the closely related problem of German reparations Americans on the whole cast their weight on the side of a general scaling down of German obligations. But Congress paid little heed to the argument, so convincing to most economists, that European nations could not repay save through dollars gained by sales of their goods in the American market, and that American tariffs continued to make such repayment impossible. Congressmen tended to reduce the complexities of international debts to President Coolidge's simple dictum: "They hired the money, didn't they?"

The spirit of isolationism also lay behind the immigration restrictions of the 1920s, which reversed the former American policy of almost free immigration. The reversal was motivated also by the widespread prejudice against the recent and largely Catholic and Jewish immigrants from Mediterranean and Slavic Europe. The act of 1924 set an annual quota limit for each country of 2 percent of the number of nationals from that country resident in the United States in 1890. Since the heavy immigration from eastern and southern Europe had come after 1890, the choice of that date reduced the flow from these areas to a mere trickle. Northern countries like Britain, Germany, and the Scandinavian states, on the other hand, did not use up their quotas.

Yet during this era of partial isolationism the United States by no means withdrew entirely from international politics. Rather, as an independent without formal alliances, it continued to pursue policies that seemed to most Americans traditional, but that in their totality gradually lined them up against the chief international troublemakers. In 1928, the Republican secretary of state Kellogg submitted to the great European powers a prosposal for a renunciation of war as an instrument of national policy. Incorporated with similar proposals from the French foreign minister Briand, it was formally adopted in August of that year as the Pact of Paris, commonly known as the Kellogg-Briand Pact. It was eventually signed by twenty-three nations, including the United States. The pact has often been dismissed as a futile denunciation of sin, and it is certainly true that it did not prevent World War II. Yet by this action the United States at least expressed a concern over the peace of the world.

During the 1920s the United States was at work in a hundred ways laying the foundations for the position of world leadership it reached after World War II. American businessmen were everywhere; American loans were making possible the revival of German industrial greatness; American motors, refrigerators, typewriters, telephones, and other products of the as-

sembly line were being sold the world over. In the Far East, the United States took the lead in negotiating the Nine-Power Treaty of 1922 that committed her and the other great powers, including Japan, to respect the sovereignty and integrity of China. When President Roosevelt in 1941 resisted the Japanese attempt to swallow China and other Far Eastern territory, he was following a line laid down under President Harding.

Boom—and Bust

In domestic affairs, the Coolidge era (1923–1929) has now become legendary. These were years of frantic prosperity; nearly everybody played the stock market, and the market value of stocks rose to fantastic heights. They were the years of "prohibition," the ban on the manufacture and sale of alcoholic beverages, enforced, in theory, by the Volstead Act of 1919 under the Eighteenth Amendment to the Constitution. And so they were also the years of the speakeasy and the bootlegger. They were the years of the short skirt (not nearly so short, however, as the "mini" of the 1960s), of sex appeal (also known as "it"), of the Charleston, "bathtub gin," and other forms of "sin." They were years which, like the "naughty nineties" of the nineteenth century, we look back on with a sort of reproving envy, years that now look colorful and romantic.

But the Coolidge era was by no means completely summed up in novels of the jazz age, like The Great Gatsby of F. Scott Fitzgerald, or even in Sinclair Lewis' half-satirical Babbitt and Main Street, with their sallies against the materialism and narrowness of provincial America. It was an era of marked industrial progress, of solid advancement of the national plant and productive capabilities, vindicating President Coolidge's contention that "the business of America is business." It was an era of the steady spreading in the United States of standards of living heretofore limited to the relatively few, standards of living that seemed to intellectuals vulgar, but that were nevertheless a new thing in the world. These were the years when, if you had a servant, you could no longer take her for granted, but had to take some pains to keep her content.

At its most glamorous, the era ended with the onset of the Great Depression in the autumn of 1929. During the preceding year, Wall Street had enjoyed an unprecedented boom. Speculators by the millions were playing the market, buying stocks on margin in hopes of quick resale at huge profits; they paid only a fraction of their cost in cash, borrowing the balance from their brokers through margin arrangements and often borrowing, too, their cash investment. Not only stocks but houses, furnishings, automobiles, and many other purchases were financed on borrowed money. Credit swelled to the point where it was no longer on a sound basis in a largely unregulated economy. Eventually, shrewd investors began to sell their holdings in the belief that the bubble would soon burst. The result was a disastrous drop in stock values, beginning in October

A soup kitchen in New York City, 1931.

1929 and continuing almost without letup to 1933. Both the speculators and the lenders from whom they had borrowed money were ruined.

The immediate cause of the depression, then, was the stock-market crash. About the more deep-seated causes the economic physicians are not wholly agreed. Yet this much seems certain: Coolidge prosperity was very unevenly distributed among the various sectors of the American economy and American society. Agriculture, notably, suffered a kind of permanent depression throughout the 1920s. At the close of World War I, farmers commanded very high prices for their produce and enjoyed an apparently insatiable market at home and abroad. They expanded their production—and borrowed to finance the expansion—often at a reckless rate. Then, as "normalcy" returned in the early 1920s, the foreign market dried up, the home market shrank, farm prices fell rapidly, and the inevitable foreclosure of farm mortgages began. Wage-earning workers, though not hard hit like the farmers, gained comparatively little increase in their purchasing power during the 1920s. The worker did often raise his standard of living, by purchasing a house or a car, but he did it on credit, by assuming the burden of a heavy mortgage or by financing a purchase on installments to be paid over a long period. The "big money" of the Coolidge era went chiefly to business, above all to big business.

The Great Depression was very severe in many countries throughout the world, but nowhere was it worse than in the United States. Its effects may be measured by the figure of sixteen million Americans unemployed at the low point in the early 1930s—something like one-third of the national labor force. In terms of gross national product (GNP), the United States Department of Commerce sets for 1929 the figure of $103,828,000,000; for 1933, $55,760,000,000.

The most remarkable thing about this grave crisis in the American economy is that it produced almost no organized movements of revolt, no threat of revolution. The intellectuals of the 1930s did indeed turn to "social consciousness," and Marxism made some converts among writers and artists. But the bulk of the population showed no serious signs of abandoning their fundamental belief that the way out lay through the legal means provided by existing American institutions. Even before the election of Franklin D. Roosevelt in 1932, local authorities and private charities did a good deal to soften the worst sufferings of the unemployed. They were helped by the establishment early in 1932 of the federal Reconstruction Finance Corporation (RFC), which advanced government credits to release the frozen assets of financial institutions severely affected by a wave of bankruptcies and bank failures. The Republican administration of President Hoover, however, was generally committed to the philosophy of laissez faire; aside from the RFC, it did little to cushion the effects of the depression. People who wanted a more vigorous attack on economic problems voted for the Democrats in 1932; most significantly, they did not vote in very important numbers for the socialist or communist presidential candidates. In the crisis of a great depression, the American two-party system continued to meet basic political needs.

The New Deal

The victory of the Democrats in 1932 seemed to give them a clear mandate to marshal all the resources of the federal government against the depression. The Democratic president, Franklin Roosevelt (1933–1945), who had succeeded Al Smith as governor of New York, took office on March 4, 1933, in the midst of a financial crisis that had closed the banks all over the country. He at once summoned Congress to an emergency session and declared a bank holiday. Gradually the sound banks reopened, and the New Deal began. Subsequently, under improving economic conditions, the American business community mostly turned with great bitterness against Roosevelt and all his works. But in those early months of 1933 the mere fact that a national administration was trying to do something about the situation was a powerful restorative to national morale. The nation emerged from the bank holiday with a new confidence, echoing the phrase from Roosevelt's inaugural address that there was nothing to fear "but fear itself."

The New Deal was in part a series of measures aimed at immediate difficulties and in part a series of measures aimed at permanent changes in the structure of American society. The distinction between its short term and its long-term measures is in a sense arbitrary, for the men who carried both through were never quite clear in their own minds exactly what they were trying to do. What must chiefly interest us is the implications of their work. In the perspective of Western history, the New Deal was the coming to the United States, under the special pressures of the Great Depression, of those measures—"socialist" to some of their opponents—that we have already seen in European countries like Great Britain and imperial Germany. They are best summed up in that value-charged term, the welfare state.

The short-term measures of the New Deal aimed, by releasing the dollar from its tie with gold, to lower the price of American goods in a world that was abandoning the gold standard. They aimed to thaw out credit by extending the activities of the RFC and by creating such new governmental lending agencies as the Home Owners' Loan Corporation. They aimed to relieve unemployment by public works on a large scale, to safeguard bank deposits by the Federal Deposit Insurance Corporation, and to regulate speculation and other stock-market activities by the Securities and Exchange Commission. The National Recovery Act (NRA) of 1933 set up production codes in industry to regulate competition and ensure labor's right to organize and to carry on collective bargaining. The historical significance of many of these innovations rested in the fact that they were undertaken not by private business or by state or local authorities but by the federal government. There was one exception to the rule of widening federal activity. The Twenty-first Amendment to the Constitution (ratified in December 1933) repealed the Eighteenth and abandoned the increasingly unsuccessful federal efforts to enforce prohibition.

The long-term measures of the New Deal were, of course, more important. The Social Security Act of 1935 introduced to the United States on a national scale the unemployment insurance, old-age pensions, and other benefits of the kind that Lloyd George had brought to Britain. Somewhat more equal distribution of the national wealth resulted from increased federal taxation, especially taxes on individual and corporate incomes. Congress passed a series of acts on labor relations, which strengthened and extended the role of organized labor in American economic life. A series of acts on agriculture, though leaving the business of farming still in the hands of several million individual farmers producing for sale in a cash market, nevertheless regulated crops and prices and provided subsidies, all on a scale that would have been incomprehensible to a nineteenth-century farmer. And finally —the showpiece of the New Deal—a great regional planning board, the Tennessee Valley Authority, used government power to make over the economic life of a relatively backward area by checking the erosion of farmlands, instituting flood control, and providing cheap electric power generated at government-built dams.

The Presidential election of 1936 gave Franklin Roosevelt an emphatic popular endorsement: Maine and Vermont were the only states he failed to carry. Yet the New Deal never regained the momentum it had had in his first term. Piqued by the Supreme Court's decisions that the NRA and some other New Deal measures were unconstitutional, Roosevelt in 1937 put before Congress legislative proposals that would have

Franklin D. Roosevelt, photographed at sea during World War II.

enabled the President to appoint additional justices to federal courts "where there are incumbent judges of retirement age who do not choose to resign." Supporters of the plan hailed it as a justified measure to emancipate the Supreme Court from the "nine old men" who were blocking progress; opponents, including many Democrats in Congress, denounced it as "court-packing," striking at the roots of the separation of powers. Congress rejected the proposal. Meanwhile, aided by the protection of other New Deal legislation, organized labor was making great gains. The drive was spearheaded by the new CIO (Congress of Industrial Organizations), which was committed to organize all workers in an industry into one union and not into a series of craft unions, as was the traditional procedure of the older AFL (American Federation of Labor). Employing the French-devised sit-down strike, the CIO won recognition for its unions from the steel and automotive industries after a hard and not entirely peaceful fight. By 1938 further major advances on the domestic scene seemed unlikely in the face of a sharp recession at home and the gathering of war clouds abroad.

In retrospect, although the New Deal is still a subject of controversy, it seems evident that the measures taken by the Roosevelt administration, combined with the resilience of American institutions and culture, pulled the United States at least part way out of the Depression. Full recovery, however, did not come until the end of the recession of 1938 and the boom set off by the outbreak of World War II. It seems evident, too, that the New Deal measures also restored a high degree of confidence to Americans. The intellectuals, whose role in modern America has generally been in opposition to the men of business, in the 1920s had found the United States a hopelessly crass and vulgar society. But in the 1930s, though some intellectuals flirted with Marxism, many of them turned to support the new American way marked out by the New Deal.

The onset of war in Europe found Americans, as we shall see in the next chapter, anxious not to jeopardize in war their still precarious prosperity, anxious to remain neutral if Europe should persist in going to war. Roosevelt and his Republican opponents had been for some time exchanging insults: the "economic royalists" fought back at "that man in the White House." Yet in the pinch of the international crisis of 1939–1941 it became clear that, although the nation was not completely united, at any rate it was not pathologically divided. As so often in American history, the violence of verbal politics masked a basic unity. When the war came to the United States in 1941, Americans were largely ready for it psychologically and—what is really remarkable in a Western democracy—not too unready for it militarily.

When the war came, moreover, the United States had already made many efforts to enlist the support of the Latin-American states. In 1930, before the so-called Roosevelt Revolution in American diplomacy, President Hoover's State Department issued the Clark Memorandum, written two years earlier by the undersecretary of state, specifically stating that the Monroe Doctrine does not concern itself with inter-American relations but is directed against outside intervention in the affairs of the Western hemisphere. The United States was no longer to land the Marines in some Central American republic at the drop of a hat but was trying to strengthen hemispheric solidarity. And so, on the foundations of the Clark Memorandum, President Roosevelt built his celebrated Good Neighbor policy toward the other American nations.

Meantime, what may be called American imperial policy was likewise undergoing some liberalization, notably with respect to the Philippines. When the United States had annexed the islands at the close of the Spanish-American War, a stubborn Filipino insurrection broke out in protest, and it took American forces three years (1899–1902) to subdue the rebels. Filipino nationalists, though partially disarmed by the conciliatory measures taken by the United States after the suppression of the rebellion, nonetheless continued to advocate eventual freedom. In 1934, Congress passed an act promising the Philippines formal independence, with some strings attached, after twelve years, and bestowing a dilute kind of dominion status on the islands during the interim.

V The Loosening of Imperial Ties

The Filipino insurrection of 1899 was a portent. Even before 1914, there were signs that many of the more advanced "colonial" peoples were already chafing under imperialism. Native nationalist movements were creating trouble for the British in Egypt and India, for the French in Morocco and Algeria, and for all the imperial powers in China. World War I itself speeded up the process of rousing national consciousness among the "natives" of the various empires, and at its end there was no doubt that the hold of the West had been loosened. Psychologically, the experience of the war gave a lift to non-Western peoples; they had often rendered important services to their white masters, and their leaders had widened their knowledge of the West. The Arab peoples of the old Ottoman Empire had raised armies of their own and had fought with European aid for their own freedom from Turkish rule. French colonial troops and British Indian troops had taken part in the conflict, sometimes in Europe itself.

The very spectacle of the masters quarreling among themselves did something to lower the prestige of the West among subject peoples. Moreover, the Allies had fought the war in the name of democratic ideals of self-determination for all peoples, and in their propaganda against the Central Powers they had stressed their opposition to imperialism. The fifth of Wilson's Fourteen Points asserted that in disputed claims to colonial territories "the interests of the populations concerned must have equal weight" with the interests of the colonial powers. It is true that the Allies did not give up any of their territories in 1919 but actually added to them under the mandate system. To many of the subject peoples, as to liberals in the West itself, the mandate was simply a disguise for the old imperialism; yet it is surely significant that a disguise seemed necessary to the imperialist powers. The West now appeared to be committed to a process of at least gradual emancipation of the colonial dependencies.

Japan

Alone among non-Western peoples, the Japanese were able to maintain themselves as a fully independent major political entity during the golden age of imperialism. More than that, as the twentieth century opened, Japan was experiencing the Industrial Revolution and advancing to the status of a great power, a full but somewhat unwelcome participant in the struggle for imperial position. As we have seen, the Japanese made these impressive accomplishments without radically altering their traditional oligarchical and absolutist political structure.

In the decade after World War I, it looked as though Japan might achieve a gradual liberalization of her political institutions. The cabinets of the 1920s included many men from the business class who favored vigorous expansion abroad but who also granted some measures of cautious liberalism at home. The suffrage was gradually extended, and in 1925 all men received the right to vote. For the first time, political parties, Western-style, began to put down roots, especially in the urban population, and seemed likely to give new vitality to the Diet, the not very powerful central representative assembly of Japan. Trade unions also took shape and began to win a following.

Japan, however, did not evolve into a parliamentary democracy on the Western model during the twenty years' truce. By the early 1930s, political power was falling more and more into the hands of army and navy officers, many of whom were descended from the feudal samurai class. This officer clique hated the prospect of liberal civilian government and envied and mistrusted the business class. They found a potent political weapon in the institution of the emperor, who was supposed to possess the kind of political infallibility that Westerners associated with a divine-right monarch. Putting their own words into the emperor's mouth, the admirals and generals used his pronouncements to further their own ends. And, to make doubly sure, they assassinated or terrorized the chief spokesmen of nascent Japanese liberalism.

The consequence was the progressive clamping of a military dictatorship on Japan during the 1930s. Although popular elections continued to be held, their results were disregarded, and the Diet lost its recently acquired vitality. Businessmen supported the new regime out of fear or in anticipation of the huge profits to be secured from its adventures abroad. A cult of.

emperor worship was concocted out of a rather innocuous traditional Japanese religion to focus popular loyalties on the divine mission of the emperor and to ensure popular submission to the will of the men who ruled in his name. A corps of ruthless agents, picturesquely named "thought police," hounded anyone suspected of harboring "dangerous thoughts." In short, Japan now had a government that exploited many uniquely Japanese traditions but in its operations also bore a striking resemblance to the totalitarian governments of Europe.

Nowhere was the parallel with European totalitarianism more marked than in the foreign policy of Japan between the two world wars. Like Hitler's Germans or Mussolini's Italians, the Japanese claimed to be a "have-not" nation. They, too, pointed to their steadily growing population—and did all they could to encourage its further growth. They, too, harped on the overcrowding of the homeland, its inadequate resources, and its restricted markets. Behind these arguments lay real economic problems of sustaining the Japanese economy in the face of the Depression and the worldwide disruption of international trade, problems of providing food and work for the sixty million Japanese in 1930. In seeking to solve these problems by imperial expansion, the militarists of the 1930s were following a pattern that had already been set by the West. And they were also following the path marked out by the Japanese officers and politicians who had secured Formosa in 1895 and annexed Korea in 1910. During World War I, Japan had tried in vain to subjugate China; by World War II, she had apparently almost succeeded in doing so. To follow the course of this Japanese imperialism we must turn to the history of its chief victim, China.

Revolution in China

China, meantime, was engaged in a great struggle to free herself from the tutelage of the Western colonial powers. The struggle was much more than a simple conflict between oriental nationalists and occidental imperialists. It was complicated by two additional elements—the increasing threat to Chinese independence from an expansionist Japan, and increasing communist intervention in Chinese politics. It is scarcely an exaggeration to say that China faced the prospect of simply exchanging one set of imperial overlords for another.

By 1900, the Chinese Empire was far gone in political decay. Nominally independent under the rule of its Manchu dynasty, it had lost much of its effective sovereignty through concessions of naval bases and economic and political privileges to the European powers and Japan. Following China's defeat by Japan in 1895, European imperialists engaged in a hectic scramble for further concessions. The Germans leased Kiaochow, the French Kwangchou Bay, the Russians Port Arthur, and the British Wei-hai-wei. In 1899, the American secretary of state, John Hay, sought to end the scramble by getting the powers to accept the principle of the Open Door, whereby all foreign goods could be marketed in China on equal terms, with no special favors to any one power. Although the interested states subscribed to Hay's policy in principle, the Open Door meant little in practice.

Meantime, a formidable reaction to the outburst of imperialist activity was gathering within China itself. The hard-pressed Manchu government encouraged the formation of an antiforeign nationalist secret society called the Boxers. The result was the Boxer Rebellion of 1900, in which more than 200 foreigners, mainly missionaries, were slain. The foreign powers, including the United States, used troops to protect their nationals and property against the Boxers. In 1901, they obliged the Manchu government to pay an enormous indemnity and to grant them further rights that, of course, further impaired Chinese sovereignty.

The next Chinese rebellion, the revolution of 1911, was directed against the Manchu regime that had proved so incapable of resisting the encroachments of imperialism. In this revolution, a factor operated that may often be found in the whole process of national self-assertion by non-Western peoples. The movement was directed against the West—against Westerners themselves or against native governors who seemed to be the agents of the West. But it was a movement inspired at least in part by Western ideas and examples and led by often thoroughly "westernized" natives, a movement that could scarcely have come into being without the influence of the West.

The Chinese revolution of 1911 was comparatively bloodless in its early stages. It was sealed by the abdication on February 12, 1912, of the six-year-old Manchu emperor, Pu-yi. From the start, the two chief revolutionary groups displayed conflicting ideas about the nature of the new society that would replace the discarded Manchu regime. One group soon formed the Nationalist party, the Kuomintang, led by Sun Yat-sen and many young intellectuals who had studied and traveled in the West. Its leaders wanted a democratic parliamentary republic of China modeled on the Western political system, though preserving as far as possible the basic Chinese family and village structure, on which Western industrial society was to be grafted. The other group, whose leader was Yuan Shih-k'ai, wanted a strong central government basically authoritarian in structure, with authority not in the hands of an emperor and the traditional and highly conservative mandarin bureaucracy, but in the hands of strongmen capable of achieving the modernization of China from above.

A struggle for power broke out between the assembly elected after 1911 and Yuan Shih-k'ai. The party of Sun Yat-sen was defeated, and by 1914, after a purge of the Kuomintang members of the assembly, Yuan Shih-k'ai issued a constitutional compact that put him in the presidential office for ten years. Sun Yat-sen and his followers had failed to turn China into a Western parliamentary democracy. Sun was, however, a gifted

leader, and the ideas for which he stood, though they were never firmly rooted in China, have never quite disappeared. Sun remains somewhat paradoxically the great hero of the Chinese revolution of 1911.

Yuan's subsequent career bears some resemblance to that of another military reformer, Oliver Cromwell. Faced with continuing opposition not only from the republicans of the Kuomintang but also from the monarchists, Yuan decided to follow the age-old Chinese pattern and set himself up as the first of a new dynasty of emperors to follow the Manchus. A revolt caused him to revoke his plans, and early in 1916 he reorganized the republic with a military cabinet. He died on June 6, 1916, leaving the new republic enmeshed in another age-old Chinese political pattern—the dissolution of all but the shadow of central control and the assumption of real power by regional strongmen. A new era of provincial warlords had begun.

In the years of crisis following 1911, China also faced the aggressive attempts of Japan to take over the Far Eastern imperial interests of European powers now at war among themselves. Early in 1915, the Japanese presented in secrecy to the Chinese government the Twenty-One Demands, which amounted to a demand for something close to a protectorate over China and for all sorts of concrete concessions. The Chinese republic, now at the nadir of its strength, countered by declaring war against the Central Powers, thus securing at least the nominal protection of two of the Allies, Britain and France. The Japanese did not feel able to defy Western objections, and so contented themselves with taking over Kiaochow and other German concessions in the Shantung peninsula. At the end of the war, the victorious Allies, with the United States in the lead, acted to check the ambitions of their recent military partner, Japan. At the Washington Conference of 1922, Japan was forced to sign the Nine-Power Treaty guaranteeing the independence of China. This rebuff to Japan was one of the first events in the long chain that aggravated the hostility of Japan toward the United States and ended, two decades later, in the attack on Pearl Harbor.

Nationalists, Communists, and the Japanese in China

During the twenty years' truce the main elements in the Chinese situation were the Kuomintang, the communists, and the Japanese invaders. The Kuomintang, after the death of Sun Yat-sen in 1925, came under the leadership of his brother-in-law, Chiang Kai-shek, an army officer trained in Japan. The Nationalists of the Kuomintang were engaged in a constant and often very unsuccessful struggle to set up an effective central government against the power of provincial warlords. They were also often locked in battle with the communists and the Japanese. The Chinese Communist movement began in the early 1920s. It was inspired by direct contacts with the Comintern in Moscow, guided by Soviet agents, and encouraged at first by leaders of the

Kuomintang. Sun Yat-sen hoped that the example and advice of the successful Russian party might help to strengthen his own faltering party organization. For a time, the Chinese Communists were no more than the left wing of the Kuomintang, but a breach soon occurred between them and the more conservative elements among the Nationalists, led by Chiang Kai-shek.

The communists lost out badly in this early struggle for power. In 1926, Chiang's forces began a campaign of persecution and assassination against them; in 1927, they were expelled from the Kuomintang. An important reason for this setback was the failure of the Chinese Communists to get effective support or help from Moscow, for these were the years of the Trotsky-Stalin feud in Russia. The conflict between the two titans was intensified by their differences over the "correct" Chinese policy for the Soviet Union to follow. Stalin, who was rapidly gaining the ascendancy, believed that China was not ripe for a proletarian revolution; therefore, he did nothing to succor his Chinese comrades.

Nationalists and communists fought in word and deed for the allegiance—or at any rate for the passive acceptance—of nearly five hundred million Chinese, for the most part peasants, and for the most part illiterate. For the most part, too, the masses of China were so far from sharing Western attitudes toward the state that it is hardly an exaggeration to say that they felt toward politics as Westerners feel toward the weather—that it is something beyond human control. In transforming the Chinese into a nation in the Western sense, the indispensable step was something more than building railroads and factories or promoting the study of modern science instead of the Chinese classics. It was getting the Chinese peasant to regard himself as an individual Chinese citizen. This indispensable process was beginning in the 1920s and 1930s. It goes far to explain why the Japanese, when they renewed their aggression in 1931, were virtually beaten from the start in the attempt to become the true masters of China. In an earlier age one can readily imagine the Japanese as military conquerors in China setting up a new dynasty, foreign in orgin, but very soon thoroughly absorbed by the Chinese. That this age-old pattern was not followed in the 1930s shows that China herself was beginning to change.

The Japanese attack came in September 1931, on Manchuria, an outlying northern province of China that was a particularly tempting target for Japanese aggression. Manchuria had good resources of coal and iron; it adjoined Korea, already a Japanese possession; and it had never been fully integrated into the structure of Chinese government and looked, therefore, as though it could easily be pried loose. Moreover, the Japanese regarded themselves as the natural successors of the Russians, whom they had driven from Manchuria in the Russo-Japanese War of 1904–1905. By 1932, the Japanese were strong enough in Manchuria to proclaim it an "independent" state, which they called Man-

Chiang Kai-Shek, 1931.

chukuo, under a puppet ruler, Pu-yi, who as a boy had been the last emperor of old China. The Chinese responded to Japan's aggression in Manchuria by a very effective boycott of Japanese goods; the Japanese countered by carrying the war to the great Chinese port of Shanghai. Given the weakness of the Kuomintang government, effective Chinese resistance would have required full support from stronger outside powers. Neither the Western powers nor the League of Nations gave China more than verbal support; the Chinese had to give up their boycott of Japanese goods, and the Japanese remained in Manchuria. Tension between China and Japan persisted and the Japanese soon decided to attempt the absorption of all the rest of China. Their invasion came in July 1937, without a formal declaration of war.

In a purely military way the Japanese did very well. By October, when the key southern Chinese city of Canton fell, they had taken the strategic points of the coastal area and the thickly populated river valleys. Chiang Kai-shek, his army, and his fellow politicians of the Kuomintang took refuge in the interior province of Szechwan, where he set up his capital at Chungking

SHANGH PORT TREATI

JAPANESE GOV'T. PROMISES

WORLD COURT

L. OF N. COVENANT

KELLOGG PACT

NINE POWER TREATY

JAPAN

An American newspaper cartoon of 1931 on the Japanese Seizure of Manchuria.

on the upper Yangtze River. There, protected by distance and a ring of mountains, receiving Western aid through India by the Burma Road and, when that was closed, by air, the Nationalist government held out until the end of World War II and the collapse of Japanese imperialism.

Yet the Japanese, even at the height of their success, had achieved no more than the stretching across China of a string of garrisons, and the control of great cities like Shanghai and Peking. They held the railroads, subject to guerrilla attack, but away from the relatively sparse lines of modern communication they were helpless. Many a Chinese village in the area nominally Japanese never changed its way during the occupation; nowhere did the Japanese win over the acquiescence, to say nothing of the loyalty, of the Chinese people.

The Nationalists of the Kuomintang led the resistance to the Japanese from the beginning, yet they too ultimately failed to win the full loyalty of the Chinese people. This was partly a military matter, for Chiang's armies were no match for the Japanese, who controlled the few industrial cities in China, so that Chiang was always relatively badly off in terms of logistics. In the long exile in Szechwan, moreover, the morale of the

Nationalists decayed. The ordeal, far from purifying and strengthening them, emphasized their alienation from the masses of the Chinese, their corruption and intrigue, their inability to live up to the early promise of Sun Yat-sen and the Kuomintang. It was the communists, not the Nationalists, who succeeded in capturing and harnessing the human emotions and aspirations, the binding power that holds people together in society with the tightness modern material culture demands.

During the 1930s and the early 1940s the relative strength of communists and nationalists underwent a gradual and decisive shift. Both parties, it should be noted, were in a sense totalitarian. Both were organized on the one-party pattern, which left no place for an opposition; neither of them was geared to the give-and-take of Western party politics. The communists, driven about over much of China during the 1930s, ended up with a base in the region of Yenan in the north; their strategic position somewhat resembled that of Chiang in his southern base of Szechwan. But there was an important difference. In the long years of Japanese occupation, Chiang remained in Chungking with his army and his bureaucracy. The communists, on the other hand, managed to string their network of organized armies and local councils in and around the Japanese in the north; they extended their apparatus right down to the sea and up through Manchuria. By 1945, the communists were ready for a successful conflict with the Kuomintang.

Southeast Asia and India

The turning point in the recent history of the Far East was World War II, with its aftermath of communist victory in China and of French withdrawal from Indochina, British from Burma and Malaya, Dutch from the East Indies, and American from the Philippines. Before World War II there were few clear signs of the spectacular changes to come in Southeast Asia, that part of the Far East stretching east from India and south from China through the islands of Indonesia. But informed observers during the twenty years' truce noted the initial American steps toward granting the Filipinos independence, and they were also aware of the slow growth of nationalist opposition to imperial rule, particularly in Indochina and the Netherlands East Indies. They saw that the British-controlled Malay peninsula, with its characteristic colonial economy of rubber and tin production, was peculiarly dependent on the economic health of the West and peculiarly vulnerable in a major depression.

In India, by contrast, it was World War I that marked a crucial turning point. India made important contributions to the British armies, particularly to their victory over the Turks. Indians, growing in numbers and educated in the Western tradition, received the full impact of Allied propaganda in favor of the war to save the world for democracy. Monetary inflation and other war dislocations favored the growing agitation for self-government. Already in the war period the British viceroy and his experts, both British and Indian, were working toward a plan of reform. Public opinion not only in India but throughout the world was sharpened in favor of the Indians by what seemed to be a throwback to the crude days of imperial force when, in April 1919, British troops fired on demonstrators at Amritsar.

The Amritsar massacre was an exception, however. One basic fact about India after World War I was the still relatively serene British rule with its slow but steady acclimatization of Indians to Western material things like railroads and hospitals and to Western ideas like equality and freedom. A second basic fact, growing out of the first, was the growing Indian demand for the termination of British colonial rule. A third basic fact, conditioning the second, was the tension between Hindus and Muslims.

A large Muslim minority, about a quarter of the total population, had grown up in the nine hundred years since the first invasion of India by Muslim peoples. In the Indus Basin and part of the Punjab in the northwest, and in part of Bengal in the east, the Muslims were actually a majority; elsewhere they lived scattered among the Hindus and other non-Muslims.

Though some of the Muslims belonged to the aristocratic classes, the bulk were peasants, and on the whole the Muslim community was outstripped financially, industrially, and culturally by the Hindu community. Although some Muslims, especially in the upper classes, were proud descendants of foreign military conquerors, for the most part the Muslims and the Hindus were roughly of the same racial mixtures, both really native Indians.

Yet Muslims and Hindus felt—and feel—toward each other in a way exceedingly difficult for most Westerners to understand. A friendly British observer has summed it up in this manner:

> What are the things which keep Muslims and Hindus apart, which make them feel that they are different races and nations, which keep them permanently potentially on edge with each other? The first perhaps is the doctrinal issue of idolatry. The Muslim has borrowed from the Semitic races both his passionate rejection of polytheism and his passionate hatred of idolatry. . . . The worship of many gods, the portrayal of the divine in human form, is something to him which is less than human, the mark of the beast. It has, I think, no counterpart in the West; for it is far stronger than our ideas of good form or fair play or the behaviour of a gentleman. . . . The ramifications of these emotions are widespread through the whole realm of Hindu-Muslim relations because of the ubiquitous working of the Hindu doctrine of incarnation. So much in Hinduism is divine. The Muslim does not mind a Hindu not eating beef, for example, but he does object to his worshipping the cow. In times of irritation there is consequently a strong urge to kill a cow out of sheer bravado. . . .
>
> But the mental anguish of mutual relations is not all on the Muslim side. Hindus suffer acutely in the ceremonial sphere. Hindu feelings about the cow are as untranslatable into Western terms as are Muslim feelings about idolatry, and they are no less strong. A Hindu may literally turn sick at the sight or smell of beef. Muslim practice in the matter of food seems to the typical Hindu to be impure, dirty, and degraded, something beneath the level of man. He cannot understand, on the other hand, what he calls Muslim fanaticism on the subject of idolatry. Orthodox Hindu and Muslim individuals can be, and often are, very good friends, but they usually take good care that their intercourse avoids these danger areas.*

It is not surprising, therefore, that after serious attempts to bring Hindu and Muslim into a unified resistance movement against the British, two separate bodies grew up in the twentieth century—the Indian National Congress and the All-India Muslim League. Immediately after World War I, the two bodies did often succeed in presenting a common front against the British, but as time went on their mutual opposition, indeed their irreconcilability, tended to increase rather than diminish.

In spite of these difficulties, the Indian drive for self-government and independence went on steadily from the end of World War I. For the Hindus, the

*Percival Spear, *India, Pakistan, and the West,* © Oxford University Press, 1967. Reprinted by permission of the Oxford University Press, Oxford.

Mahatma Gandhi, 1921.

Congress party was held together effectively and given extraordinary influence over the masses by one of the great leaders of the twentieth century, Mahatma Gandhi (1869–1948). Gandhi was not a Brahmin (a member of the highest Hindu caste) but a member of the *bania* or shopkeeping caste. Educated as a lawyer at Oxford and therefore familiar with the West, trained in the harshness of practical politics as a young lawyer serving the Indian minority in South Africa, Gandhi was admirably equipped to deal with both British and Hindus. Among his own people he appealed by his simple and austere personal life, his fasts, and his exiguous native costume. He worked out the technique of insurrection called nonviolent noncooperation, which appealed to the fundamental Hindu belief that force is illusory and therefore ineffective. Characteristic measures sponsored by Gandhi were the organized Indian boycott of British goods, backed by his own recourse to the spinning wheel to publicize the resources of native cottage industries and by his march to the sea to make salt from it illegally in defiance of British regulations. The Mahatma also defied Hindu prejudice, directing some of his hunger strikes not against the British but against the continued position of the untouchables as pariahs outside the caste system.

Other Congress leaders, especially at the local level, were willing to use more clearly Western methods of agitation, propaganda, and, it must be admitted, rather violent nonviolence. Concession after concession was wrung from the British, and as the Indians gained political experience in provincial self-government and in the civil service, dominion status appeared to be just

around the corner. This was the situation at the outbreak of World War II. By the time the war was over, however, it was evident that the mutual antagonism of Hindus and Muslims might well require the formation not of a single unified India but of two separate states.

The Middle East

The European powers had a long history of attempts to secure an imperial stake in the Near East—or Middle East, to use the term that gained currency in World War II. At the opening of the twentieth century the Middle East—Persia and the Asian and African lands that were still nominally part of the decaying Ottoman Empire—was still a poverty-stricken region. But by 1914 the first discoveries of petroleum had been made, discoveries that have gone on and on until today the Middle East contains the largest proved reserves of oil in the world. The whole of the area was not to share in this new wealth: the major fields were found in southwestern Persia, in the river valleys of Iraq (ancient Mesopotamia), and along the Persian Gulf. The newfound riches of the Middle East heightened the interest of the European powers, and in the 1930s, as American experts began to worry about the depletion of oil reserves in the Western hemisphere, the United States entered the area in something more than its older roles of Protestant missionary and benevolent educator through American schools and colleges. American oil companies joined with British, Dutch, and French companies in developing and marketing Middle Eastern petroleum.

While the Westerners tried to maintain sufficient control of the Middle East to ensure the orderly exploitation of oil, they also tried to avoid the cruder sort of political imperialism. At the close of World War I the Arab territories of the old Ottoman Empire were administered as Western mandates, not annexed as Western colonies. The French got the mandates for Syria and for Syria's half-Christian neighbor, Lebanon. The British, who already held a protectorate over Egypt, got the mandates for Palestine and Iraq. The only Arab state of significance enjoying anything like full independence was Saudi Arabia, which occupied the bulk of the desert Arabian peninsula. It was an essentially medieval state, the personal creation of a remarkable tribal chieftain, a latter-day feudal warrior, Ibn Saud (1880–1953).

The postwar arrangements, which brought so much of the Arab world under a dilute form of imperial control, frustrated the aspirations of Arab nationalists. In these nationalist movements the usual ingredients—Western education, hatred of Westerners, desire to emulate them—were mixed with a common adherence to Islam, and a vague but real feeling of belonging to some kind of common Arab "nation." Arab nationalism was already being focused on the special problem of Palestine, for by the Balfour Declaration of 1917 the British had promised to open this largely Arab-populated territory as a "national home for the Jewish people." The immigration of Jews into Palestine, especially after the Nazis took power in Germany, raised their proportion of the population from about 10 percent to about 30 and caused repeated clashes between Arabs and Jews. Caught between the irresistible force of Jewish nationalism or Zionism and the immovable object of Arab nationalist intransigence, the British mandatory regime in Palestine tried in vain to please both sides. On the eve of World War II, mindful of Nazi attempts to woo the Arabs, the British restricted Jewish immigration into Palestine and Jewish purchases of Arab lands in the mandate. The seeds were being sown for the acute Palestine problem of the postwar period.

The French made few concessions to Arab nationalism; in fact, they infuriated the Syrians by bombarding their capital of Damascus in the course of quelling an insurrection in 1925 and 1926. A decade later, the expectations aroused by the Popular Front's willingness to grant at least a degree of independence to Syria and Lebanon were nullified when the French Chamber of Deputies rejected the draft treaties.

The British attempted a more conciliatory policy by granting some of their wards nominal independence and substituting the looser ties of alliance for the older imperial ties. In Egypt a powerful wave of nationalist agitation after World War I led Britain to terminate her protectorate and proclaim the country an independent monarchy under King Fuad, the ranking member of the dynasty established by Muhammad Ali a century earlier. The British, however, still retained the right to station troops in the country and insisted that Westerners resident there continue to enjoy the special privilege of being under the jurisdiction not of regular Egyptian courts but of the "mixed courts," on which the Western judges (including one American as well as Europeans) outnumbered the Egyptians. In 1936 an Anglo-Egyptian agreement provided for the eventual termination of the mixed courts and the eventual withdrawal of British troops from the country, except along the Suez Canal. The controversial question of the future of the Anglo-Egyptian Sudan, which some Egyptians hoped eventually to annex, was left unsettled. Meanwhile, Egypt continued to be closely allied with Britain.

The British followed rather similar policies in Trans-Jordan, the half-desert area east of Palestine, and in Iraq, nominally an independent kingdom but actually much influenced by British advisers and the presence of British air bases. Until World War II, it looked as though Britain might have found a way of leading the Arabs gradually to independence and retaining their friendship. But the exacerbation of the Palestine problem after the war and the rapid intensification of Arab nationalism were to blast any hope that the Arabs would remain grateful and loyal "old boys" of the British imperial school.

In the meantime, Turkey was undergoing a political renaissance. The losses suffered by Turkey as a result of World War I reduced her territory for the first time to a cohesive national unit, the largely Turkish-populated lands of Anatolia (or Asia Minor). To defend this Anatolian core against threatened additional losses to the Greeks and to the victorious Allies, the Turks launched an ardent nationalist revival extending dramatically the reforms begun by the Young Turks before 1914. The leader of this new political revolution was a highly gifted army officer, Mustafa Kemal (1881–1938), who forced the expulsion of the Greek forces from Anatolia and negotiated more favorable terms with the Allies at Lausanne in 1923. Under his guidance, the old Ottoman Empire was abolished in 1922, and in its stead the Republic of Turkey was proclaimed, with a constitution modeled on Western parliamentary lines, though operated under a one-party system. To point up the new nationalistic focus of the republic, Kemal moved its capital from cosmopolitan Istanbul, on the western edge of Turkish territory, to Ankara in the interior of Anatolia.

Kemal also imposed rapid, wholesale, and sometimes ruthless measures of westernization. Women received the vote, began to serve as deputies in Parliament, and were, at least in theory, emancipated from Muslim restraints, though even Kemal did not dare to sponsor legislation actually banning the wearing of the veil in public. He did, however, require men to give up their traditional baggy trousers and substitute a hat or cap for the fez (a symbol of modernity when it was introduced into Turkey a century earlier but now a symbol of reaction). The whole fabric of social and political life was removed from the highly conservative influence of Islam, again in principle at least. The office of caliph, with its vague memories of medieval Muslim grandeur, was abolished along with that of Ottoman emperor. The sacred law of Islam was replaced by an advanced European law code; polygamy was banned and civil marriage required, at least in theory; the Western calendar was introduced, with Sunday, not the Muslim Friday, the weekly day of rest; and the building of new mosques and repair of old ones were discouraged, while Justinian's Santa Sophia, which had become a mosque with the Ottoman conquest in 1453, was secularized as a museum. The Turkish language experienced a radical reform by the introduction of a Western alphabet—a measure of major importance, for only a fraction of the Turkish people had ever been able to master the old Ottoman Turkish with its heavy content of Persian and Arabic words, and with its difficult Arabic script. All Turks were now required to take surnames in the Western manner, and Kemal himself appropriately took that of Atatürk, "Father of the Turks." By the time of his death in 1938, Atatürk had revolutionized his country, even though westernization was only just beginning to trickle down to the grass roots of Turkish society, where Islamic traditions remained strong. And he had ensured its independence of the West, as the neutrality of Turkey during World War II was soon to demonstrate.

The example of Turkey was followed, though less sweepingly and less effectively, by the other traditionally independent major state of the Middle East— Persia, or, as it has been officially styled since 1935, Iran (Land of the Aryans). The Iranian revolution began in 1905–1906 in response to the imperialist encroachments by Britain and Russia that were making Persia a kind of Middle Eastern China. The political structure inherited from the Middle Ages was altered in the direction of limited monarchy, with an elected parliament and with the shah as a constitutional ruler. The Iranian revolution proved to be abortive. The country, with its powerful class of wealthy landlords and its millions of poor peasants and restless tribesmen, did not adapt itself readily to modern Western political institutions. The shah was unwilling to give up his traditional powers, and the British and Russians were unwilling to give up the respective spheres of influence they had delimited for themselves in their agreement of 1907. During World War I they both stationed troops in an ostensibly neutral Persia.

The Russian revolution eased one threat to Persian sovereignty, and at the end of the war Persian nationalists were strong enough to force a supine government to reject a British attempt to negotiate a treaty that would have made the country a virtual British protectorate. The leader of the nationalists was Reza Khan, an able army officer and the closest Iranian counterpart of Atatürk. But he lacked Kemal's familiarity with the West and his sense of the possible, so that his erratic attempts to modernize his isolated and backward country often failed. He assumed the office of shah in the mid-1920s and ruled in increasingly arbitrary fashion, demonstrating also mounting sympathy for the Nazis, largely because of his fears of some new British or Russian encroachment on Iranian independence. In 1941, after Hitler's invasion of the USSR, the British and Russians sent troops into the country and forced Reza Shah's abdication in order to secure the important trans-Iranian supply route to the Soviet Union.

The fate of Reza Shah served as a reminder that some of the seemingly sovereign states of the non-Western world were not yet strong enough to maintain their independence against the might of the great powers. By the time of World War II, imperial ties had been loosened but they by no means severed or dissolved; the revolution against imperialism was yet to come.

Reading Suggestions
on the Democracies and the Non-Western World 1919–1939
The Political and Economic Climate

R. J. Sontag, *A Broken World, 1919–1939* (*Torchbooks). Comprehensive survey in the Rise of Modern Europe series, with very full bibliography.

H. S. Hughes, *Contemporary Europe* (Prentice-Hall, 1966); A. J. P. Taylor, *From Sarajevo to Potsdam* (*Harcourt). Surveys stressing intellectual and military-diplomatic history, respectively.

E. Fischer, *The Passing of the European Age* (Harvard Univ. Press, 1943), and Felix Gilbert, *The End of the European Era, 1890 to the Present* (*Norton). Reasoned defenses of the thesis that World War I cost Europe its old hegemony.

J. K. Galbraith, *The Great Crash* (*Sentry). Wall Street, 1929, revisited by an articulate economist.

L. C. Robbins, *The Great Depression* (Macmillan, 1936); H. V. Hodson, *Slump and Recovery, 1919–1937* (Oxford Univ. Press, 1938); H. W. Arndt, *Economic Lessons of the 1930s* (Oxford Univ. Press, 1944); I. Svennilson, *Growth and Stagnation in the European Economy* (United Nations, 1954). Instructive studies of the Depression and its implications.

J. M. Keynes, *Essays in Persuasion* (*Norton), and J. Schumpeter, *Capitalism, Socialism, and Democracy* (*Torchbooks). Critiques by distinguished and stimulating economists.

Great Britain

C. L. Mowat, *Britain between the Wars, 1918–1940* (*Beacon); A. Marwick, *Britain in the Century of Total War, 1900–1967* (Little, Brown, 1968); W. N. Medlicott, *Contemporary England, 1914–1964* (McKay, 1967); D. Thomson, *England in the Twentieth Century* (*Penguin); A. J. P. Taylor, *English History, 1919–1945* (*Oxford Univ. Press). Good general surveys.

R. Graves and A. Hodge, *The Long Weekend* (*Norton). Lively social history of interwar Britain.

G. E. Elton, *The Life of James Ramsay Macdonald* (Collins, 1939); K. Middlemas and J. Barnes, *Baldwin* (Macmillan, 1970). Biographies of important politicians.

France

N. Greene, *From Versailles to Vichy* (*Crowell). Lucid survey of interwar France.

D. Brogan, *France under the Republic* (Harper, 1940). Stimulating, if sometimes allusive, survey by a British scholar who knew France well.

R. Albrecht-Carrié, *France, Europe, and the Two World Wars* (Harper, 1961). Illuminating study of French difficulties against their international background.

Stanley Hoffmann et al., *In Search of France* (*Torchbooks); J. Joll, ed., *The Decline of the Third Republic* (Chatto & Windus, 1959). Insightful essays.

A. Werth, *The Twilight of France, 1933–1940* (Harper, 1942). Condensation of several detailed studies by a perceptive British correspondent.

M. Wolfe, *The French Franc between the Wars* (AMS Press, 1951). Enlightening study of France's chronic monetary difficulties.

The United States

W. E. Leuchtenburg, *Perils of Prosperity, 1914–1932* (*Univ. of Chicago Press), and *Franklin D. Roosevelt and the New Deal, 1932–1940* (*Torchbooks). Well-balanced studies.

F. L. Allen, *Only Yesterday* and *Since Yesterday* (both *Harper). Evocative social histories of the 1920s and 1930s, respectively.

A. M. Schlesinger, Jr., *The Age of Roosevelt,* 3 vols. (*Sentry). Detailed study by a sympathetic though not uncritical historian.

F. Freidel, ed., *The New Deal and the American People* (*Spectrum). Sampling of different views on the experience.

Frances Perkins, *The Roosevelt I Knew* (*Colophon). Perceptive appraisal by the secretary of labor in his administration.

J. M. Burns, *Roosevelt: The Lion and the Fox* (*Harvest). Analysis of FDR as a politician.

The Non-Western World

J. K. Fairbank, *The United States and China,* 3rd ed. (*Harvard Univ. Press); E. O. Reischauer, *The United States and Japan* (*Compass); W. N. Brown, *The United States and India, Pakistan, Bangladesh* (*Harvard Univ. Press); W. R. Polk, *The United States and the Arab World,* rev. ed. (Harvard Univ. Press, 1969); J. F. Gallagher, *The United States and North Africa* (Harvard Univ. Press, 1963). These volumes in The American Foreign Policy Library furnish scholarly appraisals of the recent history of the countries indicated.

E. Erikson, *Gandhi's Truth* (*Norton). Appraisal by the distinguished psychohistorian. May be supplemented by R. Duncan, *Gandhi: Selected Writings* (*Colophon).

F. Hutchins, *The Illusion of Permanence* (Princeton Univ. Press, 1967). Excellent critique of British imperialism in India.

G. Lewis, *Turkey,* 3rd. ed. (Praeger, 1965) and Lord Kinross (Patrick Balfour), *Atatürk* (Weidenfeld and Nicolson, 1964). Respectively, a lively survey of the Turkish revolution and a careful biography of its chief architect.

G. Antonius, *The Arab Awakening* (*Capricorn). The classic sympathetic account, stressing the rapid growth of Arab nationalism in the years during and immediately after World War I.

J. and S. Lacouture, *Egypt in Transition* (Methuen, 1958); S. H. Longrigg, *Syria and Lebanon under French Mandate* (Oxford Univ. Press, 1958); and J. M. Upton, *The History of Modern Iran: An Interpretation* (*Harvard Univ. Press). Perceptive studies of individual Middle Eastern states.

A. H. Fuller, *Buarij: Portrait of a Lebanese Muslim Village* (*Harvard Univ. Press). Beautifully written brief appraisal of the timeless round of village life.

Historical Novels

E. M. Forster, *A Passage to India* (*Harcourt). The classic novel detailing the obstacles impeding the meeting of East and West.

A. Malraux, *Man's Fate* (*Vintage). Excellent novel about Chinese communists in the 1920s.

E. Waugh, *Decline and Fall* and *A Handful of Dust* (*Dell). Two corrosive short novels, published in one volume, on English society in the interwar years.

A. Huxley, *Point Counterpoint* and *Brave New World* (*both Harper). Mordant novels written in the 1920s appraising contemporary mores in England and forecasting their future, respectively.

H. Spring, *Fame Is the Spur* (Viking, 1940). The career of the fictional hero, who is corrupted by political ambition, has many parallels with that of Ramsay MacDonald.

W. Holtby, *South Riding* (*Curtis). Sound novel of industrial England during the Depression.

A. Gide, *The Counterfeiters* (*Vintage). French middle-class values put under the microscope by a talented novelist.

F. S. Fitzgerald, *The Great Gatsby* (*Scribner's). The famous novel about the jazz age.

J. Steinbeck, *The Grapes of Wrath* (*several editions). "Okies" journeying from Oklahoma to California in the wake of drought and depression.

E. Hemingway, *The Sun Also Rises* (*Scribner's). Widely considered the classic novel about the "lost generation" of disillusioned American idealists after World War I.

E. O'Connor, *The Last Hurrah* (*Bantam). Hilarious fictional portrait of an old-fashioned American political boss.

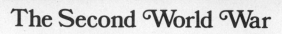

29

The Second World War

General or world wars in our state system are usually born of a previous war or, even more often, of a previous peace settlement that fails to solve certain important problems. We have already been obliged in seeking the origins of the First World War to go back to 1870, to Bismarck, to the "rape of Alsace-Lorraine" and the consequent rise of the spirit of revenge among Frenchmen. We shall now have to go back to 1919 and the grave difficulties that arose in the attempt to carry out the settlement of Versailles. So troubled were international relations for the twenty years after 1919, so closely in time did the Second World War follow on the First, that the interval between the two has been christened the "twenty years' truce." And it is not impossible that historians in the future will actually consider the two wars really one war, as they now consider the wars of the French Revolution and Napoleon essentially one war. A historian might argue that the first world wars were perhaps those of Louis XIV, if not those of Charles V and Philip II, but for the present we use the accepted terms: World War I (1914–1918) and World War II (1939–1945). Such usage has at least the advantage of emphasizing by the use of roman numerals the close relationship between these two wars. In both of them Germany appears as the perturber.

with two of its former enemies, Italy and Japan, each disappointed with its share of the spoils of victory in 1918.

Why was the peace settlement of 1919 followed in a short space of twenty years by a second great war? Why was it so unlike the last great settlement, that of 1815 following the Napoleonic wars, which had inaugurated a long period of general peace, interrupted only by localized wars? Nazi Germany maintained that the second war was the direct and inevitable result of what her leaders called the *Diktat*, the "dictated peace of Versailles that ended the first war. Supported by most Germans and many German sympathizers, the Nazis claimed that Germany was humiliated by the war-guilt clause, stripped of territories and colonies that were rightfully hers, saddled with an astronomical and unpayable reparations bill, denied the normal rights of a sovereign state in armaments—in short, so badly treated that simple human dignity made revolt against the Diktat and its makers a necessity. It is perfectly true that the settlement of Versailles did saddle the new German Republic with a heavy burden—a burden that was dictated in part by revenge and fear. A wiser Allied policy would perhaps have tried to start the new government off without too great a burden, as the Allies in 1815 had done with the France of Louis XVIII.

I International Politics, 1919–1932

During the first part of the twenty years' truce, international leadership of the democratic world rested with Britain and France. Though supported in principle and often in practice by the United States, they were increasingly unable to stem the rise of powers hostile to liberal democracy—Italy, Germany, Spain, Russia, Japan. In the end, the beaten perturber of 1918, Germany, once more waged aggressive warfare against the major Allies of 1918. This time Germany was allied

The "Era of Fulfillment"

But the Diktat thesis is very far from containing the whole truth. What breaks down the argument that the iniquities of Versailles alone explain the second war is the "era of fulfillment." In spite of the Treaty of Versailles, the Germans and their former enemies did manage to come together in the 1920s.

The great landmark of the "era of fulfillment" was a general treaty negotiated in October 1925 at Locarno in Switzerland. Germany there agreed with France and

Belgium on a mutual guarantee of their common frontiers; Britain and Italy agreed to act as guarantors—that is, to provide military aid against the violator if a violation of the frontiers occurred. Germany affirmed her acceptance of the western frontier drawn for her at Versailles, and France, for her part, affirmed the new moderate direction that her German policy had taken since the failure of her occupation of the Ruhr.

The "Locarno spirit" of reconciliation endured for the next several years. It was nourished by the general prosperity of both the French and the Germans and by the constructive policies of their respective foreign ministers, Briand and Stresemann. In 1926, Germany was admitted to the League of Nations, an event that seemed to signify not only the restoration of Germany to international respectability but also German acceptance of the peaceful purposes and duties of League membership. These hopeful impressions received confirmation when Germany signed the Kellogg-Briand Peace Pact of 1928. In 1929, the French consented to withdraw the last of their occupation troops from the Rhineland during the forthcoming year, thus ending the Allied occupation of Germany at a date considerably in advance of the one stipulated in the Versailles Treaty.

Meantime, other international developments were bolstering the "Locarno spirit." The great worldwide organization planned by Wilson, the League of Nations, began its operations in 1920. We shall soon see that the League was never able to impose its will on a determined and defiant aggressor. Yet the record of the League during the 1920s was by no means one of unmitigated failure. In the first place, the League became a going concern. Its Council, dominated by the great powers, and its Assembly, representing all its members, met regularly at the League's "capital," the Swiss city of Geneva. Second, the League played a direct part in the peaceful resolution of two crises that, had they not been resolved, might well have led to little wars—in 1920 a dispute between Sweden and Finland over some Baltic islands, and in 1925 a frontier incident involving Greece and Bulgaria.

Although the United States Senate had voted down President Wilson's proposal that America join the League, our government did take a leading part in furthering one of the League's chief objectives—disarmament. Soon after the first war, the United States invited the other principal sea powers to consider the limitation of naval armaments. Meeting in Washington during the winter of 1921–1922, the naval conference achieved an agreement establishing a ten-year "holiday" in the construction of capital ships (battleships and heavy cruisers). The agreement also set the allowed tonnages of capital ships at a ratio of 5 for the United States, 5 for Britain, 3 for Japan, and 1.67 each for France and Italy.

A conference at London in 1930, however, had less success in limiting "noncapital" ships, including sub-

marines. The partial failure of the London naval conference was a portent. Two years later, after long preparation, the League itself convoked a meeting to address the still more pressing problem of limiting military armaments. Not only the League members, but also the United States and the Soviet Union, sent representatives to Geneva. The Geneva disarmament conference of 1932, however, accomplished nothing. It was wrecked above all by a renewal of Franco-German antagonism, by the German demand for equality in armaments with France, and by the French refusal to grant the demand.

The Failure of "Fulfillment"

By 1932, then, the "Locarno spirit" was dead, and the "era of fulfillment" had ended. There is one very obvious factor in any explanation for the failure of the hopes aroused in the 1920s—the world depression that began in 1929. In Germany itself, as we have seen, the depression was a last straw, a decisive factor in putting Hitler in power. In the democracies, too, it had heavy consequences for the peace of the world, for the depression sapped their morale and made them less confident. But the great worldwide depression is no more in itself a sole explanation of World War II than is the Diktat of Versailles.

Another factor that was unsettling to international politics was Soviet Russia. In the eyes of the Western nations, Russia was a revolutionary power that could not be trusted, that could not be fully integrated into the international state system. The Soviet Union was the center of a revolutionary faith hated and distrusted by the politicians of the West, who feared, by no means without justification, communist agitation among their own peoples. Westerners simply could not trust a government which was based on the Marxist belief that all Western "capitalist" democracies were destined to collapse and become communist after a violent class war.

Still another basic factor that led to the second war was the continuing failure of the three great Western democracies, Britain, France, and the United States, to present anything like a united front. Americans of internationalist sympathies have probably exaggerated the results of the sudden American withdrawal into isolationism in 1919. It is hard to believe, especially in light of the rivalry and cross-purposes that Britain and France displayed *within* the League of Nations, that formal American membership in the League would have helped the situation greatly. Still, the isolation of the United States undoubtedly exacerbated French fears and the French sense of weakness, and pushed France toward the sort of intransigence that was illustrated by her disastrous intervention in the Ruhr in the mid-1920s.

More serious was the failure of France and Britain to work together effectively. France, exhausted and in this decade with a declining population, endeavoring to play the part of a first-rate power but supported only by second-rate resources, lived in perpetual fear of a revived Germany. She sought not only to carry out to the full the economic and political measures of the Versailles Treaty that aimed at weakening Germany and keeping Germany weak, but also to make up for Russia's defection as her Eastern ally against Germany. This she did by making alliances, beginning in 1921, with the smaller states to the east of Germany—Poland, Czechoslovakia, Romania, and Yugoslavia. All of them wanted French protection against the possible restoration of the Hapsburg Empire, whose former lands made up so much of their own territory (Czechoslovakia, of course, had been entirely formed out of Austria-Hungary). All of them except Poland were informally linked together as the "Little Entente."

To a Britain whose statesmen knew well the long story of Anglo-French conflicts from the Hundred Years' War to Napoleon, the France of the 1920s seemed once more aiming at European supremacy, seemed once more an active threat to the traditional British policy of preventing any such supremacy. Although it is now plain that the French were animated rather by fear than by ambition, and that they could never again be major aggressors, it is true enough that many of their statesmen seemed to be falling into old ways, or at least old words, of aggression. The mistaken British diagnosis was at least understandable.

Finally, something of the old British isolationism had survived the war and made the British—and especially their dominions—unwilling to commit themselves firmly to guarantees to intervene with force in continental Europe. Britain did indeed accept Locarno, but in the previous year the dominions had played a large part in her rejection of the more sweeping Geneva protocol which had been urged upon her by France and which would have committed its signatories to compulsory arbitration of international disputes.

The difficulties of the Anglo-French partnership also go far to explain the weakness of the League of Nations. The effectiveness of any piece of machinery is bound to hinge on the skill and coordination of the mechanics who operate it. The League lacked a means of enforcing its decisions. And it was somewhat top-heavy, since the fully representative Assembly counted for less than did the smaller Council, where Britain and France took a preponderant role. When these two mechanics disagreed, therefore, the machinery scarcely operated at all. One example of the way in which the grand purposes of the League suffered from Anglo-French friction is the rejection of the Geneva protocol. Another is the Corfu incident of 1923, when Mussolini for a time defied the League and set a sinister precedent for the later use of gangster tactics by the dictators. In the midst of the Corfu crisis, the League was crippled by Anglo-French discord over the Ruhr policy of France.

The Aggressors

The Corfu incident underlines the presence of one more element, the most important of all, in the rapid deterioration of the twenty years' truce. This, of course, was the fact of aggressions by Italy, Germany, and Japan. We have seen how the ruthlessly ambitious programs of fascism and Nazism steadily led Mussolini and Hitler to a foreign policy of adventure and aggression. We have seen, too, how the somewhat similar totalitarian policies of the Japanese militarists led them to begin the seizure of China by their occupation of Manchuria in 1931. Against this background of underlying tensions—the punitive features of the Versailles settlement, the disastrous effects of the depression on the Locarno spirit, the continuance of the revolutionary focus in Russia, the defensive attitude of the western democracies and their mutual mistrust, the new aggressive faiths of fascism and Nazism, and the rise of imperialist Japan—we may now consider the actual steps taken by the nations along the road to a second world war.

II The Road To War, 1931-1939
The First Step: Manchuria, 1931

It is now clear that the first step along the road to World War II was the Japanese seizure of Manchuria in 1931. Stimson, President Hoover's secretary of state, responded to the seizure by announcing that the United States would recognize no gains made by armed force. Stimson hoped that Britain and the other democracies might follow this American lead, but his hopes were largely disappointed. The League of Nations did send out a commission headed by an Englishman, the Earl of Lytton, and the subsequent Lytton Report condemned the Japanese act as aggression. Neither the United States nor the League, however, fortified verbal protests by effective action; force was not met by force. Japan, refusing to accept the Lytton Report, withdrew from the League of Nations in March 1933, making the first formal breach in the League's structure.

The Second Step: German Rearmament, 1935-1936

The next breach in the League's structure, and the next step toward war, was made by Germany. In October 1933 Hitler withdrew from the League, thereby virtually serving notice on the world of his aggressive intentions. On March 16, 1935, he denounced the clauses of the Treaty of Versailles that limited German armaments and set about the open rebuilding of the German armed forces.

The response to this illegal act set the pattern for the next few years. On April 17, 1935, the League of Nations formally condemned Germany's repudiation of treaty obligations—and Germany continued to rearm. In May 1935 France hastily concluded with the Soviet Union a treaty of alliance against German aggression—and Germany continued to rearm. In June 1935 the British realistically but short-sightedly—for their action seemed like desertion to the French—signed with rearming Germany a naval agreement limiting the German navy to one-third the size of the British, and German submarines to 60 percent of those of Britain.

It is hardly surprising that Hitler's next act drew no more than the customary protests from the signatories of Locarno. This was the "reoccupation" of the Rhineland in March 1936—that is, the sending of German troops into the western German zone demilitarized by the Treaty of Versailles. Britain and France once more did nothing, although many military critics thought then—and still think—that united British-French military action in 1936 could have nipped Hitler's career of aggression in the bud. Such action would have been fully legal in terms of existing treaties and might well have succeeded, for German rearmament was far from complete. In retrospect, this moment in 1936 seems to have been the last opportunity to avert war in Europe.

The Third Step: Ethiopia, 1935

Meanwhile, the Italians struck in Ethiopia. In that pocket of old Africa an independent state had precariously maintained itself, largely because its imperial neighbors, Britain, France, and Italy, would neither agree to divide it nor let any one of the three swallow it whole. The Italians, who wanted it most, had lost the disastrous battle of Adowa to the native Ethiopians in 1896. This humiliation rankled with the fascists, who felt they had to show the world that there was more than rhetoric in their talk about a revived Roman Empire.

In 1934, a frontier incident at Ualual, a desert post in Italian Somaliland—or in Ethiopia, for both sides claimed the place—put the matter before the international politicians. France and Britain were characteristically quite ready for appeasement of Italy, partly because they hoped to align Mussolini with them against Hitler. Over the protests of the Ethiopian ruler, the emperor Haile Selassie, they offered Mussolini rich economic concessions and virtually everything else in Ethiopia. But since Ethiopia was a member of the League, the French and the British had to insist that its formal independence be observed. This Mussolini would not accept, and in October 1935 his troops began the invasion of Ethiopia. Italian airplanes, artillery, and tanks make it impossible for the Ethiopians to repeat their victory of 1896. Mussolini's poison gas finished the task early in 1936, and the King of Italy acquired the coveted title of Emperor of Ethiopia. Once more there was an emperor—of a sort—in Rome!

The League of Nations had already formally condemned the Japanese aggression in Manchuria and the German denunciation of the disarmament clauses of the Treaty of Versailles. In 1935, it at once declared that Italy, by invading Ethiopia, a League member, had violated her obligations under the Covenant of the League. Now the League made the momentous decision to test its power to move from words to deeds. This action had the accord of most of its members and was urged on by the British, less vocally by the French, and strongly in a moving and dignified speech delivered to the League in Geneva by Haile Selassie, speaking in Amharic, the language of Ethiopia, while Italian fascists hissed and booed. On October 11, 1935, fifty-one member nations of the League voted to invoke against Italy the famous Article 16 of the League Covenant, which provided for economic sanctions against a member resorting to war in disregard of its covenants.

The sanctions thus invoked failed. There were loopholes; oil, for instance, was not included in the list of articles barred from commerce with Italy, which had only meager stockpiles of this vital war material. There was much mutual recrimination among members of the League over what articles should be placed on the prohibited list and over the fact that Britain and France did nothing to check Italian movements of troops and munitions through the Suez Canal, which Britain then in fact controlled. Germany was no longer in the League and was wholly unaffected by its decision. No major power applied these sanctions rigorously. To that extent, it is true that the method of economic sanctions was not really tried.

The Ethiopian fiasco was a disastrous blow to the League, which from then on was helpless in high international politics. Its special services as a group of trained international civil servants, its "functional groups," dealing with labor problems, international police matters like the drug traffic and prostitution, and much else, persisted, however, to be absorbed after World War II by the United Nations. But for the rest of the 1930s, the League was hardly even a formal factor in the increasing tensions. No one was surprised or greatly concerned when Italy followed the example set by the other aggressors, Japan and Germany, and withdrew from the League in December 1937.

The Fourth Step: The Spanish Civil War, 1936–1939

The next step after Ethiopia on the road to war is of great psychological and moral interest. No doubt the later direct aggressions of Hitler in Czechoslovakia and Poland were the politically decisive steps. But the Spanish Civil War, which broke out in July 1936, was the emotional catalyst that divided millions of men and women all over the Western world.

As we know, the war was fought between the fascists, monarchists, and just plain conservatives of the right against the socialists, communists, anarchists, and a few liberals or just plain democrats of the left. As in most great civil wars, there was really no center. It was a quasi-religious war, waged with the great violence and with the consecrated devotion that mark wars of

Pablo Picasso's "Guernica" (1937): the artist's protest against the Spanish Civil War.

principle. No one can say for sure how the struggle would have ended if it had remained a purely Spanish one, as the American Civil War had remained a purely American one. Certainly the "Loyalists" of the left would have been in a much stronger position if the democratic powers had followed the usual practice in international law of sending arms to the *de jure* government of Spain. Such speculation, however, is useless. Almost from the very start the Spanish Civil War engaged, not merely the vicarious emotional participation of the West, not merely individual foreign enlistments, but the active though never wholly open intervention of other nations. This intervention was decisive and effective on the part of the fascist powers, Italy and Germany; it was less determined and effective on the part of communist Russia; and feeblest of all on the part of Britain and France. Early in 1939, with the fall of Barcelona, the Civil War was in effect over. Once more a fascist group had won.

Meantime, dizzy with success, Mussolini was going on to other adventures. In October 1936 he signed a pact with Hitler, thereby formally establishing the Rome-Berlin "Axis" and committing fascist Italy to alliance with Nazi Germany. Mussolini gave strong support to Franco's rebellion in Spain. And late in 1938 he orchestrated a public outcry in Italy for the French to hand over certain territories. He wanted not only Nice and Savoy, which had been ceded to Napoleon III during Italian unification negotiations almost a century earlier, but also the Mediterranean island of Corsica, which had been French since the days of Louis XV in the eighteenth century, and Tunisia, which had never been under Italian rule and had been a French

protectorate since 1881. These demands came to nothing, but they further impaired relations between France and Italy. Finally, on Good Friday (April 7), 1939, Mussolini attacked Albania, across the Adriatic Sea from Italy and so long coveted by the Italians, and quickly subjugated this backward little Balkan state. For a few years, Victor Emmanuel was to be King of Albania as well as Emperor of Ethiopia.

The Fifth Step: Anschluss, 1938

The immediate origins of World War II lay, however, in the mounting series of German aggressions. Hitler had begun the open rebuilding of German armed forces in 1935. Three years later, he felt strong enough to undertake the first enterprise of expansion, an enterprise which, like all he undertook, he insisted was no more than a restoration to Germany of what the Diktat of Versailles had taken away. Austria, German in language and tradition, had been left a mere fragment by the disruption of the Hapsburg Empire. Ever since 1918 there had been a strong movement among Austrians for union (*Anschluss*) with Germany proper. This movement had been strenuously opposed by the victors of the first war and especially by France, but agitation for Anschluss kept on, nourished by Nazi propaganda and, in 1934, an attempted putsch.

Hitler carefully laid the ground for the success of the next Nazi attempt. The pact with Italy that formally established the Rome-Berlin Axis (October 1936) disarmed Mussolini's opposition to Anschluss. Early in 1938, Hitler began what turned out to be his standard technique of softening his victims for the final blow.

He unleashed a violent propaganda campaign by press, radio, and platform against the alleged misdeeds of the government of independent Austria. In February 1938 he summoned the Austrian chancellor Schuschnigg to his Bavarian retreat at Berchtesgaden. There he let loose a bullying tirade against the hapless Schuschnigg. In March, he moved his troops into Austria and made Anschluss a fact.

Hitler now had six million more German-speaking nationals in the fold; and in the union of Austria and Germany he had achieved something that no Hapsburg and no Hohenzollern had been able to do. But he showed no sign of being content with what he had gained. Almost at once he went to work on the acquisition of the Sudeten Germans of Czechoslovakia.

The Sixth Step: Czechoslovakia Dismembered, 1938–1939

The Czechoslovak republic was the only state in central or eastern Europe where parliamentary democracy had achieved a real success after World War I. The republic faced a difficult problem of national minorities, but it had the good fortune to inherit some of the most highly developed industrial regions of the old Hapsburg Empire. Its economy, consequently, was far better balanced between industry and agriculture than was that of the other states of eastern Europe. This healthy economy was mirrored in the social structure, where a working balance was maintained among peasants, middle classes, and industrial workers. The period immediately after the war, as well as the great depression of the 1930s, times of great suffering elsewhere, affected Czechoslovakia very lightly. Yet these advantages could hardly have preserved democracy in the republic had it not been for the enlightened policies of Thomas Masaryk, liberator and president of his country until his resignation at the age of eighty-five in 1935.

Even the enlightened Czech regime, however, could not keep the country from ultimately being smashed by outside pressures working on its sensitive minorities. The Sudeten German minority of $3\frac{1}{4}$ millions were the heirs of all those Germans who had so long opposed Czech aspirations within the Hapsburg Empire. As Germans, they looked down on the Slavic Czechs and resisted the new republic at every turn, even when the Prague government made concessions to satisfy their just grievances. Sudeten extremists early turned to Hitler, but even moderates and socialists among the Sudetens were more or less pan-German in their views. From 1933 on, Nazi agitation, supported by Hitler with men and money, became increasingly serious in Czechoslovakia. Early in 1938, having secured Austria, Hitler decided to push the Czech affair next. Henlein, his Sudeten agent, made demands on the Prague government for what amounted to complete Sudeten autonomy. The summer of 1938 was spent in negotiations and in mutual propaganda blasts. The Czechs relied heavily on their French allies and on the friendly, though not formally allied, British. But by the spring of 1938, it seems clear now, Britain and France had agreed not to defend the territorial integrity of Czechoslovakia.

By the autumn of 1938, Hitler was ready for action. On September 12 he made a violent speech at Nuremberg, insisting on self-determination for the Sudeten Germans. This was the signal for widespread disorders in Czechoslovakia and for the proclamation of martial law by its government. The situation was now a full-fledged European crisis that called for the personal intervention of heads of state. The British prime minister, Neville Chamberlain, made two preliminary visits to Hitler in Germany in an effort to moderate German demands, and finally—with the help of Mussolini—persuaded Hitler to call a full conference of the four great Western powers. This conference—Hitler, Mussolini, Chamberlain, with Daladier for France—met in Munich on September 29, 1938. Russia was not invited; her exclusion was to complete her abandonment of the "Popular Front" policy.

Munich was a sweeping victory for Hitler. Czechoslovakia was partially dismembered; her Sudeten rimlands were turned over to Germany; the Czechs were obliged to hand over Teschen and certain other areas to the Poles; the whole economy and transportation system were lamed; the defense of the frontiers was made impossible by the loss of the border mountains and their fortifications; and Slovakia was given autonomy within a federal state, emphasized by the official change in spelling from Czechoslovakia to Czecho-Slovakia. The Czech leaders had felt it impossible to resist the Germans without the aid of the French and British; their people acquiesced bitterly in the settlement of Munich. The Germans had played fully on the differences between the more industrialized Czechs and the still largely agricultural Slovaks. But even had the country been strongly united, the laming blow of Munich would have ruined its morale. Hitler acted quickly. In the very next spring, before the final lines of demarcation set at Munich had actually been drawn, he summoned the Czech president, Hacha, to Germany for another of those ghastly interviews, in which he announced that the fate of the Czech people "must be placed trustingly in the hands of the Führer." In March 1939, Hitler sent his army into Prague and took over the remaining Czech lands, meeting no real resistance. Hungary, long anxious to reclaim some of its lost territory, with German consent occupied the eastern-most province of Czechoslovakia, Ruthenia.

The most respectable defense that can be made of Munich and "appeasement" rests on the argument that the West was buying time to prepare for a war which it knew to be inevitable but for which it was not yet ready. Chamberlain may have thought so; but Winston Churchill and others have pointed out most cogently that the democracies were in a stronger military position relative to that of Germany in September 1938 than they would be in September 1939. It also seems likely that Chamberlain and Daladier, as well as mil-

**Europe on the Eve
August 1939**

Neutral countries

0   300
Miles

The Axis Powers
Areas annexed by Germany, 1935-39
Areas made "protectorates" of Germany, 1939
Annexed by Italy, 1939

lions all over the world, believed or hoped that the acquisition of Sudeten Germans would satisfy Hitler, that after Munich he would behave as Bismarck had behaved after Sedan, and that he would settle down and try to preserve the balance of power. Some Westerners even hoped that Hitler would perhaps ally himself with them against communist Russia or obligingly get himself so entangled in eastern Europe that he would bring on a Russo-German war. Hitler's words and deeds, however, had given no real foundation for the belief that he would now "play ball" with the West. And we now know that he had as early as November 5, 1937,

announced to his close advisers his unalterable intention of destroying Czechoslovakia and moving on into Poland and the Ukraine.

The actual destruction of old Czechoslovakia in March 1939 seems not to have surprised anyone. Indeed the curious mixture of resignation, condemnation, and resolution with which this action was greeted in the West marks a turning point. The days of appeasement were over. Munich had proved to be an epoch-making event, a catalyst for both professional Western diplomatists and statesmen and for Western opinion generally. Hitler's next aggression would not lead to a Munich. We cannot be sure whether Hitler and his aides realized this or thought they could take still another step without bringing on a general war. In public and semipublic, Hitler, Goering, and the other Nazi leaders made no secret of their feeling that the British and French were decadent, spineless, inefficient societies, quite unable to summon the courage needed to resist an inspired and rejuvenated Germany. Yet there is good evidence that Hitler now expected at least a local war with Poland and that he was quite prepared to face involvement with the French and the British. "Whom the gods would destroy, they first make mad."

The Final Step: Poland, 1939

Poland was inexorably Hitler's next victim. The Polish corridor dividing East Prussia from the rest of Germany was an affront to great-power psychology. So, too, was the separation from Germany of the Free City of Danzig, on the edge of the Polish corridor. Danzig was thoroughly German in language and tradition. Germans, even quite enlightened Germans, thought of the Poles, as indeed of all Slavs, as inferior people who would benefit from capable German supervision. Hitler began his Baltic adventure in March 1939, when he took the port town of Memel from Poland's northern neighbor, Lithuania.

The critical issue in the tense half-year that led up to the outbreak of war on September 1, 1939, was not at all the possibility that Poland, unsupported by Britain and France, would undergo the same fate as Czechoslovakia. The British government publicly supported Poland by signing a pact of mutual assistance with her in April. Indeed, in the midst of the final week of crisis, Chamberlain's foreign minister, Lord Halifax, sent a telegram to Hitler himself in which he made a pathetic appeal to the lessons of history:

> It has been alleged that if His Majesty's Government had made their position more clear in 1914 the great catastrophe would have been avoided. Whether or not there is any force in that allegation, His Majesty's Government are resolved that on this occasion there shall be no such tragic misunderstanding. If the need should arise, they are resolved and prepared to employ without delay all the forces at their command. . . . I trust that Your Excellency will weigh with the utmost deliberation the considerations which I put before you.*

The critical point at issue was the attitude of Russia. Hitler had an understandable fear of a war on two fronts, a war against major powers to the east and to the west, like the war on which Germany had embarked in 1914. He was in fact to be drawn within two years into just such a war. Even if he had been faced in 1939 by the united front of Britain, France, and Russia in support of Poland, it is perfectly possible that

*Documents on British Foreign Policy, 1919–1939, ed. E. L. Woodward and R. Butler (London, 1954), 3rd series, Vol. II, No. 145.

he could not have restrained himself and his followers. One is tempted to see the Nazi top command as driven on by some abnormal and obsessive motivation and quite oblivious to ordinary considerations of self-interest. Hitler perhaps could no more keep his hands off Poland than an alcoholic can keep his hands off liquor. But, as events developed, Hitler was able to seize Poland without fear of Russian intervention. Indeed, he was able to arrange with Stalin a partition of Poland that recalls the eighteenth-century partitions.

Why did the Russians make an agreement with Hitler? They resented their exclusion from the negotiations over the Czechoslovakian crisis of the year before, an exclusion that they blamed primarily on the British and the French. From the failure of the Western powers to stand up to German violations of the Versailles Treaty ever since 1934, the Russians had drawn conclusions at least as disparaging to the Western will to fight as those drawn by Hitler. In particular, they deeply distrusted the British Tories under Neville Chamberlain, believing that in many ways Tory Britain was more fundamentally hostile to communist Russia than even Nazi Germany was.

The Russians' mistrust of the West was not dispelled by the diplomatic mission that Britain and France sent, belatedly and grudgingly, to negotiate with Russia in this critical summer of 1939. The Western powers proposed a mutual assistance pact, but the efforts of their negotiators were inept and halfhearted. Moreover, Chamberlain's government made a tactless choice of negotiators. One of them, Ironside, had been involved in the British intervention against the Reds at Archangel in the early beleaguered days of the Bolshevik state—he had, indeed, been made a peer under the title "Lord Ironside of Archangel"; another was a mere professional functionary of the foreign office. The Russians like to deal with top people; they like to be made to feel important. Significantly, Hitler, who was also negotiating with Russia at the time, put Foreign Minister Ribbentrop himself on the job. So the Anglo-French overture to Moscow came to nothing. The Russian leaders had apparently reached the conclusion that, if they themselves did not come to terms with Hitler, he would attack them anyway. They possibly also calculated that the French armies would resist the Germans successfully for some time and that the Western powers would thus reduce themselves to weakness and enable the USSR to profit by the consequences, or at least gain valuable time to arm itself further.

Finally, the Russians were quite as distrustful of the Polish government as of anyone else. The Western, especially the French, policy of encouraging the smaller powers of eastern Europe to act as counterweights to *both* Germany and Russia now bore its natural fruit. The Polish government would not accept Russia as protector; it would not, in these hectic months of negotiations, consent to the passage through Polish territory of Russian troops in case of war with Germany. The

The Nazi motorized cavalry sweeps into Poland.

Russians were tempted by the opportunity to recover lands in eastern Poland that they had lost in World War I and its aftermath.

So, to the horror of the West, the USSR signed at Moscow on August 23, 1939, a nonaggression pact with Germany, the "Hitler-Stalin" or "Ribbentrop-Molotov pact," a cynical about-face of two supposedly irreconcilable ideological enemies. A week later, the German army marched into Poland. On September 3, Britain and France honored their obligations and declared war on Germany. The twenty years' truce was at an end.

Democratic Policy in Review

It is not really difficult to understand why the democracies behaved as they did in these years. Britain, France, and the United States were the victors of 1918, and by the very fact of their victory they were on the defensive. Wisdom and luck might have made their defense more effective than it was, but nothing could have altered the fact that they were on the defensive. In the long past of our state system, the defensive has always proved a difficult position, has always been—perhaps from the very nature of Western culture with its drives toward change—at a disadvantage against aggression. This disadvantage seems by no means associated with democracies as such. Absolute monarchies have suffered quite as much from the difficulties of the defensive, as the failure of Metternich shows.

In the years between the two world wars, the normal tendency of the victors to relax was no doubt increased by some of the facts of democratic life. The Western democracies were committed to an effort to secure for every citizen some minimum of material comforts; they were committed to the pursuit of happiness. Their normal tendency was to produce butter rather than guns. Their totalitarian opponents may well have been quite as "materialistic" as they, but for them the butter was to be attained in the future, and by means of the guns. In short, the German, Japanese, and Italian governments were able to get their societies to tighten their belts in order to make military preparation possible. Yet it was exceedingly difficult for democratic governments to get such sacrifices from their citizens until war actually broke out.

III The Nature of the War

The first world war of our century had, in its main theater, the western front, been one long siege. Since the military experts tended to fight it over and over again in their planning, both France and Germany in the 1930s built two confronting lines of fortifications on their common frontier. The Maginot Line, on the French side, and the Siegfried Line, on the German, were far more formidable than the improvised trenches of the war of 1914–1918. So it is not surprising that on the outbreak of hostilities in September 1939, most people expected first, that the war would be decided primarily in the area between France and Germany, and second, that it would be a closely confined war of siege in the West, with at most diversionary activity in other parts of the world.

But the war itself showed once more the perils of prediction in great human affairs. As Germany was joined by her Axis partners, Italy and Japan, and as the United States entered on the other side, this second world war became much more truly a world war than the first had been. It was decided in Russia, in the Pacific, even in the Mediterranean, quite as much as in the West. And it turned out to be one of the most extraordinarily open wars of movement in history. Indeed, the armies of the British Montgomery and the German Rommel in North Africa moved through the desert with the freedom of nomad hordes of old; but the gasoline engine had replaced the horse and camel.

It was also a war in which for the first time the airplane played a major role, a role foreshadowed in the fighting waged in Ethiopia and Spain during the 1930s. Over the water, the airplane, both land-based and carrier-based, soon established itself as a central factor in naval warfare; in the opinion of many experts, it had made the great warship obsolete. Over the land, the airplane soon established itself as an essential arm of the fire power of land armies, an arm that needed and in the end got careful integration with the ground forces. But even in this war the airplane did not live up to the advanced billing given it by its more imaginative proponents; it did not become the sole means of warfare, superseding all others. Air power by itself alone proved inadequate in the great test of 1940, when the Germans tried to reduce Britain from the air.

Aerial bombardment—toward the end of the war carried on by German pilotless aircraft and rocket missiles—did indeed bring the horrors of warfare back to the civilians of the cities. Military experts had been inclined to believe that civilians could not possibly stand aerial bombardment and that any country whose cities were subject to a few such bombardments would be obliged to sue for peace. Yet European and Asian civilian populations proved able to stand up to months of bombardment. German civilian deaths from air bombardment have been estimated at about 500,000. Organized systems of shelter, partial dispersal of populations, the obvious but not previously noted fact that much of the space of modern cities is made up of streets, parks, gardens, churches, and other public buildings not used at night (when much of the bombing was done)—all combined to make it possible for the people of heavily bombed cities like London, Berlin, and Tokyo to endure what were in effect front-line conditions.

Yet at the very end of the war a technical innovation was introduced that may have altered radically the character of war, may indeed make any future world war so unendurably destructive that it will at least be brief. This was the atomic bomb, developed in secrecy by American, Canadian, and British experts, with scientific support from German and Italian refugees from fascism, and first used on the Japanese city of Hiroshima on August 6, 1945. A single bomb destroyed something over half the city. Somewhat less material damage was done by a second and somewhat different bomb dropped on Nagasaki, a hilly city, three days later. But over a hundred thousand people were killed in the two cities by the two bombs—then the only ones in existence—an incidence of death that seems to justify fully the fears that the atomic bomb and its still more powerful hydrogen bomb successors have aroused throughout the world in our own generation.

IV Early Successes of the Axis
Polish and Finnish Campaigns

The first campaign of World War II reached a by no means unexpected conclusion. No one had seriously supposed that isolated Poland could possibly stand up for long against the German and Soviet armed forces or that Britain and France could possibly get into action rapidly enough to help their Polish ally decisively. Yet the speed of the German conquest surprised almost everyone. The German air force, the Luftwaffe, soon gained absolute command of the air and used it to disrupt Polish communications and to spread terror with its dive bombers. Special German task forces, fully motorized, swept through and around the more primitively armed Poles. This was what the Germans called a Blitzkrieg, or lightning war. The German word was later simplified by the English into "blitz," and was used by them to apply to the German air bombardment of Britain in the years 1940–1941.

Anxious to get his share of Poland, Hitler's new collaborator, Stalin, hastened to push the Russian armies in from the east on the hapless Poles. He also established Russian military bases in the Baltic republics of Estonia, Latvia, and Lithuania, which had been created out of Russian provinces at the close of World War I. "Mutual assistance" pacts between giant Russia and the tiny Baltic states were to be the entering wedge for their full occupation by the USSR in 1940 and their amalgamation, as constituent republics, into the Union of Soviet Socialist Republics.

Fear of Germany, or an imperialistic desire to expand, or both, also drove the Russian leaders into a war with neighboring Finland for bases in the Baltic (November 1939). The Russians, who had perhaps miscalculated the strength of their little opponent, did rather badly at first. For a time, the British and French were even considering massive aid to the Finns. By March 1940, however, Soviet forces had worn down the Finns; they secured their bases and annexed Finnish lands very close to Leningrad. It seems quite possible that this "winter war" with Finland pushed Hitler toward the fateful decision of 1941 to make war on Russia. The German military experts drew from Russian difficulties in this war conclusions extremely disparaging to Russian capabilities.

"Phoney War" and Blitzkrieg in the West

Meanwhile in the West, what the British called the "phoney war" was pursuing its uneventful course. The French and the British duly mobilized as in 1914, and as in 1914 the British sent a few divisions to the Continent. But the Germans refused to repeat the pattern of 1914. Busy in Poland, they did nothing in the West. Occasionally, a French patrol from the Maginot Line would exchange shots with a German patrol, but for the most part the troops exercised, ate, slept, and went on leave as though they were merely in training.

The Germans, however, had no intention of sitting out a defensive war in the West. But the German general staff was not prepared to begin a decisive campaign in the West with the winter ahead. They waited until spring. In April 1940 they made sure of their northern flank, as they had not in 1914, by making without declaration of war a sea and air invasion of neutral Denmark and Norway. Denmark, totally unprepared, was occupied almost without resistance. Norway, also unprepared, made a brave showing. But neither the British nor the French were able to help with more than token forces, and by the end of April important Norwegian resistance had been broken. The Germans now had admirable bases for air and submarine action against the British.

The great blow was struck, without warning, on May 10, 1940, when the German armies, brilliantly supported in the air, invaded the Low Countries and so went around the end of the Maginot Line. Holland, spared in 1914, was this time invaded so that the Germans might make doubly sure of their northern flank. A carefully planned attack on the key Belgian fort of Eben Emael, an attack that had been rehearsed on a dummy of the fort set up inside Germany, was at once successful, and opened the way into the Low Countries.

In the era of weakness among Western democracies in the 1930s, both the Belgians and the Dutch had been extremely anxious to avoid compromising themselves by planning for joint resistance with Britain and France against a possible German attack. They were now to suffer the full consequences of their own policy of attempting to appease Hitler. For the crucial failure to hold the Germans in actual battle came in the Low Countries. We cannot be sure that a carefully coordinated plan among French, British, Belgians, and Dutch would have stopped Hitler. But clearly the lack of such coordination was a major factor in the German success. Indeed, though much has since been written against the "Maginot mentality," it is a fact that the Germans did not take the French Maginot Line by frontal assault, but outflanked it at the critical point where it tapered off along the Franco-Belgian border in the hilly region of the Ardennes.

Through the Ardennes the Germans poured their best motorized troops into France. In a blitzkrieg that once more capitalized on the "lessons of 1914," the Germans resisted the temptation to drive at once for the prize of Paris, but instead pushed straight through northern France to the Channel, where the port of Boulogne fell on May 26, a little over two weeks after the start of the campaign. By this stroke the Germans separated the British, Belgian, and part of the French troops from the bulk of the French armies to the south. Shortly afterward the French replaced General Gamelin with General Weygand as commander in chief. Meanwhile in Britain, Neville Chamberlain had resigned after an adverse vote in the Commons on May 8 as a result of failure in Norway. He was succeeded as prime minister by Winston Churchill, whose advent was comparable to the replacing of Asquith by Lloyd George in World War I. Chamberlain was neither a man of action nor an appealing or heroic figure; Churchill was to prove himself all this and more.

In despair the new leaders attempted to work out a plan for pinching off the adventurous German motorized thrust by a concerted attack from north and south. But the Belgians, badly disorganized, decided to capitulate, and neither the French nor the British could rally themselves to carry out the movement. In the last days of May and the first days of June, the British did indeed achieve the miracle of the successful withdrawal to England of some 215,000 British and 120,000 French soldiers by sea from the beaches around Dunkirk at the northern tip of France. With protection from the Royal Air Force, an extraordinary flotilla of all sorts of vessels, including private yachts and motorboats, got the men

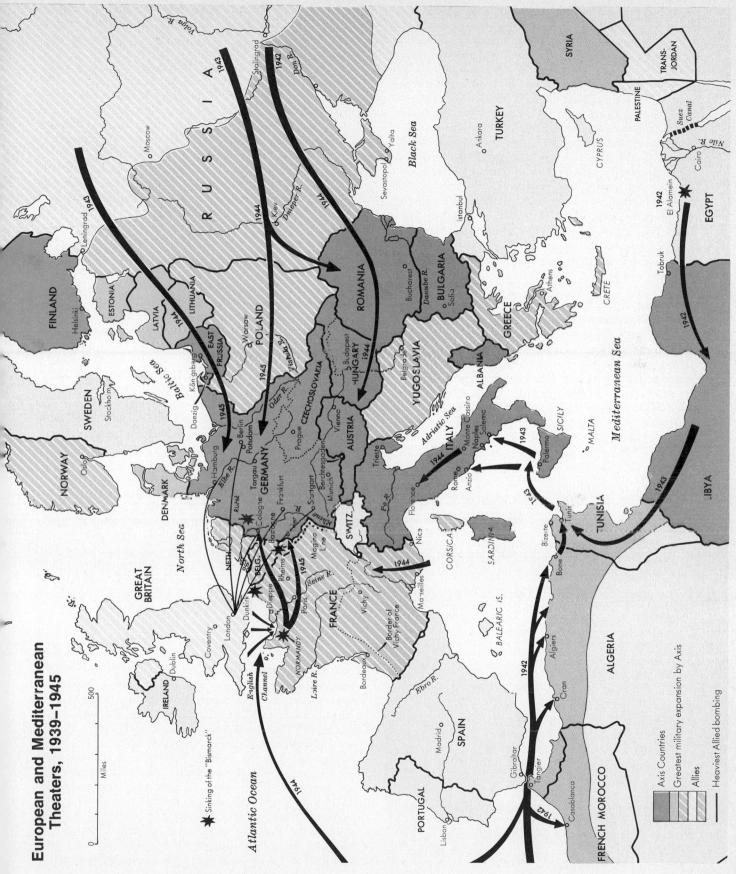

**European and Mediterranean
Theaters, 1939–1945**

★ Sinking of the "Bismarck"

★

Miles
0   500

RUSSIA

Volga R.
Moscow
Leningrad 1943
1943
1942
Stalingrad
Don R.
Kiev
Dnieper R.

FINLAND
Helsinki
SWEDEN
Stockholm
Oslo
NORWAY

ESTONIA
LATVIA
LITHUANIA
1944
1944

Baltic Sea

EAST
PRUSSIA
Königsberg
Danzig
Warsaw
POLAND
1945
Vistula R.

1944
1944

Black Sea
Sevastopol
Yalta
Istanbul

TURKEY
Ankara

SYRIA
TRANS-
JORDAN
PALESTINE
Suez Canal
Nile R.
Cairo
CYPRUS

EGYPT
1942
El Alamein
Tobruk
1942
1942

GREECE
Athens
CRETE

Mediterranean Sea

LIBYA
1943

DENMARK
North Sea
GREAT
BRITAIN
Coventry
London
Dublin
IRELAND

Hamburg
Berlin
Potsdam
Elbe R.
Torgau
GERMANY
Ruhr 1942
Cologne
Frankfurt
Stuttgart
Munich
Berchtesgaden
Rhine R.

Prague
CZECHOSLOVAKIA
Vienna
AUSTRIA
Oder R.
1945

Budapest
HUNGARY
1944

ROMANIA
Bucharest
Danube R.
Belgrade
YUGOSLAVIA

BULGARIA
Sofia

ALBANIA
Adriatic Sea

Trieste
Po R.
ITALY
1944
Florence
Rome
Anzio
Monte Cassino
Naples
Salerno
1944
1943
1943

SICILY
Palermo
MALTA

CORSICA
SARDINIA

NETH.
BELG.
Dunkirk
Dieppe
Rheims
1945
Maginot
Line
SWITZ.
NORMANDY
Paris
Seine R.
FRANCE
Vichy
Border of
Vichy France
Nice
Marseilles
English
Channel
Loire R.
Bordeaux
Ebro R.
BALEARIC IS.

TUNISIA
Tunis
Bizerte
Bone
1943
1943

Atlantic Ocean
1944

SPAIN
Madrid
PORTUGAL
Lisbon
Gibraltar
Tangier
Casablanca
FRENCH MOROCCO
Oran
Algiers
1942
1942
ALGERIA

Axis Countries
Greatest military expansion by Axis
Allies
Heaviest Allied bombing

off, though almost all their equipment had to be abandoned. Dunkirk was a courageous action and one that did much to help British morale. But from German documents that fell to the Allies after the final defeat of Germany it is pretty clear (though the point is still controversial) that the miracle of Dunkirk was possible largely because Hitler himself decided not to press home the destruction of the British forces penned on the coast, since he believed that Britain was no longer a real threat. At the last moment, moreover, Hitler did give in to the lure of Paris, and decided to push the attack on the French homeland at once. Here he was wholly and rapidly successful. The French under Weygand could not rally, and the Germans marched southward almost unopposed. The clear signal to the world that the rally of 1914 at the Marne would not be repeated was given on June 13, when the French declared Paris an "open city" and evacuated it without fighting.

"The Fall of France"

The battle of France was thus decided by mid-June 1940. But the French might yet have tried to defend the south, or, failing that, to use their navy and merchant marine to get as many men as possible across the Mediterranean into French North Africa. There, based on their great empire overseas, they might have continued with British aid the fight against the Germans. Some of the French leaders wished to do this,

Hitler in Paris, 1940.

and to persuade them to do so Winston Churchill made France the extraordinary offer of a complete governmental union of the two countries to continue the struggle. But his offer was not accepted.

On June 16 the French premier, Reynaud, was supplanted by Marshal Pétain in what amounted to a kind of coup d'état. Pétain and his colleagues were determined on peace at any price, and this they got. On June 22, 1940, an armistice was signed at Compiègne at the exact spot where the armistice of November 11, 1918, had been signed. By this armistice, the French withdrew from the war, handed over three-fifths of France, including the whole Atlantic and Channel coasts, to German occupation, and retained under strict German supervision no more than the central and Mediterranean regions. This "unoccupied France" was ruled from the little resort city of Vichy, where Pétain—the hero of the World War I Battle of Verdun against the Germans, now aged and thoroughly defeatist—set up a French form of authoritarian, anti-democratic state of which he was "chief." History has labeled his government simply "Vichy France."

Some of Pétain's collaborators were pro-German. But most of them, even men like the "collaborator" Pierre Laval, a dominant figure at Vichy, were sure that Hitler had won the war and were coming to terms with what they regarded as the inevitable German victory. They did not believe that Britain had any chance of successfully resisting the German war machine that had crushed France. In this belief they were followed at first by the great majority of Frenchmen.

The new Vichy government attempted to remake France along conservative, monarchist lines that had not been practical politics since the Seize Mai of 1877. For the slogan "Liberty, Equality, Fraternity" the Vichy regime tried to substitute a new trinity of "Labor, Family, Fatherland." From the start the Vichy regime was compromised by its association with the hated Germans; born of defeat, it could do little in the few years it had to live before it died in the Allied victory.

Even in the dark days of June 1940, a few Frenchmen, led by General Charles de Gaulle, who was flown out to London at the last moment, refused to give up the fight. With British aid, de Gaulle, a mere brigadier (one-star general) but a formidable intellectual and a scientific student of war, set up a French National Committee with headquarters in London. A nucleus of French soldiers taken off the beach at Dunkirk, and a stream of refugees who came out of France by all sorts of means in the next few years, made up the Free French or Fighting French. At home in France the Resistance movement gradually formed underground to prepare for eventual liberation. North Africa (Morocco, Algeria, Tunisia), strongest of the French colonial areas, remained under the control of Vichy. But some of the colonies rallied to the Free French from the start. Notably in Equatorial Africa, under the leadership of the black governor, Félix Eboué, a most useful base for Allied operations was secured. Weak as the fighting French groups were in the early days, they were at least a rallying point. They were able to set up an effective radio center in England from which they conducted a propaganda campaign against Vichy and the Germans, beamed across the Channel to the homeland.

On June 10 Hitler's ally Mussolini had brought the Italians into the war against France and Britain, too late to affect the outcome of the battle of France. But this "stab in the back," as Franklin Roosevelt called it, further outraged American opinion, already alarmed by the Nazi successes. And Italy was now irrevocably engaged in the struggle, anxious to secure some kind of success that would offset the great gains of her German ally. The war, up to this time confined to northern and western Europe, now spread to the Mediterranean.

The Battle of Britain

The Germans, for all their miracles of planning and execution, had not really worked out a way to deal with Britain. Hitler seems to have believed that with France out of the war he could find groups in Britain who would see the light and with whom he could make a separate peace, a peace of compromise in which Germany would dominate the continent of Europe and Britain would continue satisfied with her overseas empire. This division of the spoils, Hitler reiterated in public and in private, should be eminently satisfactory; he did not threaten the British Empire. Mixed with his hatred for England was a deep-rooted admiration and an emotional and altogether misleading idea that Germany and England were natural allies—if only the English could be made to see it. Yet for over four centuries Britain had gone to war rather than accept the kind of one-power domination over western and central Europe that Hitler exercised after the fall of France. The British, therefore, paid no attention at all to his peace feelers.

Hitler was counting heavily on the possibility that German submarines could eventually cut off British supplies of food and raw materials from overseas and thus starve her into submission. But at best this would take a long time. Hitler and his colleagues were impatient. The obvious thing to do was to attempt a landing in England ("Operation Sea-Lion"). But the Germans had made no real preparation for amphibious warfare; they had no specially designed landing craft. Moreover, the German air force and the German navy were at odds over the best way of combining for an invasion across the Channel. A hastily assembled flotilla of miscellaneous vessels was badly damaged by British aircraft, and early in August 1940 Hitler and Hermann Goering, his air marshal, made the fateful decision to try to do the job solely with air power.

The Battle of Britain that followed had two main phases. First, in August and September, the Luftwaffe attempted in daylight bombing attacks to wipe out British airports and fighter planes. The Royal Air Force, using the new detection apparatus called radar to spot the attackers early, proved just barely strong enough to check the Germans. In the critical actions of September 15–21, German official records show 120 planes lost (the British at the time claimed 268). This was, however, a rate of loss that Goering, head of the Luftwaffe, felt the Germans could not stand. This phase of the blitz was called off. In one of his imperishable phrases, Churchill said of the small group of British fighter pilots who had saved Britain, "Never . . . was so much owed by so many to so few."

The second phase began in the autumn of 1940. The Germans sought by night bombing of major British industrial centers to destroy British production and to terrify the civilian population so that the government would be obliged to sue for peace. Neither aim was successful. Even at Coventry, an important center of the automotive industry, though grave damage was done, the industry was by no means knocked out. Indeed, more damage was done to the cathedral and other buildings in the center of the city than to the great factories on the outskirts. As for civilian morale, it is clear that these bombings strengthened the British will to resist. Civilian defense measures proved adequate to protect both persons and property from that extreme of destruction which might indeed have broken the will to resist. By winter, when the weather gave the British some respite, the Battle of Britain had been won.

Mediterranean and Balkan Campaigns

Hitler now faced the possibility of a long stalemate, something that conquerors like Napoleon in the past have rarely been able to face. Like Napoleon turning to Egypt in 1798, Hitler turned at first to the obvious strategy of getting at Britain through her Mediterranean lifeline to India and the East. His ally Mussolini, already itching to expand in the Mediterranean, invaded Greece from Albania in October 1940, without previously informing Hitler of his intention. The Greeks held on valiantly and even pushed the Italians back halfway across Albania. But just as the Germans came in the first world war to the rescue of their Austrian ally, so they now came successfully to the rescue of Mussolini.

Just how far Hitler himself wanted to invest in action in this theater is not clear. Certainly he toyed with the idea of a campaign against the British fortress of Gibraltar through Spain, to be coordinated with Axis attacks in the eastern Mediterranean to clear that sea of the British. But the Spanish dictator Franco wanted too high a price from the French for his consent to a German march through Spain, and Hitler was unwilling to risk driving Vichy France, which still controlled French North Africa, too far. In the upshot, the Germans had to be content with backing up Mussolini in Greece and with an attack on Egypt from the Italian colony of Libya. Efforts to rouse native action against the British and French in the Near East were suppressed without grave difficulty by British and Free French action in Syria, and Turkey stood obstinately neutral.

Nevertheless, the German commitment to help the Italians in Greece took valuable German divisions away from another task in the spring of 1941. Though Hitler forced on a timid Yugoslav government a treaty allowing German forces free passage across Yugoslavia to Greece, a patriotic Serbian uprising overthrew the Yugoslav regime, and the Germans had thereafter to combat guerrilla resistance and to dismember Yugoslavia. In Greece the British did their best to back up their Greek allies, but once more they were not strong enough. German air power crippled British naval power in the Mediterranean and by June the Axis had conquered the Greek mainland. A spectacular attack on Crete followed, the German troops landing by glider. The British defeat appeared total, but in fact the Germans had invested far too much armament in the Balkan campaign.

The Invasion of Russia

The other task for which the German forces were to be used in the spring of 1941 was the conquest of Russia. Hitler had firmly resolved not to repeat what he thought was the fateful mistake of Germany in 1914; he would not engage in a war on two fronts. Yet by his invasion of Russia in June 1941—an invasion delayed for a perhaps decisive two months by the Balkan adventure—he committed himself to just such a war. Russia was indeed a tempting goal. The Nazi plan had always looked to the fertile areas of Poland and south Russia as the natural goal of German expansion, the Lebensraum of German destiny. With the precedents of successful blitzkrieg in Poland, western Europe, and now Greece, Hitler and his military experts believed that they could beat the Russians in a single campaign before winter set in. It was quite clear that neither Britain nor the United States—even though the latter should enter the war—could land armies in Europe in 1941. An attack on Russia, then, Hitler seems to have told himself, would not *really* create two fronts. Indeed, once Russia was conquered, as in Hitler's mind it was sure to be, the Germans would have no trouble disposing of Britain, and, if necessary, the United States.

Russia was not conquered in 1941. But it was very close—closer perhaps than the Battle of Britain. Hitler's plan almost worked. There really was a successful blitzkrieg. Within two months the Germans were at the gates of Leningrad, and in the south they had conquered the Ukraine by the end of October. Hundreds of thousands of Russian troops had been killed or taken prisoner. In sheer distance, the German armies had pushed more than twice as far as they had in France.

Yet, as the Russian winter closed in, the Germans had taken neither Moscow nor Leningrad. Russian heavy industry had been in part transferred to the remote Urals, and existing plants there and in Siberia

had been strengthened. The United States was beginning to send in supplies. The vast resources of Russian manpower were still adequate for Russian needs. The government had not collapsed, and national spirit was high. Moreover, the Germans had shown once more, as they had in the Battle of Britain, that their boasted planning was far from perfect. Their troops were not sufficiently equipped to stand the rigors of a Russian winter. Confident that one summer and autumn would be enough to finish the business, the German planners had left the winter to take care of itself. Indeed, in winter fighting between December 1941 and May 1942, the Russians regained much useful ground.

American Policy

Meanwhile, the Germans had fallen into a second fatal involvement. Impressed with what he thought were the disastrous failures of German policy in World War I, Hitler had sought to keep out of war with the United States. Although the United States had a strong isolationist element and even some Nazi sympathizers, American opinion had from the very beginning of the attack on Poland in 1939 been far more nearly unanimous against the Germans and Italians than it had been against the Central Powers in 1914. With the fall of France in 1940, anti-Axis sentiment grew stronger, reinforced by a growing belief that if Hitler had his way in Europe the United States would be marked out as his next victim.

Between June 1940 and December 1941, the Roosevelt administration, with the consent of the Congress and with the general backing of American public opinion, took a series of steps "short of war" in aid of Britain and later Russia. By conventional standards of international relations, these steps were not in accord with America's technical status as a neutral; they would have given Hitler ample legal justification for declaring war against the United States. The American government transferred to the British fifty "overage" destroyers in exchange for Atlantic naval bases in British colonies, supplied the British with all sorts of arms, and used the American navy to help get these supplies across the Atlantic. Above all, in March 1941, by the so-called Lend-Lease Act, the United States agreed to supply materials needed for defense, including foodstuffs, to "any country whose defense the President deems vital to the defense of the United States." Supplies at once began rolling into England and later to other anti-Axis powers without the unfortunate complications produced by the war-debt methods employed during World War I. This help went, as we have just noted, promptly to communist Russia. Churchill and Roosevelt recognized that, despite mutual hostility between the USSR and the West, despite even the Stalin-Hitler alliance so rudely broken up only by Hitler, it was to the Allied interest to assist the USSR vigorously. This clearly helped prevent among Britain, the United States, Russia, and the Free French the kind of actual

Fighting in the streets of Stalingrad, October 1942.

back-stabbing and desertion that characterized the failure of Europe to defeat, or even contain, the revolutionary French and Napoleon after 1792.

Yet Hitler still did not let himself get involved in war against the United States. He had, however, firm commitments to aid Japan. And the Japanese, controlled by a militarist group, had taken advantage of the fall of France and the Netherlands and the weakness of Britain to speed up vastly the policy of expansion in Asia that they had begun in Manchuria as far back as 1931. They early took advantage of the fall of France to penetrate into French Indochina (Vietnam). They continued to press their campaign on the mainland of China. The American government, which had never in the days of technical peace in the 1930s been willing to accept Japanese conquests in China, did not now abandon its policy of opposition to what it considered Japanese aggression. It is indeed highly likely that had the American government been willing to allow Japan a free hand in the Far East there would have been no Pearl Harbor. But short of such complete abandonment of the previous American policy in the Far East, it is unlikely that the United States could have kept out of war with Japan.

Pearl Harbor and After

In the summer and autumn of 1941, the American government took steps to freeze Japanese credits in the United States, to close Japanese access to raw materials, and to get the Japanese to withdraw from China and Indochina. Negotiations toward these ends were going on between the Japanese and the Americans when on December 7, 1941, the Japanese without warning struck with carrier-based airplanes at the American naval base at Pearl Harbor in Hawaii. Grave damage was done to ships and installations, but American power in the Pacific was by no means destroyed. Moreover, the psychological effect of the "day of infamy" on American public opinion was to produce in a nation of many millions an almost unanimous support for war against Japan. And the consequence was the immediate declaration of war against Japan by the United States. Germany and Italy honored their obligations to their Axis partner by declaring war against the United States on December 11. As the year 1942 began, the war was literally and fully a world war.

Although the United States was incomparably better prepared than she had been in 1917, she was still at a disadvantage. Against Germany she could for the moment do no more than continue, indeed increase, aid to Britain and Russia by Lend-Lease and take full part in the struggle against the German submarines. Against Japan she was almost as powerless. Her Pacific outposts of Guam, Wake Island, and the Philippines fell in rapid succession to Japanese arms. Nor could the British and the exiled Dutch governments protect their colonies in Southeast Asia. By the spring of 1942, the

Pearl Harbor, December 7, 1941.

Japanese had taken Malaya from the British and Indonesia from the Dutch, and had virtual control of Siam (Thailand) and Burma. They seemed poised for an attack on Australia.

V The Victory of the United Nations
The Turning Points

There were several turning points in the struggle. The earliest was a series of naval actions in which Japanese expansion was stopped. In these actions, carrier-based American airplanes played a decisive role. On May 7, 1942, in the battle of the Coral Sea in the southwest Pacific, Allied sea and air power halted a possible Japanese invasion of Australia and its protecting islands. In June, American sea and air power dispersed a Japanese fleet that was aiming at the conquest of Midway Island. Although the Japanese landed on American territory in the Aleutians, they never seriously threatened Hawaii or mainland Alaska.

In the West, the Americans and the British were as yet unwilling and unable to respond to Russian pressure for a "second front" on the European mainland. But in November 1942, they did effect a series of landings in French North Africa. Secret prior negotiations with anti-Axis elements among the French in North Africa were not completely successful, and the landings in Morocco were sharply though briefly resisted by the Vichy French. Nonetheless, the Allies were rapidly established in force in Morocco and Algeria.

The Libyan segment of the long North African coast had been held by the Germans and their Italian allies since the beginning of the war in the Mediterranean, and there had been seesaw campaigns in these desert areas, campaigns that recaptured some of the adventure, even romance, of wars of old. At the time of the North African landings, the British under General Montgomery were holding a defensive line inside the Egyptian frontier; but on October 23, 1942, the British started on a westward offensive, which was planned to coordinate with an eastward offensive by General Eisenhower, commander of the Allied forces in French North Africa, in the classic maneuver of catching the enemy in a vise. The Germans responded quickly to the threat and succeeded in reinforcing their African armies through Tunis, which was delivered to them by the Vichy authorities. The planned expulsion of the Germans and Italians from North Africa was thus delayed, but the vise closed slowly. In May 1943, Free French, British, and American troops took the last Axis strongholds of Tunis and Bizerte and accepted the surrender of some three hundred thousand Axis troops.

The North African campaign had clearly been a turning point. The Allies had successfully made large-scale amphibious landings, and they had annihilated one of the most renowned of Axis forces, commanded by one of the few German generals in this war to strike the imagination of the world, Rommel, the "desert fox." North Africa was by no means a great central operation, but it was nevertheless a major campaign in which the Allies gained confidence and prestige.

The great turning point on land was, however, the successful Soviet defense of Stalingrad (the present Volgograd). The defense turned into an attack in the same month (November 1942) that saw the Allied landing in North Africa. After their check in the winter of 1941–1942, the Germans had turned their Russian summer offensive of 1942 away from Leningrad and Moscow and toward the oil-rich regions of southeastern European Russia. The Germans were already beginning to suffer oil shortages, partly because of Allied bombing, but even more because, though they held the oil fields of Romania, they simply did not have oil enough for the ravenous demands of mechanical warfare. This push toward the Russian oil fields carried the Germans a prodigious distance inside the USSR, over a thousand miles from their original starting point. But again it failed, falling just short of the really rich oil fields of Grozny and Baku. Russian distance and Russian weather and Russian manpower, and the Russian ability to take punishment, were too much for the over-extended Germans. Their armies were pinched off at Stalingrad, and early in 1943 the Russians started the long march westward that was to take them to Berlin two years later.

The Battle of Supply

A much less spectacular turning point than the engagements in the Coral Sea, in North Africa, and at Stalingrad was the Allied victory in the battle of supply. Yet this victory was of even greater importance, since naval and military successes ultimately depend on supplies. Even for the USSR, an important source of supplies was the United States. But the United States was separated from its allies—and its enemies—by water, and all but the most precious and least bulky supplies, which could go by air, had to move across the seas. If the Germans could stop this movement, or even reduce it greatly, they might still be able to win in spite of the overwhelming resources of the Allies. They made important improvements in their submarines, notably the snorkel, a device that enabled submarines to travel submerged for great distances. Submarine crews and commanders were well trained and resourceful. But there were not enough submarines, and the counter-measures of the Allies—radar, coordination of naval vessels and aircraft, the convoy system, and others—slowly reduced the proportion of sinkings.

Early in 1942, after Pearl Harbor, the rate of sinkings had been really dangerous, and German submarines had operated close to the Atlantic coast of the United States. But by the end of 1942, the statistics showed improvement, and in the summer of 1943 the Allies were confident enough to announce publicly that the number of sinkings from U-boat action in the first half of 1943 was only a quarter of what it had been in the first half of 1942.

The Axis on the Defensive

In the last two years of the war, the Axis powers were on the defensive. Both in Europe and in Asia the Allies attacked with land forces along definite lines of march; these were "campaigns" of the traditional kind. But the way for these armies was made easier by two new factors in warfare: air power and modern propaganda, or "psychological warfare." These new methods did not "win" the war by themselves, but they were useful adjuncts, and they undoubtedly hastened the process. Air bombardment, at least until the atomic bomb at Hiroshima, was never the perfect weapon that the prophets of air power had preached. The Germans put some of their key production underground. Allied "precision" bombing rarely reached perfection. But as the superior Allied air power grew, as it was used systematically to destroy enemy capabilities in critical materials like ball bearings, machine tools, locomotives, and oil; and as American airplanes dropped incendiary bombs on the relatively flimsy Japanese cities, it did much to destroy the Axis will and power to resist.

On Germany and Italy, the attack by land was pressed in three directions—by the Russians from the east, and by the British, French, Americans, and the other Allies from the south and from the west. In the south, the Allies moved from North Africa across to Sicily in a successful amphibious operation (July 1943) within two months of their final victory in Tunisia, and from Sicily they moved in another six weeks across the Straits of Messina to the mainland of Italy. German forces were able to keep the Italian campaign going for longer than the Allies hoped. The Allied victories of the summer of 1943 were, however, sufficient to put

Churchill, Roosevelt, and Stalin at the 1945 Yalta Conference.

Italy itself for the most part out of the war. High officers of the Italian army and others close to the king, helped by dissident fascist leaders, engineered a coup in July which brought about the fall and imprisonment of Mussolini and the beginnings of negotiations between the Allies and the new government headed by Marshal Badoglio.

But the Germans were quite unwilling to abandon the peninsula, perhaps as much for reasons of prestige as for military reasons. A detachment of German troops rescued Mussolini from his Apennine prison (September 1943) and set him up as the head of a "fascist republic." The former duce continued in this post until he was executed by partisans in April 1945. Meantime, Italy had a civil as well as a foreign war on her hands. Many Italians, never really taken in by Mussolini's posturing as an imperial Roman, had never liked the war and were now heartily sick of it. Still, many were politically active in Italy in 1943–1945 and of these the pro-Axis group was far less strong than the pro-Allied group. Italy came naturally enough into the United Nations. The war in Italy went on. In June 1944 the Allies succeeded, after particularly severe fighting around Cassino, in breaking through to Rome, and by August they were in Florence. They could not effectively move further north until the final collapse of the Germans in the early months of 1945.

The Defeat of Germany

The great Allied push in the west, it was finally decided at the Teheran conference of Churchill, Roosevelt, and Stalin (December 1943), would be in France. After long preparation, the landings in France began on June 6, 1944, "D-day." The Allies had chosen the Norman coast at the base of the Cotentin (Cherbourg) peninsula and thereby gained some initial advantage of surprise, for the German high command believed the landings would come farther north and east along the Channel coast. In their four years of occupation the Germans had fortified the French coastline with great thoroughness. But the Allies had also used those four years for study, invention, and planning. In the test, Allied landing craft, amphibious trucks called "ducks," naval and air support—by now the Luftwaffe had almost been driven from the skies—artificial harbors, and a well-organized supply system proved sufficient to gain a beachhead for the allied land forces. From this beachhead, a little over a month after D-Day, they were able to break out at Avranches and sweep the Germans back across the Seine in a great flanking movement led by the American General Patton's Third Army.

A long-planned auxiliary landing on the French Mediterranean coast, to be followed by a march north up the Rhône-Saône valleys, was launched on August 15, 1944, and met very little resistance. Everywhere the

French resistance welcomed the liberating forces, some of whom were French and French colonials fighting as heirs of the Free French of 1940. Paris, a symbol rather than a mere place, was liberated toward the end of August after its inhabitants had staged an uprising, barricades and all, in the style of 1848, against the German garrison.

The Germans were beaten, but not disorganized. In July 1944 an attempt to assassinate Hitler and to pave the way for negotiations was made by conservative elements, both military and civilian. But Hitler survived the bomb intended for him, and the Nazis retained their firm grip on the German state. The Allies were encouraged by their rapid successes in July and August to try to destroy the German armies before winter, or to cut them off from their homeland. Patton's mechanized troops, however, ran out of fuel; the new German pilotless planes and rocket-propelled missiles delayed the full use of Antwerp as a port of supply;

and by late autumn it was clear that the Germans had retired in good order to their own Siegfried Line.

From the east, the Russians had been pushing on relentlessly ever since the turning of the tide at Stalingrad. In the campaign of 1943, while the Western Allies were busy in Italy, the Russians won back most of their own territories that had been lost in 1941 and 1942. They kept up the pressure during the winter and started an early spring campaign in the south. By the autumn of 1944, the Russians had been able to sweep across Romania and Bulgaria, only half-hearted allies of Hitler, to a juncture with the Yugoslav communist guerrillas under their leader Marshal Tito, and were ready for the attack on Hungary. In the center and north, they had recovered all their own territory and were ready to attack Germany itself from the east.

The year 1945 saw the rapid conclusion of the Battle of Germany. The Russians had not stopped for winter, but had pressed on through Poland to menace

Corpses of Nazi victims, Belsen concentration camp, 1945.

Berlin early in March. The Western Allies broke through the Siegfried Line in February, crossed the Rhine, and entered the heart of Germany. Early in February 1945, Stalin, Churchill, and Roosevelt met at Yalta in the Crimea and confirmed final plans for the conquest of Germany. It was plain that the Germans, whose key industries had been so riddled from the air that they no longer could support their armies adequately, and whose manpower had been reduced to the very bottom, could not hold out for long. But the Allied planners were anxious to check the race to be the first to arrive in Berlin and settle peacefully which areas of Germany each of them would occupy and govern after the German defeat. The decision to give the Russians the honor of taking Berlin is one that, with many other decisions reached in the conference at Yalta, has since been severely criticized in the West. At the time, however, it seemed a recognition of the fact that during the two years of successful offensive against the Germans the Russians had worn down many more German divisions than had the Western Allies.

The Russians fought their way into a Berlin already pulverized by the air power of the Western Allies. Hitler went down to his death, as he had long promised, in a Germanic funeral pyre at his Berlin headquarters.

The Allied advance into Germany revealed for the first time the full ghastliness of Nazi treatment of slave laborers from conquered lands, of political opponents, and of Jews, Poles, and other German-styled "inferior" peoples. One after another, the concentration camps were liberated—Auschwitz, Belsen, Buchenwald, Dachau, Nordhausen, and others. And the world was appalled at the gas ovens that had claimed so many victims, at the piles of emaciated corpses not yet cremated, and at the pitiful state of the prisoners who had survived. This was one of the horrors of war whose reality exceeded the grimmest expectations of Allied opinion.

By May 8, 1945, Churchill and Truman (who had become the American president on Roosevelt's death in April) were able to announce the end of German resistance, the day of victory in Europe, V-E Day. It was symbolic of difficulties to come that Stalin was offended because the Western Allies had accepted from some of the German army leaders a formal surrender at Reims in France. He chose to announce separately, on Russia's part, the final victory over Germany, and not until the next day.

The Defeat of Japan

V-J Day, the day of victory in Japan, was now the great goal of Allied effort. The USSR had carefully refrained from adding Japan to its formal enemies as long as Germany was still a threat. Britain and the United States, on the other hand, were anxious to win Soviet adherence as an ally against the Japanese. This natural desire—natural in the sense of historical precedent, for coalitions in the past have usually sought to rally as many allies as possible—was responsible for many of the concessions made to Stalin in the last months of the German war.

The two years of Allied successes against Germany had also been two years of Allied successes against Japan. The attack on Japan had been pressed home in three main directions. First, in a process that the American press soon christened "island-hopping," the American navy drove straight toward Japan from the central Pacific. One after another, the small island bases that stood in the way were reduced by American naval forces, which used both air support and the amphibious methods that were being worked out simultaneously in Europe and North Africa. The names of these islands are now a part of the litany of American arms— Tarawa, Eniwetok, Kwajalein, Iwo Jima, Okinawa.

Second, in a series of operations calling for the close cooperation of air, sea, and land forces, the Americans and Australians, with help from other commonwealth elements, worked their way up the southwest Pacific through the much larger islands of the Solomons, New Guinea, and the Philippines. The base for this campaign, which was under the command of the American General MacArthur, was Australia and such outlying islands as New Caledonia and the New Hebrides. The start of the campaign goes back to the first major offensive step in the Far East, the dramatic and difficult seizure of Guadalcanal in the Solomons by the United States Marines on August 7, 1942. These campaigns involved jungle fighting of the hardest sort, slow and painful work. But by October 1944 the sea forces had won the battle of the Philippine Sea and had made possible the successful landing of MacArthur's troops on Leyte and the reconquest of the Philippine Islands themselves from the Japanese.

The third attack on the Greater East Asia Co-Prosperity Sphere (the Japanese term for their conquered territories) came from the south, in the "CBI"— the China-Burma-India theater. No brief narrative can do justice to the complex interweaving of events in this theater, where the main effort of the Allies was to get material support to Chiang Kai-shek and the Chinese Nationalists at Chungking and, if possible, to damage the Japanese position in Burma, Thailand, and Indochina. After Pearl Harbor, when the Japanese seized and shut the famous "Burma Road," the only way for the Allies to communicate with Chiang's Nationalists was by air. While the Western Allies did not invest an overwhelming proportion of their resources in this CBI theater, they did help keep the Chinese formally in the fight. And, as the final campaign of 1945 drew on, the British, with Chinese and American aid, were holding down three Japanese field armies in this CBI theater.

The end came in Japan with a suddenness that the Allied peoples, perhaps even the Allied governments, hardly expected. From Pacific island bases, American airplanes inflicted crippling damage on Japanese industry in the spring and summer of 1945; the Japanese fleet had been almost destroyed; submarine

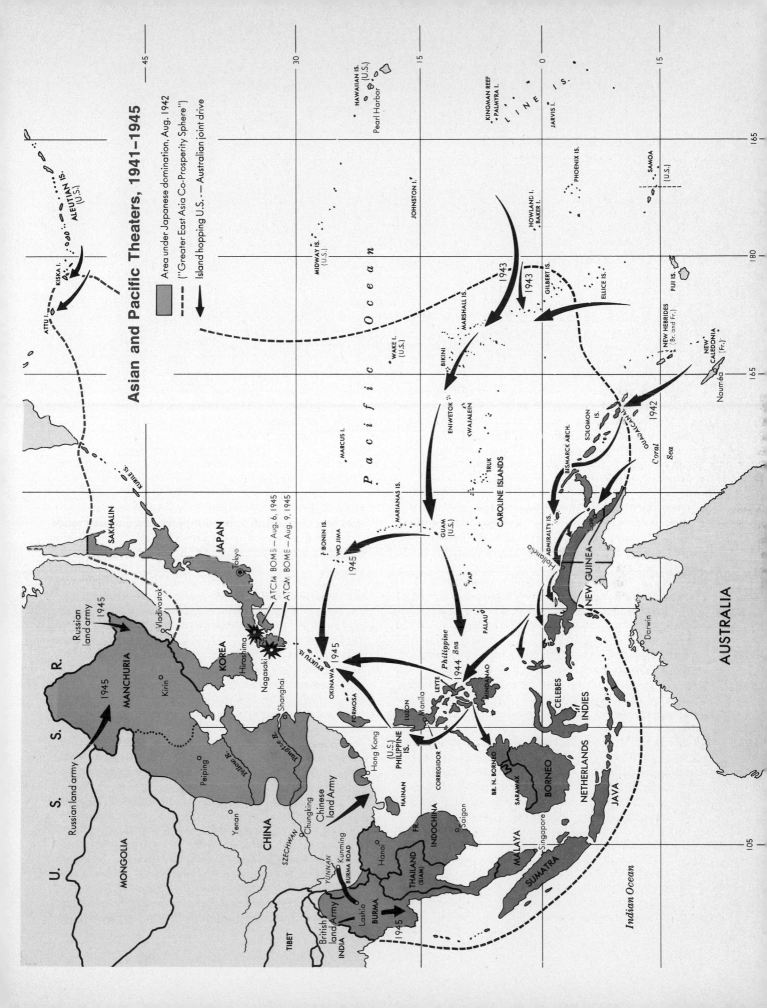

Asian and Pacific Theaters, 1941–1945

Area under Japanese domination, Aug. 1942
("Greater East Asia Co-Prosperity Sphere")

Island hopping U.S. — Australian joint drive

U. S. S. R.

MONGOLIA

MANCHURIA

Russian land army
Russian land army

1945
1945

Kirin

Peiping

Yenan

CHINA

SZECHWAN

Chungking

Yellow R.

Yangtze R.

Chinese
land Army

TIBET

INDIA

British
land Army

Lashio

Kunming

YUNNAN

BURMA ROAD

BURMA

1945

THAILAND
(SIAM)

Hanoi

FR.
INDOCHINA

Saigon

HAINAN

Hong Kong

MALAYA

Singapore

SUMATRA

JAVA

NETHERLANDS

BORNEO

SARAWAK

BR. N. BORNEO

CELEBES
INDIES

CORREGIDOR

PHILIPPINE
IS. (U.S.)

LUZON

Manila

LEYTE

MINDANAO

PALAU

YAP

Philippine
Sea

1944

CAROLINE ISLANDS

TRUK

PALAU

NEW GUINEA

Hollandia

Lae

ADMIRALTY IS.

BISMARCK ARCH.

SOLOMON
IS.

GUADALCANAL

1942

Coral
Sea

NEW
CALEDONIA
(Fr.)

Nouméa

NEW HEBRIDES
(Br. and Fr.)

FIJI IS.

ELLICE IS.

GILBERT IS.

1943

1943

MARSHALL IS.

BIKINI

ENIWETOK

KWAJALEIN

WAKE I.
(U.S.)

MARCUS I.

MARIANAS IS.

GUAM
(U.S.)

BONIN IS.

IWO JIMA

1945

FORMOSA

OKINAWA

RYUKYU IS.

1945

JAPAN

Tokyo

KOREA

Hiroshima

Nagasaki

ATOM BOMB — Aug. 6, 1945
ATOM BOMB — Aug. 9, 1945

Shanghai

Vladivostok

SAKHALIN

KURILE IS.

ATTU I.

KISKA I.

ALEUTIAN IS.
(U.S.)

MIDWAY IS.
(U.S.)

JOHNSTON I.

HAWAIIAN IS. (U.S.)

Pearl Harbor

KINGMAN REEF
PALMYRA I.

LINE IS.

JARVIS I.

HOWLAND I.
BAKER I.

PHOENIX IS.

SAMOA
(U.S.)

P a c i f i c   O c e a n

AUSTRALIA

Darwin

Indian Ocean

45

30

15

0

15

165

180

165

105

Hiroshima after the bomb.

warfare had brought the Japanese economy near to strangulation; and there was impressive evidence of the declining morale of Japanese troops. Nonetheless, American decision makers were convinced that only the use of their recently invented atomic bomb could bring a quick decision and avert the very heavy casualties likely in the proposed amphibious invasion of the Japanese home islands. The result was the dropping of the first atomic bomb, on Hiroshima, August 6, 1945. On August 8, the Russians, who had agreed to come into the war against Japan once Germany was beaten, began an invasion of Manchuria in full force. Faced, after the prompt dropping of the second atomic bomb, with what they felt was certain defeat, the Japanese government, unlike the German, decided not to make a last-ditch stand in their own country. On September 2, after brief negotiations, the Japanese made formal surrender at Tokyo. Japan gave up its conquests abroad and submitted to American military occupation. Contrary to the desires of part of Allied opinion, however, the emperor of Japan was not dethroned. Purged of most of its militarists, the Japanese government continued to rule under nominal Allied—actually American—supervision.

The Allied Coalition

The Grand Alliance, as the historian Churchill liked to call it, but mostly known in its last years as the United Nations, had mustered overpowering strength against Germany, Japan, Italy, and such collaborators as the Axis powers could secure in the Balkans, Southeast Asia, and western Europe. Britain, the USSR, and the United States were the heart of the Allied coalition. But Nationalist China, for all its inefficiencies, had occupied the attention of hundreds of thousands of Japanese soldiers, and the resources of the French Empire and the French resistance movements at home and abroad had been useful. The United Nations had been able to count on the resources of Latin America, and Brazil had been an active member of the alliance. In this truly global war, Brazilian troops had fought in Italy, which at the end had been the most cosmopolitan of theaters. There American (including Japanese-American, or Nisei), French imperial, British imperial, pro-Allied Italian, Polish, and other troops had fought, in addition to the Brazilians. At the very end of the war, Argentina too declared war on Germany and Japan.

The instruments of continuing Allied union were the conferences of the "Big Three"—Roosevelt, Churchill, and Stalin—with their political and military advisers and experts, and the more frequent Anglo-American conferences. Even before the United States entered the shooting war, Roosevelt and Churchill met off Newfoundland and issued the Atlantic Charter, on August 14, 1941, in which they declared for the freedom of the seas, equality of access to economic opportunity, abandonment of aggression, and the restoration of rights to conquered peoples. The Atlantic Charter had been attacked as no more than another empty assertion of impossible ideals, but the true realist sees in it an important step in rallying world opinion against the Axis. Later, formal conferences—between Roosevelt and Churchill at Casablanca (January 1943) and Quebec (August 1943), and among the "Big Three" at Teheran (December 1943) and Yalta (February 1945)—brought to a head consultations that had been steadily carried on at lower political and military levels. From July 17 to August 17, 1945, a final conference at Potsdam near conquered Berlin brought the United States, Britain, and the USSR, with two new figures, President Truman and Prime Minister Attlee, together to confirm in general the Yalta decisions.

There were always grave military and political matters to be ironed out. It was not easy to maintain even the Anglo-American collaboration, which was perhaps the closest military collaboration ever achieved between two major sovereign powers. For the actual direction of operations in the field, the British and Americans decided to set up, not just the sort of supreme command the Allies painfully achieved late in World War I under Foch, but a complete intermeshing of staffs. All down the line, an American in command always had a Britisher as his second, and a Britisher in command always had an American as his second. In the pinch, and in spite of normal national jealousies, the arrangement worked. An anecdote about General Eisenhower from North African days relates that he sent an American officer home, not because he called his immediate superior a so-and-so, but because he called him an *English* so-and-so. At the highest level, the Combined Chiefs of Staff, in close touch with top American and British government officials, did the overall planning. The Russians could never be brought into such close military cooperation, and in the field Soviet troops always fought on their own.

Political Issues

During the war the Allies agreed that the Axis powers were to be forced into "unconditional surrender." Past history was responsible for this policy. Hitler had simply followed widespread German opinion in insisting that in World War I Germany had not really been defeated in the field but had been betrayed by the false promises of Wilson's Fourteen Points into surrendering while still undefeated. This time the Allied leaders were determined to give the Germans no excuse for a future rallying point of this sort. The Germans must be beaten unmistakably, and Allied troops must enter Berlin as conquerors. There must be no political negotiation at all, simply unconditional military surrender. In Britain and the United States there was some opposition to this policy during the war, partly on humanitarian grounds, but also because people feared that the prospect of unconditional surrender would inevitably stiffen the

German will to resist, and would unite the nation behind Hitler. In retrospect, it does not seem that Hitler would ever have negotiated with the Allies; and after the failure of the attempt to kill him with a bomb in July 1944 there was little chance that the Germans themselves would overthrow the Nazi government.

Another political problem made a much clearer rift between the British and the Americans. The underlying issue was just how far anti-German elements in France, Italy, and other occupied lands must go in proving that they were good honest democrats in order to secure the backing of the democratic Western powers. Here the difference in the underlying tone of American and British policies was evident in the views of Roosevelt and Churchill. Roosevelt was convinced that if the Allies did not interfere to support scheming conservatives and reactionaries in the occupied lands, but instead allowed their peoples to choose their form of government freely, then they would choose democracy. Churchill was much less idealistic. He was eager to use any elements that were hostile to the Germans, even if their hostility was quite recent, and he had little faith in the capacity or desire of peoples like the Italians for Anglo-Saxon democracy. Therefore he was quite willing to back Badoglio and the monarchists in Italy; Roosevelt kept insisting that the Italians wanted and needed a republic. Yet the opposition between American support of democratic or leftist elements and British support of conservative, monarchist, rightist elements was not a clear one. We were hard on Badoglio and soft on Vichy; the British were hard on Vichy, soft on Badoglio.

In French politics the issue was further complicated by Roosevelt's suspicions of de Gaulle, whose firm resistance in June 1940 had made him the inevitable leader of the French movement for liberation. To Roosevelt, de Gaulle seemed a potential man on horseback, no better than Boulanger or Napoleon III. To Churchill, de Gaulle seemed indeed difficult, a man obsessed with the need to restore the greatness of France, but an indispensable ally. As it turned out, the Gaullists, in collaboration with the organized French resistance in the homeland, did take over the civilian administration of French territory as it was liberated, and France by free popular vote restored in the Fourth Republic a form of government essentially like that of the Third. In Italy, the liberated people voted the establishment of a republic. What had threatened at one time to be a serious difficulty between American policy and British policy was resolved by the action of the liberated people themselves. The anger aroused in de Gaulle himself, and in many other French leaders, by Roosevelt's policy of refusing solid support to de Gaulle and his plan—never fulfilled—to "occupy" France under AMGOT (Allied Military Government in Occupied Territory) embittered Franco-American relations for three decades.

But the political issue that has bulked largest since World War II was by no means so clear an issue during the war itself. This is the problem of Soviet domination in eastern and southeastern Europe. It is often said that at Yalta the Western powers took much too soft a line with the USSR, allowed Stalin to push his armies much too far westward, and relied foolishly on his promises to permit free elections in Poland, Hungary, Czechoslovakia, and the Balkans. This criticism is often accompanied by the argument—popular with Churchill during the war—about the "soft underbelly of Europe": the Western powers should have struck as soon as possible, perhaps in 1943, from the Mediterranean northward in the Danube Valley in order to get there ahead of the Russians. Had they done so, the critics maintain, the "Iron Curtain" would have been drawn far to the east of where it is now, leaving eastern and southeastern Europe democratic and on the side of the West rather than under Soviet domination.

Yet most of the smaller eastern European countries had no tradition of Western-style democracy; most of them had moved toward fascist totalitarianism before World War II. A transition to communist totalitarianism was not difficult. Nor was the "soft underbelly" really soft at all. Moreover, during the war itself it was by no means clear that the Germans and the Japanese would be beaten so readily. Churchill, who never trusted Stalin, did not dare risk losing the aid of Soviet manpower and material resources during the war. Even in 1945, at Yalta, with Japan still very much in the fight, appeasement of Stalin seemed absolutely essential, not only to Roosevelt, who hoped the USSR would collaborate with us in the postwar world, but also to Churchill, who seems to have had little if any hope of such collaboration.

In the Far East, political problems seemed less serious—at least in wartime. There was general agreement that the Chinese Nationalists, however corrupt and inefficient their government was, had to be supported against the Japanese. Nor did the final decision to accept the continuance on the throne of the Japanese emperor arouse serious opposition in the West. The critical decisions on the Far East were rather the work of the troubled period after V-E and V-J days, when to the bitter disappointment of most Western peoples it became clear that the peace was likely for some time to be no more than a continuation of war. Indeed, there was no peace, and these years deserve a term that was soon coined, the years of "cold war."

In sum, as we all know now, and as we shall see in more detail in the next chapters, the great war of 1939–1945 ended indeed, but there was no peace. From our own Western point of view, and in plain language, the defeat of the perturbers, the aggressors, Germany and Japan, was almost immediately followed by the rise of a new perturber, the USSR, which had already given clear indications of its perturbing power. And indeed, it is easy to go on to the conclusion that just because the Germans and Japanese were beaten in the way they actually were, the present menace of the USSR—pretty clearly a greater menace than the old German menace—was helped, was in fact made possible, by that defeat; from there it is all too easy to conclude that the USSR, not Germany, should have been our enemy all along.

Yet the wise student of history will not readily jump to the conclusion that any other Allied policy, and in particular a different American policy at Yalta and Potsdam, could have either kept Stalin down or turned him into a cooperative democrat. In the perspective of modern Western history the Western statesmen at Yalta were using time-honored methods to win a dreadful war as quickly and as decisively as possible. With the long record of failures of coalitions in the past before them, they were determined to hold together their extraordinary and unprecedented coalition, known hopefully as the United Nations, until *both* the mainstay powers of the Axis coalition had been beaten. This they did.

Reading Suggestions on the Second World War
General Accounts

W. S. Churchill, *The Second World War,* 6 vols. (Houghton Mifflin, 1948–1953). Magisterial account by a chief architect of Allied victory.

C. de Gaulle, *The Complete War Memoirs.* (*Simon and Schuster). Beautifully written first-hand account of de Gaulle's own experiences.

F. L. Snyder, *The War: A Concise History, 1939–1945* (Messner, 1960), and K. S. Davis, *Experience of War: The U.S. in World War II* (Doubleday, 1965). With full notes and bibliography.

J. F. C. Fuller, *The Second World War* (Duell, Sloane, and Pearce, 1949), and C. Falls, *The Second World War,* 2nd ed. (Methuen, 1948). Succinct military accounts.

D. Flower and J. Reeves, eds., *The Taste of Courage: The War, 1939–1945* (Harper, 1960). A good anthology of "war pieces."

F. Pratt, *War for the World: A Chronicle of Our Fighting Forces in World War II* (Yale Univ. Press, 1950). A good succinct American account.

United States Army in World War II (Dept. of the Army, 1947). The official history, in many detailed volumes, to be found in library catalogs under the general title above, or under "United States: Department of the Army."

S. E. Morison, *History of United States Naval Operations in World War II,* 15 vols. (Little, Brown, 1947–1962). Official but detached and professional history, with full attention to political and diplomatic problems.

C. Wilmot, *The Struggle for Europe* (Harper, 1952). Highly controversial study, critical of the American high command.

Special Studies

F. Gilbert and G. A. Craig, eds., *The Diplomats, 1919–1939* (Princeton Univ. Press, 1953). A helpful symposium.

A. Wolfers, *Britain and France between Two Wars* (Harcourt, Brace, 1940). A solid analysis of the foreign policies of the two powers.

S. R. Smith, *The Manchurian Crisis, 1931–1932* (Columbia Univ. Press, 1948). On the watershed between postwar and prewar periods.

J. W. Wheeler-Bennett, *Munich: Prologue to Tragedy* (Macmillan, 1948), and L. B. Namier, *Diplomatic Prelude, 1938–1939* (Macmillan, 1948). Good studies of the last international crises before World War II.

W. L. Langer and S. E. Gleason, *The Challenge to Isolation, 1937–1940* (Harper, 1952) and *The Undeclared War, 1940–1941* (Harper, 1953). Solid studies of America's role.

C. C. Tansill, *Back Door to War: The Roosevelt Foreign Policy* (Regnery, 1952). Alleging that Roosevelt pushed America into war.

H. F. Armstrong, *Chronology of Failure* (Macmillan, 1940); "Pertinax" (André Géraud), *The Gravediggers of France* (Doubleday, 1944); M. Bloch, *Strange Defeat* (Oxford Univ. Press, 1949). Three perceptive studies of the French defeat in 1940.

A. J. Liebling, ed., *The Republic of Silence* (Harcourt, Brace, 1947). Excellent collection of materials pertaining to the French resistance movement.

L. Collins and D. LaPierre, *Is Paris Burning?* (Simon and Schuster, 1965). Deservedly best-selling account of the liberation of Paris.

R. Wohlstetter, *Pearl Harbor: Warning and Decision* (Stanford Univ. Press, 1962). First-rate monograph.

A. Weber, *Farewell to European History; or, the Conquest of Nihilism* (Kegan Paul, Trench, Trubner, 1947). A German sociologist reviews—and regrets—his country's part in the crises of World War II.

D. L. Gordon and R. Dangerfield, *The Hidden Weapon: The Story of Economic Warfare* (Harper, 1947). A very good popular account by trained experts.

H. Feis, *Churchill, Roosevelt, Stalin* (Princeton Univ. Press, 1957). A fascinating and very fair-minded account of their wartime relationship.

There are many memoirs of actors in this great war. The following make a good beginning: D. D. Eisenhower, *Crusade in Europe* (Doubleday, 1948); H. Truman, *Memoirs*, 2 vols. (Doubleday, 1958); B. L. Montgomery, *Memoirs* (World, 1958).

30

The Cold War
and Great-Power Domestic Policy
1945-1970

Many historians would maintain that the events of the single generation since World War II are not yet history at all, but merely "current affairs." Yet these events have made up our lives, and although they are perhaps still too close to us to enable us accurately to judge their meaning, we think it would be cowardly not to face the challenge of trying to make some sense out of them. Moreover, we would be denying ourselves the pleasure of discovering where all the history we have been so solemnly considering throughout this book has been leading the human race and us with it. No doubt in some later edition of this book we shall have to eat some of the words that follow, but that too in its own way will be a pleasure.

From the vantage point of 1974, when these words were being written, the quarter-century immediately following World War II, between 1945 and 1970, seemed to take on a unity of its own, while in 1971 logjams began to break, old patterns dissolved, and a new period seemed about to begin, with characteristics as yet only vaguely discernible. For this reason, the two chapters that follow deal primarily with events through 1970. In the first of the two, we discuss the phenomenon of the cold war in general terms, and then turn to a brief account and estimate of the domestic affairs of the major Western nations and of the Soviet Union. In the second, we begin with Soviet foreign policy and its relationship to international affairs in general, and then move on to the great international confrontation to which it made such a contribution: the USSR, China, and America in Asia, of which the Vietnam war was only the most recent manifestation. Finally we deal with the emerging nations of Africa, the Middle East, and Latin America, and try to view at least a few of them both from within and from the point of view of great-power politics. The two chapters are divided for convenience only and belong together.

I The Cold War

Though it may seem ironical to take comfort in a negative and chilling fact, one can at least reflect that since 1945 the world has allowed itself longer for peace and reconstruction than the twenty-one years that separated the end of World War I from the beginning of World War II. And there are further ironies: the very existence of the atomic weapons that would probably kill off much of the human race in another great war has acted as a deterrent. Man's worst fears have not been realized; Armageddon has not yet taken place, nor does it loom on the horizon, as several times during the tumultuous years since 1945 it seemed to do. The years after 1945 have been full of anxiety, of contention, of fighting in the various parts of the globe, but the worst has not happened, and perhaps it never will happen.

During World War II, most people expected that when the shooting stopped there would be a general peace conference, as there had been after all the major general wars of modern time. But as it turned out, basic differences in outlook between the Soviet Union and its Western allies, and the tensions that arose between them during the war itself, made a peace conference impossible. So World War II bequeathed to mankind a legacy of problems to be solved one by one if at all.

The devastation wrought by the war greatly exceeded even that in World War I: at least forty million dead, more than half of them civilians, and more than $2,000 billion in damage. Despite a sharply rising birth rate and vast programs of economic reconstruction, such losses could never be fully repaired. Moreover, new and terrifying problems faced the statesmen of the world. Atomic weapons, hydrogen bombs, the possibility—and soon the development—of guided missiles, made concrete the threat that a new general war might exterminate mankind or relegate it to something like another Stone Age. The United States and the Soviet Union at first were the only powers capable of initiating or pursuing the new warfare. Given the ideology of the USSR and the suspicious and vengeful character of its supreme dictator Stalin, it was inevitable that the Russians would regard the Americans as their rivals for control of the world and that the Americans should quickly have been forced to accept the same estimate of the situation. The postwar history of international politics thus became in large part a history of Soviet-American rivalry: the cold war.

In 1945 enemy attack and occupation had caused incalculable devastation inside the Russian borders and left millions of survivors destitute, while Russia's capitalist ally, the United States, had remained intact and had invented and used atomic weapons. Stalin knew that if he had been the sole possessor of the atomic bomb, he would have used it against the capitalist world. He attributed to the Americans the strategy that he himself would have pursued. It seemed to him that all the technological advance of the Soviet period, undertaken in order to bring the USSR up to the industrialized West, had now been wiped out by the American development of the atomic bomb. It took Stalin four years (1945–1949) to catch up once again by making his own atomic bomb. No doubt scientific information given the Russians by agents and spies made some contribution to this achievement, but only the high level of Soviet science and technology and the Soviet capacity to concentrate their investments made it possible at all.

Even before the USSR could join the United States as an atomic power in 1949, the two had engaged in a series of tests of will, in Europe and in Asia, that determined where the increasingly clear boundary between a Russian sphere of influence and an American sphere of influence would run. And the confrontation continued after 1949. In Iran, in Greece, in Berlin, in Korea, the lines were drawn, tested, and redrawn, sometimes after bloodshed. Though the Soviet Union and its former Western allies were able to reach agreement on peace treaties with Italy and with three of the Axis powers' former European satellites—Hungary, Romania, and Bulgaria—no such treaty could be concluded with Germany itself or with Japan.

The United States occupied Japan alone. But defeated Germany was divided into four zones—American, British, French, and Russian. The USSR obtained the eastern regions of Germany bordering on Poland and extending considerably west of Berlin, which, as the former capital, was also divided into four occupation zones, one for each of the Allies. This arrangement was designed for temporary military occupation, but continued in effect because no treaty could be reached. It proved extremely dangerous, for it left Berlin as an island surrounded by Soviet-dominated territory, yet an island including zones to which the Western allies were entitled to have access. The failure to reach any settlement over Germany left the most serious problem in Europe without a solution.

In 1949, the three Western powers allowed their respective zones to unite in the Federal Republic of Germany, called West Germany, with its capital at Bonn, and the Russians responded by creating the

Barbed wire blocks passage through Berlin's Brandenburg Gate, postwar symbol of divided Germany.

communist German Democratic Republic—East Germany—with its capital at Pankow outside Berlin. Many if not most West Germans were naturally eager for reunion with their fellow Germans in the Soviet zone. Yet a reunion of Germany under Western capitalist auspices was precisely what the Russians feared most, believing that it would mean a revival of aggression. An all-communist Germany was equally intolerable to the Western powers. Indeed, few Frenchmen or Englishmen looked with enthusiasm upon the idea of any reunified Germany, and if there were more Americans who sympathized with reunion as an ultimate goal, there were no responsible men in high places who failed to understand the dangers of trying to bring it about unilaterally.

In Asia—with Japan under American occupation—the most grievous problem remained that of China. The communists, who had challenged Chiang Kai-shek's ruling Kuomintang (nationalist) party for power, kept their forces in being during the years of Japanese occupation. The United States tried in 1946–1947 to bring about an agreement between Chinese nationalists and communists that would end the civil war. The effort failed, and the civil war continued. By 1949, the communists had defeated Chiang Kai-shek, who took refuge on the offshore island of Formosa (Taiwan), where the communists could not follow because they had no fleet. In the last years of the struggle, Chiang had lost his hold over the Chinese people; the morale of his own forces was low, and an ever-mounting inflation ravaged the economy, already ruined by the long Japanese occupation. By 1950, mainland China had gone communist and formed part of the Soviet bloc. Only Chiang's government in Taiwan remained a part of the American bloc. American foreign policy had suffered a major defeat. Some Americans blamed the failure on a conspiracy by a few evil men, but the magnitude of the change, the huge numbers of Chinese involved, rendered this explanation unsatisfactory.

Elsewhere too the Soviet Union pursued its goal of turning the whole world communist through the agencies of individual Communist parties. In virtually every country a Communist party existed, sometimes strong—as in France or Italy—sometimes weak—as in Britain or the United States—often varying in its precise degree of subservience to the Communist Party of the Soviet Union (CPSU) and the Soviet government, but almost always prepared to act as the domestic agent for Soviet interests and policies. The United States, by contrast, had no such disciplined and reliable supporters in most of the world.

The Soviet Union thus had a certain advantage in the cold war, which consisted in part of a competition between the two superpowers for the allegiance and support of the rest of the world. Each became the leader of a great coalition, whose members were attached more or less tightly by bonds of self-interest to the senior partner.

The members of the loose American coalition in 1945 included the Western hemisphere nations, Great Britain, western Europe, Japan, the Philippines, Australia, and New Zealand. The Soviet coalition included the countries of eastern Europe and, by 1949, China. The border between the two coalitions in Europe—called the Iron Curtain by Winston Churchill in 1946—ran along a north-south line extending from Stettin on the Baltic to Trieste on the Adriatic. Yugoslavia lay in the Soviet sphere, and the frontier resumed again with the border that divided communist Albania, Yugoslavia, and Bulgaria from Greece. Turkey belonged to the Western coalition, and portions of the Middle East and of Southeast Asia were linked to it by a network of pacts. The dividing line between North and South Korea, with the USSR occupying the north and the United States the south, represented a kind of Asian extension of the long frontier between the two coalitions. Along the frontier came the aggressive Soviet probing operations that led to crises and in several cases to wars.

Repeatedly the United States sought in vain to ease the relationships between the two coalitions. In 1946, Stalin refused to join in a United Nations atomic energy commission, or to have anything to do with international control of atomic weapons. In 1947, the United States proposed an international plan of massive American economic aid to accelerate European recovery from the ruin of the war, the Marshall Plan, so called for George C. Marshall, then secretary of state. The Soviet Union refused to accept the aid for itself and would not let its satellites participate. The Marshall Plan nations subsequently formed the nucleus of the North Atlantic Treaty Organization (NATO: 1949). The Soviet coalition founded the Cominform (Communist Information Bureau) in 1947 as a successor to the former Comintern, "abolished" during the war, and created the Warsaw Pact (1955), binding eastern Europe together, as an answer to NATO. The United States and Britain sought in the 1950s and 1960s by a variety of means to prevent the spread of atomic weapons: the plan called for a joint Multilateral (Nuclear) Force in which the Germans would participate. The French rejected MLF and in 1966 withdrew their military forces from NATO and forced withdrawal of NATO headquarters from France.

In the Near East, the Baghdad Pact and its successor, the Central Treaty Organization (CENTO), proved no more than a series of agreements among the United States, Britain, Turkey, Iran, and Pakistan. With the withdrawal of Iraq from the Baghdad Pact in 1959, no direct alliances linked the Arab world with the West. In the Far East, on the other hand, the Southeast Asia Treaty Organization (SEATO) linked Australia, New Zealand, the Philippines, and Thailand to the United States.

Outside the coalitions remained the neutral nations. Some, like Switzerland or Sweden, were simply maintaining their traditional policies of not aligning themselves with any grouping of powers. But most were new nations now emerging as independent, having discarded their former colonial status. Of these India was the most influential, taking from both coalitions much-needed economic assistance. As economic aid became an instrument in the cold war, neutral nations tried, often with success, to play the Americans off against the Russians, raising the not too subtle threat that if Washington saw fit to deprive them of something they wanted, they might regretfully have to go communist. It was not until the 1960s that the United States learned to regard neutrality as often positively helpful to its interests.

Through the years of cold war and the occasional outbreaks of something hotter, the United Nations—formed during World War II from among the opponents of the Axis and chartered in 1945 at San Francisco—served as an international organization where members of both coalitions and neutrals alike could confer. As the direct successor to the League of Nations, it inherited the League's duty of keeping the peace, but like the League it lacked independent sovereignty or authority over its members. To deal with threats to the peace, its charter created a Security Council with eleven member states, five of which—the United States, the Soviet Union, Great Britain, France, and China—held permanent memberships. The other six were elected to rotating two-year terms by the General Assembly, to which all member states belonged. The secretary general, elected by the Security Council, could exert great personal influence in international affairs. But each of the five permanent members of the Security Council had a veto over any substantive question. Decisions had to be unanimous before action could go forward. Both the USSR and the United States insisted on this provision in the charter. As a result, the Security Council often found itself unable to act because of a veto: of the eighty vetoes cast between 1945 and 1955 the USSR cast seventy-seven.

In the mid-fifties new nations joined the UN: some pro-Western, like Austria and Italy (both former Axis states and so originally excluded), some pro-Soviet, like Romania, Bulgaria, former Axis satellites in eastern Europe, and some neutral and mostly former colonies, like Ceylon or Libya. Japan joined in 1956. As former colonies obtained their independence during the late fifties and early sixties, each joined the United Nations, where the "Afro-Asian bloc" came to command a majority in the General Assembly. Germany remained outside the UN, but both East and West Germany had their observers there. The United States for twenty years successfully opposed the seating of the Chinese communists, which until 1971 left the permanent Chinese seat on the Security Council in the possession of Chiang Kai-shek's representative. The first three secretaries general were the Norwegian Trygve Lie, the Swedish Dag Hammarskjöld, and the Burmese U Thant.

Though the UN could not "settle" the cold war or bring about the international control of atomic weapons, it did repeatedly manage to prevent small wars from becoming big ones. The League of Nations had never been able to put its own forces into the field, but the UN did so repeatedly: in Korea in 1950–1952 (where, because of the absence of the Soviet representative from the Security Council, the Russians failed to veto the Council's decision to intervene, and the American army fought under the sponsorship of the UN); on the Arab-Israeli frontiers (1956–1967, and again in 1974); in the former Belgian Congo; and in Cyprus.

Through its functional councils and special agencies—the Economic and Social Council, the Educational, Scientific, and Cultural Organization (UNESCO), the World Health Organization, the Food and Agricultural Organization, and the World Bank—the UN advanced loans to governments to initiate new development plans, controlled epidemics, and provided experts on modern farming techniques. The UN's international civil servants deserved well of mankind. Occasional critics disliked the organization's spectacular buildings in New York and wished that it had never left Switzerland because it might now be mistaken for an instrument of American imperialism. Occasional isolationist Americans demanded that "the U.S. get out of the UN and the UN get out of the U.S.," while those who took the opposite view urged that the UN be given more "teeth" and that the nations abandon more of their sovereignty to it. Yet with its successes and its faults the UN reflected both the diversity and the elements of unity in the world of which it was the forum, and perhaps it would have been unreasonable to ask more of it than that.

II The Major Free-World States
The United States

Instead of reverting to isolationism, as it had in the years after 1918, the United States took the lead in organizing both the United Nations and the network of alliances that constituted its own coalition. Vigorously it put through various programs of economic aid to other countries, beginning with the Marshall Plan and continuing by assisting the newly emerging countries of the former colonial world. Some of the money went for military assistance, most for economic development. Grumblings at home were many, but both political parties generally espoused these programs, and it was not until the American government began to suffer from the special strains imposed by the Vietnam War in the years after 1965 that the sums appropriated for foreign aid were substantially cut.

The rough agreement between the Republicans and Democrats on foreign policy was actually shared on domestic policies as well, although this statement would be hotly challenged by the professional politicians of either party. The stereotyped view continued to prevail that the Democrats were the more liberal and radical of the two parties and the Republicans the more conservative, yet when, in 1952, for the first time in twenty years, the Republicans elected a president, he was not really a politician at all, but General Dwight D. Eisenhower, a popular hero because of his performance as supreme Allied commander in World War II.

And during eight years (1953–1960) the Eisenhower administration not only did not repeal the New Deal enactments of the Roosevelt period, which had been continued and extended by Roosevelt's former vice-president Harry Truman in the years from 1945 to 1952, but left them intact and even expanded the system of social security. An occasional Republican politician might darkly threaten to sell the Tennessee Valley Authority to private companies, but no responsible Republican leader ever wasted his time trying to do so. Nor, despite the effort to tag the Democrats as the "war party," did the Republicans shift the bases of foreign policy: Eisenhower's secretary of state, John Foster Dulles, spoke of "rolling the Russians back" and "liberating" their satellites in eastern Europe, but when he was challenged by Soviet military intervention in Hungary in 1956 he did nothing—exactly what the Democrats would have done.

The early 1950s brought—as a kind of domestic response to the cold war—an extraordinary episode, in which a single senator, Joseph McCarthy of Wisconsin, attacked American civil servants whom he called communists. The fact that some genuine American communists had actually obtained government posts and had in some cases passed valuable information to the Russians lent some credibility to McCarthy's performances. But he himself never located a single communist in high places, while he did attack many persons on the flimsiest evidence or none at all. Bad as it was, the McCarthy period was no reign of terror: no blood was shed, the prisons were not filled, brave men opposed him, and in 1954 he was condemned by his fellow senators 67 to 22 for abuse of his powers. The spectacle of McCarthy bullying witnesses on television—then a new device—helped arouse the public against him.

In 1946, the U.S. government "freed" the Philippine Islands, which became a sovereign state. Puerto Rico, a colonial dependency until 1952, in that year became a free associated state, or commonwealth, with its own constitution and its own government. In 1958 Alaska and in 1959 Hawaii became states of the Union.

The United States was generally prosperous and productive during the quarter-century following World War II, with only occasional recessions and readjustments. So remarkable was the steady growth of the gross national product that some came to feel that the Americans had learned how to avoid depression altogether. The general affluence, which made the United States, despite its very rich men, the most nearly classless country in the world, did not, however, by any means filter down satisfactorily to the poorest members of society. In the presidency of the Democrat Lyndon Johnson (1963–1968), when a series of programs to

assist the poor was proposed, much of the planned effort had to be abandoned because of the heavy expense of the war in Vietnam. The strains imposed by the war, accompanied by increasing domestic unrest, inflation, and rising unemployment, continued to mount after the Republican Richard M. Nixon succeeded Johnson in 1969.

The fact that so many of the poor in the United States were black exacerbated what was already the gravest American social problem. Though gifted blacks had won recognition in the arts, in sports, in the field of entertainment, and often in business and the professions, the race as a whole was none the less handicapped by the failure of American society to provide its members with equal opportunities for education and for jobs. This was true not only in the South, more agricultural than the North, with memories of slavery and the northern victory in the Civil War still alive, where some whites retained bitter antiblack prejudice and refused to permit the black man to advance himself, but also in the cities of the North, where hundreds of thousands of blacks had flocked to live, and where their lot was often squalid and seemingly hopeless.

In 1954 the Supreme Court unanimously declared that the existence of separate compulsory public schools for blacks was unconstitutional. This major decision, of course, immediately affected chiefly the South, where "separate but equal" education for the two races had been the theoretical rule but where the separate black schools had usually been markedly inferior. In any case, the Court declared, separate education could not be equal education. The years that followed saw varying degrees of compliance with the new requirement: most parts of the South were determined to disobey the Court by one means or another, or, if they obeyed, to admit only token numbers of black students to predominantly white schools. The many efforts to speed compliance met with some success: black students began to study with whites in every state of the Union and in the border states, and by 1970 in some cities of the Deep South, such as Atlanta, the number was large. Southern state universities were also desegregated, after some efforts at resistance. But of course the existence in the northern cities of the black "ghettos" and the prevalence of neighborhood schools everywhere meant that public education in New York or Boston was often as segregated as it was in Mississippi. Northern whites often opposed bussing children out of their home neighborhoods to school as a method of balancing the numbers of black and white children just as vigorously as southern whites opposed desegregation in principle. Many predominantly white universities strove to find and admit qualified black students, and institutions previously black began to worry about losing their most talented pupils. Southern white support for Nixon in the election of 1968 left him with a political debt to southern politicians, and many observers felt that the diminished efforts of the federal government to enforce desegregation reflected an effort to repay this debt. The problem of equal education for the races remained a serious one.

The drive to improve conditions for blacks extended far beyond education. In the late fifties and early sixties northern whites and blacks worked to increase the registration of black voters in the South, and to liberalize real estate practices to enable blacks to buy houses wherever they wished. Both drives made considerable headway. Some blacks, feeling that justice could never be gained by gradual means, turned away from the organizations—such as the National Association for the Advancement of Colored People (NAACP)—which had traditionally preferred to work by persuasion, toward more militant groups. Even the Reverend Martin Luther King, a nonviolent black minister from the South who had sponsored a successful black boycott of busses in Montgomery, Alabama, and forced the bus lines to end segregation, lost some of his large following to other groups advocating one form or another of "Black Power."

During the summers of 1965, 1966, and 1967, severe rioting broke out in the Watts district of Los Angeles and in Newark, Detroit, and other northern cities; blacks burned large portions of their own neighborhoods, looted shops, and engaged in gunfights with the police. The passage of a federal Civil Rights Act in 1965 and the outlawing of discrimination in real estate transactions did not calm the stormy situation. Black violence aroused bitter protest even among white moderates who favored the black advance but were growing more and more anxious about public order. This anxiety was surely a factor in Nixon's victory in the election of 1968.

By that time the Black Panther party appeared to be the most influential of the black militant movements. Its founder, Eldridge Cleaver, had published a widely read autobiography, *Soul on Ice,* a fierce and shocking document that aroused both sympathy and horror among its many readers, white and black, perhaps replacing as the key book in the field the earlier

Martin Luther King, his wife, Coretta King, and an estimated 10,000 civil rights marchers on last leg of Selma-to-Montgomery March, March 3, 1965.

Autobiography of Malcolm X, the Black Muslim leader assassinated by a rival faction. Cleaver, under a prison sentence, fled the United States. From Algiers he tried, but vainly, to keep the movement unified. Panthers at home preached and engaged in violence. The conflict often narrowed down in the cities to one between Panthers and police, increasing local tensions which were mounting in any case. By the early 1970s, with the Panthers in disarray, more moderate black voices were heard once again.

The new wave of violence in American life derived not only from the race question. The Democrat John F. Kennedy, the first Roman Catholic to be elected president, succeeding Eisenhower and defeating Nixon (1960), was a young man of intelligence, personal elegance, and charm. His successor-movement to the New Deal, which he called the New Frontier, envisioned federal medical care for the aged, tax reform, civil rights, and antipoverty measures. But Kennedy was assassinated in 1963 by a psychopathic killer with a rifle. Televised details of the crime came into every American home, as did the fantastic subsequent murder of the assassin by another psychopath.

The deaths and destruction in the summer riots of 1965, '66, and '67, the murder of Martin Luther King—also by rifle—in 1968, and the murder by pistol of President Kennedy's brother, Senator Robert F. Kennedy of New York, while he was campaigning to secure the Democratic nomination for the presidency in 1968, all combined with lesser crimes to produce a major public revulsion: but not one powerful enough to persuade the Congress to enact a drastic statute against the easy public procurement of guns. Crime continued to present a severe and growing problem.

Lyndon Johnson's administration successfully put through much of the social program that President Kennedy had not been able to achieve. But the gains were outweighed in the public mind by the cost in life and money of the war in Vietnam and by the rising discontent with a society that could not better distribute its own affluence. City life, in particular, seemed to degenerate as rapidly as prosperity increased. Together with racial tension and crime, the pollution of the air and water, the intolerable pile-up of motor traffic belching poisonous fumes, the multiplication of strikes by sanitation employees, teachers, air traffic-control officers, and others made urban life a nightmare. Your garbage sometimes festered in the streets, your children failed to receive the public education for which you were paying, you were not safe if you walked home at night, you could not easily leave town by car or plane, while the railroad system had apparently suffered a total breakdown. What you ate or drank was likely to be unsafe for human consumption, and your municipal government was probably both corrupt and bankrupt. Yet your taxes rose faster than your fast-increasing income. In the suburbs, neat lawns and good public schools concealed imperfectly what some felt to be a cultural desert, while others fought to preserve what

they had so recently acquired from encroachments, aggressions, and looming threats.

Children of the well-to-do, pampered by any standard, were "opting out" of the society in large numbers. Some took drugs—the increasingly fashionable marijuana, which they insisted (against much medical evidence) was no more harmful than the alcohol their parents had always indulged in; or more addictive and dangerous drugs such as heroin, or LSD, or even the deadly "speed." Many dropouts left home, congregated in special places (San Francisco's Haight-Ashbury district, New York's East Village), living from hand to mouth or handout to handout, eccentrically dressed in American Indian feathers or beads, affecting what they believed to be Buddhist ideas, speaking a special dialect, and protesting their love for everybody, which often looked uncommonly like hate. These were the "hippies" of the late 1960s. A multiple murder committed by a roving group of dropouts served to focus public attention on the number of young men and women self-outlawed from American society, who had apparently crossed the line into a new, mad universe.

Other young people actively rebelled against the institutions of their immediate world, the university or the draft board. A few took Mao Tse-tung or the Cuban guerrilla leader Che Guevara, killed in Bolivia, as their heroes, and the difficult writings of Herbert Marcuse as their inspiration. Starting at the University of California in Berkeley and Columbia University in New York and moving then to other institutions small and large, student radical violence in 1968 and 1969 usually took the form of sit-ins or building seizures, often accompanied by the disruption of classes, the theft of documents from files, and the intimidation of individual professors or administrators. The perpetrators of these acts generally argued that this was the sole means of obtaining favorable responses to one or another set of "demands," often local but usually including some that bore on the nation's problems (abolish ROTC because the Vietnam war is wicked, build more housing for the poor, grant open admission to blacks). Since the universities as such had as a rule no power to influence national policies, the demands were usually delivered to the wrong address.

Among violent students there were a few who were eager to overthrow American society altogether and were beginning with the institution closest to their own lives. "Tear it all down first, and then discuss what should be put in its place" was an argument that Bakunin would have recognized and welcomed. Whenever university authorities summoned the police or the National Guard to quell violence, the usual effect was to turn moderate students into radicals. The universities were thus faced with a painful dilemma, as their radical enemies realized: either to submit to intimidation and violence from the left, or, in fighting the left, vastly to increase its numbers. When the National Guard fired into a student demonstration at Kent State University

National Guardsmen hurl tear gas at students of Kent State University, May 4, 1970.

in Ohio in 1970, killing four students, all white, and within a few days police in Mississippi killed two more, this time black, there was a national cry of outrage on the university campuses.

On the far left fringe of the student radical movement were those who used bombs against university buildings, banks, or public buildings. In response, outraged Americans of older generations and of all social classes grew more militant. The construction workers or "hard hats," the police in some communities, those everywhere who believed in seeking one's political and economic goals by traditional peaceful means, to some degree shared the baffled revulsion. And the most unhappy among them found their spokesman in Nixon's vice-president, Spiro Agnew, who repeatedly flailed away at rebellious youth.

Exploding in many western European countries as well as in America, the rebellion of the youth reminded many observers of the Russian nihilists and anarchists of the nineteenth century. The Russian "establishment" of the nineteenth century had not understood how to isolate the extremists among the rebels by embracing the moderates. Perhaps twentieth-century authorities would ponder the lesson.

So it was that in 1970 America seemed to many to be trapped in full domestic crisis. Even the national prosperity was shaken, as the war continued, inflation grew worse, and the stock market fell. Race relations, public order, conditions in the cities, the disaffection of the young: everywhere one turned one could read (interminably and not very helpfully) about all of them. The voices of movements for the liberation of women and homosexuals added a new note to the chorus. Outraged by injustices such as their inability to obtain equal pay for equal work, these militants

sometimes sounded as if they were determined to end the human family as an institution.

Canada

After 1945, Canada enjoyed an economic growth and prosperity proportionately even greater than that of the United States. American capital poured in, and much was raised at home and in Britain. Though still producing vast amounts of raw materials from farm, mine, and forest, Canada came now to be a great industrial nation, exploiting her remarkable hydroelectric resources and her oil and mineral wealth. In the mid-fifties, Canada took the lead in carrying out a long-discussed plan for a canal from the Great Lakes to the lower St. Lawrence, deep enough to accommodate ocean-going ships and producing in addition important hydroelectric power. In the United States, vested interests long succeeded in preventing American participation. But when Canada announced her intention of going ahead with the canal entirely on Canadian territory, the United States joined in a collaborative development; work began in 1954, and the canal was opened in 1959. Many Canadians had begun to worry over what they felt was undue cultural and economic dependence on the United States. But the three-thousand-mile frontier without a fort remained peaceful.

Until the late 1950s, Canada was politically one of the stablest of Western nations. While other parties at times held power in the provinces, the federal government except for the Conservative years of 1957–1963 remained under the control of the Liberals, who depended for their support on an effective collaboration between the English-speaking provinces and the

French-speaking province of Quebec. In addition to Conservatives and Liberals there were minority parties—New Democrats, to the left; Social Credit, favoring unorthodox economic ideas but not socialist; and a French-Canadian variant of this last. It seemed possible in the sixties that Canada was beginning to develop a splinter-party system like those of many European democracies.

One reason for this was the rise of French-Canadian nationalist feeling, chiefly in the province of Quebec. The few thousands of French left in Canada in 1763 had multiplied by the 1960s to some seven million. Since World War II they had for the first time enjoyed a vigorous economic growth and increasingly high standards of living, after lagging for decades behind the rest of Canada. Their unrest was in part a demand for a greater share in the Canadian managerial and financial worlds. It was also a demand for greater cultural participation in dominion life and especially for true bilingualism after the Swiss pattern. Many people in the rest of Canada resisted their demands. By 1967, the French extremists who actually proposed to secede and set up an independent Quebec were probably no more than a noisy few. A federal commission on biculturalism was set up.

Into this somewhat tense situation the French president de Gaulle—with typical drama and concern for French *"grandeur"*—intruded in 1967, on a state visit to Canada. By shouting *"Vive le Québec libre!"* ("Long live free Quebec!") to an enthusiastic crowd he seemed to be sponsoring secession. The Canadian federal government called his performance inadmissible, but he made a strenuous attempt thereafter to open special official cultural and economic relations with Quebec. No doubt the episode reflected in part de Gaulle's eagerness to make trouble for all "Anglo-Saxons" and for all friends of the United States. The Canadians responded by producing a brand-new political leader: a previously unknown Liberal, Pierre Elliott Trudeau, who won a smashing electoral victory in 1968. Half-French, bilingual, handsome, and intelligent, he had a free hand to cope with separatism as with all other questions that might arise. Trudeau began to cut back on Canada's international commitments in an effort to achieve a "just society" for the Canadian people. Attempting to free his country from too great reliance on the United States, he established diplomatic relations with the People's Republic of China. The Official Languages Act established French as the equal of English but did not satisfy the separatists. In 1970, one terrorist group kidnapped a British diplomat, who was freed when they were allowed to go to Cuba; while a second group kidnapped and murdered a Quebec government official and got away. Trudeau proclaimed martial law and calmed the immediate crisis.

ment, but also made real attempts to organize a "free Europe" on a level above and beyond that of the national state.

In 1952, as a first step, France, West Germany, and Italy joined Belgium, the Netherlands, and Luxembourg ("Benelux") in setting up the European Coal and Steel Community, which created for their coal and iron industries a free market area of all six nations, in which a joint administrative body could make certain final and binding decisions without the participation of any government officials. Each nation had given up some part of its sovereignty, and the plan was a success.

In 1957, these six countries, by the Treaty of Rome, established the European Economic Community (EEC), better known as the Common Market, or sometimes "the Six." This was the beginning of closer economic union under a central administration composed of delegates from each partner nation. Its administration had certain rights independent of any member government. The treaty also provided for increasing powers over trade, production, immigration, and other matters for the Common Market, according to a carefully worked-out schedule. By the 1970s, it was planned, there would be in effect one common trading and producing society, a single market free from internal tariffs, and a population of some 180 million or more, substantially equal to that of the United States and equipped with equal economic skills and experience, and with similar "mixed" economies—free enterprise under government regulation.

The years after 1957 saw substantial progress toward this goal. The tourist by car or rail, remembering prewar delays at the frontiers of the six countries, was astonished to be able to pass from one country to another almost as easily as he crossed state lines in the United States and quite as easily as he crossed the Canadian-American frontier. Yet difficulties arose in the orderly carrying out of the schedule. Twice France vetoed Britain's proposed entry into the EEC and insisted on specific provisions favoring French farmers in the Common Market. The difficulty about a British part in any European supranational arrangement was real, for many of the British regarded themselves as primarily part of the Commonwealth and not as Europeans. The British set up in 1959 the European Free Trade Association, often called the "Outer Seven," with Britain, Sweden, Norway, Denmark, Austria, Switzerland, and Portugal as members. A much looser arrangement than the Common Market, it allowed each member to set its own external tariffs as it wished, thus protecting British "imperial preference" in favor of Commonwealth countries. Not until the disappearance of de Gaulle from French political life in 1969 did the possibility of British entry into the Common Market revive.

Western Europe

After 1945, the nations of western Europe preserved the form of the sovereign state, and much nationalist senti-

Great Britain

In the United Kingdom of Great Britain and Northern Ireland (Southern Ireland being completely independent), a general election held in July 1945, after the war had ended in Europe, ousted Churchill and the Conservative party and for the first time returned the Labour party with an absolute majority in the House of Commons. The Liberal party was practically extinguished. The new prime minister was Clement Attlee, a middle-class social worker.

The new government—with a mandate for social change—proceeded to take over, with compensation to the owners, the coal industry, the railroads, and some parts of commercial road transportation, and began to nationalize the steel industry. Britain already had a well-developed system of various social insurances; this was now capped by a system of socialized medical care for all who wished it. The educational system was partly reformed in an effort to make it more democratic and to lengthen the required period of compulsory education. In accordance with Labour party philosophy, some parts of the old empire were given independence and others were granted dominion status— that is, national independence within the extraordinary British multinational system, the Commonwealth.

What emerged was a British economy pushed a little more toward collectivism than before, but still a "mixed" economy. Once nationalized, coal and railroads did not become great state trusts run by bureaucrats on the Russian model but rather public corporations with a structure not unlike that of private industries in the West, run by impartial boards not dominated by bureaucrats or politicians. Broad sectors of the economy remained in private hands, under no more than the kind of government regulation common in the United States.

When the Conservatives, with Churchill still at their head, were returned to power once more in 1951 and remained there for twelve years, they halted the nationalization of steel, which had begun, but otherwise kept intact the socialism of their opponents, including the national health scheme. Churchill was succeeded by Anthony Eden (later Lord Avon), who fell from office after the débacle over Suez in 1956 (discussed below), and Eden in turn by Harold Macmillan, who governed until 1964.

In the postwar years the British were not resilient enough to keep up with the extraordinary pace of technological innovation. The British automobile industry, for example, which immediately after the war gained a big share of the world market, in the 1950s saw the Germans, with their inexpensive, standardized light car, the Volkswagen, take the lead. Ironically enough, the British were penalized because they had been the *first* to industrialize, and so their plant was the first to become obsolescent and inefficient. Observers often found Britain's managers lacking in enterprise, unwilling to adopt new ways, and uninterested in research; while the workers were generally suspicious of any change in methods, regarded management as the perpetual enemy, and were more interested in the tea break than in the quality of the product.

And even in apparent prosperity, Britain remained in economic trouble. The pound, a currency still used as standard along with the dollar in the "free world," was always in danger. Its exchange value, already reduced in 1940 from $4.85 to $4.00, had after 1949 been pegged at $2.80. But continued pressure on the pound in the 1960s repeatedly required help from Britain's allies in the form of rather complex financial measures to maintain this value. This weakness of the pound signaled an unfavorable balance of trade: the British people were buying more from the rest of the world than they could sell to it. In the fifties and sixties, in what came to be called the brain drain, some of Britain's distinguished scientists and engineers left home to migrate to the United States, Canada, or Australia.

Under Harold Wilson, a shrewd politician often criticized for opportunism, the Labour party came to power in 1964 and governed until 1970. In 1966, Wilson froze wages and prices in an effort to restore the balance between what the British spent and what they produced. In his own party, such measures were deeply unpopular and were regarded as exploiting the poor to support the rich. Wilson had to devalue the pound once again, to $2.40, after heavy foreign pressure against it. Despite the unpopularity of his policies, by 1969 the deficits had disappeared and general prosperity continued despite high taxes and rapid inflation. Prices were rising so fast that the gains from increasing wages were largely illusory. Yet more and more English workmen were able to buy cars and take their seaside holidays. The National Health scheme and education for working-class mothers had resulted in the virtual disappearance of the thin unhealthy infant from the British scene, as all classes seemed to produce an endless new supply of bouncing, rosy-cheeked, healthy specimens.

An increasing number of new universities (often called "red-brick" to distinguish them from the older, originally medieval seats of learning with their Gothic or Jacobean or eighteenth-century stone buildings) sprang up to offer young people of all classes educational opportunities that had previously been available only to the upper and upper-middle classes. Oxford and Cambridge themselves now included large numbers of working-class young men and women on state scholarships. But English universities suffered like those in America—though not so severely—from disruptive students. A still more important issue was posed by Labour's plans for "democratizing" secondary education through a new program of "comprehensive" schools, which, it was charged, would handicap the talented and reduce schooling to a low common denominator of mediocrity. The Conservatives opposed Labour's plan, and many Labourites lacked enthusiasm for it.

In the postwar years, the race problem for the first time became a serious one in Britain. Indians, Pakistanis, West Indian and African blacks—Commonwealth subjects with British passports—left poor conditions at home and freely came to England in large numbers to take jobs in London and the industrial midlands in factories, public transportation, and hospitals. Dislike for blacks now rose markedly and affected both political parties. Despite its liberal and antiracist protestations, the Wilson government was forced to curtail immigration sharply. But the most vociferous warnings were sounded by a Conservative politician, Enoch Powell, who predicted bloody race riots—a few of which had already taken place—unless black immigration was halted and blacks already in England were deported. Many working-class people, lifelong Labourites, supported Powell, who also had the support of much Conservative opinion, despite the party's official attempts to repudiate him.

Closely related to the race issue at home was the question of official British relations abroad with South Africa (to which the Labour government had refused to sell arms because of the racial policies of the South African regime) and with the new white-dominated African state of Rhodesia (which the Labour government did not recognize and on which it had declared an economic boycott for similar reasons). Many Conservatives, Powell among them, deplored these policies and charged that Labour had forgotten England's true interests and proper close bonds with countrymen overseas.

Even the Irish problem, long quiescent, arose again in the late 1960s. In Ulster, the northern counties that were still part of the United Kingdom, an industrial area suffering from economic troubles, the Catholics by and large formed a depressed class. The first to lose their jobs in bad times in a Protestant-dominated land, and cherishing their traditional feelings as the oppressed, they were inflamed by the insistence of the Protestant extremists (the "Orangemen") on continuing to celebrate the anniversaries of those victories of William III in the 1690s that had ensured English domination over the region. Marching provocatively in parades through Catholic districts and crying out contemptuous slogans, the Orangemen in the summer of 1969 precipitated disorders that began in Derry (Londonderry) and spread to Belfast and other areas. The regular police—the Royal Ulster Constabulary or RUC—were accused by the Catholics of being mere tools of the Protestant oppressor and had to be disarmed. The British army intervened to keep order.

The clearest voices in Ulster were those of two extremists, both of whom won seats in Parliament in London: for the Catholics, Bernadette Devlin, a young university student; and for the Protestants, the Reverend Ian Paisley, minister of a sect of his own, whose irreconcilable hostility to Catholics smacked more of the sixteenth century than of the twentieth. The government of the Republic of Ireland to the south necessarily took a strong interest in the Northern Irish troubles, suggesting that the UN be given responsibility for the problem, a suggestion quite unacceptable to the Northern Irish and British governments, who regarded the matter as altogether an internal problem. When violence resumed in 1970, the British army was reinforced. The extremists of the south, the Irish Republi-

can Army (IRA), who had always claimed the northern counties for a united Ireland and who from time to time tried various illegal and terroristic methods to obtain them, now revived their activities. But the IRA itself was now split between a relatively moderate wing and the Provisionals ("Provos"), anarchists dedicated to indiscriminate bombing.

Prime Minister Wilson took advantage of the improving economic situation to call for new elections in June 1970. The polls all reported the likelihood of an easy Labour victory. But to the general surprise, even of the winners, the Conservative party won a majority of forty seats in Parliament, and its leader, Edward Heath, promptly took office as prime minister. Apparently, inflation—especially rising food prices—had irritated voters who usually voted Labour. Powell's insistent antiblack speeches also gained votes for the Conservatives, although they tried to repudiate him. And among members of the middle class at least, the Labour education program had obviously seemed to threaten much that they cherished in British schools.

With both parties pledged to push the entry of Britain into the European Common Market, the Conservatives reopened discussions with the Six. But among many Britons the long delay, and Britain's double past rejection by the French, had brought a notable cooling of enthusiasm. Powell and many other Conservatives openly opposed British entry. So did many Labourites. So did many who were not primarily political but primarily English: in their loyalty to the economic preference arrangements for the Commonwealth—which would have to disappear if the new economic union with western Europe should be achieved—or in their loyalty to their traditional insularity and dislike of Europeans generally, or even in their loyalty to their pocketbooks, since it seemed sure that food prices would rise sharply if England should join the Six. The issue was to be decided in 1971 and 1972 in a dramatic debate that we discuss in Chapter 32.

No attempt to discuss Britain in the period between 1945 and 1970 would be complete without mention of the phenomena that can be summed up in the public-relations-men's phrase "swinging London." Beginning with the enormous popularity of the four popsinging Beatles in the late fifties, England for a time set the international styles for young people in other countries, even if the young themselves often were not aware of it. The long hair for men, the "unisex" phenomenon in dress, the popularity of Edwardian, eighteenth-century, theatrical, and eccentric clothes, the whole "mod" fashion syndrome that spread across the Atlantic and across the Channel started in England. Carnaby Street, Twiggy, Mick Jagger and the Rolling Stones all had their counterparts elsewhere, but the originals were English.

Nor was this all an accident or trivial. It was connected with an extremely important cultural and social phenomenon: the apparent gradual eroding of class distinctions in England, the traditional bastion of political freedom but of social inequality. The Beatles were all working-class in origin, and all spoke (or sang) with a pure lower-class Liverpool accent. Lower class too, with variations, were all the leading English pace-setters of the new styles in song, dress, and behavior among the young of the 1960s. And these styles spread not only abroad but among the middle and upper classes of young people in England as well, illustrating the increasing impatient determination to have done with the class sentiment that had so long pervaded English life. If this change continued, it would be perhaps the most important and epoch-making change in English social history at least since the industrial revolution, if not the Norman Conquest.

France

World War II inflicted on the French what psychologists call a trauma—a deep wound in the soul. Defeat by the Germans, a brutal German occupation and economic exploitation, the spectacle of much French collaboration with the enemy, all this was succeeded by liberation, which, in spite of the part played in it by the Fighting French and the French Resistance movement, was still clearly the work of American and British and, indirectly, of Russian arms. Nor had France since the early nineteenth century kept pace with the leading industrial nations in production, in finance, in population growth. Only one fact gave cause for optimism: while the "net reproduction rate" per 100 women had in 1942 sunk to 85 (that is, 15 less than the figure needed to maintain without immigration the existing population), by 1949 it had risen to 133—that is, 33 above mere stability. The rate continued at 124 or higher through 1955. This meant that hundreds of thousands of French men and women deliberately decided to have children, a clear sign of the recovery that lay ahead.

The French government-in-exile, led by General de Gaulle, in 1944 easily reestablished in liberated France the old republican forms of government. Frenchmen called this state the Fourth Republic; but after de Gaulle, disappointed by his failure to attain real power in a state still ruled by unstable parliamentary coalitions of "splinter parties," retired from politics in 1946, the Fourth Republic began to look exactly like the Third. Cabinets lasted on an average only a few months; to the old splinter parties was added a Communist party of renewed strength, openly dedicated to revolutionary change. The problems of the old empire, now known as the French Union, seemed insoluble; its peoples were in ferment. After nine years of war, Indo-China (Vietnam) was lost in 1954 in a great defeat at Dienbienphu. In the same year an active rebellion against the French began in Algeria, which France regarded not as a colony but as an overseas portion of France itself. Morocco and Tunisia were both lost in 1956, and the crisis deepened.

In 1958, General de Gaulle took power again, as

Charles de Gaulle at a press conference, September 9, 1968.

financial instability, inflation resulting from the war costs in Indo-China and Algeria, and a rising popular disgust with the "politicians" combined to bring about the fall of the Fourth Republic. A military and rightist coup d'état in Algeria took place on May 13, 1958. De Gaulle then announced that he was willing to come out of retirement. The leaders of the coup wrongly assumed that he would carry out their policies for keeping Algeria French.

In France there was very little violence, as a plebiscite confirmed the change. The constitution of the new Fifth Republic provided for a president of France, to be elected for a seven-year term by direct popular vote. An absolute majority was required, and, if not achieved in a first election, was to be obtained in a runoff between the two candidates with the greatest number of votes. Elected outright in 1958, de Gaulle was reelected to a second term in 1965 in a runoff. Under the constitution the French president appointed the premier, who could dissolve the legislature and order new elections at any time after the first year. Thus the new constitution gave the executive more power, the legislature much less. Those who disliked the new constitution complained that it made the legislature a mere rubber stamp.

De Gaulle's enemies called him a dictator. Cartoonists enjoyed drawing him as Louis XIV, the *roi soleil,* with wig and silk stockings, the personification of French haughtiness and superiority. He was certainly an obstinate, opinionated man, but though a general and personally authoritarian, he was no Napoleon III or Boulanger or Pétain. Frenchmen still enjoyed freedom of speech, of the press, of public assembly. French journalists could and did say as nasty things about their president as American journalists could and did say about theirs. Yet the regime did control radio and television. In the general election of 1965 it yielded to the pressure of public opinion, and consented to give de Gaulle's opposition candidates some time, though hardly "equal time," on the air.

The French ruling classes believed that their colonial subjects, especially the Algerians, could be persuaded to want to become real Frenchmen. But most of the Muslim nine-tenths of the Algerian population disagreed. Against the wishes of those who had brought him to power and in the face of terrorist incidents in France itself, de Gaulle in 1962 worked out a settlement making Algeria independent, leaving France some "influence" and some rights over Saharan oil. The right regarded this as treason. Most of the leftists, on the other hand, never gave him even grudging credit for it.

Starting with the Marshall Plan aid in 1947, a great series of economic and social changes began in France. Unlike the United States and Britain and Germany, France had hitherto preserved the small-scale, individualistic methods of production and distribution characteristic of the period before the industrial revolution. Now there began a full-scale reorientation of the economy in accordance with the usual practices of modern industry. Helped by foreign investment, especially American, France began to experience a real boom. The growth rate in the sixties was about a steady 6 percent per year, ahead even of West Germany; inflation, though a problem, had until 1966 or 1967 been held down to 3 percent. Prosperity meant that for the first time Frenchmen by the hundreds of thousands got their first cars, television sets, and hi-fi record players; that they traveled in ever growing numbers; that they enjoyed fearful traffic jams and incredible highway accidents; and that many of those who found the new ways unsettling blamed all the changes, like Coca-Cola, *le drugstore,* and blue jeans, on the Americans.

In foreign policy, de Gaulle was a deeply committed old-fashioned nationalist Frenchman. His memoirs showed how much of a love affair with France his whole life had been and how deeply he identified himself personally with his country. He never forgot a slight, and a slight to him was a slight to France, to be repaid in due course. The treatment accorded him by Churchill and Roosevelt during World War II he could never forget; and when he came to power he retained a healthy personal dislike of *les Anglo-Saxons.* To him, the thought of the supranational bodies that would rob France of her sovereignty even to a small degree (the Common Market, NATO, and others) was uncomfortable, and talk of a United States of Europe, in which France would be submerged, anathema. He spoke instead of an *Europe des patries,* a "Europe of fatherlands," that would not stop at the Russian frontiers but would include Russia—at least the European part—with all its historic European associations. And within the *Europe des patries,* needless to say, France would take the lead.

To do this France must have her own atomic weapons. Therefore de Gaulle refused to join the U.S., U.K., and USSR in a treaty barring atomic tests, and France continued to test nuclear weapons in the atmosphere, exploding her first hydrogen bomb in 1968 and continuing annually thereafter. She must also have her own *force de frappe,* the striking force capable of delivering atomic weapons to their targets and so of deterring an enemy. Vigorously opposed to communism at home, de Gaulle nonetheless worked out a rapprochement with Russia. The USSR, he argued, in the 1960s no longer represented the threat to the general peace that it had represented in the fifties. Now—in balancing the scales against the industrial and military power of the United States and its special friend, Britain—France needed to be friends with Russia. To South America, to Canada, with appeals to French separatists in Quebec, to Poland, and to Romania, de Gaulle took his stately presence, and his message that France would be the leader of Europe. In the spring of 1968, however, while de Gaulle was presenting his case in Romania, Paris erupted unexpectedly. The French universities, so overcrowded that there were no classrooms for students to use and no way of their listening to their lecturers, had been disregarded by the regime in a period when the young everywhere were full of resentment against the society their parents had brought them into. Led by anarchists and others, the students occupied their buildings, fought the police, and eventually drew a reluctant Communist party into the fray. In order not to lose the support of the French workers, who had already begun to strike in sympathy with the students, the Communist leadership had to support what looked for a few days as if it just might be the beginning of a new French Revolution. De Gaulle returned to Paris, assured himself of army support, proposed a referendum, which he was obliged to abandon in favor of new elections, and won a great victory at the polls, obtaining a larger majority in the legislature than before.

Thereupon he dropped his prime minister, the chief organizer of victory, Pompidou, and embarked on a new phase of his regime. His economic and social program called for *participation* by the workers not only in the profits of industry but in its management. His new minister of education, acknowledging the justice of many of the grievances of the students, pushed through the legislature a major radical reform bill decentralizing the educational system. Having established his strength with the strong support of the right—as in 1958—de Gaulle now appeared to be preparing at least to appease the left—again, as in 1958. Perhaps the military and foreign programs would have to be slowed down; but nobody who had studied de Gaulle believed they would be abandoned.

Nobody could have predicted what actually happened. De Gaulle staked his political future on a comparatively unimportant political issue set before the public in a referendum and lost. As he had done before, he withdrew into private life. In the 1969 elections, the

Gaullists were returned to office with a substantial majority, and Pompidou became president of France. As in the remainder of the Western nations, inflation grew apace, but on the whole prosperity continued as well. Pompidou in general maintained de Gaulle's policies but pursued them far less flamboyantly. De Gaulle's death in 1970 marked the disappearance of the last survivor of the great men of World War II, but had no political implications.

West Germany

In 1970 West Germany had a population of about 61 million, some 3.5 times that of East Germany. The wartime destruction of much of Germany's industrial plant paradoxically proved beneficial: the new plant was built with the latest technological equipment. The Allied High Commission, never very severe, gradually abolished controls over German industry, save for atomic energy and a few other military restrictions. It advanced economic aid and scaled down prewar German debts. By the early 1950s, West Germany had a favorable balance of trade and was achieving industrial growth as high as 10 percent a year.

Gross national product rose from $23 billion in 1950 to $103 billion in 1964, with no serious monetary inflation. This prosperity was to a large degree spread through all classes of society. The workingman in West Germany had begun to enjoy the kind of affluence that his opposite number in the United States had had for some time. New buildings rose everywhere. The divided superhighways Hitler had built largely for military purposes grew overcrowded and had to be widened and extended.

Politically, the Allies required "de-Nazification." At the Nuremberg trials in 1946, seventy-four top Nazi leaders were convicted of war crimes. Ten were hanged, after two had committed suicide; one was sentenced to life imprisonment, others to shorter terms; and three were acquitted. To have dismissed all civil servants who had held posts under the Nazi regime would have dismantled German administration altogether. A weeding out of the most compromised Nazis was achieved, though not sufficiently to satisfy many Western anti-Nazis.

The independent West German state had a constitution that provided for a bicameral legislature, with a lower house representing the people directly and an upper house representing the states (*Länder*), together with a president elected by a special assembly for a five-year term, in practice largely a ceremonial figure. Real executive leadership was vested in the chancellor, a prime minister dependent on a parliamentary majority. The old splinter-party system did not return to plague the new republic. Under the leadership of Konrad Adenauer, the Christian Democrats, distant heirs of the old Centrist party, held power down to 1961.

A Rhineland Catholic, former mayor of Cologne, conservative, pro-French, and thoroughly democratic, Adenauer was forced to retire only because of age and continued to wield enough influence to weaken his successor, Ludwig Erhard, a Protestant, who remained in office for five more years. The twenty-year reign of the Christian Democrats was one supported by the voters, not the result of one-party totalitarian politics.

West Germany seemed to be approaching two-party democratic politics, with the Christian Democrats challenged chiefly by the Social Democrats, roughly similar to the British Labour party. The Social Democrats held power in some of the states and cities of the federal union, notably in West Berlin, whose popular mayor, Willy Brandt, ran unsuccessfully for the federal chancellorship against Erhard in 1964. A neo-Nazi minority existed in West Germany, but it achieved no very alarming successes at the polls. Militant organizations of war veterans and of refugees from the "lost" Eastern territories now included in Poland, the USSR, or Czechoslovakia at times seemed to pose more of a possible threat to stability.

The major political question remained that of an eventual reunion with communist-dominated East Germany. Neither Germany recognized the other. After long years during which East Germans, attracted by better West German living conditions, crossed the border by the tens of thousands, the East German government in August 1961 began building a wall between the two parts of the city. Though on special holidays families in West Berlin were allowed to cross into East Berlin briefly to visit relatives and friends, the wall in 1970 still stood as the visible symbol of divided Germany.

As part of the cold war, the Americans, British, and French permitted the West Germans to rearm early in the 1950s and to join NATO. Military conscription was introduced in 1957, and by 1970 West Germany had developed a sizable modern army, navy, and air force. Government and people supported the armed forces as a necessity, but the old militarism did not revive among the people at large. Access to the atom bomb was not included in this rearmament, but German public opinion apparently was not greatly exercised over the exclusion.

In the late autumn of 1966 there arose in West Germany a major political crisis. Chancellor Erhard was governing in coalition with a small right-wing party, the Free Democrats, non-Nazi conservatives opposed to "socialism." There was friction with some of the high command of the armed forces. It was hard to support American policies in Europe and yet not break with France. The slowing down of West German economic growth might, it was feared, presage a real recession. All this contributed to Erhard's downfall. In November 1966 the Free Democrats refused to support his proposals for higher taxes, and the government fell.

But the Christian Democrats came forward with Kurt Georg Kiesinger, a Catholic, who as premier succeeded in forming a "grand coalition" with his chief opponents, the Social Democrats. Willy Brandt became vice chancellor and foreign minister. Though some members of both parties disapproved, and though Kiesinger's past membership in the Nazi party aroused some alarm abroad, the grand coalition commanded popular support. It was designed to last until the elections scheduled for 1969.

When these took place the Christian Socialists lost for the first time, and Willy Brandt, the Social Democrat, became premier and formed a coalition in his turn with the Free Democrats, who obtained the foreign ministry in his cabinet. Brandt moved slowly and cautiously toward the opening of discussions with the East Germans. The chief stumbling block in the way of serious negotiations between the two Germanies lay in the Soviet fear of Western Germany. So it gradually became apparent that a treaty between West Germany and the USSR in which both renounced the use of force for the future would be at least one of the necessary preliminaries. Brandt in the summer of 1970 succeeded in reaching agreement with the Russians on the text of such a treaty. It recognized all existing European frontiers, which Germans and Russians thus both agreed never to try to alter by force. Of course the Germans could still hope that perhaps a change in the frontiers of Poland might some day be negotiated. The second step was an agreement with Poland itself, and this, too, Brandt put through during 1970. The East Germans would be next. The USSR stood to gain by the new accessibility of West German technical and industrial skills. And this prospect was creating doubts about Brandt's achievements in the very official American circles that had earlier encouraged his policies.

The Other Western Countries

In Italy a plebiscite in 1946 showed 54.3 percent of the voters in favor of a republic, and in spite of the comparative narrowness of the margin, the republic, once it was established, proved viable. There were monarchists who regretted the forced departure of the House of Savoy, and there were even some who regretted the end of the fascist regime. But neither group was able to influence parliamentary politics to any great extent. A strong Christian Democratic party (a Catholic party with a relatively liberal reform program) under a succession of leaders, Alcide de Gasperi, Amintore Fanfani, Aldo Moro, and Mariano Rumor, proved able to hold power thereafter with support from other groups. It took positive measures to break up the large landed estates in the south, with a view to redistributing the land. De Gasperi was challenged chiefly by a very strong Communist party, the largest in the West, with whom the larger faction of the Socialists—that led by Pietro Nenni—was allied. The firmly anticommunist Socialist faction led by Giuseppe Saragat participated in the government.

In the sixties a series of complicated negotiations began a process the Italians called the *apertura a sinistra*,

the opening to the left. In this process the Christian Democrats won over some Socialist support. A further weakening of the extreme left occurred in 1966, when the Socialists—long split between an anticommunist wing and a wing that often collaborated with the Communists—reunited as one party.

Italy's economic growth between 1953 and 1966 was so remarkable that the Italians called it their *"miracolo economico."* As in France, this was achieved with some government ownership and with much government regulation and planning. Italy was a mixed economy but a free society. Milan, long a busy and active city, began to look like another Chicago. Rome had perhaps the most desperate traffic problem of any great city in the world. Membership in the Common Market and freedom from the troubles of imperial liquidation gave Italian enterprise opportunities that it had never had before.

The grave problems of the *mezzogiorno*, the southern part of the peninsula, and the islands of Sardinia and Sicily, were attacked by programs of investments, by providing jobs in the north or in Germany or Switzerland for the surplus workers of the south, and by old-age pensions. In the Italian balance of payments, an income of about $1 billion annually from tourists provided a useful item on the "export" side.

Yet in the late 1960s Italian political stability apparently began to crumble. In part this was due to the severe internal political strains and feuding within the Christian Democratic party. Cooperation among Christian Democratic politicians became more and more difficult, and their negotiations with each other tended to break down. In part it was due to the uncertainty of their relationship with their supposed partners, the socialists, who, though anticommunist on the national level, often cooperated with the communists on the local political level, arousing bitter recriminations when such cooperation effectively blocked local Christian Democratic political success. In part it was due to the same sort of inflation that was plaguing the other Western countries, but that Italy, with its large poor population and its lack of any tradition of the welfare state, was perhaps less able to bear than any other advanced industrial nation. Strikes occurred sporadically and unpredictably but often. The government seemed frozen in bureaucratic incompetence. Personal vendettas were proving in many cases stronger than patriotism. A prolonged political crisis ended temporarily with the success in 1970 of an experienced economist, Colombo, in forming a cabinet.

The smaller states of "free Europe" shared the general prosperity and the common problems. In Belgium, which enjoyed great material well-being, the chronic difficulties between the minority of French-speaking Walloons and the majority of Dutch-speaking Flemings continued to worsen and to threaten stability. Spain—still in Franco's control more than thirty years after the end of the Civil War—had taken major steps toward modernization and a few mild measures to relax political tyranny. Low wages, especially to the depressed coal miners of the north, and bitter government opposition to the national sentiment of the Basques prevented full economic or political stability. Franco arranged that after his death the monarchy would be restored under Prince Juan Carlos, grandson of Alfonso XIII and son of Alfonso's still-living son Prince Juan, who, however, had not renounced the royal title. Portugal, under the rigidly conservative Salazar, dictator since 1932, lagged well behind Spain. In 1968, Salazar—crippled by illness—was replaced by Caetano. This promised to open a new chapter, though the expenditure of men and money involved in holding onto the Portuguese colonial empire made rapid changes unlikely. In Greece, the takeover of the government in the 1960s by a group of army officers ("the colonels") led to a ruthless repression of political opposition but not to a fascist state.

III The Communist Bloc: The USSR at Home

Alone among the leaders of the Big Three of the war years, Stalin remained in power immediately after the war. His remaining years, 1945–1953, marked a continuation and even a sharpening of the policies that he had made his own. Some four years of political uncertainty followed his death, but in 1957 Nikita Khrushchev emerged supreme and held onto power until 1964. He was succeeded by two co-chiefs, Brezhnev and Kosygin, who remained on top in 1970.

Facing the devastation caused by the war and what he regarded as the immediate threat of American atomic weapons, Stalin felt obliged to decree a continuation of austerity into the postwar years, at just the moment when the Russian people most yearned for new housing and a few creature comforts. The party, still his docile instrument and experiencing regular purges to prevent any relaxation, dominated political life, with the constant assistance of the secret police; while the army, still mobilized at high strength and performing a variety of occupation duties abroad, remained the third Soviet institution with power of its own.

Not long before he died, Stalin in 1952 created a new Presidium, which he planned as a larger body than the Politburo, to include the ten Politburo members and fifteen additional high-ranking Soviet officials. But he did not live to announce the membership of the new body or to summon a meeting of it. After his death, the new Presidium simply replaced the old Politburo, with the same ten members. Khrushchev later declared that, in enlarging the membership and changing the name of the Politburo, Stalin had been taking the first step toward the complete purge and liquidation of its ten existing members; so it is perhaps no wonder that, having survived this first step, they declined to take a second.

The fourth five-year plan (1946–1950) and its successor the fifth (1951–1955) continued to emphasize investment in heavy industry at the expense of consumer goods. Financial measures—the raising of prices, the wiping out of savings by the establishment of a new currency—kept severe economic pressure on the population. Reparations exacted from Germany and industrial loot from the eastern European countries gave massive stimulus to Soviet reconstruction. The fourth five-year plan saw the first Soviet atomic bomb completed; the fifth saw further advances in armaments and the building of the Volga-Don canal. In agriculture, the regime embarked on a policy of reducing the number and increasing the size of collective farms. In 1951, Nikita Khrushchev, now appearing as a leading party agricultural expert, proposed a plan to create great agricultural cities (*agrogoroda*) in order to concentrate farm labor and abolish rural backwardness.

The cultural policy of the regime was in keeping with the bleak austerity and terror of these years. The cultural boss, Andrei Zhdanov, decreed that literature had to take an active role in the "engineering" of human souls. The official school of "socialist realism" was the only permissible line for a writer to follow. Zhdanov denounced in particular Mikhail Zoshchenko, writer of witty and satirical short stories, whose tale of the adventure of a monkey accidentally set free by a bomb suggested strongly that life in a cage in a zoo was more agreeable than life at large among the Soviet people; and Anna Akhmatova, a sensitive lyric poet who had had the unpatriotic ill-judgment to lament in verse her feeling of loneliness, which no proper Soviet citizen would do. Both were silenced. Though Zhdanov died suddenly in 1948, his principles continued to reign. Violent anti-Western propaganda filled Soviet books and resounded from the Soviet stage in such a play as *The Unfortunate Haberdasher,* in which President Truman was cast as Hitler.

With the attack on the Western nations went a constant drumbeat of new (and sometimes comic) claims for Soviet, or at least Russian, "firsts" in every field of intellectual and artistic endeavor. No scholar could safely investigate a topic without paying his respects to the supreme authorities on everything: Marx, Lenin, and, chiefly, Stalin. Archaeologists, historians, students of literature began their work with a compulsory quotation from Stalin and genuflected before him as the great teacher, the "choryphaeus of the sciences."

Stalin supported the geneticist Trofim Lysenko, who maintained—contrary to all accepted biological doctrine—that acquired characteristics were hereditary, strongly implying that "new Soviet man" would emerge as a biological phenomenon and giving pseudoscientific support to the political argument that communism would change the human species. In linguistics too, Stalin personally intervened in 1950 to denounce the prevailing theories originated by Nikolai Marr, then sixteen years dead, who had implied that the world's languages corresponded to the degree of social development reached by their speakers. Neither biologist nor linguist, Stalin laid down the law for both.

As Stalin grew older, the secrecy, censorship, and conspiratorial miasma at the top of the Soviet state and society all intensified. Catering to ancient prejudices and violating Leninist precepts, Stalin now moved against the Jews. Anti-Semitic propaganda reached its peak with the publicity given an alleged "doctors' plot," in which Jewish doctors were accused of plotting to poison Stalin. When Stalin died, the stage seemed set for a full-scale anti-Semitic drive reminiscent of Hitler. Fear of the West, and detestation of Zionism—many Soviet Jews wanted to live in Israel—did not alone explain Soviet anti-Semitism. Despite their long years of preaching cultural autonomy for nationalities, many Soviet leaders were personally anti-Semitic and perhaps recognized that the population at large could be expected to welcome anti-Semitism at a moment when there was little else in the government policies that they could endorse. Official Soviet anti-Semitism would continue to wax and wane.

By the early 1950s it had become a favorite occupation in the West to speculate on Stalin's succession. Would it be the Communist party, or the secret police, or the army that would emerge supreme? Would it be some combination of two of these against the third? Was this or that member of the Politburo identified with one or another of these three chief agencies? Would the world see a new bitter rivalry comparable to the struggle between Stalin and Trotsky for the succession to Lenin? If so, would the resulting instability go so far as to disrupt the machinery of Soviet government?

When the moment actually came, in March 1953, Georgi Malenkov, personally close to Stalin, succeeded him as premier but surrendered his Communist party secretaryship to Nikita Khrushchev. It was thus clear that nobody would immediately inherit all of Stalin's power. Soon the regime began to denounce the "cult of personality" (i.e., Stalin's former one-man rule) and proclaimed a "collegial" system (i.e., government by committee). The dreaded chief of the secret police, Presidium-member Beria, was executed for treason.

But no free-for-all among the remaining members of the inner circle ensued. Malenkov vanished from the top post of premier, to be succeeded by the political general Bulganin; but Malenkov was at first simply demoted to a lower cabinet post and remained in the Presidium. It was noteworthy that when Malenkov confessed error, he took responsibility for the failure of the agrogoroda, which were actually Khrushchev's idea. Khrushchev was certainly very powerful, but his fellow members on the Politburo had great influence and showed no outward signs of fearing him as all had feared Stalin. On the whole, it appeared that the transfer of power had actually gone quite smoothly.

At a party congress held early in 1956, Khrushchev made a speech in which he denounced Stalin, emotionally detailing the ghastly acts of personal cruelty to which the psychopathically suspicious nature of the late dictator had given rise. Khrushchev thus echoed what Western observers of the USSR had been saying for years. As the details of the speech were leaked out to the Soviet public, there was of course some distress at the smashing of the idol they had worshiped so long; but a good many of them no doubt had all along suspected that Stalin was something less than godlike. So the widespread disorders that some observers were predicting failed to materialize.

Abroad, however, the speech led to turmoil in the Soviet satellites in Europe and so gave Khrushchev's opponents at home an opportunity to unite against his policies. Within the Presidium they had a majority. But Khrushchev was able to rally to his support the larger body of which the Presidium was the inner core, the Central Committee of the Communist party of the USSR. A veteran party worker, he had installed his own loyal supporters in all key party posts, repeating Stalin's performance after the death of Lenin, and he emerged from this greatest test with his powers immeasurably enhanced (June 1957). Now the Soviet press denounced the "antiparty group" of Malenkov, Molotov, and Kaganovich, three of the members of Stalin's own entourage. In Stalin's day, this would have led them to the execution block. Khrushchev, however, acted differently. All three were expelled from the Presidium and removed from their high posts, but all three were given minor positions at a safe distance from Moscow. In 1958 Bulganin followed them into the discard: he too had sided against Khrushchev, whose succession to Stalin's position of undisputed power now seemed complete.

Bureaucratic Problems

Yet there were certain differences. Already in his sixties, Khrushchev could hardly hope for a quarter-century of dictatorship such as Stalin had had. Moreover, in the very course of making himself supreme he had deprived himself of some of the instruments available to Stalin. After 1953 he had released millions of captives from prisons and slave-labor camps. Almost everybody in Russia had a relative or friend now freed. These men and women now took jobs, some of them even government jobs. Within a year or two Soviet society at every level except at the very top of the bureaucracy had absorbed these sufferers from tyranny. The secret police no longer enjoyed almost-independent power in the state, a power that might challenge the party or the army. Khrushchev himself had emotionally denounced its terror. It was still possible to prosecute and even persecute individuals by terrorist means, but Stalin's mass terror as a system of government had disappeared.

Instead of terror, Khrushchev embarked on a series of bureaucratic changes. He gave the Russian Republic, by far the largest and most populous of the republics, virtually a separate administration, and took complete control of its personnel. In 1963 he took parallel measures for central Asia and the Transcaucasus. Khrushchev was wrestling with the problems of efficiency, output, and morale. Under Stalin, centralization had reached an intolerable tightness. But how far could one decentralize so huge an operation as the Soviet economy and still retain control over local operations? How far could one centralize and still obtain local cooperation, loyalty, and especially, production? Between 1953 and 1957, responsibility for many heavy industries was transferred from the ministries of the central government to those of the individual republics. In May 1957 a decree abolished many central ministries and transferred their duties to 105 newly created regional economic councils (*sovnarkhoz*) in the hope of giving full play to informed, on-the-spot decisions, of improving the use of local resources, of consolidating overlapping services, and of reassigning experts from the central government to the grass roots. Regionalism—devotion to regional interests as against national ones—replaced what might be called devotion to one industry ahead of others. But patriots for Armenian industry (to the detriment of other regions) were no more helpful to the national economy than patriots for the cement industry (to the detriment of other industries).

By 1960, a process of recentralizing had begun. By the end of 1962, the sovnarkhozes were reduced from 105 to about 40, and new state committees appeared to oversee their work. These committees greatly resembled the old ministries and in fact were before long reorganized as ministries. The pendulum had swung back almost the entire distance. Now all lower levels of the party were divided into agricultural and industrial wings in an effort to make the political functionaries serve the economy more efficiently.

In mid-October 1964 the world learned to its astonishment that Khrushchev had been removed from power and succeeded by two members of the Presidium. L. I. Brezhnev replaced him as first secretary of the Central Committee of the Communist party and A. N. Kosygin as premier (chairman of the USSR Council of Ministers). Both were "Khrushchev men": Brezhnev aged fifty-eight, a metallurgist by training, had held posts in the Ukrainian, Moldavian, and Kazakhstan Communist parties, entering the Presidium in 1957; Kosygin, aged fifty, an engineer, commissar of the textile industry in 1938, premier of the Russian Republic throughout World War II, member of the Politburo from 1949 to 1952, and minister for light industry, went into eclipse shortly before Stalin died and reemerged as a member of the Presidium only in 1957. The published communiqués spoke of Khrushchev's ill health and advanced age, but it was clear that he had not acquiesced in his own removal. How had Brezhnev and Kosygin managed it? And what did they stand for?

Khrushchev had not practiced the kind of constant vigilance over his associates that alone could have ensured him security in office. The plotters acted in his absence and took careful steps to line up the members of the Central Committee in support of their action so that he could not appeal to the Committee over the head of the Presidium as he had done in 1957. Until his death in 1971, Khrushchev continued to live in retirement in Moscow and in his country house. No large-scale purge followed his removal.

Khrushchev was responsible for major agricultural failures at home and much more serious Soviet setbacks abroad, as we shall see. Yet he might have continued in office had it not been for his personal rudeness. The communiqué that announced his replacement referred to his "hare-brained scheming," no doubt in reference to the virgin lands fiasco (see below), and to "half-baked conclusions and hasty decisions and actions, divorced from reality; bragging and bluster; attraction to rule by fiat [literally, "commandism"]." Caustic and crude, Khrushchev had apparently tried his former supporters too far.

Industry and Agriculture

Khrushchev had faced the same problem that had faced all Soviet leaders: how much emphasis could be put on consumer goods and how much still must be devoted to heavy industry? Though temperamentally more interested in providing consumer goods than Stalin or Malenkov, Khrushchev made the same choice as they: continued emphasis on the means of production. The sixth five-year plan (1956–1960) set more ambitious goals than ever before, but the huge expenses involved in the Polish and Hungarian outbreaks forced the Soviet government to shelve the plan. By the end of 1958, it announced a new seven-year plan, to run until 1965. Starting from base figures of 500 million tons of coal, 55 million tons of steel, and 113 million tons of oil, output by 1964 had reached 554 million tons of coal, 85 million tons of steel, and 224 million tons of oil. In 1966, the regime returned to the system of five-year plans.

Most spectacular were the successes achieved in the field of rocketry and space. The USSR successfully launched the first earth satellite (Sputnik, 1957) and first reached the moon with a rocket (1959). Heavy payloads soared aloft before American engineers could get their lighter ones off the ground. Spurred to some degree by the Soviet technical advance, the United States itself embarked in the late fifties on an intensive program of research and development in space. Though the USSR got the first man into space and for some time held the lead in technical achievements, by the mid-sixties the United States had caught up in most aspects of space technology; and the American landings of manned space vehicles on the moon beginning in 1969 overshadowed Soviet accomplishments in space.

Agriculture continued to present the Soviet planners with apparently insoluble problems. In 1953, Khrushchev embarked on the "virgin lands" scheme, a crash program to plow under more than 100,000 acres of prairie in the Urals region, Kazakhstan, and Siberia. Drought and poor planning and performance led to a clear failure by 1963. By the following year, the number of collective farms was down to about 40,000 from an original 250,000, and the average size of the new units was far larger, perhaps about 5,000 acres. By 1965, the government recognized that many collectives were now too big.

To increase incentives, the regime in 1958 abolished compulsory deliveries of farm products, the most onerous of the peasants' burdens, and raised agricultural prices. Simultaneously, the government decreed the gradual abolition of the MTS's (Machine Tractor Stations) and the sale of the tractors to the individual collectives, which the government undertook to subsidize in part. In 1964, the government for the first time extended its system of old-age and disability pensions to agricultural laborers; it removed the ceilings on the private allotment of land allowed to the individual peasant in a collective and on the number of cattle that he might own privately. Yet yields continued low; animal husbandry caused grave concern, and the regime's agencies thundered against inefficiency and "fascination with administration by fiat."

In the years after Khrushchev's fall from power in 1964, the Soviet authorities engaged in an open debate about the best way to revise the statutes governing the collective farm in view of the immense changes since 1936. The party and the government ordered the collective farms to guarantee the individual farmers a monthly sum in cash for their work and to pay in addition for the produce actually received. The state bank would advance the farms the credit where necessary. Some economists were arguing for the introduction of a free market economy; others vigorously defended centralized planning (with improvements). Obviously the Soviet authorities were recognizing the importance of "capitalist" incentives in the field of agriculture as in many others.

Yet the problems of supply and production continued to be intractable, and the regime itself was often caustic in its denunciations of failures caused by stupidity and bad management. It was always difficult to decide how grave the problems really were and how far the regime's shrillness was designed to frighten the Russians themselves into making further superhuman efforts.

Education and the Arts

In 1958 Khrushchev introduced an important change in the Soviet educational system: "polytechnization," which emphasized vocational training and on-the-job experience. This represented a retreat from the goal of a ten-year general educational program for all. Khrushchev ordered the universities now to favor applicants who had had practical experience. By the mid-sixties, almost all children in the USSR finished the first four years of school (ages seven to eleven), and illiteracy had virtually disappeared. Almost as many finished the second four years (ages eleven to fifteen), which were now combined with "polytechnization." In

1964, the conventional next course of three years (ages fifteen to eighteen), usually taken by only about 40 percent of Soviet youth, was reduced to two years. Nationwide talent contests were held to discover the most promising candidates for university study in math and science.

Khrushchev extended to the field of arts and letters the same partial relaxation that accompanied de-Stalinization in other fields. It took Soviet writers some time to accustom themselves to the idea that it might now be possible to voice dissent: too many had vanished forever at Stalin's whim to make the risk an attractive one. Moreover, convinced Stalinists or party hacks who had grown up under Stalinism lay in wait to attack the innovator. Khrushchev was himself opinionated and autocratic and kept artists and writers in constant uncertainty lest new purges break forth. The dangers of self-expression continued great indeed.

In a few individual books and authors we may find indices of the new policies. Ilya Ehrenburg, veteran propagandist for the regime, in *The Thaw* (1955), hailed the relaxation of coercive measures over artists. Vladimir Dudintsev's novel *Not By Bread Alone* (1956) had as its hero a competent and enthusiastic engineer whose invention of a new pipe-casting machine was thwarted at every turn by the entrenched bureaucrats. Government-controlled writers' agencies denounced Dudintsev, who retracted his views and for six or seven years was forced to earn his living by translation only. Boris Pasternak's *Dr. Zhivago* (1958) became a *cause célèbre* throughout the world. Pasternak, a brilliant poet who had for years confined himself to translating Shakespeare, took advantage of the "thaw" to offer for publication his novel about a doctor who, through all the agonies of the First World War and the Russian Revolution, affirmed the freedom of the human soul. Accepted for publication in Russia, the novel was also sent to Italy to be published. Then the Soviet censors changed their minds and forced Pasternak to ask that the manuscript in Italy be returned to him. The Italian publisher refused, and versions in Russian, Italian, English, and other languages appeared abroad, arousing great admiration. In 1958, the Nobel Prize Committee selected Pasternak as the winner of the prize for literature. He accepted. But then the Khrushchev regime reverted to Stalinism: Pasternak's fellow writers reviled him as a pig and a traitor, and the government threatened him with exile if he accepted the prize. As a patriotic Russian he then declined it.

In the same week that a Soviet physicist accepted the Nobel Prize for physics, the regime called the Nobel Prize for literature a capitalist invention. And a few years later, Mikhail Sholokhov, author of the famous Cossack trilogy *The Quiet Don* and a personal friend of Khrushchev, accepted the Nobel Prize for literature. Pasternak's persecution revealed the limits of the thaw as of 1958. His Jewish origins, his intellectualism, his proclamation of individualism touched hostile chords in Khrushchev himself and in other Soviet officials and writers, making it impossible to publish *Dr. Zhivago* in the USSR.

But the spirit of individualism, slow to express itself even when liberated in the older generation, found in the 1960s new and more vigorous expression among the younger poets and novelists who had grown up since the Second World War and for whom the heroic age of the Revolution and the early Bolshevik struggles were ancient history. The young Ukrainian poet Yevtushenko denounced Soviet anti-Semitism in his *Babi Yar* (the name of the ravine near Kiev in which the Nazis had massacred thousands of Jews) and declared his identity with the murdered human beings. In another poem he begged the government to double and triple the guard over Stalin's tomb,

> *So that Stalin may not rise*
> *And, with Stalin the past.*

> *. . . the ignoring of the people's welfare*
> *The calumnies*
> *The arrests of the innocent.*

Former supporters of Stalin, he went on,

> *Do not like these times*
> *When the camps are empty*
> *And the halls where people listen to poetry*
> *Are crowded.* *

When Yevtushenko recited his verse, the halls were indeed always crowded with eager, excited, contentious young people, claiming the right to think for themselves. "We've found out," said another young poet, "what it leads to when somebody else does our thinking for us."

Yevtushenko's mention of "the camps" suggests another new phenomenon in the Soviet writing of the early sixties, the deep interest in the terrible days of Stalin's labor camps and in the suffering of their inmates, reflected, for example, in Alexander Solzhenitsyn's novel *A Day in the Life of Ivan Denisovich.* Khrushchev viewed with some apprehension the flood of fiction about the camps that came pouring into the publishing houses, only a little of which was published. Khrushchev tried to remind the younger generation of the glorious revolutionary past through which their elders had triumphantly lived. He declared—as if in answer to their demands for full freedom—that even under full communism it would not be possible to give complete liberty to the individual, who would continue "like a bee in a hive" to make his contribution to society.

After Khrushchev's ouster in 1964, his successors tightened the reigns of censorship and repression. In

September 1965 two writers, Andrei Sinyavsky and Yuli Daniel, were arrested for writing under pseudonyms and sending abroad anti-Soviet fiction and essays. Writing as Abram Tertz, Sinyavsky, in *The Trial Begins,* had given a candid and revolting picture of the life of the Soviet leaders under Stalin; his novel *Lyubimov* (translated into English as *The Makepeace Experiment*) dealt with a one-man revolt against communism in a small Russian town; and his essay *On Socialist Realism* damned what was still the official literary doctrine of the regime. Writing as Nikolai Arzhak, Daniel, in *Moscow Calling,* produced a fantasy in which the Soviet government set aside one day on which murder was allowed. In 1966, despite the protests of many young people, Sinyavsky and Daniel were tried and condemned to prison.

The defection in 1967 of Stalin's daughter, Svetlana Alliluyeva, to the United States and the publication in this country of her autobiography were treated vituperatively in the Soviet press as part of a plot arranged by American agents to spoil the celebrations planned for the fiftieth anniversary of the Revolution of 1917. At the Writers' Congress of 1967, old-line writers reaffirmed the theories of socialist realism and attacked all who opposed them. In 1968, the authorities arrested three young men and one young woman and charged them with treasonable contact with a foreign agent, a spy of Russian origin who had allegedly paid them to circulate anti-Soviet materials from abroad. All were imprisoned after a trial against which some of the young writers protested, thereby bringing down upon themselves vigorous rebukes. At least one of the accused and one of the chief protesters were Jews.

Solzhenitsyn whose somber and gripping novels *The First Circle* and *Cancer Ward* convinced Western readers that Russian humane values had found a spokesman of the stature of Tolstoy or Pasternak—found himself in 1970 expelled from the party's Union of Writers and silenced. When in his turn he was awarded the Nobel Prize in 1970, he accepted it, but explained that he could not come to Stockholm to receive it because he might not be permitted to return to Russia. He and others were denounced as "spiritual emigrants" from the USSR. The voices of the protesters were more clearly audible in the West than ever before, and this too infuriated the regime. Protesters in the arts and sciences were on the whole ruthlessly dealt with, and hackwork of the old Stalinist type was still rewarded. The regime continued to have severe problems in controlling its "intelligentsia," perhaps 20 percent of the Soviet working population.

* Pravda, October 21, 1962.

Reading Suggestions on the Cold War and Great-Power Domestic Policy
See the list at the end of Chapter 31.

31

Great-Power Foreign Policy and the Emerging Nations 1945-1970

I Soviet Foreign Policy: The Last Years of Stalin, 1945–1953

Eastern Europe, Iran, Greece, and Berlin

When World War II ended, the Soviet Union did not immediately terminate all forms of cooperation with its allies. The joint plan for dividing and ruling Germany went through. The four occupying powers together tried the chief surviving Nazi leaders at Nuremberg in 1946. In February 1947 came the peace treaties with Italy, Romania, Bulgaria, Hungary, and (for the USSR) Finland. These confirmed Soviet territorial gains from Romania, Bessarabia and northern Bukovina, from Finland, portions of Karelia and a long lease on the naval base at Porkkala. In addition, the USSR annexed part of former East Prussia and the extreme easternmost portion of Czechoslovakia.

In Poland, Romania, Hungary, and Bulgaria the USSR, relying on the pressure of the Red Armies, sponsored the creation of new "people's republics" under communist governments. In each country the Russians eliminated all political groups that could be accused of collaboration with the Germans. Then they formed "progressive" coalitions of parties, and next destroyed all noncommunist elements in each party by splitting off a small fragment that would collaborate unquestioningly with the communists and then denouncing and persecuting the remainder. Elections, despite the promises at Yalta, were accompanied by intimidation and brutality. Western protest uniformly failed. These four states became true Soviet satellites.

Yugoslavia organized its own communist government and had Albania as its own satellite. Soviet troops occupied about a third of Germany, roughly between the Elbe and the Oder rivers, where they organized the communist-led satellite of East Germany. The part of Germany lying east of the line formed by the Oder and Neisse rivers, save for the sections of East Prussia directly annexed to the USSR, the Russians handed over to their Polish satellite. Here a wholesale transfer of population removed the Germans and replaced them with Poles. Finland became part of the Russian security system but retained its prewar political institutions. The four Allied powers detached Austria from Germany—thus undoing Hitler's Anschluss of 1938—and divided it, like Germany, into four occupation zones. The presence of Soviet troops in Hungary and Romania was specifically guaranteed to "protect" the communication lines between Russia and its occupying forces in Austria.

In 1948, the communists took over Czechoslovakia by a coup d'état and ousted the government of Edward Beneš, brave enemy of Hitler in 1938, betrayed now for a second time. Within each satellite the communists aped Soviet policies, moving with all speed to collectivize agriculture, impose forced-draft industrialization, control cultural life, and govern by terror.

As early as 1946, the USSR refused to withdraw its forces from northwest Iran and yielded only to pressure from the United Nations. A more alarming probe of the Soviet perimeter came in Greece, where a communist-dominated guerrilla movement had already during World War II attempted to seize control and had been thwarted only by British troops. In 1946, the Greek communists tried again, backed this time by the communist governments of Albania, Yugoslavia, and Bulgaria to the north. Simultaneously, Stalin exerted pressure on the Turks for concessions in the Straits area. In response President Truman proclaimed that countries facing the threat of communist aggression could count on help from the United States. Under this "Truman Doctrine," he sent American military aid to Greece and Turkey. The threat to the Turks evaporated, and by 1949, after severe fighting, the Greeks had put down the communist uprising with the help of American advisers.

In Germany, the Russians began in 1948 one of

the most bitter phases of the cold war. By shutting off the land routes from the West into Berlin, they attempted to force the Western Allies to turn Berlin wholly over to them. The Allies stood firm, however, and in the next six months flew more than 2.3 million tons of coal, food, and other necessities into West Berlin. Though the Russians then gave up and reopened the land routes, Soviet determination to oust the Western powers from Berlin remained unaltered.

The Yugoslav Rebellion

In 1948, the Russians found themselves faced with rebellion from a country that had hitherto seemed the most pro-Soviet of all the new communist states of eastern Europe: Yugoslavia. Yugoslavia had overthrown a pro-German government in 1941 and remained throughout World War II a theater of intense guerrilla action against the Germans and Italians. There were two main groups of guerrillas, the Chetniks, led by General Mikhailovich, representing the Serb royalist domination over the south Slav kingdom, and the Partisans, led by the Croatian-born communist Joseph Broz, better known by his underground name, Tito. As the war continued, the communist-dominated Partisans gained ground against the Chetniks, who preferred to compromise with the German and Italian occupying forces rather than continue a war in alliance with communists. By 1943, Prime Minister Churchill, with his eyes fixed on the paramount need to beat Hitler, decided to support Tito with supplies, and the United States followed suit. When the Russians entered Belgrade in October 1944, they helped put their fellow communist Tito in control.

Once in power, Tito installed his own communist government, abolished the Yugoslav monarchy, and for three years adopted all the standard Soviet policies. Yet in June 1948, the world learned with surprise that the USSR had quarreled with Yugoslavia and expelled Tito's regime from the Cominform. The Soviet satellites broke their economic agreements with Yugoslavia, unloosed great barrages of anti-Tito propaganda, and stirred up border incidents. We know now that Soviet arrogance and insistence on penetrating the Yugoslav army and security organizations had aroused Yugoslav national feeling, never very far below the surface. Stalin believed that he could bully the Yugoslavs into submission. "I will shake my little finger," he said, "and there will be no more Tito."

But Tito remained in power, accepting the aid that was quickly offered him by the United States. Washington saw that a communist regime hostile to Stalin was a new phenomenon that would deeply embarrass the Russians. Gradually Yugoslav communism evolved a modified ideology of its own, declaring that Stalin was a heretic and Tito and his followers the only true Leninists. Tito decentralized the economy, beginning in the factories, where workers' committees now began to participate actively in the planning. From the econ-omy, decentralization spread to the local government apparatus, then to the central government, and finally to the Yugoslav Communist party, now rechristened the League of Yugoslav Communists. Though the regime admitted its past outrageous excesses, the police continued to be a powerful force. Tito also gradually abandoned agricultural collectivization, which, as always, was most unpopular with the peasants. Yugoslavia remained communist, however, suspicious of the Western capitalists who were helping it.

In their fear of the spread of this new "national" communism to the other satellites, the Soviets directed the other eastern European regimes in a series of ferocious purges, executing leading communists for alleged "Titoism" and thus terrorizing anyone who might hope to establish any sort of autonomy within the communist bloc. When Stalin died in 1953, his heirs gave high priority to healing the breach with Yugoslavia and eliminating the weakness it had created in their European position.

Asia: The Korean War

When balked in Europe, czarist Russian governments had often turned to Asia. After the failures in Greece and Berlin, the Soviet Union similarly embarked on new Asian adventures. Here, communists had tried and failed to win power in Indonesia, Burma, Malaya, and the Philippines, and had succeeded in China. The Korean War, which broke out in June 1950, was in some measure a Soviet-sponsored operation, although the Russians themselves limited their contribution to support and sympathy and allowed their Chinese ally to take the military lead.

Korea, a peninsula at the eastern extremity of Asia bordering on Manchuria and Siberia and close to Japan, had been a target of Russian interest in the late nineteenth and early twentieth centuries, but the Japanese defeat of the Russians in 1905 had led instead to Japanese annexation of the country in 1910. In 1945, at the close of World War II, Russian troops occupied the northern part of Korea and American troops the southern part. The country was divided in the middle by a line along the 38th parallel of latitude. A communist-inspired People's Democratic Republic of Korea was set up in the north and an American-inspired Republic of Korea in the south. When all American forces except for a few specialists were withdrawn from South Korea, the North Koreans marched south to unite the nation under communist control.

It is probable that the communists thought the operation was safe, since official American pronouncements had seemed to refer to Korea as outside the American "defense perimeter." But when the invasion began, the United States—with UN approval, for the vote was taken in the absence of the Russians—at once moved troops into Korea. They halted the North Korean drive and pushed the enemy back well north of the 38th parallel, almost to the Yalu River, the frontier of China. At this point, Communist China entered the war, and Chinese troops joined the North Koreans in pushing the Americans southward again. By 1951, the line of battle had been stabilized roughly along the old boundary between North and South Korea. After prolonged negotiations, an armistice was finally concluded in July 1953.

The Korean settlement by no means ended the tension between Communist China and the United States. Serious friction developed over Taiwan (Formosa) and the smaller offshore islands, Quemoy and Matsu, now in the hands of Chiang Kai-shek. Nor did the Korean settlement bring closer understanding between the USSR and the United States. It was at best a compromise: after all the fighting, the United States had managed to hang on to the devastated southern portion of the country, and the communists had been driven back to the north, which they governed undisturbed. Neither side could call it a victory. By the time it was reached, Stalin had been dead for more than three months.

Stalin's heirs realized that any attack that threatened the vital interests of the United States might well touch off the ultimate disaster. A policy of probing to see just which interests the United States considered vital had already led to the Korean War. Continued tension between the two superpowers required the USSR to continue to devote its resources to guns rather than butter. To relax the tension would theoretically have meant more butter but would in turn raise the danger that the USSR would lose its position as leader of the world communist movement. China, with its determination to seize Taiwan and to expand in Asia, might seize the leadership of revolutionary forces at least in Asia and would represent the Russians as old and tired, no longer true Leninists. In the end it proved to be impossible for Khrushchev to hold all these threats in balance, and the choices he eventually felt forced to make led to a major split in the communist world.

Eastern Europe

In eastern Europe, Khrushchev made a great effort to heal the breach with Tito. In May 1955 he went in person to Belgrade and not only publicly apologized for the quarrel, taking the blame upon the USSR, but openly agreed that "differences in the concrete forms of developing socialism are exclusively matters for the people of the country concerned," which seemed to echo Tito's own views. Relations between Tito and Moscow were temporarily improved, although the Yugoslavs never abandoned their ties to the West. Khrushchev even went so far as to declare that many prominent victims of the "Titoist" purges had been executed wrongly, and he abolished the Cominform, the body that ostensibly had started the quarrel with Tito. But in making these admissions and healing the

quarrel Stalin had started, Khrushchev had opened the door to new troubles.

Khrushchev's speech of 1956 denouncing Stalin and admitting so many past injustices proved far too strong a brew for the European satellites. Anticommunist riots by workers in Poznan, Poland, in June 1956, were followed by severe upheavals in the rest of that country. Though Polish national sentiment was declaring itself, the uprising remained within the grip of one wing of the Communist party, that led by Wladislaw Gomulka, who had been purged for alleged Titoism in 1951. Not even the presence in Warsaw of Khrushchev himself and other members of the Soviet Presidium prevented the rise of Gomulka to power, although at one moment the Russians seem to have contemplated using their army to impose their will by force. Yet because the new government in Poland was, after all, a communist government, they allowed it to remain in power.

In Hungary, however, the upheaval went farther. Starting, like the Polish uprising, as an anti-Stalinist movement within the Communist party, the Hungarian disturbance at first brought Imre Nagy, a communist like Gomulka, into office as premier. But popular hatred for communism and for the Russians got out of hand, and young men and women flew to arms in Budapest in the hope of ousting the communists and of taking Hungary altogether out of the Soviet sphere. They even denounced the Warsaw Pact, the Russian alliance of eastern European satellites set up by Moscow to oppose NATO. It was then that Khrushchev ordered full-fledged military action. In November 1956 Soviet tanks and troops, violating an armistice, swept back into Budapest and put down the revolution in blood and fire. A puppet government led by Janos Kadar was installed. More than 150,000 Hungarian refugees fled to Austria, to be resettled in various Western countries. Despite the Soviet charges that the uprising had been trumped up by the Western "imperialists" and "fascists," the West in fact had played no part at all, not daring to help the Hungarians for fear of starting a world war.

Soviet military intervention in Hungary showed the world how limited was Khrushchev's willingess and ability to permit free choices to other communist states. Tito denounced the Soviet intervention against Nagy, though he was frightened by the wholly anticommunist character that the Hungarian revolt subsequently took on, and he failed to oppose the decisive Soviet military operations that put an end to the uprising.

For a second time, relations between Moscow and Tito were strained. They were patched up again in the summer of 1957, but Tito flatly refused to sign a declaration of twelve Communist parties denouncing "revisionism"—as Tito's own views had come to be known. Instead he published his own counterprogram declaring that each communist nation should make its own decisions freely. The old quarrel was renewed for the third time. Tito would not reenter a world communist union led by Russia. Khrushchev's efforts had failed.

Both the harshness of the onslaught against revisionism and Khrushchev's acceptance of defeat in his efforts to win the Yugoslavs by softness reflected Chinese influence. Eager to play a leading role in formulating world communist ideology, the Chinese displayed a strong preference for Stalinist orthodoxy and repression. By the spring of 1958, the Chinese and Khrushchev himself had declared that Stalin's original denunciation of the Yugoslavs back in 1948 had been correct after all. In June 1958 the Soviet government underlined this decision in grim fashion when it announced the executions of Imre Nagy and other leaders of the Hungarian uprising, in violation of solemn promises of safe-conduct.

All the eastern European satellites were bound together in the Council for Mutual Economic Aid (Comecon), established in 1949, which took measures to standardize machinery and coordinate economic policies, and issued blasts against western European efforts at cooperation like the Common Market. Yugoslavia never was a member and after 1958 was not invited to send observers. In 1958–1959, Comecon called for a "specialization" plan, in accordance with which the more developed countries would concentrate on heavy industry, and Romania in particular on the production of raw materials (chiefly food and oil). The Romanian government, communist though it was, protested, pointing to its already considerable achievements in heavy industry; and in December 1961 Romania openly refused to accept the "principles" of the "international socialist division of labor" issued at the twenty-second congress of the CPSU.

Thus the Romanians, like the Yugoslavs, were assuming a more independent position within the communist bloc. They increased their trade with the noncommunist world, and they remained neutral in the growing Soviet-Chinese quarrel. In July 1963 the Russians gave in on the economic question and sanctioned Romania's continued efforts to build a steel industry, while postponing the economic integration of the block until 1966, by which time Romania would be entitled to the same status as Czechoslovakia and Poland.

The Soviet-Romanian disagreement widened under Khrushchev's successors. Soviet propaganda called for integrating the lower Danube region—which would have meant taking territory from Romania—and denied that the Romanians had contributed to the Allied cause in World War II. The Romanians claimed full credit for their own "liberation from fascism" and—most important—even dared to demand the return to Romania of the provinces of Bessarabia and northern Bukovina, annexed by the USSR in 1940. Yugoslav-Romanian cooperation became an important part of Romanian policy. Largely owing to the firmness and balancing skill of the Romanian Communist leader, Ceausescu, supported by the traditionally anti-Russian

sentiments of Romanians generally, the Romanian effort to avoid being swallowed by the USSR remained successful.

Elsewhere within the Soviet bloc in eastern Europe, there was a general liberalizing trend in Hungary. Increased tourism, wider trade with the West, better living conditions, even success with agricultural collectivization, a new agreement with the Vatican concerning the Hungarian church, and improved education all spoke of relaxed terror. In Poland, however, which had after Gomulka's success for some years enjoyed more freedom of discussion and contact with the West than any other communist country, the trend was reversed. In economic planning, in agriculture, in education, in religious policies, even in a return to anti-Semitism, a kind of neo-Stalinism emerged as standard. A sudden rise of prices announced by the government in 1970 precipitated serious riots, suppressed with heavy loss of life. The Gomulka government fell. Edward Gierek became premier, and the brittleness of communist control of eastern European peoples had again been demonstrated.

In Czechoslovakia, liberalization began before Khrushchev's ouster in 1964 and continued after it. Economic failure of the communist bureaucracy in a formerly prosperous industrial state and an entrenched and particularly brutal party leadership had aroused great discontent, which was to burst forth dramatically in 1968 and produce an international crisis (see below).

Berlin Again

In East Germany (DDR, the Deutsche Demokratische Republik), the USSR had created its most industrially productive European satellite, now fully geared into the Comecon. Except for a workers' riot the East Berlin in 1953, the German communist puppets had succeeded in repressing the population's aversion to Soviet and communist rule. Moreover, strategically the DDR was of great importance to the USSR; control over East Germany enabled the Russians to keep Poland surrounded, helpless to achieve more than a token autonomy. Yet the United States, Britain, and France each retained a zone of occupation in Berlin, deep in the heart of the DDR, and accessible by subway from East Berlin. Every year, thousands of East Germans showed how they felt about communism by escaping into West Berlin. The East German population actually declined by two million between 1949 and 1961. For those who stayed behind in the DDR, West Berlin provided an example of prosperity and free democratic government that acted more effectively on their minds than any mere propaganda.

This situation accounted for Khrushchev's determination to get the Western powers out of Berlin. The method he proposed in 1958 and later years was thoroughly Stalinist: he threatened to sign a peace treaty with the puppet government of East Germany, never recognized by the West; to turn over to it the communications to Berlin; and to support it in any effort it might then make to cut these communications and force the Western powers out. Western refusal to accept the abrogation of agreements concluded during World War II led to a prolonged diplomatic crisis during 1959.

The Western powers could neither permit the USSR to recreate the conditions it had fought during the airlift of 1948 nor accept the suggestion that, once Western troops were removed, Berlin would be a "free city." Defenseless and surrounded by communist territory, Berlin and its two million "free" citizens, it feared, would soon be swallowed up. Moreover, the negotiations proposed by the USSR, whereby the DDR would thereafter "confederate" with the West German Federal Republic, aroused the gravest doubts. How could a state that was a full member of the Western system of NATO federate with one that belonged to the Soviet system's Warsaw Pact? How could a state that stood for free capitalist development federate with one completely communized? How could a parliamentary state responsibly governed by a multiparty system with checks and balances federate with a communist totalitarian state? Khrushchev surely did not believe in the possibility of the confederation he was proposing and hoped instead that any possible union of the Germanies would be discredited, and that the DDR, with full control over Berlin, would emerge as a permanent Soviet satellite. But even a Soviet success in Berlin short of this complete victory would have meant that the West had in some measure at least recognized East

Germany, which in turn would have severely disturbed West German stability and disrupted NATO.

U-2, The Berlin Wall, Testing, Cuba

While the Berlin threat persisted, Vice-President Nixon visited the USSR, where he and Khrushchev had a famous confrontation in a model kitchen that was part of an American exhibit. President Eisenhower and Khrushchev agreed to exchange visits, and Khrushchev actually made a dramatic tour of the United States. When the leaders of the great powers met at the summit in Paris (May 1960), tensions, however, were once again inflamed by the U-2 incident: a Soviet missile had brought down a lightweight, extremely fast American plane that had been taking high-altitude photographs of Soviet territory, and the Russians had captured the pilot unharmed. After an initial denial, President Eisenhower found himself obliged to acknowledge the truth of the charge; and the incident ended both the summit meeting and the plans for his own visit to the USSR.

When Eisenhower's successor, John F. Kennedy, met Khrushchev in Vienna (June 1961), Khrushchev insisted that the USSR would sign the treaty with East Germany before the end of the year. Tension mounted, and the number of refugees fleeing East Berlin rose to a thousand a day. On August 13, East German forces cut the communications between East and West Berlin and began to build a barrier—the Berlin Wall—to prevent further departures. Taken by surprise, the United States realized that it could not resort to arms to prevent the closing of the East Germans' own border but protested, and sent Vice-President Lyndon Johnson to reassure the West Berliners of America's backing. The wall became the symbol of a government that had to imprison its own people to keep them at home. Occasional hair-raising escapes and poignant recaptures or shootings continued to take place along the wall's length. But the crisis proved to be over. Khrushchev had backed away from unilateral abrogation of the Berlin treaties.

But Khrushchev announced in August 1961 that the USSR would resume atomic testing in the atmosphere, which had been stopped by both powers in 1958. In the two months that followed, the Russians exploded thirty huge bombs, whose total force considerably exceeded all previous American, British, and French explosions. President Kennedy now decided that, unless Khrushchev would agree to a treaty banning all tests, the United States would have to conduct its own new tests. Khrushchev refused, and the American tests began in late April 1962. All during the months that followed, conversations on disarmament, including of course arrangements for the banning of future tests, continued with the Russians at Geneva.

It was during the summer of 1962 that Khrushchev moved to place Soviet missiles with nuclear warheads in Cuba, where an American-sponsored landing di-

Khrushchev and Kennedy at the Vienna summit meeting, 1961.

rected against the procommunist regime of Fidel Castro had failed dismally at the Bay of Pigs the year before. Castro may not have asked for the missiles, but he did accept them. Soviet officers were to retain control over their use. Their installation would effectively have doubled the Soviet capacity to strike directly at the United States, but the chief threat was political: when known, the mere presence of these weapons ninety miles from Florida would shake the confidence of other nations in the American capacity to protect even the United States. It would enable Khrushchev to blackmail America on the question of Berlin. American military intelligence discovered the sites and photographed them from the air. Khrushchev announced that the Soviet purpose was simply to help the Cubans resist a new invasion from the United States, which he professed to believe threatened.

But Kennedy could not allow the missiles to stay in Cuba. The only course of action at first seemed an air strike, which might well have touched off a new world war. Kennedy found a measure that would prevent the further delivery of missiles—a sea blockade ("quarantine") of the island—and combined it with the demand that the missiles already in Cuba be removed. He thus gave Khrushchev a way to avoid world war and a chance to save face. After several days of almost unbearable tension, Khrushchev backed down, and agreed to halt work on the missile sites in Cuba and remove the offensive weapons there, while reaffirming the Soviet wish to continue discussions about disarmament.

After the Missile Crisis; Czechoslovakia

Khrushchev had moved aggressively in an area close to the United States, where Soviet national security was not threatened. By lying about the missiles, he had destroyed whatever case he might otherwise have had in world opinion. But Kennedy exploited the American victory only to push for a further relaxation in tensions. In July 1963 the United States, the USSR, and Great Britain signed a treaty banning nuclear weapons tests in the atmosphere, in outer space, or under water. The treaty subsequently received the adherence of more than seventy nations, though France and China—a fledgling and a prospective nuclear power—would not sign it. The installation of a "hot line" communications system between the White House and the Kremlin so that the leaders of the two countries might talk to each other in case of need, and the sale of surplus American wheat to the Russians, marked the final few months of the Kennedy administration.

The administration of President Johnson saw no recurrence of a Soviet-American crisis as acute as that over the missiles. But relations between the two superpowers remained tense and suspicious. The war in Vietnam would alone have made a real relaxation of tension impossible, and the two powers found them-

selves on opposite sides in the Middle East as well. The visit of Kosygin to the United States in 1967, and his meeting with Johnson at Glassboro, New Jersey, accomplished little. The settlement in 1968 on the terms of a nonproliferation treaty, to prevent the spread of atomic arms beyond the nations that already possessed them, represented a step forward. The treaty awaited ratification by the Senate when Soviet intervention in Czechoslovakia in the summer of 1968 delayed it.

Long the most Stalinist of the eastern European governments, the Czech regime was unpopular at home. Soviet exploitation and the rigidity of communist dogma had crippled the once flourishing Czech economy. In 1968, Alexander Dubcek, a Slovak communist trained in the USSR, took over the Communist party as first secretary and ousted the repressive Antonin Novotny. The Dubcek government freed the press from censorship, and the pent-up protests of years now filled its columns. It seemed as though the regime might even allow opposition political parties to come into existence. Some army officers apparently favored revision of the Warsaw Pact, which enabled the USSR to hold military exercises in the territory of any member state. Yugoslavia and Romania encouraged the Czechs in the liberal course they were pursuing, and something very like a revival of the old Little Entente between these three countries seemed to be in the making.

The westernmost nation in the Soviet sphere, Czechoslovakia had long frontiers with both East and West Germany. Highly industrialized and with a strong Western cultural tradition, the Czechs could not put through a radical liberalization without deeply worrying the Russians and the East German government. In the spring and summer of 1968, the USSR moved from denunciation of the Dubcek regime to intimidation and bullying, and finally to armed intervention. Soviet and satellite tank divisions, more than 500,000 strong, swept into the country and met no active resistance. Unlike the Soviet attack on Hungary in 1956, that on Czechoslovakia in the summer of 1968 was not directed against a population already in armed rebellion against their communist masters. There was little bloodshed. But there was great shock. Those who had been arguing that the USSR had outgrown the Stalinist repressive measures of earlier years—and they included many of the best-informed observers of international affairs—found themselves proved wrong. The French and Italian Communist parties joined the Yugoslav and Romanian in condemning the invasion. The Soviet government kidnapped the Czech leaders and for a time sought frantically but vainly for native communists who would govern as puppets and so lend credence to the Soviet claim that their armies had only acted on an invitation from Czechs and Slovaks who feared "counterrevolution." In the end the Russians restored Dubcek and his colleagues, but only after extracting promises from them that the liberalization would be reversed. Soviet occupation of Czechoslovakia continued.

In the years that followed, the return of Stalinism to Czechoslovakia was slow but inexorable. Dubcek, a broken man, was ousted from government and party; his followers were powerless; and the Czech government was once more a mere Soviet puppet. A grim purge of Czech intellectuals threatened the very existence of the country's cultural institutions. The Russians had been so alarmed by the Czech cultural, economic, and political ferment and its military and diplomatic implications that they had been willing at least temporarily to sacrifice much of the international goodwill that they had been able to accumulate.

For the third time in thirty years—in 1938, 1948, and 1968—it was demonstrated that the sufferings of the Czechs at the hands of Nazis or communists could sadden the prodemocratic nations but could not elicit action or even prevent continuation of discussions with the great power guilty of the offense. Despite the initial American shock at Soviet behavior, in 1969 and 1970 discussions between the United States and the USSR with regard to limitations of armaments (SALT, Strategic Arms Limitation Talks) resumed. Both powers had an interest in somehow reducing their huge expenditures on weapons and obtaining more resources to deal with the disorderly state of their internal economies.

II The USSR, China, and America in Asia, 1956–1970

Between Stalin's death in 1953 and Khrushchev's denunciation of Stalin in 1956, Chinese-Soviet relations were basically amicable, and Chinese influence rose in the communist world. The Russians returned Port Arthur and Dairen to China in 1955. But when Khrushchev denounced Stalin without consulting Mao, the Chinese disapproved. They continued to denounce Tito and the Yugoslavs as "revisionists" and to try to block Khrushchev's reconciliation with them. They also wanted far more economic aid than the USSR had been able or willing to provide, especially aid in developing nuclear weapons. In 1957, Mao experimented briefly with a liberated public opinion ("Let one hundred flowers bloom"), but soon returned to, and remained on, a thoroughly leftist militant course. At home he embarked on forced-draft industrialization, the "great leap forward," with its backyard blast furnaces and its mass collectivization of the "people's communes," with disastrous results to both industry and agriculture. The Russians disapproved, and the latent disagreement between the two communist giants now began to emerge.

In 1959, Khrushchev told Peking that the USSR would not furnish China with atomic weapons and tried unsuccessfully to unseat Mao. The Chinese bombardment of Quemoy and Matsu (1958), their savage conquest of Tibet, and—as a result—their first invasion of Indian territory in Ladakh were undertaken without consultation between China and the USSR; and the

Russians publicly declared themselves to be neutral as between the Chinese and the Indians. In 1960, Khrushchev withdrew all Soviet technicians from China.

The Chinese tried to influence other Communist parties against the Russians and picked up a European satellite: Albania, smallest and poorest of the Balkan countries. The Albanian Communist party, trained and marshaled as a guerrilla movement by emissaries of Tito during World War II, had taken power, and had thrown off Yugoslav domination after Tito's rebellion from Stalin in 1948. More than anything else the Albanian communists feared a renewed subjection to the Yugoslavs. When Khrushchev made his repeated efforts to conciliate Tito, the Albanians found in the Chinese a counterweight to the USSR. Albania as a satellite was an economic liability, but the Chinese could rejoice in having subtracted a European communist state from the Russian bloc.

In the very midst of the 1962 crisis over Soviet missiles in Cuba, the Chinese chose to attack India again, apparently intending chiefly to seize the border regions in Ladakh, including important road communications. The Chinese withdrew when they had what they wanted; but the USSR, though ostensibly neutral, was clearly, like the United States, pro-Indian.

The Chinese built up their own organizations in Africa and Asia. When the test-ban treaty was signed, the Chinese called the Russians traitors to the international communist movement. Though Khrushchev tried to arrange for a general public excommunication of the Chinese by other Communist parties, he was unable to bring it off. Mao not only called for Khrushchev's removal, but accused the Russians of illegally occupying eastern European and Japanese territory.

By the time of Khrushchev's ouster in October 1964, the Chinese had won the support of the North Korean and North Vietnamese Communist parties and enjoyed a special position of strength in Indonesia and Algeria. In Africa they had established a predominant influence in two former French colonies, and they took the lead in sponsoring a major rebellion in the tormented former Belgian Congo. In South America they had supported Castroites within the pro-Soviet Latin American parties in the hope of starting active revolutionary movements. In the United States, Chinese propagandists won the support of some American blacks. They had defeated India. They had exploded an atomic bomb. They were actively supporting, as were the Russians, the communist efforts in South Vietnam.

But 1965 saw major Chinese setbacks. A congress scheduled for Algiers, in which they had expected to condemn the Russians, was canceled, in part because the Algerians overthrew their pro-Chinese premier Ben Bella. The Congo revolt was put down. An attempted communist coup in Indonesia failed after the assassination of numerous leading army officers. The Indonesian army took power and revenged itself heavily, with the help of the Muslim population, upon the Chinese minority and upon the native communists, of whom perhaps 500,000 were killed.

The Chinese threat to renew the attack on India during the Indian-Pakistani conflict of 1965 evaporated as the United States and the USSR tacitly cooperated in the United Nations to force a temporary ceasefire. Early in 1966, Premier Kosygin at Tashkent acted as mediator between India and Pakistan, achieving an agreement to seek a peaceful solution and thus depriving the Chinese of a pretext for intervention while reasserting Soviet influence in Asia.

Perhaps in part as the result of these successive setbacks abroad, the Chinese in 1966 began to behave at home in ways suggesting that the regime was undergoing unbearable tensions. Denunciations and removals of important figures at the top of the government and party were accompanied by a new wave of adulation for Chairman Mao. Youngsters in their teens, the Red Guard, erupted into the streets of the cities of China, beating and sometimes killing older people whose loyalty they professed to suspect, destroying works of art and other memorials of China's precommunist past, and rioting against foreigners and foreign influences. When in October 1966 the Chinese successfully fired a guided missile with a nuclear warhead—the third Chinese nuclear explosion in two years—it served notice that the political turmoil was not interfering with the development of military hardware. Yet the turmoil continued, and all of China apparently became embroiled. The Chinese educational system was completely halted, and something like civil war raged in some of the provinces.

The artificially induced "cultural revolution" in China lasted about three years and died down only gradually in 1969, when the ninth Chinese Communist party congress actually took place. In 1969 and 1970, the mystery that veiled China from the West only seemed to thicken. Obviously something like a fourth of the top party and government officials had been purged, leaving stagnation and disillusionment behind. Economic production had risen only to about the 1965 level. Occasional executions took place, but the crisis had eased for reasons as obscure as the reasons for its inception. Chairman Mao himself—nearing the age of eighty—disappeared from the news for months at a time, and when he showed himself it was not as the implacable foe of all heterodoxy but as a rather relaxed and even genial leader. Though Soviet-Chinese tension once or twice broke into open fighting on the frontiers, and though the hostile propaganda of both sides in 1969 reached a new pitch of shrillness, the two countries did not stop engaging in talks.

Behind the series of incidents that revealed the mounting Chinese-Soviet quarrel to the world there lay theoretical disagreements about the best way to impose communist control upon the peoples of Africa, Asia, and Latin America. The Chinese favored direct sponsorship of local communist revolutionary movements, the Russians "peaceful" economic competition with the capitalist world for the loyalty and admiration of the emerging peoples. The Russians said the communists would win the competition without world war, while helping along local "wars of national liberation"—i.e., revolutions at least partly under communist control. The Chinese refused to grant that nuclear weapons had changed war or imperialism and regarded world war as inevitable. "The bourgeoisie," they maintained, "will never step down from the stage of history of its own accord."

The Chinese insisted that communists alone must take charge of all revolutionary movements from the beginning and claimed that aid to noncommunist countries was a delusion. They particularly objected to Soviet aid to India, their own enemy. They opposed disarmament. They had wanted Khrushchev to freeze Soviet living standards at a low level and to invest the savings in helping the Chinese catch up, but of course Khrushchev preferred to let his own people enjoy some of the fruits of their own labors. Remembering their own success as a guerrilla operation that first came to control the countryside and then moved in on the cities, Chinese theoreticians extended this lesson to the whole globe, regarding Asia, Africa, and Latin America—the underdeveloped areas—as the countryside, and Europe and North America as the cities. From the massed peoples of the backward continents the communists would mount an offensive against the peoples of the developed industrial world and conquer them. How seriously even the authors of this startling theory believed what they said we cannot know.

One additional factor, seldom mentioned but extremely important in the Chinese-Russian quarrel, was simply that of race. The Russians—though they would deny the charge—disliked and feared the Chinese, the yellow peril on their borders. The huge masses of Chinese—soon inexorably to number one billion people—who were crowded into territory adjacent to the vast, sparsely populated regions of the USSR and already laying claim to some of them, would frighten any reasonable government. Because the threat came, not from fellow whites, but from yellow men, the fear increased. Despite their protestations to the contrary, the Russians were extremely race-conscious, as the experiences of many African students in Moscow testified, and they reserved for the Chinese the deepest dislike of all. The Chinese used race openly as a weapon in their efforts to win support among other Asians, Africans, and Latin Americans, lumping the Soviet Union with the United States as symbols of the evil white intention to continue dominating the colored world. Convinced of their own superiority to the rest of mankind, the Chinese were racists too.

Vietnam

A special problem for the Chinese, Russians, and Americans arose in Southeast Asia as the result of the revolt of the Viet Minh communist forces against

France that broke out in French Indochina with the end of World War II in 1945. During the Korean War, the United States, fearing that the Chinese communists would strike across the border into northern Indo-China, gave substantial assistance to the French. In 1954, when the French had been defeated after the fall of their stronghold of Dienbienphu, a conference of powers at Geneva gave independence to the Indochinese provinces of Cambodia and Laos.

Vietnam, the third and largest portion of the former French colony, was divided along the 17th parallel. The northern section, with its capital at Hanoi, was governed by the communist Viet Minh party, whose leader was the veteran communist Ho Chi Minh; the southern portion, with its capital at Saigon, was led by a Catholic nationalist leader, Ngo Dinh Diem. The Geneva agreements guaranteed free elections. Though the United States did not sign them, it endorsed their purport, and hoped that the area, in which it had already invested more than $4 billion, might not fall to the communists.

Between 1954 and 1959, Ngo Dinh Diem created the bureaucratic machinery for a new regime, restored order in territory that had long been held by communist guerrillas and was now held by dissident sects, provided for almost a million refugees from the communist North, and resettled in the countryside millions of peasants who had fled to the cities. After the departure of the French in 1956, the Americans assumed the responsibility for assisting the solution of these problems with financial aid and technical advice.

But Diem failed politically. He canceled the scheduled elections and, together with his immediate family, governed despotically. In 1958 and 1959, communist-led guerrilla activity broke out again. Now known as the Viet Cong, the guerrillas set up a National Liberation Front. In September 1960 Ho Chi Minh endorsed the Viet Cong movement, which he was already supplying with arms and training. Using terror in the villages as a weapon, the guerrillas by 1961 were moving almost at will in South Vietnam, overrunning much of the countryside, murdering, looting, and burning.

Neighboring Laos, though strategically important, was no nation but rather a collection of unwarlike Buddhist tribes, where only a small clique of families traditionally indulged in politics. In 1953, a communist-oriented political faction, calling itself the Pathet Lao and supported by Ho Chi Minh, seized the northeastern portion of the country. The United States tried with massive financial and military aid to build a national Laotian army and establish a firm regime, but succeeded largely in creating corruption and factionalism. The head of the government, Souvanna Phouma, who was the brother-in-law of the head of the Pathet Lao, reached agreement with him in 1957 to set up a coalition government and neutralize the country, absorbing the Pathet Lao into the army. This the United States resisted, ousting Phouma and introducing the right-wing Phoumi Nousavan. By 1960, Phouma was

working with the Russians, and a portion of the army under the neutralist Kong Le (not a communist) was working with the Pathet Lao. Soviet airlifts of supplies to their side enhanced the possibility that the country would fall to the communists and that Thailand and Burma—to say nothing of South Vietnam—would be endangered also.

President Kennedy sought for ways to neutralize Laos and to convince the USSR that if his efforts failed, American military intervention would follow. Although the USSR agreed to neutralization, fighting in Laos between Soviet-backed and American-backed forces continued until mid-May 1961, when Khrushchev apparently realized that the United States was preparing to send marines from Okinawa to Laos. Before an agreement was reached at Geneva in July 1962, Kennedy had to send marines to Thailand in order to stop the Pathet Lao from continuing to violate the truce. And when the decision to neutralize Laos was reached—many years too late—the Pathet Lao, now a strong force armed with Russian weapons and still supported by Ho Chi Minh, withdrew from the coalition and maintained control over its own portion of the country, which bordered on South Vietnam and included the "Ho Chi Minh trail," a road down which came supplies from Hanoi for the Viet Cong guerrillas. But a form of stability had been created in Laos itself. Phouma and Kong Le were now anticommunist, since it now was the Pathet Lao that was keeping Laos divided and in turmoil.

Incomplete and unsatisfactory as the Laos solution was, it far surpassed any arrangement that could be reached for South Vietnam. American efforts to get Ngo Dinh Diem moving politically failed. All that emerged was the "strategic hamlet" plan: a program to create fortified villages and "relocate" peasants in them in the hope that this would provide protection against the guerrillas and thus make the enemy campaigns first expensive and then impossible. In May 1963 Diem's troops fired on a crowd of Buddhists in the city of Hue, protesting against Diem's edict that they might not display flags in honor of Buddha's birthday. Riots followed, and several Buddhists soaked themselves in gasoline and set themselves afire. In August, Diem staged a mass arrest of Buddhists, and in November he and his brother were ousted and murdered in a coup led by dissident generals and countenanced by the United States.

Thereafter the South Vietnamese government changed hands several times, each time by military coup. The longest-lived regime, that of General Nguyen Cao Ky, successfully conducted elections in September 1966, Ky emerging as vice-president under President Thieu. But the hamlet program was a failure; insurgency increased; North Vietnamese regular troops appeared in South Vietnam in support of the guerrillas; more than half a million peasant families were made refugees once more by floods and by terrorism.

Between 1965 and 1967, the United States stepped

One of the impromptu factories that operated in Hanoi during the American bombing of the city, November 1967.

up the number of its troops from fewer than a single division to more than five hundred thousand and initiated a policy of bombing North Vietnamese installations. Massive American intervention made it impossible for the Viet Cong to conquer the entire country and assured the United States of certain bases along the coast. Having increased the American commitment to such a level that none could doubt his earnestness, President Johnson, in the hope of bringing Ho Chi Minh to the conference table, then assured the enemy that the United States had no long-range intention of remaining in the country and sought no military bases there. In 1966, he suspended the bombing for a time, but the enemy insisted that there could be no negotiations until all American troops had left the country. And the very act of offering to negotiate with the North aroused uneasiness in the South.

The Vietnam War was the first war in history that could be viewed on television half a world away. The blood and horror of the jungle fighting, the misery of the countless fleeing Vietnamese survivors, the corruption of the Saigon government came home vividly to the American public. The war's mounting costs wrecked President Johnson's widely hailed domestic programs. Some voices called for American withdrawal. Opposing public opinion urged that it be intensified and "won." On the one hand, continued intensification threatened a land war in Asia of unprecedented difficulty and unpredictable length and severity. On the other hand, withdrawal might mean the abandonment of the goals for which the United States had fought the Asian portion of World War II: the communists of the 1970s, like the Japanese militarists of the 1940s, would dominate the Asian continent in a spirit of hostility to the United States.

In 1968, as the time for American elections approached, Senator Eugene McCarthy, Democrat of Minnesota, challenged the Johnson administration by announcing his own candidacy for the presidency on an antiwar platform. His impressive successes in early primaries stimulated another opponent of the war, Senator Robert F. Kennedy, to enter the race on his own. The strength of the antiwar candidates brought about the withdrawal of President Johnson—who had been universally expected to run. Ho Chi Minh, who had always expected that internal American politics would force the United States out of Vietnam, then consented to open peace talks, which began in Paris but dragged on inconclusively.

The Nixon administration inherited both the increasingly unpopular war and the halting negotiations designed to end it. Nixon pledged the eventual withdrawal of all American forces and did indeed begin substantially to reduce them. Nixon planned to "Vietnamize" the fighting by continuing at a rapid rate to train and supply the South Vietnamese forces, who would replace the Americans in combat but who would continue to have American support, including massive air support, until a settlement could be reached with the North that did not involve the communization of the South. The death of Ho Chi Minh in 1969 brought no crisis to the North Vietnamese government. It seemed prepared to carry on with the war, obviously believing that the Americans had lost stomach for it and that the communist cause would gain more by continuing the war than by ending it through negotiations.

The military picture was further clouded for the United States by the increasing Viet Cong domination of Laos, where the hard-won settlement of the early sixties was placed in jeopardy, and by the overflow of Viet Cong forces into those portions of Cambodia nearest to South Vietnam, where the enemy was invulnerable to American and South Vietnamese pursuit. Cambodia had as its ruler a French-educated prince of an old native ruling house, Norodom Sihanouk, personally shrewd and vain, who made some effort to maintain Cambodian neutrality but who believed that in the end China would dominate his part of the world and so must be appeased. These beliefs made him suspect in Washington and unpopular at home with his own military and with many of his people, who, though peaceful, detested the Vietnamese in general, and the intruding Viet Cong and North Vietnamese in particular. In 1970, a coup d'état led by General Lon Nol overthrew Sihanouk, who, from Peking, announced the formation of a government in exile.

Not long afterward American and South Vietnamese troops made an "incursion" into Cambodia. The invading forces failed to wipe out the large numbers of enemy forces believed to be the chief target of the expedition. Public response in the United States to the extension of hostilities was far more negative than President Nixon had believed would be the case. Despite the capture of many North Vietnamese supplies, the American forces failed to find or destroy a (perhaps nonexistent) central enemy headquarters. Nixon withdrew the forces within the time he had promised; but there remained much doubt whether the Cambodian operation as a whole had been justifiable. During the Cambodian operations the U.S. briefly resumed the bombing of North Vietnam. Bombing, indeed, and the threat of bombing were likely to be the most effective instruments left to the United States as its land forces in Vietnam were reduced.

By 1970, many Americans regarded the Vietnam War as an interminable struggle, impossible to win. In South Vietnam, the government was surely both corrupt and cruel, but it also apparently represented the only defense against communist domination available to the thousands of South Vietnamese who had taken American pledges of help at their face value. For the United States, the Vietnam War had become the source of troubles that loomed far larger than the importance of the entire area it was being fought to protect. Despite the century of French occupation and exploitation, both America's Vietnamese allies and America's Vietnamese enemies shared the culture and the social outlook characteristic of an agricultural society in a Confucian tradition. With different values, Americans began to fear that we had been giving our aid to people who misunderstood its purposes and did not want it on our terms.

III   The Emerging Nations and World Politics

As in Indochina, so elsewhere, the process of liquidating old colonial empires and endowing new emerging nations with economic and political institutions had been greatly accelerated and intensified by the Second World War. The use of colonial troops by the Western powers during the war increased the self-esteem of the peoples providing the troops. Wartime propaganda inevitably strengthened the native wish to obtain self-government and self-determination. Wartime inflation, shortages, conscription of labor, and the enjoyment of war profits by the few added to the sense of grievance felt by colonial peoples.

Moreover, during the war Asians—Japanese—seized Western possessions in the Far East, putting an end to the myth of white Western supremacy. Even though Japan was defeated in the end, Western prestige did not recover. Everybody knew that the French and Dutch had not really won, that British power had been seriously weakened, and that the defeat of the Conservatives by the Labour party in 1945 promised new colonial policies. The only real victors in the war were the United States and the Soviet Union, each in its way anticolonial.

Deeper causes of anticolonialism lay in the five-hundred-year record of Western expansion, and in the Western tradition itself. Westerners brought with them the Bible, the American Declaration of Independence, the French Declaration of the Rights of Man, the Communist Manifesto. It was hardly possible to keep on insisting that "all men are created equal" really meant "white men are created the superiors of colored men." Western imperialism carried within itself the seeds of its own transfiguration into self-determination for all peoples. The great instrument for the spread of Western ideas was the education provided by the West to a relatively small native minority among the non-Western peoples. Though some of these men turned against this Western education and took refuge in a reaffirmation of the values of their traditional cultures, most of the educated came to feel that independence could be won only by learning the industrial, technological, and military skills of the West.

These educated non-Westerners wanted independence. Many were revolutionaries; some admired the Bolshevik revolution, and a few received training in Moscow. A great many Westerners made the mistake of assuming that these men were not representative of the native populations, and that the great colonial masses asked nothing better than to be ruled by the kindly whites. Instead, the urban masses and then, more gradually, the peasant masses began to share the feelings of nationalism and to demand that the foreigner go. Often this demand was exacerbated by the rapid increases in population made possible by the dramatically lower death rates resulting from the sanitary engineering, the medical facilities, and the law and order introduced by the imperialist powers.

The two decades following World War II saw the liquidation of the British, French, Dutch, and Belgian empires. Portugal alone of the imperial powers retained its major possessions overseas—chiefly Angola and Mozambique on the west and east coasts of Africa respectively—and this largely because the Portuguese government was a conservative dictatorship that would not yield to native pressures even when they took the form of open rebellion.

Britain, to be sure, continued to lead the Commonwealth of Nations, whose membership came to include many of the new nonwhite states. Although the Commonwealth continued to have economic significance as an association of trading partners, its political importance diminished, in part because of the further loosening of the ties between the white dominions and the mother country. South Africa severed its bonds with the Commonwealth in 1961 and declared itself a wholly independent republic. Australia and New Zealand came to look to the United States as the potential defender of their security.

The Fate of the Japanese Asian Empire

During the Second World War the Japanese had created a huge empire, the "Greater East Asia Co-Prosperity Sphere." To rule it they had relied chiefly on the time-honored Western device of setting up puppet native governments and exploiting for their own benefit the economic resources of the conquered lands. Because the Japanese were an Asian people, a colored people, they might well have acted as the emancipators of Asians that their propaganda proclaimed them to be. Instead, their armies looted and committed atrocities; they behaved like a master race. They alienated the people they might have won. When the war ended they were stripped of their overseas possessions.

The occupation of Japan was wholly American. Despite some strong opposition in American opinion,

the emperor was left on his throne, deprived of his divine status, and subjected to the close control of General MacArthur and the forces of occupation. Americans found that, on the surface, at least, the Japanese people did not take the occupation with hostility, but seemed eager to learn what democracy meant. By the time of the peace treaty in 1952, they had made a promising start on a democracy of the Western type. Their economy—the only well-developed industrial economy in the non-Western world—grew so rapidly that it overtook France and West Germany, to rank third in the world after the U.S. and the USSR.

Signs of change and of affluence multiplied. Programs of birth-control education were successful, and the birth rate dropped, to become one of the lowest in the world. Peasants migrated to the cities, especially to Tokyo, which surpassed London and New York as the world's largest city. Appalling smog settled over Tokyo, which was linked to Osaka, Japan's second city, by a new high-speed rail line, the fastest in the world. Weekend traffic jams resulted from the rush of Tokyo residents to the beaches in the summer and the ski slopes in winter. Inflation appeared to be the main threat to Japan's continued prosperity and to her social and economic westernization.

Politically, the democratic parliamentary institutions so carefully fostered by the American occupation forces flourished under successive cabinets of the essentially conservative Liberal Democratic party. The left-wing opposition, including both socialists and communists, objected to the mutual security pact binding Japan and the United States after the official restoration of full Japanese sovereignty in 1952. Left-wing demonstrations caused the last-minute cancellation of President Eisenhower's planned visit to Japan in 1960. Anti-Americanism derived from resentment over the continued United States occupation of the island of Okinawa (to the south of the main Japanese islands), from a bitterness left by the atomic blasts over Hiroshima and Nagasaki, and from left-wing mistrust of American policy and aims in Vietnam. In addition, the extreme insularity of many Japanese made Japan seem at times more nationalist and neutralist than pro-Western. To these factors in the late 1960s was added a particularly virulent case of student extremism. The Japanese university system—always intensely competitive and full of emotional strain—was now halted for months at a time by armed conflicts between rival groups of students and between radical students and police.

South Korea also attempted constitutional government in the Western manner but ran into serious difficulties. After the disruptive Korean War of the early 1950s, the government of Syngman Rhee, the perennial South Korean president, came under mounting criticism for its corruption and its arbitrary actions. In 1960, massive protests by students forced the eighty-five-year-old Rhee out of office, and inaugurated a tumultuous period marked first by the political intervention of the army and then by another attempt at constitutional rule. The economy continued to depend heavily on American assistance and boomed in the late 1960s. The South Koreans sent troops to fight in Vietnam. Pressure from communist North Korea in 1970 remained a major threat.

Once the Japanese occupation ended in Southeast Asia, the major Western colonial powers found that they could not revert to the prewar arrangements. The United States gave the Philippines independence in 1946. In 1949, the Dutch had to recognize the independence of the Netherlands East Indies as the Republic of Indonesia, with a population of a hundred million people. Britain gave Burma independence outside the Commonwealth (1948) and the Federation of Malaya independence within the Commonwealth (1957); the port of Singapore at the tip of Malaya, with its largely Chinese population, secured a special autonomous status (1958). When Malaya joined with the former British protectorates on the island of Borneo in the Federation of Malaysia (1963), Singapore at first participated, then withdrew (1965).

The Dutch in Indonesia had not prepared the people for independence by education. Nevertheless, the Indonesians at first attempted to run their government along the lines of a parliamentary democracy. Almost everything went wrong. The economy was crippled by inflation and shortages, by administrative corruption and the black market, and by the expulsion of experienced Dutch businessmen. The Muslims, who made up the bulk of the population, proved unable to form responsible political parties. The outlying islands of the archipelago, resentful of domination by the island of Java, which contained the capital (Djakarta, the former Batavia) and two-thirds of the population, rebelled against the central government. As the high expectations raised by the achievement of independence were disappointed, President Sukarno, the hero of the Indonesian struggle for independence, urged a "guided democracy" based upon indigenous rather than borrowed political institutions.

In 1959 and 1960, Sukarno suspended the ineffectual parliamentary regime and vested authority in himself and in the army and an appointive council. But "guided democracy" created still more turmoil. Inflation ran wild, necessities vanished from the market, pretentious new government buildings were left unfinished for lack of funds, and all foreign enterprises were confiscated. In external policy, Sukarno initiated an alternating hot and cold war with the new Federation of Malaysia for control of the island of Borneo, where both states had territory. By threat and intimidation he managed to annex former Dutch New Guinea (called West Irian by the Indonesians). When the United Nations recognized Malaysia, Sukarno withdrew Indonesia from membership early in 1965; he also told the United States "to go to hell with their aid" and moved closer and closer to Red China.

But a coup planned by Indonesian communists misfired at the last moment in the autumn of 1965, and the result was a wholesale slaughter of local communists. The anticommunist forces came to power under military leaders, among whom General Suharto took the lead, becoming president in 1968, reaching a settlement with Malaysia, and rejoining the UN. Inflation was brought under control, a five-year plan was launched, and parliamentary elections were held. Indonesia seemed to be gradually reviving.

Communist efforts in Southeast Asia were not confined to Indonesia and Indochina. In the Philippine Republic and Malaya too, the communists launched stubborn guerrilla campaigns, which were not checked until the late 1950s. Wherever there were large colonies of "overseas Chinese," some of these became sympathizers of Mao.

India and Pakistan

The Labour victory in Britain in 1945 made Indian emancipation a certainty. But the deep-seated tension between Muslims and Hindus now assumed critical importance. When the Hindu Congress party and the All-India Muslim League faced the need to make a working constitution for the new India, they found themselves in complete disagreement. The Muslims had long been working for a partition into separate Hindu and Muslim states, and this was in the end reluctantly accepted by the Hindus. In 1947, Hindu India and Muslim Pakistan were set up as self-governing dominions within the British Commonwealth.

Pakistan was a state divided into two parts, widely separated by intervening Indian territory—the larger, arid West Pakistan in the northwest, and the smaller, more fertile, and far more densely populated East Pakistan in East Bengal. The rest of the former British Indian Empire and four-fifths of its inhabitants became the Republic of India by virtue of its constitution of 1950. Pakistan, with its smaller population (still well over a hundred million people) and its relatively poorly developed industry, was weaker than India, and at first kept closer political ties with the British Commonwealth.

Violence accompanied partition. It was not possible to draw a boundary that would leave all Hindus in one state and all Muslims in another. Bitter Hindu-Muslim fighting cost hundreds of thousands of lives, as Hindus moved from Pakistani territory into India and Muslims moved from Indian territory into Pakistan. A particular source of trouble was the beautiful mountainous province of Kashmir. Though mainly Muslim in population, it was at the time of partition ruled by a Hindu princely house, which turned it over to India. India continued to occupy most of Kashmir, to the great economic disadvantage of Pakistan. The United Nations sought to determine the fate of Kashmir by arranging a plebiscite, but failed to secure the needed approval of both parties.

In domestic politics the two states went through

sharply contrasting experiences. The chief architect of Pakistani independence, Mohammed Ali Jinnah (head of the Muslim League), died in 1948. Thereafter Pakistan floundered in its attempts to make parliamentary government work and to attack pressing economic difficulties. In 1958, the army commander, the British-educated Ayub Khan, took full power, attacked administrative corruption and the black market, and instituted a program of "basic democracies" to train the population in self-government at the local level and thence gradually upward through a pyramid of advisory councils. For a long period Ayub's "basic democracies" proved more workable than Sukarno's "guided democracy," and led to the proclamation of a new constitution in 1962, which provided for a national assembly and also for a strengthened president, an office that Ayub continued to fill. But as Ayub grew older, charges of corruption were made against his family and his officials, and the teeming and depressed people of East Bengal more and more loudly protested against policies that discriminated in favor of West Pakistan. Disorder spread, and in 1969 a new military government under General Yahya Khan ousted Ayub. The tension between West Pakistan, whose Punjabis had a disproportionately large role in the government, and the underrepresented and miserably poor Bengalis of East Pakistan in 1970 remained an urgent unsolved problem.

Newly emancipated India suffered a grievous loss when Gandhi was assassinated by an anti-Muslim Hindu fanatic in 1948. But Jawaharlal Nehru, already a seasoned politician, at once assumed leadership. India successfully inaugurated a parliamentary democracy of the Western type. Its elections were free and hotly fought, and based on universal suffrage among voters who were in the main illiterate and rural. Understandably, Indians were proud of their accomplishment. India faced in an acute form the problem of overpopulation: by 1960, there were over five hundred million people, with approximately fifteen million added annually. The threat of famine and actual death through starvation was always present. In 1950, the government launched the first in a series of five-year plans for economic development, permitting the expansion of private industry but stressing government projects: irrigation and flood control, transport and communications, and especially agricultural education. Low yields could be improved by more fertilizers, by small local irrigation projects to supplement the showy large ones, and by modern tools, equipment, and varieties of grain. Expert opinion held that India put too much stress on industrial growth and too little on the agricultural sector. The United States helped by furnishing technicians, money, and the surplus grain needed to avert the repeated threat of famine. In the late 1960s, a new strain of high-yielding Mexican wheat was planted experimentally; the initial results were promising. But the very success of the new foods (the "green revolution") threatened a new form of crisis, as farmers displaced from the countryside by new agricultural techniques flooded into the cities of India, where there was no employment for them. Starvation and political unrest always threatened in India. Meantime, the government sponsored a campaign for birth control, which was, however, repugnant to many Hindus.

Indeed, Hindu society found it difficult to adopt Western ways. The tradition of Hinduism, an immensely complex and ancient way of life, taught that each living man, indeed each living thing, was a soul alienated by the very fact of living from the ultimate, universal soul which is peace, absence of struggle and desire, ineffable nonbeing. By turning away entirely from the world, by living without desire, the holiest of men could perhaps attain this nonbeing in the end. But most human beings—and all animals—were now living out in this world the consequences of a sinful life as another personality in the past. That is why the most orthodox of Hindus would harm no living thing. This specifically included the millions of "sacred" cattle that competed with starving people for food. Proposals for limiting the number of cattle led to widespread riots as late as 1966.

Hindus believed that man's sins in past incarnations were reflected by his status, his *caste*. The poor and humble were poor and humble because their sins had been greater; they could not improve their lot, for they could only slowly in subsequent incarnations redeem their wickedness by living as holy a life as possible. Below and outside the caste system were the "untouchables," so called because even their shadow would corrupt a caste Hindu. The Indian Constitution of 1950 abolished the outcast status of the untouchables (Harijans) as undemocratic. The legal change, however, penetrated Indian custom only very slowly.

In 1964, when Nehru died, and again early in 1966, when his successor, Shastri, fell victim to a heart attack, India chose a new prime minister by due constitutional process. The choice in 1966 was Nehru's daughter, Mrs. Indira Gandhi. The Congress party, long the spearhead of Hindu nationalism, continued to dominate the Parliament, though torn increasingly by factionalism. Several times Mrs. Gandhi had to offer to resign in order to maneuver in such a way as not to have to do so.

Political controversy arose over the question of language. There were about a dozen major regions in India each with its own distinctive tongue. Believing that a common language was essential to a common sense of national identity, the government supported a new national language, Hindi, to which it gave official status in 1965. It also recognized English as an associate language, though ardent nationalists deplored this as an "ignoble concession" to colonialism. In fact, English was indispensable, both because of its modern scientific and technical vocabulary, which Hindi could not provide, and because it was the only common language of educated Indians, who could not understand one another's native tongues. The elevation of Hindi to official status aroused especially strong opposition among the speakers of Tamil in the south, who viewed it as an instrument of the central government's hostility to regional or provincial pride in language and political home rule. The government met the problem by making some concessions but without abandoning its aim.

Relations with Pakistan continued strained. Sporadic outbreaks of religious warfare took place, especially near the line dividing Bengal between India and East Pakistan. The Kashmir question continued open, since neither side would concede anything. In 1965, war broke out briefly over the issue, until the Soviet Union invited leaders of both countries to confer at Tashkent, where they agreed on a mutual withdrawal of troops from their common frontier but not to a permanent settlement. The Pakistanis tended to measure every country by its attitude toward India. They remained suspicious of the United States because of American aid to India, despite U.S. eagerness to provide it for Pakistan as well; they were suspicious of the USSR, because the Russians also helped the Indians; and so they developed a curiously unnatural friendship with China because China at least was anti-Indian.

The Middle East

The region, formerly and properly called the Near East but since World War II always called by the meaningless term "Middle East," possessed in Arabia, in the small states along the Persian Gulf, and in Iraq and Iran the greatest oil reserves in the world. Developed by European and American companies, which paid royalties to the local governments, these oil resources directly and indirectly influenced the policies of all the powers. Dissatisfaction over the amounts of royalties led to upheavals in Iran in 1951–1953. Western European dependence on Middle Eastern oil led to general alarm over the closing of the Suez Canal by Egypt in 1956 and 1967. General de Gaulle's abandonment in 1967 of Israel, an ally of the French in 1956, and his adoption of a pro-Arab policy had much to do with oil. But except for Iran no crisis depended upon oil alone; and unquestionably the greatest single issue in the area in the postwar years was that between the Arabs and Israel.

Since the 1890s, Zionism had maintained its goal of creating a new Jewish state on the site of the ancient Jewish homeland. It received a great lift from the Balfour Declaration of 1917, after which the British admitted Jewish immigrants into Palestine. Nazi anti-Jewish policies before and during World War II left the remnant of European Jews more determined than ever to go to Palestine. But after the war Britain wished to protect its interests in the Middle East by cultivating the friendship of the Arabs, who had long been settled in Palestine and regarded it as their homeland.

Finding compromise impossible, the British turned the problem over to the General Assembly of the United Nations, which proposed to partition Palestine into an Arab state and a Jewish state. When the British withdrew their forces in 1948, the Jews proclaimed their state of Israel and secured its recognition by the UN. The Arab nations declared the proclamation illegal and invaded the new state from all directions. Outnumbered but faced by an inefficient enemy, the Israelis won the war. A truce, but not a formal peace, was patched up under the auspices of the United Nations (1949).

Israel now secured more of Palestine than the UN had proposed, and took over the western part of Jerusalem, the spiritual capital of Judaism—but also of compelling religious importance to Christians and Muslims—a city the UN had proposed to neutralize. The eastern part or "old city" of Jerusalem, however, including the site of Solomon's temple, the Wailing Wall, together with eastern Palestine, remained in the hands of the Arab state of Jordan. During the 1949 war almost a million Palestinian Arabs fled from Israel to the surrounding Arab states. The United Nations organized a special agency that built camps and gave relief to the refugees, and tried to arrange for their permanent resettlement. The Arab states, however, did not wish to absorb them, and many refugees regarded resettlement as an abandonment of their belief that the Israelis would soon "be pushed into the sea," and that they themselves would return to their old homes. This acute problem made the truce of 1949 a most uneasy affair, frequently broken in frontier incidents by both sides.

The new state of Israel could not trust its Arab minority, numbering about 200,000. It continued to admit as many Jewish immigrants as possible, some of them from Europe, but others from North Africa and Yemen, still largely living in the Middle Ages. The welding of these disparate human elements into a single nationality was a formidable task. Much of Israel was mountainous, and some of it was desert. The Israelis applied talents and training derived from the West to make the best use of their limited resources, but they depended on outside aid, especially from their many sympathizers in the United States. To most Arabs Israel appeared to be a new outpost of Western imperialism, set up in their midst under the influence of Jewish financiers, Jewish journalists, and Jewish voters. Therefore it was difficult for the United States and other Western nations to retain cordial relations with the Arabs, who were in any case passing through a highly nationalistic phase.

In 1952, less than four years after the Arab defeat in Palestine, revolution broke out in Egypt, where a corrupt royal regime was overthrown by a group of army officers chiefly sparked by Gamal Abdel Nasser. They abolished the monarchy, established a republic, encouraged the emancipation of women, and pared down the role of the conservative courts of religious law. Only one party was tolerated, elections were closely supervised, and press campaigns were orchestrated by the Ministry of National Guidance. As an enemy of the West, which he associated not only with past colonialism but with support for Israel, Nasser turned for aid to the USSR. Czechoslovak and Russian arms flowed to Egypt, and Russian technicians followed. Nasser was determined to take the lead in uniting the disunited Arab world to destroy Israel.

Nasser's chief showpiece of revolutionary planning was to be a new high dam on the Nile at Aswan. He had expected the United States to contribute largely to its construction, but in mid-1956 John Foster Dulles, Eisenhower's secretary of state, told Nasser that the United States had changed its mind. In retaliation Nasser nationalized the Suez Canal, hitherto operated by a Franco-British company, and announced that he would use the revenues thus obtained to build the dam. For several months, contrary to expectation, the new Egyptian management kept canal traffic moving smoothly. The French and British governments, however, concealing their intentions from the United States, determined to teach Nasser a lesson, and secretly allied themselves with Israel.

The Wars of 1956 and 1967: Continuing Crisis

In the fall of 1956, the Israeli forces invaded Egyptian territory, and French and British troops were also landed at Suez. The Israeli operations were skillful and successful; the British and French blundered badly. The Soviet Union threatened to send "volunteers" to defend Egypt, despite the fact that Soviet troops were at the very moment of the Suez crisis engaged in putting down the Hungarian revolution. Nor did the United States, angry at its British and French friends for concealing their plans, give them support. With the United States and the Soviet Union on the same side of the issue, the United Nations condemned the British-French-Israeli attack, and eventually a United Nations force was moved into the Egyptian-Israeli frontier areas, while the canal, blocked by the Egyptians, was re-opened, and finally bought from the company by Nasser. Nasser experienced some disillusion with Russia during the summer of 1958, when revolution broke out in Iraq, where Soviet-sponsored communists were opposing Nasser's own pan-Arab aims. Prompt American intervention in Lebanon and British intervention in Jordan may have temporarily countered the threat of the spread of Soviet influence. The Russians provided the aid that eventually made possible the high dam at Aswan and much armament for the Egyptian armies, but Nasser remained unaligned with either major bloc.

In 1958, Nasser proclaimed the merger of Egypt and Syria into the United Arab Republic. The two components of the U.A.R. were separated by the territories of Israel, Lebanon, and Jordan; Nasser was trying

Third-world leaders Nasser, Nehru, and Tito in 1956.

to prevent a coup by Syrian communists or fellow travelers. When the almost ungovernable Syrians revolted in 1961, Nasser announced that he could never fire on "brother Arabs," and permitted them to regain their independence as the Syrian Arab Republic. Yet Egypt continued to style itself the U.A.R. The Arab League, a loose association of the Arabic-speaking states of the Middle East and North Africa, proved to be little more than a forum for expressing the conflicts of views and personalities that kept the Arab world disunited.

After the Suez crisis, Nasser tried one experiment after another to create a party and other institutions that would gain support for his regime at the grass roots. His economic policy was governed by the grim struggle to support a fast-growing population (the birth rate in Egypt was double that in the United States). He undertook programs to reclaim land from the desert by exploiting underground water, and to limit the size of an individual's landholdings so that the surplus might be redistributed to landless peasants. To provide more jobs and to bolster national pride he also accelerated the pace of industrialization, often at very high cost. Most foreign enterprises were nationalized.

But the temptations of foreign adventure proved irresistible to Nasser. In far-off Yemen, a primitive kingdom in southern Arabia where republican rebels overthrew the monarchy in 1962, Nasser sent Egyptian forces to assist the revolution. The largest state of Arabia proper, the Saudi Kingdom, most of whose huge revenues came from American oil companies, disliked the Egyptian intervention as threatening the cause of monarchy and endangering Saudi stability. But not even in tiny Yemen could Nasser's modern forces score a victory, though they freely used poison gas against their brother Arabs. By 1967 the Egyptian forces had suffered a defeat, though the Yemeni republican regime continued to control part of Yemen, while monarchists continued active in the remainder.

Needing a victory, Nasser in 1967 demanded that the United Nations troops which had kept Egyptians and Israelis separated since 1956 be removed. Secretary General U Thant complied. The Egyptians began a propaganda barrage against Israel, and closed the Strait of Tiran at the northeast corner of the Red Sea that provided the only water access to the newly developed Israeli port of Elath. The Israelis struck the first blow, knocking out the Egyptian air force on the ground, and hitting also at the air forces of the other Arab states. In six days, they overran the Sinai peninsula, all of Palestine west of the Jordan, including the Jordanian portion of Jerusalem, and the Golan heights on their northern frontier with Syria, from which the Syrians had been launching dangerous and painful raids for several years. The third Arab-Israeli war in nineteen years ended in an all-out Israeli victory.

It was a humiliation not only for Nasser but for the USSR, which had supplied so much of the equipment he had now lost. The Russians moved vigorously to support the Arab position, arguing their case in the United Nations, moving token naval forces into the Mediterranean, denouncing Israel, and ostentatiously beginning at once the rearmament of Egypt. Israeli armies remained in control of all the territory they had occupied. Had it been possible to begin negotiations soon after the war, much of this territory could perhaps have been recovered. As time passed, the Israeli attitude hardened, and it became difficult to imagine that any Israeli government could ever consent to give up any part of Jerusalem, now reunited in an emotional wave of Jewish religious sentiment, or the Golan heights, whose possession ensured Israeli territory against Syrian attack. Sinai, the Gaza strip, perhaps the west bank of the Jordan, might be negotiable.

But the Arabs, led by Nasser, refused to negotiate directly with the Israelis or to take any step that would admit the existence of the state of Israel. Rearmed and partly retrained by the Russians, the Egyptians repeatedly proclaimed their intention of trying again, while occasionally leaking a suggestion that a new United Nations force might be acceptable. Since the last one had been withdrawn by Nasser's unilateral request, this had little appeal for Israel. Blocked again, the Suez Canal was now becoming less crucial because of the development of oil tankers that would have been too large to pass through the canal in any case, and that went around the Cape of Good Hope, transporting oil more cheaply because of their great capacity. Perhaps the most important result of the war of 1967, however, was not the Israeli victory but the fact that the USSR—whose ally had lost—had gained naval bases at Alexandria and even in Algeria. The Russians had a firmer position in the Mediterranean area than ever before.

In 1969 and 1970, tension mounted dangerously in the Middle East. As before the 1967 war, Arab Palestinians organized guerrilla attacks on Israeli or Israeli-occupied territory, from Jordan, Syria, and Lebanon. The Lebanon government, balanced between Christians and Muslims, and hitherto the most moderating influence among the Arab regimes in the area, was threatened by the Palestinian guerrillas, and forced to concede to them for their operations the Lebanese territory nearest the Israeli frontier. In various European airports—Zurich, Athens—Arab terrorists attacked planes carrying or thought to be carrying Israelis, and Israel tried to avenge such murderous acts and prevent their recurrence by such measures as a parchutists' raid on the Beirut airport. At times the Palestinian Arab terrorist movement took on the aspects of an independent power, negotiating with the Chinese, compelling Nasser to modify his pronouncements. In the autumn of 1970, the guerrillas hijacked four large planes in a single day, holding the passengers as hostages in Jordan for the release of certain captives of their own. In the midst of the tense negotiations that followed, full-scale hostilities broke out between the Arab guerrillas and the Jordanian government. The Syrians intervened on the side of the guerrillas, and the threat of American intervention on the side of Jordan, and of a Soviet response, was suddenly very real. Jordanian successes, Syrian withdrawal, and American and Soviet restraint helped the critical moment pass. The Arab guerrillas could no longer use Jordanian territory.

Just as grave was the continual Arab-Israeli confrontation in Egypt. Here Egyptian raids across the Suez Canal into Israeli-occupied territory in Sinai were more than overborne by Israeli commando raids into Egyptian territory on the west side of the canal, and by deep Israeli air raids into Egypt. During 1970 the installation of Soviet missile sites near the canal forced the suspension of the Israeli attacks. But Soviet operational involvement in Egyptian defense also threatened open confrontation between the Soviet Union and the United States.

To avoid this danger, and to create a situation in which the Russian military could be withdrawn from Egypt without forcing the Russians to lose face, the United States, Britain, and France held regular four-power discussions with the USSR on the Arab-Israeli conflict. With the Russians totally committed to the Arab side, and the French, even after de Gaulle's departure from office, making no change in a pro-Arab policy, with Britain balancing between the two sides, and the United States trying hard to help Israel but determined to avoid even the possibility of another Vietnam—or worse, since the Middle East was far more sensitive than Southeast Asia—the Israelis regarded with skepticism the possibility of any favorable solution emerging from the big powers' discussions, and firmly insisted that only direct talks between them and the Arabs could lead to a satisfactory settlement. Arab insistence that a return of all occupied territory must precede discussions rendered discussions impossible. In the summer of 1970, however, Egyptians and Israelis agreed to a cease-fire. But as hope renewed that discussions might at least begin, President Nasser died suddenly, to be replaced by Anwar el-Sadat, who pledged himself to regain all occupied territories.

Iraq, Iran, Turkey

Among the other Arab states, Iraq, closely aligned with the British after the war, and using its share of profits from the Western-controlled Iraq Petroleum Company to build public works, in 1958 experienced a nationalist uprising which ousted the monarchy and proclaimed a republic. Pro- and anti-Nasser factions, pro- and anticommunists, thereafter subjected the country to a series of coups and abortive coups, and the rebellious Kurdish tribes in the northern mountains contributed to the disorder and to the abrupt slackening of economic development after 1958. In 1969 and 1970, Iraq developed the most paranoid regime of all the Arab states, publicly executing from time to time amid general celebration various of its resident Jews or members of earlier Iraqi governments on charges of working for

Israel or the American CIA or both, and always surprised at the hostile response such authorized terrorism brought even from their own Arab allies. Nasser himself rebuked the Iraqis for their excesses of zeal. The Kurdish question, however, became temporarily quiescent after a grant in 1970 of at least partial autonomy to the Kurds.

In Iran, where the Anglo-Iranian Oil Company had the oil concession, the government after the war demanded that the company follow the example set in Saudi Arabia by the Arabian American Oil Company, which paid 50 percent of its profits to King Saud. Supported by a wave of antiforeign nationalism, the demagogue Mossadeq in 1951 secured the nationalization of the oil company. But the Iranian economy was badly hurt by an international boycott of the oil, and Mossadeq himself was overthrown in 1953 by a coup d'état allegedly masterminded by the American CIA. The government reached an agreement to pay foreign oil companies to assist in exploiting and marketing the oil. A measure of land reform sponsored vigorously by the Shah himself led to improved economic conditions. Iran maintained satisfactory relations with both the United States and the USSR, but the question of future influences in the Persian Gulf embittered relations with Iraq.

In Turkey, Atatürk's Republican People's party, the only one allowed in Atatürk's own day, after the war permitted the activities of an opposition, and in the election of 1950 went down to defeat at the hands of the young Democratic party. Western opinion saluted this peaceful shift of power as the coming of age of Turkish parliamentary democracy. The Democratic government of Prime Minister Menderes proceeded to promote both state and private industry, to build roads and schools, and in other ways to bring the spirit of modernization to the villages, which had been neglected in Atatürk's day but contained three-quarters of the population. To propitiate Muslim opinion, some of Atatürk's secularist policies were moderated, religious instruction was restored in the schools, and the call to prayer sounded once more in Arabic from the minarets (sometimes on amplified tape recordings made in Mecca).

But Menderes' regime became increasingly arbitrary, muzzling the press, persecuting the Republican opposition both in and out of the Grand National Assembly, and restricting more and more the free conduct of elections. In May 1960 student riots touched off a coup by the Turkish army, which overthrew the government, outlawed the Democratic party, and brought Menderes to trial and eventual execution. A new constitution, in 1961, sought to avert a repetition of the experience with Menderes by strengthening the legislature and judiciary against the executive. It was the army, however, that exercised the real power. Moreover, the new Justice party, to which followers of Menderes gravitated, won a majority of the seats in the parliamentary election of 1965. Thus tensions persisted between the urban champions of secularization and westernization, represented by army leaders and by Atatürk's old Republican People's party, and the defenders of the conservative Muslim way of life in Turkish towns and villages, who tended to support the Justice party.

Low wages and the lack of employment opportunities at home impelled tens of thousands of Turks to take jobs abroad, especially in West Germany and the Netherlands, and the marginal quality of much Anatolian farmland, with its thin soil and scanty rainfall, promoted an even greater exodus from the villages to the towns and cities. Turkey appeared to be suffering a sharp attack of social and economic growing pains. Its hopes for achieving a quick "takeoff" were thwarted by the country's meager resources, by its chronic difficulty in paying for needed imports, especially oil, and by the government's slowness in fashioning an effective organization for economic planning. Friendship for the United States, very warm down to the 1960s and cemented especially by the brave Turkish fighting in the Korean War, dwindled because of the disenchantment of sensitive Turkish nationalists with NATO and with the American refusal to support Turkey wholly against Greece in the Cyprus question. Anti-American feeling ran high, and radical student groups and others even began to look to the USSR—traditionally the bugbear of all Turks.

Africa

The revolution against imperialism reached Africa in the 1950s, although there had long been ominous rumblings, such as an uprising in 1947 on the large French island of Madagascar off the east coast, put down by the French in a bloody massacre. The independent Empire of Ethiopia was taken from its Italian conquerors after the war, and restored to the durable emperor Haile Selassie, who had been ousted in 1935. In 1952, he annexed the former Italian colony of Eritrea. He had embarked on various programs of internal modernization—though not liberalization—and he worked hard to assist in the development of African unity.

Among the northern tier of states bordering the Mediterranean, all Muslim and Arabic-speaking, the former Italian colony of Libya achieved independence in 1951, and the French-dominated areas of Morocco and Tunisia in 1956, Morocco as an autocratic monarchy, Tunisia as a republic under the moderate and intelligent presidency of Habib Bourguiba, a veteran nationalist leader, educated at the Sorbonne. The huge area of Algeria, between Morocco and Tunisia, followed, but only after a severe and debilitating war of independence against the French. Its first ruler after independence, Ahmed Ben Bella, was intimate with the Chinese communists. Colonel Houari Boumédienne, who ousted Ben Bella in 1965—perhaps in large part because of the slumping economy—seemed to favor the

USSR. Algeria and Libya strongly supported the Arab cause against Israel, distant Morocco more feebly, and Tunisia under Bourguiba hardly at all. Bourguiba's voice could occasionally be heard calling for a reasonable accommodation between Arabs and Israelis.

In Libya, a colonels' coup d'état in 1969 brought to power a group of army officers who apparently modeled their movement on Nasser's. In 1970, they confiscated Italian- and Jewish-owned property. American evacuation of a huge airbase in Libya and the purchase of French and Soviet arms by the Libyans added to the general apprehension in North Africa. And though a loose "union" of Egypt, Libya, and the Sudan formed in 1970 had little political importance, it marked the emergence of Colonel Qaddafi, the Libyan political boss and prime minister, as the purest Muslim fundamentalist and the most intransigent ruler in the Arab world. He was also one of the richest.

South of the Muslim tier lay the colonies of the French, British, and Belgians, inhabited chiefly by blacks. West African climatic conditions had always discouraged large-scale white settlement except in portions of the Belgian Congo; but in East Africa—in the British colonies of Kenya and Uganda especially—whites had settled in the fertile highlands in large numbers, farmed the land, and regarded the country as their own, as of course did the large white population of the Union of South Africa—which seceded from the British Commonwealth in 1961 and became the Republic of South Africa—and the whites of some of the lands in between, such as Rhodesia.

In the areas of small white settlement, the revolution moved swiftly. The Gold Coast—a West African British colony with a relatively well-educated population and valuable economic resources—became the nation of Ghana in 1957. Its leader, the American-educated Kwame Nkrumah, the pioneer of African emancipation, made what seemed a hopeful start on economic planning within a political democracy. But he grew increasingly dictatorial, jailing and mistreating his political enemies and insisting on being worshiped as a virtual god by his subjects. He also sponsored unrealistic and grandiose projects that enriched him and his followers personally. And he became fanatically anti-Western and determined to court Chinese communist favor in an effort to unite Africa into a kind of personal empire. He was ousted in 1966, and his successors embarked on a sober program of putting Ghana back on the track once more.

The French colonies—covering huge areas of territory often sparsely populated—all achieved independence simultaneously in 1960, except for Guinea, a small West African state that broke away in 1958 under the leadership of a pro-Russian politician, Sékou Touré. With independence, some of the colonies retained close economic ties with France, as members of the French Community. Guinea did not; all Frenchmen had left in 1958, and the country had virtually come to a stop. The neighboring states of Mali (formerly

French Sudan) and Mauritania also pursued a general pro-Russian line. In the late 1960s Touré apparently began to regret his economic dependence on the USSR, for he accepted U.S. and World Bank loans to finance a major mining complex.

Some of the newly independent French colonies—Upper Volta, Niger, Chad, Gabon—were hardly more than geographical expressions without national traditions or even tribal cohesion. Others proved stable and successful, such as Senegal—governed by Léopold Senghor, a celebrated poet who wrote in French of the beauties of négritude (being black); Ivory Coast—whose leader Houphouet-Boigny had long parliamentary experience as a deputy in Paris; and the Malagasy Republic (formerly Madagascar)—which had a flourishing economy based in large part on vanilla. In at least one case (Gabon), the French intervened with troops to save the government from a military coup d'état. In others—Togo, Dahomey, Cameroon—the coups took place unimpeded and sometimes repeatedly. In 1970, for instance, large numbers of French troops were fighting a little publicized war in Chad, while the regime in the former French Congo (Brazzaville) was thoroughly procommunist.

In 1960, Nigeria, most important of the British colonies, achieved independence. With sixty million people and large and varied economic resources, it represented a great hope for the future. The British had carefully educated and trained many thousands of Nigerians both in England and in excellent schools and universities established in the country itself. Nigeria was divided into four regions, each semiautonomous, to ease mutual tribal tensions, of which perhaps the most severe was that between the Muslim Hausa tribe of the northern region and the Ibo tribe of the eastern region. In the Hausa areas, the well-educated, aggressive, and competent Ibos ran the railroads, power stations, and other modern facilities, and formed an important element in the cities. When army plotters led by an Ibo officer murdered the Muslim prime minister of Nigeria and seized power in 1966, the Hausas rose and massacred the Ibos living in the north, killing many thousands, while others escaped in disorder to their native east. By 1967, the Ibo east had seceded and called itself the Republic of Biafra, and the Nigerian central government embarked on full-scale war to force the Ibos and other eastern tribesmen to return to Nigerian rule. The general who headed the central government and the officer who headed Biafra were both graduates of British institutions. Misery and famine accompanied the operations, and the war dragged on until 1969. Both Britain and the Soviet Union helped the Nigerian government. The Biafrans got much sympathy but no real help except from the French, who as usual were interested in future oil concessions. When the war finally ended, the mass slaughter that had been feared did not materialize, and the nation devoted its energies to the task of reconciliation and recovery.

In East Africa, the British settlers in Kenya struggled for eight years (1952–1960) against a secret terrorist society formed within the Kikuyu tribe, the Mau Mau, whose aim was to drive all white men out of the country. The Mau Mau horribly murdered white settlers and their families and also Kikuyus and other tribesmen who would not join them. Though the British imprisoned one of its founders, the educated Kikuyu Jomo Kenyatta, and eventually put down the movement, they did give Kenya independence in 1963, against the bitter protests of many white settlers. Kenyatta became the first postliberation chief of state. By 1962, neighboring Uganda attained independence, and in 1964, under the leadership of Julius Nyerere (educated at Edinburgh), so did Tanganyika—which had been German before World War I and British since. A violent pro-Chinese communist coup d'état had taken place on the offshore spice island of Zanzibar, which merged with Tanganyika as the new country of Tanzania. Nyerere, who had been pro-Western, thereafter became more notably neutralist. In 1964, Nyasaland became Malawi under Dr. Hastings Banda, who had formerly been a dentist in London, and Northern Rhodesia became Zambia under Kenneth Kaunda, a western-educated moderate.

In contrast to the British, who had at least tried to prepare the way for African independence by providing education and administrative experience for Africans and who could not be held responsible for the troubles in Ghana and Nigeria, the Belgians, who had since the late nineteenth century governed the huge Central African area known as the Congo, made no such effort. When the Belgian rulers suddenly pulled out in 1960, leaving a wholly artificial Western-style parliamentary structure, it was not long before tribal and regional rivalries between native leaders asserted themselves and virtual chaos prevailed. A leftist leader, Patrice Lumumba, was assassinated (the Russians soon named their university for Africans in Moscow after him); the province of Katanga, site of rich copper mines with many European residents, seceded under its local leader, Moise Tshombe, who was strongly pro-Belgian. Other areas revolted. Africans in rebellion murdered whites, or took them prisoner and kept them as hostages; white mercenaries enlisted in the forces of Tshombe and others. The United Nations sent troops to restore order and force the end of the Katangese secession, while the Chinese supported certain rebel factions, and the South Africans and Belgians others. By 1968, the military regime of General Joseph Mobuto seemed relatively firmly in control. Soon after, Mobutu had renamed the cities and people of his country (including himself) to get rid of all traces of the colonial past, and the Congo itself had become Zaire.

The Congolese troubles overflowed the borders of the Congo into Portuguese Angola to the south, where a local rebellion, at first supplied from the Congo, forced Portuguese military intervention. Angola, which provided Portugal with much of its oil, together with Mozambique on the east coast and the tiny enclave of

Portuguese Guinea on the west, remained under Lisbon's control despite guerrilla uprisings. Portuguese political theory regarded these countries as overseas extensions of metropolitan Portugal. Every African who had a certain minimum education obtained the status of an "assimilated" Portuguese. Nor did the Portuguese draw the color line as other colonial powers had generally done. But the guerrilla warfare they had to fight was proving expensive and unpopular at home.

Most intransigent of all were the white-dominated Republic of South Africa and its northern neighbor, the state of Rhodesia (formerly Southern Rhodesia), which broke its political ties with Britain in 1965 rather than agree to any African participation in political life. In South Africa, the whites included not only descendants of the Dutch settlers, the Afrikaners, but also a minority of English descent. But altogether the whites were themselves a minority, of about one in five of the population. The nonwhites included blacks, "coloreds," as those of mixed European and African blood were called, and Asians, mostly Indians, who were usually shopkeepers.

The Afrikaners, who had tried unsuccessfully to keep South Africa from fighting on Britain's side in World War II, and some of whom sympathized with Hitler, emerged after the war as a political majority. Imbued with an extremely narrow and reactionary form of Calvinist religion that taught that God had ordained the inferiority of the blacks, the ruling group moved steadily to impose on the black majority their policies of rigid segregation: apartheid. Separate townships to live in, separate facilities of all sorts, no political rights, no opportunity for higher education or advancement beyond manual labor, internment of black leaders including the Zulu chief Albert Luthulli, winner of the Nobel Peace Prize: these were the conditions that a succession of Afrikaner governments defended and extended. Supported by some of those of English descent, who were fearful that the black upheaval to the north would spread to South Africa, the Afrikaners also introduced emergency laws making it possible to arrest people on suspicion, to keep them incommunicado, and to punish them without trial. Severe censorship prevailed, and dissent was silenced. It was no doubt true that communist agents had been at work among the Africans, but the combination of policies known as apartheid was calculated only to make their message more credible.

The regime sought to disarm criticism by founding in Botswana and Lesotho (1966) two black states on South African territory. Lesotho was the former Basutoland, and Botswana the former Bechuanaland, both previously African reservations. Inhabited solely by blacks, but dominated by whites, these two states were not likely to produce much black enthusiasm. In 1949, defying the UN, South Africa annexed the former German colony and League mandate of South-West Africa. Here too the policies of apartheid held sway and met with bitter black hatred.

White South African writers who opposed apartheid, like Alan Paton or Nadine Gordimer, were heard and appreciated outside South Africa, and vilified and repressed at home. The Rhodesians who defied the British in 1965 rather than allow Africans to participate in politics were many of them originally emigrants from South Africa. Boycotted by the British Labour government and later by the UN, they managed to get supplies from South Africa and from Mozambique. But the 1970 victory of the Conservatives in England brought a considerable relaxation of British policy toward the country. To American observers, the whites at the southern end of the African continent seemed determined to defy what seemed to be the lessons of history elsewhere.

Latin America

Although most of the Latin American republics had by 1945 enjoyed political independence for more than a century, they had much in common economically and socially with the emerging nations of Asia and Africa. Like the Asians and Africans, the Latin Americans had traditionally been suppliers of foods and raw materials to the rest of the world. Bananas, coffee, sugar, beef, oil, nitrates, and copper fluctuated widely in price on the world market, and before the Latin Americans could raise their standards of living they would have to build on a more stable economic base. Like the other emerging nations too, most of Latin America had a racially mixed population: some native-born whites or immigrants from Europe (like the Italians in Argentina), some descended from the indigenous Indians, and some blacks (chiefly in Brazil and Haiti). Nominally governed under a democratic system of elected officials and parliaments, they had all too often lived under military dictatorships that shifted whenever a new army officer felt strong enough to challenge the one in power. Persons of mixed racial origin were of course very numerous.

Toward the United States, Latin Americans traditionally felt a mixture of envy, dislike, and suspicion. The United States was rich and powerful, "the Colossus of the North." Upper-class Latin Americans educated in Europe believed that North Americans lacked true culture. North Americans generally seemed to know little and care less about Latin America. Whenever the United States ceased to be indifferent and devoted some attention to Latin America, it did so by what seemed like intervention in Latin affairs. Upper-class Latin Americans, aware of the miserable poverty in which the majority of their people lived, often had a bad conscience. Usually they did not care whether the conditions of the poor improved or not: theirs was not the Anglo-American tradition of *richesse oblige*. By and large they cared only for their own comforts and hoped that nothing—least of all a social revolution—would disturb the system. So it made them uneasy to find North Americans worrying more about the Bolivian or Peruvian peasant than the Bolivians or Peruvians themselves had ever done. Craving attention and admiration yet at the same time longing to be left alone, the Latin Americans made it very difficult for the United States to develop consistent, satisfactory policies toward them. And by and large the Latin complaints about us were true: we were indifferent except when crises arose, and then we tended to intervene. We were tactless, we were crude, we did not understand, our motives were often questionable.

President Franklin Roosevelt's "Good Neighbor" policy after 1932 was an attempt to overcome these difficulties. The Pan-American Conference that dated back to 1890 had become a Pan-American Union in 1910; both of these were primarily cultural in emphasis. But after World War II the Pan-American Union became the Organization of American States (OAS). Somewhat looser than an alliance, the OAS provided a means for consultation among all the American nations, North, South, and Central, on all important matters of mutual concern. The United States was—quite naturally—accused by its enemies of having forged just another instrument of its imperialistic policies, yet OAS did in fact enable all the American states to reach genuine joint decisions. The Alliance for Progress, launched under President Kennedy's impulse and designed to enable the United States to help the Latin Americans to help themselves, proved a disappointment, in part because it was so difficult to allay Latin American suspicions of our intentions, in part because of the deeply entrenched oligarchies that dominated most Latin American countries.

Broad generalizations are of course subject to challenge: not every Latin American country was oligarchical or backward. Uruguay, for example, a small country with a population largely European in origin, had gone further toward creating an advanced welfare state than any other in the world, even the Scandinavian countries or Britain—so far, indeed, that the Uruguayan economy by 1970 was collapsing, largely because of the payment of state funds to individual citizens for the many types of benefits available. Venezuela, with rapidly developing oil resources, in 1959 ousted the last of its long line of military-oligarchic dictators and made the transition to moderate democratic rule, though still threatened by communists sponsored from outside.

Columbia underwent a lengthy terrorist campaign in the countryside—virtually a civil war—in which many thousands were killed, and even when this drew to an end was still experiencing extremes of wealth and poverty. Brazil, the enormous Portuguese-speaking land larger than any other Latin American country, suffered from recurrent economic crises and military coups. Its poverty-stricken northeast, where many thousands lived in virtual peonage on big plantations, contrasted sharply with the luxurious apartment-house and beach life of the big cities; but each of these, too, had its festering slums. Brazilian government was a tight military dictatorship, and stood accused of torturing its political prisoners.

Chile, too, though plagued by a continual economic crisis and by occasional military intervention, maintained democratic government. Indeed, in 1970 Chileans freely elected a Marxist, Salvador Allende, as president. Though Allende was a minority president, having won less than 40 percent of the votes, he took office in relative calm and moved gradually in expropriating foreign properties. In any case, Chile was the only country to move left by democratic processes.

Alone in Latin America, Mexico had passed through and recovered from a true social revolution. The overthrow of the emperor Maximilian in 1867 was followed only nine years later by the advent of the dictator Porfirio Diaz, who ruled in the interests of foreign investors and large landholders until 1910, when a peasant revolution broke out that lasted with interruptions for thirty years, marked by violence and insurrection, by revolutionary reformers who turned into wealthy dictators, and by radical social and economic experimentation. The Catholic church, long regarded by many Mexicans as opposed to economic and political reform and indifferent to the welfare of the masses, was the target of extreme anticlerical measures. The foreign oil companies, American and British, suffered expropriation. The revolutionary governments initially gave labor unions extensive privileges and power, expropriated great estates to emancipate the poor peasant, and began a vigorous program of educating the large and neglected population of native Indians. A remarkable cultural awakening took place, based on native traditions and crafts. Mexican revolutionary painters like Rivera and Orozco won international fame. The Mexican revolution, however, ran out of radical steam in the 1940s. The new leaders were more reconciled to the need for foreign capital, for patience in the long task of raising the standards of the masses. The Mexican regime was dominated by a single political party whose leaders in turn were elected president every seventh year, and each in turn stepped down peacefully to make way for his successors. It exerted rigorous control over the unions, and exhibited only an occasional flash of its old revolutionary zeal. Though suspecting U.S. attempts to influence it, each new Mexican government cemented further a relationship that was not only peaceful but friendly.

By contrast, Argentina, peopled almost entirely by European immigrants and their descendants, and dependent on the export of beef and grain to Europe, continued to have a social system that gave power to a small landlord class. The beginnings of industrialization, and especially the growth by 1945 of the capital, Buenos Aires, into a great metropolis of nearly five million, increased the numbers of working-class and middle-class people and deepened popular dissatisfaction with the regime.

Brought to power in the national election of 1946, Colonel Juan Perón became a dictator on the model of Mussolini, Hitler, and Franco. In 1955, he went down before a characteristic Latin American military

Prime Minister Fidel Castro signing a decree nationalizing American-owned banks in Cuba, 1960.

coup d'état. He had begun more and more to appeal to the poorer masses, the *descamisados* ("shirtless ones"), and thus lost much of his following in the conservative upper classes. Moreover, he quarreled with the Roman Catholic church and put through anticlerical measures that cost him further support. Nor could he solve the grave economic and financial problems arising out of his country's essentially colonial position; indeed, his extravagant spending on public works and welfare projects virtually bankrupted Argentina.

During the years that followed, workers and some other groups continued to look to Perón, who lived in exile in Spain. Twice (1962 and 1966) a weak elected government was overthrown by a military coup. The army regime installed in 1966 promised to purge Argentina of corruption but aroused much opposition by its repression of academic freedom. The old problems remained unsolved, indeed almost untackled. And they remained unsolved as well in Peru, which had a relatively advanced urban life at the time of the military coup of 1968, and in Ecuador and Paraguay, which were still largely rural, as well as in Haiti, which in 1970 still suffered under the brutal dictatorship of Duvalier.

It was, of course, Cuba that in the postwar years provided the new revolution. Beginning in the late 1950s, under the leadership of Fidel Castro as a guerrilla movement in the hills of the easternmost province (Oriente), it succeeded in ousting the government of Fulgencio Batista in 1959. American attitudes toward Castro had been ambivalent: on the one hand, the Batista regime was singularly corrupt and unsavory; on the other, nobody really knew how deeply Castro was committed to communism or to Soviet domination. After his success, he made a series of increasingly pro-Soviet pronouncements, and quarreled bitterly with the United States, which boycotted Cuban goods. Since the Cuban economy was dependent upon the export of sugar and tobacco, Castro soon found himself exporting largely to the USSR and its associated powers, and obtaining most of his imports from them. In 1961, the Kennedy administration backed an expedition of anti-Castro exiles, who landed at the Bay of Pigs and were thoroughly defeated.

In 1962, as we have seen, Castro opened Cuba to the installation of Soviet missiles, leading to the great crisis of October. Once the crisis was over and the missiles were withdrawn, Castro seemed to grow more and more impatient with what he felt to be the inadequate amount of Soviet assistance, and tried to take advantage of the Soviet-Chinese quarrel to extract more from the USSR. He also tried strenuously to export his revolution into the rest of Latin America: to Venezuela; to Guatemala, where communist terrorists dominated portions of the country and murdered the American ambassador in 1968; and to Bolivia, where a band of guerrillas operating under the Argentine revolutionary theorist Ernesto ("Che") Guevara, formerly a member of Castro's cabinet, was finally wiped out in 1967, but where a military coup brought a leftist government to power in 1970.

In 1965, the United States concluded, perhaps too hastily, that a revolution in the Dominican Republic, on the neighboring island to Cuba, was inspired by Castro. Between 1930 and 1961, the Dominican Republic had been ruled by General Trujillo, a ruthless, corrupt, and bloodthirsty dictator. After his assassination, the first freely elected government in a generation took office under Juan Bosch, but increasing tension between the army and the new reformers led to military coups and finally to a civil war in 1965. Fearing that communists might soon take over, President Johnson sent in a division of marines, and then tried to internationalize the intervention by appealing to the Organization of American States. By a narrow margin, the OAS responded, and five of its member states, all with conservative military regimes, sent troops to join the Americans. The Dominican Republic was pacified sufficiently for constitutional elections to be held in 1966; a moderate, Joaquin Balaguer, became president and retained his office when the next elections were held in 1970.

It would have been political suicide in 1965 for any president of the United States to allow another Caribbean country to fall into pro-Soviet hands. But the entire episode aroused much opposition among Americans; and in Latin America, where Mexico, for

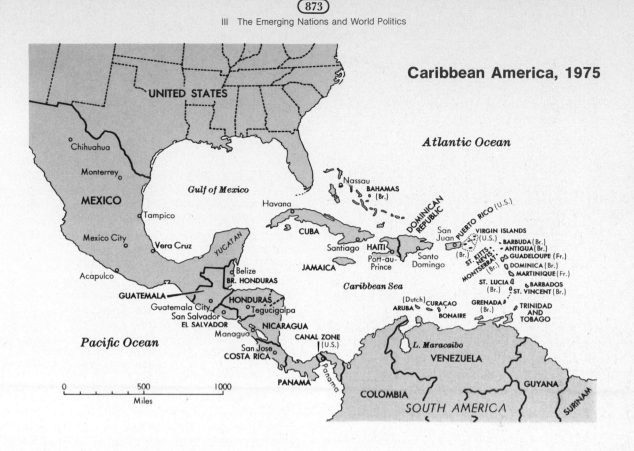

Caribbean America, 1975

example, had opposed intervention, the reappearance of American marines served to heighten the suspicion that the United States was still up to its bad old tricks.

With a population consisting chiefly of East Indians and Negroes, deeply at odds with each other, British Guiana also had a strong communist movement, led by an Indian, Cheddi Jagan. When it appeared that independence from Britain would be followed by Jagan's assuming power, the British postponed independence until an effective anticommunist coalition of Jagan's opponents was safely in office. The new state of Guyana was created in 1966.

It appeared, therefore, that there was little cause for optimism about the immediate future in Latin America. The spread of terrorist methods to Brazil, to Argentina, and even to Uruguay—where foreign diplomats or local politicians were kidnapped and sometimes murdered—added a frightening new development to a region whose problems were already grim enough.

The Cold War: Final Reflections

Not the least important aspect of the cold war was the competition between the United States and the Soviet Union for the support of the emerging nations. In their programs of foreign aid, both countries made mistakes: as when American aid enabled a Ghanian politician to buy himself a solid gold bed, or when Soviet aid supplied quantities of obsolete and inappropriate agricul-

tural machinery that rusted uselessly on a Guinean dock. In the larger sense, it was a mistake for an American or a Russian to promise that his system would promptly usher in the millennium for those who imitated it. New nations would have to wait for most of the consumer goods they yearned for until they had educated enough of their own people to do the work of modernizing that would earn the money to buy them. Then political stability and economic growth might each contribute to the other. The American experiment of the Peace Corps, launched by President Kennedy, temporarily provided a hopeful model: education by example for the hard pull ahead.

As to the cold war itself, many by the mid-sixties had for some time thought the term was obsolete, that the United States and its partners had won without realizing it, that the USSR was undergoing a fundamental change, and that a worldwide relaxation of tensions might have been in prospect, had America not—by its policies in Vietnam—forfeited such a large measure of international goodwill and weakened its ability to negotiate. These views vanished like a puff of smoke after the Soviet intervention in Czechoslovakia in 1968. The USSR would still intervene with force in its own bailiwick; if it showed signs of wanting the Vietnam War to end, this was because such a solution would hurt the Chinese; it would negotiate only when it could further its own immediate interests. In 1970, the cold war was still much with us.

Reading Suggestions on the Postwar World

General Accounts

N. A. Graebner, ed., *The Cold War: Ideological Conflict or Power Struggle?* (*Heath). Divergent interpretations.

D. Donnelly, *Struggle for the World* (St. Martin's, 1965). A history of the Cold War, tracing it back to 1917.

P. Calvocoressi, *International Politics since 1945* (*Praeger). Factual study.

C. E. Black, *Dynamics of Modernization* (*Torchbooks). Illuminating study.

S. Kuznets, *Post-War Economic Growth* (Harvard, 1964). Good analysis.

S. P. Huntington, *Political Order in Changing Societies* (Yale, 1968); L. L. Snyder, *The New Nationalism* (Cornell, 1968). Wide-ranging and provocative surveys.

The Free World

J. Freymond, *Western Europe since the War* (Praeger, 1964). Good brief manual.

T. H. White, *Fire in the Ashes* (*Apollo). Postwar economic recovery and the role of the Marshall Plan.

M. M. Postan, *An Economic History of Western Europe, 1945–1964* (*Barnes & Noble). Comprehensive review.

W. O. Henderson, *The Genesis of the Common Market* (F. Cass, 1963); L. B. Krause, ed., *The Common Market* (*Prentice-Hall). Useful works.

A. Marwick, *Britain in the Century of Total War* (Little, Brown, 1968). Assessment of the impact of war on society.

F. Boyd, *British Politics in Transition, 1945–1963* (Praeger, 1964). Solid account.

C. Cross, *The Fall of the British Empire, 1918–1968* (Hodder & Stoughton, 1968). Analysis of a central aspect of Britain's altered position.

S. Hoffmann et al., *In Search of France* (*Torchbooks). Essays on economics and politics in twentieth-century France.

D. Pickles, *Fifth French Republic*, 3rd ed. (*Praeger). Good political handbook.

P. Williams, *Crisis and Compromise* (*Anchor). Analyzing the failures of the Fourth Republic.

C. Brinton, *The Americans and the French* (Harvard, 1968). Perceptive essay on the French in the postwar world.

H. S. Hughes, *The United States and Italy*, rev. ed. (*Norton). Guide to postwar Italian politics and society.

M. Salvadori, *Italy* (*Prentice-Hall). Handy introduction.

K. P. Tauber, *Beyond Eagle and Swastika*, 2 vols. (Wesleyan, 1967). Study of German nationalism since World War II.

A. Grosser, *The Federal Republic of Germany* (*Praeger). Concise history.

G. M. Craig, *The United States and Canada* (Harvard, 1968). Guide to Canada's problems.

T. H. White, *The Making of the President, 1960; . . . , 1964; . . . , 1968; . . . , 1972* (*Signet). Highly informative analyses.

Dean Acheson, *Present at the Creation* (Norton, 1969). Beautifully written memoirs of the 1950s.

A. M. Schlesinger, Jr., *A Thousand Days* (Houghton, 1965), and

T. C. Sorenson, *Kennedy* (*Bantam). Memoirs by aides of President Kennedy.

H. Sidey, *A Very Personal Presidency* (*Atheneum). On the Johnson years.

The Communist Bloc

C. E. Black, *The Eastern World since 1945* (*Ginn). Instructive scholarly survey.

L. Schapiro, *The Government and Politics of the Soviet Union*, rev. ed. (*Vintage). Short authoritative treatment.

Z. Brzezinski, *The Soviet Bloc*, rev. ed. (Harvard, 1967). Solid study of unity and conflict by a leading scientist.

Adam Ulam, *Expansion and Coexistence: The History of Soviet Foreign Policy, 1917–1967* (Praeger, 1968).

D. Zagoria, *The Sino-Soviet Conflict, 1956–1961* (*Atheneum); W. E. Griffith, *Albania and the Sino-Soviet Rift* and *The Sino-Soviet Rift* (*MIT). Useful studies.

R. L. Wolff, *The Balkans in Our Time* (*Norton). Informed survey.

The Emerging Nations

S. C. Easton, *The Rise and Fall of Modern Colonialism* (Praeger, 1962). Sweeping survey.

V. M. Dean, *Nature of the Non-Western World* (*Mentor). Brief overview.

B. Ward, *Interplay of East and West* and *Rich Nations and Poor Nations* (*Norton). Studies by an articulate economist.

F. W. Houn, *A Short History of Chinese Communism* (*Prentice-Hall, 1973). Useful recent introduction.

J. K. Fairbank, *The United States and China*, rev. ed. (*Compass); E. O. Reischauer, *The United States and Japan*, rev. ed. (*Compass). Authoritative surveys.

D. J. Duncannon, *Government and Revolution in Vietnam* (Oxford, 1968). Authoritative political history.

B. B. Fall, *The Two Viet-Nams*, rev. ed. (Praeger, 1965), and R. Shaplen, *The Lost Revolution: The U. S. in Vietnam, 1946–1966* (*Colophon). Outstanding.

J. D. Legge, *Indonesia* (*Spectrum); W. N. Brown, *The United States and India, Pakistan, Bangladesh* (*Harvard); S. Wolpert, *India* (*Prentice-Hall, 1965). Useful introductory studies.

R. H. Davison, *Turkey* (*Spectrum); L. Fein, *Politics in Israel* (*Little); W. R. Polk, *The United States and the Arab World*, rev. ed. (Harvard, 1969); H. B. Sharabi, *Nationalism and Revolution in the Arab World* (*Van Nostrand). Introductions to the Middle East.

J. Hatch, *A History of Postwar Africa* (*Praeger). Clear and helpful guide.

B. Ward, *Africa in the Making* (Norton, 1966). Stimulating general discussion.

L. G. Cowan, *The Dilemmas of African Independence*, rev. ed. (*Walker). A mine of information.

J. F. Gallagher, *The United States and North Africa* (Harvard, 1963); W. Schwarz, *Nigeria* (Praeger, 1968); J. Cope, *South Africa* (Praeger, 1965). Good studies.

G. M. Carter, ed., *Politics in Africa: Seven Cases* (*Harcourt). Informative.

V. Alba, *Nationalists without Nations* (Praeger, 1968). Attack on the ruling oligarchies as barriers to progress in Latin America.

R. J. Alexander, *Today's Latin America,* 2nd ed. (*Anchor); T. Szulc, *Winds of Revolution: Latin America Today and Tomorrow,* rev. ed. (*Praeger). Suggestive introductions.

C. C. Cumberland, *Mexico: The Struggle for Modernity* (*Oxford); A. P. Whitaker, *Argentina* (*Prentice-Hall, 1964); A. Marshall, *Brazil* (*Walker); K. Silvert, *Chile Yesterday and Today* (*Holt); J. E. Fagg, *Cuba, Haiti, and the Dominican Republic* (Prentice-Hall); H. Bernstein, *Venezuela and Colombia* (*Prentice-Hall, 1964); M. Rodriguez, *Central America* (*Prentice-Hall, 1965).

32

The World Since 1970

1971–1972: The Ice Begins to Crack

The shape of the postwar world, which for the quarter-century between 1945 and 1970 had seemed to be hardening into a fixed mold, began to change during 1971.

Nixon's Trip to China

Perhaps the most obvious and dramatic change—and one noted by virtually every inhabitant of the globe—was the one initiated by President Nixon's decision to visit China and by the visit itself. Of course, as hostile critics claimed, the shift in American policy toward the Chinese communists was undertaken in part for Nixon's domestic political purposes at home in an election year. But once this had been conceded, one had to ask *why* Nixon, the keen politician, believed that a move toward bridging the twenty-year-old rift with China would redound to his advantage at home. Were not the Chinese communists our sworn enemies, who had shed our blood in Korea, strengthened the hands of our enemies in Vietnam, kept some of our citizens in wretched prisons, and viciously denounced us wherever they had a forum? Why then should Americans welcome Nixon's new initiative instead of repudiating it? Some, of course, did repudiate it. But more seemed to feel that the traditional policy of treating Chiang's government on Taiwan as the only legitimate Chinese government had become dangerously unrealistic. Quite possibly a Democratic "liberal" president of the United States would have found himself unable to make a friendly gesture towards Mao Tse-tung for fear of being denounced as soft on communism or worse. But Nixon was not a Democratic "liberal" president.

It was also true that both the United States and communist China disliked the policies of the Soviet Union. But while the United States had grown accustomed to tests of strength with the Russians and had the power not to knuckle under when vital American interests seemed threatened, the Chinese were frightened, and with reason, that the USSR might destroy them. With large armies poised on the Chinese frontier, armed with advanced weapons, the USSR in 1971 posed to China the kind of threat that it did not pose to the United States. Though it possessed nearly a billion people and nuclear weapons, China was not yet an advanced industrial power and was weak by comparison with either the United States or the USSR. So the opportunity obviously existed to take the first step toward overcoming Chinese suspicions, toward decreasing tensions with China, toward tipping the balance of power a bit more toward a genuine balance. And Nixon took the opportunity.

Warning the public not to expect great results immediately, Nixon and the Chinese, in a visit given maximum publicity by Chinese consent, did talk to each other about the difficult issues that still separated them, of which Taiwan was obviously the most intractable. Since Chiang shared the communist Chinese view that "two Chinas" did not exist, and that Taiwan was an inseparable part of "one China," the United States was able to make it clear that it would interpose no force to stop an eventual solution by which Taiwan would somehow join the mainland. With Chiang unable to attack the mainland and the communists unlikely to attack the island, this left future arrangements to time and to discussion. Many in the United States deplored the abandonment of old friends, but few defended as realistic an appraisal of the future probabilities different from President Nixon's. The irony was that the native Taiwanese, forming 80 percent of the population of the island, did not want to be governed by *any* Chinese regime, either nationalist or communist, and that their wishes would almost surely continue to be ignored.

In the months between the announcement of Nixon's trip and the trip itself, the United Nations reversed its position held since 1950, and gave the Chinese communists the Chinese seat on the Security Council and expelling the Taiwan regime. It was clear that the United States could not in any case have kept the Chinese communists out much longer: with the President pledged to wind down the Vietnam War and the American position in Asia obviously scheduled to undergo a major change as a result, some sort of overture to Peking could—in the national interest of the United States—hardly have been postponed.

Some students of Asia maintained that the president's trip made a far greater contribution to Chinese security than to American. At a time when the Chinese government was in a visible state of disrepair owing to the excesses of the cultural revolution of the years before 1969 and the quarrels since (which had resulted in the demotion—and death—of General Lin Piao, the man who had been named Mao's heir), the chief of the most powerful state in the world *went to China* in person. To Asians this seemed a recognition that China, to which he went, was more important than America, from which he came. Traditionally in Asian minds, an official visitor from a foreign state was a bringer of tribute from an inferior to a superior government. The Chinese were happy to publicize, therefore, what to many Asians was a clear American acknowledgement of inferiority. No doubt the American government knew that this would be the interpretation put upon the visit by millions of Asians, and had taken this fact into account. But it did not alter the fact that the Chinese—who even at the end of the visit had not agreed to return it—had been enormous gainers in prestige. Each power opened an official mission in the capital of the other.

Repercussions: The USSR, Vietnam

Like the rest of the world, the USSR was taken by surprise at the announcement of Nixon's intention to visit Peking. Although the United States assured Moscow that the American approach to China was not directed against Russia, the first Soviet reaction was naturally one of deep suspicion lest a great new diplomatic combination against the USSR might be in the making. But Nixon planned a trip to Moscow in May 1972 to follow the trip to Peking in February.

During the interval between the trips, the North Vietnamese launched a massive invasion of South

President and Mrs. Nixon at the Great Wall of China, February 24, 1972.

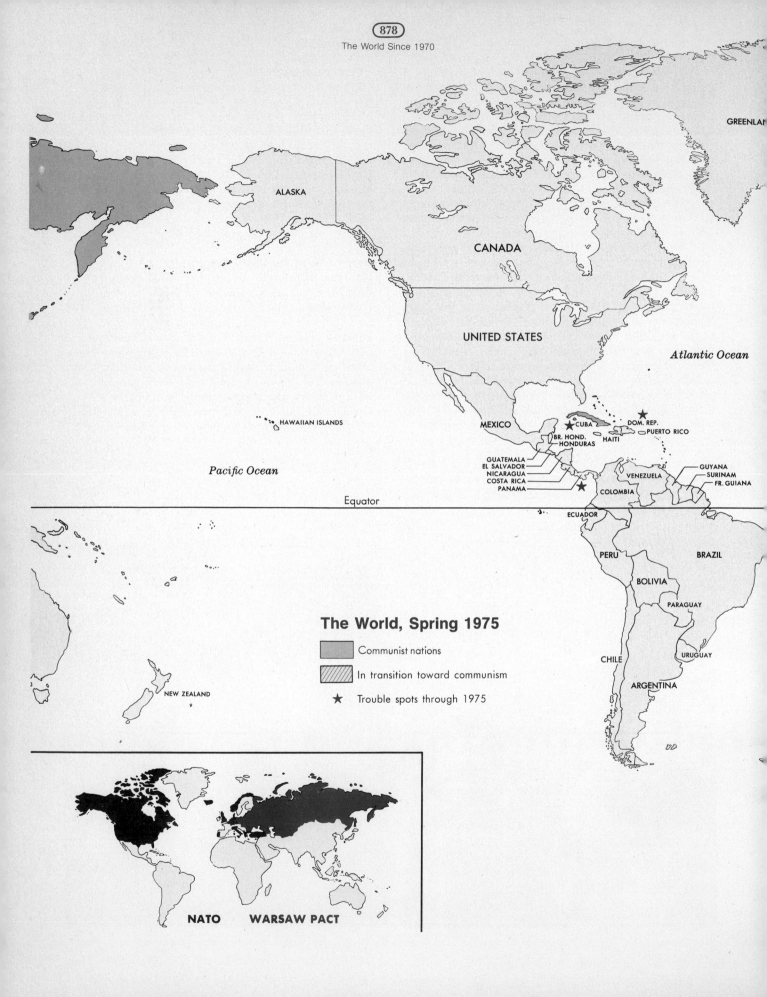

GREENLAND

ALASKA

CANADA

UNITED STATES

Atlantic Ocean

MEXICO
CUBA
DOM. REP.
BR. HOND.
HONDURAS
HAITI
PUERTO RICO
GUATEMALA
EL SALVADOR
NICARAGUA
COSTA RICA
PANAMA
GUYANA
SURINAM
FR. GUIANA
VENEZUELA
COLOMBIA

HAWAIIAN ISLANDS

Pacific Ocean

Equator

ECUADOR

PERU

BRAZIL

BOLIVIA

PARAGUAY

The World, Spring 1975

Communist nations

In transition toward communism

★ Trouble spots through 1975

CHILE
URUGUAY
ARGENTINA

NEW ZEALAND

NATO **WARSAW PACT**

ICELAND

NORWAY SWEDEN FINLAND

UNITED
KINGDOM

DEN.

EIRE

NETH.
BEL.   W. GER.   E. GER.   POLAND
L.   GER.
FRANCE SW. AUST. CZECH.
        ITALY HUN.
               YUG. ROM.
               ALB. BUL.

USSR

MONGOLIA

PORTUGAL SPAIN   TURKEY
GREECE   CYPRUS
                 LEBANON SYRIA
                 ISRAEL
MOROCCO   IRAQ   IRAN   AFGHAN.   KASHMIR   TIBET   CHINA
IFNI   PAKISTAN   NEPAL BHUTAN
SPANISH   JORDAN
SAHARA   ALGERIA LIBYA EGYPT   SAUDI   BURMA
MAURITANIA   ARABIA   INDIA   N. VIETNAM
         MALI   NIGER   CHAD   OMAN   LAOS   S. VIETNAM
GUINEA   SUDAN   YEMEN   THAI. CAM.
SAU   SOUTHERN YEMEN   CEYLON
LEONE   UPPER   MALAYSIA BRUNEI
         VOLTA   NIGERIA CENTRAL AFARS & ISSAS
LIBERIA   CAM.   AFRICAN TERRITORY
IVORY COAST   EQ.   REPUBLIC ETHIOPIA
GHANA   GUINEA UGANDA   SOMALI REPUBLIC   INDONESIA
TOGO   GABON   RWANDA   KENYA
DAHOMEY CABINDA REP.   BURUNDI
                 OF   ZAIRE   TANZANIA
                 CONGO   MALAWI   Diego Garcia
         ANGOLA   MOZAMBIQUE
                 ZAMBIA   Indian Ocean
                 RHOD.   MALAGASY
SOUTH-   REPUBLIC MAURITIUS
WEST   BOTSWANA   N.W. Cape
AFRICA   SWAZILAND
Atlantic Ocean REPUBLIC OF LESOTHO   AUSTRALIA
                SOUTH AFRICA

N. KOREA S. KOREA JAPAN

TAIWAN

PHILIPPINE IS.

NEW GUINEA
WEST IRIAN
PAPUA

OAS   CENTO
           (Incl. U.S.)

SEATO   ARAB LEAGUE

Vietnam, taking important strategic centers, and threatening to cut South Vietnam in two. The brunt of the ground attack had now to be borne by the South Vietnamese army, since American forces had been reduced from 542,000 to 36,000 men. But the United States resumed the bombing of North Vietnam on a massive scale. Moreover, Nixon mined North Vietnamese ports in order to interdict the delivery of supplies by sea. The Russians, who all during the Nixon visit to China had denounced the Chinese for having abandoned the cause of the North Vietnamese, now found themselves faced with a choice between canceling his visit to the USSR or seeming to acquiesce in his latest measures against North Vietnam. They denounced the measures but did not call off the trip, which led to the signing of a series of important agreements between the U.S. and the USSR.

The Russians attached enormous importance to the document called "The Basic Principles of Relations between the USSR and the U.S.A." because to them it was "the first document to give international legal form" to the relations between the two countries. Both accepted the principle of peaceful coexistence, committed themselves to resolve disputes by negotiation, avoiding force or the threat of force, and striving to prevent nuclear war; each recognized the complete equality of the other. To the USSR the willingness of the U.S. to sign an official document stating what had long seemed so obvious to the entire human race was in itself a triumph. Moreover, the fact that of course the two countries had "different social systems" demonstrated for the Russians the truth of the current Soviet Communist party line: that normal or even good relations must be sought with noncommunist states in order to avoid thermonuclear war.

Far more specific was the treaty between the two countries limiting antiballistic missile systems to fixed numbers of launchers, missiles, and radar installations: a technical document that was the outcome of much previous negotiation. There were also accords on cooperation in the exploration of space—with a joint docking maneuver scheduled for 1975—and cooperation in science and technology, medicine and public health, and in protecting the environment, envisioning the exchange of ecologists. And there were statements on other problems. With regard to Europe, both powers welcomed the relaxations of tension. On the Middle East, nothing but a pious wish for peace could be agreed upon; on Vietnam, each side simply restated its well-known position in opposition to that of the other.

Together with Nixon's Peking visit, and in part because of it, his Moscow visit and its communiqué were a clear sign that great-power relations, hitherto apparently eternally frozen into a pattern of three-way hostility between the United States, China, and Russia, had begun to thaw. The ice was being broken—at least between the United States and both of the communist powers—though the two communist powers remained implacably hostile to one another.

The Moscow meeting was followed later in 1972 by massive Soviet purchases of American wheat—driving up the world market price and allegedly enabling insiders in the United States to profit hugely—and by a trade pact that envisaged joint American-Soviet commercial enterprises such as the building of pipelines in the USSR in order to make possible the shipment of Soviet gas and oil to the United States and "most-favored-nation" treatment for the USSR in the American market. Soviet repressive policies with regard to Jewish emigration, discussed below, delayed the necessary Senate confirmation of this pact.

Repercussions: Japan and South Asia

In going to China, Nixon was shaking the foundations of the special American relationship with Japan. And by failing to let the Japanese know about his plan before the public announcement, Nixon offended them seriously, leading them to ask whether the Americans were preparing to abandon them and scuttle their alliance. Probably Nixon felt he had to keep the Japanese in the dark because the Chinese had been growing paranoid about Japan as well as about Russia. The enormous economic success of the Japanese had stimulated the ever-present Chinese fear that Japan would rearm, and Chinese propaganda constantly stressed "renewed Japanese imperialism." In order to allay this fear, Nixon concealed his plans from the Japanese, no doubt hoping that he could later repair the damage.

But the United States later compounded the slight by following the same tactics in proclaiming a series of surprise new economic measures. The President freed the dollar from gold, allowing it to float, and imposed a new 10 percent customs surcharge on foreign goods. Both these measures were damaging to the Japanese, who were forced to revalue their undervalued currency, and whose enormous sales of manufactured goods in the United States would no longer be so profitable. For the second time in a few weeks, Nixon had failed to take the Japanese into his confidence on matters gravely affecting them. The Japanese continued to feel betrayed despite all efforts to reassure them.

Premier Sato—living symbol of the intimate partnership with the United States—soon afterwards resigned, and his successor, Kakuei Tanaka, though a member of the same political party, was a younger man whose cabinet was more sensitive to anti-American public opinion and who was prepared to open up for reconsideration the entire question of Japan's role in international politics. After first meeting with Nixon, Tanaka went to Peking in September 1972. Regular Chinese-Japanese diplomatic relations were established, which meant that Japan would no longer recognize the Taiwan government. Tanaka apologized publicly for Japan's past misdeeds in China, and Chou En-lai publicly cautioned him against rearmament.

Alone among the potential great powers of the

world, Japan had limited its close relations since the war exclusively to the United States. And Japan's lack of powerful military forces—combined with its great economic power—also made it unique. With the exclusive dependence upon the United States no longer attractive (or perhaps even possible), with Chinese relations on a new footing, and with no real wish to rearm, the future course for Japan would perhaps consist of new diplomatic and commercial initiatives: in Asia, for example, an active sponsorship of the gradual easing of tensions between North and South Korea, leading to the eventual reunion between the two halves of that country, so close to Japan physically and culturally. Indeed, one of the most dramatic new developments in 1972 had been the opening of discussions and the exchange of official delegations between North and South Korea, hitherto implacably hostile to one another, and the assumption by the South Korean President Park of dictatorial powers.

Beyond Korea, there seemed to be possibilities for an increasingly close relationship between Japan, Indonesia, and Australia, beneficial to all three and threatening to nobody. Eventually the détente now taking shape in Europe might well be mirrored in Asia, with the Japanese playing a key role.

The timing of the plans for Nixon's Chinese trip contributed also to a major American loss of favor in India. Partly because it had been through the good offices of Pakistan that Nixon's advisers had been able secretly to get to China to make the preliminary arrangements for the trip, and partly because Nixon personally liked the Pakistani leader Yahya Khan a good deal better than he liked Mrs. Gandhi, the American government favored Pakistan in a new trial of strength with India, the most serious that had yet taken place. This was settled in the months between the announcement of Nixon's trip to Peking and the trip itself.

Having first announced that he was prepared to abide by the results of free elections in Pakistan, Yahya Khan found that the Bengali nationalist Awami League, led by Sheikh Mujibur Rahman of East Bengal, had won virtually all the seats from that populous province and that the Bengalis would thus have an absolute majority in the Pakistani Parliament. So Yahya Khan went back on his word, nullified the elections, jailed Mujib, and invaded East Pakistan. Hostility between the native Bengalis there and Bihari immigrants into East Bengal from India (both Muslim) had led to a good many Bengali atrocities before the West Pakistani troops invaded. But after the invasion, the West Pakistani atrocities against the Bengalis were on a vaster scale than anything since the Nazi exterminations of the Jews during World War II. Bengali refugees to the number of perhaps nine million poured into India. Any permanent settlement of so many Muslim refugees in India was obviously impossible.

In the last months of 1971, therefore, came a new Indian-Pakistani war, as the Indian armies drove into East Pakistan, which Yahya Khan's government could not hold. In a few days, the Indians had rounded up and captured the West Pakistani troops and for the most part protected them from the infuriated Bengali population, whose leaders proclaimed the state of Bangladesh, an independent Bengal. Yahya Khan's government fell, and a hitherto pro-Chinese and anti-American (though American-educated) politician, Zulfikar Ali Bhutto, took over in West Pakistan. Bhutto freed Sheikh Mujib from prison, and he returned to Bangladesh to head the new regime there. The refugees began to pour back into their devastated country from India.

Throughout, the United States supported Pakistan, whose troops were committing the atrocities and which was also bound to lose. No doubt American policy derived in part from the preoccupation with ensuring that Nixon's Chinese visit should come off as scheduled. But—as was clear from secret documents leaked to the press—Washington also greatly overestimated the power of the Pakistani forces in East Bengal to hold out against the Indians and underestimated the excellence of the Indian Army. Moreover, it seems to have misread Indian intentions, expecting (falsely) that the Indians intended to destroy Pakistan altogether by attacking all-out in the West as well as the East. The sending of American naval vessels into the Bay of Bengal during the height of the hostilities alienated the Indians and did the Pakistanis and the United States no visible good.

And the Russians moved swiftly to capitalize on the opportunity. They signed a treaty of alliance with India and, along with their European satellites, early recognized Bangladesh as an independent state. For the United States, regaining Indian goodwill would be a long process, made no easier by the social cordialities of Nixon's China visit when it did take place: the televised toasts at the banquets, the private conference with Mao, the almost affectionate American behavior to India's sworn enemies.

In the aftermath of the war, Mrs. Gandhi—more self-assured now than ever and in undisputed political control of her victorious country—declined to let the Russians preside over a settlement of the latest India-Pakistan war as they had done at Tashkent in 1965, and preferred instead to negotiate directly with Premier Bhutto. Reeling from defeat, Pakistan was balancing precariously close to anarchy. Bhutto would have liked to recognize Bangladesh, but his own Punjabis at home furiously opposed such a move, which would surely have led to insistent demands for more autonomy—perhaps even independence—from other minorities (Pathans, Sindhis) in West Pakistan, now all that was left of the country. The Indians still held many thousands of Pakistani prisoners, and Bangladesh wanted them handed over for trial as war criminals. But this would have made negotiations with Bhutto impossible for an indefinite period and might have led to his ouster and the imposition in Pakistan of some sort of military dictatorship, with incalculable consequences.

East Pakistani refugees fleeing to India to escape fighting between East and West Pakistani rebels, April 10, 1974.

In the poverty-stricken and devastated new independent state of Bangladesh itself, Sheikh Mujib was faced with almost insoluble problems of reconstruction. American recognition was eventually granted, but communist China, now holding the Chinese seat on the UN Security Council, vetoed Bangladesh's application for membership in the UN. Despite his popularity, Mujib's country was showing signs of political instability: freedom alone had not brought in the millennium, and disillusionment had begun to grow. The threat of famine was intense.

The U.S. Election of 1972 and the Ceasefire in Vietnam

Once again, the apparently interminable Vietnam war became in 1972 an issue in the American presidential election. With no seeming change in the North Vietnamese peace terms, which remained unacceptable to the Nixon government, Senator George McGovern, the Democratic nominee, called for their immediate acceptance, assuring the public that he could obtain the release of American prisoners after the settlement instead of as a precondition for the settlement. But President Nixon's calculation that American antipathy to the war would be sufficiently blunted by the withdrawal of America's own forces—and that much public opinion would at least tolerate, and much approve, his policy of not yielding on this and other important issues—proved justified.

Not long before the election was scheduled, in October 1972, came a sudden breakthrough in negotiations, as President Nixon's adviser on national security, Dr. Henry Kissinger, confirmed a prior announcement from Hanoi that a formula for a ceasefire had in fact been hammered out. It included American withdrawal, the release of prisoners, the freezing of the military positions, and the creation of a new political body—not a coalition government, on which Hanoi had previously insisted, but a National Council of Reconciliation and National Concord that would include representation from both sides. But whereas Hanoi believed that there was nothing left to discuss and pressed Washington to sign immediately, Kissinger explained that points remained to be settled and predicted some delay in the actual signing. Nixon won the election, and shortly thereafter negotiations were renewed.

In December 1972, they were interrupted amidst mutual charges of bad faith, and Nixon resumed intensive bombing of North Vietnam in the face of hostile opinion. Early in 1973, negotiations began again and culminated in an agreement for a ceasefire, accepted by the United States, North Vietnam, South Vietnam, and the Viet Cong. International inspection teams began their task of supervision, and the release of prisoners got under way. The cease fire was only the beginning of change, but it seemed an event of immense actual as well as symbolic importance.

East-West Détente in Europe; the Common Market

Far less sudden than the new thaw between the United States and both China and the USSR, and deriving more obviously from the events of the years just past were the continued steps during 1971 and 1972 towards a détente between western and eastern Europe. But they were no less momentous in their implications for the possibilities of a new international order.

The Brandt government in West Germany moved steadily towards a *rapprochement* with the communist powers to the east. Treaties painfully hammered out between West Germany and the Soviet Union and between West Germany and Poland—accepting the postwar frontiers—won even more painful acceptance and eventual ratification. The Christian Democratic opposition was split on the question, so that it ceased to be entirely a party issue. The implied acceptance as permanent of the postwar eastern European boundaries was a hard dose for some West Germans to swallow. Ulbricht, the aging doctrinaire communist boss of East Germany, who had steadfastly opposed any increase in intimacy with the West, was replaced by Erich Honecker—also a communist, of course—who was willing to talk. And the conclusion of a four-power pact on Berlin itself served at last to render harmless a major

Members of the 96th Infantry Brigade prepare to board a troop carrier plane at Phu Bai Airport, June 16, 1972, following the ceasefire agreement in Vietnam.

issue that had repeatedly endangered the peace of the world since 1945.

Having painstakingly moved step by step through the necessary preliminaries, Brandt in the closing months of 1972 signed directly with the East Germans a treaty looking toward the establishment of normal relations. Brandt's election in November 1972 indicated popular approval of his diplomatic achievements. The Berlin Wall still stood, but the thing that it had symbolized was in the process of disappearing.

The years 1971 and 1972 also saw the gradual and often painful progress of Great Britain toward membership in the European Common Market. After the major outstanding questions had been resolved by negotiations between Prime Minister Heath's Conservative government and the officials of The Six, Heath took the issue to Parliament. There all the Labour party politicians who had been in charge of Market negotiations under Harold Wilson's government testified that the conditions now offered were conditions that they would have accepted but had been unable to get. But Wilson himself now shifted his ground.

Keenly aware of strong anti-Market sentiment among his own trade-union constituents and indeed in the British public generally, Wilson came out against British entry, and turned the question into a party issue. Enough Labour MP's broke with their party leader and voted with the Conservatives to pass the initial motion for entry by a considerable majority.

And during 1972 each of the subsequent necessary votes on the details of the process also obtained a majority for entry, although in one critical case it was the tiny Liberal party membership—only five men strong—that provided the votes needed to get the measure through the House of Commons. Had there been a referendum it seems likely that public opinion would have voted down the Common Market; and Wilson repeatedly demanded one. But referenda on such issues are contrary to British political tradition in which responsibility rests on the duly elected members of Parliament. On January 1, 1973, Britain joined the Common Market, a tremendous break with the past, initiating a new era for the British, the Western Europeans, and, indeed, for the rest of the world as well.

With Britain, the Republic of Ireland also joined. And until late in 1972 it had seemed probable that Norway and Denmark, also members of the loose Outer Seven would enter the Common Market and turn The Six into The Ten. But in a surprising popular referendum, Norway voted against entry. Though its leading politicians, economists, and businessmen strongly favored the commitment, many farmers and fishermen were opposed. And there were enough strong nationalists who feared the loss of some national sovereignty and an influx of foreign workers, and enough left-wingers who opposed the Market on principle, to outvote those who favored entry. A few days later, the Danes, in a referendum of their own, voted to join the Market, presumably in large part because this would enable them to continue their lucrative trade with Britain.

Despite the continued maintenance of national sovereignties and of national armies, it was expected that Western Europe, including Britain, would have the economic strength of a superpower.

Exception: The Middle East

Although a thaw was under way, certain issues continued to resist all efforts at settlement, notably those of the Middle East. Premier Sadat of Egypt repeatedly threatened in 1971 and 1972 to renew the war against Israel and "reach a final settlement." But he refrained from open hostilities, while making an ominous series of more and more intimate agreements with the USSR. Then suddenly, in the summer of 1972, Sadat announced that Egypt had asked the USSR to withdraw its more than 20,000 military advisers. In Egypt the Soviet forces had insisted on maintaining control of the most advanced weapons there and had acted in an overbearing manner to the Egyptian military and to the population. And the Soviet government had refused to give Egypt still more modern missiles. The expulsion of the Russians was a popular one in Egypt, since it emphasized Egyptian sovereignty and ability to act independently. The blow to Soviet influence in the Middle East was major, although the Soviet fleet would continue to use Egyptian bases.

And the Egyptians had acted without previously securing an alternate source of military assistance, which could presumably be only the United States. No American government, especially during an election year, could consider taking on the Egyptians as a military client. And even if it were not for the domestic political considerations that surely moved Washington and that presumably Sadat understood as well as anybody, no prudent American government could have moved quickly and openly to take the place of the disgruntled Russians and emphasize the Russian loss of face. Well-armed, but somewhat weakened in its capability to use its armaments, Egypt was, it now appeared, probably readier for a settlement than at any time since the 1967 war. And well-authenticated rumors were circulated that the Israelis—as the basis for discussions—had informally offered to return to Egypt most of the Sinai peninsula.

But the vigorous revival of terrorism by the so-called Black September branch of the Palestinian liberation movement made impossible any consideration of negotiations in the Middle East. Deprived of their bases in Jordan, the guerrillas had only one frontier—the Lebanese—in common with Israel. And though southern Lebanon became "Fatah-land" and the guerrillas had units in the villages and on the hillsides there, the main attack was carried on by small groups of terrorists elsewhere. Three Japanese extremists, trained and enlisted by the movement, machine-gunned the airport at Tel Aviv indiscriminately, killing and wounding chiefly a group of Puerto Rican Catholic pilgrims. And five Arabs broke into the Israeli athletes' quarters at the Olympic Games in Munich in an episode that resulted in the deaths of eleven Israelis and three of the terrorists. In reprisal, Israel struck at the terrorists in Lebanon.

The world was faced with an unprecedentedly difficult police problem as well as a moral and political one. No Arab government except that of Jordan—already committed against the terrorists, who had assassinated King Hussein's prime minister on Egyptian soil—could take a public stand. Yet at least the Soviet-American rapprochement seemed to diminish the possibility of major-power conflict arising from a Middle East explosion.

II 1971–1972: The Nations at Home

In the domestic affairs of the nations of the world the chief issues in 1971–1972 remained very much what they had been before, although of course they often took new shapes.

The Western Nations

In the United States the familiar issue of "bussing" children out of their own neighborhoods to schools in other neighborhoods in order to achieve a more racially integrated school system remained controversial even after the Supreme Court had decided that it was permissible and loomed large in the (often not explicit) campaigning that preceded the national political conventions of 1972. Inflation—galloping ahead in spite of the Nixon government's efforts to stop it and the repeated assurances that those efforts were working—angered and plagued the citizen. And McGovern's social and economic programs promised more of it, and higher taxes than ever. Quite possibly alarm generated by the probable expense of McGovern's proposals contributed to Nixon's massive popular and electoral victory in November 1972.

In Canada, Trudeau's policies were viewed as too pro-French, and he lost his majority in the elections of 1972. But the Conservatives did not win enough seats to govern, and the balance of power rested temporarily with the Social Democrats.

In Britain, the familiar issue posed by the power of the unions to disrupt the economy was only exacerbated by a severe miners' strike in the winter of 1971–1972, forcing the curtailment of electrical services, and by two jurisdictional disputes among the dockers (longshoremen) that closed British ports for part of the summer of 1972. The weakness of the currency that forced the Heath government to free the pound from gold and let it float downward in value was an old phenomenon. Stringent controls over inflation were installed—contrary to Tory economic policies—late in 1972.

The agony caused by the worsening crisis in Ireland only deepened, as the British suspended the Northern Irish provincial government and took military and political control in the troubled province to preserve order in the face of continued IRA terrorism. William Whitelaw, appointed by Prime Minister Heath to take charge of efforts to settle the troubles, interned—as the Northern Irish constitution permitted him to do—a number of men arrested as terrorists, but the largest Catholic political group, the relatively moderate Social Democratic and Labour party, refused to enter into discussions until all interned men had been freed. Bombings continued; troops were reinforced. The British public would have liked nothing more than to withdraw but could not abandon the province to inevitable civil war and anarchic bloodshed. Cracks were appearing, however, within the IRA, as the Catholic population grew more and more restive under the military rule necessitated by IRA terror.

And in 1972 a new stimulus was given to the growing racial tension in Britain by the action of the new military dictator of Uganda, General Idi Amin, in suddenly expelling some 50,000 Ugandan Asians who held British passports, including many middle-class business and professional men and their families. Amin himself was personally and politically unstable. From the British point of view the step threatened to exacerbate the growing anti-Asian and more generally racist sentiments of the working class in Britain, to which most of the Asians would have to go. Canada, the United States, India, and other countries took a few thousand, but the main impact fell upon Britain. And Amin's wild talk made very real the threat that he would next take action against the remaining Ugandan Asians—perhaps almost as many—who held Ugandan rather than British documents. The implications of his actions within Africa itself we discuss below.

In France, when charges of corruption against government officials grew more strident in 1971 and 1972, this was nothing new: it was just that the Fifth Republic of the Gaullists, now in power for more than fourteen years, was beginning to lose its purity and to look more and more like the Third and Fourth Republics, where official corruption and public cynicism had been familiar features of the political landscape. The failure of Premier Chaban-Delmas to pay any income tax was not illegal: he was only making use of loopholes in the tax law, like many other Frenchmen (or Americans), but public response to the news so diminished his political usefulness that President Pompidou had to replace him. The choice of replacement, Pierre Messmer, widely regarded as at best a stopgap until elections, only heightened the general disillusionment: no Frenchman, however hostile to de Gaulle, could ever have entertained the notion that corruption would flourish where the General knew about it; now, things seemed to be different.

In Italy, the growth of political corruption and of crime continued to give new stimulus to extremists of the left and of the right. But Premier Giulio Andreotti's

Members of the outlawed IRA, behind a barricade in Londonderry, North Ireland.
They are masked to prevent identification.

new Christian Democratic government in 1972 seemed to be tackling immediate economic problems in a rational way that reminded spectators of Andreotti's late mentor, Alcide di Gaspari.

In Spain, right-wing forces were solidly entrenched, despite the economic desirability of Spain's entry into the Common Market and the political difficulties of doing so as an unreconstructed dictatorship. Police repression of alleged dissidents continued to be severe.

The USSR

In the USSR and in eastern Europe also, the patterns of events remained all too recognizable. Renewed agricultural failure on a scale as yet undetermined in 1972 left the Soviet Union short of food. A new recrudescence of anti-Semitism made its appearance, partly as the result of the continued wish of large numbers of Soviet Jews to emigrate to Israel. Zionism as such had always been anathema to Soviet regimes, but in 1971 and 1972, with Russian life far more open to view by foreigners, it was impossible to revert to a Stalinist policy

of total terror against Soviet Jews who wanted to leave. Terror and arrests there were, but the government did also permit Jews to leave in larger numbers than before.

Affecting fear of something like a "brain drain," however, the regime announced a new policy of requiring Jewish émigrés to pay large sums of money for permission to depart, alleging that the amounts charged were to repay the costs of the education each such émigré had received in the USSR. The more highly educated the would-be Jewish émigré, the higher the cost of emigration. Few if any Soviet Jews could find sums in the tens of thousands of dollars to pay such levies, and the only recourse would have been to raise the money in the United States. The end of 1972 saw the blackmailing emigration policies in full swing and repression mounting against Jews who wanted to stay as well as Jews who wanted to leave.

Connected with anti-Semitism was the whole question of dissent. Jews who wished to leave were by definition dissenters; so were the many Jews who stayed and openly protested against the regime's repression of writers and intellectuals. And in the years immediately after 1970 the phenomenon of dissent, which we have noted in the sixties, became even more notable. The output of the dissenting press, called by the Russian name *Samizdat*, "self-published," swelled to an unprecedented size and attracted much attention in the USSR and abroad.

On the thinnest of typing paper, usually bought surreptitiously a few sheets at a time, the Russian dissenter typed an original and as many carbon copies as possible of some document recording a recent instance of repression: censorship, the stifling of contacts between scientists and foreigners, or the like. Then he passed a copy surreptitiously to each of ten or a dozen friends, who in turn repeated the process. Many thousands of these documents appeared, varying in length from a one-page letter of Alexander Solzhenitsyn to the patriarch of Moscow, protesting against a Christian church under the dictatorial supervision of atheists, to an entire novel that could not get past the censors. *The Chronicle of Current Events,* a bulky Samizdat newspaper reporting a mass of the most recent repressive episodes and edited and "published" by men unknown to their fellow dissenters, made a regular appearance. Many of these materials reached the West clandestinely, and a large collection—twenty-four volumes—was compiled outside Russia. Already the first eleven issues of the *Chronicle* had been published in English translation in book form. *

The men and women who undertook such activities were enormously brave. But their bravery and their dislike for the regime were perhaps the chief things they had in common. Some were communists who deplored what they regarded as the regime's departure from Leninist principles. Some advocated the kind of humane communism associated with the brief efforts of Dubcek in Czechoslovakia. Some were out-and-out democrats, some monarchists and Orthodox rightwingers in the old czarist tradition. As they often declared, they were united only in their anti-Soviet sentiments: in any future non-Soviet Russia they would be deadly enemies.

Moreover, no such future non-Soviet Russia was in fact remotely conceivable, and the dissenters' own activities served to underline this fact for observers. The dissenters were all members of the intelligentsia, and all were concerned with the varying problems of intellectuals or religious groups. While the anti-Tsarist protest movements of the nineteenth-century concerned themselves with the problems of the downtrodden peas-

*Peter Reddaway, ed., *Uncensored Russia* (London: Cape, 1972).

Russian Jewish immigrants touch the ground reverently as they arrive in Israel, November 1971.

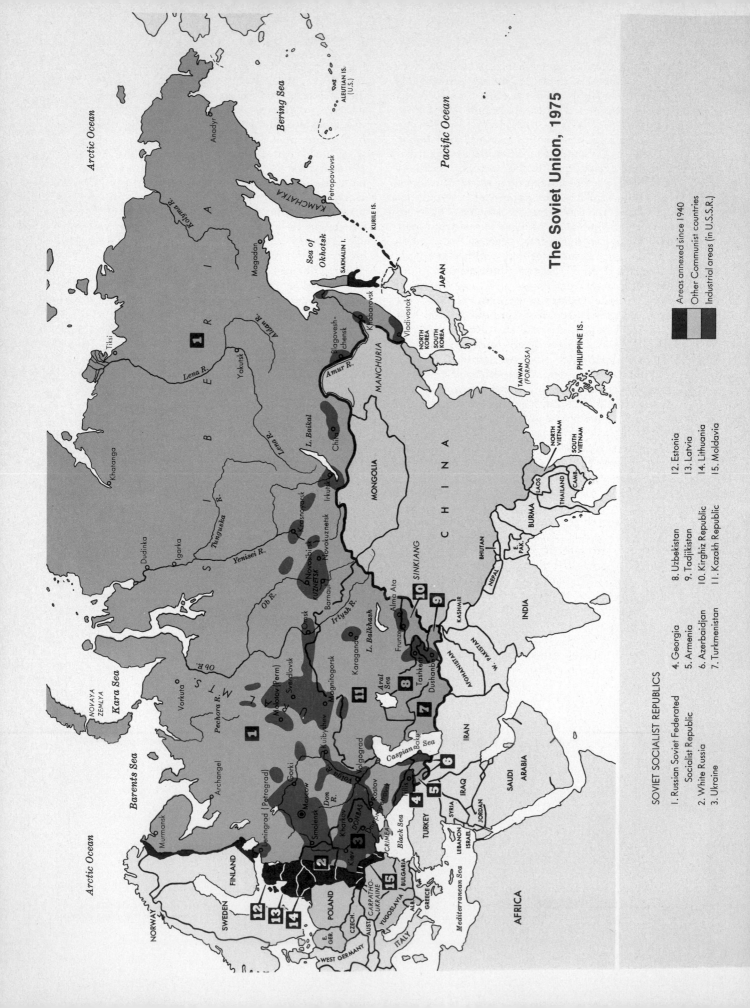

The Soviet Union, 1975

SOVIET SOCIALIST REPUBLICS

1. Russian Soviet Federated
   Socialist Republic
2. White Russia
3. Ukraine

4. Georgia
5. Armenia
6. Azerbaidjan
7. Turkmenistan

8. Uzbekistan
9. Tadjikistan
10. Kirghiz Republic
11. Kazakh Republic

12. Estonia
13. Latvia
14. Lithuania
15. Moldavia

Areas annexed since 1940
Other Communist countries
Industrial areas (in U.S.S.R.)

antry and so eventually struck a chord in the masses of the Russian people themselves, the anti-Soviet protest movement of the late 1960s and early 1970s made no effort to describe—much less prescribe for—the renewed enserfment of the Soviet peasantry, the shortages of food and housing, the prevalence of drunkenness, the social and economic inequality, the luxurious life of the favored bureaucrats: conditions which, however wretched, nonetheless marked a distinct improvement. There was apparently no likelihood whatever that the masses of Russians were interested in the troubles of the intellectuals or that the intellectuals thought they might become so. So Samizdat—however brave, however interesting, however tempting a phenomenon to westerners—could not be taken as indicating a major weakness of Soviet society.

Such weaknesses, however, did exist: the chief one was nationalism. Mistreatment of Catholic priests in the Lithuanian SSR could still produce a long petition of protest signed by many thousands, and precipitate a riot. The Ukraine had its own nationalistic Samizdat, whose newspaper and other publications echoed ancient separatist, right-wing, and anti-Semitic slogans. Indeed, the Ukrainian paper denounced the non-Ukrainian dissenters for confining their agitation to the civil rights question and failing to espouse the cause of the nationalities, and for thus seeming to approve of the status quo. The passionate vehemence of the Ukrainians was only more articulate than that of the Caucasian, Central Asian, Baltic, and other minorities. And the persistence of such national sentiment inside the USSR was the chief reason why the Soviet regime could never afford to become liberal in the ways desired by the Russian dissenters: a liberal regime would lose its non-Russian territories in short order. The Russia that would be left would no longer be a major power. So the Soviet bureaucracy would not be shaken by the dissenters, however brave.

And during 1972 arrests increased in number: some of those arrested, whether Jews or not, were given one-way tickets to Israel; others were sent to jail or to insane asylums. A leading figure of the movement for Russian civil rights, Pyotr Yakir, son of a general who had been murdered by Stalin in 1937 and later posthumously "rehabilitated," and himself a veteran of fourteen years of Stalinist imprisonment, was arrested in June 1972 despite his credentials as a victim of Stalinism. The regime was cracking down on dissent, and dissent itself seemed threatened. The deeply moving words of Solzhenitsyn's Nobel Prize address, which he could not deliver in person in Stockholm but which was published abroad, only underlined the tragic fate of art and freedom in the USSR.

In Titoist Yugoslavia too, nationalism continued to pose a major threat to the stability of the country: in this case the traditional nationalism of the Croats, reappearing now both within the Communist party and outside it. The Croatian Communist party—in Marxist-Leninist vocabulary—protested just as vigorously at what it regarded as Serb domination as Croatian non-communists had traditionally done in the past. Tito moved angrily first to purge it, and then to purge the Serbian party also. But much damage had been done to the picture the regime was trying to present of a Yugoslavia united at last.

And outside Yugoslavia, right-wing Croatian nationalists took to terrorist activities on behalf of a "free" Croatia, murdering the Yugoslav ambassador in Sweden, liberating the murderers by hijacking a Swedish plane and causing the destruction of a Yugoslav transport plane in the air. The threat of Croatian separatism left and right remained to plague a country whose proposed government after the death of Tito—now over eighty—was in any case a kind of Rube Goldberg committee that even in the most tolerant atmosphere of political understanding would seem unwieldy and unworkable.

Africa, Latin America

In Africa there were coups, even in Ghana, where the anti-Nkrumah forces had seemed firmly in control. In Morocco, for the second time in two years, the authoritarian king in 1972 escaped assassination; this time his strongman, Mohammed Oufkir—a man with a long record of political murder—was caught and executed. In Libya, Colonel Qaddafi for a few days seemed to be in trouble but emerged with his life and power intact and a reorganized government. In Rhodesia, black African opposition to the government took the form of effective public demonstrations against a negotiated agreement with the British.

In South-West Africa (Namibia), the previously docile Ovambos gave vigorous public expression to their hatred for South African rule, and the UN was once again charged with this problem, which it had fumbled for decades. Ugandan opponents of General Amin—supporters of Milton Obote, based in Tanzania—began an abortive invasion of Uganda to which Amin responded by bombing Tanzanian villages.

In Latin America the military coup continued to bring more radical forces to power (Ecuador provided a new case), while the freely elected government of President Allende in Chile seemed to be plunging the country into economic chaos. At the UN itself a fourth secretary general, the Austrian Kurt Waldheim, succeeded U Thant.

III 1973–1974: Frustration and Disarray in the West

At the end of 1972, despite the unwelcome persistence of all-too-familiar problems in the domestic life of the nations of the world, it would have taken a pessimist of no mean order to foresee the troubles that lay ahead in the next two years, making a mockery of what had seemed a promising new pattern of international rela-

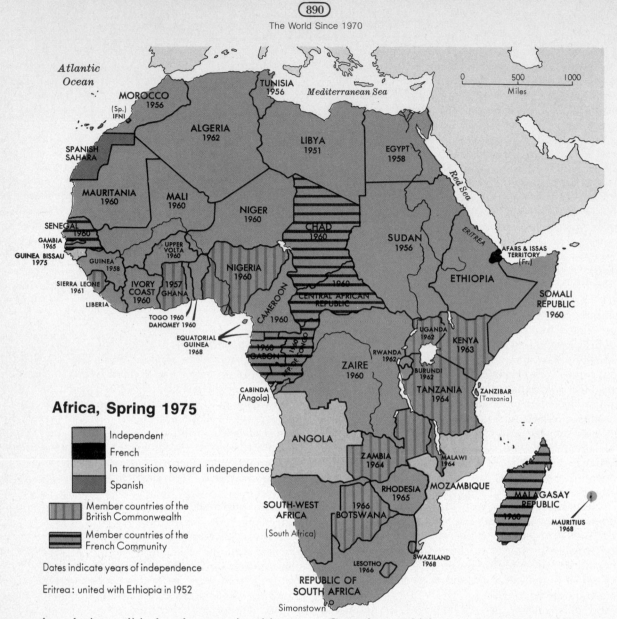

Africa, Spring 1975

Independent
French
In transition toward independence
Spanish

Member countries of the British Commonwealth

Member countries of the French Community

Dates indicate years of independence

Eritrea: united with Ethiopia in 1952

tions, and producing political and economic crisis on a global scale. In January 1975, we were too close to these events to reach anything like a satisfactory judgment or perhaps even to write a coherent and reasonably accurate account of them. But—in addition to all the human frailties, to the blunders and even crimes of politicians, to the greed and ruthlessness of governments and industries and labor unions—observers might agree that mankind during 1973 and 1974 had suffered to an unprecedented degree from sheer bad luck. A great deal of the trouble certainly could be blamed on the oil crisis, which we discuss below. But many other causes could be found.

The United States: "Watergate"

Well before Nixon's election in 1972, a guard at a housing development near the Potomac, known as Watergate, arrested a small group of men in the act of breaking into the offices of the Democratic National Committee, which were located there. The burglars proved to be in the employ of the Committee to Re-elect the President (acronym: C-R-E-E-P), but in the interval between their arrest and the election the episode was widely regarded as no more than an excess of zeal or a merry political prank. Yet the ramifications of the early investigations led to the exposure of a series of scandals that directly involved President Nixon and by 1974 were preoccupying the American government and public to the exclusion of virtually all other matters of national interest.

An investigation was launched by a Senate Committee under the chairmanship of Sam Ervin, Democrat, of North Carolina. President Nixon himself appointed a Special Prosecutor—Professor Archibald Cox of the Harvard Law School—to pursue an independent inquiry. The Watergate burglars included several with direct links to the Central Intelligence Agency. The chairman of CREEP was John Mitchell, who had been Attorney-General in Nixon's first cabinet. Some of the

Caribbean Sea

PANAMA
CANAL   Cartagena

Caracas

TRINIDAD AND TOBAGO

VENEZUELA

GUYANA

SURINAM

Georgetown

Medellín   Paramaribo

Bogotá   *DEVIL'S ISLAND*

COLOMBIA   GUIANAS   Cayenne

Orinoco R.

FRENCH GUIANA

ECUADOR   Quito

Guayaquil

Negro R.

Amazon R.

Manaos

Iquitos   Belem
(Pará)

Amazon R.

Fortaleza

B   R   A   Z   I   L   Natal

Madeira R.

Purus   *R.*

Tapajos R.

Recife
(Pernambuco)

PERU

São Francisco R.

Callao

Tocantins R.

Salvador
(Bahia)

Araguaia R.

Titicaca

La Paz   FEDERAL
DISTRICT   Brasilia

Arequipa   BOLIVIA

Tacna

Belo
Horizonte

Arica

Paraguay R.

Parana R.

Pacific Ocean

São Paulo

GRAN   CHACO

PARAGUAY

Rio de Janeiro

Antofagasta

Asunción   Santos

Tucuman

Parana R.

Pôrto Alegre   *Atlantic Ocean*

Cordoba

CHILE

URUGUAY

Valparaiso   Mendoza

Santiago   Buenos Aires   Montevideo

ARGENTINA

Rio de la Plata

Colorado R.   Bahia Blanca

0 _____ 500

Miles

⊙ Capital cities

FALKLAND IS.
(Br.)

Str. of Magellan

Punta Arenas
(Magallanes)

South America, 1975

CAPE HORN

Members of the Senate Watergate committee. Seated: Howard Baker and Sam Ervin, chairman.
Standing: Lowell Weicker, Daniel Inouye, Herman Talmadge, and Edward Gurney.

same persons who had tried to "bug" or burgle the office of the Democratic National Committee proved also to have been involved in another burglary: that of the office of a Los Angeles psychiatrist, one of whose patients had been Daniel Ellsberg. A former employee of the CIA, Ellsberg had appropriated for his own use a secret government document: a long history of the Vietnam war, written especially for former Secretary of Defense Robert McNamara and known as "the Pentagon Papers." Ellsberg had delivered it to the *New York Times* for publication. The Nixon administration had been eager to procure (no matter how) evidence derogatory to Ellsberg for the Department of Justice's prosecutors to use when the case came to trial. When the trial opened, President Nixon and his assistant John Ehrlichman secretly and improperly offered the judge the directorship of the Federal Bureau of Investigation. The prosecution's failure to inform the defense of the activities conducted in its behalf led to the collapse of the government's case. Hush-money from the CREEP proceeds had been paid to the teams of burglars.

Independently of the growing Watergate scandal, the Nixon administration found itself deeply embarrassed by the evidence produced, during an inquiry into charges of corruption in Maryland, that Vice-President Spiro Agnew, once governor of that state, had taken "kick-backs" from contractors even after accepting his high federal office, and that he was guilty of income-tax evasion. A Federal judge in Maryland before whom Agnew's case was to be tried agreed to accept a Justice Department recommendation whereby Agnew was permitted to sign a memorandum admitting the charges against him in exchange for an agreement that he not be prosecuted. He resigned as Vice-President and went free amidst a good deal of public feeling that the wealthy and powerful could command "special deals" and avoid paying the penalty for their criminal acts. Yet there were also many who agreed with the Attorney-General, Elliot Richardson, who argued that the disgrace itself was punishment enough, and that no purpose would have been served in bringing Agnew to trial. Using a new constitutional amendment for the first time in history, Nixon then appointed as Vice-President Gerald Ford, Republican leader of the House of Representatives, and both houses of the Congress confirmed him.

But Nixon too, it appeared, had at least "avoided" if not "evaded" income taxes. He had taken a large deduction for the gift to the federal government of his papers as Vice-President during the Eisenhower administration, but the papers had been donated after such deductions were illegal and the deed of gift had been back-dated. He owed the United States almost half a million dollars. He had managed altogether to avoid paying state income tax in either New York or California. Large sums of public money had been spent on his two luxurious private residences, one in Florida and the other in California. His friend Charles Rebozo, a Florida banker, had handled a large sum of money contributed to the Nixon campaign by the mysterious millionaire, Howard Hughes, in a fashion that raised serious questions. Grave public doubts were arising about the integrity of the President and his associates.

Meanwhile John Dean, Special Counsel to President Nixon, had accused Nixon himself and his two chief aides, J. R. Haldeman and Ehrlichman, as well as Mitchell, of having ordered a "cover-up" of the original Watergate break-in. For a time it was Dean's word against theirs. But then, almost accidentally, it emerged from the testimony of a relatively minor official, Alexander Butterfield, that Nixon had installed a system of tape recorders in his White House office and that verbatim permanent records of his conversations with his aides existed. Soon Special Prosecutor Cox found himself locked in battle with the White House in an effort to obtain these tapes, unprecedented sources of vital evidence. Pleading executive privilege, Nixon ordered Attorney-General Richardson to dismiss Cox. Richardson and his second-in-command, William Ruckelshaus, refused and resigned. The next-ranking officer of the Justice Department complied, and Cox was fired. But this "Saturday-night massacre," as it was quickly christened, aroused a furious outburst of public disapproval.

To appease it, Nixon consented to turn over certain tapes to the Federal Judge, John Sirica, who had jurisdiction over the original Watergate case. He also found himself obliged to appoint a new Special Prosecutor—Leon Jaworski—as successor to Cox. He had to accept the resignations of Haldeman and Ehrlichman. The first transcripts of the tapes were made public, revealing the President of the United States (despite the numerous "expletives deleted") conversing with his aides in the language of the locker-room if not of the gutter. There was an eighteen-minute gap in one of the tapes. Who had caused it? And there were hundreds—perhaps thousands—more tapes, which might or might not have recorded important conversations. For months on end, the President, hiring and firing one expert lawyer after another, continued to claim that exposure of the tapes would adversely affect national security and infringe upon presidential privilege.

By the time the Supreme Court, by an eight-to-nothing decision, ruled that Nixon would have to surrender the tapes, the Judiciary Committee of the House of Representatives was well advanced on an inquiry into the advisability of impeaching Nixon. They too had long been demanding the tapes. And before Nixon complied with the Supreme Court's decision, he was forced to admit what he had so long and so often denied: that he had not only known of the Watergate "coverup"

but had ordered it. In August 1974, the House committee voted to recommend impeachment, which the Senate would overwhelmingly have approved. Faced with the certainty of becoming the first president in American history to be ousted by the elaborate process provided by the Constitution, Nixon resigned, and retired into private life with the threat of prosecution apparently hanging over him. The openness and good humor of his successor, Gerald Ford, contrasted with Nixon's own secretive and vindictive personality, all too well known by now to the public, which had had the unparalleled experience of reading the transcripts of the tapes.

With a general sigh of relief after the apparently interminable ordeal, the American public had just exchanged a round of congratulations about how well the "system" had worked, when President Ford, contrary to an earlier undertaking, gave Nixon full presidential pardon for any acts he might have committed as president, thereby freeing him from any possible criminal prosecution. Ford explained that "no purpose" could have been served by leaving Nixon open to trial and possible punishment. Many accepted the thesis that Nixon had indeed "suffered enough." Yet Ford's popularity diminished markedly, as public cynicism about equal justice—already aroused by the Agnew case—received a tremendous new impetus. President and Vice-President, apostles of "law and order," had both been forced to resign in disgrace as law-breakers. The trial of Mitchell, Haldeman, and Ehrlichman (with two lesser figures) followed late in 1974, with some feeling that it was not "fair" to prosecute the underlings when the boss had gone free. But Nixon's serious illness and physical inability to testify, combined with the guilty verdict rendered by the jury for the three chief defendants, convinced many that in the main justice had not been thwarted.

There remained serious questions about the "system," especially after the appointment and congressional confirmation of Nelson Rockefeller, ex-Governor of New York, whom Ford selected as his Vice-President. Now neither President nor Vice-President had been elected. It was not only unprecedented; it was deeply troublesome. And Rockefeller's enormous wealth, and the immunity it gave him to the problems of mankind generally, worried many who had no doubts of his integrity or his ability. Others deplored the light sentences given John Dean and others who had collaborated with the authorities on Watergate as compared with the severe sentences served by the lesser men who had committed the burglaries. Many believed that there were other Nixon "White House horrors" (the term was John Mitchell's) that had never been discovered and now never would be.

Historians would long be puzzled over many unsolved riddles. Why, for instance, did Nixon ever order his conversations to be recorded? Of course, he did have great hopes that he would go down in history as a great president. But could he really have believed that the revelations on the tapes of his personal qualities—

coarseness and brutal overbearingness—would have given him the reputation he sought? And why—having made the tapes—did he not order them destroyed, as the net closed around him? Had he done so, perhaps there would never have been evidence enough to convince the Congress that he should be impeached. And above all, how was it that a man of such unquestioned talents and so many qualifications for public service could also have been so mean, small, deceptive, and criminal? By the time of his downfall, the United States government had been virtually paralyzed domestically and seriously handicapped abroad for almost two years, in the face of grave economic and political problems.

The Changing of the Guard: Britain and Western Europe

Nineteen seventy-three and 1974 saw a turnabout if not an actual overturn in every major country of the European Economic Community or the North Atlantic Treaty Organization. Calling an election in autumn 1973 with the expectation of victory, Prime Minister Heath lost his majority. But the labor party under Harold Wilson also failed to get one, although Wilson obtained a few more seats than Heath. Holding a balance of power, the Liberals refused to enter into a coalition with either party, and Wilson formed a minority government. Early in 1974, Wilson called a second election, this time winning a tiny majority, still too small to allow the Labourites full freedom to put through their program. To restrict them was apparently the aim of the electorate, which seemed unready for such extreme social measures as the proposed "wealth tax." A capital levy, this tax, according to its official proponents, would have required all British subjects to estimate the value of all their posessions and to pay to the government an annual percentage of the total self-assessment in addition to the already heavy income taxes. The revenue to be expected was not large, but the goals were rather social than economic. Many of those with property in land, for example, would have been compelled to pay each year in taxes a sum exceeding their total annual incomes: a measure that would soon have destroyed, as it was intended to, an entire social class.

Wilson's regime rested, he proclaimed, upon a new "social contract" between the unions and the Labour party, whereby the unions would abstain from striking so long as Wilson remained in power. But the government's ability to hold the large communist-dominated unions in line remained highly doubtful. Hamstrung by its small majority, the Labour party devoted itself merely to getting by. Inflation continued to worsen, running at an annual rate of about 20 percent in 1974, and sure to grow even more serious in 1975. Wages rose, but real wages—which depend upon productivity—lagged behind prices. The key problems: overmanning (what Americans sometimes call featherbedding), the clinging to unnecessary positions in factories, the failure to curb the dictatorship of the unions, the neglect by

management of investment for modernization while plant and equipment became ever more obsolete: all these remained notable symptoms of the "British disease." The partners in the European Economic Community viewed with dismay the Labour party's commitment to seek a popular vote in a nationwide referendum on Britain's continued membership. IRA terrorism in England itself increased in a series of horrifying bombing episodes.

Across the channel, President Pompidou of France died early in April 1974. In the enormously powerful job of President of the Fifth Republic, he had tried to combine personal direction of foreign and military policy—so long the province of de Gaulle—with his own special concern for economic development. Pragmatically he had reversed de Gaulle's veto on British entry into the Common Market and had worked energetically for industrial expansion and towards the eventual social modernization of France as well. By mid-May he had been succeeded by Valéry Giscard d'Estaing, who had first knocked out the Gaullist candidate, Chaban-Delmas, in a primary, and then gone on to triumph by a narrow margin (50.7 to 49.3 percent) over the candidate of the entire combined left, Mitterand. Not a Gaullist but the chief of his own small party, which had always collaborated with the Gaullists, Giscard was the product of the most elite French academic institutions for educating bureaucrats. Young (forty-eight), handsome, aristocratic, and articulate, he hoped to steer France on a middle course between what western Europe regarded as the unrestrained capitalism of the United States, with its inadequate public transportation and health systems, on the one hand, and, on the other hand, the morass of bureaucracy characteristic of left-wing governments. Personally Giscard proved a curious combination: technocratic, impersonal, and informal: discarding traditional formal wear for his own inauguration, abrogating de Gaulle's law against insulting the President, putting an end to wiretapping.

Giscard promised to transform society. He gave important roles in French government to women; made birth-control pills available free under the national health system; reformed the divorce laws; successfully introduced a liberal abortion law; and lowered the voting age to eighteen. To begin to reduce the ever-widening discrepancy between rich and poor, he raised the minimum wage (which still remained very low), passed an unemployment insurance law giving a full year's pay to the unemployed, and increased the income taxes on the rich. But would they pay the taxes? Frenchmen often did not. To celebrate Bastille Day, this man of the right held the celebration in the Place de la Bastille itself instead of in the traditional Champs Élysées. There remained certain key and intractable problems to wrestle with: to decentralize France so that Paris would no longer dominate the country politically and economically and drain off all the best professional personnel from the provinces; to give the regions their own assemblies with their own taxing and development programs. Yet the rigidity of French society, both social and geographical, made it difficult for any government to obtain the assent of the French to such vigorous changes. Giscard enjoyed only the very briefest honeymoon with the French people, and by the end of 1974 was already the target for general sniping.

Some of the projects chiefly associated with de Gaulle's policy of *grandeur* were abandoned or modified: French nuclear testing in the atmosphere, the mass production of the supersonic Concorde airplane, the intervention in Canadian internal affairs, even the steady series of rebuffs to the United States. At Giscard's meeting with President Ford on Martinique late in 1974, several outstanding issues left over from the Gaullist period were apparently settled. Whether the general international crisis, combined with the threat to Giscard's programs from the French left, would give him time to prove himself remained a major question in January 1975.

The West Germans, too, most stable of all the western European governments, went through a dramatic and unexpected shift in leadership when Willy Brandt resigned in mid-1974. Perhaps those foreigners who had all along taken it for granted that Brandt was the incarnation of the "good German" were most surprised. Brandt's achievements were indeed admirable: as Mayor of Berlin, with a staunch anti-Nazi and anti-communist record, he alone perhaps could have restrained his West Berliners from rising against the Soviets in sympathy with the Hungarian revolution of 1956 or in protest against the building of the Berlin Wall in 1961: uprisings that might well have had a catastrophic effect. He had easily won the premiership in 1969 and 1972, and successful détente with the USSR and East Germany had properly led to his winning the Nobel Prize for Peace. Yet domestic problems had always annoyed Brandt. Seeing himself as above the battle, he found himself embroiled with the labor unions over questions of wages, and increasingly menaced by the radical left inside his own Social Democratic party and out. A curious indecisiveness seemed to seize hold of him at moments of crisis, and he tended to postpone key decisions and to pay too little attention to detail. Perhaps it was because of these traits that he failed to see the danger latent in the presence within his inner circle of a certain Guillaume, who proved to be an East German spy. In the furor that followed the discovery, Brandt resigned and was succeeded by Helmut Schmidt.

Experienced in the two most difficult posts in the West German government—the Ministries of Defence and of Finance—an excellent debater with a keen mind, a Social Democrat standing well to the right of the center of his party, Schmidt opposed any doctrinaire program of nationalization of industry. He had coined the campaign slogan of 1972: "Five percent inflation is less of a tragedy than five percent unemployment," and the low figure in each case could serve as a token of the economic well-being of West Germany relative to any other country. Lacking Brandt's personal appeal, bored and impatient with detail, Schmidt was nonetheless by far the ablest possible choice as successor. Brandt's willingness to stay on as Party Chairman would prove immeasurably valuable to him. Nor would the East Germans quickly regain in Bonn the trust they had forfeited through the Guillaume affair.

The Italian political and economic crisis, grave enough in 1972, deepened and became chronic in 1973 and 1974. The once prosperous economy seemed sick at its very heart, and public order barely survived the constant reshuffling of the cabinet. Ostensibly the major political issue during these two years was the general referendum over the retention of the divorce law of 1970. This had negated the provision of Mussolini's Concordat of 1929 with the Vatican (still in force), according to which the state gave civil sanction to the sacrament of marriage. By the standards of most other countries the law of 1970 was still far from liberal, authorizing divorce only on the grounds of mental illness, criminal activity, or a five-year desertion. Meanwhile, the Vatican had modernized its annulment procedures by reducing the fees and eliminating the required preliminary five-year waiting period. Italian husbands tended to apply for annulments rather than divorces, since an annulment meant that the marriage had never taken place and required no alimony or support of children. After an intense political campaign, with the Church mobilizing all its forces against the confirmation of the divorce law, and the left trying to avoid the vote altogether, the referendum was held, and the divorce law approved.

But actually the Italian illness was far more deep-seated. A long postal strike cut communications, and newspapers published pictures of piles of undelivered letters being used to stoke furnaces. Sporadic activities by right-wing extremists raised the specter of a possible new fascist coup. Only massive loans of capital from abroad staved off bankruptcy. Even though it was a modern industrialized consumer society, Italy seemed to be failing in confidence, stability, and capacity to regulate itself.

In Spain, a serious illness of Generalissimo Franco in his early eighties and the temporary takeover of his duties by Prince Juan Carlos falsely aroused hopes or fears that change might at last be imminent there. Franco—it was announced—recovered, however, and his characteristically repressive policies continued unabated. What might emerge after the inevitable eventually happened was perhaps in part signalized by events in neighboring Portugal.

Overturn: Portugal and Greece

In Portugal, the continued drain on human and financial resources imposed by the interminable wars to retain the African colonies intact eventually permeated important groups among the army officers, the only force in the nation capable of precipitating a change. A coup headed by General Spinola overthrew the Caetano government—which had never managed to liberalize significantly the traditional policies of Salazar—and a junta of seven army officers came to power. An extraordinary outburst of public enthusiasm followed, with noisy parades, demonstrations of delight at the restoration of free speech after almost half a century, and prolonged meetings in public and in factories and workshops as to the proper forms that society should take. There was almost no bloodshed, although members of the hated political police were sometimes hunted down and killed.

Gradually the nation sobered up. The Communist party, so long outlawed, proved to be highly organized and well financed. Late in 1974 its influence led to an overturn within the junta. Spinola himself and three additional members were forced out. The remaining three "elected" one of their own number, Costa Gomes, as President. Their spokesman explained that "in every revolution the laws adapt to match the facts that the revolution creates." With the governmental committee of coordination dominated by the communists, the Portuguese political future seemed clouded. Elections were scheduled for spring, 1975. If they should be held and conducted democratically, it was doubtful whether the communists could win, even with strong left-wing allies. For that reason, it was widely predicted that the elections would somehow be postponed, or their impact minimized in advance.

The new government proceeded with speed to deal with the pressing problems of the colonies. The agreement to make Guinea-Bissau independent was reached in September 1974. Mozambique was far more difficult, and resentful whites there vainly protested with violence against "abandonment" by Lisbon, eliciting counter-violence from the blacks. Even for Angola, with three separate and mutually hostile black liberation groups, a preliminary settlement embracing all forces was reached early in 1975. These were revolutionary events indeed.

An equally revolutionary overturn took place in the Greece governed by the colonels' dictatorial regime. It was precipitated by events in Cyprus—80 percent Greek and 20 percent Turkish in population—an independent nation under the presidency of Archbishop Makarios, where a United Nations force was protecting the Turkish minority against Greek mistreatment, and a guerrilla movement (EOKA) in favor of union with Greece agitated in the countryside. To Cyprus the Greek government had sent a small force of a few hundred army officers, ostensibly to train the Cypriot National Guard, but in fact often engaging in pro-EOKA activities. The Greek government refused Makarios' request to recall these officers and an attempted EOKA coup followed, ousting Makarios, who fled abroad. Instantly the Turkish government intervened, to protect its fellow Turks, landing forces on the northern coast of Cyprus and fanning out. The colonels'

government in Greece—faced with the prospect of war with Turkey—collapsed, and former Prime Minister Karamanlis, long in exile in Paris, returned to head a new democratic regime. "At last we owe something good to the Turks" was apparently a typical reaction among the people of Greece.

But the Turkish advance eventually extended to 40 percent of the island, and almost two hundred thousand Greek Cypriot refugees fled into the remaining area. There was much suffering. A man of peace who had always sought good relations with Turkey, Karamanlis could not appear to recognize a conquest of so much of Cyprus by force, while the difficulties were compounded by the feebleness of the Turkish government itself, which, despite the successes of its army, remained a mere "caretaker" regime without sufficient political support to negotiate effectively. The eventual future of Cyprus remained uncertain, with some form of partition almost a certainty, in order to guarantee the safety of the Turkish minority. Meanwhile, Greek Cypriots blamed the United States for not protecting them against the Turkish invasion, and for failing to intervene to prevent Turkish Cypriot refugees from being moved into the houses and shops of Greeks who had fled from the Turkish-occupied territory.

And the continental Greeks blamed the United States for having supported the colonels' regime, and for all their other troubles. Karamanlis, meanwhile, easily won a secure majority in a free election and held a referendum on the monarchy, in which the majority favored a republic. On firm political and constitutional foundations, he then proceeded, late in 1974, to initiate orderly judicial processes against the leaders of the former dictatorial regime. Whatever the injustices that Cypriot Greeks might be suffering (and they were considerable, though Makarios returned safely to resume control of the government), much of the blame was to be laid at the door of the colonels and of the EOKA conspirators. And beyond that, of course, stretching into the deep past lay the deep memory of Christian suffering under Ottoman rule and a Greek-Turkish hatred that seemed ineradicable. In the immediate future the damage to NATO at its southeastern flank was serious indeed. But the USSR, which was caught off base by the Cypriot and Greek events, had not visibly capitalized on the situation by early 1975.

IV 1973–1974: International Tensions
The Middle East, Oil, and Energy

In October 1973, the new war in the Middle East that everybody feared actually erupted. Its outbreak took even the Israelis by surprise and contributed enormously to the difficulties of the entire world. The Egyptians attacked across the Suez Canal, pushing back the Israelis in the territory on Sinai that they had taken in 1967 and since occupied. The Syrians attacked in the Golan heights. Seriously threatened and suffering

Golda Meir and Henry Kissinger, February 1974.

large casualties, the Israelis managed to hold off the Syrians while establishing a bridgehead on the Egyptian side of the canal. They cut off supplies to the Egyptian forces on the other side, thus threatening them with collapse and capture. Then they advanced into Syria towards Damascus, capturing the city of Quneitra. Henry Kissinger, who by then had become Nixon's Secretary of State while continuing to hold his job as White House adviser on foreign policy, engaged in frenzied "shuttle diplomacy" between Israel and the Arab capitals and managed to produce a cease-fire on both fronts. The Israelis were prevented from maximizing their military advantage in Egypt and had to withdraw to the east bank of the canal. Truce lines were established between the Israelis and both the Egyptians and the Syrians, while UN forces were inserted as buffers between the belligerents on both fronts. During 1974 Golda Meir was replaced as Premier by Itzhak Rabin, the first Israeli-born politician to reach the top.

But the truce only stopped the active combat, and minimized the immediate danger of U.S.-Soviet confrontation. The Arab countries, showing a surprising unity of purpose, together with the non-Arab countries (Iran, Venezuela) in the Organization of Petroleum Exporting Countries (OPEC) agreed not only to raise the prices of oil but also initially to boycott certain nations (the United States, the Netherlands) whom they regarded as pro-Israeli. It was these steps—and chiefly the enor-

mously higher prices for all forms of petroleum products—that triggered the worldwide energy crisis that came on top of all the other economic troubles from which the nations were suffering: inflation and a simultaneous slow-down of output ("stagflation"), plus growing unemployment and recession in the developed nations, and outright misery as a result of shortages elsewhere.

Of course the nature and degree of pain varied from nation to nation. In the United States, with its wasteful habits of burning huge amounts of gasoline in overlarge automobiles occupied by one person at a time, there were shortages, annoyance, a sharp and painful rise in prices, a tendency to blame American oil companies, whose profit-statements showed all too clearly that they too were benefiting from the OPEC actions, and a severe political problem for the discredited Nixon government and for Ford's administration as its successor. The usual political and financial horse-trading went on, and early in 1975, with recession spreading and the newly-elected overwhelmingly Democratic (but not necessarily competent or public-spirited) Congress feeling its oats as it faced a tired and unimaginative Republican administration, both the short-range palliatives and the long-range measures not even yet devised or discussed remained a matter of grave doubt.

As we have seen above, the nations of western

Europe were already suffering to varying degrees from a variety of economic ills when the oil producers' actions hit them. Since none of them had immediate sources of oil outside the OPEC, the impact varied directly with the degree of existing dislocation: it was worst in Italy and in Britain, where already gravely unfavorable trade balances were now swollen grotesquely and dangerously. It was less serious in France and in West Germany. Off the North Sea coast of Britain, large resources of underseas oil were still in the process of exploitation, and would not begin to flow until approximately 1980. It was predicted that amounts sufficient for Britain's own needs would be available. But it would still be necessary to export some of this chiefly light-grade oil in exchange for heavier grades purchasable only abroad. A strongly revived Scottish Nationalist movement, moreover, was claiming for Scotland the future revenues from the oil. It seemed probable that any British government would soon have to make some concession, at least, to these demands, perhaps in the form of larger autonomy for Scotland and the use of some of the future cash in Scottish development, managed and planned by Scots. Moreover, the revenues for the future oil were being largely mortgaged in advance to meet the huge national debt, estimated at $200 billion by 1980, the interest alone on which would be $8 billion annually. Finally, once the North Sea oil should be available, it was perfectly possible for the OPEC nations to cut their prices or raise their own production or both and thus greatly reduce the beneficial effects of the new resources. Prime Minister Wilson was planning to nationalize the underseas wells, forming a British National Oil Corporation to manage them, and reimbursing the private investors by negotiation.

Outside of Europe, the actions of the oil producers fell most severely upon Japan, India, and the developing "third world" nations without oil of their own. Totally dependent on imports, and already suffering from social and economic dislocation, Japan suffered a grave setback. Japanese unions, traditionally unwilling to strike, altered their policies in 1974, when an effective transport strike won a 30 percent pay raise for transport workers. The rapidly rising standard of living of the boom years eroded the Japanese "will to work" and the proverbial discipline of the labor force. At high levels of management, profiteering, price-fixing, and tax evasion led to scandals. Weakened also by internal feuding, the governing Liberal party suffered severe damage. Premier Tanaka fell and was succeeded after much infighting by a relatively unknown figure, Miki. The growth rate of the Japanese economy—averaging between 8 and 13 percent annually for two decades—sank to 2.5 percent in 1974. Chaotic inflation made Japanese cities the most expensive in the world, and abroad Japanese industrial products were facing real competition for the first time as the costs of production in Japan forced prices up.

In India, where petroleum products formed a major ingredient in fertilizer, the rise in oil prices sharpened the always critical food position. Public opinion, always volatile, and moved by scandals within the Congress party and the government, turned sharply against Mrs. Gandhi. In two states, Gujerat and Bihar, Congress party governments were overthrown. Rival members of the Congress party built up cliques of supporters. The assassination of the Minister of Railways, Mishra, in his home state of Bihar late in 1974 reflected the emergence into the open of such a feud, as well as public resentment of Mishra's own self-aggrandizement and autocratic behavior. As a prominent disciple of Mahatma Gandhi charged, democratic values in India seemed in the process of disappearing, and the Prime Minister had become a fussy and indecisive old woman, unable to keep her corrupt machine functioning. In the usual fashion, the United States was blamed for everything that had gone wrong, while India's policy grew more and more favorable to the Arab states that had touched off the worst of the crisis. First among the nations of the world, India granted quasi-diplomatic status to the Palestinian Liberation Organization of Yassir Arafat. Even more drastically affected by the oil price rise, Bangladesh became economically a national basket case.

Immediately south of the Sahara, black Africa—where drought had caused fearful losses in human lives and in the lives of the cattle on which the region depended, and was difficult to alleviate because of the poor communications—was also dealt a severe blow by the OPEC actions. Drought extended to Ethiopia as well, where discontent flared up and Eritrean separatism was rampant. During 1974 an army officers' coup brought down the aged Haile Selassie in the name of liberty and reform. The rebel junta then executed some sixty prominent Ethiopians and killed their own leader in a quarrel that ended in a shoot-out. Except for recognizably revolutionary jargon, there was no real clue as to their future program for the country, which had been allowed for the most part to remain outside the twentieth century.

As for the Arab oil-producing nations themselves, they profited mightily from the rise in prices. Saudi Arabia, for example, with a production of 9 billion barrels a day, almost half that of the entire Middle East, moved rapidly to take over the Arabian-American Oil Company (Aramco), buying out its assets and making it a service agency for its own national company, Petromin. With $20 billion a day in revenue accruing, the problem was how to invest it. Some of it, of course, would go into development plans, notably petrochemical plants, and there was naturally a plethora of foreigners attempting to sell the Saudis one scheme or another to spend their vast sums. Moving cautiously, their government put a lot of its cash into very short-term paper in the West, producing unprecedented financial imbalances there. It was calculated that the oil producers within a finite time could, if they chose, buy out every share of stock in every stock exchange in the world, and own everything, at least nominally. How would they use their money? Tiny states like Kuwait or Abu Dhabi had even graver problems. Not all oil producers could emulate the Shah of Persia, lord over a huge country territorially, who had embarked on vast development schemes, was rapidly building up a strong army and air force, and was self-consciously laying claim to the ancient prestige and power of Persia in the Middle East as a whole. Supporting the Kurdish rebels against the government of neighboring Iraq, with which he disputed hegemony in the Persian Gulf region, the Shah was otherwise moving closer to the Arab nations, fellow Muslims, though Sunni, not Shiite like himself, in their conflict with Israel.

Peace with Israel no longer depended chiefly—as it had after the 1967 war—upon territorial settlements with respect to Israeli borders. At the heart of the question now was a settlement of the Palestinian question. In the wake of the 1973 war, Arafat and his PLO—terrorism and all—emerged as unquestionably the leading representatives of the Palestinians. In 1974 a "summit" meeting of Arab chiefs of state accepted Arafat in place of King Hussein of Jordan as spokesman for Palestine, and Hussein had to acquiesce. Promptly the UN General Assembly, dominated by the anti-American, anti-Israeli, pro-Arab states, invited Arafat to address it. With his pistol visible on his hip, he made an impassioned speech and received a tumultuous ovation. From the oil states he could count on all the financing he could possibly need. It seemed doubtful if the Israeli government had yet come to terms with the necessity of swallowing the bitter pill and negotiating with the leader of the terrorists. If negotiation did not begin reasonably soon, still another war in the Middle East seemed—early in 1975—altogether probable.

If it should come, it would raise more sharply than ever before the extent of the American commitment to help Israel. Would American public opinion, in the wake of general disillusionment with foreign adventure after Vietnam, support even the most limited armed action in the Middle East? It seemed unlikely, unless, as President Ford and Mr. Kissinger both hinted late in 1974, "strangulation" of American interests was threatened by the Arab position on oil. The reluctance of American officials to speculate on the subject was understandable, but it was certain that such speculation would continue unchecked.

The USSR and the U.S.: Middle East and Far East

Largely unaffected by the OPEC actions because of its own ample oil reserves, the USSR suffered no internal crisis in 1973 and 1974. True: its leaders were aging, and at the end of 1974 rumors of Brezhnev's ill health were circulating widely. Even Kremlin-watchers were not sure whether at sixty-eight he was merely tired, or having diplomatic illnesses that permitted him, for

Arafat, head of the PLO, addresses the United Nations, November 14, 1974

instance, not to go to Egypt or receive an Australian Premier, or whether it was something more serious. In the face of what seemed a general popular reluctance to have more than two children at most, the Soviet government embarked on a propaganda campaign for a three-child family, in order to produce enough population to inhabit the still vacant lands within the USSR, and yet not enough to burden Soviet womanhood with too many offspring. The housing shortages, the need for women to work, might well make many women reluctant to enlarge their families. Many of the uninhabited lands were in fact uninhabitable. Such increases in population as were being registered came not from Russian or Ukrainian families but from those of the Asian peoples of the USSR. Yet "opening up" the lands by 1990 formed a major goal of the regime, which urged on "shock troops" from student brigades and young communists to move northward along the Baltic and White Sea coasts. A new railroad line running parallel to the Trans-Siberian, but far to the north and away from the Chinese frontier and Chinese rockets, also had high priority.

To the student of Russian and Soviet thought it was of extreme interest in 1973 and 1974 to read the publications of the two leaders of Soviet intellectual dissent, Solzhenitsyn and the physicist, Andrei Sakharov. Solzhenitsyn denounced the Soviet state, of course, but as essentially alien to the proper Russian spirit: Marxist, hence western, and far too highly industrialized, also a western vice. He dreamed of a Russia sprinkled with small, quiet cities where cultivated Rus-

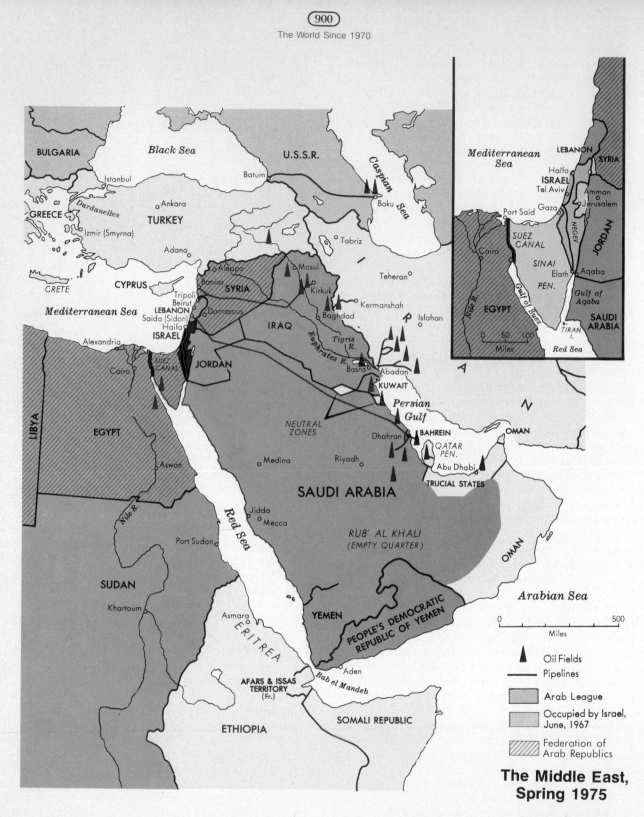

The Middle East, Spring 1975

Oil Fields
Pipelines
Arab League
Occupied by Israel, June, 1967
Federation of Arab Republics

sians might live Russian lives according to the national genius. In short, he sounded very much like a nineteenth-century Slavophile, and there could be no doubt that his exile to Switzerland with his family was extremely painful to him. Sakharov, on the other hand, urged that the Soviet authorities ease state capitalism and bureaucratic rigidity, and move toward the west in granting freedoms. Sakharov sounded like a nineteenth-century westerner, an internationalist opposing Solzhenitsyn's nationalism.

Relations between the United States and the USSR stayed pretty much on dead center, despite a visit to Moscow by Nixon in the waning days of his presidency, undertaken, like so much else in those days, because it would keep him in the public eye and there was nothing he could do at home. "Détente with cosmetics," one observer called it, as no real progress was made toward freedom of communications and the "good-neighborly relations" hailed by the official communiqué. In his turn, President Ford too visited the USSR, meeting Brezhnev at Vladivostok, a curious choice of setting in view of its immediate proximity to China. Although that meeting led to an understanding about the numbers of intercontinental missiles that each party would produce, it was not regarded as real progress toward the limitation of armaments, since the number allotted to each side was far in excess of those already in existence and of any reasonable requirement for security. It ensured the continuation of the cruelly expensive armaments race.

As for the trade agreement, it was finally wrecked after approval by the United States Senate, by the Soviet refusal to tie to its terms any published concession on the numbers of Jews who might be allowed to leave the USSR, and on the conditions to be attached to their departure. Although the Soviet authorities had been willing quietly and without publicity to relax their regulations and to continue their relaxation, they could not accept the publication of the evidence that they were acceding to American "interference" in their internal policies, and thus perhaps encourage other groups to try to leave the USSR. The wreckage of the agreement could be laid in large part at the door of Senator Henry Jackson of Washington, who insisted that the Trade Agreement include a formal provision about the Soviet Jews. He overreached himself. Moreover, the $300 million credit to be extended the USSR by the Export-Import Bank was probably too small to make the Soviet authorities swallow what they viewed as an affront. If the USSR was to sell its acquiescence and bow to American demands about the Jews, it would not do so as cheaply as that. Early in 1975 it remained to be seen how gravely, if at all, the failure to reach a trade agreement would actually affect American-Soviet trade in practice.

During the Arab-Israeli war of 1973 there occurred, as had been feared, a confrontation between the United States and the USSR, which might easily have been serious. American armed forces were put upon an emergency alert in anticipation of a Soviet troop movement that, as it turned out, did not take place. There was considerable public criticism of Nixon's and Kissinger's apparent bellicosity, but once the incident was closed it was rapidly forgotten. Kissinger's preemption of the chief, and sometimes the sole, activity as intermediary and peacemaker between the belligerents also aroused Soviet misgivings, as it became all too apparent to the world that even the left-wing Syrians preferred to keep their Soviet friends at a distance if possible, while the other Arab states, with variations, were positively pro-American. But no arrangements in the Middle East that did not have Soviet approval could possibly succeed in the long run. Gradually the differences between the two great powers simmered down to a matter of preference as to the mode of conducting negotiations between Israel and the Arabs: the United States favoring Kissinger's personal diplomacy and repeated visits between capitals while keeping the threads of the discussion entirely in his own hands, the USSR preferring an international conference at Geneva in which its own representatives would have full participation.

It was, however, clear that neither great power wanted a test of force or even a test of wills over the Middle Eastern issue. Yet, as long as a real settlement remained in suspense and the possibility of a new war grew steadily, a real chance remained for a major American-Soviet dispute over the issue. A factor not often enough taken into account, perhaps, was the new Soviet strategic position in the Mediterranean, Red Sea, Persian Gulf, and Indian Ocean. With access to Arab Mediterranean ports, complete cooperation from Somalia on the horn of Africa, friendly assistance from the republic of South Yemen including the strategic port of Aden, a naval base at the head of the gulf in southern Iraq, and free use of certain Indian port facilities, the naval strength of the USSR could for the first time in history move freely in these waters. Indeed the Soviets had largely occupied the strategic naval positions abandoned in the late 1960s by the British in their withdrawal from the Middle East. If and when the Suez Canal should be reopened, there would be an instant further quantum jump in Soviet mobility between the Mediterranean and the Indian Ocean.

The UN might, as it did in 1971, piously declare the Indian Ocean a "zone of peace forever," but the contrary—as so often with UN declarations—was in fact the case. The United States response to the potential threat was to extend the operations of the Seventh Fleet from the Pacific to include the Indian Ocean, and to utilize bases in Thailand, on the Northwest Cape in Australia, and on the small Indian Ocean island of Diego Garcia (a communications base since 1971), where desalinization plants were built and runways extended. The government of India and the Indian press made loud objection to this, with no basis in international law, since Diego Garcia lay more than 1,000 miles from India, which was directly assisting the Soviet fleet in its own ports. The real objection was Soviet, not Indian, since Indian Ocean bases put Soviet territory within the reach of submarines carrying Polaris missiles. American bases might perhaps be supplemented by remaining British installations and concessions in the Maldives, Oman, and Simonstown in South Africa. The Soviet build-up alarmed the Chinese, on whose southern flank the Russians were busily bringing together India, Afghanistan, and Iraq in a grouping opposed to Iran, Pakistan (an ally of China), and, of

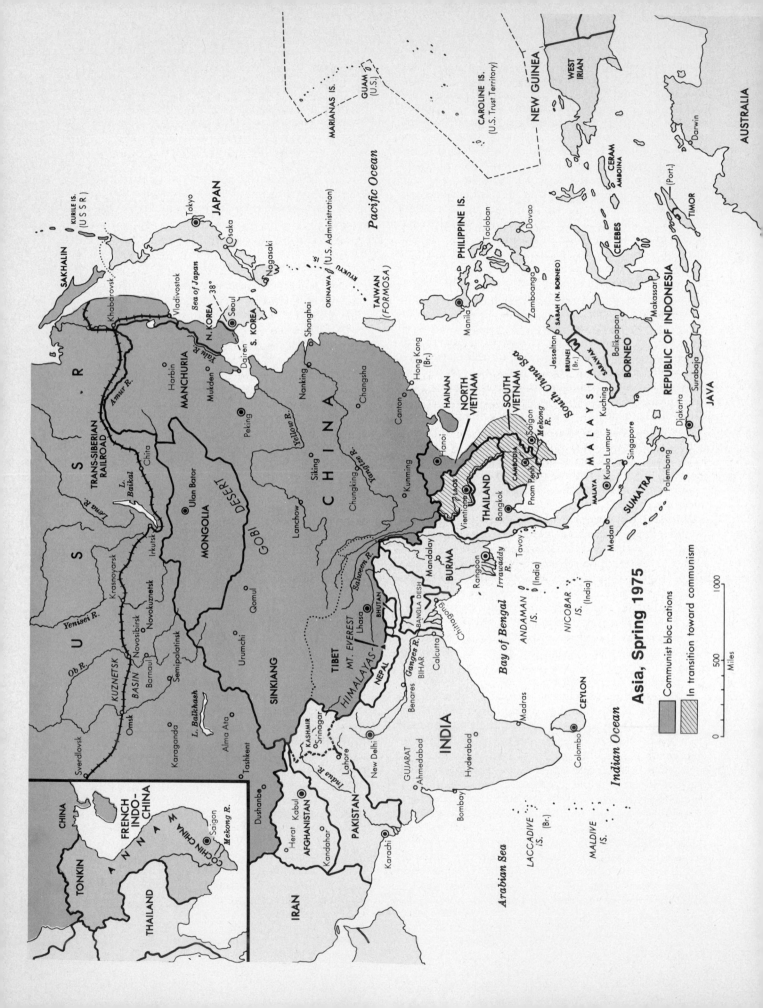

Asia, Spring 1975

Communist bloc nations

In transition toward communism

0   500   1000
            Miles

Pacific Ocean

KURILE IS.
(USSR)

SAKHALIN

JAPAN
Tokyo
Osaka
Nagasaki
Sea of Japan
38°
N. KOREA
Seoul
S. KOREA
Vladivostok
Khabarovsk

U   S   S   R

TRANS-SIBERIAN
RAILROAD
Amur R.
Chita
L. Baikal
Irkutsk
Lena R.

Yenisei R.
Krasnoyarsk
Novosibirsk
Novokuznetsk
Barnaul
Semipalatinsk
KUZNETSK
BASIN
Omsk
Sverdlovsk
Karaganda
L. Balkhash
Alma Ata
Tashkent
Ob R.

Dushanbe
Herat Kabul
Kandahar
AFGHANISTAN
IRAN
Karachi
PAKISTAN
Lahore
Srinagar
KASHMIR
Indus R.
New Delhi
GUJARAT
Ahmedabad
Bombay
Hyderabad
Madras
INDIA
BIHAR
Benares
Calcutta
Ganges R.
BANGLA DESH
NEPAL
HIMALAYAS
MT. EVEREST
Lhasa
BHUTAN
TIBET
SINKIANG
Urumchi
Qomul
MONGOLIA
Ulan Bator
GOBI DESERT
Harbin
MANCHURIA
Mukden
Dairen
Peking
Lanchow
Siking
Yellow R.
CHINA
Nanking
Shanghai
Changsha
Canton
Kunming
Chungking
Yangtze R.
Saiween R.
Mandalay
BURMA
Rangoon
Irrawaddy R.
Tavoy
Chittagong

Bay of Bengal
ANDAMAN IS.
(India)
NICOBAR IS.
(India)
CEYLON
Colombo
LACCADIVE IS. (Br.)
MALDIVE IS.
Arabian Sea
Indian Ocean

HAINAN
NORTH VIETNAM
Hanoi
LAOS
Vientiane
THAILAND
Bangkok
SOUTH VIETNAM
Saigon
CAMBODIA
Pnom Penh
Mekong R.
South China Sea
Hong Kong (Br.)

OKINAWA (U.S. Administration)
RYUKYU IS.
TAIWAN (FORMOSA)
Manila
PHILIPPINE IS.
Tacloban
Davao
Zamboanga

GUAM (U.S.)
MARIANAS IS.
CAROLINE IS.
(U.S. Trust Territory)

NEW GUINEA
WEST IRIAN

MALAYSIA
SABAH (N. BORNEO)
Jesselton
BRUNEI (Br.)
SARAWAK
Kuching
BORNEO
Balikpapan
Makassar
CELEBES
CERAM
AMBOINA
TIMOR (Port.)
REPUBLIC OF INDONESIA
SUMATRA
Medan
Palembang
Djakarta
Surabaja
JAVA
MALAYA
Kuala Lumpur
Singapore

Darwin
AUSTRALIA

CHINA
TONKIN
FRENCH INDO-CHINA
ANNAM
COCHIN CHINA
Saigon
Mekong R.
THAILAND

course, the United States. Gunboat diplomacy was assuming a new importance in these regions during 1973 and 1974, and the Chinese well understood the threat behind Brezhnev's hopes for what he called a "system of collective security in Asia."

East and Southeast Asia

As for the Chinese themselves, they continued their economic advances. With an output of 50 million tons of oil in 1973, China did not suffer from the oil crisis, but was able to export a small amount. Food and cotton were purchased from the United States. Steel production rose to 25 million tons. Complete chemical plants for fertilizers were imported, with American, Japanese, and French technical personnel reluctantly allowed to install them and launch their operations. For the first time, the Chinese government tolerated an unfavorable balance of trade and adopted a policy of deferred payments on debts, paying interest over a five-year period on the balance due. Politically, the most important factors—the increasing age and growing frailty of Mao and Chou—were difficult to assess. After some months in a hospital—while rumors circulated that he had lost his power—Chou reemerged to preside at a major party conference at the beginning of 1975, in which a new constitution was promulgated. It contained no surprises, unless it was that Chou's own "moderate" views had triumphed. After a quarter of a century, he had managed to outlive and overcome all the turmoil of intraparty rivalry. Mao himself was absent from the congress, though his giant portrait brooded over its deliberations, and quotations from his sayings rattled forth at brief intervals throughout. He had gone into a sort of retreat, and yet, perhaps, was still keeping control of China's policies. Speaking in his name, Chou predicted war between the USSR and the United States, and cast the fortunes of the Chinese once more with the "third world."

Elsewhere in Asia—in the two regions where the United States had intervened since World War II—things were going very badly indeed. In Korea, the severe repressiveness of the Park government had led to a veritable persecution of Catholics and other Christians and to an assassination attempt on the Premier, in which his wife was killed. Discussions with the North were broken off amidst gathering mutual suspicion. Each side feared an invasion from the other, and a new and potentially serious quarrel, over some offshore islands not included in the Panmunjom demarcation

agreement, loomed as a further source of possible serious trouble.

In southeast Asia, the war raged out of control in Cambodia, where the "Red Khmer" forces controlled much territory, though only a small portion of the population, and kept up severe pressure on Pnom Penh. The government forces of Lon Nol, supported by a few American military advisers, were about equal in effective numbers (perhaps 60,000) to the insurgents, but the government was inefficient. It could not capitalize on its control of the cities and of the areas nearest to Thailand, or prevent the North Vietnamese and Viet Cong from moving freely in eastern Cambodia. Although the Red Khmers were taking a long time to win, the eventual outcome was not in doubt.

In South Vietnam, where so many billions and so many lives had already been lost, the situation two years after the cease-fire agreement resembled that in Cambodia. Saigon itself was under attack; an important provincial capital had fallen, and Thieu's regime was in deep trouble. President Ford was about to ask the Congress for more money in military aid. Thoroughly sick of the horrible mess they were in, to which the Vietnam policies of the successive administrations of Kennedy, Johnson, Nixon, and Ford had so largely condemned them, the American public had as yet taken no clear position on the question of deeper new involvement. Meanwhile, in Laos, almost without attention in the American press, the Pathet Lao—with strong connections in Hanoi—had made huge gains. Not only did it control two thirds of the territory (with only one third of the population) but within the coalition government it had taken over the key ministries of justice, information, the economy, and foreign affairs. Its chief, Souphanouvong, had refused a deputy premiership and maneuvered for larger powers outside the government. The North Vietnamese operated freely from Laotian bases in their war against Saigon. Had the United States really any further military business in southeast Asia?

Conclusion

This chapter deals not with history in any long-range sense of the term, but with "current events." It reveals a spirit of rising expectations in 1971 and 1972, and one of rapidly falling expectations and increasing disorder in 1973 and 1974. And this general picture, however it might be corrected later on in detail, seemed likely to remain an accurate sketch-graph of world affairs since 1970.

Man's Fate in the Twentieth Century

I Introduction: A Confused and Confusing Age

Among the countless ideas that come to our attention through the printed or spoken word, through symbols, pictures, and musical sounds, it is almost impossible to distinguish those that are characteristic of our own age, that give its flavor or style and establish its "climate of opinion." It is tempting to conclude that this seemingly infinite variety of ideas, spread among countless millions by all the channels of mass communication, is in itself the distinguishing mark of the later twentieth century. Moreover, the historian who relied on evidence from the work of "serious" writers or artists would come to quite different conclusions from one who studied comic strips, popular music, films, and television and radio programs. Yet both sets of evidence would have some things in common, and both would show many dramatic changes between the culture of the 1870s and that of the 1970s.

If a proper Victorian were suddenly catapulted into our own day, he would be startled by the virtual disappearance of old taboos against discussing sexual activities in public and uttering or printing the four-letter Anglo-Saxon words. Perhaps even more disconcerting would be the increasing violence of twentieth-century life, the emergence of a "drug culture" (even though powerful opiates had been widely used to pacify children before the introduction of pure food and drug regulations in the late 1800s), and experiments with communal living (even though many of the nineteenth-century utopian communities had been popularly identified with "free love"). The visitor would soon become aware of the resentments, the frustrations, and the sense of desperation or disorientation that make young people especially revolt against established ways and values. Nothing seems to be sacred any more, as the family, the church, the state, and what used to be considered "civilized" or "decent" behavior all come under attack. Conventional art and classical music are

scorned as "representational" or "literal." More positively, a great premium is placed on originality and spontaneity, on youth as against the elderly or middle-aged, on the natural as against the synthetic or processed, and on full and open discussion of everyone's "hang-ups."

To the historian looking back a hundred years hence in the 2070s all this may prove to record the birth pangs or growing pains of a new and higher culture, replacing one that was outworn, overly materialistic, and increasingly hypocritical in applying its lofty standards of justice and equality. Most of us today may hope so. Meantime, many of us together with our Victorian visitor find the latter twentieth century both bewildering and terrifying. It is the purpose of this chapter to gain perspectives on our confused and confusing age by examining some of the leading innovations in thought and culture during the last three-quarters of a century.

II Main Currents of Thought

Psychology

Following leads from the biological sciences, especially the Darwinian theory of evolution, the nineteenth century emphasized process, the dynamics of change in time. The twentieth century, taking its cue from psychology, has come to put particular emphasis on the role of the unconscious in human thought and action, on the irrationality—or at least nonrationality—of much human behavior. Foremost among the thinkers responsible for this emphasis was Sigmund Freud (1856–1939). Freud was a physician trained in Vienna in the rationalist medical tradition of the late nineteenth century. His interest was early drawn to mental illness, where he soon found cases in which patients exhibited symptoms of very real organic disturbances for which no obvious organic causes could be found. Under analysis, as Freud's therapeutic treatment came to be called, the patient, relaxed on a couch, was urged to pour out what he could remember of his earliest childhood, or indeed infancy. After many such treatments the analyst, Freud argued, could make the patient aware of what was disturbing him.

Had Freud merely contented himself with this kind of therapy, few of us would have heard of him. But from all this clinical experience he worked out a system of psychology that has had a very great influence on our basic conceptions of human relations. Freud starts with the concept of a set of drives with which each person is born. These drives, which arise in the unconscious, are expressions of the id, the Latin word for "it," which Freud used to avoid the moralistic overtones in words like "desires." These drives try to get satisfaction and pleasure, to express themselves in action. The infant, notably, is uninhibited—that is, his drives well up into action from the id without restraint from his conscious mind. But by no means without restraint from his parents or nurse—and there's the difficulty. The infant finds himself frustrated. As he grows, as his mind is formed, he comes to be conscious of the fact that some of the things he wants to do are objectionable to those closest to him, and on whom he is so dependent. He himself therefore begins to repress these drives from his id.

With his dawning consciousness of the world outside himself, the child has in fact developed another part of his psyche, which Freud at first called the censor, and later divided into two phases which he called the ego and the superego. The ego is the individual's private censor, his awareness that, in accordance with what Freudians call the reality principle, certain drives from his id—for example, the wish of the male child to become his mother's lover—simply cannot succeed. The superego in a way is what common language calls conscience; it is the individual's response as a member of a social system in which certain actions are proper and others are not. Now these drives of the id, and indeed in most of its phases the dictates of the superego, are for Freud a sort of great reservoir of which the individual is not normally aware—that is, they are part of his unconscious. In a mentally healthy individual, enough of the drives of the id succeed so that he feels contented. But even the healthiest of individuals has had to repress a great deal of his drives from the id. This successful repression the Freudians account for in part at least by a process they call sublimation. They think that the healthy individual somehow finds for a repressed drive a new and socially approved outlet or expression. Thus a drive toward sexual relations not approved in one's circle might be sublimated into the writing of poetry or music or even into athletics.

With the neurotic person, however, Freud held that drives, having been driven back down into the unconscious without a suitable outlet or sublimation, continue, so to speak, festering in the id, trying to find

Sigmund Freud, photographed with his fiancee, Martha Bernays, in September 1885.

some outlet. They display themselves in all sorts of neuroses and phobias, which have in common a failure to conform to the reality principle. The neurotic individual is maladjusted, and if the failure to meet the reality principle is really complete, he is insane, psychotic, living in an utterly unreal private world of his own.

Freud's therapy rested on the long slow process of psychoanalysis, in which the patient day after day sought in memories of his earliest childhood for concrete details and the listening analyst could pick from this stream of consciousness the significant details that pointed to the hidden repression, the blocking that came out in neurotic behavior. Freud gave special importance to the patient's dreams, in which, Freud thought, the unconscious wells up out of control, or but partly controlled, by the ego. Once the patient got beneath the surface of his conscious life, and became aware of what had gone wrong with his hitherto unconscious life, he might then adjust to society and lead a normal existence.

What is important for us is the wider implications of Freud's work, particularly his concept of the very great role of the individual's unconscious drives. Ordinary reflective thinking is for the Freudian a very small part of our existence. Much even of what we consider the exercise of reason is, according to the Freudian, what psychologists call rationalization, thinking dictated, not by an awareness of the reality principle, but by the desires of the id. One can get a good measure of the difference between eighteenth-century rationalism and Freudian psychology by contrasting the older belief in the innocence of the child, or at least the moral neutrality of the "blank slate" of Locke's newborn infant, with the Freudian view of the child as a bundle of unsocial or antisocial drives, as in fact a little untamed savage.

But second, and most important, note that the Freudians do not wish to blow out the candle of human reason. They are moderate, not extreme, antirationalists; they are chastened rationalists. Their whole therapy is based on the concept, which has Christian as well as eighteenth-century roots, that "ye shall know the truth, and the truth shall make you free." Only, for the Freudian, truth cannot be distilled into a few simple rules of conduct that all men, being reasonable and good, can use as guides to individual and collective happiness. It is on the contrary very hard to establish and can be reached only by a long and precarious struggle. Many will not reach it and will have to put up with all sorts of maladjustments and frustrations. The Freudian is at bottom a pessimist, who does not believe in the perfectibility of man.

Freud, to whom religion was an "illusion," was himself a cult leader. His faithful disciples still form an orthodox nucleus of strict Freudian psychoanalysts. Other disciples parted with the master. The Austrian Adler (1870–1937) rejected the master's emphasis on the sexual and coined the familiar phrase "inferiority complex." The Swiss Jung (1875–1961) attempted to expand the horizons of psychology by studying the evidence of man's past, his literature, his mythology and religious faith. His studies convinced him that there was a "collective unconscious," a reservoir of the entire human experience that we all tap and that is reflected symbolically in the archetypes, such as prophets, seers, and saviours, that appear and reappear in art, literature, legend, and religion.

Full psychoanalysis has usually remained an extremely lengthy and expensive treatment limited to relatively few patients. Modified and less costly forms of analytical therapy have developed, such as group therapy and experiments with "sensitivity sessions."

The Freudian influence on imaginative writing has been very great, as evidenced by "stream-of-consciousness" fiction; it has also deeply affected philosophy and the arts generally. Freud reinforced the intellectual reaction against scientific materialism and against nineteenth-century bourgeois optimism and strengthened the revival of intuition and sensibility in a kind of neo-Romantic and neo-Stoic protest against unbridled reason.

The Freudians hold no monopoly of the field of psychology. Indeed, the eighteenth-century tendency to regard human nature, if not as wholly rational, at least as wholly malleable by those who could manipulate the human and nonhuman environment, still had representatives in the mid-twentieth century. The Russian psychologist Pavlov (1849–1936), Nobel prizewinner in 1904, gave us the term "conditioned reflex." Pavlov's laboratory dogs, after being fed at a given signal, came to water at the mouth at this signal even when no food was within sight or smell. Training or conditioning can produce automatic responses in the animal that are essentially similar to the kind of automatic responses the animal is born with. Pavlov's experiments confirmed eighteenth-century ideas about the way in which training can be manipulated to produce specific responses from organisms. But they also contradicted eighteenth-century optimism by suggesting that once such education has taken hold, further training becomes difficult if not impossible. Pavlov, after having trained some of his dogs, tried mixing his signals, frustrating and confusing the dogs by withholding food at the signal that had always produced food for them. He succeeded in producing symptoms of a kind close to what in human beings would be neurosis.

The Social Sciences

In the social sciences, the twentieth century has continued to develop the critique of our eighteenth-century inheritance of faith in the basic reasonableness and goodness of human nature. In fact, the very term "human nature" seemed to some social scientists to be so all-embracing as to make no sense. The specific programs and the values of twentieth-century thinkers in this broad sociological field were very varied. Yet most of them had a sense of the subtlety, the complexities, the delicacy—and the toughness and durability—of the forces that bind human beings together in society but also hold them apart. The Swiss writer Denis de Rougemont puts the same kind of challenge to our conventional notions of what makes sense when he speaks of tensions between two terms that are "true, contradictory, and essential." * The distinguished American sociologist Talcott Parsons, in his *The Structure of Social Action* (1937), found in the work of many different thinkers, such as the German Max Weber, the

*Man's Western Quest (New York, 1957), p. 116.

Frenchman Durkheim, the Englishman Alfred Marshal, the Italian Pareto, a common aim to put the study of man in society on a basis that takes full account of the difficulties of "objectivity" and gives full place to the role of the subjective and nonrational in human life.

We may take as an example Pareto (1848–1923), a trained engineer who tried hard to establish a genuine science of sociology. In *The Mind and Society* (1916) he was concerned chiefly with the problem of separating the rational from the nonrational in human actions. What interested Pareto was the kind of action that is expressed in words, ritual, symbolism of some kind. Buying wool socks for cold weather is one such action. If they are bought deliberately to get the best socks at a price the buyer can afford, that is rational action in accord with the doer's interests; it is the kind of action the economist can study statistically. If, however, they are bought because the buyer thinks wool is "natural" (as compared with synthetic fibers) or because he finds snob value in imported English socks, or because he wants to help bring sheep-raising back to Vermont, we are in a field less "rational" than price. The practical economist will still study marketing and consumer demand, but he will have to cope with many complex psychological variables.

It is these that Pareto studied under the name of "derivations," which are close to what most of us know as rationalizations. They are the explanations and accompanying ritualistic acts associated with our religion, our patriotism, our feelings for groups of all kinds. Prayer, for instance, was for Pareto a derivation; he was a materialist, at bottom hostile to Christianity, though he approved of it as a means of social concord and was fascinated by its hold over men. It is irrational, or nonrational, to pray for rain, because we know as meteorologists that rain has purely material causes quite beyond the reach of prayer. Derivations, while a factor in human social life, do not really move men to social action.

What does move men and keep them together in society, says Pareto, are the residues. These are expressions of relatively permanent, abiding sentiments in men, expressions that usually have to be separated from the part that is actually a derivation, which may change greatly and even quickly. For example, pagan Greek sailors sacrificed to Poseidon, god of the sea, before setting out on a voyage; a few centuries later, Christian Greek sailors prayed, lighted candles, and made vows to the Virgin Mary just before sailing. The derivations are the contrasting explanations of what Poseidon and the Virgin respectively do; the believer in the Virgin thinks his pagan predecessor was dead wrong. The residues are the needs to secure divine aid and comfort in a difficult undertaking and to perform certain ritual acts that give the performer assurance of such aid and comfort. The residues are nearly the same for the two sets of sailors, who have similar social and psychological needs and satisfy them in much the same

ways, though with very different explanations of what they are doing.

Two of the major classes of residues Pareto distinguished help form his philosophy of history. These are first the residues of "persistent aggregates," the sentiments that mark men who like regular ways, tradition and habit, men like the Spartans, the Prussians, or any rigorously disciplined military class. Second, there are the residues of the "instinct for combinations," the sentiments that mark men who like novelty and adventure, who like to cut loose from the old and the tried, men not easily shocked, men who hate discipline, men like most intellectuals and inventors—and many entrepreneurs and businessmen. Like most philosophers of history, Pareto was far from clear on just how a conservative society where the residues of persistent aggregates predominate changes into one dominated by the residues of the instinct for combinations. But he did have the conception of a pendulum swing, even a struggle of thesis and antithesis.

The nineteenth century in the West was for Pareto a society in which the residues of instinct for combinations played perhaps the greatest role of which they are capable in a human society. It was a century of competition among individuals full of new ideas, inventions, enterprises, convinced that the old ways were bad, that novelty was the great thing to strive for at the expense of everything else. But since it was also a society notably out of equilibrium, it had to run toward the other kind of residues, toward the persistent aggregates, toward a society with more security and less competition, more discipline and less freedom, more equality and less inequality, more uniformity and less variety. It had to move toward the totalitarian state.

The main influence of the newer psychological and sociological approach to the study of man in society has by no means been exclusively in the direction of authoritarianism. The psychology of motivation interested not only Mussolini and Hitler, both of whom had pretensions to philosophy, but also many democratic politicans as well as a host of experts employed by advertising agencies to persuade consumers. Early in our century Graham Wallas, a British leftist, wrote a most influential book, *Human Nature in Politics.* Wallas, campaigning as a Progressive for a seat in the London County Council, discovered by experience that the voters he canvassed were more pleased and influenced by little tricks of baby-kissing, chitchat, and personal flattery than by appeals to reason or even to self-interest. Something of the same emphasis on the need to go beyond abstractions to practical psychology in politics appears in the earlier writings of the American Walter Lippmann, whose *Preface to Politics* appeared in 1913. It has, of course, always been known to politicians.

Some American intellectuals, however, still reject adopting a Machiavellian strategy, even in a righteous cause. It seems to these good children of the Enlightenment that reason and high principles must and will

Soren Kierkegaard: a caricature by Wilhelm Marstrand.

prevail together, and that catering to the elements in
human nature so emphasized by modern psychology
is yielding to the evils of existing society. Since active
politicians seldom have such scruples, a gap often remains between the idealistic theorist and the practical
man who wants to get things done. Yet perceptive
political leaders know that more and more planning
is needed to deal with such essentials as education,
health care, social security, and the conservation of
natural resources and the environment. All are bound
to cost a lot of money, and the planners know that in
a democracy the government cannot simply impose
their plans. Ideas from the social sciences can help with
the problem of persuading the electorate to want, ask
for, and pay for what the planners think they ought
to want. Such concerns may be found in the writing
of the American economist J. K. Galbraith, author of
The Affluent Society.

Philosophy

In the field of formal (which nowadays tends to mean
also university-supported) philosophy the latter twentieth century displays once more its variety. It is safe to
say that in the West at least there are today representatives of just about every philosophical system that
has ever existed, from extreme idealism to extreme
materialism and complete skepticism. In addition, a
philosophy known as existentialism developed from
such nineteenth-century sources as Nietzsche and the
Danish theologian Kierkegaard (1813–1855), who assailed the depersonalizing and dehumanizing effects of
the secularized materialistic society of his day. Twentieth-century existentialists continue to find reality
pretty depressing—"chaos" and "nothingness" are
terms they use to describe it—but they are determined
to face this reality as heroically as possible.

The central theme of existentialism has been stated
by the French writer Sartre (1905–   ) as "existence
precedes essence." This cryptic pronouncement seems
to mean that human awareness of living, of being,
precedes in time, and is therefore somehow more important than, our thinking or our mental ticketing of
reality by means of words. Clearly existentialism, which
has been aptly described as more a mood than a systematic world view, is part of the anti-intellectualism
of the twentieth century. Yet the existentialists are sensitive artists and by no means simple anti-intellectuals
who want us to think with our blood or our hormones.
They respect the instrument of thought and use it
themselves in making the hard choices and commitments they feel that being demands. But they do not
quite trust thought or its chief representatives in our
day, the conventional scientists.

The most original, and in a sense the most typical
and vital, philosophic movement of the twentieth century is called variously logical analysis, logical positivism, linguistic philosophy, and, in some of its phases,
symbolic logic. It looks to an outsider as though the
movement accepted most of the strictures the new psychology made on old-fashioned rationalism and then
went ahead to insist that, although only a tiny bit of
human experience could be brought under rubrics of
rational thought, that tiny bit should be protected and
explored carefully. This somewhat varied school can be
considered as beginning early in the twentieth century
in Vienna, the city of Freud. Such distinguished pioneers of the school as Ludwig Wittgenstein (1889–1951)
and Rudolf Carnap (1891–1970) emigrated, the first to
England, the second to the United States.

The American physicist P. W. Bridgman put one
of the school's basic positions clearly. When, on the
pattern of scientific practice, a problem can be answered by the performance of an "operation" and the
answer validated by logical and empirical tests or ob-
servations, knowledge can be achieved. But when no
such "operation" is possible, as in such problems as
whether democracy is the best form of government,
whether a lie is ever justifiable, or whether a given poem

is a good one or a bad one—in short, almost all the great questions of philosophy, art, literature, history—the problem is for the logician "meaningless." Most of these logical positivists would admit that nonlogical or pseudological methods for getting at such problems, though they could not result in the kind of finally accepted answers the scientists expect to get, are nonetheless useful and necessary for normal human living. Some of the popularizers of this philosophy, however, pretty explicitly held that all mental activity save logical analysis and empirical verification is a waste of time.

Appoaching their problems in a very different way from Freud and Pareto, these logical analysts nevertheless came to a similar conclusion about the reasoning capacity of most human beings. Most human beings, they conclude, are at present incapable of thorough, persistent, successful logical thinking, and they cannot be taught to do this kind of thinking in any foreseeable future. Of course, just as there are radical Freudians who hold that if everybody could be psychoanalyzed all would be well, there are radical positivists, usually labeled semanticists, who hold that semantics, the study of meaning, if available to everyone, would cure all our troubles. The leading expert of this rather naïve semantic therapy was the Polish-American scientist Alfred Korzybski (1879–1950), author of *Science and Sanity* (1933). By a quite different approach, summed up in the phrase "the medium is the message," the Canadian Marshall McLuhan (1911–   ) came to the conclusion that if we all really understood communication and the mass media we would all get along together happily.

Probably the most widespread philosophical movement of our century developed on the margin of formal philosophy. This movement may be called historicism, the attempt to find in history an answer to those ultimate questions of the structure of the universe and of man's fate the philosopher has always asked. At bottom, the transfer of Darwinian concepts of organic evolution from biology to this great, sweeping field of philosophical questions contains the essence of twentieth-century historicism. Once Judeo-Christian concepts of a single creation in time and of a God above nature were abandoned along with the rest of the traditional world view, men in search of answers to their questions about these ultimates had to fall back on the historical record. Man is not made by God, but by nature, which amounts to saying that *man makes himself* in the course of history. We get our only clues as to man's capacities here on earth, clues as to how he ought to behave, clues as to that future that so concerns him, from the record of the past.

But "clues" is a modest and misleading word here. Many of the thinkers who appealed to history found much more than indications of what *might* be, much more than the always tentative, never dogmatic or absolute "theories" the scientist produces in answer to the less-than-ultimate questions he asks. Many of these philosophers of history, to simplify a bit, found in what

they held to be the course of history a substitute for the concepts of God or Providence. They found substantially the equivalent of what Christians found in revelation—the explanation of man's nature and destiny.

Of these historicisms, the most important and most obviously a substitute for Christianity is Marxism. The theological parallels have been frequently noted by non-Marxists: for God, absolute and omnipotent, the Marxist substitutes the absolutely determined course of dialectical materialism; for the Bible, he substitutes the canonical writings of Marx, Engels, and Lenin; for the Church, the Communist party; for the Christian eschatology of divine judgment and heaven or hell, the revolution and the "classless society."

Another type of historicism was put forward by the German Oswald Spengler (1880–1936) in *The Decline of the West*, published just at the end of World War I. Spengler found from the historical record that societies or civilizations have an average life span, a thousand years or so for a civilization being the equivalent of seventy years or so for the individual human being. He traced three Western civilizations, a Hellenic from 1000 B.C. to about the birth of Christ, a Levantine or Middle Eastern from then to about A.D. 1000, and our own modern Western, which began (according to him) about A.D. 1000 and was, therefore, due to end about A.D. 2000. Some critics have argued that because Spengler saw Germany about to be defeated in 1918, he consoled himself by forecasting the imminent end of Western civilization itself. Most historians would say that, though Spengler has real insights into the growth and decay of civilizations, what he wrote is not history but metaphysics or "metahistory," a kind of Wagnerian commemoration of the twilight of another set of gods.

Somewhat paralleling *The Decline of the West* but written by a trained historian is the multivolumed *Study of History* (1934–1954) by the Englishman Arnold Toynbee (1889–   ). Toynbee has a Christian background along with a strong family tradition of humanitarian social service (a Victorian Arnold Toynbee, who coined the term *industrial revolution,* was an active Christian socialist). World War I aroused in Toynbee a great hatred for war, and a conviction that nationalism, which he once declared to be the real if unavowed religion of our Western society, is the villain of the piece. His great opus is an attempt to trace the causes of the rise and fall of dozens of societies in the past, and owes a good deal to Spengler. But Toynbee is a gentle English Christian humanist, not a German Romantic racist brought up on what was no doubt a perversion of Nietzsche. He does, like the majority of contemporary philosophers of history, conclude that our Western society is facing a very serious challenge, that in terms of the cyclical rise and fall of societies he has traced it looks as if we were about to give ourselves the "knockout blow." But he refuses to abandon hope. Though the facts of historical development may indicate destruction for us, we may transcend history and, under the influence of a revived or Buddhist-influenced Christianity of gentleness and love, pull ourselves out of the hole.

Almost all professional historians in the West, nowadays mostly conventionally democratic in their values and skeptics in religion, simply give these philosophers of history the cold shoulder. Existentialists are firm in their contention that, though we may not neglect history as a record of human experience, we must find in ourselves something—salvation, perhaps—quite beyond history. And as for the logical analysts, history is far too lacking in precise data to make it a subject worth their while.

III Science

In the twentieth century each science, each branch of each science, has continued its cumulative course. The cooperation (not without rivalry) among pure scientists, applied scientists, engineers, bankers, businessmen, and government officials has produced in all phases of human control over material things the kind of exponential increases that send the lines of graphs quite off the paper. Man's attained rate of travel is no doubt an extreme example, one not achieved in the same degree, for instance, in such fields as those of medicine and genetics. In 1820 the fastest rate was still 12 to 15 miles an hour; railroads made it 100 miles or so by 1880; piston-engined airplanes made it 300 miles or so by 1940; jet planes broke the sound barrier only yesterday in 1947, making speeds of close to 1,000 miles per hour possible; and starting in 1969, rockets propelled men to the moon at speeds exceeding 20,000 miles an hour.

Each science is highly specialized, so that the active scientist usually masters only part of a given science. Nonetheless, at a broad, nonspecialist's level of understanding many educated men in the West have a good idea of what modern science is trying to do and how it does it. Scientific respect for nature and natural laws, and scientific skepticism toward the supernatural, have added powerfully to the modern drive toward rationalism, positivism, materialism. Science continues to promote the world view we have seen arising in early modern times and culminating in the Enlightenment of the eighteenth century. Indeed, many scientists have managed to make of the pursuit of scientific knowledge itself a kind of religion.

The Revolution in Physics

The great scientific event of the twentieth century has been the revolution in physics symbolized for the public in the figure of Albert Einstein (1879–1955) and made possible by the contributions of many experts in addition to Einstein himself. The revolution centered on the radical revisions made in the Newtonian world machine, the mechanistic model of the universe that had

been accepted for more than two centuries. It will be recalled that many nineteenth-century scientists were convinced that light moved in waves and was transmitted through the ether, which supposedly filled outer space. In the 1880s, however, experiments demonstrated that there was no ether. If the ether did exist, then it would itself be set to moving by the motion of the earth, and a beam of light directed against its current would travel with a velocity less than that of a beam directed with its current. But the experiments showed that light traveled at 186,284 miles per second whether it was moving with or against the hypothetical current.

In 1905, Einstein, who was then twenty-six years old, published a paper asserting that since the speed of light is a constant unaffected by the earth's motion, it must also be unaffected by all the other bodies in the universe. The unvarying velocity of light is a law of nature, Einstein continued, and other laws of nature are the same for all uniformly moving systems. This was Einstein's Special Theory of Relativity, which had many disconcerting corollaries. In particular, it undermined the idea of absolute space and absolute time and made both space and time relative to the velocity of the system in which they are moving. If a rod moves at a speed approaching that of light, it will shrink: at 90 percent of the velocity of light, it will contract to half its "normal" length. The motion of a clock carried aboard the rod will slow down commensurately; if men should ever travel at such speeds through space for what seemed to them six months, they would discover on returning to earth that they had been absent for a year!

Space and time, therefore, are inseparably linked, and time is "the fourth dimension." An air-traffic controller needs to know the position of an airplane not only in longitude, latitude, and altitude but also in time, and the total flight path of a plane must be plotted on what Einstein called a "four-dimensional space-time continuum," a term he also applied to the universe.

Einstein equated not only space and time but also mass and energy. His famous formula—the most famous in the twentieth century—$E = mc^2$ means that the energy in an object is equal to its mass, multiplied by the square of the velocity of light. It means also that a very small object may contain tremendous potential energy. Such an object, for example, can emit radiation for thousands of years or discharge it all in one explosion, as happened with the atomic bomb in 1945 when a way was found to unlock the potential energy in uranium.

The problem of mass also involved Einstein in reviewing the Newtonian concept of a universe held together by the force of gravity—the attraction of bodies to other bodies over vast distances. Einstein soon concluded that it was erroneous to suppose that the gravity—that is, the weight—of an object had anything to do with its attraction to other objects. After all, the famous experiment of Galileo had demonstrated that light and heavy bodies fell from the leaning tower in

Pisa at the same speed. Einstein proposed that it would be more useful to extend the concept of the magnetic field, in which certain bodies behaved in a certain pattern, and speak of a gravitational field in which bodies also behaved in a certain pattern. Einstein did not penetrate the mystery of what holds the universe together, but he did suggest a more convincing way of looking at it. This was the essence of his General Theory of Relativity (1916), which stated that the laws of nature are the same for all systems regardless of their state of motion.

One of these laws of nature had been formulated in 1900 by Max Planck (1858–1947), a German physicist, who expressed mathematically the amount of energy emitted in the radiation of heat. He discovered that the amount of energy divided by the frequency of the radiation always yielded the same very tiny number, which scientists call Planck's Constant. The implication of this discovery was that objects emit energy not in an unbroken flow but in a series of separate little units, each of which Planck called a quantum. Quantum physics suggested a basic discontinuity in the universe by positing that a quantum could appear at two different locations without having traversed the intervening space. It seemed almost absurd: as Bertrand Russell noted, it was as if a person could be twenty years old or twenty-two, but never twenty-one.

Other physicists, however, made discoveries reinforcing the idea of continuity, with all physical phenomena behaving like waves. The old dilemma of whether light consisted of particles or of waves was therefore greatly extended. Einstein and others suggested that the only useful procedure was to grasp both horns of the dilemma—and teach wave theory Mondays, Wednesdays, and Fridays, as one distinguished British physicist put it, and particle theory Tuesdays, Thursdays, and Saturdays. Since the correlation of space and time and also of mass and energy had been demonstrated, why not assume the correlation of particles and waves and speak of "wavicles"? During the 1920s it became evident that man might never be able to answer ultimate questions about the universe. He could not fully understand the behavior of the individual electron, the basic component of the atom, because in the act of trying to observe the electron he created effects that altered its behavior. Study of the electron led Werner Heisenberg (1901–   ), a German physicist, to propose the principle of "indeterminacy" or "uncertainty," which concludes that the scientist will have to be content with probabilities rather than absolutes. While an individual electron can jump from one orbit to another quite unpredictably, the behavior of many, many electrons remains predictable. Although the universe is no longer the world machine of Newton, its activity is by no means random or wholly indeterminate and can still be expressed in the mathematical language of probabilities.

The development of twentieth-century astronomy has been closely linked to that of physics. To the layman, such modern astronomical concepts as that of a finite but expanding universe, curved space, and perhaps above all the almost inconceivable distances and quantities such as light years and galaxies, have made astronomy the most romantic of sciences. And these distances and quantities *are* almost inconceivable. A light year is the distance traversed by light in one year, or roughly 5,880,000,000,000 miles; our own Milky Way galaxy has some thirty thousand million stars and nebulae, in the form of a disk with a diameter of about a hundred thousand light years.

Science and the Quality of Life

Chemistry, which made possible plastics, synthetic fibers like nylon, and many other innovations, has greatly affected our daily lives by its impact on our foods, our clothing, and almost all the other material objects we use. Chemistry has also assisted the very great gains made by the biological sciences and their application to medicine and public health. Not only in the United States and the other countries of the West but also elsewhere, infant mortality and many contagious diseases have been conquered so successfully that the average expectancy of life at birth has increased by twenty years since 1900. In the economically backward areas of the globe, however, more children are born and more live, so that the problem of feeding a burgeoning population remains acute. Some alleviation of the problem has resulted from the extension of irrigated farming, the use of new chemical fertilizers, and the planting of highly productive new hybrid strains of wheat and corn developed by experts. On the other hand, the problem is compounded by the inability of poor countries to pay for fertilizer and other scientific advances and by the vagaries of climate. In the early 1970s, for example, the Sahel, the band of grazing and crop land stretching across several states in West Africa south of the Sahara, suffered a severe famine when the usual rains failed to materialize for several years running.

Thus, the advance of science has created problems as well as solving them. Some of the problems have been comparatively minor, like the fashionable doctrines of moral and aesthetic relativism of only yesterday, which resulted from a misapplication of misunderstood doctrines of relativity in physics. And some have been of the very first magnitude, notably the prospect that the uncontrolled Frankenstein monster of modern military technology, with its hydrogen bombs, its missiles, and its biological warfare, could literally destroy humanity. In addition, pesticides, detergents, and plastics, which were originally thought to be purely beneficial to the quality of life, have also proved to threaten it by their harmful effects on ecology. Even scientists and technicians have come under attack as cold, inhuman, and unable to control properly the awesome gadgets they have created. Merely to finance proper scientific education and research in this very complex and very, very expensive age is a major problem. Yet the fact remains that the twentieth century has accomplished many wonders, not least of which is to demonstrate the continued vitality and inventiveness of the Western civilization that so many prophets of doom have already consigned to a Spenglerian twilight.

IV Literature and the Arts

Literature

Twentieth-century writers, too, have surprised the prophets of doom. The century's poetry remains, for the most part, what it had become in the late nineteenth century, difficult, cerebral, and addressed to a small audience. An occasional poet, like the American Robert Frost (1874–1963), broke from the privacy of the little magazines and the limited editions to wide popularity and a place enshrined in old-fashioned anthologies. But Frost was no more esoteric in form or substance than Wordsworth. More remarkable and more symptomatic is the wide attention given to T. S. Eliot (1888–1965), born in St. Louis, but as an adult wholly Anglicized, an abstruse and allusive poet, an intellectual of intellectuals. The figure of speech with which he began "The Love Song of J. Alfred Prufrock" in 1917, which once seemed strange, "advanced," is now tame enough for any anthology:

> Let us go then, you and I,
> When the evening is spread out against the sky
> Like a patient etherised upon a table.*

The novel remains the most important form of contemporary imaginative writing. Critics have long bemoaned its exhaustion as an art form, and the French have even invented what they call the antinovel, but the novel does not die. Although it is difficult to predict which novelists of our century are likely to be read in the twenty-first century, the American William Faulkner (1897–1962), who wrote existentialist novels about darkest Mississippi, the German Thomas Mann (1875–1955), and the Frenchman Camus (1913–1960) seem already enshrined as classics. Mann, who began with a traditionally realistic novel of life in his birthplace, the old Hanseatic town of Lübeck, never really belonged to the avant-garde. He is typical of the sensitive, worrying, class-conscious artist of the age of psychology. Camus, too, was sensitive and worrying, but with an existentialist concern in his novels and plays over man's isolation and his need to engage himself in life.

The most innovative novelist of the twentieth century is surely the Irishman James Joyce (1882–1941). Joyce began with a subtle, outspoken, but formally conventional series of sketches of life in the Dublin of his youth, *Dubliners* (1914), and the novelist's inevitable,

*T. S. Eliot, *Complete Poems and Plays* (New York: Harcourt Brace Jovanovich, 1952), p. 3.

and with Joyce undisguised, autobiography, *Portrait of the Artist as a Young Man* (1916). Then, mostly in exile on the Continent, he wrote the classic experimental novel *Ulysses* (1922), an account of twenty-four hours in the life of Leopold Bloom, a Dublin Jew. *Ulysses* is full of difficult allusions, parallels with Homer, puns, rapidly shifting scenes and episodes, and is written without regard for the conventional notions of plot and orderly development. Above all, it makes full use of the then recently developed psychologies of the unconscious as displayed in an individual's "stream of consciousness." The last chapter, printed entirely without punctuation marks, is the record of what went on in the mind of Bloom's Irish wife as she lay in bed waiting for him to come home. What went on in her mind was in large part too shocking for contemporaries, and *Ulysses,* published in Paris, long had to be smuggled into English-speaking countries. It is now freely available everywhere, and it has been faithfully adapted as a film.

Ulysses, though it took attentive reading and, even for those most fully abreast of the avant-garde culture, was often puzzling, is still a novel in English. Joyce's final big work, *Finnegans Wake* (1939), is one of those radical experiments about which, like many modern paintings, the ordinary educated layman simply has to say that it means nothing, or very little, to him. The continuities and conventions of narration and "plain English," not wholly flouted in *Ulysses,* are here quite abandoned. *Finnegan's Wake* is a dream novel, compounded of puns and free association. There are words and even sentences; but meaning has to be quarried out by the reader and may when quarried turn out to be quite different from what Joyce intended. But there are keys to *Finnegans Wake*—we cite one in our reading list for this chapter—and the reader who wants to try can get his start there.

Painting

Even more than literature, the fine arts confront the cultivated Westerner with the problem of aesthetic modernism. There are still a few very popular painters in the representational tradition, such as Andrew Wyeth in the United States. But the mainstream of painting has flowed on and on into the many channels first explored by Manet, Monet, and their contemporaries a century ago. No painter can better serve as an introduction to the endless variety and experimentation of twentieth-century painting than the versatile and immensely productive Pablo Picasso (1880–1973).

A native Spaniard and an adopted Frenchman, Picasso painted in many "styles" or "periods." For example, the paintings of his "blue period" in the very early 1900s, with their exhausted and defeated people, have a melancholy lyrical quality that reflects the struggling young artist's own poverty. These pictures are said to have been influenced by the work of El Greco, the sixteenth-century Spanish master; certainly both artists conveyed a sense of concentrated emotion

Picasso's "Les Demoiselles d'Avignon."

by exaggerating and distorting human proportions. Around 1905–1906 Picasso turned to more daring innovations and distortions, much influenced by exhibitions of primitive masks from black Africa and of large-eyed reduced-to-essentials archaic sculptures recently discovered in the Mediterranean world. Picasso strove, as Cézanne had striven, to transfer to the two dimensions of a picture the three dimensions of the real world. Sometimes he used the techniques of abstractionism, the reduction of figures to a kind of plane geometry, all angles and lines; and sometimes those of cubism, a kind of solid geometry, all cubes, spheres, and cones; and sometimes *collage* (pasteup), in which he glued onto a picture fragments of real objects, a bit of newspaper or of caning from a chair.

Perhaps the most arresting of these innovative paintings was *The Demoiselles d'Avignon* (the demoiselles were prostitutes, and Avignon was the name of a street in the red-light district in Barcelona). Some of the women have the huge eyes and simplified features and outlines of archaic sculpture, and two have the distorted faces and magnified noses of primitive masks. In later years Picasso often returned to more traditional representational painting, as in the almost classical portraits

of his "white period" after World War I and in innumerable on-the-spot sketches of friends. Yet he also persisted in his more radical vein of showing the human or animal figure from two or more angles simultaneously, hence the misplaced eyes and other anatomical rearrangements that he employed with such telling effect in *Guernica* (1937), depicting the havoc wrought by fascist planes upon an undefended town during the civil war in Spain.

Anyone worried by contemporary art can take some comfort in the fact that one of its most extreme manifestations occurred more than half a century ago and has never been quite equaled for its extraordinary defiance of all rules and traditions. This was the protest made by a very alienated group of intellectuals, the Dadaists, the "angry young men" of World War I and its aftermath. They reacted against a world so much sillier than their Dada—a deliberately meaningless name, babytalk for *hobbyhorse*—that it could slaughter millions in warfare. Here are some characteristic passages from an account of Dada written by a sympathetic observer:

In Berlin as elsewhere we notice the persistent desire to

destroy art, the deliberate intent to wipe out existing notions of beauty, the insistence upon the greatest possible obliteration of individuality. Heartfield works under the direction of Grosz while Max Ernst and Arp sign each other's paintings at random. . . .

In the first New York Independents' exhibition, 1917, he [Marcel Duchamp] entered a porcelain urinal with the title *Fontaine* and signed it R. Mutt to test the impartiality of the executive committee of which he himself was a member. By this symbol Duchamp wished to signify his disgust for art and his admiration for ready-made objects. . . .

At an exhibition in Paris among the most remarkable entries sent by the poets was a mirror of Soupault's entitled *Portrait of an Unknown*. . . . Certain paintings by Duchamp supposed to be in this exhibition were replaced by sheets of paper marked with numbers which corresponded to the Duchamp entries in the catalog. Duchamp, who had been asked to take part in the exhibition, had just cabled from New York: "Nuts."*

Although it has been argued that the Dadaist protest was more political and social than aesthetic, most of the men mentioned in the quotation above made distinguished contributions to the arts. Jean Arp (1887–1966), who fled his native Alsace for Switzerland to avoid service in the German army, was a pioneer in abstractionist painting and sculpture. Max Ernst (1891–   ) experimented with surrealism, the attempt to transfer to canvas the Freudian world of dreams and nightmares, and George Grosz (1893–1959) made mordant sketches satirizing the foibles of German society between the two world wars. Marcel Duchamp (1887–1968) was already the *enfant terrible* of art before 1914: he created a sensation at the New York Armory show of 1913, which introduced avant-garde art to the American public, by exhibiting his *Nude Descending a Staircase*, a cubist attempt to depict the human figure in rapid motion.

Duchamp, Grosz and Ernst all eventually moved from Europe to the United States as part of the wave of artistic emigration that reached its peak in the late 1930s and early 1940s and ended the century-old dominance of Paris as the center of the avant garde. In the 1940s and 1950s New York became the capital of abstract expressionism, which communicated ideas or moods by entirely nonrepresentational means through color, form, and a sense of movement or action. The American Jackson Pollock (1912–1956) dripped or even hurled automobile enamel on huge canvases, which he laid on the studio floor, to create an arresting spattered effect. In the 1960s the New York spotlight shifted to pop art, a neo-Dadaist reaction to mass-produced and mass-marketed commodities. Pop artists depicted over and over again boxes of Brillo, cans of Campbell's soup, road signs, incidents from low-brow comic strips, and blurred pictures of movie stars from magazines or the television screen. Claes Oldenburg, the Scandina-

vian-American sculptor, explained pop art by noting brashly that "I am for an art that does something other than sit on its ass in a museum" and "embroils itself with the everyday crap."*

The Other Arts

Pop sculpture featured plaster casts of real people surrounded by copies of actual pieces of furniture, a three-dimensional comic strip of devitalized, defeated humanity. At the other pole, sculpture in the grand manner experienced a rebirth, thanks above all to the work of two talented Britishers. Barbara Hepworth (1903–1975) made classically-fashioned standing abstract forms of great beauty, like the memorial to her friend Dag Hammarskjold outside the United Nations headquarters in New York. Her sometime fellow student Henry Moore (1898–   ) is widely considered the ranking sculptor of the century, possibly the greatest practitioner of the art since Michelangelo. His powerful renditions of monumental human figures, not realistically copied but simplified and reduced to essentials, create an effect not unlike that of a cubist or expressionist painting. Altogether, in sculpture as in painting, the variety and vitality of innovations are remarkable—from the highly polished rhythmic abstractions of the Romanian Brancusi (1876–1957) to the disturbing, greatly emaciated figures of the Swiss Giacometti (1901–1966) and on to the suspended abstract or whimsical mobiles of the American Calder (1898–   ) and their larger sometimes menacing brothers, his stabiles.

In architecture the twentieth century produced the first truly original style since the end of the eighteenth century. This "functional" style is no revival of the past, no living museum of eclecticism like most nineteenth-century building. It prides itself on its honest use of modern materials, its adaptation to its site and to the demands of twentieth-century living, and its dislike of waste space and overdisplay. One of its pioneers was the American Frank Lloyd Wright (1869–1959), who spent an apprenticeship with the designers of early Chicago skyscrapers and then developed at the turn of the century the "prairie" style of house, emphasizing the planes and the uncluttered simplicity that Wright admired in Japanese houses. Toward the end of his life Wright made a radical experiment in designing the Solomon Guggenheim Museum in New York, which consists mainly of one vast, high space through which visitors descend along a ramp that permits them to see the works displayed both close at hand and at several different removes of distance. There is in modern architecture a touch of austerity, even puritanism, that is a healthy reaction against nineteenth-century vulgarity but that can also lead to sterile uniformity. Travelers complain that the world over they find the same un-

*Alfred H. Barr, Jr., ed., *Fantastic Art, Dada, Surrealism*, 3rd ed., pp. 23, 19, 33. © 1947 by the Museum of Modern Art, New York. The essay on Dada was translated by Margaret Scolari Barr.

*Quoted in J. Russell and S. Gablik, *Pop Art Redefined* (Praeger, 1969), p. 97).

"King and Queen": sculpture by Henry Moore.

Barbara Hepworth's "Single Form": memorial to
Dag Hammarskjold at the United Nations.

Alexander Calder's stabile "Whale."

ornamented steel and glass boxes, which seem to have
been put up with no regard for the physical site or the
traditions of the country.

Modern music, unlike modern architecture, has
never quite crystallized into a distinctive style. The
twentieth century has produced a great many attempts
to transcend classical music and its rules of harmony—
by using a twelve-tone scale rather than the conventional eight-tone one, by stressing dissonance and discord, by borrowing the insistent rhythms of jazz, by
incorporating all kinds of electronically produced
sounds, and in extreme cases by abandoning all nota-
tion and directing the players to bang on pipes or tin
pans. Half a century ago, the general public came to
identify musical innovation most closely with the Russian Igor Stravinsky (1882–1971), who on the eve of
World War I composed two ballet scores, *Petrouchka* and
The Rite of Spring, that were far removed from the polite
and formalized ballet of tradition. Stravinsky may
prove to have been the musical counterpart of the successful artistic pioneer Picasso; significantly, however,
although he continued to compose experimental works,
none of them has equaled his great ballets in impact
or popularity.

A Final Word

In sum, the creative arts seem to get more complex and
difficult all the time, so that they are only very gradually becoming "understood of the people." While a
retrospective show of Picasso's work may be thronged,
critics are forever complaining that the concertgoing
public couldn't care less about contemporary music. Yet
there is little point in worrying unduly about the gulf
between the tastes of the many and the tastes of the

The John Hancock Building, Chicago.

few in the Western world. It seems to be an evidence of the tolerance of diversity possible in a society.

By contrast, the three great attempts to impose a really totalitarian society in our century have, to phrase it mildly, not exactly favored intellectual or artistic innovation. Communist China appears to employ very traditional forms of dance, gymnastics, and music to further its new political goals. In Nazi Germany, although science prospered despite the departure of Einstein, intellectual life was stultified and the artistic avant garde, which had flourished in the 1920s and early 1930s, could exhibit only in a museum of "decadent" art. In Soviet Russia, too, though science has thrived, literary and artistic innovation have often been equated with "bourgeois decadence," particularly since the heyday of Stalin when such promising cultural beginnings as the movies of Eisenstein and the more advanced music of Russian composers came under censorship. For it is clear from the Russian experience that when the proletariat gets power, it wants and, in the arts at least gets, about what the conventional bourgeois of an earlier generation thought desirable and lovely. No doubt tastes will change one day. The French revolutionaries, too, shared the artistic preferences of the Old Regime they had overthrown, but their official enshrining of neoclassicism only delayed and did not prevent France's reemergence as the leader of the avant garde in the arts.

Reading Suggestions on Man's Fate in the Twentieth Century

Psychology

J. Rickman, ed., *A General Selection from the Works of Sigmund Freud* (*Anchor). A well-chosen anthology.

E. Jones, *The Life and Work of Freud,* 3 vols. (Basic Books, 1953–1957). Detailed study by a great admirer; available also in an abridged version (*Anchor).

R. L. Schoenwald, *Freud: The Man and His Culture* (Knopf, 1956), and P. Rieff, *Freud: The Mind of the Moralist* (*Anchor). Two good studies stressing Freud's place in contemporary culture.

B. F. Skinner, *Science and Human Behavior* (*Free Press). A clear and extreme statement of behavioristic psychology.

Sociopolitical Thought

H. S. Hughes, *Consciousness and Society* (*Vintage). Excellent study treating not only social thought but also other facets of intellectual history, 1870–1930.

V. Pareto, *The Mind and Society,* 4 vols. (Harcourt, 1935). A major work in general sociology. Also available are briefer *Selections* from Pareto's writings (*Crowell).

T. Parsons, *The Structure of Social Action,* 2nd ed. (Free Press, 1949). A landmark in American sociological thinking.

G. Wallas, *Human Nature in Politics* (Constable, 1908) and *The Great Society* (*Bison). Pioneering studies of the psychology of politics.

W. Lippmann, *A Preface to Politics* (*Ann Arbor). Another pioneering study.

J. K. Galbraith, *The Affluent Society* (*Mentor). Lively assessment by an economist.

Philosophy

M. G. White, ed., *The Age of Analysis: Twentieth-Century Philosophers* (*Mentor). Excerpts and comments, very well chosen.

A. Naess, *Modern Philosophers* (Chicago, 1968). Carnap, Wittgenstein, and Sartre are among those discussed.

R. Harper, *Existentialism: A Theory of Man* (Harvard, 1949). A sympathetic introduction.

W. Kaufmann, ed., *Existentialism from Dostoevsky to Sartre* (*Meridian). Instructive selections from existentialist writings, with helpful editorial comments.

A. Camus, *The Stranger* (*Vintage) and *The Plague* (*Modern Library). Moderately existentialist novels by a gifted writer.

P. W. Bridgman, *The Way Things Are* (*Compass). Moderate logical positivism expressed by a leading physicist.

A. Korzybski, *Science and Society,* 3rd ed. (Non-Aristotelian Library, 1948). The name of the publisher is indicative of the tone of this work on "general semantics" and "human engineering."

M. McLuhan, *Understanding Media* (*Signet). Controversial appraisal of the significance of communications.

O. Spengler, *The Decline of the West* (Knopf, 1932). By a prophet of doom.

A. J. Toynbee, *A Study of History,* 12 vols. (*Galaxy). This classic of historicism is also available in a faithful abridgment by D. C. Somervell, 2 vols. (*Laurel).

M. F. Ashley-Montagu, *Toynbee and History* (Porter Sargeant, 1956), and I. Berlin, *Historical Inevitability* (Oxford, 1954). Criticisms of Toynbee in particular and historicism in general, respectively.

Science and Technology

R. Taton, ed., *Science in the Twentieth Century* (Basic Books, 1966). Translation of a comprehensive French survey.

I. Asimov, *The Intelligent Man's Guide to the Physical Sciences* and *The Intelligent Man's Guide to the Biological Sciences* (*Pocket). Informative surveys by a prolific popularizer of difficult material.

C. T. Chase, *The Evolution of Modern Physics* (Van Nostrand, 1947), and L. Barnett, *The Universe and Dr. Einstein,* rev. ed. (*Bantam). Helpful popular accounts of key developments in twentieth-century science.

G. Gamow, *Mister Tompkins in Paperback* (*Cambridge). "Mr. Tompkins" explores the atom and other areas in a scientific wonderland; by an accomplished popularizer.

Literature and the Arts

C. Mauriac, *The New Literature* (Braziller, 1959). Essays translated from the French, and treating mainly French writers.

E. Wilson, *Axel's Castle* (*Scribner's). A study in imaginative literature from 1870 to 1930, extending down to Joyce and Gertrude Stein.

H. Slochower, *Literature and Philosophy between Two World Wars* (*Citadel). Originally called *No Voice Is Wholly Lost;* an informative study of the relations between intellectual and literary history.

F. J. Hoffman, *Freudianism and the Literary Mind,* 2nd ed. (Louisiana State, 1957). A suggestive exploration.

J. Campbell and H. M. Robinson, *A Skeleton Key to Finnegans Wake* (*Compass), and W. P. Jones, *James Joyce and the Common Reader* (Oklahoma, 1955). Two guides to a baffling writer.

H. H. Arnason, *History of Modern Art* (Abrams, Prentice-Hall, 1969). Encyclopaedic introduction to twentieth-century painting, sculpture, and architecture.

G. H. Hamilton, *19th and 20th Century Art* (Abrams, Prentice-Hall, 1972). A lucid and less detailed survey.

H.-R. Hitchcock, *Architecture: 19th and 20th Centuries* (Penguin, 1958). A meaty volume in "The Pelican History of Art."

The Armory Show, 1913 (Arno, 1972). Three volumes reproducing the catalogues and other documents of the famous New York exhibition.

H. Richter, *Dada: Art and Anti-Art* (McGraw-Hill, n.d.); P. Waldberg, *Surrealism* (*McGraw-Hill); J. Russell and S. Gablik, *Pop Art Redefined* (Praeger, 1969). Useful introductions to particular movements.

L. Wertenbaker, *The World of Picasso* (Time-Life Books, 1967) and C. Tomkins, *The World of Marcel Duchamp* (Time-Life Books, 1966). Very informative attempts to relate two artistic pioneers to the cultural world of the twentieth century.

P. Collaer, *A History of Modern Music* (*Universal). A helpful guide.

J. Cage, *Silence: Lectures and Writings* (*MIT). By a great experimenter in extending musical frontiers.

Illustrations

Index